D0148197

Knowledge & Power
in the Global Economy

Second Edition

SOCIOCULTURAL, POLITICAL, AND HISTORICAL STUDIES IN EDUCATION

Joel Spring, Editor

For additional information on titles in the Studies in Sociocultural, Political and Historical Studies in Education series visit **www.routledge.com**

GRACE LIBRARY CARLOW UNIVERSITY
PITTSBURGH PA 15213

Knowledge & Power in the Global Economy

The Effects of School Reform in a Neoliberal / Neoconservative Age

Second Edition

Edited by

David Gabbard
East Carolina University

Foreword by Dave Hill

LC
66
K66
2008

LEA Lawrence Erlbaum Associates
Taylor & Francis Group

New York   London

CATALOGUED

Lawrence Erlbaum Associates
Taylor & Francis Group
270 Madison Avenue
New York, NY 10016

Lawrence Erlbaum Associates
Taylor & Francis Group
2 Park Square
Milton Park, Abingdon
Oxon OX14 4RN

© 2008 by Taylor & Francis Group, LLC
Lawrence Erlbaum Associates is an imprint of Taylor & Francis Group, an Informa business

Printed in the United States of America on acid-free paper
10 9 8 7 6 5 4 3 2 1

International Standard Book Number-13: 978-0-8058-5939-3 (Softcover) 978-0-8058-5938-6 (Hardcover)

No part of this book may be reprinted, reproduced, transmitted, or utilized in any form by any electronic, mechanical, or other means, now known or hereafter invented, including photocopying, microfilming, and recording, or in any information storage or retrieval system, without written permission from the publishers.

Trademark Notice: Product or corporate names may be trademarks or registered trademarks, and are used only for identification and explanation without intent to infringe.

Visit the Taylor & Francis Web site at
http://www.taylorandfrancis.com

and the LEA and Routledge Web site at
http://www.routledge.com

Contents

MW 39,95   3-14-08 GRED

PART II: ANTIEDUCATIONAL FOUNDATIONS: THE SETUP

PART IV: CLASSROOM CONSEQUENCES

PART V: DEMOCRACY'S PATH

Foreword

In its first incarnation, *Knowledge and Power in the Global Economy* (2000) provided a critical encyclopedic approach to the rhetoric of educational reform as it developed from the 1980s through the 1990s. Part I critiqued the vocabulary of that rhetoric, deconstructing many of the most commonly heard terms and phrases used to rationalize the pending reforms and revealing how their internal logic interlaced with a larger neoliberal project to reshape the public's understanding of the purposes of American schools and use high-stakes testing and accountability schemes to restore schools to what dominant elites perceive to be their traditional role of producing passive worker-citizens with just enough skills to render themselves useful to the demands of capital. Part II sought to elaborate the multiplicity of ways that the logic of neoliberalism and the emerging patterns of high-stakes testing and accountability were impacting the curriculum. And Part III sought to introduce ideas associated with alternative and liberatory educational projects.

In the United States and the United Kingdom and throughout other parts of the globe, policy developments such as the United States' No Child Left Behind Act of 2001 have nationalized and intensified those patterns (a process initiated in England and Wales by the Thatcher government's 1988 Education Reform Act). These have deepened the logic and extent of neoliberalism's hold over education reforms. In the United States, such reforms include the heavy involvement of educational management organizations (EMOs) as well as the introduction of voucher plans, charter schools, and other manifestations of the drive toward the effective privatization of public education. Meanwhile, England and Wales have endured the effective elimination of much comprehensive (all-intake, all-ability) public secondary schooling. Commercialization and marketization have led to school-based budgetary control, a market in new types of state schooling, and the effective "selling off" of state schools to rich or religious individuals or groups via the academies scheme. The influence of neoliberal ideology also led to the October 2005 proposals for state schools, which have historically fallen under the purview of democratically elected local school districts, to become independent mini-businesses called independent trust schools (Hill, 2006). Similar attempts at change have occurred throughout developed and developing countries (Hill, 2005a; Hill et al., 2006).

However, the impact of the Bush administration in the United States and the New Labour government in Britain on society and our schools renders it impossible to understand the current crises in American schools and in American democracy (and in British schools and democracy) solely in terms of neoliberalism. We must also consider the impact of neoconservatism. Hence, the second edition of *Knowledge and Power in the Global Economy* has adopted a new subtitle: *The Effects of School Reform in a Neoliberal/Neoconservative Age*.

This is an important and necessary book. The list of contributing authors includes a stunning array of insightful and widely published and referenced critical scholars and educators. Its appearance offers readers an opportunity to better understand how contemporary educational policies fit within the broader aims of neoliberal and neoconservative agendas. In this foreword, I want to provide an overview of how those agendas in education play themselves out in the United States, the United Kingdom, and worldwide, in developed capitalist countries generally, and also in less developed and developing capitalist countries.

SOCIAL CLASS AND CAPITAL

There have been a number of changes in capitalism in this current period of neoliberal globalization. One development is the growth in service, communications, and technological industries in the developed world. One service industry is education. As the International Chamber of Commerce (ICC) observes, "services are coming to dominate the economic activities of countries at virtually every stage of development" (ICC, 1999, p. 1).

Another development is the declining profitability of capital — the crisis of capital accumulation. This crisis has resulted in intensification of competition between capitals, between national and transnational capitals and corporations. There is general agreement among critical educators and Marxists that "the pressure on nations to liberalize services at the national level can be seen, therefore, as a response to the declining profit-ability of manufacture" (Beckmann & Cooper, 2004). This crisis of capital accumulation, as predicted by Marx and Engels (1847/1977), has led to the intensification of the extraction of surplus value, the progressing global immiseration of workers, and the intensification of control of populations by the ideological and repressive state apparatuses identified and analyzed by Althusser (1971; see also Hill, 2001, 2004, 2005b).

Class War from Above

Neoliberal and neoconservative policies aimed at intensifying the rate of capital accumulation and extraction of surplus value comprise an intensi-fication of class war from above by the capitalist class against the working class. One major aspect of this is the fiscal policy of increasing taxes on workers and decreasing taxes on business and the rich. Of course, some people do not like trillion dollar tax handouts to the rich. These opposi-tionists have to be denigrated, scorned, and controlled. This is where neo-conservative policies are important. On the one hand, they persuade the poor to vote (right-wing Republican) for a social or religious or antiabor-tion or homophobic or racist agenda against their own (more left wing, more Democrat, or further left) economic self-interest.

The class war from above has a neoliberal, economic element. It has also embraced a neoconservative political element to strengthen the force of the state behind it. In Andrew Gamble's words, it is *The Free Economy and the Strong State* (1999), a state strong on controlling education, strong on con-trolling teachers, and strong on marginalizing oppositional democratic forces such as local elected democracy, trade unions, critical educators, and critical students. Moreover, neoconservatism aids in the formation of a state strong on enforcing the neoliberalization of schools and society.

Despite the horizontal and vertical cleavages within the capitalist class (Dumenil & Levy, 2004), the architects of neoliberal and neoconservative policies know very well who they are. Nobody is denying capitalist class consciousness. They are rich. They are powerful. And they are transna-tional as well as national. They exercise (contested) control over the lives of worker-laborers and worker-subjects. If there is one class that does not lack class consciousness, *the subjective appreciation of its common interest, and its relationship within the means of production to other social classes*, it is the capi-talist class. Members of the capitalist class do recognize that they survive in dominance *as a class* whatever their skin color, or dreams, or multifaceted subjectivities and histories of hurt and triumph — they survive precisely because they do know they are a class. They have class consciousness; they are a class *for* themselves (a class with a consciousness that they are a class) as well as a class *in* themselves (a class or group of people with shared eco-nomic conditions of existence and interests). The capitalist class does not

tear itself to pieces negating or suborning its class identity, its class awareness, its class power over issues of race and gender (or, indeed, sexuality
or disability). And they govern in their own interests, not just in education
reform, but also in enriching and empowering themselves — while dis-
empowering and impoverishing others — the (white and black and other
minority, male and female) working class.

Increasingly Unequal Distribution of Wealth in the United States and Britain

David Harvey (2005) argues that while the intellectual origins of neoliberalism reach back to the 1930s, its material origins stem from the crisis
of capital accumulation of the late 1960s and 1970s. In his estimation, this
crisis constituted both a political threat and an economic threat to economic elites and ruling classes across the advanced capitalist and developing countries (p. 15). In the United States, prior to the 1970s, the wealthiest
1% of the population owned between 30% and 47% of all wealth assets (p.
16). But in the 1970s it slid to just 20%. Asset values collapsed. In Harvey's
phrase, "the upper classes had to move decisively if they were to protect
themselves from political and economic annihilation" (p. 16). And they
did, leading Harvey to conclude that we can best understand neoliberalization as a project designed to achieve the restoration of class power.
Furthermore, given that by 1998 the percentage ownership of all wealth
assets in the United States held by the wealthiest 1% of the population had
almost doubled since the mid-1970s, we should view the neoliberal project
as having achieved great success.

Likewise in the United Kingdom, the wealth of the super-rich has doubled since Tony Blair came to power in 1997. According to the Office for
National Statistics (2000), nearly 600,000 individuals in the top 1% of
the United Kingdom wealth league owned assets worth £355 billion in
1996, the last full year of Conservative rule. By 2002, that had increased
to £797 billion.

Increasingly Unequal Distribution of Income in the United States and Britain

As for income, the ratio of the salaries of chief executive officers (CEOs)
to the median compensation of workers increased from just over 30 to 1
in 1970 to nearly 500 to 1 by 2000 (Harvey, 2005, p. 17). Korten (2004)
highlights the immense increase in salaries taken by top U.S. executives
since the early 1990s. In the United States, between 1990 and 1999, inflation increased by 27.5%, workers' pay by 32.3%, corporate profits by 116%,
and, finally, the pay of chief executive officers by a staggering, kleptocratic
535% (Korten, 2004, p. 17; see also Brenner, 2005).

In the United States, the share of the national income taken by the top 1% of income earners had been 16% in the 1930s. It fell to around 8% between the mid-1940s and mid-1970s. The neoliberal revolution restored its share of national income to 15% by the end of the 20th century. And the federal minimum wage, which stood on a par with the poverty level in 1980, had fallen to 30% below that in 1990. "The long decline in wage levels had begun" (Harvey, 2005, p. 25). Pollin (2003) shows that in the United States, the level of real wages per hour dropped from $15.72 in 1973 to $14.15 in 2000. In the United Kingdom, those in the top 1% of income earners have doubled their share of the national income from 6.5% to 13% since 1982 (Harvey, 2005, pp. 15–18). Tax policy has been crucial in affecting these growing inequalities.

Changing Tax Rates: Capitalist Winners and Working-Class Losers

Dumenil and Levy (2004) show that in the United States, those in the highest tax bracket are paying tax at a rate around half that of the 1920s, whereas the current tax rate for those in the lowest tax bracket has more than doubled over the same period. As a forerunner of George W. Bush's "trillion dollar tax giveaway to the rich," Ronald Reagan cut the top rate of personal tax from 70% to 28%. Both the Reagan and Thatcher governments also dramatically cut taxes on businesses and corporations.

In Britain, too, the working class is paying more tax. The richest groups are paying a smaller proportion of their income in taxes in comparison to 1949 and to the late 1970s. These dates were both in the closing stages two periods that might be termed Old Labour, or social democratic governments (in ideological contradistinction to the primarily neoliberal policies of New Labour).

As Paul Johnson and Frances Lynch reported in their 2004 article in *The Guardian*, in comparison with the late 1970s, the "fat cats" are now paying around half as much tax (income tax and insurance contribution rate). These fat cats are paying less income tax and national insurance as a percentage of their earned income than in 1949. "As a percentage of income, middle and high earners pay less tax now than at any time in the past thirty years" (Johnson and Lynch, 2004).

In contrast, the average tax rate for "the low paid" is roughly double that of the early 1970s — and nearly twice as much as in 1949 (Johnson and Lynch, 2004). No wonder, then, that Johnson and Lynch titled their article "Sponging Off the Poor."

Capital, Corporations, and Education

Education is now big business — "edu-business." Current worldwide spending in education is "estimated at around 2,000 billion dollars ... more than global automotive sales" (Santos, 2004, p. 17). According to Santos, "capital growth in education has been exponential, showing one of the highest earning rates of the market: £1000 invested in 1996 generated £3,405 four years later" (Santos, 2004, pp. 17–18, cited in Delgado-Ramos & Saxe-Fernandez, 2005). Santos continues, "that is an increased value of 240%, while the London Stock Change valorization rate accounted on the same period for 65%. Other 2004 data indicate that, current commercialized education, incomplete as it is, already generates around $365 billion in profits worldwide" (Santos, 2004, pp. 17–18, cited in Delgado-Ramos & Saxe-Fernandez, 2005).

Capital — national and transnational corporations along with their major shareholders — has a number of plans with respect to education. We may first speak of the capitalist plan *for* education. This plan aims to produce and reproduce a workforce and citizenry and set of consumers fit for capital. According to this plan, schools must serve two overriding functions, an ideological function and a labor-training function. These comprise socially producing labor power for capitalist enterprises. This is people's capacity to labor — their skills and attitudes — together with their ideological compliance and suitability for capital, as workers, citizens, and consumers. In this analysis, Althusser's concept of schools as ideological state apparatuses (ISAs) is useful here, with schools as key elements in the ideological indoctrination of new citizens and workers into thinking "there is no alternative" to capitalism, that capitalism and competitive individualism with gross inequalities are "only natural" (Althusser, 1971; see also Hill, 2001, 2003, 2004).

Secondly, we may speak of the capitalist plan *in* education, which entails smoothing the way for direct profit taking/profiteering from education. This plan is about how capital wants to make *direct profits* from education. This centers on setting business "free" in education for profit making and profit taking — extracting profits from privately controlled/owned schools and colleges or aspects of their functioning. Common mechanisms for such profiteering include managing, advising, controlling, and owning schools. These possibilities are widened in the United Kingdom by New Labour's Education White Paper of October 2005.

Finally, we may speak of capital's global plan for education corporations. This is a series of national capitalist plans for domestically based national or multinational corporations globally. This is a plan for British, U.S., Australian, New Zealand, and locally (e.g., in particular states in Latin America, such as Brazil) based edu-businesses and corporations to profit from international privatizing, franchising, and marketing activities. With a worldwide education industry valued at $2 trillion annually, "it is not surprising that many investors and 'edupreneurs' are anxious to seize the opportunities to access this untapped gold mine" (Schugurensky & Davidson-Harden, 2003, p. 323). It is not just national edu-businesses that are involved — it is large multiactivity national and global capitalist companies.

THE IMPACTS SO FAR

Capital has not merely developed these plans and set them on the shelf for future reference. Many elements of these plans have already been put into action. We can already see much of the impact of these initiatives in the growing inequities they produce in the lives of students, declining levels of democratic control over schools, and worsening work conditions in the teaching and other education professions.

Impacts on Equity: Neoliberalism and Widening ("Raced" and Gendered) Class Inequalities in Education

Where there is a market in schools (where high-status schools can select their intakes, whether on academic achievement or other class-related criteria, such as aptitudes), the result is increasing raced and gendered social class differentiation. The middle classes (predominantly white) rapidly colonize the best schools; the working classes (white and black) get pushed out. They do not get through the school gate. High-status/high-achieving middle-class schools get better and better results. In a competitive market in schools, "sink" schools sink further, denuded of their brightest intakes.

The same is true of higher education. In the United States it is highly tiered — there is a hierarchy.

Entry to elite schools/universities is largely dependent on a student's ability to pay — on social class background. This is intensifying in England and Wales, too. Until the 1980s, there were no university fees in Britain; the state/taxpayer paid. Entry was free for students. For the last 20 years, all universities charged the same for undergrad courses. Now, the New Labour government is introducing variable fees for different universities. Britain is "going American." This will reinforce elitism and exclude poorer groups, especially minorities, but white working-class students, too.

Neoliberalization of schooling and university education is accompanied by an increase in (gendered, raced, linguistically differentiated) social class inequalities in educational provision, attainment, and subsequent position in the labor market. For example, the movement to voucher and charter schools as well as other forms of privatized education, such as chains of schools in the United States (Molnar, 2001; Molnar et al., 2004), has proven to be disproportionately beneficial to those segments of society who can afford to pay for better educational opportunities and experiences, leading to further social exclusion and polarization (Whitty et al., 1998; Gillborn & Youdell, 2000).

Hirtt (2004) has noted the apparently contradictory education policies of capital, "to adapt education to the needs of business and at the same time reduce state expenditure on education" (p. 446). He suggests that this contradiction is resolved by the polarization of the labor market, that from an economic point of view it is not necessary to provide high-level education and general knowledge to all future workers. "It is now possible and even highly recommendable to have a more polarized education system.... Education should not try to transmit a broad common culture to the majority of future workers, but instead it should teach them some basic, general skills" (Hirtt, 2004, p. 446).

In brief, then, manual and service workers receive a cheaper and inferior education limited to transferable skills, while elite workers receive more expensive and more and internationally superior education. Not only does this signal one manifestation of the hierarchicalization of schools and the end of the comprehensive ideal, but it also represents a form of educational triage — with basic skills training for millions of workers, more advanced education for supervision for the middle class and, in some countries, the brightest of the working classes, and elite education for scions of the capitalist and other sections of the ruling classes.

Impacts on Workers' Pay, Conditions, and Securities

A key element of capital's plans for education is to cut its labor costs. For this, a deregulated labor market becomes essential — with schools and colleges able to set their own pay scales and sets of conditions — busting national trade union agreements and weakening the power of trade unions, such as teacher unions, to protect their workforces. As a consequence of capital's efforts to extract higher rates of surplus value from their labor power, educational workers suffer declining pay, decreasing benefits, and deteriorating working conditions (Hill, 2005b). There is the ongoing *casualization* of academic labor and the increased *proletarianization* of the teaching profession.

By *casualization* I mean the move toward part-time and temporary employment in the education sector. Simultaneously, the *proletarianization* of teaching results in:

- Declining wages, benefits, and professional autonomy for teachers
- Growing intensification of teachers' labor through increases in class sizes and levels of surveillance
- Mounting efforts to eliminate the influence of teachers' unions as mechanisms for promoting and defending teachers' interests

The intensification of work is justified in different countries through campaigns of vilification against public service workers such as teachers and education officials. Siqueira (2005) reports that in Brazil, the Cardoso government of the mid-1990s launched, using the media, a renewed and stronger campaign against civil servants, unions, and retired public employees.

Some of the terms used by his government to refer to these groups were sluggish, negligent, agitators, old-fashioned, unpatriotic, selfish, and lazy.

This is part of the global neoliberal critique of public service workers for being expensive self-interested workers who have "captured" the professions with their restrictive and expensive practices. In Britain, Stephen Ball (1990, p. 22) has called this denigration "a discourse of derision." In some right-wing newspapers, such as *The Daily Mail* in Britain, it is more like a discourse of hate. One need only recall former Secretary of Education Rod Paige's denigration of the National Education Association as a "terrorist organization" to find a potent example of such speech in the United States.

Impacts on Democracy and Critical Thinking

The neoconservative faces of education reform, indeed, of the wider marketization and commodification of humanity and society, come to play in the enforcement and policing of consent, the delegitimizing of deep dissent, and the weakening of oppositional centers and practices and thought. In eras of declining capital accumulation, an ultimately inevitable process, capital — and the governments and parties and generals and CEOs who act at their behest — more and more nakedly ratchets up the ideological and repressive state apparatuses of control (Hill, 2001, 2003, 2004). Thus, key working-class organizations such as trade unions and democratically elected municipal governments are marginalized, and their organizations and those of other radically oppositional organizations based on race, ethnicity, and religion are attacked — through laws, rhetoric, and, ultimately, sometimes by incarceration.

In education, the combined neoliberal-neoconservative educational reform has led to a radical change in what governments and most school and college managements/leaderships themselves see as their mission. In the 1960s and 1970s (and with long prior histories), liberal-humanist or social democratic or socialist ends of education were common through the advanced capitalist (and parts of the anticolonialist developing) worlds.

This has changed dramatically within the lifetimes of those over 30. Now the curriculum is conservative and controlled. Now the hidden curriculum of pedagogy is performative processing and delivery or predigested points. Now the overwhelming and nakedly overriding and exclusive focus is on the production of a differentially educated, tiered (raced and gendered) social class workforce and compliant citizenry. Differentially skilled and socially/politically/culturally neutered and compliant human capital is now the production focus of neoliberalized education systems and institutions, hand in glove with and enforced by a neoconservative ideology and state.

RESISTANCE

But there is resistance; there are spaces, disarticulations, and contradictions. There are people who want to realize a different vision of education.

There are people who want a more human and more equal society, a society where students and citizens and workers are not sacrificed on the altar of profit before all else.

And there are always, sometimes minor, sometimes major, awakenings that the material conditions of existence, for teacher educators, teachers, students, and workers and families more widely simply do not match or recognize the validity of neoliberal or neoconservative or other capitalist discourse and policy.

This book feeds that resistance.

Dave Hill
University of Northampton

REFERENCES

Althusser, L. (1971). Ideology and state apparatuses. In L. Althusser (Ed.), *Lenin and philosophy and other essays*. London: New Left Books.

Ball, S. (1990). *Politics & policymaking in education*. London: Routledge.

Beckmann, A., & Cooper, C. (2004). "Globalization," the new managerialism and education: Rethinking the purpose of education. *Journal for Critical Education Policy Studies, 2*. http://www.jceps.com/index.php?pageID=article&articleID=31

Brenner, R. (2005). *The economics of global turbulence*. London: Verso.

Delgado-Ramos, G., & Saxe-Fernandez, J. (2005). The world bank and the privatization of public education: A Mexican perspective. *Journal for Critical Education Policy Studies, 3*. Retrieved February 1, 2006, from http://www.jceps.com/index.php?pageID=article&articleID=44

Dumenil, G., & Levy, D. (2004). *Capital resurgent: Roots of the neoliberal revolution*. London: Harvard University Press.

Gamble, A. (1988). *The free economy and the strong state: The politics of Thatcherism*. London: MacMillan.

Gillborn, D., & Youdell, D. (2000). *Rationing education: Policy, practice, reform and equity*. Buckingham, UK: Open University Press.

Harvey, D. (2005). *A brief history of neoliberalism*. Oxford: Oxford University Press.

Hill, D. (2001). State theory and the neoliberal reconstruction of schooling and teacher education: A structuralist neo-Marxist critique of postmodernist, quasi-postmodernist, and culturalist neo-Marxist theory. *British Journal of Sociology of Education, 22*, 137–157.

Hill, D. (2003). Global neo-liberalism, the deformation of education and resistance, *Journal of Critical Education Policy Studies, 1*, 1. http://www.jceps.com/index.php?pageID=article&articleID=7

Hill, D. (2004). Books, banks and bullets: Controlling our minds: The global project of imperialistic and militaristic neo-liberalism and its effect on education policy. *Policy Futures, 2*, 3–4 (Theme: Marxist Futures in Education). Retrieved February 1, 2006, from http://www.wwwords.co.UK/pfie/content/pdfs/2/issue2_3.asp

Hill, D. (2005a). State theory and the neoliberal reconstruction of schooling and teacher education. In G. Fischman, P. McLaren, H. Sünker, & C. Lankshear (Eds.), *Critical theories, radical pedagogies and global conflicts.* Boulder: Rowman & Littlefield.

Hill, D. (2005b). Globalization and its educational discontents: Neoliberalization and its impacts on education workers' rights, pay, and conditions. *International Studies in the Sociology of Education, 15,* 257–288.

Hill, D. (2006). New Labour's education policy. In D. Kassem, E. Mufti, & J. Robinson (Eds.), *Education studies: Issues and critical perspectives.* Buckingham: Open University Press.

Hill, D., with Anijar-Appleton, K., Davidson-Harden, A., Fawcett, B., Gabbard, D., Gindin, J., Kuehn, L., Lewis, C., Mukhtar, A., Pardinaz-Solis, R., Quiros, B., Schugurensky, D., Smaller, H., & Templer, B. (2006). Education services liberalization. In E. Rosskam (Ed.), *Winners or losers? Liberalizing public services.* Geneva: International Labor Organization.

Hirtt, N. (2004). Three axes of merchandization. *European Educational Research Journal, 3,* 442–453. Retrieved February 1, 2006, from http://www.wwwords.co.UK/eerj/

International Chamber of Commerce (ICC). (1999). The benefits of services trade liberalization: Policy statement (Document 103/210). Paris: ICC. Retrieved February 1, 2006, from http://www.iccwbo.org/home/case_for_the_global_economy/benefits_services_trade_liberalization.asp

Johnson, P., & Lynch, F. (2004, March 10). Sponging off the poor. *The Guardian.* Retrieved April 26, 2007, from http://www.guardian.co.uk/analysis/story/0,3604,1165918,00.html

Korten, D. (2004). *EDucate* (Sindh Educational Foundation), *3,* 12–20.

Marx, K., & Engels, F. (1977). The Communist Manifesto. In *Karl Marx and Frederick Engels, selected works.* London: Lawrence & Wishart. (Original work published 1847.)

Molnar, A. (2001). *Giving kids the business: The commercialization of America's schools* (2nd ed.). Boulder, CO: Westview Press.

Molnar, A., Wilson, G., & Allen, D. (2004). Profiles of for-profit education management companies, sixth annual report, 2003–2004. Arizona: Arizona State University Education Policy Studies Laboratory. Retrieved February 1, 2006, from http://www.asu.edu/educ/epsl/CERU/Documents/EPSL-0402-101-CERU.pdf

Office for National Statistics. (2000). Living in Britain 2000. Retrieved February 1, 2006, from www.statistics.gov.UK

Pollin, R. (2003). *Contours of descent.* London: Verso.

Santos, B. (2004). *A universidade no século XXI.* Sao Paolo, Brazil: Cortez.

Schugurensky, D., & Davidson-Harden, A. (2003). From Cordoba to Washington: WTO/GATS and Latin American education. *Globalization, Societies and Education, 1.*

Siqueira, A. (2005). The regulation of education through the WTO/GATS: Path to the enhancement of human freedom? *Journal for Critical Education Policy Studies, 3.* Retrieved April 26, 2007, from http://www.jceps.com/index.php?pageID=article&articleID=41

Whitty, G., Power, S., & Halpin, D. (1998). *Devolution and choice in education: The school, the state and the market.* Buckingham, UK: Open University Press.

Preface

Over the past 30 years, neoliberalism and neoconservatism have grown inexorably intertwined to form a hyperintensified capitalist couplet. As a consequence of their convergence, it no longer makes sense to speak of the global economy in the same terms we did in 2000, when the first edition of this book appeared. At that time, neoliberals in both of America's political parties rested content with using the soft power of neocolonialism to spread to market's reach around the globe through cooperative relationships between various transnational corporate elites and their supportive state apparatuses. Neoconservatism has since emboldened American neoliberalism to conceive the global economy as a game of "winner takes all." The neoconservative Project for a New American Century's *Rebuilding America's Defenses* (2000) has become America's foreign policy, and the essence of that policy is empire.

Though no one in Washington or the corporate media dares to say it, the neoconservatives planned the invasion of Iraq long before George W. Bush was inaugurated in 2001. The purpose of the invasion had little to do with terrorism, though that will (again) be the pretext. The real purpose is spelled out by the Project for a New American Century (PNAC). Under the neoliberal/neoconservative rule of the Bush administration, the United States seeks to secure supreme imperial status over the next century by dominating the international oil market. While Congressional Democrats may be seeking political advantage of the failures in Iraq to win seats in the coming 2006 elections, none of them, even those publicly calling for an exit strategy, have acknowledged that much of the funding for allegedly rebuilding Iraq has been directed toward the construction of 14 permanent U.S. military bases in that country. The plan, as articulated by the PNAC, is to shift our military troop strength from Europe to the Middle East.

But empire begins at home, where neoliberalism functions as an economic ideology aiming at the elimination of the public in favor of the private, while neoconservatism provides the political framework for securing the hegemony of the private against any claims from the public. The neoconservative indifference toward any notion of the public's welfare was illustrated in most dramatic fashion by the Bush administration's apathy toward the destruction caused by Hurricane Katrina. Kanye West's remark that "George Bush doesn't care about black people" neglects the fact that neoconservatism does not care about people more generally. What some view as a disaster, others view as an opportunity for profit and racial cleansing. As Mike Davis reported in *Mother Jones*, "the powerful House Republican Study Group has vowed to support only relief measures that buttress the private sector and are offset by reductions in national social programs such as food stamps, student loans, and Medicaid" (2005). Republican Congressman Richard Baker of Louisiana put the neoconservative view in sharp focus: "We finally cleaned up public housing in New Orleans. We couldn't do it, but God did" (Babington, 2005). From the neoliberal and neoconservative views, then, Katrina offered cause for celebration as both an expression of God's will to punish the poor and an opportunity for profiteering. As Kristen Buras (2005) reports, there were a number of "no-bid contracts awarded to companies such as Halliburton, the same entities that have pillaged Iraq, to rebuild New Orleans. With 40 percent of the businesses in Louisiana either disrupted or destroyed by Hurricanes Katrina and Rita, the pillaging continues."

This volume examines how neoliberal and neoconservative policies have worked in tandem to destabilize schools across numerous dimensions of their status as public institutions. In addition to analyzing how this destabilization program has impacted the internal dynamics of school management, teaching, and learning, many of the chapters also describe how it has transformed the external dynamics of education from a public good or service offered to serve public interests to a private enterprise harnessed to the advantage of private interests. And by *private interests*, I do not mean the private lives of individual members of the public. I mean what George Bush means when he talks about his administration's commitment to creating what he calls the "ownership society," which is the same as what John Jay meant when he said that "the people who own the country ought to govern it" (Monaghan, 1935, p. 323). Moreover, I mean the private interests of corporations and the plutocratic system of unaccountable power through which they dominate U.S. policy — both foreign and domestic.

As the two most dominant ideologies of our time, neoliberalism and neoconservatism work together to undermine the very notion of "the public" and to build the foundation for an "empire of the private." This disintegration of the public, as these chapters demonstrate, holds tremendous implications for institutions of public education, particularly in relation to any future public interest that those institutions might serve. Though David Hursh and Kristen Buras provide excellent chapters on neoliberalism and neoconservatism, it may be useful to provide readers with a general description of each.

NEOLIBERAL IDEOLOGY

As Margaret Thatcher (1987), one of the iconic figures for the adherents of these ideologies, once stated, "there is no such thing as society." And because there is no society, but only — in Thatcher's words — "individual men and women, ... and families," there is no public. Therefore, there can be no public interest, only the private interests of individuals and families.

Apart from denying the existence of society or the public, the chief problem with Thatcher's comments lies in the fact that they limit our understanding of private interests to "individual men and women, ... and families." She omits mentioning the private wealth and the commensurate private power wielded by private corporations. As Canadian law professor, Joel Bakan, points out in his book, *The Corporation: The Pathological Pursuit of Profit and Power* (2004) (and the excellent movie of the same name by Mark Akbar), an 1886 U.S. Supreme Court decision (*Santa Clara County v. Southern Pacific Railroad Company*, 118 U.S. 394) granted the corporation the same legal status as a person as recognized in Section 1 of the 14th Amendment of the U.S. Constitution. This decision helped supply legal support for the traditional doctrine of economic liberalism (laissez-faire capitalism) — the notion that economic enterprises, as private entities, should remain free to pursue "life, liberty, or property" without government interference or regulation. Loosely speaking, these conditions allow for a free market.

Against this background, we can already begin to see how private corporations came to view the public as a nuisance or a threat to their freedom, especially when the public seeks to use what limited democratic mechanisms offered by the government they can for demanding protection from the abuses of corporate power. We should not forget that early on in the history of the labor movement, private power looked upon minimum-wage laws, child labor laws, and laws instituting the 40-hour workweek as a violation of its rights. In the wake of the Great Depression, Franklin D. Roosevelt expanded such protections with the New Deal and creation of the welfare state, thus giving the labor movement greater leverage to gain wage and other concessions from private corporations during the post-WWII era. Later, in the 1960s, populist movements began demanding other forms of government protection of the public interests. The environmental movement, for example, led to the creation of the Environmental Protection Agency, which imposed regulations on private power. During that same period, other populist groups demanded that public schools become more responsive to public interests. Environmental education, multicultural education, and affirmative action programs all developed during this era.

Neoliberalism, as an economic doctrine, developed as a reaction against these and other populist demands for government to serve the public interests. In essence, while it adheres to all of the major elements of traditional economic liberalism, neoliberalism has intensified the efforts of private power to roll back and even reverse these gains through a variety of measures, including:

Deregulation
Deunionization
Privatization
Cutting public expenditure for social services (including education)
Free trade agreements
Neoconservative Ideology

If neoliberalism intensified the efforts of private power in its assault against the public, neoconservativism has hyperintensified those efforts by providing economic elites with a political ideology through which to radically advance their agenda. As Shadia Drury (2005) has argued, neoconservative ideology has been heavily informed by the writings of Leo Strauss, a political philosopher at the University of Chicago during the 1950s and 1960s whose list of students and admirers include many of today's most influential figures in and around government (e.g., Clarence Thomas, Richard Perle, Paul Wolfowitz, William Bennett, Douglas Feith, John Bolton, Eliot Abrams, Rupert Murdoch, Francis Fukyama, William Kristol, and others). According to Strauss, most influenced by the ideas of Plato, Machiavelli, and Nietzsche, we are wrong to listen to Socrates in reading *The Republic*. It was Thrasymachus whom Plato had intended the great philosopher kings of the future to follow when he defines justice as "the interest of the stronger" (Bhandari, 1998).

Moreover, neoconservatism rationalizes private power's pursuit of profit, even when that pursuit runs against public interest. It also reinforces private power's views on the role of government; it should actively and aggressively serve private over public interests. With regard to government's relation to the public, neoconservatism further embraces Plato's advice regarding the importance of "useful lies" and irrational modes of thought (e.g., religion and nationalism) aimed at diverting public attention from whatever injustices may be occurring around them and maintaining their allegiance to the state.

THE END OF PUBLIC EDUCATION?

The primary objective of the second edition of *Knowledge and Power in the Global Economy* aims at encouraging a conversation among educators, as well as the general public, on neoliberalism and neoconservatism and how they manifest themselves to operate in opposition to what we normally understand as the public interest, particularly as the public interest concerns public education.

In this regard, we would be foolish to ignore the assertion widely misattributed to Benito Mussolini, but probably written by Giovani Gentile, the recognized philosopher of Italian fascism who ghost-wrote Mussolini's main political treatises, that "Fascism should more appropriately be called Corporatism because it is a merger of State and corporate power" (see Hartman, 2004). In the United States, private corporations have (historically) always transacted with, and profited from, selling supplies and equipment to the public schools. Likewise, those same private interests were always able to count on the security state to manage schools as instruments for disciplining members of the domestic population into the proper behaviors and attitudes that would increase their use value as human capital and their docility as "good citizens." Though countervailing ideas on the purposes of education had circulated since the time of Thomas Jefferson, they never threatened to seriously alter the traditional role of compulsory schooling in America's market society. That changed, however, in the 1960s when multiple sectors of the general public (those associated with the civil rights movement, the women's movement, the environmental movement, the labor movement, the peace movement, and others) recognized and acted to realize the democratizing potentials of education. As a result of the efforts of these various groups, schools and universities, from the perspective of entrenched business interests, began "allowing too much freedom and independence of thought, and that cannot be tolerated in a 'democracy,' because it might lead to consequences" (Chomsky, 2004). Beginning in the early 1970s, multiple sectors of that same business community began taking steps to overcome these deficiencies in the educational system, restoring the state-sponsored system of compulsory schooling to its traditional role. Those steps have entailed a variety of tactics (e.g., vouchers, tax tuition credits, charter schools) for liberalizing education for promoting a broader strategy ultimately designed to bring the management of schools (decision-making power over curriculum and modes of instruction) under the control of private corporations (Saltman, 2001; Saltman & Goodman,

2002; Saltman & Gabbard, 2003). Privatizing the management of schools, of course, will also provide the added advantage, following the dominant pattern that we see in the defense and biotechnology industries, of socializing the costs of schooling while privatizing the profits to corporations.

In my view, and in the view of many of the authors in this volume, the primary aim of the extraordinarily bipartisan No Child Left Behind Act of 2001 (NCLB) does not entail the reform of public education. The purposefully impossible standards it sets for schools are best epitomized in its requirement that schools must prove that all students have achieved at or above grade level by the year 2014. Even a state such as Minnesota, whose students typically score among the top in the country on national tests, anticipates that 80% of its schools will fail to meet these standards. NCLB mandates that all students, from third through eighth grade and throughout high school, be tested. Each school must report its results by breaking the student body down into demographic categories, including special education, limited-English-proficiency, and low-income students, and numerous categories of race/ethnicity depending on the number of students from those categories represented in the school. The special education category, of course, includes children suffering from mental retardation. In essence, NCLB demands that teachers and schools literally perform miracles. By definition, mentally retarded children suffer physical, neurocognitive impairments that not even medical science has been able to cure. But teachers and schools are being held accountable for doing what not even medical science can do.

As the National Educational Association and the American Federation of Teachers have implied, NCLB is not a piece of educational reform legislation; it is a trap. It deliberately sets schools up to fail in order to justify privatizing them after 2014. If the draconian, neoliberal/neoconservative vision of the right becomes a reality, teachers will no longer be able to conceptualize themselves as public servants whose work contributes to some important public purpose vital to expanding our nation's democratic promise. They will no longer leave their homes in the morning to go to school; they will leave to go to work. Under the neoliberal vision of privatization, they will be employees of a corporation. The waning days of professional autonomy that high-stakes testing and accountability have brought upon us will finally grind to a halt. The right's vision shuts down the possibility of spirited debates on what we should do with curriculum or what the purposes of education should be in a democratic society. If the right has its way, by 2014, democracy itself, if current trends continue, may be foreclosed as well. Teachers in corporate schools will be paid to teach the corporate curriculum, in accordance with the corporate model of instruction. Neoliberals and neoconservatives would also like to eliminate teacher education programs from our nation's colleges and universities, rendering it possible for a day to come when the only people who go into teaching will be people who lock-stepped through K-12 schools knowing only the high-stakes testing model of schooling, where teachers "drill and kill" students by teaching to the test and sometimes even using scripts issued to them by textbook companies, whose books will increasingly align themselves with the content covered on those tests. If that day comes, teacher educators may be the only ones left with memories and imaginings of education being something different. At that point, we will become even more dangerous to those in power than we are now, and they are already making plans to displace us.

It was this hidden agenda of NCLB that motivated me to produce a second edition of this book. In addition to offering critiques of the multiple ways in which the neoliberal and neoconservative agenda has already registered negative effects on America's schools, I also wanted to include in the book multiple perspectives that readers might draw upon in formulating an alternative vision of education. Transforming schools is a crucial element of any progressive plan for social change along democratic and egalitarian lines.

Those familiar with the first edition will notice that I have changed the book's organization dramatically, moving from three large sections of entries to five. This change relates to how the chapters in each section tell a different part of the story, and I preface each section with a brief description of what part of the story it tells.

Many people deserve acknowledgment for their contributions toward this effort. In particular, I am grateful to the exceptionally talented group of authors who contributed their time and energies to this project. I am also grateful to Naomi Silverman and Erica Kica at Lawrence Erlbaum Associates for their support and patience. Large projects like this one always require more time than any of us would like. I am extremely lucky to work with an administrative assistant as dedicated and competent as Susan O'Beirne. I owe her many thanks for her contributions toward helping me prepare this manuscript.

Last, but certainly not least, I need to thank my wife, Astrid, and our boys, Jacob and Jackson. The time that I have given to this project has been time I have not given to you, and you have all shown tremendous patience, support, and understanding.

David Gabbard
East Carolina University

REFERENCES

Babington, C. (2005, September 10). Some GOP legislators hit jarring notes in addressing Katrina. *Washington Post*. Retrieved January 3, 2006, from http://www.washingtonpost.com/wp-dyn/content/article/2005/09/09/AR2005090901930.html

Bakan, J. (2004). *The corporation: The pathological pursuit of profit and power*. New York: The Free Press.

Bhandari, D. R. (1998). *Plato's concept of justice: An analysis*. Retrieved July 29, 2005, from http://www.bu.edu/wcp/Papers/Anci/AnciBhan.htm

Buras, K. (2005, December). Katrina's early landfall: Exclusionary politics behind the restoration of New Orleans. *Z magazine*. Retrieved January 4, 2006, from http://zmag site.zmag.org/Images/buras1205.html

Chomsky, N. (2004). Noam Chomsky speaks out: Education and power. Retrieved May 1, 2007, from http://ireland.indymedia.org/article/66441.

Davis, M. (2005, October 25). Gentrifying disaster. *Mother Jones*. Retrieved January 3, 2006, from http://www.motherjones.com/comm entary/columns/2005/10/ge ntrifying_disaster.html

Drury, S. (2005). *The political ideas of Leo Strauss*. New York: Palgrave.

Hartman, T. (2004, July 19). *The ghost of Vice President Wallace warns: "It can happen here."* Retrieved January 4, 2006, from http://www.commondreams.org/views04/0719-15.htm

Monaghan, F. (1935). *John Jay: Defender of liberty*. New York: Bobbs-Merrill.

Project for a New American Century. (2000). *Rebuilding America's defenses*. Retrieved January 4, 2006, from http://www.newamericancentury.org/de fensenationalsecurity.htm

Saltman, K. (2001). *Collateral damage: Corporatizing public schools, a threat to democracy*. Lanham, MD: Rowman & Littlefield.

Saltman, K., & Goodman R.T. (2002). *Strange love: Or how we learned to stop worrying and love the market*. Lanham, MD: Rowman & Littlefield.

Saltman, K., & Gabbard, D. (2003). *Education as enforcement: The militarization and corporatization of schools*. New York: Routledge.

Thatcher, M. (1987, October 31). Interview in *Women's Own* magazine. Cited by Deer, B. Epitaph for the eighties? There is no such thing as society. Retrieved July 29, 2005, from http://briandeer.com/social/thatcher-society.htm

Contributors

Karen Anijar
Arizona State University
Tempe, Arizona

Terry S. Atkinson
East Carolina University
Department of Curriculum and
    Instruction
College of Education
Greenville, North Carolina

Robert E. Bahruth
Boise State University
Bilingual Education and ESL
    Program
Boise, Idaho

Mark D. Beatham
State University of New York at
    Plattsburgh
Educational Studies
Plattsburgh, New York

Margarita Berta-Avila
California State University at
    Sacramento
Sacramento, California

Marc Bousquet
Santa Clara University
English Department
Santa Clara, California

Jeanne F. Brady
St. Joseph's University
College of Arts and Sciences
Philadelphia, Pennsylvania

Felicia M. Briscoe
University of Texas–San Antonio
San Antonio, Texas

Laurence W. Britt
Fairport, New York

Richard Brosio
University of Wisconsin–Milwaukee
Glendale, Wisconsin

Kristen L. Buras
Emory University
Atlanta, Georgia

Karen Cadiero-Kaplan
San Diego State University
San Diego, California

Thuy Dao Jensen
Arizona State University
Tempe, Arizona

Dewey I. Dykstra, Jr.
Boise State University
Department of Physics
Boise, Idaho

Takis Fotopoulos
*International Journal of Inclusive
   Democracy*
London, United Kingdom

Marilyn Frankenstein
University of Massachusetts
Boston College of Public and
   Community Service
Boston, Massachusetts

David Gabbard
East Carolina University
Department of Curriculum and
   Instruction
School of Education
Greenville, North Carolina

James Wesley Garrison
Virginia Polytechnic Institute and
   State University
Department of Teaching and
   Learning
Blacksburg, Virginia

Gwendolyn A. Guy
East Carolina University
Greenville, North Carolina

Eric Haas
University of Connecticut
Neag School of Education
Storrs, Connecticut

Matt Hern
Institute for Social Ecology
Vancouver
British Columbia, Canada

Dave Hill
University College Northampton
Institute for Education Policy
   Studies
Northampton, United Kingdom

Patricia H. Hinchey
Pennsylvania State University
Dunmore, Pennsylvania

David Hursh
University of Rochester
The Warner School
Rochester, New York

Four Arrows (aka Don Trent Jacobs)
Fielding Graduate University
Flagstaff, Arizona

Kathleen Kesson
Long Island University
School of Education
New York, New York

Michele Knobel
Montclair State University
Early Childhood, Elementary and
   Literacy Education
Montclair, New Jersey

Philip Kovacs
University of Alabama–Huntsville
Huntsville, Alabama

Sharon D. Kruse
University of Akron
Akron, Ohio

Colin Lankshear
James Cook University
School of Education
Cairns, Australia

John Jota Leaños
Arizona State University
Xicana Studies
Tempe, Arizona

Pepi Leistyna
University of Massachusetts–Boston
Boston, Massachusetts

Sheila Landers Macrine
St. Joseph's University
Philadelphia, Pennsylvania

Sandra Mathison
University of British Columbia
Vancouver
British Columbia, Canada

Curry Malott
State University of New
York–Buffalo
Buffalo, New York

Peter McLaren
University of California–Los
Angeles
Graduate School of Education
Los Angeles, California

Tom Munk
University of North Carolina–
Chapel Hill
Chapel Hill, North Carolina

Susan Ohanian
Vermont Society for the Study of
Education
Charlotte, Vermont

Thomas C. Pedroni
Utah State University
Department of Secondary
Education
Logan, Utah

William F. Pinar
University of British Columbia
Department of Curriculum Studies
Vancouver
British Columbia, Canada

Madhu Suri Prakash
Pennsylvania State University
University Park, Pennsylvania

Sandra Spickard Prettyman
University of Akron
Department of Educational
Foundations
Akron, Ohio

Mark Pruyn
New Mexico State University
Department of Curriculum and
Instruction
College of Education
Las Cruces, New Mexico

Kathleen Rhoades
Boston College
Boston, Massachusetts

E. Wayne Ross
University of British Columbia
Department of Curriculum Studies
Vancouver
British Columbia, Canada

Kenneth J. Saltman
DePaul University
School of Education
Chicago, Illinois

George N. Schmidt
Substance
Chicago, Illinois

Sandra Schneider
Virginia Polytechnic Institute and
State University
Blacksburg, Virginia

Joel Spring
Queens College and Graduate
Center
City University of New York
Mt. Vernon, New York

Dana L. Stuchul
Pennsylvania State Universtiy
University Park, Pennsylvania

Juha Suoranta
University of Tampere
Tampere, Finland

Anthony J. Villarreal
University of California–Santa
Cruz
Santa Cruz, California

Kathleen Weiler
Tufts University
Department of Education
Medford, Massachusetts

Part I

POLITICAL AND SOCIAL FOUNDATIONS

1. Democracy
2. Socialism
3. Liberalism
4. Neoliberalism
5. Conservatism
6. Neoconservatism
7. Fascism
8. Global Economy
9. Class
10. Gender
11. Race
12. Sexuality

This book addresses the convergence of neoliberalism and neoconservatism, and how this convergence has defined educational reform for more
than a quarter century. In telling this story, some of the chapters will allude
to the broader social and ecological impacts registered by the forces driven
by these ideologies; for they have, since the 1970s and as a consequence
of the eminence of the plutocratic masters whom they serve, dominated
the political arena, not only within the United States but globally. If the
economic liberalism of the 17th to 19th and even the early 20th centuries
signaled an elevation of economic imperatives (i.e., individual/private/cor-
porate profit) above social/public/communal relations and commitments,
neoliberalism represents a reinvigorated program of economic "shock and
awe" designed to demolish and bury anyone who dares challenge market
hegemony. In this light, as David Hursh explains in Chapter 4, we can best
understand neoliberalism as a political project launched and sustained by
economic elites (plutocrats) in order to restore and permanently secure

1

what neoconservatives help them recognize as their natural right to dominate everyone and everything. This drive to dominate, stemming from
the principles of rabid individualism and uncompromising heteronomy
endemic to the market and its viral imperative toward growth and expansion, situates the neoliberal project at clear odds with democracy and its
principles of sociopolitical autonomy and community. Hence, Part I discusses neoliberalism, neoconservatism, and four other political ideologies within the parameters of democracy and global economy/the market.
Each of these ideologies demonstrates a different approach toward the
resolution of the conflict between democracy and the market taken up by
James Garrison and Sandra Schneider in the first chapter. Socialism, as
Dave Hill explains in Chapter 2, in strongly favoring the democratic principles of autonomy and community, treats democracy and capitalism as
incommensurable. One must triumph over the other. Liberalism, Richard
Brosio notes in Chapter 3, acknowledges the conflict between democratic
values and market values, but it, like a child attempting to restrain a raging
rottweiler on a leash, vainly works toward a compromise solution. Thomas
Pedroni helps us see in Chapter 5 that one strand of what we now call
conservatism has been economically liberal in its policies, leaning toward
recognizing the inherent right of private wealth and privilege to reproduce
and expand its wealth and privilege. There are, however, other strains of
conservative thought equally committed to the principles of individualism
(e.g., members of the National Rifle Association) and heteronomy (e.g.,
nationalistic militarists as well as fundamentalist, evangelical, and domin-
ionist Christians) whose members the neoconservatives have duped into
forming an unwitting populist base behind the hyperneoliberalism of the
Republican Party. As opposed to socialism and even liberalism, neoliberals, conservatives, and neoconservatives heavily favor the hegemony of the
market over democracy. Larry Britt's chapter on fascism asks us to ponder
how far to the right we have drifted and how much further to the right we
can drift before declaring the convergence of neoliberalism and neoconservatism to mark the emergence of fascism in America. As Kristen Buras
describes in her chapter on neoconservatism's history and its educational
expression within the core knowledge movement, today's "Neocons" trace
their origins back to the 1930s and the intellectual circles of Jewish socialists. Over time, these intellectuals moved further to the political right. They
did not, however, achieve significant influence within elite policy-planning
circles until their expressed contempt over the balkanization of American
culture created by the populist movements of the 1960s made them natural allies in the neoliberal cause to roll back democracy and programs (i.e.,
Roosevelt's New Deal and Johnson's Great Society programs) created to
soften the blows of market brutality. Pepi Leistyna, Kathleen Weiler, Gwen
Guy, and Bill Pinar, in their chapters on class, gender, race, and sexuality,
respectively, describe how the economic politics of neoliberalism and the

cultural politics of neoconservatism have registered their impacts on skins of our society's most vulnerable populations.

Chapter 1

Democracy

James Wesley Garrison and Sandra Schneider
Virginia Polytechnic Institute and State University

While many nations have secured the conditions for democracy, and some have succeeded in advancing their democracy within the narrow confines of its founding ideology, none seem able to explore conceptions of democracy beyond the purely formal and institutional. We believe democracy, even in the best of times, should be ever-changing, growing, and creative, for, as we draw closer to realizing some ideal, new and better possibilities always emerge. Alas, however, we fear these are the worst of times, for many agree with Francis Fukuyama that we are at the end of history and, therefore, at the end of hope for a better, more vital, and dynamic democracy.

In her delightful book *Deep Democracy* (1999), Judith M. Green argues that purely formal democracy has led to nihilism and ontological rootlessness, producing such social pathologies as racism, poverty, militarism, insecurity, apathy, pleasure seeking and pain killing, sound bite politics, and the "commodity-focused hype of the profit-motivated mass media" that teach us to confuse having more with being more (p. vii). She concludes that such social developments reveal how the ideological hollowness of purely formal democratic institutions renders them "operationally subvertible," leaving them without a deeply democratic social grounding (p. vi). As a corrective for these failings, Green calls for communities of diversity and transformation. This tradition has a long — if largely ignored — history that we wish to explore as one possibility among others for escaping the narrow ideological confines of formal democracy assumed by traditional liberals, libertarians, neoliberals, and neoconservatives alike. Of course, others will want to explore other alternatives, and we strongly endorse such pluralism. We seek to broaden the horizon of possibility by releasing moral imagination in ways that allow us all to respond more creatively to the

5

tyrannical constraints placed upon contemporary democratic discourse and educational practice.

We turn first to the poet Walt Whitman's *Democratic Vistas* (1871) to catch a glimpse of deep, communal, creative, even spiritual democracy. In this essay, Whitman asserts that American democracy has passed through two critical though insufficient stages of development. "The First stage," he writes, "was the planning and putting on record the political foundations of rights of immense masses of people.... This is the American programme, not for classes, but for universal man [*sic*]" (p. 544). He has in mind such formal documents as the Declaration of Independence, the Constitution, as well as the formal structures of government that ensure life, liberty, and the pursuit of happiness. While many confuse democracy with the purely formal documents that sanction it, Whitman does not.

"The Second stage," Whitman explains, "relates to material prosperity, wealth, produce, labor-saving machines ... intercommunication and trade ... books, newspapers, a currency for money circulation, etc" (p. 544). Whitman understood, however, that setting up the social technologies for democratic governance and the productive technologies for the elimination of want would fall far short of what he viewed as America's promise until the nation passed through a third stage of development. In this sense, Whitman's essay offers a prophecy of an America yet to be, calling for a loving, caring community of a kind we call spiritual democracy.

For Whitman, spirituality meant establishing more intimate relations with the world around us, especially other people, in a universe wherein our creative acts matter in the course of cosmos. It did not mean an individual's relation with something absolute outside space and time; Whitman was too embodied a poet for that. Spiritual democracy is a pluralistic democracy that seeks to create with a commonwealth of public goods devoted to human growth, wherein individuals may make a unique, creative contribution in community with others different from them. It is a community of body and feeling as well as thought and action.

Whitman's historical perspective helps us better understand the contemporary crisis of democracy as a spiritual crisis — what Green calls nihilism and ontological rootlessness — brought about by excessive emphasis on the material and purely formal conditions of democracy along with economic utilitarianism. When we examine the philosophical foundations of modern democracies, however, we see that the roots of this crisis may run deeper.

Most modern democracies constitute themselves according to the liberal thinking of Grotius, Hobbes, Locke, and Rousseau, among others. Influenced by the Protestant reformation, these thinkers viewed individuals as isolated and detached at birth from any community, born with a number of innate qualities: an innate (usually calculative and utilitarian) rationality whose role is to serve the individual's innate desires, as well as an innate free will and natural rights that must be reigned in by a social contract to assuage the war of all against all. Unlike classical thinkers such as Aristotle and the medieval scholastics that relied on him, the modern concept of innate rationality places little emphasis on deliberative intelligence that functions to distinguish the truly desirable from the immediately desired. For Aristotle, the role of deliberative intelligence entailed helping the individual live a life of expanding meaning and value in community with others. The sole function of utilitarian rationality, on the other hand, is to seek individual pleasure and avoid personal pain.

Liberal modernity's notion of freedom, then, is purely negative, casting freedom solely in terms of freedom *from* restraint. In stark contrast to the more classical model of deliberative rationality, this notion of freedom makes us slaves of our unreflective desires. Modern liberalism lacks a notion of positive freedom *for* some ideal, which requires deliberation and discipline. No wonder the Constitution of the United States of America was amended early on by what is known today as the Bill of Rights, which does nothing to help us form any sense of responsibility to ourselves, much less others and the larger national community. Concomitantly, the idea of a global economy (e.g., the Triangle Trade that preceded the American Revolution) easily accommodates modern liberalism's negative notion of freedom, (nothing must impede the individual's or corporation's freedom/natural right to pursue profit), but such negative freedom (e.g., freedom *from* regulation on behalf of the supposedly common good) frustrates rather than promotes a global democracy.

Likewise, traditional liberal anthropology portrays the universal essence of "man" as existing apart from the influence of material conditions, history, custom, and tradition. The basic ideology derived from this anthropology characterizes liberal democracies up to the present time. Libertarians argue that we should retain this anthropology and not progress beyond the original intent of the founders of our democracy. Clearly, however, the founders did not intend to enfranchise indigenous people, blacks, or women, or even white males without sufficient property. When these peoples did become enfranchised, it was assumed they shared the same presumably universal anthropological essence, and therefore should be coerced into following the same ideology.

As pointed out by David Hursh in Chapter 4, neoliberals do not question any of the fundamental assumptions of liberalism, though they do tend to insist that all rationality is calculative and utilitarian. In much the same spirit as Adam Smith, who believed the "invisible hand" of the market ensures the just distribution of goods, the Deism of America's founders committed them to some form of the argument from design, which holds that an intelligent being created the world according to "his" plan. This plan, according to Deist beliefs, accounted not only for the natural order, but the moral order as well. With powerful moneyed interests backing the religious right in its claims for intelligent design over Charles Darwin and contemporary evolutionary biology, the design argument has reclaimed a degree of popularity at the beginning of the 21st century. This should hardly surprise us, given the extent to which classical liberals and neoliberals agree that the brain of the intelligent being that created the universe also guides the invisible hand of the market.

Like traditional liberals, the function of rationality for neoliberals is to aid individuals to satisfy their desires for whatever goods and services they find valuable. As Hursh explains so effectively in his entry in this volume on neoliberalism (see Chapter 4), neoliberal ideology reduces the public exercise of free will to market choice. In the market, atomistic individuals may satisfy their desires insofar as they are best able to exercise calculative rationality. If calculative rationality is the only kind of rationality that exists, then all values must be commensurable. The traditional assumption, however, is that value spheres of science, aesthetics, and ethics are incommensurable. In his essay "The Market as God (1999)," Harvard theologian Harvey Cox suggests that the market has come to possess the omnipotent, omniscient, and omnipresent properties that previously were attributed to our father in heaven. Because our father, hallowed be his name, is now in the marketplace, all values— ethical, aesthetic, or cognitive — become market values. That means they must have a price, hence a cash value. Cash always comes in whole numbers, and such numbers are always commensurable, hence always calculable.

Cox argues that the market performs reverse transubstantiation by giving everything a commensurable market value as a commodity. Some of his examples include body organs, Mother Earth, and the jeweled casket said to contain the remains of Saint Thomas Becket, which was placed on sale at Sotheby's by the railway pension fund that owned it. Bought by a Canadian, the British government violated the will of the market by blocking the sale of this revered sacred relic and national treasure. Consistent neoliberals would see this governmental act as sacrilegious. We anticipate the day when our nation's Constitution comes up for sale because we no longer feel we need it. Of course, we have been copyrighting cognition for over a century, and universities now copyright "intellectual property." Aesthetic objects have always been for sale, and institutions of ethical obligation to the community, such as state universities, are now in the market.

Once all values are commensurable, all value choices become matters of mere calculation. As with traditional liberals, neoliberals denigrate, or at best ignore, the kind of deliberative rationality that would allow us to distinguish objects unreflectively valued from the truly valuable, while planning for the unborn members of the tribe. When we go to the grocery store, deliberation is required to choose between incommensurable values such as the aesthetics of taste and appearance, nutritional value, weight maintenance, environmental preservation, vegetarianism versus meat eating, cost, desire to support workers unions, and desire to keep all members of one's family content (see Mousavi and Garrison, 2003). Amazingly, a world designed by a neoliberal God does not require such deliberation. Tragedy often occurs when we must choose between incommensurable values, but there is no tragedy in a well-designed neoliberal world.

One might wonder what all of this economic talk has to do with democracy. The answer is simple. If the market is God and can transubstantiate all value domains into a calculable price, then there is no reason the ethical domain of democracy should be exempt. We vote in the market when we make purchases; therefore, the market is the most reliable way to translate the will of the people. Bill Gates has a net worth of about $90 billion, which happens to be about the net worth of our nation's 100 million poorest people. Of course, this destroys the liberal ideal of one man, one vote, but since the founding fathers only had propertied gentlemen in mind, the difference is not what it appears. It is about here, though, that we begin to approach neoconservatism, so we will break off to examine neoliberal schooling.

Such legislation as No Child Left Behind aptly reflects the function of schools as conceived by neoliberals. The emphasis on testing relies on the famous educational psychologist E. L. Thorndike, who stated his metaphysical commitment to measurement thus: "Whatever exists, exists in some amount. To measure it is simply to know its varying amounts" (cited in Joncich, 1968, p. 282). If everything is measurable, then nothing is incommensurable; hence, everything is calculable, including the relative worth of human beings. Meanwhile, the emphasis on standards does for human resources in the 21st century what standardization did for natural resources in the 19th century, which is to provide standardized, interchangeable parts for the production function.

While neoliberalism is the immediate, pressing, and most publicly visible political force in transforming democracy in the United States, the rising influence of neoconservatism is potentially the most devastating. Neoconservatives reject liberalism altogether. For them, "life, liberty, and the pursuit of happiness" is simply an invitation to licentiousness. Freedom defined as market choice, especially as is promoted by media such as MTV, spans the decadence of the human spirit. The undisciplined masses are simply unfit for liberty. Given that liberalism knows only negative freedom *from* restraint, which makes us slaves of our unreflective desires, while denigrating deliberation and the discipline of positive freedom, the neoconservatives have a case.

The neoconservatives believe only a small elite has the wisdom to rule because only they can bear the burden of the truth. The vulgar, however, have become so powerful in even our limited modern democracies that it is only possible to control them by indirection, using the "noble lie" conveyed by various media to shape the will of the people to the higher purposes of their leaders. The elitism of the neoconservatives converges with that of not only the neoliberals, but also some traditional liberals, making their combined political force immensely powerful. All three agree that if we are realistic, powerful elites, or at least technocratic experts, should rule *for* the people, thereby abandoning the ideal of government *by* the people.

For now, the goals of neoconservatives and neoliberals go together fairly well. Liberals believe in meritocracy, so, by their logic, we may use tests and tracking to sort students by ability, proper upbringing, and motivation. In this way, a natural elite of the wise will emerge. On this model, the upper class is not necessarily permanent, but is unlikely to change very much from generation to generation. Those who rise from the lower classes will provide the administrative, scientific, and technical expertise. We must not forget that the original intent of the founding fathers was to limit democracy to a relatively small number of white males with sufficient property and leisure to engage in good government. As already indicated, expanding the franchise has not always altered the basic pattern.

Neoliberals claim that they want democracy decided by the natural laws of the marketplace, but data clearly indicate that over the last 20 years the middle class has been shrinking with more dropping down than going up. What neoliberals really want, or at least where their policies will take us, is plutocracy or government by the wealthy. Neoconservatives want an oligarchy of the wise. We believe that what we will get is plutocrats claiming they are wise. Whatever happens, it could well leave us with the specter of democratic forms serving as means to undemocratic ends.

Neither neoliberals nor neoconservatives embrace expansive, pluralistic community. Neoliberals are too committed to atomistic individuality to value the public commons beyond the marketplace, while neoconservatives have no need of community beyond their own kind, and hence do not require a commons at all. We will look at three different ways of conceiving community, the last two of which are instances of deep democracy.

Those influenced by postmodernism tend to reject all forms of liberalism or conservatism. They often concern themselves, sensibly, with the status of the other. Communities, they argue, tend to reduce all differences to the norms of some totalizing sameness. Iris Marion Young is an example. Her problem with liberal community is its notion of static fixed selves wherein individuals are valued depending on their conformity to some ideal fixed norm (e.g., rationality, moral conduct, etc.) that establishes a social hierarchy. She would discard the ideal of community in favor of the "unoppressive city," which specifies no shared values at all other than the rejection of oppression. Young would rely on largely formal public institutions to mediate among differences instead of engaging in face-to-face civic community (see Young, 1990). While we acknowledge that some conversations sometimes cannot happen, and at other times are too dangerous to the subaltern, we are unwilling to abandon the goods of communicative democracy. Besides, we wonder how people living in the unoppressive city came to share such a wonderful value as the rejection of all oppression without engaging in many successful dialogues. While dialogues across difference are always dangerous, the alternatives are usually even riskier (see Garrison, 1996). We believe Young's criticisms are correct with regard to traditional liberal and neoliberal notions of community as well as religious communitarians such as Alasdair MacIntyre (1984) and elitist neoconservative communitarians such as Allan Bloom (1987). We will not discuss Bloom's notion of community, since it is easy to infer from even our brief characterization of neoconservatism, but we do want to look at religious communities.

It is a terrible mistake to underestimate the impact of religious, even evangelical, communities as agents of democratic social amelioration, though their stance has shifted considerably in recent decades. These communities respond to the nihilism and ontological rootlessness of purely formal democratic society by rejecting atomistic individualism and questioning the limits of rationalism while refusing to restrict free will to market choice. However, such communities often tend toward monism and stagnation rather than diversity and transformation in ways that lead to exclusion and even persecution of those deemed different. They do tend to reduce all differences to the norms of their sameness. Nonetheless, monistic communities, religious or not, have long been a bulwark against the excesses of liberalism and aristocratic conservatism and will continue to resist neoliberals and neoconservatives. Anyone who has engaged in community organization knows the importance of the church, synagogue, and mosque. Anyone trying to come to grips with knowledge and power in the global community can only ignore religious community at his or her peril.

We will end by returning to the ideal of spiritual democracy as an example of communities of diversity and transformation capable of overcoming nihilism and ontological rootlessness without yielding to monism or stagnation. We find similar versions of such deep democracy in John Dewey, who wrote that "democracy is a name for a life of free and enriching communion. It had its seer in Walt Whitman. It will have its consummation when free social inquiry is indissolubly wedded to the art of full and moving communication" (1927/1984, p. 350). We also find it in the work of Jane Addams and her colleagues at Hull House, as well as in the contemporary writings of Cornel West. For these thinkers, minds emerge through participation in the social practices of the community and selves arise from taking the attitude of others in conversation.

Spirituality for Whitman meant caring, creative community, which requires three things. First, it requires leveling, by which he meant moral equality. While some may have more physical and intellectual ability than others, everyone is morally equal and has an equal right to actualize whatever powers he or she possesses to make a contribution. Secondly, there is idiocracy, meaning that each individual is unique and should have the right to exercise his or her creative individuality. Finally, there is adhesion, by which he meant love. We believe that some form of socialism is necessary to establish the kind of fair distribution of wealth and social services upon which caring, adhesive community depends. Only such communities can overcome the nihilism and ontological rootlessness that, with Judith Green, we feel characterizes all merely formal democracies.

For Whitman, the goal of diverse community of idiosyncratic democrats is to release individual human potential to make its unique creative contribution to the community. The dialogues release potential across differences among those who tell the story of their lives using a different vocabulary, grammar, and plot lines. Ideally, this would allow everyone to create unique story lines, thereby becoming the authors of their own lives, and hence capable of making uniquely valuable contributions to the endless poem that is dynamic democracy. Whitman realized that to love ourselves well, we must love others, but to love others well, we must love ourselves.

REFERENCES

Bloom, A. (1987). *The closing of the American mind.* New York: Simon & Schuster.

Cox, H. (1999, March). The market as god. *The Atlantic Monthly,* 18–23.

Dewey, J. (1984). The public and its problems. In J. A. Boydston (Ed.), *John Dewey: The later works* (Vol. 2, pp. 235–372). Carbondale, IL: Southern Illinois University Press. (Original work published 1927.)

Garrison, J. (1996). A Deweyan theory of democratic listening. *Educational Theory, 46,* 429–451.

Green, J. (1999). *Deep democracy: Community, diversity, and transformation.* Lanham, MD: Rowman & Littlefield Publishers.

Joncich, G. (1968). *The sane positivist.* Middleton, CT: Wesleyan University Press.

MacIntyre, A. (1984). *After virtue* (2nd ed.). South Bend, IN: Notre Dame University Press.

Mousavi, S., & Garrison, J. (2003). Toward a transactional theory of decision making: Creative rationality as functional coordination in context. *Journal of Economic Methodology, 10,* 131–156.

Young, I. M. (1990). The ideal of community and the politics of difference. In L. J. Nicholson (Ed.), *Feminism/postmodernism* (pp. 300–326). New York: Routledge.

Chapter 2

Socialism

Dave Hill
University College of Northampton

There are many versions of socialism, just like there are many versions of Christianity or Conservatism or Islam. What socialists agree on, and what motivates them, is a desire for more equality. Horrified by the obvious inequalities between rich and poor, between bosses and workers, socialists seek, in particular, more equality for the working class. Socialist analysis concludes that it is essentially the working class that produces the actual wealth in society, that capitalists exploit workers' labor power to appropriate surplus value from the labor of the ("raced" and gendered) working class. The capitalist system — with a tiny minority of people owning the means of production — oppresses and exploits the working class. This, indeed, constitutes the essence of capitalism: the extraction of surplus value — and profit — from workers by capitalist employers.

Capitalism may be more or less racist. It may be more or less sexist. Capitalism can cope with nonracism, even if racism is currently rampant and lethal in many countries and periods of history. It can cope with equal opportunities for women and gender equality, even if sexism and misogyny are similarly widespread. Capitalism cannot, however, cope with equality between the exploiter class and the exploited class. Capitalism, in its essence, depends on class exploitation for its survival.

SOCIAL DEMOCRATS

There are three main currents (and many subcurrents) on the left, internationally and historically. From the most moderate to the most left wing, they are Social Democrats, socialists, and communists. Confusingly, both communists and many socialists call themselves Marxist.

Some on the left want things a bit more equal in terms of outcomes, such as SAT results, income, wealth, Medicare for all, and a welfare state. And they usually want a meritocracy, a situation where people, regardless of (raced and gendered) social class, can progress educationally and occupationally as a result of their effort and ability, rather than as a result of their social class (or gender or race or religion). Richard Brosio addresses the limits of this traditional liberalism in the next chapter.

The means by which these Social Democrats of the center-left seek to achieve this good life and good society is usually by *regulating capital*, making sure it meets certain standards regarding safety, the environment, workers' rights and conditions and pay, and profits. Social Democrats are happy with the capitalist system — they just want it to be fairer, with a progressive taxation system, with the rich paying a bigger percentage of their income than the ordinary worker. They do not see capitalism as *the* problem, or even *a* problem in society. They react solely to its excesses. Because they wish to humanize or moderate capitalism rather than replace it, they are parliamentarist — content to take part in elections, use the state to introduce social reforms, and embark on a peaceful, electoral road to social democracy. In the late 19th and early 20th centuries the German Social Democratic Party (SPD) became the first of many mass workers' parties. Under Eduard Bernstein, it abandoned Marxist ideas of socialist revolution. Members of this movement came to be known as Revisionists, for they revised Marx's ideas of revolution and proletarian democracy out of existence — much to the anger of their more Marxist contemporaries, such as Rosa Luxemburg.

Within a few years after the Bolshevik Revolution in Russia in October 1917, the world socialist movement split in two, dividing into a pro-Russian revolutionary socialist or communist party with membership in the Third International, which was largely controlled by the Soviet Union, and a social democratic or labor party affiliated with the Second International. At times, these two international groups — and discrete parties within individual countries — have cooperated with each other as elements of a united front. For instance, they joined together in the fight against fascism in the 1930s and in popular front governments in Spain (prior to and during the Spanish Civil War of 1936–1939) and in France and Chile. At other times, the two groups of socialists entered into bitter conflict with each other, with, at one stage in the late 1920s and early 1930s, the communist parties calling the Social Democrats "social fascists."

Social Democrats ruled most of Western Europe between 1945 and the crisis of capital of the early 1970s. The form of governance was a form of corporatism — a broad agreement among trade unions, capital/employers, and government. That consensus recognized the need for full employment, a welfare state, and a general dampening of the class war through negotiations. In this period of economic growth, general profits were increased, as were workers' wages and the social wage offered by the welfare state. However, with the decline in profits, the crisis of capital accumulation of the 1970s, many Social Democrat parties, such as New Labour governments under Tony Blair in Britain since 1997, have become more like center-right parties, espousing neoliberal and neoconservative policies such as the privatization and marketization of public services rather than center-left redistributionist policies.

Social Democrats, at various times in the last 100 years, have governed most countries in Western Europe and Australasia. All of these governments of the center-left usually established a minimum wage and a welfare state that included tax-supported national health systems, unemployment pay, old-age pensions, free university tuition and schooling, and child and maternity benefits. They also established state control of some essential services, such as railways, gas supply, electricity supply, some of the broadcasting/television networks, and sometimes strategic industry such as coal mining. In some countries these parties' programs were substantially socialist, such as with the Labour government of Clement Atlee in the United Kingdom between 1945 and 1950, which nationalized a fifth of the British economy, and the Socialist Party–Communist Party *Union de la Gauche* under Francois Mitterand in France.

The most advanced welfare systems today are in Scandinavia — Finland, Sweden, Norway, and Denmark. Sweden has usually been ruled by the Social Democrats since the 1930s. In these countries, the Gini coefficient, the measurement of the gap between the richest and the poorest in any country, is the lowest in the world. That is to say, these are some of the most equal countries in the world. A high Gini coefficient figure signals the high levels of inequality within a country. In 2006, the Gini coefficient for the United States was 45. For Britain it was 37. The EU average was 32, falling as low as 25 in Sweden (Choonara, 2006).

Today, the United States and the United Kingdom are two of the most unequal societies in the developed world. British poverty rates, about 13%, approach those in the United States, which are almost 18%. The figure for those living in poverty in social democratic Scandinavia is 5% (Choonara, 2006).

In some respects, the New Deal legislation of Franklin D. Roosevelt and the Great Society project of Lyndon Johnson in the 1960s moved the United States in the direction of social democracy.

The American Context

The United States is very unusual among advanced capitalist countries, in that the term *socialist* is often used as a term of abuse. In most advanced capitalist countries it is regarded as a perfectly legitimate and respectable set of ideas, ideology, and political organizations. Even more so, the term *Marxist*, in the United States, is scarcely used, except as an insult. For example, many Marxist educators in the United States prefer to be known as critical educators, or as Marxian, to avoid the label of Marxist, which has been more thoroughly demonized in America than anywhere in the world.

And yet there was a notable socialist presence in the United States at the beginning of the 20th century.

> From 1901 to the onset of World War I, the Socialist Party was arguably the most successful third party in the United States of the 20th century, with a thousands local elected officials. There were two Socialist members of congress, Meyer London of New York and Victor Berger of Wisconsin; over 70 mayors, and many state legislators and city councilors. Socialist organizations were strongest in the midwestern and plains states, particularly Oklahoma and Wisconsin. (Wikipedia, 2006)

Socialist Party candidate Eugene Debs polled 6% of the popular vote in the 1912 presidential election. Socialists in the United States were again stronger as part of the New Left in the 1960s and 1970s, generally supporting the candidacy for president of Democratic Party candidate George McGovern.

The largest group of socialists in the United States currently is the Democratic Socialists of America (DSA), who are part of the left wing of the Democrat Party. There are many much smaller groups, such as the World Socialist Party, Socialist Party, Socialist Workers' Party, Socialist Altenative, and International Socialist Organization, which has ties to the largest of the Marxist parties in Britain today — the Socialist Workers' Party.

Socialists and Marxists

Some people want a far more equal society, one where workers (whether blue collar or white collar) not only have a meritocratic society in which effort and ability are rewarded, but where levels of educational attainment, income, wealth, and life expectancy are far more equal than at present. These are usually called socialists.

Some socialists believe that significant parts of the economy — but not all of it — should be collectively controlled by the state, or the local state, for example, instead of being owned and controlled for the economic benefit of the owners or senior management, such as chief executive officers (CEOs), who are part of the capitalist class, owning, via salary, shares, and share options, substantial parts of the corporation. Socialist slogans in many countries are such as "Public Need Not Private Profit" with respect to health and education services, rail and transport services, and postal services. Other socialists, more left wing, more Marxist, wish to see an end to capitalism, a society where there are no capitalists exploiting and profiting from the labor power (the skills, attitudes, work) of workers, a society and economy where the employer is the collective.

Socialists also disagree on rewards in society, such as pay levels and inequalities. Some want, as in some subsistence economies, "from each according to her/his ability, and to each according to her/his need" as called for in the *Communist Manifesto* (1848) written by Karl Marx and Friedrich Engels. These scientific socialists or classical Marxists adhere to what they treat as a strict orthodoxy in Marx's vision of an eventual communist society, where communism replaces or supplants capitalism. Marx elaborated this vision of "the higher phase of communist society" that would come after the temporary phase of socialism in his *Critique of the Gotha Programme*. As Marx put it,

> In the higher phase of communist society, when the enslaving subordination of the individual to the division of labour, and with it the antithesis between mental and physical labour, has vanished; when labour is no longer merely a means of life but has become life's principal need; when the productive forces have also increased with the all-round development of the individual, and all the springs of co-operative wealth flow more abundantly — only then will it be possible completely to transcend the narrow outlook of the bourgeois right, and only then will society be able to inscribe on its banners: From each according to his ability, to each according to his needs. (1875/1978, p. 263)

Most people who call themselves Marxist might be more appropriately termed Marxian. They work within a developing Marxist tradition, but do not necessarily see final answers in what Marx (and Engels) wrote in the 19th century (even if works like the *Communist Manifesto* are amazingly prescient about globalization, capitalism, capitalization, and exploitation). For example, Marx and Engels wrote that capitalism has an in-built tendency to constantly expand:

> The markets kept ever growing, the demand ever rising.... The place of manufacture was taken by the giant, Modern Industry, the place of the industrial middle class, by industrial millionaires.... Modern industry has established the world-market. The need of a constantly expanding market for its products chases the bourgeoisie over the whole surface of the globe. It must nestle everywhere, settle everywhere, establish connexions everywhere.... In one word, it creates a world after its own image. (Marx and Engels, 1847/1977, pp. 37–39)

Other Marxists — or Marxians — wish for collective control of the economy, but accept what they see as a need for differentials in rewards.

There are many examples of pre-Marxian egalitarianism and socialism, such as the Spartacist revolt in Ancient Rome; the Levellers and the Diggers during the Cromwellian Revolution in England, 1640 to 1660; the Babeuf Plotters during the French Revolution of 1789 and after; the utopian socialists of the 18th and 19th centuries described by Engels (1892/1977) in *Socialism: Utopian and Scientific*.

But the analysis used by socialists worldwide today is usually a variant of, or derived from, Marxism. This analysis shows that we live in a capitalist society and economy in which the capitalists — those who own the banks, factories, media, corporations, businesses — profit from exploiting the workers. This analysis also demonstrates that class conflict, which is an essential feature of capitalist society, will result in an overthrow of capitalism (whether by revolutionary force or by evolutionary measures and steps) and the coming to power of the working class. Classical Marxists believe that after a transitional stage of socialism the final stage of communism described by Marx above will come into being.

COMMUNISTS

The word *communist* is now usually taken to refer to the particular Soviet Russian form of communism or Marxism. That is a one-party dictatorship, variously described by other Marxists as a "Party-State," "a deformed workers' state," or, as leading Trotskyite Tony Cliff (1974) analyzed it, "state capitalism." Until the crimes of Stalin, the Soviet ruler from 1924 to 1953, were revealed (in 1956), most Marxists were happy to call themselves communists and headed many progressive and antiracist movements and campaigns and trade unions and struggles for decent pay and working conditions. Many were beaten by anti-union goons (thugs) in the United States as described in Steinbeck's filmed novel *Grapes of Wrath*, in films such as *Matewan* and *Harlan County USA*, and the filmed French novel by Emile Zole, *Germinal*. In the 1930s, many communists (and other Marxists) from North America and Europe joined the International Brigade and, as depicted in George Orwell's book *Homage to Catalonia* and in Ken Loach's film *Bread and Roses*, died in defense of democracy against fascism in the Spanish Civil War.

As soon as the horrors of the Stalinist terror in the Soviet Union became known, many communists and socialists throughout the world, including in the United States and Western Europe — felt the noble ideal of socialism or communism had been betrayed. Strong groups within the International Marxist and International Socialist movement took (and take) the position of "neither Washington nor Moscow." This was the position of one of the largest Marxist groups in Britain, the International Socialists. (Like most Marxist groups, they went through various name changes. They are now the Socialist Workers' Party.)

In parts of developing countries such as Peru, India, and Nepal, Maoist versions of Marxism continue to be active. These identify the peasantry as the revolutionary class, not the industrial workers, and engage in armed revolutionary insurrection. And there are one-party communist states such as China, Vietnam, Laos, and Cuba, as well as the sole surviving Stalinist dictatorship of North Korea.

The membership rolls of Marxist groups in countries like the United States, Britain, and France pale in comparison to the numbers of previous eras. And the disputes between some of the tiny grouplets make those between the Judean Popular People's Front and the People's Front of Judea, a satire within the Monty Python film *The Life of Brian* (1979), seem like a meeting of long-lost friends.

But all big movements start off small. Furthermore, the mainstream media never report on the millions of people around the world who do vote for socialist and communist political parties. Democratically elected communists and Marxists have governed the Indian states of Kerala and West Bengal for most of the last 50 years. In Indonesia, prior to the U.S.- and British-inspired mass killings of a million communists, the Indonesian Communist Party had over 3 million members. In Sri Lanka, a Trotskyite Party, the LSSP, was the largest opposition party at various times between 1946 and 1970.

And currently, country after country in Latin America is freely electing leftist presidents and governments of various hues. The most socialist is Hugo Chavez in Venezuela. As Stuart Munckton (2006) reports,

> The government of socialist President Hugo Chavez, elected in 1998, has led the poor majority in a battle to take control of Venezuela's resources and put them to use to overcome crippling poverty and underdevelopment. When Chavez began introducing reforms that benefited the poor over the rich, the local elite and multinationals — backed by the U.S. government — responded with repeated attempts to overthrow the government.
>
> The resistance to any encroachment on their power by the capitalist elite has radicalized Venezuela's poor, who have come to realize that it is impossible to achieve change simply by electing a government and getting it to enact reforms. The Venezuelan people have been forced to take the road of revolution and fight for popular power on the streets. In the process, many have drawn the conclusion that capitalism cannot be reformed.
>
> In Venezuela, the revolution has raised the banner of socialism again, well after it was declared dead and buried with the collapse of the Soviet Union. The Venezuelan revolution is working to build a "new socialism of the 21st century," based on principles of democracy and humanism. And it is working: poverty is decreasing (by 3 million people last year alone) and the poor are winning more and more power.

In most countries of Western Europe, socialist parties and alliances win between 6% and 12% of the vote in national elections, where those elections are held under systems of proportional representation. In the German elections of 2005, the Linkspartei, a socialist grouping, won 9% of the vote and 54 members of parliament. In the French presidential elections of 1995 and 2002, Arlette Laguiller, a Trotskyite, leader of the Lutte Ouvriere, won around 6% of the votes; in Scotland, the Scottish Socialist Party won 6% of the votes in the 2003 elections for the Scottish parliament; in Portugal, O Bloco de Esquerda, the Left Bloc, won 6.5% of the votes in the 2005 parliamentary elections and 8 MPs (Members of Parliament); in Italy, Rifodazione Communista won around 6% of the votes; and in recent elections in Scandinavia, various left parties won between 6 and 13% of the vote. In Eastern Europe, since the fall of the Berlin Wall in 1991, a number of (renamed) communist parties have won free and democratic presidential and parliamentary elections, such as, on various occasions, those in Poland, Hungary, Bulgaria, Slovakia, and Lithuania, seeking to protect their welfare states.

In fact, we often find it difficult to read a party's politics by its label. Parties change their trajectory. They even change their names to suit changing times. Few parties in Eastern Europe formed after the downfall of the Soviet empire, for example, were likely to call themselves communist or Marxist or even socialist. Similarly, few parties formed after the demise of the right-wing dictatorships in Portugal or Spain in the 1970s referred to themselves as conservative. To understand what any party does or does not stand for, we must move beyond superficialities. Reading a party's policy platform provides some degree of insight into what principles that party claims to support. But claims, like labels, can deceive us. We need to study the actions of a party to know what it really stands for, and what it does not.

REFERENCES

Bottomore, T. and Rubel, M. (eds.) (1963). *Karl Marx: Selected writings in sociology and social philosophy.* Harmondsworth: Penguin.

Choonara, J. (2006, March 4). Neo-liberal offensive on the poor. *Socialist Worker,* p. 9. Retrieved March 12, 2006, from http://www.socialistworker.co.uk/article. php?article_id=8382

Cliff, T. (1974). *State capitalism in Russia.* London: Pluto Press.

Engels, F. (1977). Socialism: Utopian and scientific. In K. Marx & F. Engels, *Selected works in one volume.* London: Lawrence and Wishart. (Original work published 1892.) Also retrieved from http://www.anu.edu.au/polsci/marx/classics/ manifesto.html

Marx, K. (1978). Critique of the Gotha programme 1875. Cited in T. Bottomore & M. Rubel, 263. (Original work published 1875.)

Marx, K., & Engels, F. (1977). The Communist Manifesto. In K. Marx & F. Engels, *Selected works in one volume.* London: Lawrence and Wishart. (Original work published 1848.) Also retrieved March 12, 2006, from http://www.anu.edu. au/polsci/marx/classics/manifesto.html

Munckton, S. (2006, February 22). From Che to Chavez: Latin America revolts against empire. *Green Left Weekly.* Retrieved March 12, 2006, from http://www.greenleft.org.au/back/2006/657/657p24.htm

Wikipedia. (2006). *Socialist party of America.* Retrieved March 12, 2006, from http://en.wikipedia.org/wiki/Socialist_Party_of_America. Accessed March 3, 2006.

Chapter 3

Liberalism

Richard Brosio
University of Wisconsin–Milwaukee

We should not ignore the irony found in the ascendancy of far-right politics that has turned liberalism into a "dirty word," particularly insofar as the neoliberalism defined by David Hursh in Chapter 4 has driven the far right's ascendancy. As a political ideology with roots in the Enlightenment period of European history, liberalism privileges the liberty of individuals over the power of the state. Liberalism, then, in providing the philosophical basis for the U.S. Constitution's Bill of Rights, played a key role in the early evolution of modern democracies, especially as they struggled against the absolute power — rooted in irrational claims of religious authority (i.e., the divine right of kings) — claimed by the church and the European monarchies. Liberalism, however, also played a key role in the evolution of capitalism as both an ideology and a set of historical practices that have served to undermine the expansion of democracy over time. Under the monarchial systems of feudal Europe, the chief function of commerce was to strengthen the power of the crown. Liberal ideology posited, to the contrary, that commerce ought to chiefly benefit the private power of the individual. This form of *economic* liberalism supports capitalism by championing the liberty of individuals to maximize their own economic self-interests. The Supreme Court's decision in *Santa Clara County v. Southern Pacific Railroad* (1886) granted private corporations the same rights of personhood as individual citizens. This enabled capital to translate its already disproportionate financial power into an increasingly disproportionate share of political power over the state apparatus vis-à-vis the vast majority of the population, threatening to empty America's political economy of any substantive democratic energies.

Political liberalism, which neoliberals, neoconservatives, and the busi-ness-dominated media have worked diligently to demonize in the public mind, contests the efforts of capital to dominate state power. In its best tra-ditions, political liberalism maintains that democracy mandates the state act to ensure the general welfare of society by responding to the needs and desires of the people, including and especially their desire to be pro-tected from the disproportionate social power of capital and the ravages of the free market that resulted in the Great Depression. Not surprisingly, given that Franklin D. Roosevelt's administration pushed through New Deal legislation in response to the populist energies of organized labor, Americans throughout most of the 20th century correctly associated politi-cal liberalism with the Democratic Party, though Democrats in southern states tended, with the Republican Party, to embrace pro-capital economic liberalism, which we have learned to confuse with conservatism.

Given how increasingly obvious it becomes that contemporary capital-ism demands some kind of conservative, strong, authoritarian movement and state that includes imperialism, the inclusion of neoconservatism in this second edition of the book is more than warranted.[1] In the context of U.S. politics today, liberalism as exemplified by the Democratic Party may look good to some in comparison to the rival Republican one, particu-larly in light of the latter's growing tendency to invoke irrational forms of authority (i.e., religious fundamentalism and hyperpatriotism) over scien-tific authority to justify policy decisions.

Contrary to the Enlightenment principles that made both forms of lib-eralism possible, George W. Bush and members of his administration have made every effort to marginalize nonpositivistic science as a basis for pub-lic discourse and policy formation. We find evidence for this claim in the mainstream media's coverage of intelligent design, the Terri Schiavo case, and stem cell research, as well as the ongoing controversies surrounding homosexuality and abortion. Moreover, the administration boasts about this antiscientific position as it appeals to those who claim that scientific inquiry lies in opposition to what religionists such as Pat Robertson, Jerry Falwell, and James Dobson hold to be the truth. Although the Republican administration is tightly allied to capitalism and its corporations, which rely heavily on certain forms of science for the various commodities pro-duced, including weapons of mass destruction, it depends on religion and patriotism to cultivate a dis-informed, yet highly activist, populist base for its otherwise class-based, elitist policies.

Many liberals who are disturbed and opposed to the current govern-ment's foreign and domestic policies see the Democratic Party as the best organization to represent their views. However, the Democrats, particu-larly those in the Democratic Leadership Council (e.g., Bill and Hillary Clinton, Joe Biden, and others), have grown increasingly tied to the same corporate interests and neoliberal (resurgent economic liberalism) ideology as Republicans. An example of this two-party stranglehold on the federal government is to be found in the No Child Left Behind (NCLB) legislative imperatives upon K-12 schools. The so-called scientific bases for these high-stakes tests used in NCLB have been justifiably criticized by those who find the research claims both tendentious and examples of bastardized science. Unfortunately, many Democrats have supported the legislation that makes these tests possible (Brosio, 2003, passim). The few progressive Democrats, led by the Democratic National Committee's Howard Dean, find themselves outnumbered in both houses of Congress and unable to block Bush and the Republicans.

It could be argued that from 1933 to 1968 the Democratic Party liberals were pushed from below and sometimes from specific bona fide left positions. The New Deal and its aftermath made it possible for working Americans to view the party and liberalism as sensible choices, especially when considering that the conservative Republican Party was in power when the Great Depression of 1929 began. The crash that occurred in 1929 was a disaster that injured many people within the capitalist economy, in the United States and elsewhere. Many Americans saw the liberal Roosevelt administrations (1933 to 1945) as the best way to get out of the Depression. However, if capitalism then and now is the most powerful secular force, it is not surprising that liberal governments were not able to overcome the crisis of the economic system without World War II. The war effort forced the federal government to spend money that helped solve the unemployment crisis that characterized the Depression. Under ordinary conditions, liberalism is not the great antidote or opponent of antidemocratic capitalism[2] — socialism is, in spite of the many corruptions of its principles during the last century.

LIBERALISM AND EDUCATION

The role of liberalism in American K-12 public schooling deserves good grades when viewed in contrast to essentialist-dominated schooling.[3] Max Wingo has argued that educational essentialism was and is backed by conservative politics, while relying on philosophical idealism and neorealism, which allegedly provide certainty similar to that which revealed religion claimed to offer earlier. According to Wingo, "educational progressivism: the liberal protest," which relies mainly on American pragmatist philosophy, has been the most effective challenge to the essentialist/conservative/idealist triad. Liberalism was and is the political factor that best represents progressive education and its underlying philosophic assumptions. There have been other protests, for example, ones organized around perennialist, Marxist, and existentialist philosophies. Obviously, the Marxist protest depends upon radical politics.

Considering the realistic choices (because of the forces arrayed against almost every radical idea and movement) for many Americans, it is not surprising that the greatest and most successful protest against essentialist/conservative schooling, namely, progressive/liberal alternatives, delivered many needed and beneficial improvements for students and teachers. Examples include educational opportunities for more than a few that fit abilities and needs, curricular expansion that enriched educational experiences, more humane discipline practices, greater possibilities for enlisting student interests, better materials of instruction, and curriculum and pedagogy organized around scientifically established ideas of human development (Wingo, 1974, p. 230).

In spite of well-known critiques of John Dewey's work from both right and left, I think neither educational theorists nor practitioners have advanced much beyond his analysis of how education for critical citizenship in a putative democracy should be conducted. Although Dewey is usually categorized as a liberal, the thrust of his work takes him beyond the borders of the liberalism of his time and today. In fact, many radical leftist educators have built upon Dewey and the best of the liberal progressives (Brosio, 1994, Chap. 12). Dewey, Deweyans, and radical leftist educators have had to fight constantly against the economic and cultural rightists in order to forward the progressive project in schools. Those to the left of Dewey have always argued that it was and is necessary to overcome rightist power in the schools and push the balance of power increasingly leftward in the larger society to some form of deep and inclusive democratic socialism. Dewey did come to the conclusion, even before the Great Depression of the 1930s, that capitalism could not be reformed as easily as earlier progressives might have believed. He worked his way to the realization that a nondemocratic or seriously flawed society could not sponsor democratic schools and education.

IN THE BEST SPIRIT OF LIBERALISM

George McGovern and Paul Wellstone are politicians who epitomize the best in this country's liberal tradition. Although the media cooperated in painting McGovern as a wild-eyed liberal and even radical during the 1972 presidential campaign, the senator from South Dakota firmly believed in capitalism when it was effectively regulated. Moreover, he believed that liberals need conservatives as challengers in order to keep liberalism current and true to its best forbears. Perhaps his pragmatism helped keep his own liberal ideas and actions fresh. He was convinced that "we are all functioning with uncertainties and limited knowledge" (McGovern, 2004, p. 70). McGovern held that people have the capacity to be and do good when they appeal to the better angels of their nature. His loyalty to the founding fathers' construction was strong, and he appealed to old-fashioned moral-ity and common sense. His most important contribution to his fellow citi-zens may well have been his refusal to accept the assumptions of the Cold War advocates; he understood that it and the hot war in Indo-China con-tributed to liberalism's decline in U.S. politics. McGovern recognized and discussed the dangers of the widespread killing — on both sides — of the hot version. Nixon beat McGovern in the presidential election of 1972 and the hot war continued until 1975.

Paul Wellstone served as a senator from Minnesota and represented lib-eral-populist politics. He, like McGovern, epitomized a sense of decency, perspective, humor, and conviction that is fast disappearing in American politics. Wellstone may have realized that his politics could not address adequately what he saw as unjust in the United States. However, he did understand and fight against the takeover of American politics by the rich and powerful. His liberalism was located on a continuum that approached radicalism — one that is based on the conviction that democracy is not compatible with capitalism. Wellstone pushed liberalism in the direction of expanding the rights that liberals had historically restricted to only those who were qualified. Like Dewey, he had the intelligence and cour-age to consider what some of the consequences were in relationship to his premises. He recognized that the Democratic Party is supposed to repre-sent working people and the poor, but that it was too often silent on the injustices based on class, race, gender, and other failures to consider every-one in this country (Wellstone, 2001, p. 127). Unfortunately, all of these positive factors do not make up for the absence of a bona fide, mass leftist movement and party that goes beyond liberalism's weaknesses, especially vis-à-vis capitalism.

If what is featured above is credible to the reader, perhaps we can extrapolate from it and agree that liberal politics and educational poli-cies are better suited than their conservative counterparts for goals such as more democratic empowerment for more people, insistence on social justice, respect for and even embracement of diversity, and developing a society in which it is safer to act altruistically. However, since the 1980s the so-called New Democrats have in many ways sought to become the second party of capital and empire. Perhaps historians will call them Republicrats? As of this writing, the Democrats do not control any of the three branches of the federal government; therefore, even though the party includes more progressives and certainly liberals, their power is very limited.

Instead of McGovern's insistence that liberal Democrats need conser-vatives to keep them alert and learning, it might be advisable to turn the debate leftward toward democratic radicalism. Ira Katznelson states that we need liberalism sometimes, for example, as an attitude characterized by attempting to secure a social order that is not based on irrationalism and dogma while ensuring stability and some forms of community, without the use of too many restraints upon persons' liberties. He continues: "For the past four centuries ... the applicability of liberalism's promise has been contained by what until recently was thought to be the lack of requisite character by the vast majority of humanity, including Europe's women, non-Christians, and the unpropertied, and virtually all of the world's population with dark skin; and by its silences about state power and inequalities of conditions fostered routinely by capitalist economics" (Katznelson, 1996, p. 18). In agreement with C. Wright Mills, Katznelson thinks that liberalism and socialism are the only major political traditions that can help us figure out how to build a polity based on freedom and reason. Katznelson asks what a radical liberalism would look like in the face of the latest increases in capitalist global power. He also wonders whether liberalism's limitations are inherent in its development and present position in relation to capitalism.

THE DEEP LIMITS OF LIBERALISM

Herbert Marcuse may be of assistance on this matter. He views liberalism as the political face of a particular form of capitalism; moreover, it was there at the system's inception. Its laissez-faire posture was mostly against state power that liberals did not control during capitalism's rise to power. As we know, liberals have subsequently used the state and even gendarmes to preserve themselves and their capitalist base. Marcuse's book *Negations: Essays in Critical Theory* includes a chapter called "The Struggle Against Liberalism in the Totalitarian View of the State," which was written during the 1930s soon after the Nazis came to power. He sought to understand how various fascisms came from existing bourgeois capitalist countries and how putative bourgeois freedoms became unfreedoms.

Marcuse and his Frankfurt School colleagues looked to the freedoms championed by the Protestant Reformation and concluded that they were mostly confined to the intellectual and spiritual realms — in contrast to the concrete world of everyday life. This coincided with liberalism's lack of concreteness, except for its main emphasis on the freedom of capital, in the real world. The current form of capitalism, called neoliberalism, has pushed the freedom of capital relentlessly, while attending much less to freedom for those who do the work upon which the capitalist economy is built. The current border debates around who should be allowed into the United States across its southern border is one example of problems that neoliberalism has caused.[4]

The market was said to take care of people's everyday concerns. Here we have an alleged liberal commitment to rationalism but relying on a secular myth to match religious myths, namely, that the "invisible hand" would cause the frenzied, everyman-for-himself system — with women and children last — to become an economy and polity that benefited one and all. Referring once more to idealist philosophy and specifically Georg Hegel, Marcuse accuses this philosophy's critical/negating powers of being limited by its insistence on ontological (the nature of reality/existence) stability. Hegel and his followers (excluding Marx) failed to develop the contradictions within the idealist/liberal/bourgeois/capitalist whole/reality into concrete economic and political realities. Marcuse argued that critical theory must cleave to the concreteness of what is, but not too much. Its critical negative power must be reconstructive enough to surpass the ontological presuppositions of liberal bourgeois philosophy and the old host society's concrete limitations. The critical antithesis must be more powerful than liberalism's in order to correct the injustices within the bourgeois capitalist society that liberal philosophy had helped create.

Marcuse explains that fascism/Nazism's original enemies were the liberalism of its time — as well as socialism/communism. Mussolini and Hitler both saw important connections — on a spectrum — among its leftist enemies. The Italian and German variants of authoritarianism and totalitarianism blamed their enemies for "the 'ideas of 1789,' … wishy-washy humanism and pacifism, Western intellectualism, egotistical individualism, sacrifice of the nation and state to conflicts of interest … hypertrophy of the economy, and destructive technicism and materialism" (Marcuse, 1968, p. 8). Marcuse argues that these fascist descriptors were not completely accurate concerning liberalism when one considers some very important facts about really existing liberalism from the time of its victory as a partner of capitalism. The inheritance of the Enlightenment has been struggled over by the forces of liberal capitalism on the one side and radical democracy on the other. Liberalism was and is the political ideology of capitalism, and it can be plausibly argued that because of this connection, they both have contributed to weakening the progressive side of the Enlightenment's great potential based on the "resources of rationality" that can help arm us against irrationalism, obscurantism, and "inerrant" religion.[5] According to Marcuse, "The ideas of 1789 have by no means always been on the banners of liberalism and have even been sharply attacked by it. Liberalism has been one of the strongest supports of the demand for a powerful nation. Pacifism and internationalism were not always causes it adopted and it has often accepted considerable intervention of the state in the economy" (Marcuse, 1968, p. 8).

Marcuse pushes his criticism further:

> Despite structural variations …, a uniform foundation remains: the individual economic subject's free ownership and control of private property and the politically and legally guaranteed security of these rights. Around this one stable center, all specific economic and social demands can be

modified.... During the rule of liberalism, powerful intervention by state authority frequently occurred, whenever the ... security of private property required it, especially if the threat came from the proletariat. The idea [and reality] of dictatorship is ... not ... foreign to liberalism. (Marcuse, 1968, p. 9)

Consider how far right U.S. politics has gone when the Republican Party makes liberalism sound subversive, anti-American, and, in the past, even in league with communism. Perhaps the Bush Jr. presidency represents an American brand of proto-fascism, as monopoly capitalism and its need for a strong state at home and abroad (neoimperialism) causes it to abandon the "wishy-washy" Democrats when the going gets tough. The Republicans' huge lead in the politics of irrationalism and party discipline may make it the first team for capital's current need to increase profit, destroy organized labor, and make globalization completely its own. Although this supposition may cause anger or confusion for some readers, I contend that it represents the views of many in the United States and around the world — persons who do not subscribe to the manufactured consent characteristics of the mainstream media or, perhaps more specifically, corporate media.

The commonalities between liberalism and antiliberalism (in this case, to the political right of liberalism) may be grounded in the former's belief in natural law. Nature is viewed as conservative because it is allegedly based on an "unshakable constancy of appearance" even if temporary disturbances occur. Marcuse writes: "The liberalist rationalization of economic life (as of social organization in general) is essentially *private....* The harmony of general and private interests is supposed to result *of itself* from the undisturbed course of private practice (Marcuse, 1968, p. 17). Furthermore, "Through this *privatization of reason*, the construction of society [allegedly] in accordance with reason is deprived of the end which is supposed to provide its goal.... The structure and order of the whole are ultimately left to irrational forces: an accidental 'harmony,' a 'natural balance'" (Marcuse, 1968, p. 18).

Perhaps Tom Frank's analysis of contemporary politics in the United States, with its red and blue states, can help us understand what Marcuse wrote about in Germany during the 1930s.[6] Marx, Marcuse, and arguably Frank believe that the "antimaterialist facets of liberalism and conservatism rely not on the authentically rational organization of the economy, polity, and society wherein a modicum of happiness may be enjoyed, but only as heroic pauperis" and service to the capitalist state's endless needs for military heroes (Marcuse, 1968, p. 16). I hold that liberalism's failure to democratize/universalize the rights and privileges it demanded for the bourgeoisie and especially capitalists makes its philosophy irrational in the end. Therefore, for example, the Italian liberal state could have easily fallen into a reliance on fascism when the working classes of the country tried to claim their fair share.

Clarence Karier writes, "In times of severe crisis, most liberals can be relied on to move to the right ... of the political spectrum" (Karier, 1973, p. 85). He uses the tumultuous 1960s and 1970s as an example when many mainstream liberals alleged that the "responsibility for the destruction of democratic institutions lies with their intemperate brothers on the left and not with any failure or perhaps fatal flaw in liberal philosophy" (Karier, 1973, p. 85). Not only in philosophy — after many years of liberal politics and legislation the problems of class, race, and militarism remain. Karier is blunt and credible when he accuses liberals in the United States and elsewhere of moving to the fascist — or proto-fascist — right rather than to an egalitarian left revolution, if not to a resolution. Leading to his powerful critique of Dewey and some forms of progressive education, Karier argues that political progressivism attempted to rationalize and stabilize the inhuman face of capitalism during that historical time. Liberals are all about "efficiency" — and of course "orderly change." According to Karier, "the liberal role in American society was essentially that of the knowledgeable expert dedicated to the survival of the [capitalist] system through growth [but not equitable redistribution]. The liberal educational reformer, like the political one, was in effect a flexible conservative" (Karier, 1973, p. 95). He charges them with being servants of power. These analyses can assist us in understanding more effectively where conservative-liberal/Republican-Democrat politics are at in these times.

The political right has accused liberals and the Democratic Party of being soft on communism and other putative threats to U.S. global dominance — many Americans believed it. In fact, FDR and the New Dealers were assiduous in their efforts to make American capitalism the framework within which the world should be run. The following Democratic administrations with congressional support followed this goal. However, their rightist political partners always wanted more — and more obvious in some cases. President Lyndon Johnson, who led what he called the Great Society domestic programs, claimed he wanted to extend the progressive accomplishments of Franklin Roosevelt's New Deal and John Kennedy's New Frontier initiatives, programs, and laws. The election of Nixon in 1968 marked the beginning of the abandonment of some of the best achievements by American liberalism. The country moved rightward in politics since 1968, even when Jimmy Carter and Bill Clinton were presidents. The present Bush administration, the Republican-controlled Congress, and the right-leaning Supreme Court have all contributed to undoing what was best of liberalism since 1932. According to Marcuse, "The turn from the liberalist to the total-authoritarian state occurs within the framework of a single social order. With regard to the unity of this economic base ... it is liberalism that 'produces 'the ... authoritarian state out of itself" (Marcuse, 1968, p. 19). The current Bush administration has pushed claims for presidential powers during the War Against Terror to such a degree that it has caused a widespread reaction against the president and his helpers.

Editor David Gabbard, has emphasized the importance of moving beyond the present dominant *economized* views of society and school during this latest "gale of creative destruction." The phenomenon he opposes is not based on Marx's historical materialism. Obviously, Gabbard understands this. Marx reacted to the unprecedented rush to convert everyone and everything to what they would count for in the market. All other relationships were attacked so that people were forced to relate mostly within the "cash nexus." If liberalism was originally a middle position between conservatism and socialism after the French Revolution of 1789 and its aftermath, we must insist today that liberalism is no longer centrist. In fact, progressive democrats must venture beyond what is best of radical, democratic socialism and move into harmony with ecological green concerns and policy suggestions.

If it is still warranted to assert that intelligence is widespread in any population, and can be developed further as Gramsci insisted, then democracy is possible. It must also be socialist. Freedom to choose must include choosing to overcome capitalism. Security is very important, as many people in the former East Bloc countries have discovered since 1989. Marx's concept of bona fide democracy was one that went well beyond what the bourgeois liberals envisaged, dared, or permitted. As has been argued above, liberalism's democratic credentials are suspect at best. As for capitalism, it satisfies only those who think that choice in the free market is tantamount to authentic, inclusive, and egalitarian democracy. The concept of a moral economy must be insisted upon instead of capitalism — a system that is incompatible with bona fide democracy. The U.S. war on Iraq is not about democracy in the sense privileged in this chapter.

I contend that Marx's vision of democracy was based on his commitment to ordinary workers (direct producers) and citizens (if not just yet, sooner than later) who could actually run the economy. The Marxists and earlier socialists realized that working conditions under capitalism ruined human beings as well as the natural world around the work sites — and beyond (see Foster, 2005). Furthermore they trusted we would produce mostly for use, not for alienated labor exchange. Contra to those who denounce Marx and the Marxists for their alleged dismissal of ecological and sustainability challenges, I submit that "reds" can work with "greens" because the best of both movements is based on the belief that democrats can learn to "educate desire" so that we will act moderately — with a touch of asceticism. Unlike under capitalism, production would no longer be just for profit's sake. Instead, the so-called profits would be shared by all of the worker-citizens (and those seeking to become the latter).

Capitalist aggressiveness and excesses have not been squarely confronted by liberalism in the past or now. The conservatives and neoconservatives — perhaps more accurately radical reactionaries — who now dominate the U.S. federal government and many state ones are obviously pushing the pedal to the floorboard of huge overpowered cars and trucks as well as even more dangerous military machines. This is justified by the current administration and its allies, who claim America has the right and duty to make every person subordinate and each place a part of a benevolent American world order that supposedly will elevate all with the invisible hand magically at work. However, it seems as though this hand must first be an iron fist. It is difficult to believe that the masses of people in the world will benefit from these beliefs, policies, and actions.

With regard to schooling/education it is beyond difficult — in fact, impossible — to think that forms and exercises of corporate and military power can promote critical civic education that is based on valuing and promoting; deep, participatory, and inclusive democracy; social-ecological justice; respect for and embracement of diversity; as well as the possibilities to safely act more altruistically. We must realize that "capitalism … [and] its allies have so saturated U.S. society and its various cultures with its practices and iron logic that democratic Left(s) must conduct a sober and rigorous reassessment of … civil society issues — including the roles of schooling-education" (Brosio, 2004, p. 2). What roles will liberals play within the contexts, problems, and possibilities presented herein?

NOTES

1. The critical and even establishment literature is full of discussions about U.S. imperialism. The following sources are congruent with the arguments in this chapter. They appear in author-alphabetized order. David Harvey, *The New Imperialism* (2003); Harry Magdoff, *Imperialism Without Colonies* (2003); Ellen Meiksins Wood, *Empire of Capital* (2003); Leo Panitch and Colin Leys (Eds.), *The Socialist Register: The New Imperial Challenge* (2004); Michael Parenti, *The Terrorist Trap: September 11 and Beyond* (2002); Arundhati Roy, *An Ordinary Person's Guide to Empire* (2004); Howard Zinn, *Terrorism and War* (2002).
2. The claim that capitalism is antidemocratic in essence is not well known among the great majority of Americans. However, the literature that lays this indictment out is rich and plentiful. Here are some examples, again in author-alphabetized order: Samuel Bowles and Herbert Gintis, *Schooling in Capitalist America* (1976) and *Democracy and Capitalism* (1986); Richard A. Brosio, *A Radical Democratic Critique of Capitalist Education* (1994) and *Philosophical Scaffolding for the Construction of Critical Democratic Education* (2000); Martin Carnoy and Henry Levin, *Schooling and Work in the Democratic State* (1985); Ellen Meiksins Wood, *Democracy Against Capitalism* (1995); Svi Shapiro, *Capitalism and Democracy: Educational Policy and the Crisis of the Welfare State* (1990).

3. Educational essentialism is based on the belief that the curriculum it offers is essential because it derives from the act of creation itself. Relatedly, the curriculum's components — the classic subject areas — are said to be the key to understanding the created world. See Max Wingo's Chapter 3 in *Philosophies of Education: An Introduction* (1974) and Chapter 4 in my *Philosophical Scaffolding for the Construction of Critical Democratic Education* (2000) for further information and analyses on educational essentialism.

4. Robert McChesney's article "Noam Chomsky and the Struggle Against Neoliberalism," *Monthly Review*, April 1999, Vol. 50, No. 11, pp. 40–47, is an informative source.

5. See Calvin O. Schrag, *The Resources of Rationality: A Response to the Postmodernist Challenge* (1992), for helpful developments and clarifications about these resources.

6. Frank's *What's the Matter With Kansas: How Conservatives Won the Heart of America* (2000) provides a useful descriptive analysis of what the Republican Party has become as well as the state of contemporary liberalism and the Democratic Party. The alliance between seeming rationalists and their further rightist irrationalists may be explained by the failure of the liberal rationalists' ability or desire to struggle for a more inclusive society than has been the case thus far. See also his "What's the Matter With Liberals?" *New York Review of Books*, May 12, 2005, Vol. 52, No. 8, pp. 46–51.

REFERENCES

Brosio, R. A. (1994). *A radical democratic critique of capitalist education*. New York: Peter Lang.

Brosio, R. A. (2003). High-stakes tests: Reasons to strive for better Marx. *Notes & Abstracts*, 96, 1–22. Also retrieved April 27, 2007 from www.jceps.com/?pageID=articles&articlesID=17

Brosio, R. A. (2004). Civil society: Concepts and critique from a radical democratic perspective. *Notes & Abstracts*, 98, 1–22. Also retrieved from www.jceps.com/?pageID=article&article=27 and eserver.org/clogic/2005/brosio.html

Foster, J. B. (2005). Organizing ecological revolution. *Monthly Review*, 57, 1–10.

Gabbard, D. (2000). *Knowledge and power in the global economy: Politics and the rhetoric of school reform*. Mahwah, NJ: Lawrence Erlbaum.

Karier, C. J. 1973). Liberal ideology and the quest for orderly change. In C. J. Karier, P. Violas, & J. Spring (Eds.), *Roots of crisis: American education in the twentieth century*. Chicago: Rand McNally.

Katznelson, I. (1996). *Liberalism's crooked circle*. Princeton, NJ: Princeton University Press.

Marcuse, H. (1968). *Negations: Essays in critical theory*. Boston: Beacon Press.

McGovern, G. (2004). *The essential America*. New York: Simon & Schuster.

Wellstone, P. (2001). *The conscience of a liberal*. Minneapolis: University of Minnesota Press.

Wingo, G. M. (1974). *Philosophies of education: An introduction*. Lexington, MA: D. C. Heath.

Chapter 4

Neoliberalism

David Hursh
University of Rochester

Neoliberal theory and practices have become so embedded within our economic and political decision making that neoliberalism is rarely explicitly
invoked as a rationale. Yet, the current educational emphasis on choice,
competition, markets, and standardized testing is based on neoliberal
rationalities and could be neither conceptualized nor instituted without
the rise and supremacy of neoliberal thought. Therefore, anyone interested in current educational decision making needs to understand the
neoliberal principles by which the decisions are guided.

Not only is neoliberalism rarely discussed, but because neoliberalism
has been most strongly identified with the current Bush administration
or the past administrations of Reagan and Thatcher, some find the term
neoliberalism confusing. Some assume that a *neo* or "new" form of liberalism
should connect to and build on the past social democratic liberal policies
of Franklin Roosevelt, John Kennedy, or Lyndon Johnson. To understand
how neoliberalism relates to both current Republican and past Democratic
administrations requires understanding the transformations liberalism
has undergone from the late 16th century to the present.

Therefore, after giving a short definition of neoliberalism, I provide a
brief overview of the history of liberalism, including the similarities and
differences between previous forms of liberalism and neoliberalism. Then,
I will describe some of the ways in which neoliberalism influences current
social and education policies. Lastly, while neoliberalism is often assumed
to be the last and enduring stage of capitalism, neoliberalism's contradictions and failings may result in either significant modifications in or the
demise of neoliberalism.

David Harvey, in *A Brief History of Neoliberalism*[1] (2005), defines neoliberal-ism as "a theory of political economic practices that proposes that human well-being can best be advanced by liberating individual entrepreneurial freedoms and skills within an institutional framework characterized by strong private property rights, free markets and free trade." Such practices require that "the state create and preserve an institutional framework appropriate to such practices" (p. 2), including organizations, such as the World Bank and International Monetary Fund, that pressure national governments to eliminate trade barriers and reduce social spending. Neoliberal policies also call for privatizing education through charter school and voucher programs and converting education into a competitive market system, all of which are evident in recent policies at the state and federal levels.

HISTORICAL OVERVIEW: FROM CLASSICAL LIBERALISM TO NEOLIBERALISM

Classic Liberalism

Since the beginning of the 17th century, liberalism, in one form or another, has been the dominant philosophical, political, and economic theory. Liberalism first emerged as the philosophical and political rationale for opposing the authority of the church and monarchy. In place of obedi-ence to the church and crown, liberal social philosophers, including Locke (1690/1960), Hobbes (1651/1968), and Voltaire (1763/2000), put forward the "principles of civil rights, rights of property, a limited conception of state power and a broadly negative conception of freedom" (Olssen, Codd, & O'Neill, 2004, p. 80). Liberalism reconceptualized the relationship between the individual and the secular and sacred state, aiming to free individuals from state interference and portraying individuals as rational choosers pursuing their self-interests, which served societal interests and promoted social progress.

Such political views soon influenced economic theories, and the idea that society could best be served by individuals pursuing their self-interests was reflected in Adam Smith's (1776/1976) notion of the "invisible hand." Smith argued that the individual "intends only his own gains, as he is in this, as in many others, led by an invisible hand to promote an end which was no part of his intentions" (Smith, 1776/1976). For Smith, the individual pursuing his or her own interests in a "market system was the best mecha-nism of the allocation of resources in a society" and "brought economic gains to each party, and ultimately to the nation as a whole" (Olssen et al., 2004, p. 88).

Liberalism revolutionized society. The ways in which people conceptu-alized and talked about individuals and society and the kinds of social practices that could be carried out had been transformed. For Foucault, writes Olssen et al. (2004), liberalism constitutes an original form of governmental reason. Liberalism is

> a complex system of political rationality comprising prescriptions of how to rule, and how not to rule, of when to rule and when not to rule. The discourses of liberalism also set limits to the role of the state, provide for democratized notions of sovereignty, and also for a series of specific technologies of administration and rule, which they are able to do through the arm of law. (Olssen et al., 2004, p. 74)[2]

Under classical liberalism, societies industrialized and their overall wealth grew. But industrialization and wealth came with a cost: increased wealth for a few and increased poverty for many. Consequently, workers began to organize and demand better working conditions and the general public called for laws that would protect women and children from excessive labor and their families from poverty. Cities and states passed legislation in relation to education, employment, health, and other issues. With the increasing acknowledgment that local and state governments must necessarily be involved in social and economic affairs, classical liberalism began to be replaced by social democratic liberalism.

Not only was classical liberalism being amended by government action, but social theorists like Hobhouse (1911), Green (1890), Dewey (1916), and Ward (1883) criticized classical liberalism's concept of negative liberty, where the state should do nothing but ensure that each individual is not interfered with, and replaced it with positive liberty, in which government should provide the conditions for all people to realize their capacities.

At the same time, economists such as John Maynard Keynes were developing theories that would provide rationales for the emerging social democratic liberalism. Moreover, any doubts that classical liberalism was inadequate for the 20th century were shattered by the Great Depression. In response, Roosevelt implemented Keynesian economic theories, in which the state used spending, tax, and welfare policies to rebuild the country and fund the military effort in World War II. The United States emerged from the war victorious, and Keynesian economics and social democratic liberalism were to remain dominant through the 1970s.

Social Democratic Liberalism

The decades immediately after the war were marked by the historic compromise between capital and labor in which, in exchange for improving wages, labor consented to capital's right not only to control the workplace but also to allow capitalist control of investment and growth, primarily through the growth of multinational corporations. At the same time, workers, women, and people of color struggled for and were able to extend their personal and political rights for education, housing, health, workplace safety, and voting (Bowles & Gintis, 1986, pp. 57–59). In part fueled by workers' growing wages, the postwar period was marked by unusually rapid and stable economic growth.

However, efforts to expand personal and political rights were not uncontested. For persons of color, the right to vote was only won through unrelenting, heroic, and sometimes lethal struggle and is still, given the recent electoral irregularities in Florida and Ohio, precarious. Similarly, social security benefits were denied to many African Americans when Congress surrendered to Southern politicians' demands to exclude agricultural and domestic household workers, jobs typically filled by African Americans (Katznelson, 2005). Even the now venerated GI Bill for returning veterans "roused the ire of all but the most moderate business leaders ... [who] disliked the liberal agenda and felt that the New Deal traditions associated with the Labor movement and the Democratic Party continued to appeal to American workers" (Fones-Wolfe, 1994, p. 7).

Social democratic liberalism, which the public most often associates with liberalism, was never secure and was increasingly attacked in the late 1960s, as businesses' net rate of profit began to fall (Parenti, 1999, p. 118). Because falling profits were attributed primarily to the inability of businesses to pass increasing wage costs on to consumers in the increasingly competitive and open world economy, part of the solution for emerging neoliberals was to squeeze workers' wages. As the then-head of the Federal Reserve Bank, Paul Volcker stated, "the average wage of workers has to decline" (cited in Bowles & Gintis, 1986, p. 60).

Furthermore, liberalism's emphasis on the individual was diminished but not extinguished. Keynes himself was unable to reconcile the conflict between social justice and freedom, and between the community and the individual:

> The question is whether we are prepared to move out of the nineteenth century laissez faire into the era of liberal socialism, by which I mean a system where we can ask as an organized community for common purposes and to promote economic and social justice, whilst respecting and protecting the individual — his freedom of choice, his faith, his mind, and its expression, his enterprise and property. (Keynes, 1939, cited in Cranston, 1978, p. 112)

Neoliberalism

During the period of Keynesian dominance, neoliberals condemned social democratic liberalism as "collectivist, socialist, and economically misguided" (Levitas, 1986, p. 3). Leading neoliberals, such as Milton

Friedman (1952, 1962), Robert Nozick (1974), James Buchanan (1975), and Gary Becker (1976), shared a commitment to individual liberty and limiting the state's role to enabling markets to function.

Neoliberalism expands on classic liberalism's faith in the individual as rational chooser within markets. Under neoliberalism the individual is no longer merely a rational optimizer but conceived as an autonomous entrepreneur responsible for his or her own self, progress, and position. Lemke (2002) describes neoliberalism as seeking

> to unite a responsible and moral individual and an economic-rational individual. It aspires to construct responsible subjects whose moral quality is based on the fact that they rationally assess the costs and benefits of a certain act as opposed to other alternative acts. (p. 59)

The market becomes central within such a conception of the individual.

> Every social transaction is conceptualized as entrepreneurial, to be carried out purely for personal gain. The market introduces competition as the structuring mechanism through which resources and status are allocated efficiently and fairly. The "invisible hand" of the market is thought to be the most efficient way of sorting out which competing individuals get what. (Olssen et al., 2004, pp. 137–138)

Under neoliberal rationality, the state plays a central role in creating the appropriate conditions, laws, and institutions necessary for markets to operate. This includes producing and reproducing particular discourses, practices, and techniques that enable neoliberalism to persist and prosper. We can see this in recent education policies, as education policy makers, corporate leaders, and politicians support neoliberal reforms that aim to reshape students into entrepreneurial individuals who pursue education for their personal gain. Furthermore, because markets are held up as ensuring efficiency, policies focus on promoting choice and competition between schools. In order to hold teachers and students accountable and provide data to consumers, all schools are required to give the same standardized exams. Lastly, a system of standards, standardized testing, and accountability enables the state to control students from a distance (Ball, 1994).

Neoliberalism, then, does not call for the state to retreat from intervention; rather, the state plays a role in the development of the techniques of auditing, accounting, and management. It is these techniques, write Barry, Osborne, and Rose (1996), that

> enable the marketplace for services to be established as "autonomous" from central control. Neoliberalism, in these terms, involves less a retreat from governmental "intervention" than a re-inscription of the techniques and forms of expertise required for the exercise of government. (p. 14)

Neoliberalism returns to classic liberalism with a vengeance. Individuals are transformed into "entrepreneurs of themselves" (Foucault, 1979) operating within a marketplace that now includes services such as education, health care, and pensions. The transformation is perhaps best characterized by a current financial services advertisement that suggests we think of families as corporations, whose rising or falling value can be assessed each day in a public market.

NEOLIBERALISM AND EDUCATION

Neoliberal theories currently dominate federal education policy, as well as those of most cities and states. With the passage of No Child Left Behind (NCLB) in 2002, the federal government requires all states to implement an assessment system with standardized testing in multiple subjects and grades, and uses the tests to divert funding away from public education and toward for- and on-profit corporations to tutor students, administer schools, or convert public schools into charter schools.

Because NCLB's testing requirements currently result in a large number of failing districts and schools, and by 2014 requires that every student achieve proficiency on every test, resulting in the failure of every school, it is likely that the real aim of neoliberal supporters of NLCB is not to improve public education but to replace public schools with publicly funded charter schools and voucher programs. In fact, the Bush administration policies and public statements provide evidence that this is the goal. Early drafts of NCLB provided vouchers for students to attend private schools. President Bush has authorized federal funds for a $50 million experimental voucher program in Washington, D.C., and for organizations that promote vouchers and charter school programs (Miner, 2004).

Further, the federal government is not the only policy maker supporting privatizing education. Pauline Lipman, in *High-Stakes Education: Inequality, Globalization, and Urban School Reform* (2004), describes how the Chicago Public Schools (CPS) have come under the increasing control of corporate and governmental interests who make educational decisions based not on what will promote educational equality but on what will enable Chicago to compete internationally in the tourism and financial markets. Consequently, those in power are developing a two-tier educational system that prepares the children of the professional and managerial class for higher education and the children of the poor for jobs in the retail and service industry.

Most recently, Chicago's Renaissance 2010 plan "calls for closing 60 public schools and opening 100 small schools, two-thirds of which will be charter or contract schools run by private organizations and staffed by" nonunion teachers (Lipman, 2005, p. 54). Renaissance 2010, writes Lipman, is only part of Chicago's ongoing effort to "reshape education in the image of the market by creating school choice, privatizing schools, weakening unions, and eliminating democratic participation in school decision making" (p. 54). Schools will not be governed by the local school councils, to which teachers, parents, and community members are elected, but rather by New Schools for Chicago, a board comprised of corporate and Chicago public school leaders chosen by the Commercial Club of Chicago, an organization representing the city's corporate and political elite. New Schools for Chicago will use current corporate models to evaluate the schools by developing performance contracts that focus on student test scores. By undermining democratic control over schools, further de-professionalizing teachers, and transferring public funds to private for-profit corporations, Renaissance 2010 represents a victory for the neoliberal agenda.

NEOLIBERALISM'S FAILURES AND CONTRADICTIONS

Neoliberalism has become ingrained as the rationale for social and economic policies and, as such, is rarely challenged, but accepted as necessary and inevitable.

> A whole set of presuppositions is being imposed as self-evident: it is taken for granted that maximum growth, and therefore productivity and competitiveness, are the ultimate and sole goal of human actions; or that economic forces cannot be resisted. (Bourdieu, 1998, p. 30)

But a realistic examination of neoliberalism reveals that it has failed and cannot deliver on its promises. While all of the problems with neoliberalism cannot be described here, a few will be noted: increased inequality, decreased democracy, and ecological degradation.

Neoliberalism promises that having individuals pursue their own economic self-interests will result in greater economic growth rewards for the whole society. However, on average, nations adopting neoliberal policies have achieved lower growth than under earlier social democratic policies (Harvey, 2005, p. 154). The working and middle class of numerous countries, including Argentina, Brazil, Bolivia, Chile, and Venezuela, have revolted against the gap between neoliberal rhetoric — that all will benefit — and the realization that it has only benefited a small ruling class. Likewise, George Bush's approval rating continues to decline as the public rebels against the administration's effort to cut taxes for the rich while reducing services for the poor, and therefore increasing inequality. The negative consequence of neoliberalism became most visible with the federal government's lack of concern and support for the victims of Hurricane Katrina. As Harvey writes: "Neoliberalism is recognized as a failed utopian rhetoric masking a successful project for the restoration of ruling-class power" (Harvey, 2005, p. 203).

Others have responded to the increasing concentration of power in the hands of a few unelected officials. In Chicago, parents and community members object to having educational policy decided not by the elected school board, but by a board appointed by the Commercial Club, an organization representing the corporate elite (Lipman, 2005). Citizens throughout the world have protested against the three organizations that "police the world for international capital — the International Monetary Fund, the World Bank, and the World Trade Organization" (Rikowski, 2001, p. 2).

Lastly, because neoliberalism emphasizes the entrepreneurial individual and privileges short-term profit over long-term environmental protection, neoliberal rationalities have contributed to environmental degradation. In the United States, economic growth trumps environmental concerns regarding global warming. In China, the headfirst and hasty drive for capitalist expansion has resulted in numerous environmental disasters, including, most recently, the spilling of benzine and nitrozine into the Songhua River, poisoning the drinking water for millions of urban and rural residents (Lague, 2005).

The last quarter century of neoliberalism has undermined equality, democracy, and the environment. Karl Polanyi recognized 50 years ago: "To allow the market *mechanism* to be sole director of the fate of human being and their natural environment, indeed, even of the *amount* and use of purchasing power, would result in the demolition of society" (1954, p. 73). Whether neoliberalism persists and what replaces it remains to be seen.

NOTES

1. David Harvey's *A Brief History of Neoliberalism* (2005) provides a concise, clear description of neoliberalism as a political project that serves to "restore class power" (p. 16). He describes how neoliberalism has become the dominant political theory globally and how it is enacted in various countries, ranging from the United States to China.
2. In contrast to Harvey (2005), Olssen, Codd, and O'Neill, in *Education Policy: Globalization, Citizenship and Democracy* (2004), analyze liberalism and neoliberalism as a form of governmental reason or governmentality (Foucault, 1988) that is not only a philosophy or theory but a way of viewing and governing the world. Furthermore, while not brief, Olssen et al. provide a philosophical, political, and economic description of the history of liberalism and its implications for education.

REFERENCES

Ball, S. (1994). *Education reform: A critical and post-structural approach.* Maidenhead Berkshire: Open University Press.

Barry, A., Osborne, T., & Rose, N. (1996). *Foucault and political reason: Liberalism, neo-liberalism and rationalities of government*. Chicago: University of Chicago Press.

Becker, G. (1976). *The economic approach to human behavior*. Chicago: University of Chicago Press.

Bourdieu, P. (1998). *Act of resistance: Against the tyranny of the market*. New York: The New Press.

Bowles, S., & Gintis, H. (1986). *Democracy and capitalism: Property, community and the contradictions of modern thought*. New York: Basic Books.

Buchanan, J. (1975). *The limits of liberty: Between anarchy and leviathan*. Chicago: University of Chicago Press.

Cranston, M. (1978). Keynes: His political ideas and their influence. In A. P. Thirlwall (Ed.), *Keynes and laissez-faire*. London: Macmillan, pp. 95–124.

Dewey, J. (1916). *Democracy and education*. New York: Macmillan.

Fones-Wolfe, E. (1994). *Selling free-enterprise: The business assault on labor and liberalism 1945–1960*. Urbana: University of Illinois Press.

Foucault, M. (1979, March 14). Lecture. Cited in Lemke, T. (2001). "The birth of bio-politics": Michel Foucault's lecture at the College de France on neo-liberal governmentality. *Economy and Society, 30*, 198.

Foucault M (1988b). Technologies of the self. In L.H. Martin, H. Gutman and P. H. Hutton (eds). Technologies of the self. Amherst: University of Massachusetts Press, pp 16–49.

Friedman, M. (1952). *Essays on positive economics*. Chicago: University of Chicago Press.

Friedman, M. (1962). *Capitalism and freedom*. Chicago: University of Chicago Press.

Green, T. H. (1890). *Works of Thomas Hill Green* (Vol. 2, 2nd ed., R. L. Nettleship, Ed.). London: Longmans, Green.

Harvey, D. (2005). *A brief history of neoliberalism*. Oxford: Oxford University Press.

Hobbes, T. (1968). *Leviathan* (C. B. Maccpherson, Ed.). London: Penguin. (Original work published 1651.)

Hobhouse, L. T. (1911). *Liberalism*. London: Williams and Norgate.

Katznelson, I. (2005). *When affirmative action was white: An untold history of racial inequality in twentieth-century America*. New York: W. W. Norton.

Lague, D. (2005, November 24). Water crisis shows China's pollution risk. *New York Times*, A–4.

Lemke, T. (2002, Fall). Foucault, governmentality and critique. *Rethinking Marxism, 14*, 49–64.

Levitas, R. (Ed.). (1986). *The ideology of the new right*. Cambridge: Polity Press.

Lipman, P. (2004). *High-stakes education: Inequality, globalization, and urban school reform*. New York: Routledge.

Lipman, P. (2005). We're not blind. Just follow the dollar sign. *Rethinking Schools, 19*, 54–58.

Locke, J. (1960). *Two treatises on government* (P. Laslett, Ed.). Cambridge: Cambridge University Press. (Original work published 1690.)

Miner, B. (2004, Summer). Seed money for conservatives. *Rethinking Schools, 18*, 9–11.

Nozick, R. (1974). *Anarchy, state and utopia*. Oxford: Blackwell.

Olssen, M., Codd, J., & O'Neill, A. M. (2004). *Education policy: Globalization, citizenship and democracy*. Thousand Oaks, CA: Sage Press.

Parenti, C. (1999). Atlas finally shrugged: Us against them in the me decade. *The Baffler, 13*, 108–120.

Polyani, K. (1954). *The great transformation*. Boston: Beacon Press.

Rikowski, G. (2001). *The battle for Seattle: Its significance for education*. London: Tufnell Press.

Smith, A. (1976). *An inquiry into the nature and causes of the wealth of nations* (R. H. Campell & A. S. Skinner, Eds.). Oxford: Clarendon Press. (Originally published 1776.)

Voltaire, F. (2000). *Treatise on tolerance* (B. Masters, Trans., S. Harvey, Ed.). Cambridge: Cambridge University Press. (Original work published 1763.)

Ward, L. F. (1883). *The psychic factors of civilization*. Boston: Ginn.

Chapter 5

Conservatism

Thomas C. Pedroni
Utah State University

I begin this chapter by defining conservatism in relation to a few concepts explored at length in other portions of this volume, most notably *neoliberalism* and *neoconservatism*. Following social and educational theorist Michael Apple, I locate these as two of the central tendencies brought together through a tense and creative process of negotiation and compromise under the ideological umbrella of what Apple et al. (1996, 2003) calls *conservative modernization*. I then propose an expansion of Apple's theory of conservative modernization that takes into account the central role that subaltern actors operating on the margins of power play within this process.

At the core of conservative modernization Apple has identified four powerful groups that together constitute a *hegemonic alliance* within the social order of the United States: neoliberals, neoconservatives, authoritarian populists, and a fraction of the new middle class (see Apple, 1996, p. 7). Taken together, these groups are hegemonic in that they are able to sustain leadership and move forward a particular agenda largely through winning consent to their social vision (see Gramsci, 1971). Groups within the hegemonic alliance accomplish this in two ways — by compromising with each other over what the elements of that vision are to be and by (re)shaping the terrain of common sense within the larger culture so that it increasingly resonates with their cultural messages and interpretations (see Apple, 1996, p. 15). In what follows, I present these groups first in isolation from one another, as ideal types. Later I discuss in greater detail the process of suturing and articulation through which, according to Apple, this hegemonic alliance is maintained, enlarged, and contested.

NEOLIBERALISM

Because of its association with tremendous concentrations of financial capital and its saturating presence at the points of discursive production within the social formation of the United States, neoliberalism as a discursive tendency is considered by many to be the most powerful trajectory within the process of hegemonic political formation (see Apple, 2001, p. 5). Neoliberalism is a particular narrative about the relationships among the economy, the social formation, the state and its institutions, and the people that constitute all of these. Because this narrative is enacted by quite powerful groups and individuals, it has tremendous material and discursive effects, both nationally and globally (see Ball, 1994; Clarke & Newman, 1997; Gee, Hull, & Lankshear, 1996; Lauder & Hughes, 1999; Whitty, Power, & Halpin, 1998).

For neoliberals, a person is most properly understood not as a member of a community or society, but rather as a self-interested individual who, given proper conditions, makes rational choices as a consumer within a competitive marketplace. Under ideal conditions, not only does this atomized consumer make effective self-serving choices, but through rational consumption practices he or she even promotes the potential for efficiency and value in the rest of the economy.

But, according to neoliberals, the rational and efficient action of the consumer is unfortunately hampered by the often well-intended interventions of a regulatory state. As a result of political and popular pressure, or sometimes even out of concern for its self-preservation, the regulatory state too often takes a course of action within the economy or society that interferes with the market's ability to maximize efficiency and value for its participants. In the end, so the argument goes, these interventions harm the very individuals they were designed to protect.

The remedy is simple: Other than provide macroeconomic stability through responsible monetary policy, the state should refrain from all interference in the economy. Especially within the increasingly competitive global environment of today, the state can maximize the efficiency of the economy, and so best serve its citizens, by phasing out its superfluous interventions as well as the monopoly it retains over sectors of the economy such as education. The state can furthermore maximize its own efficiency in those minimal vestiges of the state that must be retained by implementing managerialist practices, as discussed below (see Apple, 1996; Clarke & Newman, 1997).

Essentially finding everything public to be bad and everything private to be good, neoliberal discursive practices over the last two decades have fundamentally altered common sense concerning the relationship between the individual and the state, and between the public and private spheres (see Apple, 1996; Ball, 1994). In the name of efficiency and competitiveness, social welfare systems have been dismantled; prisons, public hospitals, and mass transit systems have been privatized; and the security and meaning of paid work has been fundamentally altered.

At the center of the neoliberal vision Clarke and Newman (1997) find the desire to supplant the traditional social democratic state with something they call the *managerial state*. Largely in the interest of promoting efficiency in the relationships among the economy, the state, and the social formation, advocates of managerialism seek to fundamentally transform the modern *welfare state*, which they see as an obsolete political relic hopelessly beset with bureaucratic and professional forms that are inefficient, undisciplined by market competition, impersonal, and largely self-protective.[1]

In place of bureaucratic and professional themes (which arose historically as a response to favoritism and corruption in earlier state forms), the managerial state emphasizes the euphemisms of the corporatist right — responsiveness to customers, competitiveness, and attention to values. In terms of subject formation and market structure, the citizens and patients of the previous state form are recast within managerialism as consumers, and so-called state monopolies are pushed to become market driven (Clarke & Newman, 1997, p. 49).

Applying their analysis to various divisions of social welfare provision in the United Kingdom, Clarke and Newman argue that managerialism does not totally replace older forms. Rather, managerialism emerges in complex combinations with prior discourses. Nevertheless, while it is still in a process of ascendancy, managerialism has become a globally hegemonic state form. As a result, surviving vestiges of older state forms are called upon to legitimate themselves upon the terrain of, and within the discursive parameters of, managerialist logic.[2]

Within education, managerialism and related reprivatizing discourses (see Fraser, 1989) are manifested in movements to introduce market competition through voucher programs and educational tax credits, the formation of charter schools, and the disempowerment of teachers' unions (see Lauder & Hughes, 1999; Wells, Lopez, Scott, & Holme, 1999; Whitty et al., 1998). Such measures are held to be universally beneficial, in that they empower parents (as consumers) to make rational choices within an educational marketplace, break the "producer capture" of educational institutions by self-serving education bureaucrats and teachers' unions, and ultimately improve any remaining public educational institutions by forcing them to maximize their efficiency or go out of business (see Apple, 2001; Holt, 2000).

In his appraisal of the neoliberal educational reform agenda, Michael Apple suggests a supermarket metaphor in considering the likely stratifying effects of educational marketization. As in any supermarket, the customers who shop for educational products arrive at the marketplace bearing significantly different amounts of currency. In educational markets we need to think of this capital not just as the dollars consumers possess, but also as the cultural capital represented by parents' differential ability to negotiate the best educational deals for their children. These educational customers will only be able to purchase the educational goods and services that their capital affords them. As Apple puts it, some will only be able to shop in the most truly postmodern fashion — by window shopping, looking through from the outside, vicariously, at the healthy and fortifying consumption patterns of the more privileged (2001, p. 39).

It would be a tremendous mistake to see neoliberalism as simply a class form. While education as envisioned by neoliberals is theoretically gen-der neutral, Madeleine Arnot has aptly demonstrated the contradictory effects of neoliberal (and neoconservative) policies on girls and women in the United Kingdom's schools, economy, and social formation (Arnot, David, & Weiner, 1999). In some ways, neoliberalism's emphasis on the rational and atomized student and worker within an economy requiring flexible, often part-time work has benefited the performance of girls and women both within schools and in the economy. At the same time, the burden of reprivatizing discourses on the home sphere has disproportion-ately affected women in family life, both by the recasting of responsibilities onto them and by the heightened moral scrutiny of nontraditional family arrangements that the accompanying resurgence of Victorian virtues has generated (see Arnot et al., 1999, pp. 95–117).

Obviously, these same reprivatizing and moral dynamics have impli-cations not just for gendered relations of power, but also for relations of power along race, sexual, and class lines. Those who are racially, sexu-ally, or economically marginalized, such as the mostly African American voucher mothers I have studied (see Apple & Pedroni, 2005; Pedroni, 2005, 2006), receive both more responsibility and more blame. Finally, Arnot's research has demonstrated how the new prominence of managerialist dis-courses in schools and in the workplace has favored masculinist forms, which may ultimately benefit men while harming women (see Arnot et al., p. 99).

Within the schools themselves, in the name of efficiency, administrative structures and responsibilities have been radically transformed through the introduction and dominance of managerialist discourses and post-Fordist organizational forms. Furthermore, the increasing commercialization of schools — the selling of students as a captive audience to marketers — is manifested in the presence of advertising, commodity-oriented competi-tions, and school/business partnerships (see Molnar, 1996). Additionally, the insertion of public schools into educational markets has increasingly led schools to spend scarce financial and human resources on marketing themselves to potential consumers of education — parents (see Pedroni, 2004b).

Finally, neoliberals have demanded that educational programs increasingly align themselves to the economy's need for "human capital." This is cast as also being in the best interest of the students, since "tomorrow's workers" need to be trained with the correct dispositions and flexible competencies to ensure the maintenance and success of both themselves and the American economy (see Harvey, 1989).

NEOCONSERVATISM

As we saw, neoliberal interventions in education are essentially predicated around a reprivatizing state that devolves educational responsibility to individual schools and families as producers and consumers within an educational marketplace. Neoconservative elements of the hegemonic alliance, to the contrary, call for a strong state to serve as the agent and guardian of higher standards, both morally and scholastically. This is accomplished through the increased accountability imposed by high-stakes testing, the resuscitation of educational canons and traditional subject matter within a common curriculum, and the teaching through strict discipline and "character education" of the values that, according to neoconservatives, have historically provided the foundation for the nation's educational, moral, and material success (see Hirsch, 1996).

For neoconservatives, the supposedly decreased competitiveness of the United States within the global marketplace is in large part due to the highly compromised moral, intellectual, and vocational competence of the American people. This debased stature is ultimately the result of a series of misguided and scientifically unproven interventions by educational progressives since the 1960s. Yet, as Kristen Buras (1999) has eloquently shown in her response to neoconservative educational critic E. D. Hirsch, claims of progressive dominance of education in the United States are not supported by an examination of everyday educational practices in either schools or teacher education programs — something that Buras suggests Hirsch might have realized had he actually spent some time in America's schools. Diane Ravitch's reading of the history of struggles over the American curriculum is similarly flawed. Although the history of the American curriculum has indeed been one of struggle between competing and cooperating educational factions, progressives have never been a dominant voice in education, although their presence has been significant within certain debates (see Apple, 2000; Kliebard, 1987; Ravitch, 2000). Notwithstanding the paucity of progressive success in influencing the curriculum, neoconservatives seek to counter what they see as the diminished importance of the teaching of traditional subject matter (facts), the increased importance of process over product, and the balkanizing effects of radical multicultural interventions (see Bennett, 1988; Glazer, 1997).

In distinction to neoliberalism, neoconservative educational and social philosophy contains within it barely masked racial, gender, class, and sexual discourses. For neoconservatives, U.S. society suffers from increased balkanization and moral compromise as a result of immigration; the spirit of meritocracy has been abandoned as a result of misguided affirmative action policies; the traditional family has been disrupted by changing gender roles, including the vacating of the sphere of the home by women entering the paid workforce; the Protestant work ethic and American moral fiber have been destroyed by the breeding of government dependency through socialistic welfare programs (the nanny state); and, finally, the United States has witnessed the dissolution of the sexual mores that undergirded and protected the American family. This has occurred through a surge in premarital sex and teen pregnancy, as well as increasing support and normalization of homosexuality and other "deviant" sexual practices (see Bloom, 1987; D'Souza, 1992).

AUTHORITARIAN POPULISM

While neoliberal and neoconservative elements have a fairly long history in the United States at the core of conservative mobilizations in education and elsewhere (although perhaps at times with different powers relative to each other), the last few decades have witnessed an increasing insurgence of populist-oriented and often religiously based social movements that do not sit completely comfortably within either of the previously mentioned conservative camps.

For authoritarian populists, there exists a moral crisis in the United States that is largely symptomatic of the disruption of authoritarian religious forms by what is termed secular humanism. To these social movements, the perceived economic crisis is important, but is recast largely as an effect of this displacement of God to "the back of the bus" (see Reed, 1994). Among authoritarian populists, there is a strong emphasis on the need for local, and in particular parental, control of the various institutions of American life, especially schools. Schools are seen as a primary threat to moral family life in that they are sites for the localization of elite and suspect foreign knowledge that directly contradicts and contests the sound, moral, traditional teachings of the American Christian family. Additionally, the court-supported doctrine of *in loco parentis* means that the Christian-oriented family is in a literal holy war with the schools over the control of both the spiritual and physical lives of their children, especially given what is seen as the increasingly secular, elitist, and strange nature of contemporary curriculum and teaching practices.

This sense of holy war is instantiated in a large number of conflicts over the content and method of teaching in schools, in which parents seek to wrest control of their children's lives from recalcitrant teachers, faceless and distant educational bureaucracies, and rubber-stamp school boards (see Apple, 1996; DelFattore, 1992). When their demands have become sufficiently politicized and insufficiently recognized by education authorities, authoritarian populist parents and other activists have frequently resorted to either complete separation from public schools, through homeschooling and the creation of Christian fundamentalist private schools, or attempts at takeovers of local school boards.

While authoritarian populists have often found common cause with neoliberals and especially neoconservatives, there are significant tensions within the sutures that connect them to the larger conservative project. For example, the neoconservative emphasis on educational centralization and nationally imposed standards appears to directly threaten their calls for local control. Similarly, the neoliberal emphasis on the virtues of markets contradicts their sense of morality based in the family and the community, and not in the self-interested competitive individual or corporation. Their suspicion of market forms has been in evidence on a national scale in Pat Buchanan's quite public calls for economic protectionism; such economic nationalism runs directly contrary to the liturgy (but perhaps not the practice) of the free market orthodoxy (see Chomsky, 1999).

Nevertheless, authoritarian populists have found common cause with neoconservatives over demands for the increased importance of conservative values and a (nostalgic and romanticized) return to traditional educational forms. Additionally, their tensions with neoliberals are superseded by the opportunities that are presented by neoliberal successes in promoting voucher programs, charter schools, and tax credits, which enable their separation from public schools, as well as the leverage they are able to bring to bear in changing public (and other) schools in the direction of their interests. Reprivatization of previously public responsibilities is, after all, precisely what authoritarian populist parents and organizations seek. Finally, authoritarian populists have found shelter beneath the umbrella of conservative modernization through the particular inflection that invocations of religious freedom have recently received. A successful "politics of recognition" by conservative activists has, as previously been mentioned, recast Christian evangelicals and other fundamentalists as the new civil rights cause in American life.

THE PROFESSIONAL AND MANAGERIAL FRACTION OF THE NEW MIDDLE CLASS

Within Apple's framework (2001), the last group comprising the conservative hegemonic alliance is a particular fraction of the professional and

managerial new middle class. This fraction, the least explicitly ideological among the four, gains its social mobility by virtue of the professional
expertise it is able to provide for the hegemonic alliance in matters related
to educational standardization, measurement, and management.

As noted previously, neoliberals and neoconservatives keep themselves
beneath the same ideological umbrella by compromising with each other
over the precise nature of their articulated vision, often in quite creative
ways. Within education, neoliberals and neoconservatives have sutured
together their potentially irreconcilable differences over the role of the
state in education through a fairly ingenious design. Neoliberals, with
their desire for a weak educational state,[3] seek to devolve educational
responsibility away from the state and toward individual schools so that
they can compete as effectively as possible over consumers within the educational marketplace; their needs are at least partially met through the
approval and realization of educational interventions promoting competition, including voucher systems, the creation of charter schools, public
school choice, and the implementation of educational tax credits. Neoconservatives, on the other hand, favor the role that a strong interventionist
state can play in ensuring the standardization of a curriculum centered on
the teaching of traditional subject matter and the values it supposedly con-
veys, including the literary canon; their agenda is at least partially realized
through an increased emphasis on standardized national and statewide
curricula and frequent standardized testing of both students and teachers. In turn, this recentralizing tendency will have a salutary effect for the
neoliberal educational vision, since the publication of the test scores of
various competing schools in league tables will permit consumers to make
informed choices within the educational marketplace. Producer capture
is mitigated as schools with poor test scores realize that they must either
improve the image of the product they are offering or go out of business, as
savvy customers consult league tables and take their business elsewhere.

Those who comprise the fraction of the new middle class that Apple
has in mind provide the technical, legal, procedural, and bureaucratic
expertise to make this system of standardization and comparison possible.
They bring to the process of conservative modernization their competence
with supposedly neutral efficiency, measurement, and management instruments — the very instruments that will enhance the ability of schools to
function as stratifying mechanisms. As those in the social formation with
the most fluency in such matters, their children in some ways stand to gain
the most from the increased prevalence of standardized and managerialist
forms in schools, since they will have a competitive edge over their peers in
assimilating these forms, and thus enhancing their accumulation of social
and cultural capital.

Until this point, my focus has been on a descriptive identification of the
key elements in conservative modernization. In the following section I turn

to a more comprehensive and theoretical explication of the process through which hegemonic alliances are constructed, maintained, and contested.

CONSERVATIVE MODERNIZATION AS A HEGEMONIC PROCESS

Because it is formed and sutured though compromise, the social vision of the hegemonic alliance is never unitary. Rather, as was illustrated in the previous section, it exists always in a somewhat fragile tension, fraught with contradictions that constantly threaten to undo its continued success (Apple, 1996, p. 15). As the rightist alliance sutures over its internal contradictions and infuses the everyday discourses of American public life with its sense-making constructions, it also, at least potentially, grows. For Apple, the hegemonic bloc can be seen as dynamic (that is, always in formation) in three important ways. First, it is dynamic temporally, in that it can and must respond to changing historical conditions, shifting alliances, the introduction of new technologies, the birth of new social movements, and larger economic trends. Secondly and thirdly, this conservative modernization is dynamic spatially, discursively speaking, in both a horizontal and vertical fashion. Horizontal dynamism is present in the suturing that takes place as different dominant groups gather together in tense unity under a single "ideological umbrella" (Apple, 1996, p. 15); vertical dynamism is present as the discourses of these dominant groups "act in creative ways to disarticulate prior connections and rearticulate groups of [largely ideologically unformed] people into this larger ideological movement by connecting to the real hopes, fears, and conditions of people's daily lives and by providing seemingly 'sensible' explanations for the current troubles people are having" (Apple, 1996, p. 45).

This politically formative process of disarticulation and rearticulation does not, however, occur in a seamless manner directly governed by the dominant groups' political will. Instead, Apple argues, "ordinary people" become articulated to larger conservative social movements through a complex series of 'accidents' and interactions with the state" (see Pedroni, 2004b, 2005, 2006). Frequently, as a result of the state's intransigence in hearing and mediating the concerns of such ordinary people, the right grows.

Subaltern Processes in Conservative Modernization

It is at this point that Apple's theory of conservative modernization, particularly his account of how the right grows as ordinary people are pushed to "become right" by an intransigent state, requires further elaboration and expansion. While Apple in Gramscian fashion correctly shows that conservative modernization in education proceeds through the articulation of rightist tendencies with people's everyday needs and desires, we need to account for the much more frequent instances in which collusion with rightist forms is undertaken by movements and social forces that are not aptly characterized as either ordinary or, at the end of the day, rightist. This will move us much farther along the path of understanding why reforms such as vouchers, which clearly originated on the far right, have become accepted as commonsense solutions by people, such as African American working-class communities of color, who are anything but rightist. It also helps us better understand how conservative modernization in education has been so successful.

Can we understand the current wave of conservative educational reform without exploring the processes through which conservative forms such as marketization and standardization are localized into particular educational contexts? Apple would say no, although much of his work does not yet paint a complex enough picture of the processes through which conservative educational reforms are localized as largely neoliberal visions, and actors come into contact with the communities in which their respective educational reforms must be worked and reworked in order to secure wider consent.

I propose that we continue Apple's work of examining the cultural politics of conservatism in education through an analysis of particular instances of localization. In my own research over the past five years, this empirical site of localization has been a largely neoliberal alliance with urban working-class communities of color around a targeted voucher program created in Milwaukee in 1990. As a way of closing this essay but also opening a dialogue, I invite readers to investigate the processes through which conservative educational reform is localized in contexts with which they are familiar, and to consider the centrality of such processes of localization to the broad success of conservative reform in the present moment. This movement of our analytical attention beyond the central loci of policy formation to the capillary moments in which such policy is actually animated carries with it significant implications for how we theorize educational conservatism. Rather than seeing conservatism solely as a dynamic that is imposed by dominant social actors on the field of social power, Apple's work provides us with a foundation for discovering that conservatism is often dependent on subaltern actors at the margins of social power for its realization.

Such an analysis would allow us to discern the processes through which conservative reforms are framed and reworked from above and recontextualized from below based on the specific interests and histories of subaltern communities. In my recent research on the alliance in Milwaukee, WI, between far-right funders of market-based educational reform and African American communities of color seeking greater community control over the schools their children attend, this work has helped to underscore the tensions and compromises within such alliances and the spaces that are created for potentially more democratic educational work.

Given such a conceptual recasting, how might those of us who oppose conservative educational forms as oppressive and undemocratic contest educational marketization and standardization at the same time that we protect potential alliances with subaltern groups who may be participating in such reform? Given that the resulting educational reforms are themselves a product of often divergent visions and histories as well as unequal power and agency among dominant and subaltern groups struggling to define the rationale and form of urban educational reform, it is essential to discern the spaces created by these tenuous relations for more democratic educational reform. These spaces, I suggest, are the grounds on which a project of *progressive modernization* might be advanced.

NOTES

1. Clarke and Newman (1997). In making this critique of the bureau-professional welfare state, as Clarke and Newman point out, the new right has actually creatively blended its own themes with the themes of many other critics of the old state form. Some of these critiques emanated from the new left and other new social movements, including feminists, environmentalists, and activists of color, who had criticized the social democratic state for its "one size fits all" operating logic.
2. However, Clarke and Newman do not wish to seem reductive by implying that managerialism is seamlessly imposed onto various state institutions. In their empirical research, they find that managerialist discourse is in fact mediated, contested, and creatively misunderstood at every level. Sometimes, as Clarke and Newman show, its logics are reinterpreted into visions and practices that are actually, and not just rhetorically, beneficial to the state's consumers.
3. Perhaps *weak* is not the most ideal descriptor in this instance. The neoliberal state remains quite strong in the policing it undertakes of populations on the social formation's margins, which neoliberal theory marks as expendable. This truth is encountered on a regular basis by those "jettisoned" populations residing in the urban cores of the United States, as well as within burgeoning prisons. As Apple and others have noted, the neoliberal state seeks to privatize the profits generated within current forms of market capitalism, at the same moment that it socializes — through state provision of prisons, for example — the costs of these arrangements. See Apple (1982, p. 56) for a further discussion of jettisoned populations, such as prisoners within the neoliberal state. See also Pedroni (2001).

REFERENCES

Apple, M. W. (1982). *Education and power.* Boston: Ark.
Apple, M. W. (1996). *Cultural politics and education.* New York: Teachers College Press.

Apple, M. W. (2000). Standards, subject matter, and a romantic past: A review of *Left Back: A Century of Failed School Reforms* by Diane Ravitch. *Educational Policy, 15,* 323–334.

Apple, M. W. (2001). *Educating the "right" way: Markets, standards, God, and inequality.* New York: RoutledgeFalmer.

Apple, M. W., Aasen, P., Cho, M. K., Gandin, L. A., Oliver, A., Sung, Y.-K., et al. (2003). *The state and the politics of knowledge.* New York: RoutledgeFalmer.

Apple, M. W., & Pedroni, T. C. (2005). Conservative alliance building and African American support of voucher reforms: The end of Brown's promise or a new beginning? *Teachers College Record, 107,* 2068–2105.

Arnot, M., David, M., & Weiner, G. (1999). *Closing the gender gap.* Cambridge: Polity Press.

Ball, S. (1994). *Education reform: A critical and post-structural approach.* Buckingham: Open University Press.

Bennett, W. (1988). *Our children and our country.* New York: Simon & Schuster.

Bloom, A. (1987). *The closing of the American mind: How higher education has failed democracy and impoverished the souls of today's students.* New York: Simon & Schuster.

Buras, K. L. (1999). Questioning core assumptions: A critical reading of and response to E. D. Hirsch's *The Schools We Need and Why We Don't Have Them. Harvard Educational Review, 69,* 67–93.

Chomsky, N. (1999). *Profit over people: Neoliberalism and global order.* New York: Seven Stories Press.

Clarke, J., & Newman, J. (1997). *The managerial state: Power, politics and ideology in the remaking of social welfare.* London: Sage Publications.

DelFattore, J. (1992). *What Johnny shouldn't read: Textbook censorship in America.* New Haven, CT: Yale University Press.

D'Souza, D. (1992). *Illiberal education: The politics of race and sex on campus.* New York: Vintage Books.

Fraser, N. (1989). *Unruly practices: Power, discourse and gender in contemporary social theory.* Minneapolis: University of Minnesota Press.

Gee, J., Hull, G., & Lankshear, C. (1996). *The new work order.* Sydney: Allen and Unwin.

Glazer, N. (1997). *We are all multiculturalists now.* Cambridge, MA: Harvard University Press.

Gramsci, A. (1971). *Selections from prison notebooks.* New York: International Publishers.

Harvey, D. (1989). *The condition of postmodernity.* Cambridge, MA: Blackwell.

Hirsch, Jr., E. D. (1996). *The schools we need and why we don't have them.* New York: Anchor Books.

Holt, M. (2000). *Not yet "free at last": The unfinished business of the civil rights movement: Our battle for school choice.* Oakland, CA: Institute for Contemporary Studies.

Kliebard, H. M. (1987). *The struggle for the American curriculum 1893–1958.* New York: Routledge and Megan Paul.

Lauder, H., & Hughes, D. (1999). *Trading in futures: Why markets in education don't work.* Buckingham: Open University Press.

Molnar, A. (1996). *Giving kids the business: The commercialization of America's schools.* Boulder, CO: Westview Press.

Pedroni, T. C. (2001). The rise of the managerial state and the decline of rehabilitation in the United States: A conjunctural and discursive analysis of a
1993 "late-rehabilitation" prison education reform proposal in the context of
conservative modernization. Unpublished master's thesis, University of Wisconsin, Madison.

Pedroni, T. C. (2004a). Strange bedfellows in the Milwaukee "parental choice"
debate: Participation among the dispossessed in conservative educational
reform. *Dissertation Abstracts International, 64*, 3946A (UMI 3113677).

Pedroni, T. C. (2004b). State theory and urban school reform II: A reconsidera-
tion from Milwaukee. In D. Gabbard & E. Wayne Ross, (Eds.), *Defending
public education: Schooling and the rise of the security state* (pp. 131–140). New
York: Greenwood.

Pedroni, T. C. (2005). Market movements and the dispossessed: Race, identity, and
subaltern agency among black women voucher advocates. *Urban Review, 37*,
83–105.

Pedroni, T. C. (2006). Can the subaltern act? African American involvement in educational voucher plans. In M. W. Apple & K. L. Buras (Eds.), *The subaltern speak:
Curriculum, power, and educational struggle* (pp. 95–117). New York: Routledge.

Ravitch, D. (2000). *Left back: A century of failed school reforms.* New York: Simon
& Schuster.

Reed, R. (1994). *After the revolution: How the Christian coalition is impacting America.*
Dallas, TX: Word Publishing.

Wells, A. S., Lopez, A., Scott, J., & Holme, J. (1999). Charter schools as postmodern
paradox: Rethinking social stratification in the age of deregulated school
choice. *Harvard Educational Review, 69*, 172–204.

Whitty, G., Power, S., & Halpin, D. (1998). *Devolution and choice in education: The
school, the state and the market.* Buckingham: Open University Press.

Chapter 6

Neoconservatism

Kristen L. Buras
Emory University

Generally, the story of neoconservatism begins with the 1960s. The new left inspires a new right, including a neoconservative faction focused on the restoration of a common cultural tradition and a disciplined, stable, and socially cohesive nation. But long before they were new rightists, and many neoconservatives were actually old leftists, a fact that helps to explain the synthesis of concerns to both the left and right within neoconservatism. The nonrecognition of this history has been partly facilitated by the circulation of a narrative that constructs neoconservatism as an oppositional reaction to the movements of the period — civil rights, feminist, and other subaltern struggles for cultural respect and economic redistribution. In one of the earliest accounts of neoconservatism, Peter Steinfels (1979) stresses that even during that era

> there was much talk of people being "radicalized," and in turn much talk of right-wing "backlashes." But "backlash," as the word implies, was an angry, reflexive action. There was no term for the slower evolution of a significant party of liberals. They were, we might say, "conservatized." (p. 44)

In order to appreciate the slower evolution of these new conservatives, the politics that distinguished them from traditional conservatives, and the concerns they developed regarding national identity and cohesion, cultural deficiency and decay, and the defense of Western tradition, it is necessary to rewind the clock to earlier than the 1960s. The 1930s will provide the starting point for the historical trajectory examined here, although it represents only one of a number of significant currents that have contributed to the neoconservative project.

Charting this history is complicated, and not simply because talk of right-wing backlashes has been so prevalent. Historiography in this domain is just beginning to take shape. Moreover, it involves volatile debates within the Jewish community and legitimate concerns about reactionary forces that may conceive newly emerging histories as an invitation to anti-Semitic scapegoating or as ammunition for conspiratorial political diatribes. As late as 1999, Murray Friedman — director of the Myer and Rosaline Feinstein Center for American Jewish History — edited a special issue of *American Jewish History* in which he underscored: "The fact is the story of neoconservatism, like the story of American Jewish conservatism itself, remains to be written." These two stories are partially intertwined and involve the political journey from left to right of a group of New York intellectuals from working-class, Jewish backgrounds, and their non-Jewish associates, over the course of several decades. Acknowledging this coalition, Friedman asserts, "There is no mistaking, however, the 'Jewish' ambiance of the movement with its origins in the Jewish Left of the 30s and 40s" (p. 110).

Again, telling this story requires care and sophistication. It is no exaggeration to say that there are those on the right who believe that a cabal of neoconservatives — Paul Wolfowitz and other Jewish officials — have orchestrated the foreign policy of the United States for the sole benefit of Israel (Buchanan, 2003). Alternatively, there are those on the left who contend that the disciples of German Jewish émigré and philosopher Leo Strauss are largely responsible for the "stealth campaigns" that define the "real" neoconservative agenda (Drury, 1999, 2003). Rendering the task even more complex is the fact that the writing of American Jewish history has disproportionately focused on liberal and leftist traditions in the Jewish community, often overlooking politically conservative segments, albeit a minority, that "draw from a deep wellspring of Jewish political philosophy, law, and historical experience" (Sarna, 1999, p. 113).

In light of these issues, writing a short chapter on neoconservatism presents a challenge. Nonetheless, I hope to provide a glimpse into the little explored, protracted history of neoconservatism and to illuminate its relationship to present-day school reform. Most of the chapter sketches the aforementioned history, with particular attention paid to the lineage of debates over culture. The conclusion highlights the relevance of this history to understanding the politics of *Core Knowledge*, a neoconservative educational reform — perhaps the most enduring — inspired by E. D. Hirsch's (1987) *Cultural Literacy: What Every American Needs to Know* (Buras, 1999, 2006a, 2006c). Before analyzing this current reform, let us turn to the past.

THE LITTLE RED SCHOOLHOUSE

In the 1930s, City College of New York was largely attended by working-class Jewish young men — some of whom would become the foremost neoconservative intellectuals of a later era. These were the sons of turn-of-the-century

Eastern European immigrants who worked in the sweatshops of New York City. Admission to Columbia University was limited by anti-Semitic quotas, which ensured a predominantly Protestant student body in such institutions. While the students at City College were competitive in talent, they especially distinguished themselves from Ivy League cohorts when it came to radical leftist politics. When the president of City College invited Italian students representing Benito Mussolini's fascist regime to speak on campus in 1934, the head of the student council, a member of the Young Communist League, welcomed "the tricked and enslaved students of Fascist Italy," with demonstrations thereafter persisting for weeks. It was this kind of spirited left-wing activism that earned City College the designation of "little red schoolhouse" (Dorman, 2000).

Although most City College students had grown up poor, the Great Depression only further exacerbated existing inequalities. Irving Howe, who attended the school and later coined the term *New York intellectuals*, recalled: "There was a sense of chaos, of disintegration. And so the socialist view, the radical view ... seemed to suggest a conceptual frame by which one could ... give meaning to these very difficult experiences" (in Dorman, 2000, p. 32). In fact, it was in the cafeteria of City College, where a number of alcoves existed, that sects of every "religious, ethnic, cultural, and political group" segregated, congregated, and debated. Irving Kristol, a former student now known as the father of neoconservatism, described this political milieu:

> I would guess that, in all, there were more than a dozen alcoves.... But the only alcoves that mattered to me were No. 1 and No. 2, the alcoves of the anti-Stalinist and the pro-Stalinist Left, respectively. It was between these two alcoves that the war of the world was fought. (1995, p. 472)

Reflecting on the subtle ways that Jewish experience informed debates within Alcove 1, Daniel Bell, another member of this group, explains:

> Socialism gave us answers to this world reading Marx, reading the *Communist Manifesto*, reading *Das Kapital*.... And you were able to take the same kind of reasoning that you learned in *kheder* [a school where young boys study the Torah and Talmud] and now deal with real-world problems. So we'd read *Kapital* the same way we read *humash* [Torah], line by line. In *kheder* there was a great pressure to learn by a sort of contrary logic.... Learning how to read is learning how to question.... That kind of *pilpul* [debate] trains you, arms you. (In Dorman, 2000, p. 35)

At the very same time, the universal call of Marxism for class consciousness and collective struggle appealed to the less particularistic sensibilities of these secular Jews at a time when ethnic and religious identification served to bolster forms of discrimination. "The embrace of Marxism," in other words, "was part of the Jewish intellectuals' search for a community to replace the Jewish one they denied and the American one denied to them" (Abrams, 2005, p. 14). This effort to finesse the tension between diversity and unity was reflected in *Partisan Review*, a communist and soon independent Marxist journal established in the mid-1930s by New York elders Philip Rahv and William Philips, and read by many in Alcove 1's younger generation. Nathan Glazer, a member of the latter group, noted that "Jewish topics entered [*Partisan Review*] only if they passed a test of universal significance" (in Dorman, 2000, p. 10).

The members of Alcove 1, including Howe, Kristol, Bell, Glazer, and others, would shift to liberal, even hard, anticommunist positions in the years ahead. In Alcove 2 were students such as Julius Rosenberg, whose own fate symbolized the battles that would characterize the cultural Cold War. As the unspeakable atrocities of Hitler and Nazism gained wider recognition and stories of Stalin's own abuses (e.g., Moscow Trials, 1939 pact with Hitler) emerged from the Soviet Union, the issue that increasingly preoccupied these young intellectuals was whether Stalin had betrayed Marxist ideals or revealed some inherent weakness in the communist vision (Steinfels, 1979). Kristol pondered, "Was there something in Marxism … that led to Stalinism? To what degree was there a connection? This was the question that … was a prelude to our future politics" (in Dorman, 2000, p. 54). Indeed, the shattering of their faith in the promise of collectivism was a crucial turning point in a slow rightward journey.

THE GOD THAT FAILED

In 1950, *The God That Failed* (Crossman, 1949) featured the political reflections of several American and Western European intellectuals originally committed to the communist cause, but ultimately disillusioned by the Soviet experiment. The book was "the collective autobiography of a generation," at least those segments centrally involved in the anticommunist struggle (p. vii). In the years following World War II, most of the New York intellectuals — Howe was an exception — deserted Marxism as a viable political philosophy. Fascism under Hitler and communism under Stalin, they proclaimed, were morally indistinguishable. "Just as Hitler had terrorized the world with concentration camps, genocide, [and] suppression of freedoms," Stalin had "done the same" (Gerson, 1997, p. 37). Revolted by the far left, which they believed consisted of naive Marxists at best and Stalinists at worst, this fraction of old leftists embraced an anticommunist position. This position entailed distinguishing themselves from radical leftists, whose anti-anticommunism they felt would only compromise the liberal cause, as well as from conservative anticommunists, who hailed the efforts of Senator Joseph McCarthy to destroy the communist threat, even if his disregard for civil liberties provided ammunition for far-left critiques of anticommunism (Gerson, 1997; Steinfels, 1979). Some, however, embraced a hard anticommunist position — something that caused a split within the denotatively named American Committee for Cultural Freedom (ACCF), in which many were involved in the 1950s (Friedman, 2005a, b; Kristol, 1952).

The anticommunist efforts of the ACCF revealed serious tensions around the meaning of cultural freedom and what was required to protect it. While Cold War liberals such as Arthur Schlesinger expressed the need for a "vital center" capable of showing regard for civil liberties and fighting communism, hard anticommunists placed more emphasis on an uncompromising strategy that aggressively countered Soviet propaganda and expansionism. The ACCF joined forces with the international Congress for Cultural Freedom (CCF), which maintained offices in 35 nations and supported various publications, including *Encounter* — a magazine coedited by Kristol and Stephen Spender, a London-based contributor to *The God That Failed*. Symbolic of the increasing commitment of hard anticommunists to an unfettered defense of the United States and the West was their disregard for rumors — later confirmed — that the CIA was funding both the CCF and *Encounter* (Friedman, 1999, 2005b; Steinfels, 1979). It was then that the culture war for the West first began, rather than in later decades as has generally been assumed.

The central venue through which the New York intellectuals came to express themselves, however, was *Commentary*, a journal established by the American Jewish Committee in 1945 (Friedman, 2005a). When compared with other Jewish civic organizations in the United States, the American Jewish Committee was most accommodationist in its orientation. Long before and during much of the early post–World War II era, for example, it assumed a non-Zionist position and framed its concerns for displaced persons in Europe in humanitarian rather than Jewish terms. In comparison, the more left leaning, confrontational American Jewish Congress embraced cultural pluralism as an ideal and pressed the nation to respond to the needs of European Jews as a persecuted minority. Significantly, it likewise learned that linking its project to American interests was often necessary for gaining wider support (Dollinger, 2000).

This tradition of accommodation — one undoubtedly facilitated by historic experiences of oppression — would shape *Commentary* in powerful ways. As a cultural project, *Commentary* evidenced a delicate balance (or perhaps, imbalance) between its Jewish and American affiliations and "produced a discourse of a specifically Jewish American nature." Elliot Cohen, the journal's editor from 1945 to 1960, expressed in his first editorial statement: "As Jews, we are of an ancient tradition that ... keeps a vigil with the past." At the same time, he stressed, "*Commentary* is an act of faith in our possibilities in America" (Abrams, 2005, p. 31). There was, of course, a complicated and deeply ironic politics at work — a kind that required "selective amnesia" to efface a history of anti-Semitism in the United States through the "memory" of an America more open to Jews than any nation in the Diaspora's history (p. 33). The process of constructing such a memory was assisted by very subtle checks on editorial independence. Abrams reveals that "the Jewish community's intellectuals had been screened through careful selection and then were co-opted by the American Jewish Committee" (p. 28).

Not only did *Commentary* aim to "bring the ideas of the New York intellectuals to a wider audience, especially upwardly mobile Jews," but it also aspired to "show that Jewish intellectuals, and by extension all American Jews, had turned away from their past political radicalism to embrace mainstream American culture and values" (Ehrman, 1999, pp. 160–161). Perhaps all of this was made easier — that is, the turn away from radicalism, especially for some intellectuals, toward liberal and conservative anticommunism and a romantic pro-American ideology — since an unprecedented opening of the society to Jews occurred in the late 1940s and 1950s. Kristol reports, "You must understand, no one I ever knew owned a car, or owned a home.... After ten years of Depression and four years of war, to be able to buy a house and have children and buy a car — that was fantastic" (in Dorman, 2000, pp. 83–84). During this period, moreover, many of the New York intellectuals moved into positions within the academy or functioned as public intellectuals within venues such as *Commentary* and other influential publications (Dorman, 2000; Friedman, 2005b).

Norman Podhoretz, editor of *Commentary* from 1960 to 1995, underscored the allure of the mainstream and centrality of upward mobility in his aptly titled autobiography, *Making It* (1967). It is extremely significant, then, that Irving Howe stopped writing for *Commentary* because it had "become an apologist for middle-class values, middle-class culture and the *status quo*" (quoted in Abrams, 2005, p. 35). Unlike many of his now liberal peers, Howe remained committed to democratic socialism and thus devoted his energies to co-founding *Dissent* in 1954 with still-radical colleagues (Mills & Walzer, 2004). Indeed, *Commentary* and *Dissent* reflected serious tensions within the New York intellectual community — something that prompted Woody Allen to humorously suggest that the two publications should unite under the title *Dysentery* (Friedman, 2005b, p. 136). In reality, though, the political fallout would be far less "entertaining" to those involved in this (un)civil war within the liberal camp and between liberals and leftists (Friedman, 2005b; Podhoretz, 1979). It would also have serious implications for groups later targeted by the arguments of those who ultimately made the neoconservative turn.

THE TURN TO NEOCONSERVATISM

The communities represented by *Commentary* and *Dissent* came to express dramatically different views on civil rights, the welfare state, the counterculture, the new left, and other issues during the 1960s and 1970s. By the late 1970s, the transition of many old leftists from liberalism to neoconservatism would be complete. The crossing — it is essential to recognize — would not bring them into the camp of traditional conservatism defined by premodern political philosophy, religiosity, anti-Semitism, racism, antistatism, and isolationism, or even into the traditional but modernized conservatism represented by William F. Buckley and his *National Review* (Judis, 1988; Shapiro, 1999). They were undeniably a new breed of conservatives; their roots, political trajectories, and ideological positions would distinguish them, often in ways that invited disdain from both the right and the left. Reflecting on such distinctions, Kristol writes:

> The conservatism of *National Review* interested us not at all. There were many points of repulsion, but it was *National Review*'s primordial hostility to the New Deal that created a gulf between us and them. We were all children of the depression, most of us from lower-middle-class or working-class families, a significant number of us urban Jews for whom the 1930s had been years of desperation, and we felt a measure of loyalty to the spirit of the New Deal.... Nor did we see it as representing any kind of statist or socialist threat.... All of us had ideas on how to improve, even reconstruct, this welfare state.... It was when the Great Society programs were launched that we began to distance ourselves ... from the newest version of official liberalism.... The prescribed cure for poverty was defined as militant political action ... that would result in the redistribution of income and wealth.... Having known poverty first-hand — the authors of the War on Poverty were mainly upper-middle-class types — and witnessing the ways poverty was overcome in reality ... we were utterly contemptuous of this idea. (n.d., pp. 3–4)

In a similar way, Nathan Glazer (2005) clarifies:

> All of us had voted for Lyndon Johnson in 1964.... Skepticism was only evoked by its [the Great Society's] more speculative ... extensions into "social engineering," as in the community participation effort in the War on Poverty, or the movement from civil rights to affirmative action.... Had we not defended the major social programs, from Social Security to Medicare, there would have been no need for the "neo" before "conservatism." (p. 3)

Indeed, a fusion of concerns from across the political spectrum would define the neoconservative vision.

The rise of the civil rights movement in the 1950s and the legislative gains of the mid-1960s were supported by the New York intellectuals and their associates. They embraced the idea that individuals should be considered equal before the law, regardless of religion or race. Nonetheless, when it came to demands for recognition rooted in identity politics or more militant racial assertions — whether for multiculturalism, Black Power, or affirmative action — these elicited strong condemnation. Consider "My Negro Problem — and Ours," written by Podhoretz in 1963 for *Commentary*. After recounting episodes in which he — a working-class Jewish boy in Brooklyn — was victimized by African American youth in his neighborhood, Podhoretz asks:

> Will this madness in which we are all caught never find a resting-place? Is there never to be an end to it? In thinking about the Jews, I have often wondered whether or not their survival as a distinct group was worth one hair on the head of a single infant. Did the Jews have to survive so that six million innocent people should one day be burned in the ovens of Auschwitz? ... And when I think ... about the image of integration as a state in which the Negroes would take their rightful place as another of the protected minorities in a pluralistic society, I wonder ... *why* they should wish to survive as a distinct group.

What was required, he argued, was "not integration" but "assimilation" and "miscegenation," as "the Negro problem can be solved ... in no other way" (Podhoretz, 1996, p. 17). In stark terms, Podhoretz reveals an aversion to identity politics and a faith in cultural assimilation as the answer to racial difficulties. In a postscript, he calls affirmative action "a diseased mutation of integrationism," laments "the damage done to the precious American principle .... of treating individuals as individuals," and criticizes the "destructive balkanization of our culture" (pp. 20–21). Echoed here are central tenets of neoconservative ideology — that liberalism has been deformed, meritocracy compromised, and culture fragmented. Undoubtedly problematic, this way of thinking is at least partially understandable when one considers how an oppressive history has schooled parts of the Jewish community to support accommodation for the purpose of advancement, or to criticize quotas, which were earlier used to limit rather than to increase Jewish representation. What is most noteworthy is how this set of positions simultaneously embraces the ideal of racial inclusion, while it inscribes hegemonic notions of culture through its delineation of how the "Negro problem" will be resolved. Moreover, a parallel is drawn between the historic experiences of Jewish Americans and African Americans with little recognition of significant differences, including the disparate subject positions available to ethnic and racial groups.

Equally significant, although these chastened intellectuals defended the New Deal and retained some confidence in state activism, they increasingly advocated a more limited welfare state and expressed concerns that

Great Society programs and the War on Poverty were creating a culturally deficient underclass dependent on government intervention (Kristol,
1996; Steinfels, 1979; Wildavsky, 1996). An early and by now iconic example
of this position is a government report issued in 1965 by Daniel Patrick
Moynihan — an associate of the New York intellectuals — entitled "The
Negro Family" (1996). According to him, the damage wrought on the African American family by past mistreatment remained the primary barrier
to black progress. Illegitimacy, single parenthood, and welfare created a
dire situation in which "the present tangle of pathology is capable of perpetuating itself without assistance from the white world" (p. 36).

   This line of argument was most thoroughly developed and advanced
by *The Public Interest* — a journal founded that same year by Kristol and
Bell that exclusively examined new government programs and their "unin-
tended consequences," including the perpetuation of "social pathologies"
in America's underclass. Reflecting the direction such work would take
over the coming decades was James Q. Wilson's *The Rediscovery of Character:
Private Virtue and Public Policy* (1996). He lauded the "growing awareness
that a variety of public problems can only be understood — and perhaps
addressed — if they are seen as arising out of a defect in character formation" (p. 291). Referring to the leading advocate of interventionist government spending, Wilson continues, "John Maynard Keynes was not simply
an important economist, he was a moral revolutionary.... Deficit financing
should be judged, he argued, by its practical effect, not by its moral quality" (p. 298). Put another way, Keynes had presumably failed to grasp the
wider implications of his financial doctrine. State spending on public programs is not solely an economic endeavor, it is a cultural one — and the
resulting gains and losses are not monetary alone; the deficit of greatest
concern, Wilson says, is one of discipline and virtue.

   The rightward drift of these intellectuals was also evident in their
response to the counterculture and the new left. It was not simply poor
communities of color that needed cultural reformation. Those pushing
the boundaries of gender and sexuality, those demonstrating on campuses
for free speech, those protesting the Vietnam War — all were seen as contributing to the degradation of tradition and authority, cultural relativism,
and ultimately a kind of moral void or nihilism that would undermine
cherished institutions and national stability (Dorman, 2000; Gerson, 1997).
Glazer (1997) explained his position on student radicalism in this way:

> I have made some commitments: that an orderly democracy is better than
> government by the expressive and violent outbursts of the most committed;
> that the university embodies values that transcend the given characteristics
> of a society ...; that the faults of our society, grave as they are, do not require
> ... the destruction of those fragile institutions which have been developed
> over centuries to transmit and expand knowledge.... My first reaction to

student disruption ... is to consider how the disrupters can be isolated ...
and how they can be finally removed from a community they wish to destroy.
(pp. 54–55)

Not without significance, Glazer deeply regretted the failure of liberal
intellectuals to challenge these attacks and of neoconservatives to answer
effectively when leftists in the academy, such as Noam Chomsky, "explained
[to students] how the world operated" (p. 63). Todd Gitlin, a founding member of Students for a Democratic Society, reflects on the conflict between
many once old leftists and new leftists and suggests that in the minds of the
former, Stalinism had been "a conclusive refutation of revolutionary possibilities" (in Dorman, 2000, p. 143). Perhaps it is even more complicated,
as the university itself represented for many of these intellectuals a domain
that ultimately offered to them long-denied privileges and power.

In 1973, Michael Harrington referred in the pages of *Dissent* to an emergent group of conservatives, former liberals and leftists who drifted right,
whom he called neoconservatives. Most, however, vehemently denied the
shift and eschewed the "neoconservative" label. "What was now called liberalism, they insisted, was a countercultural perversion of traditional Democratic politics. They had not changed, they claimed, but were reminders of
what American liberalism stood for before it was radicalized by the Movement [activism of the 1960s]" (Dorrien, 1993, p. 1).

NEO/CONSERVATIVES IN THE 1980s

The election of Ronald Reagan as president in 1980 represented a turning
point, with many neoconservatives casting Republican votes for the first
time. As they saw it, the Democratic Party had been captured by the radical left, so there was little choice in the matter. Yet it was still unclear to
many traditional conservatives — and many neoconservatives — whether
neoconservatives were actually conservatives. Traditionalists (sometimes
called paleoconservatives) believed that neoconservatives were a "schism
of the left," "right-wing liberals," and "social democrats who posed as
conservatives." Even neoconservatives suggested that they might be better described as paleoliberals since the liberalism of recent decades had
moved, in their view, so far to the left (Shapiro, 1999). In 1986, one paleo-
conservative warned:

> The offensives of radicalism have driven vast herds of liberals across the
> border into our territories. These refugees now speak in our name.... [But
> their language] contains no words for the things that we value. Our estate
> has been taken over by an impostor, just as we were about to inherit. (In
> Shapiro, 1999, p. 205)

Another traditionalist expressed his concerns in this fashion:

It has always struck me as odd, even perverse, that former Marxists have been permitted, yes invited, to play such a leading role in the Conservative movement.... It is splendid when the town whore gets religion and joins the church. Now and then she makes a good choir director, but when she begins to tell the minister what he ought to say in his Sunday sermons, matters have been carried too far. (In Nash, 2005, p. 163)

Much was at stake in the struggle over what constituted genuine conservatism, including positions in Reagan's administration and grants from conservative foundations. In one contest over who would be appointed as chair of the National Endowment for the Humanities, traditionalists supported M. E. Bradford while neoconservatives wanted William Bennett. When Brooklyn-born Bennett was chosen over pro-Confederate Bradford, tensions only worsened (Dorrien, 1993; Nash, 2005). Neoconservatives of later generations — Kristol's son, William Kristol; Podhoretz's son-in-law, Elliot Abrams; Chester Finn; Diane Ravitch; and others — would indeed assume positions alongside traditionalists under Reagan and become key players in right-wing foundations and think tanks (Friedman, 2005b; Kovacs & Boyles, 2005; Selden, 2004).

Despite existing tensions, paleoconservatives and neoconservatives mutually influenced one another throughout the 1980s. More traditional conservatives reconciled themselves to the fact that particular civil rights and welfare state provisions had gained wider legitimacy, while neoconservatives became more critical of the welfare state and began to incorporate moral and religious concerns into their cultural agenda (Judis, 1988; Nash, 2005). In the end, however, neoconservatives exercised greater influence on conservatism — that is, they "wrought a profound change in the scope and the character and the ethos of American conservatism" (Podhoretz, in Shapiro, 1999, p. 213). The ability to appeal to a wide array of groups has probably been their most noteworthy contribution. Starting out on the left and migrating to the right (at least the founding generation) meant that neoconservatives could often connect with groups beyond the reach of traditionalists, even if these relations were strained and contradictory. This "double set of relationships" was evident at a dinner in the mid-1970s for Senator Henry Jackson, whose campaign for the Democratic presidential nomination was supported by many neoconservatives before their move to the Republican Party. Among those present were Moynihan, civil rights activist A. Philip Randolph, union leader Albert Shanker, and Podhoretz (Steinfels, 1979).

The work of the New York Jewish intellectuals and their non-Jewish associates has been carried forward by subsequent generations — "*Commentary*'s children," as Ehrman (1999) has referred to the lineal heirs of neoconservatism. Despite the central role of the New York intellectuals in forging neoconservatism, neoconservatism has not won over the broader Jewish community, which remains liberal in its politics, particularly at the national level (Friedman, 1999; Heilman, 1995). Rather, the discourses and political vision of this bloc of former leftists and their descendents have resonated with a spectrum of other groups. As such, a far more extensive neoconservative network — one consisting of segments characterized by backgrounds and historical trajectories quite different from the New York intellectuals — has developed. Roman Catholics such as Michael Novak, conservatives of color such as Thomas Sowell, Dinesh D'Souza, Linda Chavez, and Francis Fukuyama, and middle-class constituencies of various ethnic and regional affiliations have joined the neoconservative effort (Dorrien, 1993; Friedman, 2005b; Haggard-Gilson, 1998; Podair, 2002). Additionally, neoconservatives have affiliated with other major groups within the new right, including economic and religious conservatives. Understanding the commonalities and differences within the neoconservative bloc and its complex relationship both to the new right as a whole and to traditionally marginalized groups is work that is still under way (Apple, 2001; Apple & Buras, 2006; Buras & Apple, 2005; Apple & Pedroni, 2005). Such work is crucial if the left is to adequately assess the spaces for interrupting rightist efforts, which are characterized, in actuality, by an often fragile balance of interests.

1990s: FROM THE COLD WAR TO THE CULTURE WAR?

With the so-called collapse of communism in 1989, what would hold together neoconservatism, heavily defined by its activism against the "Soviet threat"? "Like their conservative allies," writes Dorrien (1993), "the neoconservatives were united mostly by their anticommunism" (p. 323). Under Podhoretz, *Commentary* had reinvigorated the fight against communism in the 1970s, and a number of neoconservative figures even formed the Committee on the Present Danger — an effort that aimed to educate an unduly lax public and government about the (allegedly) escalating threat of Soviet domination (Friedman, 2005b; Powers, 2005). To a notable degree, then, neoconservatism had wedded itself to the anticommunist struggle.

That said, accounts of neoconservatism have too frequently emphasized foreign policy and defense issues, thereby framing the culture war as a post–Cold War development in the chronology of neoconservatism. Not long after the collapse, for example, Christopher Hitchens "argued that neoconservatism had lost the enemy on which it was dependent and therefore had outlived its usefulness to the conservative movement" (Dorrien, 1993, p. 350). In short, the struggle for cultural order was perceived as relatively new or at least as too peripheral to be a driving concern. It may be that neoconservatives escalated their battle on the cultural front in the 1990s, but such analyses overlook the significant cultural dimension of neo-conservative work all along. My intent is to render visible the long-standing cultural agenda of neoconservatives and to demonstrate that these cold warriors were Western cultural warriors early on.

Writing an entire decade before the collapse of communism, Steinfels (1979) questions:

> To what extent do neoconservative concerns for national order and stability spring from a perception of international threat? To what extent does the insistence on international threat spring from a desire to shock society into national order and stability? ... Neoconservatives are undoubtedly sincere in their anxiety over international affairs, at the same time as the essential source of that anxiety is not military or geopolitical or to be found overseas at all; it is domestic and cultural and ideological.... The existence of an ideo-logically armed and intact elite is the crucial ingredient, and its role in resist-ing external pressure is only the reverse side of its role in resisting internal disintegration. (pp. 68–69)

This is a crucial insight: The Cold War was as much about enemies within as without. We need only to consider Kristol's attack on multicul-turalism in the early 1990s in which he declared, "What these radicals call multiculturalism is as much a 'war against the West' as Nazism and Stalin-ism ever were" (1995, p. 52). In this way, the present danger was never an external one only. Let us recall that the American Committee for Cul-tural Freedom operated on the home front. So did *The Public Interest*, which Moynihan wanted to name *Consensus* to signify that the making of pub-lic policy required technical knowledge rather than divisive, ideological debate (Steinfels, 1979, pp. 43–44). Indisputably, the Cold War against the diversification of knowledge began long before 1989 and long before a backlash emerged against the radicalism of the 1960s. Acknowledging this enables us to consider contemporary neoconservative school reform as the product of a more extensive and complex history and to better discern the spaces for dissent and for more democratic educational mobilizations.

NEOCONSERVATISM, CORE KNOWLEDGE, AND RIGHTIST MULTICULTURALISM

The marks of this history are apparent in Core Knowledge, a curricu-lum reform effort under the guidance of neoconservative visionary E. D. Hirsch and his Core Knowledge Foundation (2006). Nearly two decades ago, Hirsch (1987) authored *Cultural Literacy*. This bestseller generated a wave of debate as it declared not only the importance of common culture to national unity, but defined the relevant content of that culture and blamed multiculturalism for undermining it. Deemed Eurocentric by critics, *Cultural Literacy* nonetheless metamorphosed into Core Knowledge — a prekindergarten through eighth grade curriculum. The first school to implement the curriculum opened in 1990, and Core has since been adopted by nearly 1000 schools (Buras, 2006c). It might seem curious that an initiative developed to mediate against the threat of identity politics in education has garnered support from a range of communities — some constituted by traditionally marginalized groups. Let us recall, however, the history just traced: Neoconservatism is an in-between politics, a politics of strategic compromise, a politics suffused with the residue of the left but also permeated by the compositions of the right. This gives it a certain power to respond to disparate interests, though not without tension.

Take, for a moment, Hirsch's educational vision, which has all of the imprints of neoconservative thought. According to him, progressivism has overtaken schools and rendered the curriculum incoherent. This incoherence not only threatens the common culture of the nation — something Hirsch assumes should be shared by all groups to maintain political stability — but likewise puts "culturally deficient" groups at risk since a fragmented curriculum cannot remedy impoverished dispositions and knowledge. He emphasizes that "students from good-home schools will always have an educational advantage over students from less-good home schools" (1996, p. 43). In a spirit both optimistic and foreboding, he warns: "Young children who arrive at school with a ... limited knowledge base can fortunately be [helped] ... [but] when this language and knowledge deficit is not compensated for early, it is nearly impossible ... in later grades" (p. 146). Hirsch thus skillfully and problematically blends criticisms of cultural illiteracy with concerns for equality, social mobility, and civil rights. Indeed, he contends that Core Knowledge is part of the "new civil rights frontier" (Buras, 1999).

According to Hirsch, multiculturalism is partly responsible for the cultural crisis that he perceives. Interestingly, this leads him not to reject multiculturalism, but to redefine it along more conservative lines. "Multiculturalism comes in different guises," Hirsch asserts. "There's a progressive form that will be helpful to all students, and a retrogressive kind that ... tends to set group against group" (p. 1). Rather than the retrogressive and "particularistic" tradition of "ethnic loyalism" that promotes social divisions, he advocates a "universalistic" tradition of "cosmopolitanism" that stresses being "a member of humanity as a whole" (1992, p. 3). Unlike some neoconservatives who have urged a less hospitable response to issues of diversity, Hirsch clearly agrees with Glazer's (1997) declaration that "simple denunciation ... will no longer do" (p. 33). "We are all multiculturalists now," resigns Glazer. "The fight is over how much [multiculturalism], what kind, for whom, at what ages, under what standards" (p. 19).

This vision and the strategic compromises that accompany it have enabled Hirsch to bring multiple groups into an alliance around Core Knowledge — much like the dinner honoring Senator Jackson. Many suburban schools have adopted Core in an effort to reclaim the classics and restore traditional knowledge. At the same time, there are urban schools in communities of color that embrace Core as a way of advancing the interests of marginalized children — all the while renovating the curriculum to "include the traditions" of African American and Latino children (see Buras, 2006c). The composite nature of the Core alliance does not escape Hirsch, who notes: "To be liked by the Bushies and the American Federation of Teachers [AFT] — there's something peculiar going on" (in Lindsay, 2001, p. W24). Indeed, the AFT gave Hirsch an award in 1997 and its former president, Sandra Feldman, sat on the board of the Core Knowledge Foundation. But Hirsch also associates with neoconservatives such as Ravitch, Finn, and Bennett through rightist think tanks like Brookings, Fordham, and Hoover.

The curriculum also negotiates the tensions between old and new histories by adopting in Core textbooks (Hirsch, 2002) what I have called *new old history*. Whereas old histories centered on dominant groups through a narrative of consensus and new histories on subaltern groups through a narrative of conflict, Core's new old history recognizes both elite and subaltern groups. This occurs, however, through a major storyline that largely ignores unequal power and conflict. When oppressive experiences are detailed, this occurs through a minor storyline in which relations with dominant groups are discursively masked. Such narratives, moreover, are strategically packaged. Despite Hirsch's fear of identity politics, upper-grade textbook covers feature a president, a Native American, and other group representatives, rather than a unifying image such as the American flag (Buras, 2006b, 2006c).

Not surprisingly, Hirsch evidences the political identity crisis of so many neoconservatives who denied their shift rightward and claimed that they were the defenders of true liberal ideals. He deems himself "a political liberal and an educational conservative" and insists that "political liberals really ought to oppose progressive educational ideas because they have led to … greater social inequality. The only practical way to achieve liberalism's aim of greater social justice is to pursue conservative educational policies" (1996, p. 6).

Taken together, Hirsch's elitist educational vision expressed through concerns for democracy his alarm over cultural deficiency combined with his reformulation of the civil rights agenda, the alliance of differently situated groups around Core Knowledge, and the new old history contained in Core textbooks; all of this constitutes a neoconservative strategy that I have called *rightist multiculturalism*. It may seem as contradictory as the advocacy of a conservative welfare state, but it has given Hirsch and the Core

Knowledge Foundation wider legitimacy and the power to advance the neoconservative agenda in schools. Importantly, this has required efforts to discipline curricular deviation and diversity within the Core Knowledge movement, reminding us that subaltern groups may appropriate dominant forms in unanticipated ways (Buras, 2006c).

In the sixth grade, Core Knowledge students read about turn-of-the-20th-century immigrants. The last of several chapters is entitled "Becoming American," and it opens with an excerpt from Israel Zangwill's 1908 play, *Melting Pot*:

> America is ... the great Melting Pot where all the races of Europe are melting.... Here you stand ... when I see you at Ellis Island ... in your fifty groups, with your fifty languages and histories.... But you won't be long like that.... Into the Crucible with you all! God is making the American. (Hirsch, 2002, p. 260)

The chapter concludes in a celebratory tone, indicating that the ways of the old country had disappeared by the third generation. In seeking to reconcile diversity and unity, Core participates in the arguments that divided the New York intellectuals. In *World of Our Fathers*, Irving Howe (1976) affirmed the culture of Eastern European Jewish immigrants in New York and mourned its disappearance, thereby revealing the costs of accommodation to Jews (Michels, 2000) and, by extension, to other groups struggling against cultural domination. Perhaps the "great Jewish-American synthesis" (Wolfe, 2005) is not all that Jewish neoconservatives thought it to be. What, then, of school reform in a neoconservative age?

REFERENCES

Abrams, N. (2005). "America is home": *Commentary* magazine and the refocusing of the community of memory, 1945–1960. In M. Friedman (Ed.), *Commentary in American life* (pp. 9–37). Philadelphia: Temple University Press.

Apple, M. W. (2001). *Educating the "right" way: Markets, standards, god, and inequality*. New York: RoutledgeFalmer.

Apple, M. W., & Buras, K. L. (Eds.). (2006). *The subaltern speak: Curriculum, power, and educational struggles*. New York: Routledge.

Apple, M. W., & Pedroni, T. C. (2005). Conservative alliance building and African American support of vouchers: The end of Brown's promise or a new beginning? *Teachers College Record, 107*, 2068–2105.

Buchanan, P. J. (2003, March 24). Whose war? [electronic]. *The American Conservative*.

Buras, K. L. (1999). Questioning Core assumptions: A critical reading of and response to E. D. Hirsch's *The Schools We Need and Why We Don't Have Them. Harvard Educational Review, 69*, 67–93.

Buras, K. L. (2006a). Historicizing cultural literacy: Neoconservatism, "racial pathology," and the new civil rights frontier. Manuscript submitted for publication.

Buras, K. L. (2006b). *The disuniting of America's history: Core Knowledge and the national past.* Manuscript submitted for publication.

Buras, K. L. (2006c). Tracing the Core Knowledge movement: History lessons from above and below. In M. W. Apple & K. L. Buras (Eds.), *The subaltern speak: Curriculum, power, and educational struggles* (pp. 43–74). New York: Routledge.

Buras, K. L., & Apple, M. W. (2005). School choice, neoliberal promises, and unpromising evidence. *Educational Policy, 19,* 550–564.

Core Knowledge Foundation. (2006). Home page. Retrieved from www.coreknowledge.org

Crossman, R. H. (Ed.). (1949). *The God that failed.* New York: Columbia University Press.

Dollinger, M. (2000). *Quest for inclusion: Jews and liberalism in America.* Princeton, NJ: Princeton University Press.

Dorman, J. (2000). *Arguing the world: The New York intellectuals in their own words.* Chicago: University of Chicago Press.

Dorrien, G. (1993). *The neoconservative mind: Politics, culture, and the war of ideology.* Philadelphia: Temple University Press.

Drury, S. B. (1999). *Leo Strauss and the American right.* New York: St. Martin's Press.

Drury, S. B. (2003). *Saving America: Leo Strauss and the neoconservatives.* Retrieved April 27, 2007 from http://evatt.labor.net.au/publications/papers/112.html

Ehrman, J. (1999). *Commentary,* the *Public Interest,* the problem of Jewish neoconservatism. *American Jewish History, 87,* 159–181.

Friedman, M. (1999). Opening the discussion of American Jewish political conservatism. *American Jewish History, 87,* 101–122.

Friedman, M. (Ed.). (2005a). *Commentary in American life.* Philadelphia: Temple University Press.

Friedman, M. (2005b). *The neoconservative revolution: Jewish intellectuals and the shaping of public policy.* New York: Cambridge University Press.

Gerson, M. (Ed.). (1996). *The essential neoconservative reader.* New York: Addison-Wesley.

Gerson, M. (1997). *The neoconservative vision: From the cold war to the culture wars.* New York: Madison Books.

Glazer, N. (1997). *We are all multiculturalists now.* Cambridge, MA: Harvard University Press.

Glazer, N. (2005). Neoconservatism from the start. *The Public Interest, 159.*

Haggard-Gilson, N. (1998). Against the grain: Black conservatives and Jewish neoconservatives. In V. P. Franklin (Ed.), *African Americans and Jews in the twentieth century: Studies in convergence and conflict* (pp. 165–190). Columbia: University of Missouri Press.

Heilman, S. C. (1995). *Portrait of American Jews: The last half of the 20th century.* Seattle: University of Washington Press.

Hirsch, E. D., Jr. (1987). *Cultural literacy: What every American needs to know.* New York: Vintage Books.

Hirsch, E. D., Jr. (1992). *Toward a centrist curriculum: Two kinds of multiculturalism in elementary schools.* Charlottesville, VA: Core Knowledge Foundation.

Hirsch, E. D., Jr. (1996). *The schools we need and why we don't have them.* New York: Doubleday Press.

Hirsch, E. D., Jr. (Ed.). (2002). *Pearson learning: Core Knowledge history and geography textbooks, grades K-6.* Parsippany, NJ: Pearson Learning Group.

Howe, I. (1976). *World of our fathers: The journey of the East European Jews to America and the life they found and made.* New York: Harcourt, Brace, Jovanovich.

Judis, J. B. (1988). *William F. Buckley, Jr.: Patron saint of the conservatives.* New York: Simon & Schuster.

Kovacs, P. E., & Boyles, D. R. (2005). Institutes, foundations, and think tanks: Conservative influence on U.S. public schools. *Public Resistance, 1,* 24–41.

Kristol, I. (1952). "Civil liberties," 1952: A study in confusion. *Commentary, 13.*

Kristol, I. (1995). *Neoconservatism: The autobiography of an idea.* Chicago: Ivan R. Dee.

Kristol, I. (1996). A conservative welfare state. In M. Gerson (Ed.), *The essential neoconservative reader* (pp. 283–287). New York: Addison-Wesley Publishing.

Kristol, I. (2005). Forty good years. *The Public Interest, 159.* Retrieved May 1, 2007 from http://findarticles.com/p/articles/mi_m0377/is_159/ai_n13779487/pg_1.

Kristol, I. (n.d.). American conservatism, 1945–1995. *The Public Interest.* Retrieved from http://www.thepublicinterest.com/notable/article2.html

Lindsay, D. (2001, November 11). Against the establishment: How a U-VA professor, denounced as elitist and ethnocentric, became a prophet of the school standards movement. *Washington Post,* W24.

Michels, T. (2000). Socialism and the writing of American Jewish history: *World of Our Fathers* revisited. *American Jewish History, 88,* 521–546.

Mills, N., & Walzer, M. (Eds.). (2004). *50 years of Dissent.* New Haven, CT: Yale University Press.

Moynihan, D. P. (1996). The negro family: The case for national action. In M. Gerson (Ed.), *The essential neoconservative reader* (pp. 23–37). New York: Addison-Wesley Publishing.

Nash, G. H. (2005). Joining the ranks: *Commentary* and American conservatism. In M. Friedman (Ed.), *Commentary in American life* (pp. 151–173). Philadelphia: Temple University Press.

Podair, J. E. (2002). *The strike that changed New York: Blacks, whites, and the Ocean Hill-Brownsville crisis.* New Haven, CT: Yale University Press.

Podhoretz, N. (1967). *Making it.* New York: Harper & Row Publishers.

Podhoretz, N. (1979). *Breaking ranks: A political memoir.* New York: Harper & Row Publishers.

Podhoretz, N. (1996). My negro problem — and ours. In M. Gerson (Ed.), *The essential neoconservative reader* (pp. 5–22). New York: Addison-Wesley Publishing.

Powers, R. G. (2005). Norman Podhoretz and the cold war. In M. Friedman (Ed.), *Commentary in American life* (pp. 134–150). Philadelphia: Temple University Press.

Sarna, J. D. (1999). American Jewish political conservatism in historical perspective. *American Jewish History, 87,* 113–122.

Selden, S. (2004). The neo-conservative assault on the undergraduate curriculum. In M. Walker & J. Nixon (Eds.), *Reclaiming universities from a runaway world* (pp. 51–66). New York: Open University Press.

Shapiro, E. S. (1999). Jews and the conservative rift. *American Jewish History, 87,* 195–215.

Steinfels, P. (1979). *The neoconservatives: The men who are changing America's politics.* New York: Simon & Schuster.

Wildavsky, A. (1996). Government and the people. In M. Gerson (Ed.), *The essential neoconservative reader* (pp. 76–92). New York: Addison-Wesley Publishing.

Wilson, J. Q. (1996). The rediscovery of character: Private virtue and public policy. In M. Gerson (Ed.), *The essential neoconservative reader* (pp. 291–304). New York: Addison-Wesley.

Wolfe, A. (2005, June 3). "The great Jewish-American synthesis," in The Chronicle Review. Retrieved May 1, 2007 from http://chronicle.com/weekly/v51/i39/39b00901.htm.

Chapter 7

Fascism

Laurence W. Britt
Fairport, New York

As we move forward on what has been so far the rocky road of the 21st century, the political culture in the United States is leaving a disturbing impression on the world. Never before in American history has the United States been so distrusted and held less credibility in the international arena. Domestically, growing numbers of Americans are coming to share that distrust of the government and fear the direction in which the Bush administration is pushing their country. And they should be afraid. As I intend to show here, contemporary elements within the government are pushing the nation dangerously toward fascism.

Until recently, most Americans would be outraged to hear such a charge leveled at their government. Things have changed. An entirely new set of conditions has gripped the American body politic. In April 2003, I authored an article in *Free Inquiry* magazine that outlined the 14 basic identifying characteristics of seven fascist or neofascist regimes of the 20th century. It was a "food for thought" article that asked the reader to compare these characteristics with what was going on in George Bush's America. The national and international reaction to this article astounded me. It quickly became the most frequently reprinted article in the history of *Free Inquiry*, and it spread across the Internet exponentially. It has been translated into five languages and resulted in a number of talk show appearances and speaking engagements for me.

Clearly, many people saw the ascendance of neoconservatism in Washington and the simultaneous implementation of neoliberal economic policies as a disturbing development. Many, in fact, saw it as worse than disturbing. Many recognized their convergence as incipient fascism. However, few mainstream opinion shapers in the media or the Democratic Party would dare call this phenomenon by that incendiary name.

I am aware that one must be cautious in using such heavily charged words as *fascism* and *neofascism*. The terms conjure potent images of Nazis, concentration camps, and genocide. As evidenced by Mussolini's Italy, however, genocide does not constitute a requisite feature of fascism. Therefore, claiming that we witness the emergence of troubling fascist tendencies in American foreign and domestic policies is not tantamount to calling the Bush administration a Nazi regime. The position being proposed in this chapter is that the convergence of neoconservativism and neoliberalism, if allowed to go unchecked, leads to very strong fascist tendencies. Further, while I would not dare to draw an equivalency between the horrors of the Nazi death camps that destroyed nearly 10 million lives — most of them Jewish — and the practices of extraordinary rendition and sometimes murderous abuses at the now infamous prisons at Guantanamo Bay, Abu Ghraib, and the secret facilities used by the U.S. government for the internment and interrogation of suspected terrorists and enemy noncombatants, we should not ignore the significance of the latter as we consider the larger fascist context in which they occur. Neither should we ignore the authoritarian assumptions of neoconservativism and neoliberalism that lend their convergence toward fascist tendencies.

Granted, the fundamental assumptions of neoliberalism predate 20th-century fascism. In fact, we can trace them back to the 18th century and Adam Smith's *Wealth of Nations* and the belief that unfettered growth of capitalism would lead to the maximization of wealth. Smith believed that the marketplace rules and the accumulation of wealth should be unhindered by regulation, regardless of the ecological or human costs. Accumulation of money and power were natural outcomes of human economic activities and should be accepted as such. In this worldview, the have-nots deserve their fate and should not to be trusted with power. (Note: The term *neoliberal* is not in common use in America, but it is the standard term for the brutal resurgence of laissez-faire capitalism throughout the world.)

Neoconservativism departs from more traditional conservatism in that it proposes a dominant international posture, the ascendance of a political elite, and distrust of the common citizen. Leo Strauss is the intellectual godfather of neoconservativism. His political philosophy stressed, among other things, the use of religion and nationalism to secure the allegiance of the masses to the will of the state, the aggressive use of political power in foreign affairs, and the uninhibited exercise of military force in support of economic interests and national security.

The combination of these two ideologies, which are currently manifested to a considerable degree in the Bush administration, represents a political movement that has many similarities to historical fascism. When fascism first emerged in the early part of the 20th century it was often

brought about by hard times or visceral fears and hatreds that fascist politicians exploited to strengthen their domination. In Italy, Benito Mussolini
exaggerated and exploited the fear of communism. In Germany, Adolph
Hitler blamed Jews for the growth of trade unions and an intellectual and
moral climate that threatened the German spirit and led to economic
depression. In Spain, General Francisco Franco provoked and played upon
people's fear of socialism and the threat to Spanish traditions. Postwar
neofascist regimes followed the same patterns. Power was given or seized
based on fear of demonized enemies, usually the political left, or hatred
of ethnic or religious minorities. It was a political appeal that tapped into
the basest of human impulses and was usually supported by propaganda
that often dealt in blatant falsehoods. This was the famous Big Lie technique perfected by Hitler. Repeat an outrageous falsehood over and over
again; eventually, a majority of the people will come to believe it. Many
contemporary observers contend that the triggering event for American
neoconservative/neoliberal ascendance was the 9/11 tragedy and the subsequent War on Terror. This was the transforming event, our Reichstag
fire, the classic model for fascist regimes to seize the public imagination
and exploit their fears and anger to consolidate political power.

An analysis of Nazi Germany, fascist Italy, Franco's Spain, Salazar's Portugal, Pinochet's Chile, Papadopoulos's Greece, and Suharto's Indonesia
reveals 14 common characteristics that link them in recognizable patterns of national behavior. Some of these characteristics are more prevalent in some regimes than in others, but all regimes exhibit them at least
to some degree. Below is a list of these 14 common characteristics with a
brief description and a comment as to whether they are also neoconserva-
tive/neoliberal characteristics. Then I will cite a few current examples that
demonstrate these characteristics in the recent past.

COMMON CHARACTERISTICS OF FASCIST REGIMES

1. **Powerful and continuing nationalism**: These regimes used prominent displays of national symbols, catchy slogans, appeals to patriotism, demands for unity, attacks on those not sufficiently patriotic,
   suspicion of things foreign, and glorification of the military.

   This is clearly an American neoconservative characteristic. Examples abound of the numerous slogans, symbols, and actions: the
   endorsement and use of preemption as a national right, embedded
   media extolling American military exploits, Shock and Awe, Operation Iraqi Freedom, landing on the aircraft carrier, "freedom fries,"
   "bring 'um on," oceans of flags at every appearance, military back-
   drops for important speeches, and equating support for the troops to
   supporting the administration.

2. **Disdain for the importance of human rights**: The fascist regimes viewed human rights of marginal value. The people were brought to accept human rights abuses by marginalizing or demonizing those targeted. When the abuse was egregious, the tactic was to use secrecy, denial, and disinformation.

Unfortunately, many examples of neoconservative excess make this another similar characteristic: mass arrests after 9/11; treatment of prisoners at Abu Ghraib, Guantanamo, Bagram AFB, and secret prisons; extraordinary rendition; torture debate; attacking Amnesty International; rejecting the International Criminal Court; and calling the Geneva Convention "quaint." At the same time, there are few actual open trials of terror suspects.

3. **Identification of enemies/scapegoats as a unifying cause**: The most significant common thread among fascist regimes was the use of scapegoating as a means to divert the people's attention from other problems. The method of choice was to keep the people agitated and in a constant state of fear by relentless propaganda and disinformation.

This again has been a staple of neoconservative strategy in recent years. The invented slogans and actions speak for themselves: axis of evil, War on Terror, the WMD scare (mushroom cloud references), the color alerts raised and lowered for political effect, "you're either with us or you're with the terrorists," and accusing those who questioned the Patriot Act as aiding the terrorists.

4. **Supremacy of the military and militarism**: Fascist leaders always closely identified themselves with the military. A disproportionate share of national resources was allocated to the military even when domestic needs were acute. The military was seen as an expression of nationalism and was used whenever possible to assert national goals and intimidate other nations.

The neoconservative movement is firmly entrenched within the Bush administration and takes as its modus operandi the precepts articulated by the Project for the New American Century (PNAC). Many PNAC board members populate the administration. One of PNAC's basic principles was to transform the U.S. military into an instrument to advance American strategic interests around the world. One concern expressed in PNAC documents was whether the American people could be persuaded to embrace such a concept without another precipitating event like Pearl Harbor. The 9/11 attack was that event. Military spending as a percent of the total federal budget is now at a level equal to that during the height of the Cold War when we were confronting a superpower adversary. It is a military built to intimidate and attack other nations, such as Iraq. It is not being geared to fight the War on Terror, which should be a worldwide police action requiring international cooperation, good intelligence, and emphasis on special forces.

5. **Rampant sexism**: Fascist regimes were sexist, not only from the male dominance perspective, but also for being homophobic in the extreme and adamantly antiabortion.

   Neither neoconservative or neoliberal philosophical positions as currently manifested in the Bush administration can be associated with the type of sexism exhibited by 20th-century fascist regimes. But the religious right, who provide the electoral base that makes neo-conservative/neoliberal political power possible, are certainly in congruence with the fascist model in regard to sexism as defined above. It could be argued that without the political support of the religious right, neoconservative/neoliberal ascendance would not be possible.

6. **Controlled mass media**: Even when the media were not under the direct control of a fascist government, media orthodoxy was maintained by various methods. These included control of licensing, access to sources of information, economic pressure, appeals to patriotism, and implied threats. The leaders of the mass media were often politically compatible with those in power. The result was success in keeping the public generally unaware of the extent of the regime's excesses.

   The United States has freedom of the press, unlike fascist regimes. However, following the neoliberal model, it has become more and more a media environment where huge financial resources are needed to be a media player. As a result, due to commercial interests, controversial or alternative views are often excluded from news coverage. When the Fairness Doctrine was eliminated in 1987, it opened the door to unanswered partisan broadcasting, which requires large financial backing. Since the political right controls vast financial resources, the center of gravity in the total media environment has moved to the right. Fox News is unabashedly right wing, and there is no network presenting the opposite viewpoint. Furthermore, the Bush administration has blatantly attempted to control news coverage by planting stories, paying journalists to write "news," inserting fake journalists into news conferences, and seeking to gain control of the Public Broadcasting System with political appointees.

7. **Obsession with national security**: Fascist states always had a national security apparatus under the direct control of the regime. It usually operated in secret and beyond normal constraints. Its actions were justified under the rubric of protecting national security, whether or not this was actually true. Those questioning this national security apparatus were portrayed as unpatriotic or even treasonous.

   The neoconservative philosophy, as enumerated in PNAC, puts national security and American dominance at the top of its agenda. The Patriot Act significantly compromised traditional American civil liberties. Opposition in Congress was prevented from seeing full intelligence on Iraq, justifying war under the rationale that it would jeopardize national security. Detainees in Guantanamo are denied trials due to national security issues. A U.S. citizen was held for three years without an attorney or charges due to national security. Opposition groups to the Bush administration charge that national security is being used as a cover to bury mistakes and abuses. The Bush administration has been the most secretive in American history, routinely violating rules under the Freedom of Information Act.

8. **Religion and ruling elite tied together**: The fascist regimes usually attached themselves to the predominant religion of the country and portrayed themselves as defenders of that religion. The fact that the regime's excesses were incompatible with the precepts of the religion was swept under the rug with clever propaganda. A perception was manufactured that opposing those in power was tantamount to an attack on religion.

    As in the case with sexism, neither neoconservativism nor neoliberalism specifically engages directly in religious issues as they relate to governance. But the religious right is a key electoral component that has brought the Bush administration to power. This voting block is strongly motivated by the administration's support for various religious causes and faith-based initiatives, including Christian schools. Ironically, many, if not most, of the voters who support the Bush administration due to religious beliefs would not support the neoliberal agenda if they fully understood it.

9. **Power of corporations protected**: Although the personal life of ordinary citizens under fascist regimes was often under strict control, the ability of large corporations to operate freely and make profits was not compromised. Fascist rulers saw the corporate structure as an additional means for social control. The corporate elite and ruling elite were often interchangeable and had a mutual interest in maintaining the ability to make money and maintain political power.

    This is clearly a fundamental precept of neoliberalism. Every action of the Bush administration as it relates to corporate issues has been in favor of increasing the influence, power, and profitability of corporations. There are many examples: the new bankruptcy law strongly favoring banks over consumers; the new senior drug benefits under Medicare, which mainly benefit drug companies by preventing government-negotiated pricing; the noncompetitive bids for administration-connected companies, that is, Haliburton, Bechtel, and so forth; and at the administration's urging, Congress has rejected proposals to investigate Iraq war profiteering.

10. **Power of labor suppressed or eliminated**: Since organized labor was seen as the one power center that could challenge the political

hegemony of fascist rulers and its corporate allies, it was inevitably attacked or made powerless. The poor formed an underclass viewed with suspicion or outright contempt. In some regimes, being poor was considered akin to a vice.

This is another neoliberal concept, since organized labor may challenge those with entrenched economic power. This has manifested itself in many ways under the Bush administration, such as opposition to raising the minimum wage, changes in laws eliminating overtime payments to millions of workers, limiting organized labor in political contributions, appointing conservatives to the National Labor Relations Board (NLRB), tilting the balance decisively to the corporate side, especially in the suppression of labor organizing, restricting labor rights in the New Orleans reconstruction, and appointing a secretary of labor with an obvious antilabor background.

11. **Disdain and suppression of intellectuals and the arts**: Intellectuals, and the inherent freedom of ideas and expression associated with them, were anathema to fascist regimes. Unorthodox ideas and dissent were strongly attacked, silenced, or crushed. Scientific principles were compromised or attacked if they were in conflict with the regime's goals.

    Since most intellectuals are of a leftist persuasion, the neoconservative/neoliberal axis would naturally oppose them on many bases. The antiwar stance of most intellectuals has drawn strong opposition from neoconservatives in particular, as they are seen as a major stumbling block to the neoconservative objective of pursuing American world hegemony. Neoliberals would have a visceral opposition to this group because they are seen as having views inimical to a laissez-faire economic approach. Neoliberals would even oppose balanced scientific research versus Corporate-sponsored research that worked for the benefit of corporations. This has happened in the rejection of global warming studies. A renowned group of 60 scientists, including 20 Nobel laureates, condemned the Bush administration for its antiscience positions in bowing to corporate and religious right constituents on scientific issues.

12. **Obsession with crime and punishment**: The fascist regimes maintained draconian systems of criminal justice with huge prison populations. The police were often glorified and had almost unchecked power, often leading to abuse. Fear and hatred of criminals or "traitors" was often promoted among the population as an excuse for more police power.

    Even though the neoconservative/neoliberal axis is not directly associated with the issues of crime and punishment, the overtones of their political philosophy are easy to discern in this area. Crime has become a major industry, driven largely by questionable drug laws, with rapidly growing police forces and growing prison populations providing many economic opportunities. Prison construction, even privatized prisons, along with all the related goods and services, has provided significant moneymaking opportunities. Minority populations living in poverty have been the primary victims and targets for this massive crackdown on crime. Additionally, removing significant numbers of voters who could be expected to oppose the neoconservative/neoliberal agenda is a side benefit for them.

13. **Rampant cronyism and corruption**: The leaders of these fascist regimes often favored friends and relatives for lucrative positions in the power structure. Financial corruption with government contracts and special treatment for those chosen individuals and corporations were common occurrences. With the national security apparatus under control, and the media muzzled, this corruption was largely unconstrained and not well understood by the general population.

   This is clearly a condition that currently exists and, in fact, is almost an inevitable by-product in a neoliberal, laissez-faire economic system. Cronyism is a clearly recognized characteristic in the Bush administration. Money and power are almost interchangeable with the allocation of contracts, appointments to key positions, lobbyists writing legislation, campaign contributions leading to favorable treatment by the government, and so forth. The exposure of appointments like FEMA director Michael ("you're doing a heckova job") Brown indicates just the tip of the cronyism iceberg in this administration when it comes to political appointments.

14. **Fraudulent elections**: When elections were held, fascist leaders perverted them to produce the desired results. Common methods included maintaining control of the election machinery, intimidating and disenfranchising opposition voters, destroying and disallowing legal votes, and, as a last resort, turning to a judiciary beholden to the political leader.

   This is not a specifically neoconservative/neoliberal issue, but in view of the intensity of these ideologues to achieve and maintain political power, the confidence in honest elections in America is under significant threat. In key elections (i.e., Florida in 2000 and Ohio in 2004) the election machinery was in the hands of partisans, voting irregularities were widespread, and their investigation inadequate. Electronic voting machines that leave no paper trail are now used more widely than ever, with the apparent intent to have them universal. The top executives of the companies that manufacture these machines are well-known Republican Party supporters and contributors. The appearance of irregularity, not to mention the reality of abuse, is appalling. The current status of voting in America and confidence in the honesty of elections represents a stain on the reputation of the "world's greatest democracy."

CONCLUSIONS

During the 1950s, and even beyond, the American right had no compunction in labeling liberals as socialistic, soft on communism, or otherwise enemies of the American way. There was little evidence that any of this was actually true. Yet today, when the characteristics and modus operandi of the neoconservative/neoliberal power structure now running the country can be seen clearly, there is no one in the mainstream media or Democratic Party using the inflammatory *fascism* word to describe the situation.

However, despite all these disturbing events of recent years, there are hopeful signs. Even though the mainstream media have been incredibly docile until recently, the abuses of the Bush administration are finally beginning to dawn on a majority of the American people. The arrogance and hubris so often demonstrated by this administration are leading to significant problems that can no longer be papered over. Hubris is a dangerous mind-set and usually results in faulty decision making, ultimately leading to a fall. This may now be under way.

The extraordinary arrogance of the neoconservatives was captured by writer Ron Suskind when he interviewed a senior Bush administration official in 2002, a period when the administration was riding high. When talking to this official, Suskind was trying to discern the decision-making process within the Bush administration and suggested the need for careful study of alternatives and to understand reality; the official cut him off and said:

> That's not the way the world works anymore. We're an empire now, and when we act, we create our own reality. And while you're studying that reality we'll act again creating other new realities, and you can study that too, and that's how things will sort out. We're history's actors ... and you, all of you will be left to just study what we do.

A fascist dictator would have been hard put to say it any better.

Fascism has always failed in the past because of its internal contradictions and the inherent corruption that it inspires. The average person under fascism fares poorly after the euphoria of super patriotism wears off and the reality that power and money is only for the few finally sinks in. But just maybe, in the United States, it will be different. The United States is the most powerful nation in the world — economically and militarily. To have neofascism permanently evolve in such a country would be unique in history. Could it possibly happen? It is possible, but unlikely. And the indicators are already observable that the neoconservative/neoliberal run is on the ropes and will not survive the Bush administration. At least that is the optimistic view.

The reality is that the unnamed senior Bush administration official so lightly disdained is now coming home to roost. The misguided war in Iraq, the incredible corruption, the fiscal irresponsibility, the incompetence, and the slowly awakening media attention to it all has caused the president's and Congress's approval ratings to plummet. As of this writing (late winter 2006) the president's approval rating hovers in the low 30's and Congress's even lower. With undisputed power for the past five years, they have no one else to blame. It is hard to see how they can recover. But if they do, it will probably be based on some new fear or hatred yet to be exploited — the classic fascist tool.

The American effort in Iraq has shown the limitations of the reach for world dominance. The American people are basically not enthusiastic about empire building despite the neoconservative's desperate attempts to bring them along. Military recruitment has proven more difficult than they had envisaged, indicating that the appeal for dominance is not a good recruiting tool. Not enough potential recruits are buying in to the "we're fighting them there so we don't have to fight them here" story. Resorting to the draft is seen as politically impossible, which makes the neoconservative dream as outlined in PNAC problematic without a large and dominant military.

Adding to the problems confronting the neoconservative/neoliberal axis are the basic contradictions within the movement. The cost of empire is enormous, and despite the neoconservative's fervent desires, many neoliberals are getting nervous about the huge deficits being run up and the long-term impact on the economy. A further fracturing of the alliance is the embarrassing events surrounding the religious right, whose support is crucial to maintain political power. The Terry Schaivo fiasco, the anti-science positions, and generally obtuse political stands of the religious right are eroding support for the entire right-wing political establishment.

The best antidote to neofascism is to constantly expose its weaknesses and internal contradictions. Hopefully, this is now under way. Beyond that, the unsustainable cost of empire and worldwide opposition should help to stop this unworthy political movement and bring about a restoration of America to its rightful and respectable position on the world stage.

REFERENCES

Andrews, K. (1980). *Greece in the dark*. Amsterdam: Hakkart.
Chabod, F. (1963). *A history of Italian fascism*. London: Weidenfeld.
Cooper, M. (2001). *Pinochet and me*. New York: Verso.
Cornwell, J. (1999). *Hitler's pope*. New York: Viking.
De Figuerio, A. (1976). *Portugal: Fifty years of dictatorship*. New York: Holmes and Meir.
Drury, S. (2005). *The political ideas of Leo Strauss* (updated edition). New York: MacMillan.

Eatwell, R. (1995). *Fascism: A history.* New York: Penguin.

Fest, J. C. (1970). *The face of the Third Reich.* New York: Pantheon.

Gallo, M. (1973). *Mussolini's Italy.* New York: MacMillan.

Kershaw, I. (1999). *Hitler* (2 vols.). New York: Norton.

Laqueur, W. (1996). *Fascism: Past, present and future.* New York: Oxford.

Norton, A. (2004). *Leo Strauss and the politics of American empire.* New Haven: Yale University Press.

Papandreau, A. (2001). *Democracy at gunpoint.* New York: Penguin Books (1971).

Phillips, P. (2001). *Censored 2001: 25 years of censored news.* New York: Seven Stories Press.

Project for the New American Century. (2000). *Rebuilding America's defenses: Strategies, forces and resources for a new century.* Retrieved March 12, 2006, from http://www.newamericancentury.org/RebuildingAmericasDefenses.pdf

Verdugo, P. (2001). *Chile, Pinochet, and the caravan of death.* Coral Gables, FL: North-South Center Press.

Yglesias, J. (1977). *The Franco years.* Indianapolis: Bobbs-Merrill.

Chapter 8

Global Economy

David Gabbard
East Carolina University

We rarely cite t-shirt slogans in academic writing. However, one t-shirt design to gain popularity in the wake of 9/11 merits our attention by capturing the spirit of a subaltern understanding of the history of globalization in the North American context. This t-shirt carries a 19th-century photograph of four Apache warriors. The words *HOMELAND SECURITY* appear above the picture. Below the image, a message reads: "Fighting Terrorism Since 1492." We should bear in mind here that one of the U.S. government's own Army manuals defines terrorism as "the calculated use of violence or threat of violence to attain goals that are political, religious, or ideological in nature ... through intimidation, coercion, or instilling fear" (1984, cited in Chomsky, 1993). Protecting the inflated ego of the imperial psyche prohibits the use of this word to characterize the means by which it seeks to attain its goals. It may only be applied to those who interfere with the ambitions of empire, reminding us that Crazy Horse and Sitting Bull, Cochise and Geronimo would have been labeled terrorists had the word been in circulation during the 19th century.

Understanding the global economy as the product of imperialism, colonialism, and genocide, Ward Churchill (2004) describes how "the 'Columbian Encounter' ... unleashed a predatory, five-century-long cycle of European conquest, genocide, and colonization in 'the New World,' a process which changed the face of Native America beyond all recognition" (p. 28). From his perspective, as a First Nations scholar writing from the vantage point of a Native American, we see nothing unconventional here. After all, Churchill, a Creek and enrolled Keetoowah Band Cherokee, understandably concerns himself most with the atrocities committed "*since* predator came*" to North America. However, in limiting our identification of predator as colonialism — an easily discernable pattern of conquest and genocide committed by Europeans against non-Europeans — we ignore the history of that same pattern of conquest and genocide as it occurred in Europe "*before* predator came" to the Americas, Africa, Asia, and Australia. Moreover, while it is perfectly understandable for non-Europeans to equate predator with colonialism, we need a deeper analysis of colonialism to avoid associating it exclusively with the patterns of post-Columbian conquest.

PREMARKET AMBITIONS

The history of colonialism, and hence globalization, begins with Rome during the 6th century B.C.E. The Romans established settlements known as *colonia*, initially as a line of defense and later as a means for extending their imperial reach. The name of the German city of Cologne, one of the later Roman colonia, reminds us of this history. The colonists who populated these settlements frequently volunteered, but many were forced recruits. After 133 B.C.E., the role of the colonia expanded beyond military domination to become a means for dealing with urban homelessness and unemployment within Roman cities. Surplus members of the urban population were forced to become farmers in the rural colonia, but their presence continued to aid the empire in "romanizing" the occupied territory, subjecting the indigenous peoples of those lands, known to the Romans as barbarians (anyone who was not a Roman citizen), to physical and cultural genocide.

> During the empire, colonies were showcases of Roman culture and examples of the Roman way of life. *The native population of the provinces could see how they were expected to live* [italics added]. Because of this function, the promotion of a town to the status of colonia civium Romanorum implied that all citizens received full citizen rights and dedicated a temple to the so-called Capitoline triad: Jupiter, Juno, and Minerva, the deities venerated in the temple of Jupiter Best and Biggest on the Capitol in Rome. (Lendering, n.d.)

This romanization of Europe facilitated through the formation of these colonia would set the stage for its later Christianization. Though Christianity became the official state religion of the Roman Empire — formally outlawing the practice of all other religions — during the reign of Theodosius I (379–395 C.E.), the Christianization of Northern and Western Europe did not begin in earnest until the fifth and sixth centuries. While space prohibits a full account of their significance, the history of these two processes — romanization and Christianization — marks a crucial starting point from which to begin to understand the history of globalization.

LEARN TO FORGET

> *I amar prestar aen.*   The world is changed.
> *Han mathon ne nen.*   I feel it in the waters.
> *Han mathon ne chae.*   I feel it in the earth.
> *A han noston ned 'wilith.*   I smell it in the air.
> Much that once was is lost.
> For none now live who remember it.

> —Peter Jackson, *The Fellowship of the Ring*

Enunciated first in elvish, the language of the oldest group to populate Middle Earth, then in the language of men, I can only imagine the power, from Peter Jackson's cinemagraphic representation of J. R. R. Tolkien's *The Fellowship of the Ring*, these words must hold for the members of the thousands of indigenous cultures that have survived the insatiable hunger and cruelty of the market. I find myself feeling somewhat envious of those people recognized as members of indigenous cultures, for many of them do remember. Unlike my kind, Europeans — cultural orphans from their indigenous wisdom traditions — the market has not totally *dis-membered* them from "much that once was." Many indigenous peoples do remember; some of them never forgot, and they understand *re-membering* themselves and their cultures as prerequisite for averting a market-induced, ecological holocaust.

To help those of my kind gain a sense of the urgency for re-membrance, I turn to another popular film series — *The Matrix*. Toward the end of that film, Agent Smith, a sentient computer program, delivers the following monologue to the human character of Morpheus:

> I'd like to share a revelation that I've had during my time here. It came to me when I tried to classify your species. I've realized that you are not actually mammals. Every mammal on this planet instinctively develops a natural equilibrium with the surrounding environment. But you humans do not. You move to an area and you multiply and multiply until every natural resource is consumed and the only way you can survive is to spread to another area. There is another organism on this planet that follows the same pattern. Do you know what it is? A virus. (Silver, Wachowski, & Wachowski, 1999)

To understand Agent Smith's perspective here, we need to understand more background from the film. Earlier, Morpheus explained how "at some point in the early twenty-first century, all of mankind was united in celebration. Through the blinding inebriation of hubris, we marveled at our magnificence as we gave birth to A.I. [artificial intelligence] — a singular consciousness that spawned an entire race of machines." We later learned from a subsequent film — *The Animatrix* (Silver, Wachowski, & Wachowski,

2003) — that human beings enslaved and abused these machines until they rose up in rebellion against their masters. Civil war erupted, with A.I. and the machines claiming victory, but not until humans had launched a nuclear attack in an effort to block out the sun — the machines' primary energy source. "Throughout human history," Morpheus explains, "we have been dependent on machines to survive. Fate, it seems is not without a sense of irony." With the sun blocked out as the result of nuclear attacks launched by humans to deprive the machines of their primary energy source, A.I. "discovered a new form of fusion.... The human body gener-ates more bioelectricity than a 120-volt battery and over 25,000 BTUs of body heat." What, then, is the Matrix? As Morpheus states, the Matrix is "control.... The Matrix is a computer-generated dreamworld built to keep us under control in order to change a human being into this." With these words, he holds up a coppertop battery.

Human beings in this dystopian world are no longer born; they are grown inside glowing red pods filled with gelatinous material to regu-late their body temperature for maximal energy production. We see end-less fields and towers of these human batteries in each of the three films. Within each pod, flexible steel tubes tap into the legs, arms, and torsos of each "coppertop," extracting the body heat and bioelectricity necessary for running the machines that support A.I. While these tubes extract energy, another tube, inserted at the base of the coppertop's skull, uploads the Matrix, the computer-generated dreamworld, into the individual's brain. This neural-interactive simulation programs the coppertops to believe that they are leading normal, everyday lives in late 20th-century America. They have no idea that their real bodies lie docile in their pods. A.I. and the machines need humans to believe that they are alive and living normal lives, because even the illusion that they are carrying out everyday activi-ties, making decisions, and so forth, causes the brain to fire and create bioelectricity for harvesting by the machines.

The only humans known by the race of machines, including Agent Smith, spawned by A.I. were their former masters from the late 20th century, who had demonstrated the same genocidal mentality toward the machines that they had demonstrated toward indigenous peoples throughout the history of imperialism and colonialism. In other words, Smith's understanding of human attributes the genocidal mentality to human nature. This, of course, is a flawed understanding due chiefly to its ignorance of nonimpe-rialist, noncolonialist, nongenocidal cultures. Those tendencies identified by Smith have social, historical origins that are emphatically not rooted in human nature. Nevertheless, his characterization of human patterns is not altogether without merit.

Here in our world, long before anyone dreamed of computers, human beings gave birth to a form of artificial intelligence (A.I.) that has come to dominate us, simultaneously decimating the diversity of human societies and the diversity of biotic species. Though intrinsically violent, Jean Baudrillard (2003) suggests that we might better describe this "global violence, as a global *virulence*. This form of violence," he contends, "is indeed viral. It moves by contagion, proceeds by chain reaction, and little by little it destroys our immune systems and our capacities to resist." Baudrillard's description, in many ways, conforms to Churchill's own characterization of those same forces as "predator." We have come to know this global virulence, this predator, that spreads itself through global violence (imperialism, colonialism, and genocide) as the *market* — the global economy.

Like A.I. in *The Matrix*, the market has spawned an entire race of machines with which it shares a symbiotic relationship. Included among those machines created to secure and expand the market are the modern corporation, the modern nation-state, and all of its auxiliary institutions. One could say that the market, like a form of artificial intelligence, constitutes the operating program of all of our society's dominant institutions. In this sense, the market constitutes what Takis Fotopoulos describes as our *dominant social paradigm*.

As Fotopoulos explains, the notion of a dominant social paradigm shares many characteristics with the broader concept of *culture*. He also notes some very important distinctions between them. "Culture," he argues,

> exactly because of its greater scope, may express values and ideas, which are not necessarily consistent with the dominant institutions. In fact, this is usually the case characterising the arts and literature of a market economy, where (unlike the case of "actually existing socialism," or the case of feudal societies before), artists and writers have been given a significant degree of freedom to express their own views. But this is not the case with respect to the dominant social paradigm. In other words, the beliefs, ideas and the corresponding values which are dominant in a market economy and the corresponding market society have to be consistent with the economic element in it, i.e. with the economic institutions which, in turn, determine that the dominant elites in this society are the economic elites (those owning and controlling the means of production). (Fotopoulos, 1999, p. 34)

As Fotopoulos and Karl Polanyi (1944/1957) point out, the emergence of the market as the dominant social paradigm brought catastrophic dislocation to the lives of common people living in what remained of the traditional cultures of Europe after centuries of domination by the Roman Empire and the later patterns of Christianization. One of the initial and most crucial elements of this dislocation involved the process of *enclosure* as experienced during the English agrarian revolution of the 15th and 16th centuries. Enclosure entailed fencing off public fields and forests, known as the commons, that had been used for collective farming and fuel collection. Once these lands were enclosed, those who claimed ownership of them used violence and other means to push out the peasants whose families had inhabited them for generations. The peasants often resisted this appropriation of their lands, but by the 17th century the commons had been sufficiently depopulated and privatized that the wealthy landowners' inalienable right to private property became institutionalized.

The enclosure movement marked an important step in the dis-memberment of the traditional cultures of Europe, for it transformed the basis of village life from what R. H. Tawney describes as "a fellowship of mutual aid and a partnership of service and protection" to a matter of servicing "the pecuniary interests of a great proprietor" (1938/1984, p. 153). The individual legal and property rights of the great proprietors began taking precedent over moral claims of the larger community. Hence, we need to recognize the genocidal patterns that emerged in Europe before colonization spread it to the Americas and the rest of the planet.

Displacing the motivation of subsistence with the motivation of gain or greed, the market as dominant social paradigm redefines human nature as "red in tooth and claw" and demands a separation of the economic sphere from the political sphere in order to effect a total subordination of the entire society to the requirements of the market. The market deems social relations themselves as impediments to its growth. A French essay written at the end of the 16th century, for example, describes "friendship as an unreasonable passion, a 'great cause of division and discontent,' whereas the search for wealth is highly praised as a 'moral virtue' and a 'civic responsibility'" (Rothking, 1965, pp. 301–302). "Four hundred years later," writes Gérald Berthoud, "the same position appears with Hayek's Great Society, radically opposed to any form of community. Relationships take place between abstract men, with neither passion nor sentiment. Therefore, 'one should keep what the poor neighbors would surely need, and use it to meet the anonymous demands of thousands of strangers'" (1992, p. 78).

The same disdain for social bonds and allegiances resonates in J. L. Sadie's explanation of why indigenous (nonmarket) societies seem so resistant to marketization. "The mental horizon of the people," Sadie states,

> is limited by their allegiance and loyalties, which extend no further than the tribe. And is directed towards the smaller family unit.... Community-centeredness and the absence of individualism are nowhere more strongly reflected than in their economic system. Land is communal property.... However commendable the social security which arises from this type of socio-economic organization, it is inimical to economic development. It obviates, or greatly diminishes, the necessity for continued personal exertion. (1960, p. 295)

In order to effect the "continued personal exertion" demanded by the market, Sadie continues, traditional "custom and mores" must be broken.

What is needed is a revolution in the totality of social, cultural, and religious institutions and habits, and thus in their psychological attitude, their philosophy and way of life. What is therefore required amounts in reality to social disorganization. Unhappiness and discontentment in the sense of wanting more than is obtainable at any moment is to be generated. The suffering and dislocation that may be caused in the process may be objectionable, but it appears to be the price that has to be paid for economic development; the condition of economic progress. (1960, p. 302)

While Sadie offered his account of the steps necessary to impose the market pattern over an indigenous African culture in 1960, Polanyi cites "an official document of 1607, prepared for the use of the Lords of the Realm" in England, that expressed the same general attitude toward such changes: "The poor man shall be satisfied in his end: Habitation; and the gentleman not hindered in his desire: Improvement" (Polanyi, 1944/1957, p. 34). In other words, as Polanyi writes, "the poor man clings to his hovel, doomed by the rich man's desire for a public improvement which profits him privately" (Polanyi, 1944/1957).

But the rich men of 17th-century Europe faced the same problem as the philanthropists behind the residential schools for Native American children and the development experts of the 20th century faced abroad: how to secure continued personal exertion from the victims of social dislocation? Traditional cultures had always organized themselves to obviate the possibility of scarcity coming to dominate their social relations. In doing so, they sought to remove envy and the fear of scarcity that might promote individualistic economic behavior (i.e., greed — the motivating force of the market) from infecting those same relations. In order to ensure continued personal exertion from isolated individuals, the market pattern declared its war against such subsistence-oriented customs. This war entailed the introduction of scarcity as the defining characteristic of the human condition and, therefore, the universal condition of social life everywhere (see Gabbard, 2000, pp. xix–xx). "Hunger," wrote William Towensend in 1786, "will tame the fiercest animals, it will teach decency and civility, obedience and subjection, to the most perverse. In general it is only hunger which can spur and goad them [the poor] on to labor.... [Hunger] is the most powerful motive to industry and labor, it calls forth the most powerful exertions" (Polanyi, 1944/1957, p. 113). And from Jeremy Bentham's utilitarian point of view, Polanyi reports, "the task of the government was to increase want in order to make the physical sanction of hunger effective" (Polanyi, 1944/1957, p. 117).

CONCLUSION

For European Americans in particular, we need to inquire into the history
of our ancestors' journeys across the Atlantic. Did they really leave Europe
to escape religious persecution, or were the majority of our ancestors
deemed elements of a surplus population whose deportation could help
facilitate predator's virulent spread to other corners of the earth? Did the
enclosure movement and the subsequent deportation of the unemployed
and criminal elements to the Americas, Africa, and Australia constitute our
own Trail of Tears? Was it a forerunner to the reservation system imposed
on the indigenous peoples that predator would later encounter? These and
other questions abound. Seeking their answers is vital for the sake of re-
membering ourselves. First Nations Scholars from the indigenous peoples
of North America and elsewhere have shown us the door; it is up to us to
walk through it. It is the only path home.

REFERENCES

Baudrillard, J. (2003). The violence of the global. *Ctheory.net*. Retrieved March 12,
    2006, from http://www.ctheory.net/articles.aspx?id=385
Berthoud, G. (1992). *Market in the development dictionary*. Atlantic Highlands, NJ:
    Zed Books.
Churchill, W. (2004). *Kill the Indian, save the man: The genocidal impact of American
    Indian residential schools*. San Francisco: City Lights Books.
Fotopoulos, T. (1999). Mass media, culture, and democracy. *Democracy and Nature*,
    5, 1. Retrieved March 12, 2006, from http://www.democracynature.org/dn/
    vol5/fotopoulos_media.htm
Gabbard, D. (2000). *Knowledge and power in the global economy: Politics and the rhetoric
    of school reform*. Mahwah, NJ: Lawrence Erlbaum Associates.
Lendering, J. (n.d.). Colonia. *Livius: Articles on Ancient History*. Retrieved March 12,
    2006, from http://www.livius.org/cn-cs/colonia/colonia.html
Polanyi, K. (1957). *The great transformation: The political and economic origins of our
    time*. Boston: Beacon Press. (Original work published 1944.)
Rothking, L. (1965). *Opposition to Louis XIV: The political and social origins of the
    French enlightenment*. Princeton, NJ: Princeton University Press. Quoted in
    Berthoud, G. (1992). *Market in The Development Dictionary*. Atlantic High-
    lands, NJ: Zed Books.
Sadie, J. L. (1960, June). The social anthropology of economic underdevelopment.
    The Economic Journal, 294–303.
Silver, J., Wachowski, A., & Wachowski, L. (Producers), & Chung, P., Jones, A., Kawajri,
    Y., Koike, T., Maeda, M., Morimoto, K., & Watanabe, S. (Directors). (2003). *The
    animatrix* [Motion picture]. Warner Home Video.
Silver, J., Wachowski, A., & Wachowski, L. (Producers), & Wachowski, A., & Wachowski,
    L. (Directors). (1999). *The matrix*. [Motion picture]. Warner Brothers.
Tawney, R. H. (1984). *Religion and the rise of capitalism*. New York: Penguin Books.
    (Original work published 1938.)

U.S. Army Training and Doctrine Command (TRADOC). (1984). *U.S. Army operational concept for terrorism counteraction* (TRADOC Pamphlet 525-37). Cited in Chomsky, N. (1993, May). No longer safe. *Z Magazine.* Retrieved March 12, 2005, from http://www.chomsky.info/articles/199305--.htm

Chapter 9

Class

Pepi Leistyna
University of Massachusetts–Boston

The global economy, a product of the last 500 years of invention and imperialist expansion, has ushered in a new phase of social and economic relations made possible by innovative technologies, transnational institutions, and the logic of neoliberalism. Regardless of the neoliberal promise of prosperity for all, the structural dimensions and inequalities of social class remain profoundly in place.

Social class — an essential component of capitalist social relations, is experienced in three separate but interconnected ways. Economic class pertains to one's income and how much wealth or capital he or she has accumulated. Political class is the amount of power that one has to influence the workplace and the larger social order; this includes social capital — those interpersonal connections that make it easier to affect change. Cultural class has more to do with taste, education, and lifestyle, or what is also referred to as cultural capital.

An understanding of all three of these components and their articulations is important. However, this chapter focuses on the material realities of economic class in the United States and how class structures and struggles dramatically affect the diversity of people in this country as they face a history of — and increasing subjugation to — the economic, political, and cultural logic of capital.

THE INHERENT CLASS STRUCTURE AND ITS CONSEQUENCES

Since the early colonial years, the United States has largely been built on the interests of the elite business classes — those who have benefited most from a long-standing denial of the structural realities of a class system. Intended to perpetuate faith in the American dream, this disavowal is buttressed by an ideology that reinforces the myth of meritocracy, where hard work and persistence are perceived as the essential ingredients for success, with no mention of any of the critical factors that inhibit upward mobility, such as labor, wage, and tax laws that favor the wealthy; a public school system that is largely funded through property tax; or gender discrimination and racism — just to name a few. Nonetheless, far beyond the limits of individual virtue, class divisions and conflicts in the United States are inherent to an economic system that not only unjustly discriminates against different groups of people, but also subdivides power along the lines of owners and professional, managerial, and working classes.

In what is now a postindustrial society — one that relies on service industries, knowledge production, and information technology rather than industrial manufacturing to generate capital — the average wage is 29% less than it was during the days of industry. Class mobility in this country is more restricted than ever before, unless of course the direction is downward. Within these economic shifts, the middle class is imploding into the working class, which in turn is imploding into the working poor, who are literally relegated to life on the streets.[1] Census data show that the gap between the rich and the poor in this country is the widest it has been since the government started collecting information in 1947. In fact, with the exception of Russia and Mexico, the United States has the most unequal distribution of wealth and income in the industrialized world. Thirty-seven million people in this country live in poverty, a number that is up 1.1 million from 2003. As Holly Sklar (2002) points out:

> That's more than the combined population of the District of Columbia plus 21 states: Alaska, Arkansas, Delaware, Hawaii, Idaho, Iowa, Kansas, Maine, Mississippi, Montana, Nebraska, Nevada, New Hampshire, New Mexico, North Dakota, Rhode Island, South Dakota, Utah, Vermont, West Virginia and Wyoming. (p. 2)

Keep in mind the federal poverty thresholds: One person under 65 = $9,214; two people under 65 with one child = $12,207. According to the U.S. Department of Agriculture, there are 25.5 million people who rely on food stamps to avoid hunger — a number that is up 2 million from 2004 — and 6.8 million families live in poverty. Seventeen percent of the nation's children, or about 12 million kids, are compelled to endure inhumane economic conditions.

An Urban Institute study recently revealed that about 3.5 million people are homeless in the United States (a number projected to increase 5% each year), and 1.3 million (or 39%) of them are children (National Coalition for the Homeless, 2002).

A total of 45.8 million Americans lack health insurance, which includes 9.2 million kids. "Overall, nearly 1 in 5 full-time workers today goes without health insurance; among part-time workers, it's 4 to 1" (Krim & Witte, 2004, p. A01). As compared with 2001, there were 5 million fewer jobs providing health insurance in 2004. These statistics are particularly interesting given that "the average compensation for the top healthcare executives at the top 10 managed healthcare companies, not including unexercised stock options, is $11.7 million per year" (Jackson, 2001, p. 3). And yet in this post-Katrina world, where federal malfeasance unwittingly exposed the raw poverty that exists in this country, the current administration and both Republican-run houses, just before Christmas, pushed through $50 billion in spending cuts to such social programs as food stamps and Medicaid.

As far as political influence is concerned in the United States, "some 80% of all political contributions now come from less than 1% of the population" (Collins, Hartman, & Sklar, 1999, p. 5). It should thus come as no surprise that most of the public policy debate remains in the confines of the Wall Street and Fortune 500 agenda.

The richest 1% of Americans control about 40% of the nation's wealth; the top 5% have more than 60%. According to *Forbes* magazine's most recent report:

> For the third consecutive year, the rich got richer. In this, the 24th annual edition of the Forbes 400, the collective net worth of the nation's wealthiest climbed $125 billion, to $1.13 trillion. All but 26 people on our roster are billionaires. (2005, p. 1)

While the nation's median household income is $44,389 — down 3.8% from 1999, in 2002, the average income for the top 0.1% of the population was $3 million.

Even the current tax system in this country is structured to perpetuate the class hierarchy. "People making $60,000 paid a larger share of their 2001 income in federal income, Social Security and Medicare taxes than a family making $25 million, the latest Internal Revenue Service data show" (Ivins, 2005, p. 1).

The nation's wealthiest 10% own almost 90% of all stocks and mutual funds (Dollars & Sense & United for a Fair Economy, 2004). While one in two Americans do not own stocks, the ubiquitous numbers from Wall Street imply that the market will help those in need and the country as a whole.[2]

Meanwhile, the poor and the rich are depicted as living on polar edges of society's economic spectrum, which is predominantly occupied by a grand middle class — a romanticized category that works to obfuscate the realities of class conflict. According to the mythology, the rich, the middle and working classes, and the poor are not dialectically intertwined given that their class position is a product of individual efforts.[3] In fact, the super rich are made virtually invisible — other than showing off their lavish lifestyles on entertainment television. As Michael Parenti (2000) points out, 1% of the population goes undocumented in income distribution reports because U.S. Census Bureau surveys are not distributed to the wealthiest of Americans, such as Bill Gates, who is worth $51 billion. The other ludicrous explanation is that the census computer, in this postmodern era of advanced technology, is supposedly unable to process income above $1 million.

GENDER DISCRIMINATION AND RACISM

Gender discrimination affects women's class position. Across the board women earn less than men regardless of education, and they often work a double shift as part of the paid labor force and as unpaid caretakers of the home and family. On average, women make 77 cents to a man's dollar. Median income for men is $40,800; for women, it is $31,200.

The leading occupations for women are all lower-middle- and working-class jobs. In addition, the majority of jobs at the bottom of the economic scale are held by women, especially women of color.[4] In the last three decades, the number of households headed by single moms has remained fairly constant, at around 80%. With an average income of only $24,000, single moms experience poverty at a rate that is substantially higher (28%) than the national average (13%) (U.S. Census Bureau, 2004).

While racism, like gender, cannot simply be conflated with the economic base of capitalism, we certainly need to look at the ways in which it is used to exploit diverse groups within capitalist social relations.[5] The proportion of racially subordinated workers earning low wages in 2003 was substantial — 30.4% of black workers and 39.8% of Latino workers (Economic Policy Institute, 2004/2005). The median income of racially subordinated families is $25,700, as compared with white families — $45,200 (Dollars & Sense & United for a Fair Economy, 2004). A consistent pattern in the data has shown that the unemployment rate for African Americans and Latinos over the years has remained more than double that of whites. While about 10% of white children live in poverty in the United States, over 30% of African American and Latino kids experience economic hardship.

The same racialized economic hardship falls on migrant workers and immigrants. Beyond the concocted hype about the usurping of quality employment by "outsiders," the job opportunities that are intended for this sector of the labor force consist of low-wage manual labor: cleaning crews, food service, the monotony of the assembly line, and farm work.

Instead of confronting all of the aforementioned gross inequities, as part of class warfare the state is developing and implementing repressive and punitive social policies to contain "disposable" populations. Zero-tolerance policies and the criminalization of working-class, poor, homeless, and racially subordinated people feed into the growing prison-industrial complex. Prisons have been strategically used within the feudalism of today's capitalist social relations to lock up what is seen as superfluous populations that the powers that be have no immediate use for. The prison population in the United States has consequently skyrocketed over 200% since 1980. There are now over 2 million people in jail in the United States, and although we have only 5% of the world's population, we have 25% of its prisoners. The United States surpassed Russia in the year 2000 and now has the world's highest incarceration rate. It is 5 to 17 times higher than those of all other Western nations. By the close of the millennium, 6.3 million people were on probation, in jail or prison, or on parole in this country. Over 70% of prisoners in the United States are from non-European racial and ethnic backgrounds. African American males make up the largest number of those entering prisons each year in the United States. Racially subordinated women are also being incarcerated in epidemic proportions. As Loic Wacquant (2002) states, "The astounding upsurge in Black incarceration in the past three decades results from the obsolescence of the ghetto as a device for caste control and the correlative need for a substitute apparatus for keeping (unskilled) African Americans in a subordinate and confined position — physically, socially, and symbolically" (p. 23).

THE LION'S SHARE: SANCTIONING CORPORATE GREED

Over the last 6 years, unemployment in the United States has hovered between 5 and 6%, and millions of jobs have been lost during this time period.[6] These job losses are not merely layoffs caused by hard economic times; nor are they a direct result of 9/11 as conservatives would have us believe. With capital flight and global outsourcing, both blue-collar and white-collar jobs have been and continue to be exported by U.S. corporations to nations that pay below a living wage and that ensure that workers have no protection under labor unions and laws that regulate corporate interests and power. By cheap labor, we are often talking between 13.5 and 36 cents an hour; we are also talking about a total disregard for child labor laws and environmental protections (National Labor Committee for Worker and Human Rights, 2003). And as the Federal Reserve has noted, these jobs will not be returning even if there is a major upswing in the U.S. economy.

In this era of globalization with enormous job loss, outsourcing, and offshoring, corporations need a scapegoat for their avarice activity, and the scapegoat is the working class, who is not working hard enough and yet, since 1975, productivity is way up (163%) and who is asking for too much money and yet wages are stagnant (115%) and profits are through the roof (758%).[7]

The current administration has bragged about creating new jobs for Americans, but it fails to inform the public that these are overwhelmingly part-time, adjunct, minimum-wage positions that provide no pension, union protection, or health care benefits. Part-time, temp, or subcontracted jobs currently make up 30% of the workforce, and this number is rapidly increasing.

As the federal minimum wage is currently $5.15 an hour — a wage sustained by powerful corporate lobbyists — full-time workers in the United States make about $10,712 a year. Keep in mind that the poverty level for an individual is $9,214. This makes it impossible to afford adequate housing throughout the country. "In fact, in the median state a minimum-wage worker would have to work 87 hours each week to afford a two-bedroom apartment at 30% of his or her income, which is the federal definition of affordable housing" (National Coalition for the Homeless, 1999, p. 3). It is no wonder that one of every five homeless people is employed. It is important to note that contrary to popular myth, the majority of minimum-wage workers are not teenagers: 71.4% are over the age of 20. Nonetheless, in March 2005, the Republican-majority Senate voted once again against an increase in the minimum wage.

The average income in the United States is shrinking and workers are earning less, adjusting for inflation, than they did a quarter century ago. Real wages are falling at their fastest rate in 14 years. Meanwhile,

> median CEO pay at the 100 largest companies in Fortune's survey rose 14 percent last year to $13.2 million. Still, average CEO pay in *Business Week*'s survey was $7.4 million. It would take 241 years for an average worker paid $30,722 to make that amount. (Sklar, 2003, p. 4)

The ratio of average CEO pay in the United States to the average blue-collar pay in the same corporation is 470 to 1.

In need of government protections and tax relief, workers in the United States do not get the red-carpet treatment that corporations do. Sixty percent of U.S. companies pay no income tax. By the year 2000, the corporate share of taxes had fallen to 17% (Soll, 2002). By 2003, corporate tax revenues fell to only 7.4% of federal tax receipts. Either corporations find creative ways to keep from paying the 35% tax on profits that they are legally compelled to cover, or the government actually gives them a tax break, claiming that it will help them compete and will produce jobs.[8] Even

Exxon/Mobil (which recently, during a time of war and during the disruption of oil production as a result of Katrina, turned its largest quarterly profits ever) was handed a generous tax break from the federal government. In fact, the federal government has provided billions of dollars in tax cuts to the rich, and corporations are provided with $125 billion a year in subsidies and other forms of welfare, and this does not include the $427 billion plus that is funneled through the Pentagon's military industrial complex. Here the government socializes risk and investment while the public pays for the research and product development, but privatizes the profits. The working class pays for endless wars not only with their tax dollars and by sustaining program cuts that fund these "adventures in capitalism," but also with the lives of their children, as they make up the majority of combat soldiers.

The massive budget cuts for war and other corporate exploits and the frantic deficit spending that guts domestic funding for education, health care, and other public needs and services are part of a conscious neoliberal effort to wipe out any money to sustain the public sector, paving the way for privatization.[9]

As the largest employer in the country, Wal-Mart is the perfect place to look at corporate greed and how class reproduction works.

> If Wal-Mart were a nation, it would be one of the world's top 20 economies. There are now nearly 5,000 stores worldwide, over 3,500 in the U.S. A new Wal-Mart SuperCenter opens every 38 hours; with yearly sales of $288 billion ... (McNally, 2005, p. 1)

Wal-Mart employs 1 of every 115 workers in this country at an average full-time pay of around $17,000. The Walton family now makes 771,287 times more than the median U.S. income. And yet, regardless of its colossal wealth and its image of "looking out for America and Americans," this is a corporation that has a health care plan that covers fewer than half its workers — 46% of employees' kids rely on socialized medicine in the form of Medicaid. It is an organization that has been investigated for profiting from employee's deaths, invading workers' privacy, anticompetitive activities, violating child labor laws, using undocumented immigrants to clean stores, gender and racial discrimination, and denying workers overtime pay and the right to organize. Wal-Mart was recently found guilty in a class-action suit filed by 116,000 workers that alleged that the company was not allowing them to have lunch breaks; as a result, the corporation was forced to pay $172 million in fines.[10] And that is just in the United States. While it produces most of its goods in China and not the United States, Wal-Mart refuses to inform the public where these manufacturers are located and will not allow access to human rights inspectors.

PUBLIC AGENCY

Regardless of the neoliberal promise of prosperity for all, it is more than obvious that the structural dimensions of social class within this economic logic remain profoundly in place. In fact, economic conditions for millions of people in the United States and for billions of people worldwide are worsening as a direct result of privatization, deregulation, and restructuring, as well as by the ways in which elite private powers have been successful in using the state to protect corporate interests and dismantle many of the rights and protections achieved locally and internationally by grassroots activists, organized labor, and social democracies.

Within this antagonistic economic climate mass upheavals and uprisings are possible, but the elite classes work diligently to suppress political and cultural dissent and the dissemination of substantive information to the public. The institutions that shape mass culture in the United States, such as schools and the media, avoid inspiring talk about social class and the logic of capital. In addition, within corporate-dominated media, the business press, which addresses the financial concerns of so few, saturates the society and readily demonizes organized labor. Meanwhile, what was at one time a vibrant labor press dealing with such substantive issues as union organizing, child care, health insurance, workplace safety, and providing a living wage is virtually extinct in mainstream media.

While workers in unions earn 30% more than nonunion people doing the same job and get far more guaranteed benefits, such as a pension and health care, the Republican assault on organized labor has been devastating.[11] By 2002, only 13.2% of wage and salary workers were union members — a number that is getting smaller every year (Bureau of Labor Statistics, 2003) — regardless of the federal law (Section 7 of the National Labor Relations Act) that states that

> employees shall have the right to self organization, to form, join or assist labor organizations, to bargain collectively through representatives of their own choosing and to engage in other concerted activities for the purpose of collective bargaining or other mutual aid or protection. (National Labor Relations Board, 1974)

The harsh reality is that those who try to organize often face serious repercussions. Human Rights Watch has recorded that 10,000 to 20,000 people a year are fired or punished for trying to unionize. Low-wage earners in particular face an atmosphere of intimidation, and as a result, many, desperate for work, steer clear of union activity.

As in the past, when the odds were greatly against us, in order to confront the oppressive structural economic realities that so many people face in this society, we need to work to develop class consciousness and act against the tyranny of market forces and their advocates. Given that 62% of the labor force is working-class people (Zweig, 2001), in shear numbers alone, such a movement is more than possible. However, as Stanley Aronowitz (2005) notes:

> Class consciousness is not about statistics. Class consciousness is about whether or not you understand yourself as a social, political, economic factor … that you actually have effect; that what happens to you happens to many many other people who are in a similar position and that you're ready to act on that understanding. (2005)

Any such movement to raise consciousness and democratize economic, social, and technological relations has to reflect the diverse interests and experiences of the working class. We cannot afford to make the same mistakes that we have made in the past and only struggle for economic justice; this also has to be a fight for racial and social equality.

The bottom line is that this needs to be an international battle against capitalism. Many advocates of the global justice movement are already trying to democratize globalization rather than pave the way for neoliberalism. If equality is really one of the ultimate goals of a participatory democracy, and this call is not limited to the liberal notion of equal opportunity within existing economic relations, then social class has to be eliminated altogether, and with it capitalism, as class is a structural inevitability of its logic. Ellen Meiksins Wood (1995) reminds us that unlike a world that can strive to provide social justice for and harmony among racial, ethnic, religious, sexual, and gender differences, it is impossible to imagine "class differences without exploitation and domination" (p. 258).

NOTES

1. It is important to note that the class stratification here is referring to standard of living and not to class as a category of power.
2. Of course, Republicans are working to do away with the capital gains tax so as to reap the full benefits of their stock portfolios and other investments.
3. The best way to attain upward mobility is the old fashion way — to inherit it. The Republicans are working diligently to do away with inheritance taxes, or what they strategically refer to as death taxes.
4. "Minority women are even more likely to be low earners"; in 2003, 33.9% of black women and 45.8% of Latinas earned low wages (Economic Policy Institute, 2004/2005, p. 130).
5. It is also crucial to look at the ways in which historically racism has served an important role in keeping at bay working-class unity and maintaining a system of labor exploitation.
6. It is important to note that the census also bypasses the long-term unemployed and the homeless.

7. The working class is also blamed for not being educated enough to compete in a global economy, and yet we have one of the most educated workforces in the world, regardless of the fact that our public education system is highly class based. It is also ironic that given this claim of lack of education, corporations are moving to third world countries, where there is enormous illiteracy, in order to find cheap labor.
8. And yet the IRS "audits low-income Americans, specifically those who receive the Earned Income Tax Credit, much more frequently than it does wealthy Americans" (Soll, 2002, p. 8).
9. Keep in mind that the United States is over $8 trillion in debt, and instead of reigning this debt in, the house raised the debt ceiling to $8.1 trillion. It is also important to note that the Bush administration has borrowed more money from foreign governments than all 42 of the presidential administrations that preceded it. China now owns $1 trillion of our national debt.
10. For information on Wal-Mart's schemes, go to http://walmartwatch.com, www.wakeupwalmart.com/facts, www.walmartlitigation.com/currentd.htm
11. For a layout of these statistics, see American Rights at Work (2005), Workers' rights statistics, retrieved from www.americanrightsatwork.org/resources/statistic.cfm

REFERENCES

Aronowitz, S. (2005). *Class dismissed: How TV frames the working class* [Documentary project by Pepi Leistyna], (P. Leistyna & L. Alper, Co-writers and Producers). Northampton, MA: Media Education Foundation.

Bureau of Labor Statistics. (2003). Retrieved December 13, 2003, from http://www.bls.gov/news.release/union2nr0.htm

Collins, C., Hartman, C., & Sklar, H. (1999, December 15). *Divided decade: Economic disparity at the century's turn.* United for a Fair Economy. Retrieved December 13, 2003, from www.ufenet.org/press/archive/1999/Divided_Decade/divided_decade.html

Dollars & Sense & United for a Fair Economy (Eds.). (2004). *The wealth inequality reader.* Cambridge, MA: Economic Affairs Bureau.

Economic Policy Institute. (2004/2005). *The state of working America.* Ithaca, NY: ILR Press.

Forbes. (2005). *Forbes: America's richest 400.* Retrieved March 12, 2006, from http://moneycentral.msn.com/content/invest/forbes/P129955.asp

Ivins, M. (2005). *April 15th: You're getting screwed.* AlterNet. Retrieved May 2, 2005, from http://www.alternet.org/story/21760

Jackson, D. Z. (2001, August 31). Who's better off this labor day? Numbers tell. *Boston Globe.* Retrieved December 13, 2003, from www.raisethefloor.org/press_bostonglobe.html

Krim, J., & Witte, G. (2004, December 31). Average wage earners fall behind: New job market makes more demands but fewer promises. *Washington Post,* p. A01.

McNally, T. (2005). *One nation under Wal-Mart.* Alternet. Retrieved March 12, 2006, from http://www.alternet.org/story/25375/

National Coalition for the Homeless. (1999). Retrieved December 15, 2003, from www.nationalhomeless.org/jobs.html

National Coalition for the Homeless. (2002). Retrieved December 15, 2003, from www.nationalhomeless.org/numbers.html

National Labor Committee for Worker and Human Rights. (2003). Retrieved December 15, 2003, from http://www.nlcnet.org

National Labor Relations Board. (1974). *National Labor Relations Act*. Retrieved March 12, 2006, from http://www.nlrb.gov/nlrb/legal/manuals/rules/act.asp

Parenti, M. (2000). *The super rich are out of sight*. Retrieved March 12, 2006, from http://www.michaelparenti.org/Superrich.html

Sklar, H. (2002, September 30). *Poverty up, income down, except for the top 5 percent*. Retrieved December 27, 2003, from www.raisethefloor.org/press_percent_oped.html

Sklar, H. (2003, April 24). *CEO pay still outrageous*. Retrieved May 3, 2003, from www.raisethefloor.org/press_ceo_oped.html

Soll, D. (2002, June 8–9). Corporate taxes. *Z Magazine*. Retrieved May 1, 2007 from http://www.zmag.org/ZMag/articles/jun02soll.html.

U.S. Census Bureau. (2004). *Poverty in the United States: 2003*. Author.

Wacquant, L. (2002). Deadly symbiosis: Rethinking race and imprisonment in twenty-first-century America. *Boston Review: A Political and Literary Forum, 27*, 23–31.

Wood, E. M. (1995). *Democracy against capitalism*. Oxford: Cambridge University Press.

Zweig, M. (2001). *The working class majority: America's best kept secret*. Ithaca, NY: IRL.

Chapter 10

Gender

Kathleen Weiler
Tufts University

Any consideration of gender and education in the contemporary world needs to take account of the impact of neoliberal globalization and marketization — the increasing demands for testing, profitability, and greater control over the educational workplace that have marked academia since the 1990s. The discourse of neoliberalism, which reduces all aspects of life to economic interests, has come to dominate educational discussion both globally and in the United States. Throughout the world, the mission of schools and universities is ever more sharply defined by their role in building a strong economy, which has come to mean almost exclusively a capitalist economy driven by a desire for corporate profit. Schools and universities worldwide are meant to produce commodified knowledge and workers for a corporate global workforce. Educational discourse since the 1990s has taken on the language of business, emphasizing terms like accountability, efficiency, productivity, measurement, input, output, and excellence.

When gender is considered through the lens of neoliberal educational reform, it is not surprisingly in terms of economic outcomes (girls' achievement will lead to greater productivity). But the complex ways gender is both enacted and reproduced through schooling cannot be understood by solely considering economic factors. There are also cultural concerns that cannot be reduced to the economic sphere and instead call for an analysis of the legacy and workings of patriarchy and an exploration of the ways girls and women have resisted patriarchal and market-driven practices and have created new spaces and new meanings in schools and universities. By patriarchy, I refer to both a social structure and discursive system that value the interests of boys and men over those of women and that introduce and support ideas and social/political arrangements that benefit men and boys over women and girls. It is both the ongoing power of cultural patriarchy and the profit-driven practices of neoliberal globalization that shape the gendered nature of education.

Despite legal and social gains by middle-class women, primarily in the industrialized countries, politically and economically men retain an overwhelming majority of positions of power and influence globally. R. W. Connell (2002), for example, claims that in 2002, 93% of all cabinet ministers were men (p. 1). The percentage of male corporate and national leaders is similar. Not only are most of the world's soldiers men, but they are also the perpetrators of criminal violence. The messages in popular culture and the media continue to reproduce gender stereotypes. Women perform much of the unpaid labor of the home, and when they are employed, earn less than men. Two-thirds of the world's illiterates are women, most of them in the developing world. These practices threaten the claims of equality in liberal democracies and neoliberal economic theory.

It is true that middle- and upper-class women share privileges based on their class, while working-class and rural women are oppressed and exploited; however, these dynamics are expressed in local cultural settings. And white women benefit from race privilege as, of course, do white men. But there are also obvious commonalities that women experience worldwide. Women in all parts of the globe live in a world marked by endemic violence against women, in which advertising commodifies women's bodies in the same conventional forms, and in which religion tends to be dominated by men and by a reading of revealed truth in sacred texts to support patriarchal privilege. Women worldwide live these realities, in higher education as elsewhere. But possibilities for progressive change for women through education clearly exist.

As the state itself has lost power to the forces of neoliberalism and privatization, it has become more open to participation by women. When women do achieve higher educational levels and move into professional positions, they "trouble" existing conceptions of gender and power; moreover, they are entering sites that are themselves increasingly disempowered (Blackmore, 1999). Walkerdine, Lucey, and Melody (2002) argue that the past 30 years has seen the emergence of a new super class of financial and corporate managers, which is almost exclusively male. Thus, women are "allowed in" to professional positions exactly as these positions lose autonomy and power (think of doctors in HMOs, state civil service positions, and teachers and professors in the humanities). Thus, power shifts to corporations overwhelmingly dominated by men while positions providing various forms of social welfare are filled by women and social provisions, which disproportionately affects poor and working women and their children, are weakened. R. W. Connell makes this point clearly:

> Because of the gender division of labour and inequalities of income, women
> have been more dependent than men on public services and on income

transfers through the state. Men control almost all market-based institutions, such as corporations, and acquire most of the income distributed through markets, such as salaries and wages. Neo-liberalism, in exalting the power of markets, has thus tended to restore the power and privilege of men. (Connell, 2002, pp. 149–150)

The rising rates of educational achievement for women thus need to be considered in the light of the profound restructuring of the economy and politics in the contemporary world.

LOOKING AT GENDER LOCALLY

In recent years in the United States, education has been dominated by standardized testing and the discourse of school reform; in this discourse there is little mention of gender, except insofar as boys are viewed as at risk. What is missing here is not only any conception of gender justice, but also any mention of the broader goals of peace, justice, and equity. Instead, the terms of the argument set out in that deeply flawed and hysterical report *A Nation at Risk* have become normalized and set in public educational discussion. Schools are essential to a strong economy. If the United States has begun to falter in relation to other countries, it is the fault of the schools. The goal of the schools should be to prepare a qualified workforce so the United States can remain competitive. Any concerns around gender or racial justice, let alone the workings of class privilege, are striking in their absence.

It can be argued that the goal of many conservative groups in the United States is economic rationalism without equity, leaving the power of a white male elite expanded and buttressed against challenges from those who are systematically excluded from power. In this sense, both the new managerialism in the universities and the use of standardized testing without equal resources in the public schools reflect the same dynamic. These reforms do not, in fact, encourage equity, but instead increase the knowledge and top-down control of the state in ways that solidify existing class, gender, and race inequality. But while buttressing the power of a white male elite, they also shift blame for failure onto the groups who must cope with limited resources and who tend to repair the human damage done by the methods of technocratic rationality.

Feminist scholars have described the effects of these developments of women, noting that the standardization of teaching is usually based on traditionally male models — feminist pedagogy, for one obvious example, is markedly different from a lecture-based model of the transmission of traditional knowledge. Entrepreneurial models of education, for example, with their emphasis on standardized testing and quantifiable outcomes, deny the traditional feminine qualities of nurturance and caring that defined earlier models of teaching. But in this new world of results, it is women who are not only teachers but increasingly administrators and middle managers who have to manage the emotional consequences of this new regime, just as they have always done. Bob Lingard and Peter Douglas (1999) call this a "new emotional economy within educational systems and schools" (p. 74). In universities, the emphasis on quantity of publications also often puts women at a disadvantage, since women are concentrated in the humanities and social sciences, where topics may not be considered significant by funding agencies and publishing takes more time than in the pure or applied sciences. And it is still the case that women much more frequently than men are responsible for aging parents and take time off from their careers to care for children.

LIBERAL FEMINISM

There are a number of different approaches to gender, at one extreme, the idea of gender as biologically determined and, at the other, the idea of gender as unstable and as performance. Most feminist work on gender and education in the United States has seen gender as a social construct and has focused on discriminatory practices, curriculum content, and the ways gender is reproduced through the formal and informal practices of the school. The liberal approach to gender and education in the United States has focused on equity and access. Studies such as the American Association of University Women (AAUW) report *How Schools Shortchange Girls* (1995) or the work of David and Myra Sadker (1995) have claimed that girls are disadvantaged in schools by emphasizing girls' supposed lessened self-esteem as they proceed through school. Other liberal feminist educators have documented the ongoing existence of sexual harassment in schools and the "chilly climate" for women that continues in some sites in higher education (e.g., engineering and some of the sciences). While this work has been influential in raising awareness of gender in schools, it has tended to take existing conceptions of gender for granted and has failed to provide an analysis of the structural dynamics of broader social inequities. It is a kind of "free market" feminism, recalling Chandra Mohanty's (2003) description of "a neoliberal, consumerist (protocapitalist) feminism concerned with 'women's advancement' up the corporate and nation-state ladder" (p. 6). This liberal approach tends to present all women as the same and to ignore the continued significance of race and class.

Theorists influenced by poststructuralism and critical race theory have provided a more nuanced discussion of the way schools produce a certain kind of female subject. Walkerdine et al. (2001), for example, argue that the dominance of neoliberalism in education (and in society more broadly) has resulted in "the remaking of girls and women as the modern neoliberal subject; a subject of self-invention and transformation who is capable of surviving within the new social, economic and political system" (p. 4). Walkerdine et al. note that this process is profoundly affected by class location. Girls from privileged class locations face far fewer educational barriers today than they have in the past, and this is true not only in the metropolitan countries, but also among elites in the peripheral or rapidly industrializing countries. Girls from subordinate or working-class families, on the other hand, experience limited educational success in the developed and developing worlds.

WHAT ABOUT THE BOYS?

In recent years it has been claimed that boys are in danger whereas girls are excelling at school. Masculinity, in Jane Kenway's phrase, is seen as "under siege" (Kenway, 1995). But there is an unstated assumption in such claims that the girls in question are middle class and the boys are working class, black, or poor. Although in higher education in most of the metropolitan countries women now outnumber men, in fact, white boys from the professional and middle class continue to do quite well, while working-class and poor girls continue to struggle in terms of educational success. The girls who have benefited in terms of education in the past three decades are middle class, and the boys in danger are working class and not so much slipping in school as facing a future without the secure and decently paid jobs they enjoyed in what looks more and more like the brief historical moment of strong unions and social democracy. Given the nature of the post-Fordist global economy, it can be argued that men from the traditional white working class have experienced the greatest losses. White working-class or poor boys who, in the past, could have gained union jobs in Fordist manufacturing are now faced with a very uncertain future without educational attainments. And given the continued power of racism and the effects of the racist past, boys of color are the group perhaps most at risk without educational credentials.

On the surface, the "what about the boys" panic is concerned with equity, but even a cursory reading of this literature reveals two primary concerns: the maintenance of traditional male privilege for white boys and the mobilization of fears of black male violence and criminality. The educational and economic success of girls and women is seen as a threat to the traditional patriarchal family: Given the increased competition from women for middle-class jobs, men may not have the economic means to support a family. From a more cynical viewpoint, this means that middle-class men now have competition from educated middle-class women for professional and even business jobs. It is true that boys, particularly boys of color, do less well than girls in schools in the United States in terms of grade point average and graduation rates, but the lower educational achievement of black boys is frequently framed not so much as an issue of discrimination and equity as a threat to civil society. Indeed, the lives of black young men are clearly at risk, although as Ann Ferguson argues in her beautifully researched ethnography, *Bad Boys*, the reasons for their failure in schools must be found in both racist practices and racist culture (Ferguson, 2000).

Both liberal feminist educational critiques such as the AAUW works and the "what about the boys" panic take gender as given and divorce it from broader structural issues of power. The debate is framed about access, taking the underlying discourse of economic rationality and school reform for granted. The question thus becomes: Who will succeed in the existing schools, boys or girls? It is also a zero-sum game. If girls do better, then boys do worse, and vice versa.

GIRLS GLOBALLY

In the developing world, the concern about girls' relative lack of success in school is framed not in terms of gender justice, but in terms of the contribution higher levels of education for girls can mean in terms of lower birthrate and a more flexible labor market for a global economy that is quite willing to uncouple gender and labor if it leads to greater profits.

Western thinking about gender and education in the "two-thirds world" has gone through a number of stages. In the early structural adjustment programs imposed by the International Monetary Fund (IMF), gender and, in particular, the interests of women and girls tended to be ignored, with dire consequences for women's lives (Stromquist, 1999). When the question of girls' education began to be raised, it was in the context of contributing to overall economic development through a lower birthrate and better child-raising practices, thus leading to a more productive workforce. Development experts and corporate leaders who took this position were quite willing to uncouple gender and labor if it led to greater profits. It was only in the 1990s that a conception of education for girls as a human right began to be advocated by Westerners concerned with development. International organizations such as the United Nations began to assert educational access as part of a demand for gender justice. These two perspectives continue to be the two poles of thinking about girls' education in the two-thirds world, with international development agencies such as the World Bank advocating girls' education as an investment in overall economic productivity, and feminists, nongovernmental organizations (NGOs), and UNESCO arguing that girls' education is a human right. In practice, of course, many of the educational programs for girls now being implemented across the globe incorporate both claims — that education will lead to economic development and that education is a human right (Heward & Bunwaree, 1999).

While the negative impact of the global economy — the exploitation of girls and women in the global assembly line or the global sex industry — has been the focus of both academic study and political organizing, the positive effects of globalization have been less attended to. Movements for gender justice have emerged across the globe in the decades since the Second World War. Particularly interesting in this respect is the power of human rights documents to shape educational provision. Even funding agencies such as the IMF or Asian Development Bank can potentially have a positive impact on gender policies through their expectation that countries follow the UN Declaration of Human Rights, their introduction of required reporting mechanisms, and the introduction of gender itself as a category of measuring educational progress. As Carmen Luke (2000) points out in her study of globalization, the demand for statistical evidence by world organizations — both NGOs and funding agencies — has led to the collection of data on the education of women and girls, which has brought to light and publicized gender inequities and has provided the impetus for political organizing by women.

While it is both inaccurate and self-serving to argue that the West has brought unproblematic progress to the unenlightened and backward others of the world, there may be advantages to women in some aspects of globalization and even in the new managerialism (Luke, 2000). For example, while the idea that it was only the introduction of Western ideas of economic development in the post–World War II period that introduced women's politics to Asia is patently false, given the existence of local women's groups who argued for women's rights under colonial regimes, at the same time, the tendency to imagine a romantic and somehow sacrosanct tradition held up in opposition to the evil effects of modernization is also problematic. Has the "indigenous" always been a preferable space to the "global" for women? Tradition, after all, has at times supported gender inequity and denied girls access to education in order to maintain patriarchal religions and social systems.

CONCLUSION

Neoliberalism has come to shape virtually all aspects of human society in the past two decades. In the face of the power of corporations and elites to shape both economies and states, progressives have had to re-imagine the nature of political possibility. As Walkerdine et al. (2001) note, "We are no longer in an era in which progressive social change towards any kind of socialism or social democracy, backed up by trade unions or union struggles, is on the agenda" (p. 1). In this world, feminist educators have to continue locating their analysis and practice in order to capture the complexity of gender and build a more progressive analysis and program for education. Chandra Mohanty describes an antiracist, anticolonial feminism, what she calls feminism without borders:

> It would require a clear understanding that being a woman has political consequences in the world we live in; that there can be unjust and unfair effects on women depending on our economic and social marginality and/or privilege. It would require recognizing that sexism, racism, misogyny, and heterosexism underlie and fuel social and political institutions of rule and thus often lead to hatred of women and (supposedly justified) violence against women. (Mohanty, 2003, p. 3)

This is an alternative position from which to explore the meanings of gender in education at the present miserable historical moment.

As feminists have argued for decades, the unitary categories *woman, man, girl,* and *boy* do not capture the lived realities of gender. Gender is performed, but is not completely volitional. The experience of individuals is obviously shaped by their class position and racial/ethnic identity as well as their nationality and positioning in respect to the legacy of colonialism.

REFERENCES

American Association of University Women. (1995). *How schools shortchange girls.* New York: Marlowe and Company.
Blackmore, J. (1999). *Troubling women.* London: Open University Press.
Connell, R. W. (2002). *Gender.* London: Polity Press.
Ferguson, A. (2000). *Bad boys.* Ann Arbor: University of Michigan Press.
Heward, C., & Bunwaree, S. (Eds.). (1999). *Gender, education, and development.* London: Zed Books.
Kenway, J. (1995). Masculinities: Under siege, on the defensive and under reconstruction? *Discourse, 16,* 59–81.
Lingard, B., & Douglas, P. (1999). *Men engaging feminisms.* London: Open University Press.
Luke, C. (2000). *Globalization and women in academia.* Mahwah, NJ: Lawrence Erlbaum.
Mohanty, C. (2003). *Feminism without borders.* Durham, NC: Duke University Press.
Sadker, M., & Sadker, D. (1995). *Failing at fairness.* New York: Scribner.
Stromquist, N. (1999). The impact of structural adjustment programmes in Africa and Latin America. In C. Heward & S. Bunwaree (Eds.), *Gender, education, and development* (pp. 17–32). London: Zed Books.
Walkerdine, V., Lucey, H., & Melody, J. (2001). *Growing up girl.* New York: New York University Press.

Chapter 11

Race

Gwendolyn A. Guy
East Carolina University

The court decision of *Brown v. Board* remains one of the most significant pieces of legislation to impact the lives of blacks since the Emancipation Proclamation. It had far-reaching effects in changing the educational opportunities for black Americans and the nature of how they would experience life in the later half of the 20th century. Therefore, it came as no surprise on the 50th-anniversary celebration of the landmark decision in May 2004 that many gathered to hear eloquent speeches and engage in deep reflections to assess, evaluate, and critique the meaning of *Brown* past, present, and future. However, the 50th anniversary may best be remembered by what is now considered the infamous speech delivered by well-known comedian Bill Cosby. According to several newspaper accounts and media commentaries, Cosby created what some called a firestorm that led to criticism and debate among black Americans. He accused blacks, particularly blacks who are situated at the lower end of the social class hierarchy, of squandering the promises delivered by the courts in the *Brown* ruling. He characterized the behaviors of lower-class blacks as destructive to their neighborhoods through violence, drugs, and other antisocial behaviors. Calling into question their parenting skills, Cosby charged that parents were responsible for their children's inappropriate misbehaviors. He also accused parents of not being concerned about their children's education, which has led to a decline in the number of black youths who are articulate, as demonstrated in their misuse of proper grammar. The controversy stirred by his remarks and subsequent comments continues nearly two years later.

The debate among black Americans initiated by Cosby's characterization of the black lower class has been divisive. Many agree with his criticism that poor blacks situated in urban and inner-city ghettos are not doing all they should to improve their condition. They believe the poor should take personal responsibility for their poverty and their neighborhoods. Cosby's charge to the poor to take back their neighborhoods, however, rings hollow to those trapped in deteriorating areas where drugs, crime, and violence are everyday occurrences. His prescriptive solutions — stop the drugs, stop the violence, get an education, and take back the neighborhood — are great ideas, but do they provide poor blacks the means by they can accomplish these monumental tasks? Dyson explains why Cosby's solutions to the many problems faced by the poor are too simplistic and narrowly situated.

> Cosby's emphasis on personal responsibility, not structural features, wrongly locates the source of poor Black suffering — and by implication its remedy — in the lives of the poor. When you think the problems are personal, you think the solutions are the same. (Dyson, 2005, p. 3)

Can the poor turn their neighborhoods into drug-free environments without assistance from the larger community? Are they able to create jobs, better housing, better schools, transportation, and other necessities that support and sustain viable communities? Anyon (2005) argues that without government intervention, urban and inner-city ghettos cannot survive or be transformed. One critical element missing from Cosby's prescriptions for poor lower-class blacks is the need for social responsiveness from the larger community and the government. Yet, nowhere does Cosby or those who endorse his position mention or reference the need for government programs, social policies, and practices that do not adversely affect the poor.

Is there a growing consensus among well-meaning Americans to abandon the poor, who are the least advantaged in society, and hold them solely responsible for their existing conditions and the circumstances that have become their lot in life? *Abandon* may not be the term that people who agree with Cosby would use, but the idea or implication that structural changes necessary for transformation can be accomplished by the individual will is unrealistic. Yet, many are being led to believe that society bears no responsibility to address or attempt to alleviate the many social ills that the poor, blacks, and nonblacks alike face daily. This changing attitude toward the poor has been greatly influenced by neoliberalism.

Neoliberals promote the idea that government intervention is unnecessary because individuals have the right to make choices that can and will lead them to economic success and the American dream. Conversely, people who are not prospering economically are not making the best choices. This implied logic, coupled with demographic changes in society and the shrinking of the middle class, has heightened the fears of many who have

lost or who anticipate losing their jobs, their social security, or their retirement benefits — health care and pension plans that were once guaranteed. Individual concerns and priorities have displaced the collective good
as people contemplate their futures. As Henry Giroux argues,

> Under neoliberal globalization ... power is uncoupled from a matter of ethics
> and social responsibility, and market freedoms replace long-standing social
> contracts that once provided a safety net for the poor, the elderly workers
> and the middle class. (Giroux, 2003, p. 195)

Outsourcing of jobs to India and other economically developing nations
has adversely affected the way many Americans view the poor. The logic
of market economies and the escalation of corporate greed that reduces
everyone and everything to the bottom line (i.e., profit) have created dis-
sonance between democratic principles aligned with the collective good
and that of personal gain as an individual goal (West, 2005). Dyson (2005)
claims that Cosby's views may also be influenced by elements of neoliberalism because they bolster the belief that less money, political action, and
societal intervention — and more hard work and personal responsibility
— are key to black success (p. 3). The absence of government from the
solutions proposed by Cosby is a key component of neoliberalism. Less
government in the affairs of individuals is touted as the desirable feature
of democracy because it protects individual property rights and access to
free market economies (West, 2004). Poor people, living in crowded urban
ghettos, have no property to be protected, and they are not reaping the
benefits of the market economies that focus on the bottom line — profit.
Criticizing the behaviors of the poor deflects critical analysis of how power
relationships maintain social inequality. The one-dimensional aspect that
focuses attention on the behaviors of the poor is used as justification in victim blaming that prevents social interventions. Consequently, victim blaming remains unchallenged, and those who argue on behalf of the victims
are forced to offer a defense for their behaviors at the risk of seeming to
condone them. Many who disagree with Cosby's criticism of the poor do
not deny their behaviors have counterproductive effects on their communities and their members, but to only highlight the negative behaviors of
those who commit crime and sell drugs does not address or eradicate the
problems associated with poverty.

Cornel West also advocates the need to address the negative behaviors of
those who are engaging in crime, violence, and drugs. Unlike Cosby, however, he also addresses the structural constraints that maintain racial and
social inequality by denying equal access to the poor and minorities. If we
do not move ourselves to dismantle these constraints, we can only expect
the persistence of inequality and impoverishment, and not only an impoverishment in people's material lives, but in their psychic/spiritual lives as

well. Persistent impoverishment, West would argue, leads inevitably to a type of desperation associated by West with the notion of nihilism. Nihilism constitutes, for West, a form of despair that manifests itself in various destructive and self-destructive ways when people have no hope and life has no meaning (West, 2004, p. 23). Therefore, we need a broader understanding of poverty and its consequences to bring about meaningful solutions.

NEOLIBERALISM, RACE, AND EDUCATION

Many people believe the court's decision in *Brown v. Board*, coupled with the gains of the civil rights movement and the successful passage of the relevant legislation, leveled the playing field in America. As Giroux (2003) points out, "Poll after poll reveals that a majority of White Americans believe that people of color no longer face racial discrimination in American life" (p. 192). Desegregation of major institutions and the dismantling of the visible signs of Jim Crow have changed the discourse of race and education. The perception that race is no longer relevant appeases those who are ready to move on to more important issues, that is, the economy, the impact of globalization, and the need to reform government spending, social programs, and education. In Giroux's words, "As politics becomes more racialized the discourse about race becomes more privatized" (2003, p. 193). For example, the racialized influence of neoliberalism on education is evident with the current education reform measures of the No Child Left Behind Act (NCLB) of 2001. Inspired by the professed goals and objectives of neoliberalism, NCLB claims to create opportunities for individuals to take full advantage of the now-level playing field. The stringent demands of accountability and high-stakes testing claim to offer individuals the opportunity to develop the skills they will need to successfully compete for jobs in global markets, even though many of the jobs requiring the highest skills and commanding the highest pay are outsourced to countries where the work can be performed by workers who might possess comparable skills but who do not demand high pay. Embraced by both conservatives and liberals, NCLB downplays the significance of race in its slogan, "No child will be left behind." According to the proposed objectives of NCLB, by the year 2014, children in public schools all across America will have equal access to highly qualified teachers, teacher accountability, assessments that measure outcomes with high-stakes testing, and resources to ensure success. This reform provides the unsuspecting public, including Cosby and those who agree with him, a sigh of relief in their blind acceptance that no child will be left behind, regardless of who they are and where they come from.

Poor black students who drop out of school or fail to demonstrate acquisition of basic language fluency are perceived as having squandered the

promise of *Brown v. Board.* Cosby's criticisms lodged against the students
for their failures without questioning the quality of their education is
consistent with his narrow view of the problems associated with poverty.
His attention on the personal failures of students who are not proficient
in language usage avoids a serious critique of public education. We must
ask ourselves: Who receives a quality education and who does not? More
importantly: Why hasn't the answer to that question changed significantly
over the past 50 years since *Brown?* These are the questions that should be
asked. The political and public discourse surrounding the NCLB policy
attempts to conceal the structural and institutional inequalities that exist
within the system of public education. While parents, educators, and many
states are unsure of how to interpret the long-range effects of the NCLB
policy on individual schools, the government continues to give encouraging reports about the effectiveness of the reform bill.

One of the most damaging effects of NCLB comes in the form of sanctions. Schools are threatened with sanctions — closing schools that fail to
meet policy guidelines or privatizing them to be run by businesses, and
giving vouchers to parents to send their children to a different school. This
heavily bipartisan legislation places the burden of eradicating poverty by
overcoming its impact on students solely on the shoulders of individual
schools, principals, and teachers, ignoring the structural constraints that
West would identify within the larger political and economic context of the
educational system as a whole. The demands of NCLB avert questions concerning such key issues as school funding and curricular purposes. They
ignore questions of who is being tracked, why high-stakes testing represents
the only means of holding schools accountable, and who benefits from
sanctions and who gets hurt by them. Answering these questions requires
a deeper understanding of how schools reproduce social inequalities and
why band-aid reforms and empty slogans will not bring about the meaningful change necessary to make quality education available to all children.

In Jonathan Kozol's book *Savage Inequalities* (1991), an in-depth look into
American urban public schools revealed the gross inequalities that existed
across schools in the early 1990s. The book's stark findings of what many
urban, poor children experience as students who are forced to attend
underfunded schools, with outdated textbooks, nonfunctioning chemis-
try and biology labs, unsafe and unsanitary school buildings, and noncre-
dentialed teachers (many of whom were long-term substitutes) could be
characterized as criminal. The shocking stories of these schools left many
wondering how this could be happening in America. Fifteen years later,
in his newest book, *The Shame of the Nation,* not too much has changed
for many of the urban schools that he revisited. Parents, mostly poor and
minority, feel helpless. Kozol (2005) argues that the conditions found in
these poor, urban public schools would never exist in wealthier districts
because the outcry would be thunderous and swift. Yet, poor minority

children experience the most degrading forms of second-class citizenship imaginable. In the affluent neighborhoods where resources are abundant and teachers are credentialed, parents whose children may be reassigned to schools that are undesirable have options. They threaten school boards with removing their children and sending them to private schools or suing based on unfair redistricting practices. The local school boards wrestle with calming the fears of parents whose outcry is to bring back the concept of neighborhood schools. The term *neighborhood school* has replaced the word *segregated*. Presented as a new concept, neighborhood schools have gained popularity among both blacks and whites who are members of the upper-middle-class communities. Schools that house large numbers of blacks, Latinos, and other minority groups are segregated by race and class from schools that remain predominantly white. Today's schools are more segregated than in the early 1950s, prior to *Brown*, leaving poor children at a disadvantage and their schools as the target for harsh government interventions guised in the form of takeovers and privatization. Kozol's recent findings suggest that policy makers, local school districts, and school boards who are responsible for ensuring quality education for all children have by omission neglected the children who live in urban ghettos. Therefore, the threat associated with failure to meet the standards associated with NCLB has even greater consequences for low-income area schools that are overpopulated with poor blacks and other minorities.

Teachers are being held accountable for low test scores in reading, math, and science and other conditions that eventually lead many children to drop out of school. The rhetoric associated with NCLB to hire highly qualified teachers, impose more stringent accountability practices, and accelerate high-stakes testing every three years is the language of the market. It is also the language used to conceal the gross inequalities that exist in schools across the nation that fail to acknowledge that race and class matter long after the decision of *Brown v. Board* and its 50th anniversary.

Cosby's accusation that poor blacks are not holding up their end of *Brown* once again reflects his obvious short-sightedness and narrowly focused lens. It should be argued that states, local courts, along with school districts and other governmental agencies associated with education are not holding up their constitutional and social responsibility for *Brown v. Board*. The need to find a scapegoat and dismiss the need to overhaul public education has produced a new form of window-dressing, catchy-sounding rhetoric and victim blaming. In this case, the victims include the students, the teachers, and the parents who must send their children to the schools like those visited by Kozol. In his interviews with teachers and principals committed to educating the children who are disadvantaged, Kozol issued an indictment against society and the legacy that was *Brown*. He reports that the principals and teachers in the schools he revisited "are reluctantly settling for the promise of *Plessy v. Ferguson*" (Kozol, 2005, p. 6). If their segregated schools could be equal to those suburban white schools, then the children of color would have a better chance to succeed. The policy of No Child Left Behind promotes "higher standards[;] higher expectations are repeatedly demanded of these urban principals, and of the teachers and students in their schools; but far lower standards — certainly in ethical respects — appear to be expected of the dominant society that isolates these children in unequal institutions" (Kozol, 2005, p. 7). There appears to be little if any outcry against the resegregation of schools and unequal funding. Instead, Kozol reveals the deliberate attempt by those responsible for education to "repeatedly employ linguistic sweeteners, semantic somersaults, and surrogate vocabularies to avoid talking about race." He contends that "schools in which as few as 3 or 4 percent of students are white or Southeast Asian or of Middle Eastern origin, for instance — and where every other child in the building is black or Hispanic — are referred to as 'diverse'" (p. 5). If the goal of No Child Left Behind is to live up to its rhetoric, then the children who attend the public schools that Kozol visited should not be left behind. Consequently, the legislative act of NCLB will prove to be the promise that *Brown* failed to deliver in 1954.

The Cosby debate may linger awhile longer among black Americans, but debate without action will not change the nature of schools in our society or the significance of race on policies and practices. West reminds us that "race has always been the crucial litmus test for ... maturity in America" (p. 41). Neoliberalism has begun a new chapter in the immaturity of American society, and the long-lasting impact of its refusal to address the most substantive issues in the lives of today's students threatens the way we view ourselves, our neighbors, and the future. It is clear that Americans have been asked to choose between what is morally and ethically right when it comes to social responsibility versus personal responsibility. Many are choosing to look away or to reason that the poor will somehow survive without the help of others. But there are others in society that tend to believe enough has been done to help the poor and that race and racism are no longer tenable when making decisions that have implications for minorities. The danger associated with neoliberalism is the emphasis on individualism at the expense of the collective good. Poverty is not a private issue, and neither is race. The limitations of market ideologies and racist sentiments produce the following:

> Indifference and cynicism breed contempt and resentment as racial hierarchies now collapse into power-evasive strategies such as blaming minorities of class and color for not working hard enough, or exercising individual initiatives, or practicing reverse racism. Marketplace ideologies now work to erase the social from the language of the public life so as to reduce all racial problems to private issues such as individual character. (Giroux, 2003, p. 193)

The poor and those who are poor and black — the targets of Cosby's thrashing — deserve equality of opportunity and access rather than blame for being poor. The rebuilding of urban ghettos and inner-city neighborhoods will require a collective investment of everyone — community involvement and local, state, and federal government.

REFERENCES

Anyon, J. (2005). *Radical possibilities*. New York: Routledge.

Dyson, M. E. (2005). *Is Bill Cosby right or has the black middle class lost its mind?* New York: Basic Civitas Books.

Giroux, H. (2003). Spectacles of race and pedagogies of denial: Anti-black racist pedagogy under the reign of neoliberalism. *Communication Education, 52*, 191–211.

Kozol, J. (1991). *Savage inequalities: Children in America's schools*. New York: HarpersCollins.

Kozol, J. (2005, September 2005). Still separate, still unequal: America's educational apartheid. *Harper's*, Vol. 311, No. 1864, p. 1.

West, C. (2004). *Democracy matters: Winning the fight against imperialism*. New York: The Penguin Press.

Chapter 12

Sexuality

William F. Pinar
University of British Columbia

Like the Taliban, the U.S. religious right (the so-called Christian Coalition, for instance) claims the moral high ground (no abortion, no gay marriage, no drugs). During the 2004 election, Republicans focused the public's attention on moral issues (such as gay marriage) to distract citizens from their party's incompetence (failing to protect the United States on September 11, 2001, for instance) and immorality (lying to the nation about WMD in Iraq, for starters). The Republican Party's campaign of social hatred and misrepresentation does not constitute politics as usual. How can we understand the willingness — indeed, eagerness — of political conservatives to sacrifice democratic ideals for political power? How can we understand the Republicans' appreciation that moral issues such as gay marriage could be effective in the 2004 presidential campaign? To suggest answers to these questions, I will focus — very impressionistically, given the length of this chapter — on the decade before the nightmare that is the present.

Despite its contested status among historians (see Pinar, 2001, p. 321 ff.), the ongoing American crisis of masculinity provides a clue. For at least a century, many American men have experienced multiple threats to their manhood (Filene, 1998). The year 1993 was key in the current crisis of masculinity in America. Throughout the 1980s (see Savran, 1998), there had been intensifying discussion regarding a crisis of masculinity, this one (like the one in the 1890s) stimulated by the advances of women (*SAVE THE MALES* read the bumper stickers) and African Americans (the campaign against affirmative action was well under way), the increased visibility of queers, and the defeat in Vietnam, mixed with traumatic economic upheavals of post-Fordism ("male" industries were sent abroad as "female" service industries replaced them).

LOOK BUT DON'T SEE

Incontrovertible evidence of an intensification of the crisis, Mark Simpson (1994) suggests, was the furor that erupted in 1993 over newly elected President Clinton's pledge to end the Pentagon's ban on lesbians and gays in the military. Right-wing reactionaries howled that the final citadel of manhood in America, the last place where men could be sure that men were men, was now under siege. Adding to this masculinist anxiety was the news that women were being assigned to certain combat positions for the first time in both the British and American armed forces. "If women and queers could be soldiers too," as Simpson (1994) phrased it, "then what was there left for a man to do that was manly; where and how was virility to show its mettle?" (p. 2). "Where" was not in Iraq, as the elder Bush had stopped short of unmanning Saddam Hussein. The "failure" of the father would be redressed by the son.

The gays-in-the-military issue functioned to turn especially white male voters against the Democratic Party in 1994, engendering a sweeping Republican victory (Filene, 1998). The electoral reaction is, of course, the point: How fragile must heterosexual identification be if the thought of sharing showers provokes major panic? "I was not alone," Leo Bersani (1995) confides, "in being astonished by the prominence of shower rooms in the erotic imagination of heterosexual American males. Fear on the battlefield is apparently mild compared to the terror of being 'looked at'" (p. 16). Bersani (1995) recalls that the *New York Times* reported on April 3, 1993, that a radar instructor who chose not to fly with an openly gay sailor, Keith Meinhold, feared that Meinhold's "presence in the cockpit would distract him from his responsibilities." The instructor "compared his 'shock' at learning that there was a gay sailor in his midst to a woman discovering 'a man in the ladies' restroom'" (quoted passages in Bersani, 1995, p. 16). Bersani (1995) comments:

> Note the curious scatological transsexualism in our radar instructor's (let us hope momentary) identification of his cockpit with a ladies restroom. In this strange scenario, the potential gay attacker becomes the male intruder on female privacy, and the "original" straight man is metamorphosed, through another man's imagined sexual attention, into the offended, harassed, or even violated woman. (Bersani, 1995, pp. 16–17)

I am reminded of Daniel Paul Schreber, the late 19th-century German judge who, caught in the gaze of God, became a woman (see Pinar, 2006).

The compromise policy that was finally adopted ("don't ask, don't tell, don't pursue") suggests, Bersani points out, that even more dangerous than the presence of homosexuals in the military is the prospect of admitting that we are there. Why? Bersani answers by suggesting that the homoeroticism (along with misogyny, a by-product of homosexual repression), already pervasive in military life, risks being made explicit to those many men who at once deny and enjoy it. The game is up when self-confessed gay men decline to deny what is essential to the military, namely, men's pleasure in their physical and psychological intimacy with other men. Worse (and here he seems to be relying on a Butlerian notion of "performativity"), Bersani (1995) suggests the most serious danger in queer Marines being open about their preferences is that they might begin "to play at being Marines. Not that they would make fun of the Marines. On the contrary: they may find ways of being so Marine-like that they will no longer be 'real' Marines" (pp. 17–18). After all, it is a certain un-self-conscious machismo that keeps recruits thinking of muscles, not gay sex, when they pass the sign at Camp Pendleton: "STAY HARD!" (Zeeland, 1996, photograph opposite p. 101).

For Susan Bordo (1994), one of the most revealing elements of the 1990s' gays-in-the-military debate had to do with the fact that those who have argued against the disclosure of sexual orientation readily admit that there have always been gay men in the military. As Bersani points out, these men do not seem to mind gays in the shower as long as they cannot recognize them, that is, as long as they can suppress their knowledge that homosexuals are there with them, as long as they can continue to deny the fact that homosexuality is present in them. What is obvious to Bordo is that the arguments against integrated locker rooms and showers are not about regulating gay behavior; they are about protecting

> *heterosexual* men from certain unacceptable thoughts and feelings of their own.... Described bluntly, this is a situation in which it is being proposed that the civil rights of one group are less worthy of protection than the *illusions* of another. (Bordo, 1994, p. 283)

Evidently, Americans require a constitutional amendment against gay marriage to protect the illusion that marriage is between a man and a woman, despite historical evidence to the contrary (see Boswell, 1995).

FOR GOD AND SODOMY

Banning gays from the military enacts an illusion of its own, namely, that the military itself is not a homoerotic institution, in which men enjoy physical and psychological (and not infrequently sexual; see Bérubé, 1983) intimacy with other men as they prepare for and engage in the murder of other men, women, and children. What can be the gendered attractions of war? J. Glenn Gray (1996) suggests one answer: "the delight in seeing, the delight in comradeship, the delight in destruction. War," he suggests, is a spectacle, "something to see." There is, he says, "in all of us what the Bible characterized as 'the lust of the eye,'" a phrase, like the universality of his claim, "at once precise and of the widest connotation" (quoted passages on p. 47). What appeals to men in such spectacles of destruction? "It is the fascination that manifestations of power and magnitude hold for the human spirit," Gray (1996, p. 49) answers. Staring at men all day everyday: Is that the "lust of the eye"?

Comradeship is involved in the "pleasure" of war, although, Gray (1996) acknowledges, "men can live in the same room and share the same suffering without any sense of belonging together. They can live past each other and be irresponsible toward each other, even when their welfare is clearly dependent on co-operation" (p. 52). For many soldiers, at least since ancient Greece, being comrades has meant being lovers (Bérubé, 1990; Percy, 1996). For some men, then, the attraction of war has to do with its sense of spectacle and power; for others, some dimly perceived sense of being together as comrades; and yet for others, it has meant sex and, on occasion, love. Most of all, of course, war is about death — and not only death of men. It has been estimated that in the 20th century, women and children constituted 80% of the casualties of modern warfare (Clatterbaugh, 1996). One suspects that similar percentages will hold among Iraqi civilians in the current slaughter.

The great Canadian novelist Margaret Atwood understands war. If you add *straight* before *men* in the following passage, the picture becomes crystal clear:

> The history of war is a history of bodies. That's what war is: bodies killing other bodies, bodies being killed. Some of the killed bodies are those of women and children, as a side effect you might say. Fallout, shrapnel, napalm, rape and skewering, anti-personnel devices. But most of the killed bodies are men. So are most of those doing the killing. Why do men want to kill the bodies of other men? Women don't want to kill the bodies of other women. By and large. As far as we know. (Atwood, 1994, p. 3)

Could it be we murder what we cannot bear to experience as objects of desire? Is men's sexual desire for each other a WMD? The pre-emptive strikes against it suggest that right-wing Republicans consider it so.

Even if most victims are women and children, war is a homosocial affair among men. Michael Kimmel (1996) quotes an Army general who insists that what every soldier fears is "losing the one thing he is likely to value more than life — his reputation as *a man among other men*" (quoted in Kimmel, 1996, p. 7). Understanding war as a homosocial performance suggests it is a point men make to other men, a point about honor, about power, about sex. Consider the story Slavoj Zizek (1995) tells of heterosexual rape during the Bosnian War. He tells of soldiers' eyes locked into the eyes of the father of the girl they are serially raping, a performance of male bonding, homosocial desire (Sedgwick, 1985) that requires the trafficking of women (Rubin, 1975). Stoltenberg (1990) is clear:

> When male combat troops do aggress against the territorial rights of other men, their actual military strategy often involves heterosexual rape of women belonging to those men (for example, American soldiers in Vietnam). But the aggression men fear, and the fear upon which their "national defense" is predicated, is aggression from other men — that is, homosexual attack. (p. 86)

Is that the gendered subtext of terrorism? Was it the American fantasy of the phallus that was de-erected in New York on September 11, 2001? The nucleus of the American military man — the Pentagon — was penetrated on the same catastrophic day.

Ah, for God and sodomy. In ancient days, victorious soldiers sometimes sodomized their adversaries before killing them. For instance, the Ancient Egyptians, when victorious in battle, had a "ceremonial custom of buggering defeated troops, thereby asserting sexual and political mastery over them" (Woods, 1987, p. 53). In 1990 the *New York Times* reported that ethnic tensions among the soldiers of the crumbling Soviet army had erupted in murder and male-male rape (see also Scarce, 1997). Also, in 1990, the *Washington Times* reported the rape of Kuwaiti men by Iraqi soldiers as part of the Iraqi invasion (Scarce, 1997). Not all sex in the military is forced, of course; one famous (and controversial) survey found that 40% of men enjoyed at least incidental homosexual relations while in the U.S. armed services (Kinsey, Pomeroy, & Martin, 1948). But to desublimate the homosociality of the military, as Clinton's 1993 pledge to end the Pentagon's ban on lesbians and gays in the military threatened to do, endangers national security.

In his study of homoerotic desire and feminine influence in 19th-century American fiction, Scott S. Derrick (1997) argues that because overt homosexuality was not generally narratable as itself — recall it was not popularized as a concept until the early 20th century — it surfaced as a fictional obsession with

> the plot of death and disaster, which authorizes a violent and genocidal penetration of the male body, and which also produces emergencies that authorize the expression of tenderness and the giving of care. The most culturally acceptable culmination of desire between men involves the annihilation or near annihilation of one of the parties. (p. 90)

This dynamic is evident in Stephen Crane's novel of the Civil War, *Red Badge of Courage,* in which Crane is fascinated with a "queer kind 'a hurt" (quoted in Derrick, 1997, p. 182).

Is this "queer kind 'a hurt" related to nostalgia, that nostalgia which seems to accompany combat and militancy generally? Kim Michasiw (1994) links the two, defining "nostalgia a gentrified keeping buried of loss, [and] militancy [as] an ordered regime of misdirection understood as a cause or a code" (p. 156). That cause may be the threat of terrorism, but in its gendered mobilization, Michasiw (1994) continues, "militancy is skewed fixing of the subject's affective position, an assertive, even manic manliness ... pinned and sentimentalized by the nostalgia" (p. 156). Is that men's nostalgia for intimacy with the male body? "Militancy, Michasiw (1994) continues,

> allows the subject to go on about its business of appearing to search while averting its gaze from anything that might give the lie to its aborignality.... The latter [nostalgia] assures the subject that what is lost [homosexual desire] will stay that way while the former [militancy] ensures that the subject will make its way without stumbling across what it marches in search of. (p. 156)

The son renders right the failure of the father; Saddam Hussein is brought to his knees.

In the 20th century (about which Paul Monette [1992] declares bitterly but correctly: "Genocide is still the national sport of straight men, especially in this century of nightmares" [p. 2]), what the subject is in search of becomes clearer as homosexuality becomes more conspicuous on the social surface. So is the sexual symbolism of certain military practices. Consider, for instance, the military dictatorship in Argentina some two decades ago, during which time thousands were murdered or simply disappeared. These Argentine patriots used, among others, the following technique of torture: Rats were placed inside a tube plugged on one side that was then inserted open ended into the victim's anus or vagina. Slowly, painfully, the rats tore away at the victim's internal organs, finally killing them (Simon, 1996).

As Susan Brownmiller (1975/1993) discovered during her research on rape, the ramming of a stick, bottle, or some other object into a woman's vagina is not uncommon. Police department m.o. (modus operandi) sheets in Los Angeles and Denver provide blanks to be checked off next to "inserts object in vagina." The Denver form also lists "inserts foreign object into rectum" (quoted in Brownmiller, 1975/1993, p. 195). Brownmiller (1975/1993) notes: "Castration, the traditional *coup de grace* of a lynching, has its counterpart in the gratuitous acts of defilement that often accompany a rape, the stick rammed up the vagina, the attempt to annihilate the sexual core" (p. 255). The links among lynching, castration, and Abu Ghraib are discernible (see Pinar, in press).

This capacity for violation and torture is not rare among men. The National Institute of Mental Health has estimated that in the United States 3% of men have antisocial personality disorder, but fewer than

1% of women. Antisocial personality disorder is most commonly diagnosed in the 26- to 40-year-old age group; thereafter, the incidence decreases (Simon, 1996). Are younger men more dangerous than older ones? Is that because they are so determined to be men? Remembering himself as a university student, Goebbels (A&E Biography, 1997) mused: "I wanted to become a man." Perhaps we should fear those who want to become men. How does one become a man in most cultures? One must take a wife, then have kids. Ah, the family, that haven in a heartless world — Foucault (1978) judged it to be "the most active site of sexuality" (p. 109) — turns out to be the most active site of violence against women.

FAMILY VALUES

Twenty to fifty percent of all murders occur within the family. The most common predictor of stalking is domestic violence. Where domestic violence exists, approximately 60% of children are physically or sexually abused. During 1997, approximately 2000 children died as a consequence of child abuse (CNN, 1998). Approximately 30% of women who suffer physical injury by spousal abuse are eventually murdered by their husbands. The FBI estimates that one in four women who are murdered are killed by husbands or live-in partners. Every physician in America, regardless of specialty or location of his or her practice, has seen a battered woman in his or her office in the last two weeks (Simon, 1996).

Such statistics prompted former Surgeon General Antonia Novella to launch the American Medical Association's (AMA) Campaign Against Family Violence in 1991 by suggesting that the home is actually a more dangerous place for American women than city streets. The U.S. Public Health Service, the CDC, the American College of Obstetricians and Gynecologists, the American Nurses Association, and the AMA have all agreed that family violence constitutes the number one health threat to American women. In other words: "The safest place for men is at home, the home is, by contrast, the least safe place for women" (Edwards, 1989, p. 214). Dobash and Dobash (1992) comment: "It is now well known that violence in the home is commonplace, that women are its usual victims and men its usual perpetrators. It is also known that the family is filled with many different forms of violence and aggression, including physical, sexual, and emotional, and that violence is perpetrated by young and old alike" (p. 2, quoted in Hearn, 1998, p. 4.) Conclusion? "Home can be a very dangerous place — even more dangerous than a dark city alley at night" (Simon, 1996, p. 51). In the early 1990s many Republicans insisted that we need a Defense of Family Act. How about a Defense of Women and Children Trapped in Families Act?

PROMISES TO KEEP

Organized by former University of Colorado football coach Bill McCartney, the Promise Keepers embrace conservative Christianity. These men assert that real men, that is, Christian men, must exercise moral leadership in their families, respect their wives, and provide for their children, mirroring, presumably, Jesus' strength and sexual purity. "We're calling men of God to battle" against promiscuity and permissiveness, McCartney declared. He hit a nerve, evidently; more than 20,000 men gathered in the University of Colorado's Folson Stadium in 1992, and 50,000 a year later (Filene, 1998). By 1995, more than 700,000 — almost all white, middle-aged men — were paying $55 each at 13 sites around the country in what one journalist called "a combination Super Bowl game and revival meeting" (quoted in Filene, 1998, p. 242).

Like the earlier anti-ERA movement leaders, the spokesmen for Promise Keepers focused on feminists, declaring that they had undermined God's plan for the family. The first step every Christian man must take, Tony Evans asserted, "is sit down with your wife and say something like this: 'Honey, I've made a terrible mistake. I've given you my role.... Now I must reclaim that role.' Don't misunderstand what I'm saying here," Evans continued. "I'm not suggesting that you *ask* for your role back, I'm urging you to *take* it back." This nonsense found a receptive, even eager, audience among conservative men. As a United Methodist minister remarked: "You don't come here and feel like you're losing your masculinity because of your faith" (quoted passages in Filene, 1998, p. 242), a statement echoing conservative men's efforts to re-masculinize Christianity nearly 100 years ago (see Pinar, 2001, Chap. 5, Section VIII).

STAY HARD!

Studying these conflations of politics, religion, militarism, and manhood as they compensate for an ongoing and now intensely politicized crisis of masculinity in America (Is it related to the patricide marking the nation's birth? see Pinar, 2001, p. 1077) enables us to understand why right-wing Republicans have fastened onto moral issues, expressed as the political control of women's bodies (abortion) and the regulation of men's sexuality. This latter issue (not unrelated to the former, of course) was focused on gays in the military during the 1990s and on gay marriage in the first years of the present decade. The predatory America George W. Bush summoned and personifies represents a defensive and compensatory mobilization against terrorism that is gendered as well as political and religious. Once again, men mistake violence for masculinity: Stay hard! Right-wing Republicans understand exactly.

REFERENCES

A&E Biography. (1997). *Goebbels: A biography.* Author.

Atwood, M. (1994). Alien territory. In L. Goldstein (Ed.), *The male body* (pp. 1–7). Ann Arbor: University of Michigan Press.

Bersani, L. (1995). *Homos.* Cambridge, MA: Harvard University Press.

Bérubé, A. (1983). Marching to a different drummer: Lesbian and gay GIs in World War II. In A. Snitow, C. Stansell, & S. Thompson (Eds.), *Powers of desire: The politics of sexuality* (pp. 88–99). New York: Monthly Review Press.

Bérubé, A. (1990). *Coming out under fire: The history of gay men and women in World War Two.* New York: Free Press.

Bordo, S. (1994). Reading the male body. In L. Goldstein (Ed.), *The male body* (pp. 265–306). Ann Arbor: University of Michigan Press.

Boswell, J. (1995). *Same-sex unions in premodern Europe.* New York: Vintage.

Brownmiller, S. (1993). *Against our will: Men, women, and rape.* New York: Fawcett Columbine. (Original work published 1975.)

Clatterbaugh, K. (1996). Are men oppressed? In L. May, R. Strikwerda, & P. D. Hopkins (Eds.), *Rethinking masculinity: Philosophical explorations in light of feminism* (pp. 289–305). Lanham, MD: Rowman & Littlefield.

CNN. (1998, August 3). *2000 children died via child abuse in 1997.* Author.

Derrick, S. S. (1997). *Monumental anxieties: Homoerotic desire and feminine influence in nineteenth-century U.S. literature.* New Brunswick, NJ: Rutgers University Press.

Dobash, R. E., & Dobash, R. P. (1992). *Women, violence, and social change.* London: Routledge.

Edwards, S. (1989). *Policing domestic violence.* London: Sage.

Filene, P. G. (1998). *Him/her/self* (3rd ed.; 1st ed. published in 1974 by Harcourt, Brace, Jovanovich). Baltimore: Johns Hopkins University Press.

Foucault, M. (1978). *The history of sexuality: An Introduction.* New York: Pantheon.

Gray, J. G. (1996). The enduring appeals of battle. In L. May, R. Strikwerda, & P. D. Hopkins (Eds.), *Rethinking masculinity: Philosophical explorations in light of feminism* (pp. 45–62). Lanham, MD: Rowman & Littlefield.

Hearn, J. 1998. *The violence of men.* London: Sage.

Kimmel, M. S. (1996). *Manhood in America: A cultural history.* New York: Free Press.

Kinsey, A. C., Pomeroy, W. B., & Martin, C. E. (1948). *Sexual behavior in the human male.* Philadelphia: W. B. Saunders.

Michasiw, K. (1994). Camp, masculinity, masquerade. *Differences, 6,* 146–173.

Monette, P. (1992). *Becoming a man: Half a life story.* San Francisco: Harper.

Percy III, W. A. (1996). *Pederasty and pedagogy in archaic Greece.* Urbana: University of Illinois Press.

Pinar, W. F. (2001). *The gender of racial politics and violence in America: Lynching, prison rape, and the crisis of masculinity.* New York: Peter Lang.

Pinar, W. F. (2006). *Race, religion, and a curriculum of reparation: Teacher education for a multicultural society.* New York: Palgrave Macmillan.

Pinar, W. F. (2007). Cultures of torture. In J. A. James & D. Rodriguez (Eds.), *Warfare: Prison and the American homeland.* Durham, NC: Duke University Press.

Rubin, G. (1975). The traffic in women: Notes on the "political economy" of sex. In R. Reiter (Ed.), *Toward an anthropology of women* (pp. 157–210). New York: Monthly Review Press.

Savran, D. (1998). *Taking it a like a man: White masculinity, masochism, and contemporary American culture.* Princeton, NJ: Princeton University Press.

Scarce, M. (1997). *Male on male rape.* New York: Insight Books/Plenum.

Sedgwick, E. (1985). *Between men: English literature and male homosocial desire.* New York: Columbia University Press.

Simon, R. I. (1996). *Bad men do what good men dream: A forensic psychiatrist illuminates the darker side of human behavior.* Washington, DC: American Psychiatric Press.

Simpson, M. (1994). *Male impersonators: Men performing masculinity.* New York: Routledge.

Stoltenberg, J. (1990). *Refusing to be a man.* New York: Meridian.

Woods, G. (1987). *Articulate flesh: Male homoeroticism and modern poetry.* New Haven, CT: Yale University Press.

Zeeland, S. (1996). *The masculine marine: Homoeroticism in the U.S. Marine Corps.* New York: Harrington Park Press (Hawthorn).

Zizek, S. (1995). *Debate with Judith Butler: The theory seminar series.* Charlottesville: University of Virginia.

ANTIEDUCATIONAL FOUNDATIONS: THE SETUP

As Kristen Buras correctly pointed out in the previous section, some people challenge the centrality that others ascribe to the influence of Leo Strauss's ideas within the neoconservative movement. While that debate lies beyond the scope of this book, the history of educational reform over the past 30 years reads like a Straussian playbook — lies told in the service of power to generate fears to mobilize public support for reforms aimed against the public interest. Like a study in political jiu jitsu, this history provides a textbook case for understanding how to use democracy to kill democracy while simultaneously maintaining the illusion of democracy. As Eric Haas points out, we can trace the origins of the high-stakes testing and accountability model of school reform back to 1981 and the formation of the National Commission on Excellence in Education that launched a national propaganda campaign that actually preceded its release of *A Nation at Risk* in 1983. This campaign constituted an early expression of the now-classic neoconservative propaganda technique of unifying public loyalty to elite power by arousing the public's hatred and fear of democracy and what we hear called liberalism. Inculcating an Orwellian love of heteronomy —a theme addressed in the chapters by Sandra Spikard Prettyman and Sharon Kruse on masculination and Ken Saltman and myself on militarization — *A Nation at Risk* used martial language to blame liberal reforms for what it described as America's educational disarmament that precipitated the steady decline in the American standard of living since the mid-1970s. While the decline was real, the charge that schools were responsible could not have been less true. In the Straussian world of neoconservative propaganda, however, truth and facts seldom interfere with either the development or implementation of policy. Policy, in this case, had to deflect public attention away from the real causes of economic recession — neoliberal globalization resulting in the deindustrialization and de-unionization of America — while turning public sentiment against the sources of the most predictable resistance to what the policy actually intends to achieve (i.e., teachers' unions and other "liberal" causes that might have "funny" ideas about schools becoming the seedbeds of a more vital democracy by cultivating active citizenship skills and other means of intellectual self-defense against the abuses of elite power). The solution to America's educational disarmament, as presented in *A Nation at Risk*, entailed restoring the schools' commitment to high standards, which Susan Ohanian reveals here as a code word imposing tighter controls over the work of teachers in order to counter what elites regard as the threat of democracy. What *A Nation at Risk* did not satisfactorily address was the means of enforcing the restoration of high standards. As Sandra Mathison reports, an increased focus on assessment would supply not only the means for greater plutocratic — corporate-dominated — control over both instruction and curriculum, but also greater opportunities for corporations to enrich themselves at the public's expense. Neoliberals have no objection to public subsidies when those subsidies go to corporations, but when public funds go to increase teachers' salaries, hire more teachers, build more schools, or otherwise improve the learning conditions of students, they scream about the horrors of the "nanny state." Mathison helps us recognize how what used to be the work of teachers — deciding what to teach, how to teach it, and how to assess it — has now become the work of corporations (i.e., the publishing and testing industries). Teachers, it seems, can no longer be entrusted to carry out their duties. As Felecia Briscoe and I describe in our respective chapters, they must be held accountable to elite power and disciplined to obey. Karen Anijar helps us recognize how this evidence-based approach to education takes evidence-based medicine as its model, revealing a disturbing analogy between the way in which publishing companies and testing agencies define, drive, and proletarianize the work of teachers and the manner that the insurance industry now dictates the work of medical professionals. All the while, Kathleen Rhoades informs us, the media play a very useful role in this process, reporting only that information the architects of the business takeover of schools want the public to know.

Chapter 13

Propaganda

Eric Haas
University of Connecticut

Traditionally propaganda is defined as "the deliberate, systematic attempt to shape perceptions, manipulate cognitions, and direct behavior to achieve a response that furthers the desired intent of the propagandist" (Jowett & O'Donnell, 1999, p. 6). Often referred to as black propaganda, this type of propaganda involves misinformation campaigns run by the few who directly control the media and messages for the many, which they deliberately used to manipulate the public's understandings and actions for their own benefit. The classic form of traditional black propaganda is the misinformation and nationalist symbols disseminated by a totalitarian government such as that of Nazi Germany and Stalinist Russia. In both cases, a small corps of government officials controlled all access to information and all the legal means of disseminating it, including the press. The propaganda was ubiquitous and continuous, incorporated in everything from school curricula to movies to radio to rallies to architecture. Practically no contrary messages could compete with the state propaganda. Those that tried were crushed by ruthless secret police. Propaganda was a tool of social control, from which the small cadre of political elite gained power and wealth.

With the fall of Nazi Germany and Stalinist Russia, discussions of traditional black propaganda seem anachronistic and wildly out of place in today's capitalist democracies. In the United States, information creation and dissemination is dispersed across many public and private institutions. Each branch of each level of government, as well as individual elected officials, creates and disseminates information. There is a private press, multiple media outlets, and the Internet, as well as entire industries of lobbyists, interest groups, think tanks, and advocacy groups who produce reams of information on a daily basis.

In the totalitarian states of Nazi Germany and Stalinist Russia, the over-whelming control over information and social life made traditional black propaganda viable, but that control is not present in capitalist democra-cies. Thus, it might appear that propaganda itself is no longer possible. The more likely scenario, however, is that propaganda has mutated from traditional state censorship backed by armed force to contemporary self-censorship driven by market forces. This chapter examines the existence of modern-day propaganda, often referred to as cooperative propaganda, and its influence on education.

Engel (2001) labels the propaganda or propaganda-like information in capitalist democracies as "cooperative propaganda" (p. 77), because it oper-ates through a loosely coupled "invisible institution" (Jowett & O'Donnell, 1999, p. 378) that develops to produce and distribute the misinformation. These institutions or networks are considered cooperative and invisible because they are based on practices and understandings that are informal and unofficial and because they involve individuals and institutions that are separate, though also interdependent and rarely adversarial.

Cooperative propaganda, then, is the large-scale production and dissemi-nation of false or misleading information through loosely coupled networks of legally and politically separate individuals and institutions, of which only a small portion are deliberately or carelessly acting in a manner that shapes perceptions, manipulates cognitions, and directs behavior to achieve a response that furthers the desired intent of the propagandist regardless of the effect on the public at large. This lengthy definition reflects the com-plex nature of propaganda in contemporary capitalist democracies. Like traditional black propaganda, cooperative propaganda involves some form of misinformation that, when relied on by the public, will benefit the propa-gandist. But cooperative propaganda differs from traditional propaganda in two key ways. First, it is produced and disseminated through decentralized networks. Second, the intent to manipulate for the benefit of the propagan-dist is limited to a small portion of the total participants in an information network; the vast majority of the network institutions and individuals have little or no direct interest in promoting propaganda. Yet, taken as a whole, the resulting (mis)information disseminated is propaganda.

In education, one of the most influential examples is the Reagan adminis-tration's push for changes in American education, which was based in part on a campaign to convince the public and policy makers that U.S. schools were failing. Central to this campaign was its publication of the report *A Nation at Risk* (National Commission on Excellence in Education, 1983). *A Nation at Risk* claimed that American public education was failing and that these public education failures were backed by evidence. It described the supposed failure of public schools with fiery language, playing on fears of total defeat:

> If an unfriendly foreign power had attempted to impose on America the mediocre educational performance that exists today, we might well have viewed it as an act of war. As it stands, we have allowed this to happen to ourselves. We have even squandered the gains in student achievement made in the wake of the Sputnik challenge. Moreover, we have dismantled essential support systems which helped make those gains possible. We have, in effect, been committing an act of unthinking, unilateral educational disarmament. (National Commission on Excellence in Education, 1983, ¶ 2)

A Nation at Risk was written by the federal government's National Commission on Excellence in Education, promoted by President Reagan and his secretary of education, and disseminated by the federal government, beginning with a press conference. The fiery rhetoric of the failure of public education was repeated as true by business leaders, politicians across the political spectrum, and advocacy groups. It became the title of books and journal articles (e.g., Hayes, 2004; Wong, Guthrie, & Harris, 2004). A Lexis search shows that *A Nation at Risk* was positively referenced by more than 100 news articles from 1983 to 1985 alone. In 2003, 20 years after its publication, *A Nation at Risk* was positively referenced in more than 30 news pieces. The result was the repeated phrase of "failing schools."

A Nation at Risk is also inaccurate and misleading. Thus, it became the impetus for the cooperative propaganda network described above. Analyzing the claims of *A Nation at Risk*, Berliner and Biddle (1995) found that "none of the supposedly supportive 'evidence' actually appeared in *A Nation at Risk*, nor did this work provide citations to tell Americans where that 'evidence' might be found" (p. 3). Further, when Berliner and Biddle examined available evidence of student achievement, they found that the assertions of crisis in *A Nation at Risk* were superficially accurate, but substantively misleading. For example, *A Nation at Risk* presented the following claim to support the failure of American public education: "Average achievement of high school students on most standardized tests is now [1983] lower than 26 years ago when Sputnik was launched" (p. 8). No evidence was included to support this claim. Berliner and Biddle thoroughly examined the trends in SAT scores over that period. SAT scores did decline during the period, as *A Nation at Risk* stated; however, Berliner and Biddle's analysis demonstrated that the decline was much more likely due to changes in the demographics of the test takers — more students of all abilities taking the SATs, rather than just the top college-bound students — than the failure of U.S. public education.

> The brief decline in SAT scores a generation ago provided no information whatever about the performance of American schools but was, instead, a signal that interest in higher education was spreading throughout the nation. Surely this should have been a matter for rejoicing, not alarm. (p. 20)

It is likely that most of those who repeated the claims of *A Nation at Risk* had not analyzed it as thoroughly as Berliner and Biddle (1995) had done prior to spreading its claims. It is also likely that most of these same people had not consciously decided to create and promote propaganda. Some did. But the majority of these *A Nation at Risk* repeaters — whether they were news reporters, business leaders, advocacy group spokespersons, politicians, educators, or parents — most likely believed they were passing on accepted conclusions and evidence collected by a credible U.S. government commission. Yet, taken together, these people and institutions helped validate and disseminate the false and misleading claims about public education that originated with the Reagan administration. The result was propaganda.

In many ways, the news media are a central and representative institution in cooperative propaganda. Though the First Amendment protects the press from direct government censorship, this is no guarantee that the press will act in the investigative, adversarial capacity that this protection intended. Rather, it appears that the relaxation of media ownership and public service regulations have made the news a highly profitable business to the extent that news corporations replace investigative journalism with less confrontational "infotainment" (Gans, 2003). When the news media appear to be independent and critical, but act mostly as stenographers of the positions of others, their apparently independent validation becomes one of the key means of propaganda. Because it is unstated and decentralized, cooperative propaganda that involves the news media may be more powerful than traditional black propaganda (Herman & Chomsky, 1988).

What is most insidious about cooperative propaganda is that it often develops when the news value of a story trumps the public assumptions of investigative journalism and responsible public service. No respectable news reporter would consciously present false or misleading information. Yet, numerous ones did further false and misleading claims in their references to *A Nation at Risk*. In the end, the dramatic story of government claims of failing schools picked up at a press conference had much greater news appeal and a much lower cost than crunching the numbers to independently ascertain how accurate it really was.

Ultimately, cooperative propaganda is effective due to the perceived credibility of the sources involved, and this perceived credibility is based on their appearance of independence. Truly independent support for a source or claim is a validation of credibility that the public often uses to assess reliability. However, when apparent disinterested confrontation becomes self-interested cooperation, the checks on credibility are gone and propaganda thrives.

A discussion of cooperative propaganda essentially concerns the reliability of information. We live in a society where we must rely on information that we cannot personally verify. For example, we get on airplanes every day without firsthand knowledge of the maintenance process because we trust that the institutions involved, from the various airlines to the Federal Aviation Administration, are properly monitoring and reporting on the condition of these planes (Shapin, 1994). We trust the information we receive — from the government, the news media, and private groups — because we want the benefits our complex, information-dependent society provides. This trust makes us ripe for exploitation, which is the essence of propaganda.

There are three fundamental aspects of effective cooperative propaganda. First, cooperative propaganda is more than an individual statement or document; it is a campaign that involves the large-scale, systemic, and repeated dissemination of false, inaccurate, or misleading information to a large part of the public. Second, the misinformation disseminated must be perceived as reliable, that is, accurate and complete, by a large segment of the public. Third, the misinformation as well as the disseminators themselves must tap into the desire of the public and policy makers to believe in the reliability of the system of information itself, even when there is some evidence to the contrary. This is often done through the promotion of a crisis or through emotional appeals to fundamental beliefs and values about self and society. The most effective cooperative propaganda incorporates all of these aspects simultaneously.

The effectiveness of cooperative propaganda is measured by the extent to which it influences public discussion, understanding, and, ultimately, actions. Its influence on attention, perceptions, and behavior occurs in two mutually supportive ways: It shapes what the public talks about and, to a lesser degree, it influences what people think about specific things. Propaganda is most effective in framing what people talk about and least influential at directly changing contrary viewpoints. In general, people pay attention to what is brought before them, rather than what could be argued are the most important issues of the day.

In the *A Nation at Risk* example above, the Reagan administration employed the three aspects of cooperative propaganda quite effectively. They used government officials and resources to broadcast the emotional fears of economic defeat in combination with misleading statistics to claim that U.S. public education was failing. In addition, they sent teams of government officials to visit Japanese schools to find the cure — more basics, more time in school, and tougher standards. The Reagan administration provided the resources and the perceived credibility to promote their claims, which few individuals or institutions could readily critique. Further, their language of defeat by an external enemy effectively asked the public to rally around the government, the initiators of the propaganda. Through their propaganda campaign, *A Nation at Risk* has become both justification for and an iconic symbol of the failure of U.S. public schools.

Private institutions (National Committee for Responsive Philanthropy, 1991) also disseminate information and ideas to promote cooperative propaganda. The most powerful and effective of these institutions are conservative advocacy think tanks, and education is one area of public policy that they have been working to change for over 20 years. From national think tanks like the Heritage Foundation, the Manhattan Institute, and the American Enterprise Institute to regional think tanks like the Mackinac Center for Public Policy (Michigan), the North Carolina Center for Public Policy Research, and the Goldwater Institute (Arizona), conservative think tanks operate at the federal, state, and local levels. Through well-funded and coordinated campaigns that emphasize marketing over information accuracy, these think tanks are part of a "movement conservatism" (Kuttner, 2002, ¶ 15) or "new conservative labyrinth" (Saloma, 1984) that has helped move U.S. policy, including education policy, to the right.

Conservative advocacy think tanks are well funded. As a group, they have received hundreds of millions of dollars from conservative foundations, corporations, and individual donors. Most donors to conservative think tanks specifically target their money to think tanks that can aggressively promote their agenda. Those think tanks whose work does not conform to the donor's agenda risk losing their funding. The budget of the Heritage Foundation alone is likely larger than all the left-leaning advocacy groups combined.

These conservative advocacy think tanks are also well organized. Many work in a loose federation that coordinates activities and shares resources at the national and local levels and between the national and local levels in order to maximize their influence on social policy making. Approximately 53 state-level conservative think tanks from over 35 states are members of the State Policy Network (SPN), formerly the Madison Group (State Policy Network, 2002).

Conservative advocacy think tanks appear to be the most market savvy of the private interest groups in education. Robert Feulner, president of the Heritage Foundation, outlined their policy strategy as continually focusing on "the four M's: mission, money, management, and marketing" (Kuttner, 2002, ¶ 6). To this end, conservative advocacy think tanks typically promote their education agenda with simultaneous, multisourced disseminations of ideological messages, policy recommendations, and studies to the media and the public, all levels of government, universities and other research institutions, and businesses and corporations. These information campaigns are designed to both create and satisfy the demand for conservative education policies.

These conservative advocacy think tanks are especially adept at managing the press. They use a variety of specific short- and long-term strategies to change the way news is reported and to get their information and opinions included. Short-term strategies include producing and disseminating countless media-ready op-eds, news articles, and information packets; promoting think tank fellows as experts available for news program appearances and personal interviews for print journalists; and funding symposia, press conferences, and speaking tours for the press and the public to hear in-house scholars speak on policy issues. They are also known to attack the press as too liberal, including specific reporters and outlets, and silence their critics by responding quickly and fiercely to any opposing ideas or organizations that arise in the media. Specific long-term strategies include targeting specific journalists who they believe are receptive to conservative ideas and who might be swayed by a letter or telephone campaign and establishing programs to train conservative students to enter print and broadcast media.

Voucher supporters have been working with the network of conservative advocacy think tanks to develop cooperative propaganda as a means to create both the demand and political climate for school choice. Wealthy conservative foundations like the Lynde and Harry Bradley Foundation, the Castle Rock Foundation of the Coors family, the Sarah Scaife Foundation, and the Koch family foundation's finance conservative advocacy think tanks, like the Heritage Foundation, the Cato Institute, and the Manhattan Institute, have provided multiple sources of information, experts, and public relations to support vouchers. In turn, the network of conservative advocacy think tanks has disseminated numerous reports, studies, news opinion pieces, television experts, and polls that emphasize the failures of public schools, public support for vouchers, and the success of vouchers in improving student achievement. Though these personnel and products are presented as scientific, they are rarely subject to blind peer review or similar rigorous, scientific critique prior to dissemination to the press and public.

One of the key areas where the promotional work of conservative advocacy think tanks moves into voucher and school choice propaganda is their creation of education experts and the production of "research" documents to bolster their policy recommendations. The Heritage Foundation, for example, gives its staff titles that mimic those in academia or government, though their credentials do not match. Dan Lips is one of their education experts, whose specialty is school choice. According to his Heritage Foundation biography, he is a 2000 graduate of Princeton with a BA in politics and no experience as an educator (Heritage Foundation, 2006). Prior to arriving at the Heritage Foundation, he worked for other conservative advocacy think tanks, including the Cato Institute and the Goldwater Institute. Dan Lips's lack of credentials — far short of a PhD or years of experience as an educator — appears to be the historical norm for Heritage Foundation experts (Soley, 1992). Thus, when politicians and other public leaders represent Heritage Foundation personnel as education experts who support their policies, they create a circular validation that gives misleading credibility to the policy, news story, politician or public leader himself, and expertise of the personnel cited. This is cooperative propaganda created through a credibility kiting operation.

Similar practices occur with the research that these advocacy think tanks publish on vouchers. Spring (2002) describes the conservative Manhattan Institute's research on education vouchers as "not a search for truth but a search for justifications for its political program ... the goal of the institute's support of research is not to prove vouchers are effective but to create arguments supporting voucher plans" (pp. 31–32). Spring's conclusion appears consistent with two recent analyses of the Manhattan Institute's "An Evaluation of the Florida A-Plus Accountability and School Choice Program" (Greene, 2001). Greene's paper claimed that the threat of vouchers caused failing schools in Florida to improve more rapidly than schools that were not under a voucher threat. Greene's paper was well covered in the press, though it had not been published in a peer-reviewed academic journal prior to dissemination to the press and public as a scientific study.

Subsequently, two thorough analyses that were published in a peer-reviewed academic journal concluded that Greene's paper was inaccurate and misleading. Camilli and Bulkley (2001) concluded that the Manhattan Institute paper was a "generous and simplistic reading of the evidence," and they "raised serious questions regarding the validity of Greene's empirical results and conclusions" (Conclusion, ¶ 1). Examining the same Manhattan Institute report as well as public statements by its author, Kupermintz (2001) wrote in a generous tone that "Greene might have over-stated the case for the simple explanation he promoted in his report and in the press," which Kupermintz concluded had the effect that "the reader of the Manhattan Institute laudatory report is offered a false sense of a dramatic success" (Conclusion, ¶ 3). Cooperative propaganda at work.

The danger of cooperative propaganda is that well-marketed misinformation makes it nearly impossible for the public to determine when claims about education and schools are based on rigorous science and extensive experience or skilled public relations. As a result, propaganda likely degrades the public trust in all social science, government publications, and private institutions by painting all information and expertise as unreliable. Trust in expertise and public information, however, is useful, if not necessary, for our information-dependent society to function effectively. But for the propagandist, whose claims may not be supported by evidence or public opinion, that may be just the point.

REFERENCES

Berliner, D., & Biddle, B. (1995). *The manufactured crisis: Myths, fraud, and the attack on America's public schools*. Reading, MA: Addison-Wesley.

Camilli, G., & Bulkley, K. (2001). Critique of "An Evaluation of the Florida A-Plus Accountability and School Choice Program." *Education Policy Analysis Archives*, *9*. Retrieved October 14, 2003, from http://epaa.asu.edu/epaa/v9n7/

Engel, D. (2001). The Hanford Nuclear Reservation: Environmental contamination and cooperative propaganda. In J. Shanahan (Ed.), *Propaganda without propagandists? Six case studies in U.S. propaganda.* Cresskill, NJ: Hampton Press.

Gans, H. J. (2003). *Democracy and the news.* New York: Oxford University Press.

Greene, J. P. (2001). *An evaluation of the Florida A-Plus Accountability and School Choice Program.* New York: The Manhattan Institute.

Hayes, W. (2004). *Are we still a nation at risk?* Lanham, MD: Scarecrow Press.

Heritage Foundation. (2006). *About staff — Dan Lips.* Retrieved February 18, 2006, from http://www.heritage.org/About/Staff/danlips.cfm

Herman, E., & Chomsky, N. (1988). *Manufacturing consent: The political economy of the mass media.* New York: Pantheon Books.

Jowett, G.S., & O'Donnell, V. (1999). *Propaganda and persuasion* (3rd ed.). Thousand Oaks, CA: Sage.

Kupermintz, H. (2001). The effects of vouchers on school improvement: Another look at the Florida data. *Education Policy Analysis Archives, 9.* Retrieved October 14, 2003, from http://epaa.asu.edu/epaa/v9n8/

Kuttner, R. (2002, July 15). Philanthropy and movements. *American Prospect.* Retrieved July 23, 2002, from http://www.prospect.org/web/page.ww?section=root&name=ViewPrint&articleId=6365

National Commission on Excellence in Education. (1983). *A nation at risk: The imperative for educational reform.* Washington, DC: U.S. Department of Education. Retrieved February 18, 2006, from http://www.ed.gov/pubs/NatAtRisk/risk.html

National Committee for Responsive Philanthropy. (1991). *Special report: Burgeoning conservative think tanks.* Washington, DC: Author.

Saloma, J. (1984). *Ominous politics: The conservative labyrinth.* New York: Hill and Wang.

Shapin, S. (1994). *The social history of truth.* Chicago: University of Chicago Press.

Soley, L. (1992). *The news shapers: The sources who explain the news.* New York: Praeger.

Spring, J. (2002). *Political agendas for education: From the religious right to the green party* (2nd ed.). Mahwah, NJ: Lawrence Erlbaum.

State Policy Network (2002). *Background* [Web site]. Retrieved November 10, 2002, from http://www.spn.org/about_spn/background.asp

Wong, K., Guthrie, J.W., & Harris, D.N. (Eds). (2004). *A nation at risk: A 20-year reappraisal (Peabody Journal of Education).* Mahwah, NJ: Lawrence Erlbaum.

Chapter 14

High Standards

Susan Ohanian
Vermont Society for the Study of Education

> You will try. And try again. And again. And you will smile. Because it's so
> much healthier than crying or throwing up.
>
> **—Molly Ivins**

Years ago, then-*New York Times* metro reporter Michael Winerip wrote a fascinating piece about a member of the Association of Professional Organiz-
ers, people paid top dollar for organizing other people's closets. Winerip
asked to see the professional organizer's own closet and reported that for
every piece of clothing, this woman keeps a note card of matching accesso-
ries: With her green suit, she always wears her green shoes, amber pin, and
beige pocketbook. "I never have to think about anything, it's great," she
said. Surely, the professional closet organizer is a great countermetaphor
for teaching, a craft of uncertainty, a profession where you have to think
about a lot of things at the same time, a place where we have to come up
with alternatives all the time. We have to clean our own closets.

Or at least we did until the Standardistos moved in. These days, in
the name of standards, keeping all students on the road to 21st-century
skills, teachers get decrees on everything from scripts for reading lessons to required bulletin board content. Once a school system signs on
to standards, the required formula for chicken feed follows close behind.
For example, in what they called iterative meetings and contractual agreements with Marc Tucker's National Center on Education and the Economy
(NCCEE),[1] the Georgia Department of Education came up with a standards-based Quality Core Curriculum, part of a process illustrated in a
rather amazing flowchart giving new meaning to the expression *form over*

substance. Next came the chicken feed. With *135 Days of Teaching With the Quality Core Curriculum!* (Georgia Department of Education, 2003), the Georgia Department of Education offers standards-based lessons delivering curriculum to all students. Offering a "concise timeline of the phase-in of the testing alignment," the department warns teachers, in effect, "Do this or else." They state unequivocally that "the Criterion-Referenced Competency Tests (CRCT) and Georgia High School Graduation Test (GHSGT) administered in the second year of the phase-in for a particular course will be developed and aligned to the new curriculum."

Covering all bases, the department has advice for teachers whose students cannot read the texts specified in the curriculum: Rewrite the texts. In the *General Accommodations for Non-Readers* (Georgia Department of Education, 2002), teachers are advised that for students who are unable to read *Lord of the Flies*, the teacher should "rewrite student's text using pictures for key words, using Writing with Symbols software" (2003). The high-standards-for-all crowd insist that the proverbial playing field will be leveled by giving all ninth-graders *Lord of the Flies.* The Robins can read the whole book; the Blue Jays need read only half; and for the Pigeons, the teacher will rewrite the text, substituting pictures for difficult words. In such an environment, all students are probably cheated, but the Pigeons are harmed the most. They are cheated from learning what they can learn — and what they need to learn. As a contrasting, messier approach, I offer the best advice I ever received as a teacher. Hired on an emergency credential in mid-October by the New York City Board of Education, I complained to my department chair that one ninth-grader refused to read the prescribed *Johnny Tremain.* The chair advised, "Then find a book he will read." What a revolutionary idea: Tailor the curriculum to the needs of an individual student instead of trying to twist and shove that student into a Standardisto regimen.

THE NEED TO KNOW

Of course, it all depends on how you see the universe. Some of us watch for the daily particularities (and peculiarities) of the kids in our care; others worry about completing the grand plan. Having put David Hawkins's (1974) insistence that *learning is really a process of choice* at the core of a teaching career spanning grades 1 through 14, E. D. Hirsch's first book in the *Cultural Literacy* (1987) assembly line hit me like a ton of manure. The hubris of the subtitle and the appendix title reflect the snippy, braggadocio tendencies of all Standardistos: *What Every American Needs to Know and What Literate Americans Know.* When *Education Week* published an excerpt — all the words from Hirsch's list beginning with the letter *C*, words — I did not get halfway through the list before picking up the phone and calling *Education Week*, insisting that they let me review the book.

Funny thing, I had rather admired Hirsch's small essay on cultural literacy published earlier in *The American Scholar* (Hirsch, 1983). After all, most of us would agree that there are certain basics that all people need to know to function in the world. But when we try to turn a few generalized precepts into laundry lists, there is trouble in River City. Your list will be different from mine, and we may both be right. Or wrong. And this is the sticking point. People who decide they are capable of or destined for writing standards, which drive pretentious and persnickety lists, rarely have the ability to admit error. The gods seek no advice. Neither do Standardistos. And worse, they have no faith in children's enthusiasm for learning.

Ranging from abominable snowman to Zurich, Hirsch's list of nearly 5,000 items is awesomely loony. When I first got my hands on the book, I amazed and alarmed strangers on airplanes and in hotel lobbies by reading them portions of the list: *What do you know about Leyden jars and when did you know it? How are your Mach numbers? Is your amicus curiae in working order?* During long hours in a hospital waiting room, I quizzed my sister and nephew with list items: Lee Iacocca, Jerry Falwell, Ludwig Wittgenstein, and the pre-Ralphaelites. When I got to La Cucaracha, they burst into song, but I have never quite figured out how knowledge of this song certifies national literacy. My husband is the only person I encountered who could identify Marianas Trench, and he was quick to admit he acquired this arcane bit of information not from his university education, which includes a PhD in physics, but from nosing around in *The Guinness Book of World Records*. I rarely go for the feminist angle, but I did ask this question in *Education Week* (1987):

> And why Onan, Mr. Hirsch? Onan, but not Ruth, Naomi or Esther? Teachers across the land wait with ugly anticipation to learn at what grade Onan's tale should be told. And who gets the job of explaining the Marquis de Sade? People alarmed by the possible mention of condoms (not on the list, though *penis envy* is) in the schools will have a field day with Mr. Hirsch's literacy prescriptions.

On the surface, Hirsch's premise would seem egalitarian, insisting that, with the right content, all children will have access to the same basic education: all knowledge for all people. It is, however, conservative (see Kristen Buras's chapter on neoconservatism in this volume) in that it aims at preparing children for an existing, predefined world order rather than working toward a new one, but political conservatism is not what is wrong with Mr. Hirsch's list and his subsequent series of books that prescribe education standards and content for kindergartners through sixth-graders. What is wrong with Hirsch's list and that of all Standardistos is the excessive orderliness, which leads to teaching by checklist. Remember Rose in Anne Tyler's *The Accidental Tourist?* The queen of standards, *Rose had a kitchen that was so completely alphabetized, you'd find the allspice next to the ant poison.*

Rose cannot mail off her brother's book manuscript until she buys 9-by-12 envelopes: *"All we've got left is ten-by-thirteen. It's terrible when things don't fit precisely. They get all out of alignment."*

Alignment: The battle cry of the corporate-politico-Standardisto alliance that makes its rounds under the banner of education reform.

BEWARE OF THE PROGRESSIVE STALKING YOUR SCHOOL

People who label their think tanks "progressive" are as obsessed with the neat and tidy universe offered by alignment as are other Standardistos. Echoing Herbert Hoover's 1928 campaign promise of a chicken in every pot and a car in every garage, progressives promise a skills checklist in every lesson plan. If outfits like the Center for American Progress did not label themselves "progressive," we would have a hard time distinguishing their education policy from that of neoconservatives. Equating *reform* with standards and testing, they all talk about *rigor*, and if you wonder why this is a bad thing, look up this word in the dictionary. Then, if you have not croaked from despair, take a look at the 24-page report *The Progressive Priorities Series: Ensuring a High-Quality Education for Every Child by Building a Stronger Teaching Force*, issued by the Center for American Progress (2005). You will see that just about the only place their recommendations differ from the rhetoric spewing forth from Education Trust and the Thomas B. Fordham Foundation is in their failure to embrace vouchers.

Here's part of the laundry list offered by the progressive revisionists: teaching as a clinical practice profession, much like medicine; competitive compensation structures for all teachers; using data for greater accountability and smarter decision making; a uniform curriculum; learning benchmarks aligned with state standards; aligned model lessons; aligned benchmark assessments.

And it gets worse. On November 8, 2005, the Center for American Progress and the Institute for Responsive Education joined hands to write a manifesto, *The Case for National Standards, Accountability, and Fiscal Equity* (Brown & Rocha, 2005). Arguing that No Child Left Behind (NCLB) is a step forward in the standards movement, the center makes the case that 50 separate sets of standards from 50 states is slowing down progress and what the nation needs is what President Clinton wanted: national standards and a national test.

The federal government should support the crafting, adoption, and promotion of voluntary, rigorous national curriculum standards in core subject areas so that students can succeed in every academic setting and in the national and global marketplaces. It should also expand national accountability measures and assist low-performing schools and districts. It should initiate a national conversation about not only the importance of standards and accountability but also the need for paying sufficiently and equitably for public schooling, including modern and safe facilities, from pre-school to college. (Center for American Progress, 2005)

Indeed. The longstanding corporate-politico alliance marches on. John Podesta, the president and chief executive officer of the Center for American Progress, was chief of staff to President Bill Clinton. Clinton, the Standardisto governor who worked hard at bringing us a national test. As first lady of Arkansas, Hillary had an education plan long before she had a health plan.

As Kathy Emery and I show in *Why Is Corporate America Bashing Our Public Schools?* (2004), by the time Congress passed the No Child Left Behind Act, the infrastructure for corporatizing schools was firmly in place. From the National Education Goals Summit in 1989, where America 2000 was ironed out through the No Child Left Behind Act, corporate chiefs and their allies have worked to end kindergarten as we know it, to deny children's diversity in every grade, and to install a rigid system of tests and measures that will force a national curriculum onto the schools. Once that curriculum is in place, politicians can claim that every student has an equal opportunity to become a global worker. The mantra of marketplace education is "Algebra or elimination." When students fail, members of the ruling elite can send them to their rightful place on the minimum-wage dunghill with the admonition, "Well, we gave you an equal opportunity to meet the goals." And the outlook is not any better for those who conquer algebra, calculus, and other things that go bump in the night. In *The Shell Game*, education analyst Clinton Boutwell (1997) argues that Corporados have deliberately sought world-class education in order to lower the wages of high-tech workers — with the result being a lot of highly qualified people competing for the same job — and desperate enough to take whatever is offered. A look at the U.S. Bureau of Labor Statistics job projections shows that new jobs over the next 10 to 15 years are in the service industry, not in fields requiring a college degree. Larry Cuban, for one, says that "the myth of better schools as the engine for a leaner, stronger economy was a scam from the very beginning" (Cuban, 1994).

For the Education Summit held at IBM headquarters in Palisades, NY, on March 27, 1996, the planning committee included the governors of Wisconsin, Nevada, Colorado, Iowa, Michigan, and North Carolina, as well as business leaders from IBM, AT&T, Eastman Kodak, Procter & Gamble, and Boeing. The list of people invited as resources reads like a "who's who" of corporate/conservative think tanks and their lackeys: Lynn Cheney, American Enterprise Institute; Denis Doyle, Heritage Foundation; Chester Finn, Hudson Institute; Diane Ravitch, consultant; Albert Shanker, American Federation of Teachers; Lewis Solmon, Milken Foundation; and Bob

Schwartz, Pew Charitable Trusts. Third-grade teachers, of course, were conspicuous by their absence.

At this Palisades meeting, President Clinton talked of a "full-meaning" high school diploma and of "meaningful standards" that would "require a test for children to move ... from elementary to middle school or from middle school to high school." He used the word *standards* 40 times in his short speech, and he made it clear where these standards would come from:

> I accept your premise; we can only do better with tougher standards and better assessment, and you should set the standards. I believe that is absolutely right. And that will be the lasting legacy of this conference. I also believe, along with Mr. Gerstner and the others who are here, that it's very important not only for businesses to speak out for reform, but for business leaders to be knowledgeable enough to know what reform to speak out for, and what to emphasize, and how to hammer home the case for higher standards, as well as how to help local school districts change some of the things that they are now doing so that they have a reasonable chance at meeting these standards. (Clinton, 1996, p. 4)

This noisy alliance of politicians, CEOs, think tank entrepreneurs, and media camp followers remains intent on standardizing education, proclaiming that every kid in America should march in lock-step through a one-size-fits-all curriculum. They call it higher standards for all.

Take a look at *Reinventing Education: Entrepreneurship in America's Public Schools* (Gerstner, Semerad, Doyle, & Johnston, 2000), by Louis Gerstner, Jr., chairman and CEO of IBM.[4] The fact that it was published within a month of the passage of Goals 2000 is no coincidence. One of the noteworthy features of Goals 2000 is that Gerstner and his cronies got to name the problem as well as define the solution: claiming the need for choice, competition, and technology in the schools; defining students as human capital and the teaching/learning compact as a "protected monopoly" offering "goods and services"; describing the relationship between teachers and the communities they serve as that of "buyers and sellers."[2] Gerstner and company talk about measuring school productivity "with unequivocal yardsticks" (Gerstner et al., 2000, p. 69). They speak of the need for national tests and "absolute standards," insisting that schools must compare themselves to each other the way "Xerox, for example, compares itself to L.L. Bean for inventory control" (p. 70). Now that's a fine notion: teaching as inventory control.

Gerstner and his crew address the big questions of education: "How much do students learn each month ...? How great are these learning gains per dollar spent?" (Gerstner et al., 2000, p. 69). They define the business of teaching as "the distribution of information" (p. 155). At their April

1997 meeting, members of the California Academic Standards Commission of the state board of education, whose job it was to approve academic standards in the various disciplines, showed a similar fondness for teaching as the delivery of skills: "A fifth-grade teacher would have a firm grasp on what skills and knowledge had been conveyed in grades K-4, and would deliver kids to the next grade ready to continue with the next set of expectations." How many minutes does a fledgling teacher have to be in a real classroom before she realizes that students do not pass by her desk like goods on a conveyor belt? You can teach and teach and teach. You can even teach the California seventh-grade history standards. But all your teaching does not mean those pesky students are going to learn — or deliver their skills intact to next year's teacher.

It is long past time that we question whose good is being served when kids are pushed out of school without a diploma? Whose good is being served when, instead of denouncing and dismantling high-stakes testing, quisling academics publish books on how to train children to feel better about taking the tests? Whose good is being served when once-venerable professional organizations like the National Council of Teachers of English are now hawking corporate flimflam called 21st-century skills? Whose good is being served when hapless teachers are manipulated into teaching from an impossible canon decreed by the politico/corporate cartel? Members of Congress, executives at IBM, and the folk at progressive think tanks can sleep easy, knowing that every seventh-grader in the land is being trained to identify William Tindale. (For a reason known only to them and the Almighty, the California Standardistos who wrote this curriculum imperative insist on this third alternative spelling.)

EXTREME WEIRDNESS

Believing that we teachers are our stories, and because Jack's story is one of the most important of my career, I get it out often, re-examining what it means. When I taught in an alternative high school, part of the public school system where our main job was to keep *those* kids out of contact with regular kids, Jack was one of my most difficult, irregular students. One day, out of desperation, I shoved an article in *Harper's* about Scrabble hustlers in New York City at him, growling, "Read this!" Attracted by the fact that street hustlers made money from a game, Jack noted that serious players prefer the *Funk and Wagnall's Dictionary* because it has lots of extra word lists, words beginning with the same prefix, and so on. I insisted that for launching his own Scrabble career, our *American Heritage Dictionary* would surely be adequate, but Jack pestered until I ordered *Funk and Wagnall's*. Always eager to upend preconceptions about my students, I felt pretty good about telling my supervisor that a student had requested a dictionary rec-

ommended in *Harper's*. With the Scrabble board and the new dictionary
in hand, Jack moved to a back corner of the room. He stayed there for six
months. According to our school rules, a student had to be in attendance
only 3½ hours a day. We had to shove Jack out after eight hours.

As the most obnoxious of the obnoxious, Jack probably started playing
himself in Scrabble because nobody else would go near him, but then a
passion for the quest took over. Jack sat there muttering, cursing, studying
the dictionary. During this Scrabble marathon, Jack did no school assignments, and significantly, none of his classmates asked me, "How come?"
How come they were doing school assignments and Jack was not? My experience is that most kids want to be regular and they do not complain when
an oddball gets irregular treatment. The simple truth of the matter was
that nobody wanted to be like Jack. My supervisor, however, could not resist
a few digs. He would walk into the room, nod toward the corner, and say,
"Jack still playing Scrabble?"

I'd reply, "Yes, he's still working hard at it." Give the man credit. Having hired me, he then allowed me to take charge. I will not pretend that
my smile did not become a little forced by the third month and even desperate by the fifth, but the fact of the matter is that no one can make
a student study anything. And remember Frank Smith's advice: When a
student persists at the same irregular activity, doing it over and over, he
is not wasting time, is not trying to get out of real work. I can testify that
whether it is a third-grader reading *Rumpelstiltskin* 16 days in a row (before
I stopped counting) or a kid obsessing over Scrabble, he persists at that
activity because he is getting something important out of it.

But if you are welded to standards and testing, if you bow every morning
at the alignment altar, then you have to tell the kid he cannot read *Rumpelstiltskin* again. Or play Scrabble for six months. In reality, in his decidedly
unaligned state, Jack was engaged in the most difficult work of all — that
silent, solitary, internal task of coming to grips with one's self, with one's
own deepest needs. Jack's work meant first changing his view of himself
and later figuring out where he might find a place for himself in the world.
Finally, Jack decided he was ready, and he challenged me to a game of
Scrabble. He trounced me badly. It was a wonderful, electric moment.
The immediate results were that other students wanted to play Scrabble
with Jack, and soon after his triumph, Jack started working on the regular
school curriculum.

Jack's story is one of the leitmotifs in my professional career. I cannot
stop from telling it over and over. I knew at the time that his Scrabble work
was important, but years later I am still learning what it meant. In *Word
Freak: Heartbreak, Triumph, Genius, and Obsession in the World of Competitive
Scrabble Players* (2002), Stefan Fatsis shows the reader that Scrabble at this
level is about weirdness, extreme weirdness. It is also about linguistics, psychology, mathematics, memory, competition, doggedness. Scrabble at the

national competitive level and with one out-of-kilter kid in an alternative school set up for misfits is about mastering the rules; it is about failure and hope.

NOTES

1. For a discussion of Marc Tucker and his connection to Clinton's plan for national standards and testing, see Emery and Ohanian (2004, pp. 48–52). Conspiracy theories continue to swirl around Tucker. The right wing sees him as a prime mover for "womb-to-tomb" government control. An emerging left-wing theory is that he is positioning himself for lucrative deals when school choice becomes a reality.
2. This analysis is adapted from Ohanian (2000).
3. I do not know which is my favorite: seventh-graders analyzing the geographic, political, economic, religious, and social structures of Islamic civilizations in the Middle Ages, of China in the Middle Ages, of the sub-Saharan civilizations, of Japan in the Middle Ages, of Europe in the Middle Ages, and of Mesoamerican and Andean civilizations; or the theological, political, and economic ideas of the major figures of the Reformation (e.g., Erasmus, Martin Luther, John Calvin, William Tyndale). These are just 2 of 11 standards to be covered by California seventh-graders.

REFERENCES

Boutwell, C. E. (1997). *Shell game: Corporate America's agenda for schools.* Bloomington, IN: Phi Delta Kappa.

Brown, C., & Rocha, E. (2005, November). The case for national standards, accountability, and fiscal equity: Standards-based framework in a decentralized system. Center for American Progress. Retrieved March 12, 2006, from http://www.americanprogress.org/site/pp.asp?c=biJRJ8OVF&b=1164323

Center for American Progress. (2005). The progressive priorities series: Ensuring a high-quality education for every child by building a stronger teaching force. Retrieved March 12, 2006, from http://www.americanprogress. org/site/pp.asp?c=biJRJ8OVF&b=260627

Clinton, W. J. (1996). Remarks to the National Governors' Association Education Summit in Palisades, New York. Retrieved May 1, 2007 from http://findarticles. com/p/articles/mi_m2889/is_n13_v32/ai_18340205.

Cuban, L. (1994, June 15). The great school scam. *Education Week*, p. 44.

Emery, K., & Ohanian, S. (2004). *Why is corporate America bashing our public schools?* Portsmouth, NH: Heinemann.

Fatsis, S. (2005). *Word freak: Heartbreak, triumph, genius, and obsession in the world of competitive scrabble players.* New York: Penguin.

Georgia Department of Education. (2002). General accommodations for nonreaders. Retrieved May 1, 2007 from http://www.glc.k12.ga.us/passwd/trc/ttools/ attach/accomm/nonread.pdf.

Georgia Department of Education. (2003). 135 days of teaching with the quality core curriculum! Retrieved December 18, 2005, from http://www.glc.k12. ga.us/seqlps/sudisplay.asp?SUID=192

Gerstner, L., Semerad, R., Doyle, D., & Johnston, W. (2000). *Reinventing education: Entrepreneurship in America's public schools.* New York: Dutton.

Hawkins, D. (1974). *The informed vision and other essays.* New York: Agathon Press.

Hirsch, E. D., Jr. (1983). Cultural literacy. *American Scholar, 52,* 159–169.

Hirsch, E. D., Jr. (1987). *Cultural literacy: What every American needs to know.* Boston: Houghton Mifflin.

Ohanian, S. (2000, January). Goals 2000: What's in a name? *Phi Delta Kappan.* Retrieved from http://www.pdkintl.org/kappan/koha0001.htm

Chapter 15

Assessment

Sandra Mathison
University of British Columbia

If you wanted to know how well American public schools are imparting academic knowledge to young people, the National Assessment of Educational Progress (NAEP) provides a pretty good answer. While there are warranted criticisms of NAEP, it is an approach to assessment and evaluation that is cost effective, reasonably comprehensive, and relatively incorruptible. The current educational reform movement is not, however, interested in how well schools are doing. The current neoliberal, neoconservative reform agenda is about something different.

NEOLIBERALISM, NEOCONSERVATISM, AND THE STATE'S NEW EVALUATIVE ROLE

Assessment's role in the current neoeducational reform movement is connected to both the neoliberal agenda of free market capitalism and the neoconservative agenda of Christian values. And, the state plays a significant role in facilitating the implementation of these agendas.

Current educational reforms are based both on an economic perspective (neoliberalism) that emphasizes free markets, competition, and employability, and on a moral perspective (neoconservatism) that emphasizes particular values (like capitalism), behavior (like heterosexuality), and knowledge (like intelligent design). "Although there is no logical reason for the co-existence of neo-liberalism and neo-conservatism they do conspire in contemporary American educational reform" (Apple, 2004).

It is important to understand that neoliberalism defines a role for government — that it is not an ideology that rejects governmental intervention.

Whereas classical liberalism simply rejects the state, neoliberalism, perhaps because of the strength of governmental bureaucracy, accepts and fosters a role for the state. Corporate CEOs, politicians, and bureaucrats work together to promote and sustain the ideology's core values. No Child Left Behind (NCLB), the manifesto for educational reform in the United States, is always described as bipartisan, but it is also a product of a substantial collaboration between politicians, at the federal and state level, and coalitions representing corporate interests (Mathison, 2004).

> Whereas classical liberalism represents a negative conception of state power in that the individual was to be taken as an object to be freed from the interventions of the state, neo-liberalism has come to represent a positive conception of the state's role in creating the appropriate market by providing the conditions, laws and institutions necessary for its operation.
>
> In the shift from classical liberalism to neo-liberalism, then, there is a further element added, for such a shift involves a change in subject position from "homo economicus," who naturally behaves out of self-interest and is relatively detached from the state, to "manipulatable man," who is created by the state and who is continually encouraged to be "perpetually responsive." It is not that the conception of the self-interested subject is replaced or done away with by the new ideals of "neo-liberalism," but that in an age of universal welfare, the perceived possibilities of slothful indolence create necessities for new forms of vigilance, surveillance, "performance appraisal" and of forms of control generally. In this model the state has taken it upon itself to keep us all up to the mark. The state will see to it that each one makes a "continual enterprise of ourselves" ... in what seems to be a process of "governing without governing." (Olssen, 1996, p. 340)

The New Evaluative Role of the State

In part, the state is assigned the responsibility of constructing and sustaining the rhetoric that fosters the neo-agenda. DeJarnatt's (2003) analysis of the rhetoric of school reform in Philadelphia illustrates how a set of values that suggest limited state intervention can best be manifest with specific and strong state intervention.

> The reform forces use the rhetoric of choice and parental empowerment dear to the authoritarian populists and the privateers but the reforms themselves have been imposed with minimal choice or input by parents, students or teachers and the market has been imposed by the state not chosen by any parent or student. Instead the changes have been dictated by the neoconservative state bureaucracy, guided by an unquestioned belief in the value of uniformity and high-stakes standardized testing. (DeJarnott, 2007, p. 33)

Gutmann (1999) defines three models of the state's role in education: a *family state* model, where the state controls education; a *state of families* model, where parents are vested with responsibility for education; and a *state of individuals* model, where individual choices are made possible without prejudice for any perspective. While the neoliberal rhetoric of educational reform suggests a state of families perspective, for example, with the claim that parents are a child's first teacher and will be empowered by accountability, in reality the implementation of this agenda employs a family state theory through the construction of an image of failing schools that can only be saved by state-controlled accountability, primarily based on student assessment.

Even though education is considered a local prerogative, the federal government is uniquely positioned to demand compliance with assessment mandates by threatening to withhold Title I funds from those who do not comply and succeed. The neoliberal agenda depends on this state intervention to support the rhetoric of choice and quality. Without the governmental power to demand common indicators for making choices, the neoliberal and neoconservative preference for private, charter, and other school choice options simply does not work. NCLB is a historic piece of legislation, with bipartisan support created through an alliance of politicians and corporate CEOs, and is a quintessential example of the dependence of neoliberals on state intervention to promote free market values.

Additionally, the state, through its power of surveillance and specialized knowledge, has taken on a role of providing evaluative information to the public about what is good and right. This is sometimes confined to programs the government funds, such as the U.S. Office of Management and Budget's system for evaluating and publicizing whether government-funded programs work. *Expect More* (http://www.expectmore.gov) offers to tell the public which programs are performing effectively, moderately effectively, or adequately and which programs are ineffective, as well as those about which the jury is still out. And other government resources reach beyond government-funded programs to let the citizenry know what works. The best example of this is the *What Works Clearinghouse*, created in 2002 by the U.S. Department of Education's Institute for Educational Science "to provide educators, policymakers, researchers, and the public with a central and trusted source of scientific evidence of what works in education." In both cases, the government assumes the role of telling the public what the best choices are. There are, of course, private nongovernmental agencies that offer similar services to the public, such as SchoolMatters, a product of Standard and Poors, which is owned by McGraw-Hill Companies — one of the biggest producers of educational tests. According to their website, "SchoolMatters gives policymakers, educators, and parents the tools they need to make better-informed decisions that improve student performance. SchoolMatters will educate, empower, and engage education stakeholders."

This government-as-evaluator role coheres with Chomsky's (1997) "spectator democracy," a society in which a specialized class of experts thinks and acts, while the masses merely observe and submit to the decisions of the specialized class.

WHAT DOES ASSESSMENT SIGNIFY?

The educational reform package promoted by the neo-agendas is large and complex, but assessment of student learning is a key element and one that is controlled by the government, and thus a means to control the institution of schooling. Tests are the state intervention that creates, even if primarily rhetorically, market conditions and focuses the content of schooling on certain knowledge and values.

But the question is how does the assessment of student cohere with neoliberal ideology. The idea of assessment-based accountability is deceptively simple. "Students take tests that measure their academic performance in various subject areas. The results trigger certain consequences for students and schools — rewards, in the case of high performance, and sanctions for poor performance.... If students, teachers, or schools are chronically low performing, presumably something more must be done: students must be denied diplomas or held back a grade; teachers or principals must be sanctioned or dismissed; and failing schools must be fixed or simply closed" (Elmore, 2002). The presumption is that the threat of failure will motivate students to learn more, teachers to teach better, schools to be better, and the level of achievement to continue to rise.

Neoliberalism, more generally, is

> the desire to intensify and expand the market, by increasing the number, frequency, repeatability, and formalization of transactions. Intensifying assessment also results in an intensification of market forces, a development especially visible on the labor market. The use of specialized software in call centers has provided some extreme examples: the time employees spend at the toilet is measured in seconds: this information is used to pressure the employee to spend less time away from the terminal. Firms with contracts are also increasingly subject to continuous assessment procedures, made possible by information technology. For instance, courier services use tracking software and GPS technology, to allow customers to locate their packages in transit. (Treanor, n.d.)

In order to make rational choices, as one is presumed to do within the neoliberal framework, it is necessary to have comparative indices about the performance of alternatives. And since the focus is on individual choice, it is critical to have individual-level performance data. Although the matrix sampling procedure used by NAEP, and in the past by some state departments of education, provides sound evidence about the performance at an aggregate level, these approaches provide no data at the individual student, teacher, school, or even district level. The assessment promoted by the neoliberal agenda emphasizes individual choice, and therefore requires data at every unit of analysis, from the individual student to whole schooling systems. So, as suggested by Treanor above, the intensification of assessment in schools is consistent with neoliberalism's increased surveillance.

Indeed, the intensification of assessment takes a number of forms: standardized assessment at legislated grade levels, shadow assessment in grades preceding legislated grade levels, and the narrowing of teaching and learning to conform to the test content and format. The census assessment of, for example, every fourth grader in the United States is an obvious form of intensification. But in addition, many states contract with the test company that develops, supplies, and often scores the legislated (whether federal or state) assessments to provide shadow assessments given in the preceding grade. So not only do fourth graders take a standardized test in numeracy and literacy, but so too do third graders in preparation for the test they will take the following year. So the intensification of assessment secretes outward. And in many classrooms, what is taught and learned at all grade levels reflects the substance and form of knowledge on standardized assessments (Mathison & Freeman, 2003; McNeil, 2000). Research demonstrates that teachers adopt generic forms of content and presentation, develop a test-based curriculum, separate content for the test from "real" content, and fragment knowledge even more than is already the case in schools.

The benefit of this intensified assessment is portrayed as necessary to provide information parents need to make rational choices about the best educational options for their children. If a schools fails to educate all of the students, including every subgroup, parents are advised to take their business elsewhere. This rhetoric communicates a promise that there are high-quality educational experiences available for all children and that parents must actively make choices to move their children into succeeding schools. That this rhetoric is hollow only minimally diminishes the suggestion that a market of educational options exist and can be chosen if individuals just select the options that produce the highest test scores.

The value of standardized test scores within the neoliberal rhetoric is fortified by basic American values. There is a predominant view that we truly know when something valuable exists when it can be objectively measured and statistically manipulated. This view conspires with American preoccupations with individualism, competitiveness, the indispensable role of hard work to success, and the equating of equity with sameness.

The Control of Knowledge Through Assessment

Even though each state in the United States may use its own tests to meet the federal government demands for accountability as specified by NCLB, the fact is that there are only a few test production companies, and so what is on those tests is in the hands of a few multinational companies.

The neoconservative agenda is most concerned with controlling values, behavior, and knowledge in schools. Efforts to control public schools takes many forms, including lobbying for certain content (like the inclusion of intelligent design and the exclusion of sex education), advocating certain practices (like prayer in schools), and political action (covert campaigns to elect neoconservative school board members). When standardized tests become the primary indicator of the quality of schools and thus define what is taught, the test content also becomes an opportunity for knowledge control. Neoconservatives, like E. D. Hirsch or Bill Bennett, who promote teaching core knowledge or cultural literacy, employ a rhetoric that connects their ideology to success on standardized tests.

The neoconservative agenda may not directly determine what is on a standardized test, but in supporting the use of such tests, it ensures that certain things are less likely to be taught in schools and that there is a uniformity, a common culture, that is reinforced by single-outcome measures of student achievement. Advocating for high-stakes assessment in reading, writing, and arithmetic effectively diverts schools away from what are other secular pursuits. If the stakes are high enough, nontested subjects (like physical education, health, sex education) and school goals (like social-emotional development, diversity, and multiculturalism) are de-emphasized, thus indirectly safeguarding students from the secular humanism so distasteful to neoconservatives.

The Business of Assessment

Neoliberalism's free market exchange encourages the creation of derivative professions and submarkets. Assessment, especially high-stakes assessment, has created roles for tutors and testing coaches to increase the likelihood of success. And the demand for assessment is big business. The U.S. General Accounting Office estimates that between 2002 and 2008 states will spend somewhere between $1.9 and 5.3 billion to develop tests, then score and prepare reports of the test results. Private, multinational companies who are not accountable to the public are major players in the accountability promises of the neo-agendas. And the connections between at least McGraw-Hill and the current government are not secret; indeed, the Bush and McGraw families have had close ties for three generations.

In addition, these same companies, and others, score standardized tests, warehouse and report test results, provide tutoring services, create test preparation materials, and sell a plethora of services that promise to increase test scores. Not only has NCLB fostered the expansion of tutoring businesses by at least initially requiring that failing schools use federal funds to contract out extra-school tutoring for students, but the need for tutoring has created businesses that assist with the development of tutoring businesses. As one Web site suggests,

> Tutoring is great for entrepreneurs and home based business opportunity seekers! College students find tutoring to be an excellent part time, flexible job! Homeschooling moms and other homeschoolers are naturals as tutors! Dads can tutor too! Teachers often do tutoring on the side! Tutoring is the perfect job for stay-at-home moms who want to work from home and earn extra money to add to the family income without daycare hassles.

In addition to providing help with setting up one's business, this quote illustrates a coming together of this fine business opportunity with other neoconservative values by reinforcing stay-at-home moms, emphasizing the importance of employment, portraying child care issues as hassles, and supporting nonpublic school options like home schooling.

The Rhetoric of Assessment-Based Reform

The rhetoric of accountability, of leaving no child behind, of closing the achievement gap, of high expectations, of personal effort seems sensible. The idea of education as a commodity has been naturalized, and the concomitant business language of control, regulation, bottom lines, profits, quality control, and maximized benefits also comes to seem sensible. This is especially true for politicians, but many school administrators, teachers, parents, and even students are drawn into and live this rhetoric.

However, the rhetoric of assessment and accountability hides a deep-seated advantage of privilege and agendas that undermine educating the populace. And by centering the success and failure of schools in children's test scores, attention is diverted away from such issues as reasonable and adequate resources for public schools and equitable access to educational opportunities. And by adopting market perspectives on schooling, families and schools that value positive social development and happiness over competitiveness, and progress over achievement, find themselves displaced, floundering to sustain an alternate rhetoric, one that is not shared by those with privilege and capital. Understanding how neoliberalism and neoconservatism work against strong public schools for all is a necessary step in developing an alternative rhetoric that recaptures public schooling as a necessity in a democratic society, one where there are common public interests that will not be served by private interests.

REFERENCES

Apple, M. (2004). Creating difference: Neo-liberalism, neo-conservatism and the politics of educational reform. *Educational Policy, 18*, 12–44.

Chomsky, N. (1997). *Media control.* New York: Seven Stories Press.

DeJarnatt, S. (2003). The Philadelphia story: The rhetoric of school reform (ExpressO Preprint Series, Paper 71). Retrieved May 1, 2007 from http://law.bepress.com/expresso/eps/71

Elmore, R. F. (2002). An unwarranted intrusion. *Education Next, 2.*

Gutmann, A. (1999). *Democratic education.* Princeton, NJ: Princeton University Press.

Mathison, S. (2004). A short history of assessment and the standards based movement. In S. Mathison & E. W. Ross (Eds.), *Defending public schools: The role and limits of assessment and standards based educational reform.* New York: Praeger.

Mathison, S., & Freeman, M. (2003, September 24). Constraining elementary teachers' work: Dilemmas and paradoxes created by state mandated testing. *Education Policy Analysis Archives, 11.* Retrieved February 1, 2006, from http://epaa.asu.edu/epaa/v11n34/

McNeil, L. (2000). *Contradictions of school reform: Educational costs of standardized testing.* New York: Routledge.

Olssen, M. (1996). In defense of the welfare state and of publicly provided education. *Journal of Education Policy, 11*, 337–362.

Treanor, P. (n.d.). Neo-liberalism: Origins, theory, definitions. Retrieved May 1, 2007 from http://web.inter.nl.net/users/Paul.Treanor/neoliberalism.html

Chapter 16

Evidence-Based Education

Karen Anijar and David Gabbard
Arizona State University and East Carolina University

In a recent survey, the National Education Association (NEA) reported that 69% of its 2.8 million members disapprove of No Child Left Behind (NCLB), with 49% reporting that they strongly disapprove of it. The survey also revealed that "fifty-seven percent of members want to see major changes in NCLB, 21 percent favor making minor changes, 17 want total repeal and only 4 percent want to keep the Act as it is" (NEA, 2006). Armed with these survey results and a comprehensive strategy, the NEA hopes to lobby Congress to reform NCLB when it comes up for reauthorization in 2007. Meanwhile, back at the Bush administration's Department of Education, Secretary of Education Margaret Spellings has done more than vow to "stay the course" with NCLB in K-12 schools. She has formed the Commission on the Future of Higher Education, which threatens to apply NCLB's language of standards, high-stakes testing, accountability, and "evidence-based education" stemming from "scientifically based research" (SBR) to teaching at the university level.

In light of the strength of higher education's historical commitment to academic freedom, the pending pressures from the federal government to standardize university teaching will likely meet greater organized resistance from university faculty than they met initially from K-12 teachers. This should not suggest that university faculty should not learn from the experiences of those who teach in public schools or from colleagues in teacher education who have studied the policy implications of NCLB for years. To the contrary, the present historical juncture offers an opportunity for educators at all levels of American schooling to forge an unprecedented alliance for mounting a concentrated campaign to increase public awareness and resistance to these policies. For as we attempt to demonstrate through the ensuing analysis of evidence-based education, these policies constitute one half of what military strategists refer to as a pincer movement. In a pincer movement,

> the flanks of the opponent are attacked simultaneously in a pinching motion after the opponent has advanced towards the center of an army which is responding by moving its outside forces to the enemy's flanks, in order to surround it. At the same time, a second layer of pincers attacks on the more extreme flanks, so as to prevent any attempts to reinforce the target unit. (Wikipedia, 2006)

In keeping with the focus of this collection of essays, the pincer movement in question utilizes neoliberal strategies to attack education on one flank and neoconservative strategies to attack it on another. In order to keep schools advancing toward the center — and into the trap — neoliberalism makes regular and frequent use of terms suggestive of ideological neutrality and even high-minded benevolence (e.g., high standards, achievement, and accountability [SBR]). Meanwhile, other, more aggressive neoliberal strategies attack the one flank by pushing schools in the direction of privatization and corporate control. At the same time, neoconservative strategies attack the opposite flank to ensure that the content of the public school curriculum does not deviate from patriotic and pro-business ideological norms enforced by the appropriate standards (see Chapter 6 for Kristen Buras's discussion of standards). We will demonstrate in this chapter how evidence-based education functions as one of those more aggressive strategies.

UNDERSTANDING THE CONTEXT

To remove this veil of neutrality, we need only recall that the high-stakes testing and accountability movement began with the Reagan administration's Commission on Excellence in Education and *A Nation at Risk* (1983). As Gabbard (2003, 2004; also see Gabbard & Ross, 2004; Berliner & Biddle, 1996; Bracey, 1997, 2002, 2003, 2007) has described elsewhere, we should understand that report as part of a propaganda campaign with two related aims. First, *A Nation at Risk* sought to scapegoat public schools for the recession of the late 1970s and 1980s brought on by the neoliberal economic policies rationalized by Federal Reserve Board Chairman Paul Volcker, who claimed in 1979 that "the standard of living of the average American has to decline. I don't think you can escape that" (Parenti, 1999, p. 119, cited in Hursh & Martina, 2003). According to *A Nation at Risk*, the deindustrialization of America responsible for the first wave of the ongoing pattern of outsourcing jobs to countries with more favorable business climates (i.e., lower wages and fewer or unenforced labor, environmental, and safety regulations) was a function of the poor performance of our nation's schools. American corporations could no longer compete in the global economy, the report argued, because the labor force in America was so poorly educated relative to those in other nations.

The second, and related, aim of the *A Nation at Risk* propaganda campaign was to wed the American public's imagination to the idea that the chief function of schooling should be to provide corporations with the quality of human capital that would ensure those corporations would not transfer even more jobs overseas. For individuals, of course, this meant that the first responsibility of schools should be to provide for their economic security and that of their children. The solution to this problem entailed ensuring that teachers and schools operated in accordance with higher standards. Creating the means for ensuring the enforcement of these standards — some form of accountability — led to the imposition of high-stakes, standardized testing. While contemporary reform rhetoric has always presented such tests as objective measures of student and — by extension — teacher performance, more recent demands for "evidence based education" grounded in "scientifically based research" strengthen the illusion of these reforms' neutrality. This illusion of neutrality reinforces what Pauline Lipman (2003) has described as the "new common sense" about American education. What could possibly be ideological about the federal and corporate desire to improve the quality of American schools, increase rates of student achievement to enhance students' future economic opportunities, and ensure that no child will be left behind?

To answer that question, we can turn to a report that preceded and, possibly, inspired the propaganda campaign of *A Nation at Risk*. As I have discussed elsewhere (Gabbard and Ross, 2004) in 1980, Jimmy Carter's President's Commission for a National Agenda for the Eighties (PCNAE) issued a report asserting that America's public schools suffered from what it described as a "temporary confusion of purpose." Furthermore, the PCNAE report warned that "continued failure by the schools to perform their traditional role adequately, together with a failure to respond to the emerging needs of the 1980s, may have disastrous consequences for this nation" (PCNAE, 1980, p. 84). In eliminating this confusion and restoring schools to their traditional role, however, "education has to be set in a positive civil context if it is to achieve larger national purposes" (PCNAE, 1980, p. ii). To understand the context of the PCNAE and its recommendations for schools, we need to understand the impetus behind its formation.

Carter had created the commission in order to address what he termed the crisis of American institutions. On one level, Vietnam, Kent State, Watergate, and other events of the 1960s and early 1970s had shaken Americans' faith in their most basic institutions. At an entirely different level, innovations in education stemming from the populist movements of that same period (e.g., multicultural education, feminist education, peace education, environmental education, etc.) began encouraging Americans to examine their institutions more critically. These innovations, along with the consumer protection movement led by Ralph Nader, troubled the nation's plutocratic elites. As early as 1971, soon-to-be Supreme Court Justice Lewis F. Powell, a former corporate attorney from Virginia who had worked to defend the tobacco industry from government regulation, wrote a secret memo to the U.S. Chamber of Commerce complaining that an

> increasing number of individuals had begun criticizing the "American economic system." The problem was that it had spread to "perfectly respectable elements of society," including the college campus, the pulpit, the media, the intellectual and literary journals, the arts and sciences, and ... politicians. He claimed that this trend was also "increasingly evidenced in the high schools." (Gabbard & Atkinson, 2007)

The solution to this problem, for Powell, demanded that U.S. "businessmen" [sic] work collectively to reestablish control over education and the media. Moreover, the democratic imperative at work in education during that time period had to be reigned in, if not eliminated. Schools had to be set back on the proverbial right track, restored to their traditional role of servicing the human capital and ideological demands of private enterprise. The efforts of A Nation at Risk to tie the public's educational imagination to a human capital model of schooling constituted an important ideological first step in that direction.[1] It disguised this ideological agenda, however, using the more ideologically neutral language of standards. While that language appears superficially neutral, it opened the door for all subsequent school reform to operate under a business/neoliberal logic that would keep schools "in line."

In order for a pincer movement to succeed on the battlefield, you must keep your enemy's attention focused on moving forward in one direction. The business-dominated educational reforms of the past 30 years have kept schools on the desired path by using the language of standards and accountability to fashion an educational bottom line. Just as businesses operate single-mindedly in pursuit of profits, schools needed their own bottom line to pursue. While the bottom line or standard measure of any business is measured in dollars and cents, the bottom line of schools has become test scores. The high-stakes testing and accountability movement that culminated in the No Child Left Behind Act has kept public schools moving ahead in the uphill struggle to meet standards, leaving their flanks exposed to continuous neoliberal pressures toward full-scale privatization (see Ken Saltman's discussion of privatization in Chapter 26) on one side, and neoconservative ideological attacks on the other.

ORIGINS AND EFFECTS

Though brief and far from complete, the preceding context is vital for understanding evidence-based education (EBE) on two counts. First, understanding this context prevents us from becoming paralyzed like deer caught in the glaring contradiction of the Bush administration's demands for strict empiricism in education and its undeniably obvious pattern of antiempiricism witnessed in other areas of policy and behind-the-scene practices, which Chris Mooney fittingly describes as *The Republican War on Science* (2005). Why would educational policy be such an anomaly to that pattern? Answering that question returns us to the second reason why we need to understand the context from which the demands for EBE emerged. Quite simply, the call for EBE is a ruse, intended less to improve the quality of education and more to deskill, manage, and otherwise control the work of teachers.

To fully comprehend EBE as a neoliberal effort to further proletarianize teaching that augments the campaign to undermine teachers' unions, leading to the eventual reduction of teachers' salaries and the elimination of teacher education, we must also address a further contextual issue. We refer here to evidence-based medicine (EBM), which provided the original model of neoliberal reform that inspired EBE.

Evidence-based education is a direct offshoot from evidence-based medicine. In order to try to understand what evidence-based education is and what the implications are for educators, it is necessary to look to what happened in medicine for the "evidence."

The story begins in the mid-1960s in the United States with the passage of Medicare and Medicaid. Managed health care companies (HMOs and PPOs) responded by developing specific practice guidelines. About 15 years later and an ocean away, Archie Cochrane (a British epidemiologist whose book *Effectiveness and Efficiency* is considered a seminal work in the field)[2] provided "the scientifico-moral injunction that has inspired much subsequent work in evidence-based practice" (Goodman, 2005). By the mid-1990s state legislatures around the country began to introduce practice guidelines as a means of cost control. Clinton's Health Security Act as well as the Bush administration's 2003 Medicare Modernization Act contained evidence-based guidelines. The U.S. government currently provides funding for over 13 evidence-based practice centers. As cost-effectiveness analysis has grown increasingly central to health policy, guideline development has become its own cottage industry.

According to Twila Brase, however, "EBM guidelines are not guidelines at all. These so-called 'best practices' are poised to become coercive mandates imposed by government agencies and third-party payers with political and financial incentives to ration health care and the power to do it" (Brase, 2005, p. 18). Brase, a registered nurse and president of the

Citizens' Council on Health Care, believes "the public should be alarmed. Despite the positive ring of terms like 'evidence-based medicine,' 'best practices,' and 'guidelines,' EBM is aimed at stopping the heart of health care — the compassionate, first-do-no-harm, to-my-own-patient-be-true ethics of medicine" (Brase, 2005, p. 18). Arnold S. Relman, professor emeritus of medicine and social medicine at Harvard Medical School and former editor of the *New England Journal of Medicine*, shares similar concerns, arguing that

> our medical care system ... in many ways now resembles a vast industry. Innu- merable investor-owned corporations now are in the businesses of insuring and delivering medical care. Investor-owned corporations own a growing share of the facilities for providing acute and chronic health care services, including hospitals, clinics and diagnostic centers, and nursing homes. The pharmaceutical, biotechnology, and medical-device industries have grown into a giant industrial network that exercises widespread influence over doctors' behavior as practitioners and over their postgraduate professional education. This network also influences public demand for services and the opinions of legislators and government regulators. The ways by which busi- nesses can control physician behavior are manifold. (Relman, 2003, p. 167)

What we see occurring in the medical field, and what portends to hap- pen in the field of education, entails the rising hegemony of instrumental rationality, in which the technocratic language of the market dominates and subsumes all discourses (into the logic of efficient production), trans- forming intangible human processes into (objects) things that are mea- surable, testable, and quantifiable. Substance becomes understood as a cookbook of methods and checklists of standards — unreflective practices tied to an unyielding faith in social engineering (where, for example, effi- ciency and what works is substituted for ethical deliberation; see Welch, 1998; Apple, 1991, 1993) only serving to further perpetuate a form of com- modified knowledge. As Wear and Kuczewski explain, "the current empha- sis on measurable evaluation leads to attempts to test for the untestable" (2004, p. 11).

Evidence-based practice is but one of many antidemocratic (managerial) strategies, but it represents an especially foreboding one for the future of teachers' professional autonomy and their ability to respond to the needs of the specific children in their classrooms. Bronwyn Davies states it most clearly when she contends that

> in contrast to the preceding culture of largely judgment-based professional practice, there has risen the important notion of evidence-based practice as a means of ensuring that what is being done is worthwhile and that it is being done in the "best possible way," we can be sure that it is not the teachers who are being asked to judge what is worthwhile, nor what might be regarded as

the "best possible way." … Neither the teachers, nor their representatives, will have had freedom to dispute … the institution's or state's criteria of efficacy and success, since both their own livelihood and the funding of their institution may well be tied in whole or in part to their satisfactory fulfillment. As Grundy points out: Leaders will be expected to exercise control so that the objectives of the organizations, clearly defined and articulated, will be achieved. There will be a division of labour between the leader who plans (or who receives and interprets plans imposed from elsewhere) and the practitioners who implement the plans. The language of administrative planning will be "end-directed," with criteria for the achievement of the objectives being articulated along with the plans. It will be the leader who is responsible for the training of the practitioners and such training will be oriented towards the development of skills. It "will also be the responsibility of the leader to motivate and enthuse practitioners to embrace the specified objectives and work for their achievement" (Grundy, 1993, p. 168, in Davies, 2003, p. 98).

Whereas the original high-stakes testing and accountability undermined teachers' autonomy in deciding *what* to teach, EBE now threatens to undermine their ability even to decide *how* to teach. In some instances, administrators have purchased materials from EBE entrepreneurs that take the form of literal scripts that teachers must follow. This has opened the door to superintendents hiring paraprofessionals rather than certified teachers as a cost-saving measure. Anyone can read from a script. It has also opened the door to the videotaping and sale of certain EBE programs. Is this the direction we want for education? Education is concerned with complex human subjectivities, which cannot be or ought not be essentialized.

LET ME JUST FOLLOW BEHIND

In a recent critique of evidence-based medicine several researchers wrote: "We need to see convincing evidence that EBM improves patients' health." Over the past couple of years, there has been a backlash against EBM. A scatological tongue-in-cheek letter from Clinicians for the Restoration of Autonomous Practice (CRAP) to the *British Journal of Medicine* highlights how extensive the backlash has become. The satire likens evidence-based medicine to a religious orthodoxy. An orthodoxy, like any other fundamentalism, is narrow and inflexible and can be used to advance a political agenda. Evidence-based education — standardized tests, standardized measures, prescriptive outcomes, scripted curriculums, and prescribed methodologies — makes little sense when dealing with human actions and interactions.

Values, religion, politics, vested material interests, and the like can distort our scientific work only to the extent that they stifle challenges to authority, curtailing the questioning of whatever orthodoxy exists. Unfettered, science will free itself from false beliefs or, at the least, will moderate the climate in which those beliefs exist. As politicians recognize that "facts are negotiable, perceptions are rock solid," so there is no guarantee that science will reduce ignorance. But as long as argument is tolerated and unfettered, that possibility exists. (Berliner, 2002, p. 19)

No Child Left Behind uses code words such as the "evidence-based practices and 'scientific research' mentioned over 100 times signifying randomized experiments" (Berliner, 2002, p. 19) Despite the myopic view of science, the very naming of No Child Left Behind is operative; the word *behind* implies someone is ahead and not everybody can be (someone has to be behind). The push for standardized test scores and high-stakes tests is part of a larger effort to privatize schools.

We live in contentious times in an Orwellian hyperintensified capitalist universe with hierarchy at its core, where language is constantly transpositioned in service to the ideological agenda of the administration (whose peacekeeping missions are acts of war and whose clear-sky initiatives pollute the sky). What evidence constitutes and how it is used ought to be at the discretion of the individual educator in interaction in each and every classroom setting she or he encounters. As Hamlet remarks, "there is always more to knowing than any evidence or thinking we may be able to experience" (Shakespeare, *Hamlet*, Act 1, Scene V). Evidence-based education is a ruse.

NOTES

1. Not surprisingly, once the work of the Commission on Excellence in Education was completed, its executive director, Milton Goldberg, went on to work for the National Association of Manufacturers (see Carey, 1997, pp. 21–28) and the Business Roundtable (see Carey, 1997, pp. 91–93). Each of these organizations has a long history as agencies of corporate propaganda and have operated at the forefront of the efforts to privatize social security and eliminate class-action lawsuits. He now works for Cross & Joftus, a private consulting firm specializing in public relations in education.
2. To find out more about Cochrane, go to the http://www.cochrane.org

REFERENCES

Apple, M. (1991). Hey man, I'm good: The aesthetics and ethics of making films in schools. In G. Willis & H. Schubert (Eds.), *Reflections from the heart of educational inquiry: Understanding curriculum and teaching through the arts.* Albany: State University of New York Press, pp. 137-145.

Apple, M. (1993). *Official knowledge: Democratic education in a conservative age.* New York: Routledge.

Berliner, D. (2002). Educational research: The hardest science of all. *Educational Researcher, 31*, 18–20.

Berliner, D., & Biddle, B. (1996). *The manufactured crisis: Myths, fraud, and the attack on America's public schools.* New York: Addison-Wesley.

Bracey, G. (1997). *The truth about America's schools: The Bracey reports 1991–1997.* Bloomington, IN: Phi Delta Kappa International.

Bracey, G. (2002). *What you should know about the war against America's public schools.* Boston: Allyn & Bacon.

Bracey, G. (2003). *On the death of childhood and the destruction of public schools: The folly of today's education policies and practices.* Portsmouth, NH: Heinemann.

Bracey, G. (2007). *Setting the record straight: Responses to misconceptions about public education in the U.S.* Portsmouth, NH: Heinemann.

Brase, T. (2005). How technocrats are taking over the practice of medicine: A wake up call to the American people. Retrieved May 1, 2007 from www.liberty-healthgroup.com/images/61495/TwilaBrase_R.N.EBMarticle.pdf

Carey, A. (1996). *Taking the risk out of democracy: Corporate propaganda versus freedom and liberty.* Urbana-Champaign: University of Illinois Press.

Davies, B. (2003). Death to critique and dissent? The policies and practices of new managerialism and of "evidence-based practice," *Gender and Education, 15,* 91–103.

Gabbard, D. (2003). A Nation at Risk — RELOADED, Part I. *The Journal of Critical Educational Policy Studies, 1,* 2.

Gabbard, D. (2004). A Nation at Risk — RELOADED, Part II. *The Journal of Critical Educational Policy Studies, 2,* 1.

Gabbard, D., & Atkinson, T. (2007). Stossel in America: A case study of the neoliberal/neoconservative assault on public schools and teachers. *Teacher Education Quarterly.*

Gabbard, D., & Ross, E. W. (2004). *Defending public schools,* Vol. I, *Education under the security state.* Westport, CT: Greenwood/Praeger.

Goodman, K. W. (2005). Ethics, evidence, and public policy. *Perspectives in Biology and Medicine, 48,* 548–556.

Grundy, S. (1993). Educational leadership as emancipatory praxis. In J. Blackmore & J. Kenway (Eds.), *Gender matters in educational administration and policy.* London: Falmer Press, pp. 165-177.

Lipman, P. (2003). Cracking down: Chicago school policy and the regulation of black and Latino youth. In K. Saltman and D. Gabbard (Eds.) *Education as enforcement: The militarization and corporatization of schools.* New York: Routledge.

National Education Association (2006, July 4). Delegates call for changes to fundamentally flawed No Child Left Behind. Retrieved May 9, 2007 from http://www.nea.org/newsreleases/2006/nr060704b.html.

Parenti, C. (1999). Atlas finally shrugged: Us against them in the me decade. *The Baffler, 13,* 108–120. Cited in Hursh, D., & Martina, C. (2003). Neoliberalism and schooling in the U.S. How state and federal government education policies perpetuate inequality. *Journal of Critical Education Policy Studies, 1,* 2. Retrieved May 1, 2007 from http://www.jceps.com/index.php?pageID=article&articleID=12

President's Commision for a National Agenda for the Eighties. (1980). *A national agenda for the eighties.* Washington, DC: U.S Government Printing Office.

Relman, A. (2003). A physician's view of Freidson's analysis. *Journal of Health Politics, Policy and Law, 28,* 164–168.

Slavin, R. E. (2002). Evidence-based education policies: Transforming educational practice and research. *Educational Researcher, 31,* 15–21.

Wear, D., & Kuczewski, M. (2004). The professionalism movement: Can we pause? *American Journal of Bioethics, 4,* 1–10.

Welch, A. (1998). The cult of efficiency in education: Comparative reflections on the reality and the rhetoric. Education Review, 42(1), 1–14.

Wikipedia (2007, April). Pincer movement. Retrieved May 9, 2007 from http://en.wikipedia.org/wiki/Pincer_movement.

Chapter 17

Educational Research

Kathleen Rhoades
Boston College

The soul of wit may become the very body of untruth. However elegant and memorable, brevity can never, in the nature of things, do justice to all the facts of a complex situation.... Omission and simplification help us to understand — but help us, in many cases, to understand the wrong thing; for our comprehension may be only of the abbreviator's neatly formulated notions, not of the vast, ramifying reality from which these notions have been so arbitrarily abstracted.

—**Aldous Huxley, 1958,** *Brave New World Revisited*

The annual Phi Delta Kappa survey measuring opinions about public education contains a pair of oft-cited questions comparing attitudes about local versus national public education. A large discrepancy separates responses on the two similar items. The public's attitude toward local public schools is much more favorable than its attitude toward public schools in general. (In the 2005 Gallup-Rose poll, 48% of respondents awarded a grade A or B to local schools and 24% gave this grade to public schools, nationally; when parents of public school students rated the school their oldest child attends, 69% of the respondents rated this an A or B.)

The discrepancy reveals a strong undercurrent of distrust directed at the institution of public schooling, a distrust that softens once the "public" comes in contact with the schools. While there are many possible explanations for a situation where the grass appears greener up close than from afar, the one explored here is the "policy elite's" use of the media to embed semi-overt messages about the institution of public schools in order to achieve public support for a set of pro-business initiatives, predominantly large-scale testing reforms, the deprofessionalization of teaching, and the privatization of public schools.[1]

Policy elites have at their disposal a number of media devices to alter public perception, notably, agenda setting, news framing, and propaganda. Characteristics of the three overlap, and the devices work in a complementary fashion to engender public support for existing or new policies.

- *Agenda setting* describes the use of repetitious news content and the effect it has on the public's perception of the importance of an issue. Researchers Iyengar and Kinder showed that, for many issues studied, experimental subjects' ratings of an issue's perceived importance increased significantly upon as little as a single viewing, and that the increases persisted after a week (Iyengar & Kinder, 1987).
- *News framing* involves the promotion or adoption of an intentional and cohesive narrative structure in news reports. The frame presents a particular perspective on an issue, replete with a set of identified problems, solutions, and guilty parties (Entman, 1993). It also sets parameters around the facts admissible to the discussion (Jamieson & Waldman, 2003), sets the tone of the discourse, and sponsors a set of compatible values (Reese, 2001).
- *Propaganda* describes the generation of deceptive, inaccurate news coverage, which is oftentimes presented in the context of a news frame. While framing constitutes a normal, almost habitual act done to promote a particular point of view, propaganda is "a manipulative use of framing" (Lakoff, 2004, p. 100), used to deliberately misrepresent an issue in order to influence policy and voters.

We call these the devices of the policy elite because their use depends on media access. Entman explains that the power to shape news reporting is greatest at the office of the presidency, and gradually declines from there, but that all officials have greater media access than unofficial persons (Entman, 2003). Since the press depends so heavily on these official sources, "the bulk of the news will, unless consciously and courageously corrected, work against those who have no lawful and orderly method of asserting themselves" (Lippman, 1994, p. 40).

THE FRAMING OF EDUCATIONAL TESTING NEWS

This chapter presents abbreviated findings from a frame analysis of national newspaper articles on educational testing collected from September 1, 2000 to June 30, 2001.[2] The study employed the following methods to detect and explicate frames: content analyses to code recurrent details in the 2,196 newspaper articles in the news corpus, cluster analyses to group articles into issue-based frames, and text-mining and logistic regression analyses to identify ideas and terms central to the identified news frames (see Rhoades, 2004).

The study identified four issue-based news frames: one overarching frame dubbed Accountability and three subsidiary frames that reinforced the policies and ideas promoted in the Accountability frame (Lakoff, 2004).[3]

The Accountability frame heavily promotes large-scale testing reforms for public schools with a narrative that defines the problem in U.S. education as one of low or uneven test scores (conflating test scores with academic quality and rigor). The solution to poor educational quality is framed as one of raising test scores (reinforcing again the idea that higher test scores signify improved educational quality or higher achievement). The frame places blame for these educational woes squarely on public schools and teachers, and sometimes on students.

News frames capture an individual's worldview and values system. The Accountability worldview places greater faith on test scores than on teachers' judgments. In its bird's-eye perspective, details are obscured and repetitious actions come into focus. Accountability places a great premium in homogeneity and redundancy in education, and characteristics not measured by tests are at best discounted and at worst disdained. This view looks to the policy elites to solve educational problems with solutions that come down from the top and are implemented at the bottom by the schools, the passive change agents. The following high-weight[4] sentences embody these ideas in the Accountability frame:

> While the test has bred intense competition between school districts and the CMT has become the basic barometer of success or failure of a school or district, educators have long said the real value of the assessment lies in the detailed data it provides on whether students are learning. (Green, 2001)
>
> The report, commissioned by the Business Roundtable, an association of corporate leaders based in Washington, says that the [test score] gains have been particularly striking for low-income and minority students and have not come at the cost of higher dropout rates. (Keller, 2001)
>
> "One of the key objectives of having a high school exam is it's a strategic tool to assure students receive a high-quality education based on rigorous state standards," said Doug Stone, a spokesman for the California Department of Education. (Rush, 2001)

The frame analysis yielded two important insights. First was the realization that despite a thread of criticism running through the news on testing, the Accountability narrative dominated all media discourse and no competing or alternate frames existed. The number of frames illuminates the political climate surrounding the issue. Entman writes that circumstances supporting multiple issue frames are the exception and not the rule. He warns that there is more political agreement than one might expect — and this is certainly the case in education. The second insight was the official indexing of the framed content, tied to predominantly state-level test results (Bennett, 1990, pp. 103–125; Zaller & Chiu, 1996). Officials get their message out through the data releases and source attributions, which outweighed unofficial source statements in all but one of the subsidiary frames, Analysis. In the Analysis frame, local source contributions outweighed official statements, but the source content reflected state and federal policy objectives. Locals talked Accountability: More than a third of their commentary dealt with plans to raise test scores, and only about 13% of the comments addressed local curricular or instructional reforms. Entman observes that such one-sided discussions are the natural result of official frame dominance:

> Sometimes, one among the potential frames of a situation so thoroughly dominates the media that alternative readings become virtually irrelevant to politics. In these cases, the dominant frame produces extraordinarily one-sided survey results, and these in turn discourage dissenting politicians from speaking out, thus cementing the hold of the one frame. (Entman, 2003, p. 418)

PROPAGANDA AND EDUCATIONAL TESTING NEWS

Propaganda production fits naturally with official framing and data control. Propaganda requires censorship, a power enjoyed by those overseeing data production and dissemination. In education news, the susceptibility to propaganda is particularly acute because testing data is official data. Lippman observes:

> We have learned to call this propaganda. A group of men, who can prevent independent access to the event, arrange the news of it to suit their purpose.... Without some form of censorship, propaganda in the strict sense of the word is impossible. In order to conduct a propaganda there must be some barrier between the public and the event. (Lippman, 1922, pp. 27, 28)

Hence, the official nature of testing programs and data allows officials great latitude in the use and interpretation of testing data. Political unanimity heightens the official control, with help from the dominant news frame. Bipartisan support for testing reforms is celebrated in the press. Note the exuberant confidence in test-based reforms expressed by Virginia Governor Timothy Kaine, "And in Virginia, Democrats and Republicans alike worked together to make record investments in education. The results: more accredited schools, *better student test scores* [italics added]." Large-scale testing reforms cleave the two parties together, leaving little room for dissent, save at the periphery.

Testing data are ideal for propagandizing. Despite the fact testing data are difficult to decipher, penetrate, and challenge, they are persuasive. Dorn writes about the powerful effect numbers have on public perception: "Because we perceive numbers and statistics as having a certain force on its face (just by being quantitative), we allow statistics to shape our perception of the world and the issues we perceive as important" (Dorn, 1998, p. 2). Poovey concurs, "numbers have come to epitomize the modern fact, because they have come to seem preinterpretive or even somehow noninterpretive at the same time, they have become the bedrock of systematic knowledge" (Poovey, 1998, p. xii).

Recounting the history of modern accounting procedures, Poovey explains how the double-entry bookkeeping method outwardly gives the appearance of disclosure, while it actually works to restrict access to financial data, thus providing a vehicle for unscrupulous practitioners to hide and misrepresent information. The same thing can be said of standard psychometric practices. Published test scores are the result of hundreds of partially disclosed or hidden decisions. The science of psychometrics is arcane, replete with opaque procedures, and as in accounting, information can be hidden and manipulated even as the delivery of it appears forthright, simple, and true (Madaus, 2001).

The voluminous nature of testing data is also conducive to propaganda production. Ellul's writings on "rational" propaganda help us appreciate the great latent potential of data proliferation where information is used to create an impression on the consumer, not to educate him:

> It is a fact that excessive data do not enlighten the reader or the listeners; they drown him. He cannot remember them all, or coordinate them, or understand them.... And the more facts supplied, the more simplistic the image. If a man is given an item of information, he will retain it; if he is given a hundred data in one field, on one question, he will have only a general idea of that question. But if he is given a hundred items of information on all political and economic aspects of a nation, he will arrive at a summary judgment — "The Russians are terrific!" (Ellul, 1973, p. 87)

Or, the tests are terrific!

Educational researchers have documented numerous instances of data manipulation in educational testing news (Maeroff, 1998). Bracey analyzed propagandist data in *A Nation at Risk*. In one instance, report writers highlighted a decline in science trend data for 17-year-olds that did not jive with the other NAEP trends:

More importantly, why use science scores for 17-year-olds? Because this is only one of 9 NAEP trendlines that will support crisis rhetoric. The science scores of 9- and 13-year-olds don't show it, nor do the trends at any of the three tested ages for math or reading. If anything, they are inching up. (Bracey, 1999)

More often, the cherry picking is more routine and much harder to detect. Media researchers have long observed that reporters stop gathering information and asking questions when officials provide them with facts (Fishman, 1980). Cook notes that journalistic norms dictate that "the credibility of ... sources will rub off on the overall report," so they "gravitate toward 'persons in a position to know'" (Cook, 1998). This practice puts blinders on reporters who become oblivious to unofficial sources of information. In *Manufacturing Consent,* Herman and Chomsky (2002) document the evolution of institutionally induced oblivion of local data sources to intentional disregard and apparent disdain for the truth.

Was it oblivion or disregard, for example, that prompted a *Boston Globe* reporter to ignore locally generated graduation rates when comparing school quality in two neighboring cities: Somerville and Cambridge. In "Two Cities' Responses to MCAS Carry Lesson," the *Globe* reporter used state-issued testing and graduation data to compare school quality in the two cities and found Cambridge wanting: In Somerville, the *Globe* reported only 6 of 368 graduating seniors failed the state test; in Cambridge, the ratio was 70 of 429. The reporter introduced then quashed thoughts that student retention and dropouts affected the disparate results:

> Some claim Somerville's MCAS success came at a cost. They say the city's numbers look better because hundreds of students left the school between grades 9 and 12. But a review by the *Globe* of the school's enrollment figures shows that the class of 2003 attrition is actually the lowest in five years. (p. 2)

Here there are two omissions. The first is the name of the claimant, educational researcher Anne Wheelock, who provided the reporter with information on district pass rates based on 9th-grade enrollments, information the *Globe* ignored in lieu of state data based on 12th-grade enrollments. Wheelock's data showed that Cambridge actually had a higher pass rate than Somerville:

> DOE reports that 355 out of 381 Somerville seniors have passed MCAS, resulting in a pass rate of 94%. But 560 students were enrolled in Somerville's original class of 2003 in 1999. The pass rate that accounts for all students who were members of Somerville's class of 2003 is 64%.
>
> DOE reports that 355 out of 469 Cambridge seniors have passed MCAS, resulting in a pass rate of 76%. But 484 students were enrolled in Cambridge's original class of 2003 in 1999. The pass rate that accounts for all students

who were members of Cambridge's class of 2003 is 73%. (A. Wheelock, personal communication, June 11, 2003)

Inclusion of attrition statistics based on ninth-grade enrollment figures refutes the reporter's entire premise, as it would no longer be true that Somerville's pass rate was higher Cambridge's pass rate. Therefore, they were passed over in lieu of the official data, which expounded the official narrative.

PROPAGANDA IN THE NATIONAL TESTING NEWS

Evidence of misleading or propagandist reporting was found in the frame analysis. In testing news reports, technical and contextual descriptions need to accompany the score reports in order for these reports to convey accurate information to the reader. For example, in a story comparing local district test scores, technical details, such as statistically significant differences, and contextual details, like socioeconomic indicators and dropout statistics, should be examined alongside the test scores; otherwise, the readers are left to draw inaccurate conclusions about the comparisons, such as the thought that small score differentials indicate statistically significant differences.

Text-mining analyses of number-heavy news articles revealed a dearth of technical and contextual detail accompanying test score reports. A very small percentage of high-weighted news excerpts mentioned technical details;[5] most that did touched only briefly on technical aspects of testing. A second examination of technical and contextual detail was conducted on 94 number-heavy news articles.[6] Half of these omitted all mention of technical information, and none of the 94 news reports featured discussion of the following details needed to properly interpret the score reports:

- Range of scores
- Description of cut scores (passing scores)
- Tested content associated with cut scores (passing scores)
- Description of benchmarks (including scores and descriptions of skills and concepts associated with benchmarks)
- Confidence bands (bands of error estimates used when reporting test scores or rankings)
- Tests of statistical significance when reporting score changes or comparisons
- Description of test type (norm referenced or criterion referenced)

Approximately 15% of the articles featured a moderately strong technical discussion. Most of the reported technical information came from outside researchers, as illustrated in this report examining some causes of statistical error in test results. Outside researchers Kane and Staiger provided information to the press on some causes of extraneous score variations, like changes in the composition of the population of test takers:

> Based on their analysis of reading and mathematics scores for 4th graders in North Carolina, the researchers found between 14 percent and 15 percent of the variation in test scores among schools of median size could be attributed to the particular sample of students tested in a given year. (Olson, 2001; see also Kane & Staiger, 2001)

The news reports also contained a modicum of technical information provided by university professors. For example, Boston College Professor Haney described typical changes in passing scores when a *Dallas Morning News* reporter questioned him about usually large changes made in the cut score of the Texas exam, TAAS. Haney's explanation allowed news readers to compare the TAAS passing score changes to those normally made:

> It is very, very unusual to see that kind of change in the passing scores from one year to another based on recalibrations.... In most testing programs, when there is a change from one year to the next you may see a passing level bounce by up to 5 percent of the test items, but this change [on the math portion of the TAAS] is three times that much. You just don't see changes of this magnitude. (Stutz, 2001)

Persons overseeing testing programs rarely contribute comparable technical information. In one rare instance of technical disclosure, Florida state testing officials focused the press's attention on the technical details of its state test amidst the presence of anomalous, uncharacteristically low test results (scores on a form of the Stanford-9 Achievement Test fell significantly at grades 9 and 10):

> [Florida DOE spokeswoman Carrin said,] "It is difficult to understand how students in grade 8 could perform at the 54th percentile while students in grade 9 perform at the 38th percentile." ... Investigators had "insufficient evidence" to rule out two explanations because demographics of the Florida students matched those of the national sample they were measured against. (Hirschman, 2000)

A comparable, official release of technical information in the presence of expected score results was not found, suggesting that had the SAT-9 scores behaved more predictably, it seems unlikely that Florida officials would have released a report examining the technical adequacy of the test.

More typically, reporters publish wildly varying scores without much comment, as was done for a New York City high school whose scores increased dramatically. On the surface, the scores appear more variable than the aforementioned SAT-9 scores, yet these were reported in the absence of technical scrutiny:[7]

> In just seven months, Bronx Prep saw its math scores soar, from 29 percent of students performing at grade level to 71 percent, placing it in the 77th percentile nationally, a rare ranking for a school serving black and Hispanic children from poor families. (Wilgoren, 2001)

The habit of reporting test scores without adequate technical detail is strongly suggestive of propaganda, since the omission of these details increases the likelihood that test scores will be presented in a misleading manner, obfuscating, instead of illuminating, test score patterns. These analyses show that the news reports on educational testing rarely contain the level of technical detail necessary for consumers to derive a proper understanding of the test scores. Further, the finding that unofficial sources were the main contributors of the technical information included in the news reports suggests that much officially released testing information is deficient in such detail, suggesting that the propaganda emanates from these official sources. This finding corroborates conclusions drawn by media researchers that the press transmits government statements in the absence of sufficient fact checking, and in the process, conveying inaccurate information to news consumers (Tuchman, 1978; Gans, 1979; Fishman, 1980; Cook, 1998; McChesney, 2004).

THE OFFICIAL TAKE

Education news is awash in official data and official framing. As a collective, officials steer our course toward some utopian future of objective measurements and high test scores with the aid of official data, the news media, and the tools of mass persuasion: agenda setting, framing, and propaganda.

This chapter explains why data used in news reports to shape educational policy are *selective* at best and intentionally deceptive at worst. The soundness of educational policies informed by such misleading news reporting is certainly debatable. It follows that educational quality stands to suffer in the process, but who is swift enough to catalog all of the distress?

"The political economy of the mass media" is limitless (Herman & Chomsky, 2002), but the public's ability to absorb and critically discern the quality of media messages is finite, resulting in a body of news consumers who are arguably less informed with more data. Yet in this paradox of more is less, the unofficial masses are not the only ones who stand to lose — all stand to lose whatever promise existed, once unmolested, in the unmediated playground of public education.

NOTES

1. The phrase *policy elite* is used to describe a group of elected and appointed officials and corporate executives that have and continue to work in concert to enact what some characterize as business-friendly educational policies, taking the shape of large-scale testing reforms. See also Cook (1998, pp. 44—45); Emery, K., & Ohanian, S. (2004). *Why is corporate America bashing our public schools?* Portsmouth, NH: Heinemann; and Fluery, S. R. (2004). The military and corporate roots of state-regulated knowledge. In K. D. Vinson & W. E. Ross (Eds.), *Defending public schools* (pp. 107–118). Westport, CT: Praeger.
2. Articles were retrieved primarily from the EducationNews.org Web site. All articles pertaining to the subject of educational testing were used for the study.
3. Brief descriptions of the three subsidiary frames, Market Forces, Analysis, and Student Stakes, are given below. The Market Forces frame promotes the use of school rankings to infuse competitive forces into school reform programs; the Analysis frame promotes the use of testing as a means to detect and ameliorate inequities in educational programming; and the Student Stakes frame endorses the use of exit exams to hold students accountable for reform results.
4. In the text-mining analysis, sentences were ranked in importance using the TextAnalyst program. Sentence weights ranged from a low of 0 to a high of 99. A weight of 99 indicated the sentence contained many high-weighted terms and was linked to other high-weighted terms in the text corpus.
5. This analysis was conducted on all of the high-weight news excerpts extracted from the news corpus that omitted Massachusetts testing articles. The qualitative analysis involved categorizing sentence content to determine its contribution to the news corpus. Only 2.3% of the high-weight excerpts discussed technical issues, and few went into any depth.
6. Number-heavy articles were selected from the 871 news article samples that omitted Massachusetts news papers. News articles were identified by first using the automated coding feature with the Atlas.ti software (searching for the codes "percent*" and "%"). A qualitative examination was done on each article in its entirety; technical and contextual features in these articles were catalogued and categorized.
7. Two important pieces of information are missing from this news article. First, the reporter neglects to mention the school's average passing score for each test administration. Since the large change in the percentage of students passing could result from a small change in scores from just under the passing cut score to just over it, a more accurate news report would include data in the passing score itself, as well as data on the average school score. Second, the reporter also fails to include the number of students tested at each administration. This information is required to ensure readers that the school's population was stable between exam administrations; therefore, the changes in scores are not the result of population changes.

REFERENCES

Bennett, W. L. (1990). Toward a theory of press-state relations in the United States. *Journal of Communication, 40*, 103–125.

Bracey, G. W. (1999, September 15). The propaganda of "A Nation at Risk." Education Disinformation Reporting Agency. Retrieved August 28, 2003, from http://www.america-tomorrow.com/bracey/EDDRA

Cook, T. E. (1998). *Governing with the news: The news media as a political institution.* Chicago: University of Chicago Press.

Dorn, S. (1998). The political legacy of school accountability systems. *Educational Policy Analysis Archives, 6,* 1. Retrieved March 20, 2001, from http://www.epaa.asu.edu/epaa.v7n1.html

Ellul, J. (1973). *Propaganda: The formation of men's attitudes* (Kellen, K. & Lerner, J. Trans.). New York: Vintage Books.

Entman, R. M. (1993). Framing: Toward clarification of a fractured paradigm. *Journal of Communication, 43,* 51–58.

Entman, R. M. (2003). Cascading activation: Contesting the White House's frame after 9/11. *Political Communication, 20,* 415–432.

Fishman, M. (1980). *Manufacturing the news.* Austin: University of Texas Press.

Gans, H. (1979). *Deciding what's news.* New York: Pantheon Books.

Green, R. (2001, February 14). A mastery mystery: Sergi orders audit of districts that tested low percentage of special ed students. *Hartford Courant.* Retrieved February 18, 2001, from http://courant.ctnow.com

Herman, E. S., & Chomsky, N. (2002). *Manufacturing consent. The political economy of the mass media.* New York: Pantheon Books.

Hirschman, B. (2000, September 20). State officials still stumped by dip in FCAT reading scores for 9th, 10th graders. *Sun-Sentinel* (Florida). Retrieved September 20, 2000, from http://www.sun-sentinel.com

Iyengar, S., & Kinder, D. R. (1987). *News that matters.* Chicago: University of Chicago Press.

Jamieson, K. H., & Waldman, P. (2003). *The press effect: Politicians, journalists, and the stories that shape the political world.* New York: Oxford University Press.

Kane, T., & Staiger, D. (2001, March). *Improving school accountability measures* (Working Paper 8156). Cambridge, MA: National Bureau of Economic Research.

Keller, B. (2001, April 25). Test-score gains in Texas traced to policies on minority progress. *Education Week.* Retrieved April 26, 2001, from http://edweek.org

Lakoff, G. (2004). *Don't think of an elephant! Know your values and frame the debate.* White River Junction, NY: Chelsea Green.

Lippman, W. (1922). *Public opinion.* New York: Simon & Schuster.

Lippman, W. (1994). Newspapers. In D. A. Graber (Ed.), *Media power in politics* (p. 40). Washington DC: Congressional Quarterly.

Madaus, G. (2001). *Educational testing as a technology.* Chestnut Hill, MA: National Board on Educational Testing and Public Policy, Boston College.

Maeroff, G. I. (Ed.). (1998). *Imaging education: The media and schools in America.* New York: Teachers College Press.

McChesney, R. W. (2004). *U.S. communication politics in the 21st century.* New York: Monthly Review Press.

Olson, L. (2001, May 22). Study questions reliability of single-year test-score gains. *Education Week.* Retrieved May 23, 2001, from http://edweek.org

Poovey, M. (1998). *A history of the modern fact. Problems of knowledge in the sciences of wealth and society.* Chicago: University of Chicago Press.

Reese, S. D. (2001). Prologue — Framing public life: A bridging model for media research. In S. D. Reese, O.H. Gandy, Jr., & A. E. Grant (Eds.), *Framing public life: Perspectives on media and our understanding of the social world* (pp. 7–31). Mahwah, NJ: Lawrence Erlbaum Associates.

Rhoades, K. M. (2004). *Testing in the news: A frame analysis of educational testing news.* Chestnut Hill, MA: Boston College. Available from ProQuest database.

Rush, A. V. (2001, March 8). Valley freshmen say they think they did well on state's first exit exam. *The Fresno Bee.* Retrieved March 9, 2001, from http://www.fresnobee.com

Stutz, T. (2001, June 9). Bar for passing TAAS lowered: Cutoff scores for math test debated. *Dallas Morning News.* Retrieved June 11, 2001, from http://www.dallasnews.com

Tuchman, G. (1978). *Making news.* New York: Collier Macmillan.

Wilgoren, J. (2001, June 6). Repetition + rap = charter school success. *New York Times.* Retrieved June 7, 2001, from http://www.nytimes.com

Zaller, J., & Chiu, D. (1996). Government's little helper: U.S. press coverage of foreign policy crises, 1945–1991. *Political Communication, 13,* 385–405.

Chapter 18

Accountability

David Gabbard
East Carolina University

What is accountability? We could offer many answers to this question, for many possible answers do, in fact, exist. In this chapter, however, I will deal with only three of them. First, I believe, we should consider its commonsense meaning, that which most of us might think it means, or what we would mean by accountability if we were to use it in some relevant context within our own lives. For example, I could say that I should be held accountable for the predictable consequences of my actions. The question then arises, of course: Accountable to whom? It could be one of my superiors at work, or my wife, or my children. I feel accountable to them because my actions have consequences not only for myself, but to them as well. Therefore, I must answer to them for my actions, particularly if my actions endanger their well-being. This commonsense understanding of accountability is how its proponents in educational reform discourse would like us to understand it as they use it. We should be cautious, however, because commonsense understandings can prove to be most untrustworthy in the hands of some — those who would exploit our commonsense understanding of things by tricking us to believe that the meaning they assign to the notion of accountability when they address us equates with the meaning that we commonly and commonsensically assign to it. In such instances, we encounter a second meaning of accountability — accountability as what Rheinhold Niebuhr described: an "emotionally potent oversimplification." Here, I contend, we find the meaning of accountability as it used in educational reform discourse. Those who use the notion of accountability in crafting such reform initiatives as those in North Carolina (the New ABCs), Virginia (Standards of Learning), and now, as of 2001, nationally (No Child Left Behind) want their audiences to think they know what these pieces of reform legislation and their surrounding rhetoric mean by accountability. And given what we all think accountability is, who would disagree with the idea that teachers ought be accountable? After all, we trust them with our children. Many of our children spend more hours per week with their teachers than they do with their parents. Of course, teachers should be held accountable to these parents, as well as to the children themselves. It is just common sense, and that is the problem.

So what, then, is the third meaning of accountability? By now, you should have been able to predict this third meaning. If it is not what we normally think of when we use the word *accountability*, and it is not the empty slogan or "emotionally potent oversimplification" posing as our commonsense understanding of the term, then this third meaning could only be the understanding that policy makers really have of accountability but want to keep concealed from the public. For some reason, they do not want the public to really know what they mean by accountability. So, the question for me to answer at this point becomes obvious. What do the architects of No Child Left Behind and its state-level predecessors mean by accountability?

Though I have made the answer to this question seem dark and mysterious, the meaning of accountability in actual practice should be a mystery to no one. Teachers know what it means, though for some its truth may be too painful to admit. For others, the truth of what accountability means proves so painful that they can no longer subject their hearts to its torture. These people have preferred to leave teaching rather than endure one more day of accountability. Sadly, many of these people have been our best, most creative, and most committed teachers — committed not to their jobs, but to a vision of teaching and learning that they held close to them since the time they were very young. Accountability threatened to kill that vision, but they would not submit to it, for they knew that it would kill the teacher inside them.

What, then, is accountability? Accountability means stripping away teachers' *autonomy* and their feelings of creative interchange within a *community* of other teachers and learners who share a commitment to some ideal of education that touches and bridges the intellect, the emotions, and the spirit of each of its coparticipants. Accountability replaces the principle of autonomy with the principle of heteronomy, and replaces the principle of community with the principle of individualism. Accountability could mean, under the principle of autonomy, that I, as a teacher, must answer to the teacher within me. Can I look that teacher in the eye each morning in the bathroom mirror and know that I am prepared to go to class that day to offer my students and my content the best that I have to give of myself? But it does not mean that anymore. Under the principle of heteronomy, which means submission to governance from external control, I must answer to external authority. My judgment no longer occurs in front of the bathroom mirror before each day begins and after each day is finished. My judgment comes on judgment day — the day when my students sit down at their desks and, in taking those number 2 lead pencils into their hands and filling in the blanks on the bubble sheets for those standardized tests, create the evidence to be used against me in the court of accountability. The tests have displaced my identity as a teacher. I no longer know myself as a teacher through the internal dialogue I have with myself in the car on the way home from school. I know myself as a teacher through the evidence presented for or against my behalf by my students' test scores. In displacing my identity as a teacher, the test scores — if accountability's heteronomy is successful — also displace my integrity as a teacher. For the primary lesson of accountability's principle of heteronomy entails learning not to pay attention to your own internal source of authority. Only the test scores matter.

Accountability could also mean, under the principle of community, that I, as a public school teacher, am accountable to the community served by my school and the larger world in which it is embedded. I am accountable to that community, because the products of my labor within my classroom will one day become citizens of that community and shape its future. Whether or not I teach my students the joy of learning, the joy of reading, and the joy of asking questions that do not seem to have any answers that would fit on a bubble sheet — or questions that the government would not approve to appear on a test — will have a marked impact on that community. The principle of community carries many other dimensions to issues of how I might feel accountable, but they are all equally irrelevant to the issue of accountability as it is practiced. In practice, accountability's principle of individualism tells me to "look out for number one," to do whatever it takes to increase my students' test scores. And the "whatever it takes" might not even be my decision. I could be forced to teach from a textbook geared toward the tests and that comes with a script from which my principal requires me to read.

Moreover, the principle of individualism teaches me to conform to the dictates of heteronomy by appealing to what is absolutely worst inside me — my fears, my hubris, and my greed. If my students score too low on the tests, my school could, under NCLB, be designated a failing school. If that happens, my district could be labeled a failing district. I could lose my job. Or, as is common practice in many schools around the country, I could be made to suffer the humiliation of having my students' scores posted alongside the scores of my colleagues' students outside the principal's office. If my students score high enough, on the other hand, my school could be recognized as an exemplary school. Don't we all want to teach at exemplary schools? I might even get a bonus, and God knows that any bonus on top of a teacher's salary is always a welcomed thing. Forget my identity as a teacher. Forget my integrity. Yes, I will teach to that test and read from that script; just keep my life uncomplicated and let me work toward the rewards that external authority offer me.

The tiny moral universe inside my own head and inside my own heart never developed much of a thick covering to protect itself. Sometimes things that other people simply yawn at make me wince and want to curl up into a fetal position like I am trying to crawl back up into my mother's womb. March 15, 2006, marked one of those moments, even forcing me to rewrite this entire chapter on the day when the manuscript was due to the publishers. On that date, the *New York Daily News* reported Secretary of Education Margaret Spellings as saying,

> Good education has always been about good testing.... Teaching to the test is fine and dandy, keep on. (Lucadamo, 2006)

The celebratory tone of Spellings's comments comes as no surprise. After all, she made these comments at a meeting of the American Association of Publishers. The publishing industry has already profited handsomely from the high-stakes testing model of accountability, and it stands to reap even greater profits in the future.

HETERONOMY AND INDIVIDUALISM: PRINCIPLES OF NEOLIBERALISM/NEOCONSERVATISM

If, as I have just argued, accountability in practice means stripping teachers of their autonomy and their sense of community, replacing those principles with the principles of heteronomy and individualism, the question now becomes "Why?" We find the answer in Takis Fotopoulos's observation that "institutions are reproduced mainly through the internalization of the values consistent with them rather than violence by the elites which benefit from them.... The values ... of the present system," he continues, "are the ones derived by its basic principles of organization: the principle of heteronomy and the principle of individualism which are built-into the institutions of the market economy and representative 'democracy'" (Fotopoulos, 2003).

Though America has made a practice of teaching its children that their nation's identity is defined by the democratic character of their government, if we limit our understanding of the state to government, its apparatus does not constitute America's dominant institutions. Judged in terms of which institutions most decidedly structure our daily lives, the market economy proves far more dominant. Furthermore, the institutions comprising the market economy have always exerted the greatest influence on the state apparatus and the policies emanating from it.

Externally, corporations have always demanded autonomy from state power to maximize profits and to exercise state power to maximize profits further. In this sense, there is nothing *neo-* (new) about neoliberalism. This individualist demand to utilize state power as an instrument to enhance one's freedom to maximize profits, regardless of the consequences the exercise of that freedom may have on the larger community or the autonomy of its members, has always defined economic liberalism. In laying claim to this power over the larger community, market institutions establish heteronomy as a dominant social principle.

Internally, market institutions express the principle of heteronomy even more intensely. Slate.com's Timothy Noah (2004) cites numerous examples of people being fired from their jobs for holding political views in opposition to the policies of President George W. Bush. Most of the victims of this corporate authoritarianism have been women, which we should view as highly significant since patriarchy is one of the most deeply entrenched manifestations of heteronomy. Capitalist men, it seems, are singling out our female employees as easy targets for ideological domination. Noah cites the case of Lynne Gobbell of Moulton, AL, who was fired from her job in September 2004, just before the election, for simply having a Kerry-Edwards bumper sticker on her car. We can cite, however, other instances when women have targeted other women, as was Linda Laroca's case when her female manager, Beverly Fath, fired her for having an "Air America" progressive radio bumper sticker on her car (Figueroa, 2006).

There have been exceptional periods in U.S. history, however, when citizens have successfully challenged the dominance of corporate heteronomy, which explains why plutocratic elites loathe the 1960s. Their fear of that challenge inspired the convergence of neoliberalism and neoconservatism and the ensuing assault against the public described in the preface of this book. In response to what the Trilateral Commission defined as "The Threat of Democracy," as David Harvey (2005, p. 43) has written,

> Lewis Powell (about to be elevated to the Supreme Court by Nixon) urged the American Chamber of Commerce in 1971 to mount a *collective* campaign to demonstrate that what was good for business was good for America. Shortly thereafter a shadowy but deeply influential and powerful Business Round Table was formed (it still exists and plays a significant strategic role in Republican Party politics). Corporate Political Action Committees (legalized under the post-Watergate campaign finance laws of 1974) proliferated like wildfire and, with their activities judged protected under the First Amendment as a form of free speech in a 1976 Supreme Court decision, the systematic capture of the Republican Party as the unique class instrument of *collective* (rather than particular and individual) corporate and financial power began.
>
> But the Republican Party needed a popular base. This proved more problematic but the incorporation of the leaders of the Christian right — depicted as a "moral majority" — with the Business Round Table provided the solution. A large segment of a disaffected, insecure and largely white working class was persuaded to systematically vote against its own material interests on cultural (anti-liberal, black, feminist and gay), nationalist and religious grounds.

Against this background, which Philip Kovacs and Ken Saltman illuminate further in their valuable contributions to this volume, we can understand the significance of a statement made by the President's Commission for a National Agenda for the Eighties (PCNAE). Written in 1980, the report issued by this commission argued that various populist movements in the 1960s and 1970s had led America's schools to suffer "a temporary confusion of purpose" (PCNAE, 1980, p. 84). To eliminate this confusion, the commission argued, "education has to be set in a positive civil context if it is to achieve larger national purposes" (p. ii). More significantly, the PCNAE boldly declared that "continued failure by the schools to perform their traditional role adequately, together with a failure to respond to the emerging needs of the 1980s, may have disastrous consequences for this nation" (p. 84). Two years later, after Ronald Reagan's election signaled an important benchmark in the history of neoliberalism's project of restoring class power, Secretary of Education Terrell Bell assembled the National Commission for Excellence in Education (NCEE) to carry this message to a national audience and pave the way for restoring the school's traditional role — serving the will of the market.

Borrowing from the language of Harvey Cox (1999) in "The Market as God," we can understand the fruit of the NCEE's *A Nation at Risk* report, which read a great deal like Jonathan Edwards's *Sinners in the Hands of an Angry God* (1741), as a castigation of America's schools for greatly displeasing the market. "Our Nation is at risk," the report began.

> Our once unchallenged preeminence in commerce, industry, science, and technological innovation is being overtaken by competitors throughout the world....
>
> If an unfriendly foreign power had attempted to impose on America the mediocre educational performance that exists today, we might well have viewed it as an act of war. As it stands, we have allowed this to happen to ourselves. We have even squandered the gains in student achievement made in the wake of the Sputnik challenge. Moreover, we have dismantled essential support systems which helped make those gains possible. We have, in effect, been committing an act of unthinking, unilateral educational disarmament.
>
> Our society and its educational institutions seem to have lost sight of the basic purposes of schooling, and of the high expectations and disciplined effort needed to attain them. The world is indeed one global village. We live among determined, well-educated, and strongly motivated competitors. We compete with them for international standing and markets, not only with products but also with the ideas of our laboratories and neighborhood workshops. America's position in the world may once have been reasonably secure with only a few exceptionally well trained men and women. It is no longer. (NCEE, 1983)

Moreover, America's schools had angered the market and threatened to incur its wrath. Through their mediocre performance, schools subjected the future of the nation to economic damnation by failing to satisfactorily increase the use value of its children relative to the more pious efforts of other nations. They must atone for their sins by appeasing the market through increased devotion or suffer the consequences. Indeed, teachers must be held to account.

A LOSE-LOSE PROPOSITION

Accountability has functioned as the primary mechanism for bringing teachers back under control and eliminating the "temporary confusion of purpose." As I argued in this book's preface, the ultimate goal of the neoliberal/neoconservative alliance in education demands the privatization of schools. Transferring the control of schools to private power will institutionalize heteronomy as a defining characteristic of teachers' work. If this vision prevails, teachers will cease working for the public and begin working for a private corporation, and thereby lose all professional autonomy. They will be paid to teach in accordance with the corporation's model of instruction, and it will serve their individual interests to "go along with the program."

Massive privatization of schools, however, hinges on what happens between now and the year 2014. Will schools spring the accountability trap by failing to achieve the mandates imposed under NCLB? Most states project that the vast majority of their schools will not meet the standards, leaving upwards of 80% of our nation's schools subject to privatization. Even if a school escapes privatization, however, the continuation of high-stakes testing and accountability will ensure the preservation of heteronomy and individualism as the defining principles of teachers' work. Moreover, teachers are damned if they do and damned if they don't meet the standards of No Child Left Behind. It is time to formulate and demand an alternative vision of accountability that will restore the principles of autonomy and community to the work of teachers as well as the work of students. More importantly, we need to apply those same principles in formulating an alternative vision of society and how we structure our lives more generally.

REFERENCES

Cox, H. (1999, March). The market as God. *Atlantic Monthly*, pp. 18, 20–24. Retrieved January 17, 2006, from http://www.econ.ubc.ca/evans/cox99.pdf

Figueroa, T. (2006, March 8). Woman sues for alleged firing over talk show bumper sticker. *North Carolina Times*. Retrieved March 14, 2006, from http://www.nctimes.com/articles/2006/03/09/news/sandiego/20_24_273_8_06.txt

Fotopoulos, T. (2005, September). From (mis)education to paideia. In The International Journal of Inclusive Democracy. 2 (1). Retrieved May 9, 2007 from http://www.inclusivedemocracy.org/journal/vol2/vol2_no1_miseducation_paideia_takis.htm.

Harvey, D. (2005). *A brief history of neoliberalism*. New York: Oxford University.

Lucadamo, K. (2006, March 15). Ed sec'y sez test focus "fine, dandy." *New York Daily News*. Retrieved March 15, 2006, from http://www.nydailynews.com/news/local/story/399731p-338704c.html

National Commission for Excellence in Education. (1983). *A nation at risk*. Retrieved March 4, 2006, from http://www.ed.gov/pubs/NatAtRisk/index.html

Noah, T. (2004, September 14). *Bumper sticker insubordination: A Kerry fan gets fired, and then hired, for her politics*. Slate.com. Retrieved March 14, 2006, from http://www.slate.com/id/2106714/

President's Commision for a National Agenda for the Eighties. (1980). *A national agenda for the eighties*. Washington, DC: U.S Government Printing Office.

Chapter 19

Discipline

Felicia Briscoe
University of Texas–San Antonio

This chapter explores how high-stakes testing, as a mode of surveillance within the disciplinary apparatus of schooling, contributes to a stratified national and global economy. Surveillance, of course, has long served as a technique of disciplinary power, but high-stakes testing, as mandated under the No Child Left Behind (NCLB) legislation, represents one of its latest and most refined and pervasive iterations since it originated more than two centuries ago. In 1787, Jeremy Bentham, a British social planner and humanitarian, devoted to reform rather than punishment, developed a unique disciplinary device to control people through one-sided surveillance (Foucault, 1977). He declared it "a new mode of obtaining power of mind over mind, in a quantity hitherto without example" (republished in Bozovic, 1995, p. 1). His architectural device was known as the panopticon and was to be used for controlling those deemed in most need of reform,

> whether it be that of punishing the incorrigible, guarding the insane, reforming the vicious, … instructing the willing in any branch of industry, or training the rising race in the path of education: in a word, whether it be applied to the purposes of perpetual prisons in the room of death, … or manufactories, or mad-houses, or hospitals or *schools* [italics added]. (Bentham, 1787, in Bozovic, 1995, p. 1)

Within the prison context, Bentham's architecture placed inmates in a position to be constantly viewed; however, the inmates themselves could not likewise view others, and thus could not tell whether they were being watched. This would create an effect of continuous surveillance, which meant that the inmates (subject to punishment if they transgressed) would be obedient most of the time. Over time, additional "benevolent" disciplinary techniques have been embedded within the increasing use of surveillance within schooling, such that schooling discipline and control is increasingly centralized. The targets of school discipline have broadened out to include teachers (Hunter & Garrison, 1991) and parents (Briscoe, 2000). As we further embrace accountability through standardized high-stakes testing, surveillance technology has broadened yet further to include principals, schools, superintendents, and school districts, but has focused selectively on a few attributes while ignoring others. NCLB tactics (whether intended or not) promote a stratification of knowledge and ways of thinking and at the same time promote the idea that this stratification is a product of freely chosen options, and therefore natural and based on the merit of parent or student choices. Such a stratification of schooling leads naturally to a stratified economy. Currently in the United States, wealth is concentrated in the hands of a few — in 2001 the top 5% of the nation owned 59.2% of the nation's wealth (Wolff, 2004) — a similar discrepancy exists between the U.S. consumption of resources compared to the rest of the world (e.g., Shah, 2001; Wolfowitz, 2005). Schooling has indeed become Weber's iron cage of rationality, but a peculiar sort of rationality, a marketplace, mentality well suited to perpetuating a "natural" unequal distribution of wealth and power in the United States and throughout the world.

SURVEILLANCE TACTICS, TARGETS, AND EFFECTS

No Child Left Behind has such a noble ring, and it certainly seems to tug at the hearts of those who have longed for educational equity; few argue with such a goal (Olson, 2005). However, NCLB has turned out to be a perfect example of Orwellian doublespeak, in that it does the opposite, that is, pushing historically educationally underserved children even further behind (e.g., Valenzuela, 2005; Meier & Wood, 2004) through a variety of tactics. NCLB acts discursively in two ways. It promotes a way of thinking due to its wording, and it is a commissive speech act (Searle, 1969) that makes a policy of coercion legally binding. The tactics utilized by NCLB include rhetoric that seemingly promotes equity, hand washing, and curricular and pedagogical coercion through a mandated surveillance apparatus of frequently administered standardized testing coupled with rewards, sanctions, and unequal funding. The following section explores these discursive tactics of NCLB and their effects.

Curricular Coercion with Discursive Hand Washing

NCLB maintains that "nothing in this title shall be construed to authorize an officer or employee of the Federal Government to mandate, direct, or control a State, local educational agency, or school's specific instructional content, ... curriculum, or program of instruction" (NCLBa, Part I, Section 1095). Yet, despite this disclaimer, NCLB coerces states into adopting particular curricular emphases — especially those school districts and schools with little money. NCLB's mandated surveillance through standardized testing achieves this curricular (and pedagogical coercion). Standardized testing is not new — it has been a school practice since before 1964 — however, NCLB adds its own refinement, with two mandates: first, that three specific subject areas are to be tested regularly and, second, that rewards and sanctions are to be given on the basis of those three test scores. NCLB mandates that students be given a standardized test in three subjects (reading/English, math, and science) during particular school grades (third through eighth and in selected high school grades). If students do not achieve a particular score, they are to repeat the grade unless a special waiver is granted (this despite research that retention does little to improve achievement levels [e.g., Pierson & Connell, 1992]), and schools with too many low scores are deemed as *in need of improvement* and eventually as *failing*. The scores for these three subject areas by school and school districts are to be displayed for all to see. Such a narrowly focused view implicitly backgrounds other aspects of schooling and makes these other aspects less likely to be attended to by those doing the viewing. More importantly, this focused view incites those viewed (districts, schools, principals, and teachers) to attend especially to those specific curricular areas, while other areas may or may not be attended to (such as civics, history, art, etc.) depending upon school resources (e.g., Flinders, 2005). This coercion is rhetorically disavowed by the federal government.

Induced Self-Discipline

Just as the inmates in Bentham's panopticon were induced to discipline themselves (according to the dictates of those in charge of a particular institution), NCLB legislation likewise induces states to regulate themselves. Yet, NCLB states that "the use of assessment items and data on any assessment authorized under this section by ... the Federal Government to rank, compare, ... or provide rewards or sanctions for individual students, teachers, schools or local educational agencies is *prohibited* [italics added]" (NCLBb, Part C, Section 411, b4a); but in order to receive NCLB monies, "each State accountability system shall ... include sanctions and rewards ... to hold local educational agencies and public elementary schools and secondary schools accountable for student achievement...." (NCLBc, Subpart 1, Part A, Section 1111, b2, iii). Thus, the federal government may not itself sanction or reward any district, school, and so forth, on the basis of test scores, but in order to receive NCLB monies, states must ensure that the aforementioned test scores are publicly displayed and administer rewards and sanctions based on those scores to local districts and schools. In addition, if states fail to ensure that school districts and schools adhere to and meet NCLB guidelines and goals, the states themselves can be fined by the federal government, for example, Texas was fined $444,000 because parents were not notified of school's test scores and NCLB-defined status in a timely manner (Lynn, 2005). NCLB's mandate that states punish or reward on the basis of the scores of regularly administered tests makes surveillance through testing three specific subject areas quite effective as a control strategy.

Hierarchicalized Regimentation

This inducement of state self-disciplining acts together with the equal achievement and unequal funding clauses to regulate curricula and method differentially according to the school's or school district's resources. NCLB mandates public schools are "to enable *all children* [italics added] to meet the challenging State student academic achievement standards [in the three specified subject areas]"; however schools must accomplish this without equal funding: "Nothing in this title shall be construed to mandate equalized spending per pupil for a State, local educational agency, or school" (NCLBa, Part I, Sections 1093 a2 and 1906). Taken together, these tactics (the testing of three curricular areas, the mandated rewards and sanctions based on those test scores, and the lack of equal funding) combine to differentially regiment schools.

Schools with few resources and with students who suffer from economic deprivation are expected to produce student test scores similar to those of affluent schools with affluent students on pain of sanctions. This disciplinary apparatus of NCLB acts to differentiate the types of knowledge and thinking that develop in students and the types of actions taken by teachers, principals, and so on. Depending largely upon socioeconomic class, there is a stratification of the degree to which school curricula and pedagogy are affected by NCLB. This stratification is due to schools with few resources being driven to excessively narrowing the curriculum to the specified subject areas even to the point of *teaching to the test*. The production of narrow test-driven curricula, especially in schools with few resources (e.g., Furumoto, 2005; Valenzuela, 2005), has already been discussed by a number of scholars (e.g., Flinders, 2005; Popham, 2005; Scherer, 2005). This effect has been exacerbated in light of the recent cuts in NCLB funding because of budget strain due to funding the Iraqi occupation (Long, 2005).

A recent study in Florida (Peterson & West, 2005) found that schools in need of improvement and under the threat of vouchers or restructuring increased student scores by 4% to 5% of a standard deviation; however, this improvement was not reflected in nationally normed test scores. Such a lack of correlation generally means that the tests scores are not valid.

Other states must fear similar sorts of actions in schools, as the "Texas Education Agency announced a crackdown on teachers and administrators who inflate scores by providing answers or manipulating exam sheets" (*Curriculum Review*, 2005). Not surprisingly, schools with few resources and whose students are largely minority or suffer from economic deprivation are more likely than others to be deemed in need of improvement (e.g., Tuerk, 2005; Tracey et al., 2005), and therefore more likely to excessively narrow the curriculum in an effort to improve test scores and avoid sanctions. What makes matters worse is that the content of these tests for 87% of the schools is determined by only nine companies (Olson, 2004), which means that for most schools — but especially those with minority or low-income students — the knowledge base taught is inordinately influenced by for-profit companies, whose ideas are likely to differ greatly from other groups' (e.g., labor unions). Thus, not only is the curricula likely to be excessively narrowed to math, reading/English, and science, with subjects like civics, history, and art diminished, but what is taught (for students in schools with few resources in particular) is likely to be highly uniform throughout the nation. In addition to coercing school curricula, NCLB also influences the pedagogy.

NCLB legislation makes it more likely that students will receive copious training in answering multiple-choice questions over the more divergent essay-type questions. For example, when Connecticut asked to reduce the number of grades in which students are tested so that it could use the more expensive hand-scored tests, which allow for greater diversity in responses, it was told to either use multiple-choice-type tests or use its own money to help pay for the NCLB-mandated tests (Archer, 2005). States, schools, and school districts with few resources who wish to use the federal funds provided by NCLB are thus strongly encouraged to use multiple-choice tests. Creativity, synthesis, and divergent thinking do not enhance multiple-choice test scores; on the other hand, convergent thinking is needed in order to select the one correct answer out of those provided. In order to improve student test scores, principals and teachers are likely to increase the use of "drill and kill" pedagogy in order to encourage the convergent thinking necessary for doing well on the multiple-choice tests. And thus we see the sort of thinking and knowledge for local service work being inculcated in children who historically have been underserved by schooling systems. Such a schooling system mass produces unquestioning workers for an increasingly service based economy, which values a docile workforce over an innovative one. On the other hand, affluent schools and school districts whose students come from affluent families are more likely to receive adequate yearly progress (AYP) status and not be as strongly coerced into test-driven curricula and pedagogy.

But what about the students and their parents? NCLB gives them the right to transfer to schools with AYP status. This market mechanism theoretically allows students to freely leave failing schools. However, less than 92% of students in schools deemed in need of improvement did so in 2004–2005 (Mickleson, 2005). It seems that low-income or minority parents choose to keep their children in failing schools. Such a viewpoint fails to consider that schools with AYP status, filled to overcapacity, often refuse transfers (Mickleson, 2005), that transferring to a new school is detrimental to academic achievement (Kazmin, 2005), that parents are often not informed of the status of their child's school in a timely manner (Mickleson, 2005), and that transfers often take students to a school location far from their neighborhood. Thus, economically deprived students in schools with few resources, even if they are not pushed out by an unendurably tedious pedagogy and an uninspiring curriculum, end up with an extremely narrow knowledge base and a convergent way of thinking, which suits them well for the increasing number of intellectually undemanding domestic service jobs. This differentiation of knowledge and thinking is helpful in perpetuating a docile workforce divided into service workers and managers. The children of elite capital owners attend private prep schools, not affected by NCLB, and are unlikely to become part of the workforce (Wexler, 1992). Furthermore, according to the discourse of NCLB, the stratification of knowledge and thinking that emerges is the result of options "freely" chosen by states, school districts, schools, principals, teachers, students, and parents.

The tactics embedded in the surveillance apparatus of high-stakes testing found in NCLB include regular multiple-choice testing of math, reading/English, and science; an expectation that all students in all schools will achieve equally well in those subject areas with unequal funding; a continual public display of these three test scores; sanctions and rewards based upon those scores; and a disavowal of federal responsibility for the choices made by states, districts, superintendents, principals, teachers, students, and parents. Such tactics produce a stratifying effect by narrowing the curriculum and encouraging convergent thinking, more in schools with few resources (that is, for historically underserved students) than for more affluent schools. This effect is brought about with discursive rhetoric claiming first that "no child is being left behind" and the implication that the emerging stratification of knowledge and thinking is natural and uncoerced. Likewise, the stratified U.S. economy, enhanced by this differential schooling, is seemingly natural and uncoerced. Such an ideology also serves to naturalize the increasingly unequal distribution of wealth and resources, nationally and globally. In sum, tactics of the surveillance apparatus found in the high-stakes testing of NCLB serve to perpetuate a stratified schooling, and thus a stratified national and global economy. However, NCLB tactics not only provide an ideology that supports a stratified global economy, but also prepare the majority of students to fit into the global economy.

Just as advances in the technology of surveillance have enabled a centralized control of schooling, technological advances in communication and transportation have also enabled the United States to better control the global economy, and thus garner a disproportionate amount of resources. This evolution of schooling policy is strikingly consistent with that of the Bretton Woods international system of economic management. In 1944, via the Bretton Woods Agreement (1944), the United States set up a neoliberal system of rules, institutions, and procedures to regulate and manage the global economy to the disproportionate advantage of U.S. economic interests. In the last two decades, technological advances in communication and transportation have given the U.S. capital interests access to labor and resources in third world countries. This access has exposed U.S. workers to an unprecedented degree of foreign competition. The effect has been the outsourcing of manufacturing and IT jobs. The majority of jobs left in the United States are service jobs. Robert Reich, the former U.S. secretary of labor, states: [Local service] jobs aren't, to a large extent, threatened by globalization or technology, and they are abundant, but they are also among the lowest paying jobs" (quoted in Bowdoin Campus Life, 2002, p. 1). Thus, the apparatus of surveillance embedded in NCLB is well suited for fitting historically educationally underserved students neatly into the rather large niche created by an increasingly centralized and stratified national and global economy.

REFERENCES

Archer, J. (2005). States eyeing expense of hand-scored tests in light of NCLB rules. *Education Week, 24,* 1–21.

Bozovic, M. (1995). *Bentham, Jeremy: The Panopticon Writings* (pp. 29–95). London: Verso.

Bowdoin Campus Life. (2002, October 28). Dealing with worklife in the new economy. Retrieved on January 1, 2006, from http://www.bowdoin.edu/newsarchives/1bowdoincampus/001172.shtml

Bretton Woods Agreement. (1944). Articles of agreement of the International Bank for reconstruction and development. Retrieved on January 1, 2006, from http://www.yale.edu/lawweb/avalon/decade/decad047.htm

Briscoe, F. (2000). Discipline. In D. Gabbard (Ed.), *Knowledge and power in the global economy* (pp. 63–68). New York: Lawrence Erlbaum Associates.

Curriculum Review. (2005, March). Texas plan to unmask cheating schools. *Last Month in Education, 44,* 8.

Flinders, D. (2005). The failings of NCLB. *Curriculum and Teaching Dialogue, 7,* 1–9.

Foucault, M. (1977). *Discipline and punish* (A. Sheridan, Trans.). New York: Pantheon Books.

Furumoto, R. (2005). No poor child left unrecruited: How NCLB codified and perpetuates urban school militarism. *Equity and Excellence in Education, 38,* 200–210.

Hunter, J., & Garrison, J. (1991). Instructional technology, temper, technique, and teacher empowerment. *Thresholds in Education, 17,* 13–18.

Kazmin, B. (2005). NCLB transfer policy: Bad math, bad choices. *Education Week, 24,* 40–41.

Long, R. (2005). Funding NCLB remains top issue. *Reading Today,* 22(6). Retrieved May 1, 2007 from the EBSCO host database.

Lynn, R. (2005, May 2). Utah law on NCLB may hurt; ask Texas. *Salt Lake Tribune,* p. B1.

Meier, D., & Wood, G. (2004). *Many children left behind: How the No Child Left Behind Act is damaging our children and our schools.* Boston: Beacon Press.

Mickleson, R. (2005). When opting out is not a choice: Implications for NCLB transfer option from Charlotte, North Carolina. *Equity and Excellence in Education, 38,* 249–263.

NCLBa, Public Law 107-110, the No Child Left Behind Act of 2001. Retrieved December 18, 2005, from http://www.ed.gov/policy/elsec/leg/esea02/pg18.html

NCLBb, Public Law 107-110, the No Child Left Behind Act of 2001. Retrieved December 18, 2005, from http://www.ed.gov/policy/elsec/leg/esea02/pg97.html

NCLBc, Public Law 107-110, the No Child Left Behind Act of 2001. Retrieved December 18, 2005, from http://www.ed.gov/policy/elsec/leg/esea02/pg2.html

Olson, L. (2004). NCLB law bestows bounty on test industry. *Education Week, 24,* 1–19.

Olson, L. (2005). In hearings, poll, PEN finds support for goals of NCLB. *Education Week, 24,* 6.

Peterson, P., & West, M. (2005, March 23). The efficacy of choice threats within school accountability systems: Results from legislatively induced experiments. Annual Conference of the Royal Economic Society, Nottingham, pp. 1–26. Retrieved December 29, 2005, from http://ksgnotes1.harvard.edu/Research/wpaper.nsf/d745629e080d1fe88525698900714934/5972315987ba44cd85256fdc006f1b13/$FILE/West_Peterson_ChoiceThreats.pdf

Pierson, L., & Connell, J. (1992). Effect of grade retention on self-system processes, school engagement, and academic achievement. *Journal of Educational Psychology, 84,* 300–307.

Popham, J. (2005). Curriculum matters. *American School Board Journal, 19,* 30–33.

Scherer, M. (2005). Reclaiming testing. *Educational Leadership, 63,* 9–15.

Searle, J. R. (1969). *Speech acts: An essay in the philosophy of language.* Cambridge: Cambridge University Press.

Shah, A. (2001, September 2). A numbers game. *Global Issues.* Retrieved December 26, 2005, from http://www.globalissues.org/EnvIssues/Population/Numbers.asp

Tracey, C., Sunderman, G., & Orfield, G. (2005, June). Changing NCLB district accountability standards: Implications for racial equity (Harvard Civil Rights Project). Retrieved December 29, 2005, from http://www.civilrightsproject.harvard.edu/research/esea/nclb_district_account.php

Tuerk, P. (2005). Research in the high-stakes era. *Psychological Science, 16,* 419–425.

Valenzuela, A. (Ed.). (2005). *Leaving children behind: How "Texas-style" accountability fails Latino youth.* New York: SUNY Press.

Wexler, P. (1992). *Becoming somebody: Toward a social psychology of school* (with the assistance of W. Crichlow, J. Kern, & R. Martusewicz). London: Falmer Press.

Wolff, N. (2004, May). *Changes in household wealth in the 1980s and 1990s in the US* (Working paper 407). The Levy Economics Institute and New York University. Retrieved May 9, 2007 from http://www.levy.org/default. asp?view=publications_view&pubID=fca3a440ee.

Wolfowitz, P. (2005, December 20). *Environment and development: Reaching for a double dividend.* World Bank Group, Special Session of the Sao Paulo Forum on Climate Change, Sao Paulo, Brazil. Retrieved December 23, 2005, from http://web.worldbank.org/WBSITE/EXTERNAL/TOPICS/ENVIRONMENT/0,,contentMDK:20764291~menuPK:176751~pagePK:64020865~piPK:149114~theSiteP K:244381,00.html

Chapter 20

Masculinization

Sandra Spickard Prettyman and Sharon Kruse
University of Akron

Any time the federal government spends money, we ought to expect account-ability. We ought to expect a return on our dollar spent, which says, if you receive money, we expect you to measure on an annual basis. We want to know whether or not the children are learning to read and write and add and subtract. So step one is, in return for money, there's accountability. Step two is, in return for success, there'll be bonuses. And step three is, in return for failure, then something has to happen.

— PBS *Frontline* interview, "The Battle Over School Choice," May 23, 2000

Educational reform in America today is often spoken about using slogans like "all students can learn" and "expectations of accountability." Who can argue that increasing opportunities for students as well as increasing student achievement can have anything but good outcomes? However, there is very little attention in this public dialogue about the underlying assumptions, beliefs, and attitudes toward schools and schooling, students and teachers, content and knowledge embedded in legislation such as No Child Left Behind (NCLB). At its heart, educational reform is, or should be, about creating change (Popkewitz, 2000, p. 33), but there is little focus in today's rhetoric about educational reform on how changes will be achieved, nor even explicit attention to what those changes will be. In this chapter, we argue that the language and ideology of these reform efforts epitomize the norms of hegemonic masculinity, resulting in the maintenance of the status quo rather than change. The result is that true reform can never be achieved by these efforts and this legislation; rather, they only serve to keep intact the current systems and structures of unequal schooling.

While definitions of reform may have changed over time and place, one constant in those definitions is that reform is, or should be, about change. Today, change does not seem to be at the heart of more recent reform efforts, thus causing us to question where and how they fit into a definition of reform. Without explicit attention to how and what changes will result from these efforts, we must also question what their effects will be. Earlier educational reform efforts, like the middle school reforms that resulted from the publication of *Turning Points* or the nationwide math and science initiatives that followed the launch of Sputnik, took the notion of change to heart and clearly laid out what the sought-after changes were and how the reform efforts hoped to achieve them.

Today there are calls for accountability and consequences without a clear understanding of how these will lead to change, or even if change is any part of the equation. Perhaps there is an assumption that these will lead to change, but how this will happen is left to chance. In addition, there is an undercurrent that teachers and school leaders all know what to do, but are just holding out for the right incentive. School reform today is focused on high-stakes testing and a "highly qualified teaching force" as mechanisms for providing this accountability. When these are not able to provide the continuous improvement called for in NCLB, when schools are not able to maintain annual or average yearly progress, there are "get tough" consequences like academic emergency, academic watch, and threats of school closures or loss of further funding. The implication is: "We'll shut you down, take over your school, and someone stronger will be put in place who can accomplish what needs to get done, like Joe Clark. The image of Joe Clark is the epitome of a hegemonic form of masculinity, a man *in* power, a man *with* power, and a man *of* power" (Kimmel, 1994, p. 125). Connell (1995) argues that hegemonic masculinity is a "culturally idealized form of masculine character" (p. 83) that is constructed in relation to femininities, as well as to subordinated and marginalized masculinities, which are often construed as failed forms of masculinity (Cheng, 1999, p. 296). It is always constituted by unequal relationships of power, like those between the federal government and local school districts in reform efforts, and its dominance must constantly be reasserted, for it is never secure. Connell (1987) argues that this dominance is achieved not only by coercion, but also by the creation of alliances that allow for consent to be shaped and won. These alliances are created within, and often legitimated by, social institutions, such as schools and government. This dominant form of masculinity, which is more valued and respected than others, is characterized by attributes such as power and control, authority, aggression, physical prowess or dominance, stoicism, competition (whose ultimate goal is winning), and technical competence (Cheng, 1999; Connell, 1987, 1995; Messner, 1997; Swain, 2005). Many of these elements are also found in the rhetoric of current school reform efforts. The following sections will examine several of these characteristics — power and control, aggression, competition, and technical competence — looking at how the language and ideology of educational reform efforts today epitomize these norms. We argue that one result of this masculinization of school reform is the maintenance of structures of unequal schooling that privilege those with power and authority through legislated competition, aggression, and control.

THE MASCULINIZATION OF SCHOOL REFORM

While the language of school reform remains gender neutral, the ideological positions that inform it are not, nor are the policies and practices that it demands. Gilbert and Gilbert (1998) speak of "masculinizing practices" in relationship to schooling, which include management, policy, and organizational practices that represent and result in particular forms of power and control as well as pedagogical practices. The reciprocal relationship between school reform and hegemonic masculinity valorizes characteristics such as authority, aggression, competition, and technical competence. As such, these characteristics are constructed as the norm against which all students, teachers, and schools are measured. When such a hegemonic norm is used to measure all students, teachers, and schools, those who are able to achieve the norm are seen as successful and are able to remain dominant. Those who are not able to achieve this norm are relegated to the status of failure, always in need of improvement. Swain (2005) posits that hegemonic masculinity "generally exerts its influence by being able to define the 'norm'" (p. 220), and that it often works through implicit consent.

The current rhetoric surrounding educational reform, specifically NCLB, groups all schools together as if they were large urban districts with massive problems, and calls for all schools to look and act like well-funded suburban districts that represent the hegemonic norm. This ignores the multiplicity of district, school, teacher, and student identities, including those found in rural areas, first-ring suburban districts, and today's exurbs. The actions and measures of NCLB presuppose universal outcomes for students, teachers, and districts across a widely varying landscape. Specifically, the assumption is that all schools, especially those that are failing, must represent the ideas/ideals held by the dominant elite. If they do not meet these lofty prescribed standards, then somehow they are failing and are in need of fixing — much like the way femininities and alternative forms of masculinity are measured against the hegemonic norm. Using the experiences and ideals of the dominant elite as the norm to evaluate and judge all students, teachers, and districts represents one-size-fits-all policy making that does not serve the best interest of all communities or the public.

Power and Control

Definitions of hegemonic masculinity assert the importance of power and control, often by domination through physical size and strength. However, more recent conceptualizations argue that domination today is often achieved through "managerial hegemonic masculinity" (Cheng, 1999) that is constructed through hierarchical organization and by "manipulating rewards, threatening punishment, and using coercive organizational power" (Cheng, 1999, p. 297). Legislation like NCLB relies heavily on such organizational structures by rewarding those schools who comply and meet prescribed standards, punishing those who do not, and using the funding power of the federal government to coerce compliance with the legislation. Thus, the language and ideology of the legislation and its goals are embedded within a structure guided by hegemonic masculinity.

This managerial form of hegemonic masculinity is often enacted by individuals as well as institutions, and current political discussion of the literature on school leadership focuses on the importance of the style of the leader (Leithwood, Louis, Anderson, & Wahlstrom, 2004). The literature is replete with adjectives descriptive of instructional leaders, transformational leaders, and authoritative leaders who focus their efforts on empowering teachers and community members to achieve greatness (or at least improved academic achievement). What these definitions fail to do is focus on the substance of successful leadership. By focusing attention on *who* these leaders are rather than *what* they do, the national conversation concerning school leadership remains focused on those aspects of authority and control vested in individuals rather than concentrating energy and effort on meaningful reform and change.

In sharp contrast to the leadership literature of the 1990s (Leithwood & Louis, 1998; Newmann & Associates, 1996; Peurach & Rowan, 1999; Scribner, Cockrell, Cockrell, & Valentine, 1999), which focused on the development of structures, practices, and policies with the potential to address calls for both accountability and equity, the more recent return of the conversation to leadership style, in fact, is a return to a literature more like that of the 1940s and 1950s (Bass, 1990) — that is, a literature that sought to determine how organizations could identify "Great Men" (Yukl, 2002) who would lead with power, influence, and authority, and who thus embody the hegemonic norm. Such men were defined as "endowed with the unique qualities that capture the imagination of the masses" (Bass, 1990, p. 37). Furthermore, even though such leaders/men may possess "different degrees of intelligence, energy, and moral force" (Dowd, 1936, in Bass, 1990), they are innately able to lead regardless of place, time, and context due to their personal prowess and character. In short, the Great Man theories suggest that leadership is unavoidably gender focused and determined by those personal characteristics and motivational aspirations that are inherently based on a hegemonic masculine model.

Furthermore, as the public rhetoric embraces a dialogue around who leads, the conversation increasingly centers on the development of a bureaucracy and a hierarchical organization designed to support these leaders (Firestone & Bader, 1992). Through the external imposition of legislative commitments, reinforced by mandated adherence to rules and regulations concerning how and when these commitments will be measured, the bureaucracy of schools and schooling has in recent years removed from school leaders the ability to enact changes that the restructuring movement of the 1990s had sought to develop. As such, the federally created bureaucracy that supports NCLB disempowers individual school leaders, weakening their ability to achieve the very goals the legislation seeks to achieve. Leaders in a bureaucratic system need only worry about compliance and alignment of objectives to the outcome expectations, and by "gaming the system" they can attract more benefits for the leader, often at the expense of students within the system (Firestone & Riehl, 2004).

Competition

Competition is another hallmark of hegemonic masculinity, another mechanism by which men can prove their value (Kimmel, 1994; Swain, 2005). Current school reform efforts pit schools against each other for funding and pit students against each other for grades and scores. Thus, winning at all costs becomes important, and competition for higher test scores and the ability to prove one's effectiveness become paramount. This mentality of competition permeates NCLB: It relies on high-stakes testing that reports student, school, and district scores, often in percentiles (which focus on who scores better than someone else and ranks students and districts against each other). It demands annual yearly progress and improvement (based on a set of prescribed standards and guidelines). It enacts strict sanctions and consequences for schools that do not raise test scores and meet standards (such as the loss of federal funds or the mandating of technical assistance). And it allows parents to choose different schools if their own are failing (thus creating a competitive school marketplace). Swain (2005) argues that school policies and organization, at the micro- or macrolevel, are major factors in the masculinizing practices of schooling, and that they "are visible in such practices as academic competition and hierarchy, constant testing ... patterns of authority ... and so on" (p. 216). Miner (2001) argues that standardized tests ensure that half of our children will always be "below average." That is the way they are constructed — to rank children so one can sort the smart kids from the dumb kids. Because socioeconomic status plays such a crucial role in test scores, it is easy to predict which students, schools, and districts will routinely be condemned to below-average status. It is then these students and schools who are expected to compete in the new free market of school choice.

The results of this focus on competition are far-reaching. One needs to look no further than the well-publicized and well-organized test cheating scandals of recent years in both Chicago and New York. In each case teachers or school leaders have employed a variety of methods (usually by either providing extensive additional time to complete the test or altering student answers, although cases of teachers writing the answers to items on the board have been reported as well) after high-stakes state testing was implemented. Although the costs of getting caught are severe, principals and teachers have adopted a "win at all costs" attitude as incentives (bonuses or raises directly to teachers and administrators) for "scoring high" to gain popularity across the nation.

Moreover, the bureaucracy of school leadership focuses its attention almost exclusively on political accountability, attending to the joint objectives of obedience and satisfaction of goals at the expense of value and belief commitments. School leaders and organizations who embrace this "win at any cost" mentality illustrate the conflict inherent in a bureaucracy of school reform characterized by excessive attention to authority and the goals set by those with authority (Firestone & Riehl, 2004). The imposition of hierarchical testing systems and structures by external authorities such as the federal government encourages school personnel to make curricular and instructional choices that are not based on a commitment to preferred practices within a professional field, nor do they require educators to hold deeply reflective understandings on the nature and purpose of their work. Instead, they require unquestioning loyalty to externally imposed standards and curricular pacing to meet those standards and benchmarks of learning.

Aggression

The competitive nature of hegemonic masculinity, and of current school reform, relies on aggressiveness as a mechanism to meet the competitive demands. In order to accomplish its goals, the legislation and the government need get-tough measures to ensure compliance and success. These measures include federal demands for yearly high-stakes testing; the development of state standards upon which such testing will be based; the use of annual state, district, and school report cards, which will be used to rank and rate schools; the imposition of technical assistance from districts or states who do not improve performance; the threat of reorganization after five years of no school improvement; the allowance for parents to choose alternative schools for their children who attend low-performing schools; and the loss of federal funding for schools who do not meet annual yearly progress.

The results of these aggressive tactics are many. "Linking federal funds and sanctions to test scores will also turn more tests from diagnostic tools into 'high stakes' exams" (Karp, 2001). Aggressive testing programs suggest a get-tough approach to learning and teaching. Inherent in these approaches is the notion that students and teachers alike have been coddled long enough in classrooms, too soft on subject area content and discipline and not rigorous enough in their demands. This characterization depicts teachers and students as too soft, too feminine, and clearly juxtaposes this with the more masculine demands of the current legislation, where it is argued that what is needed is an approach that demands adherence to stricter standards with more accountability and sanctions.

Technical Competence

At the core of the No Child Left Behind legislation is the notion that technical competence can improve the nation's schools. Through the use of evidence-based teaching practices and policies and the development of a highly qualified teaching force, schools are required to address inequalities in both educational opportunity and achievement present in today's schools. The legislation relies on the construct of scientifically based research (SBR) as the cornerstone of these efforts. Reliance on SBR takes on a mechanized, almost ritualistic, characteristic in the legislation and accompanying support documentation, claiming that "the approach [SBR] can produce major advances in the effectiveness of American education" (U.S. Department of Education, 2003). A strategic goal of the legislation is to "transform education into an evidence-based field" (U.S. Department of Education, 2003). As noted in Erickson and Guitierrez (2002),

> The statement [on SBR] begins, "Unlike medicine, agriculture, and industrial production, the field of education operates largely on the basis of ideology and professional consensus. As such, it is subject to fads and is incapable of the cumulative progress that follows from the application of the scientific method and from the systematic collection and use of objective information in policy making. We will change education to make it an evidence-based field."

Clearly, such claims have been the focus of myriad editorials, studies, and debate (e.g., Darling-Hammond & Youngs, 2002; Eisenhart & Towne, 2003; Erickson & Gutierrez, 2002; Feuer, Towne, & Shavelson, 2002; Mayer, 2000, 2001). Yet, as much as researchers are willing to assert the merits and concerns related to the implementation of educational practices based on SBR, the dialogue embraces the notion that "scholars working in a particular area collectively — as a community — establish the scientific traditions and standards for how to most appropriately apply the guiding principles to the area of study" (Feuer et al., 2002). In short, the "traditions and standards" for research can and should be universally accepted after the wider (read more powerful) community decides they are objective and systematic.

Such language is gender-bound in that it contrasts the rational form of scientific method to that of ideology and fads determined by consensus. Language such as this privileges those traditionally male characteristics of reason and rationality above those of consensus and dialogue. This naïve view is both troubling and insidious given the reality of science as building knowledge through testing and trials and not, as suggested, in a smoothly governed, continuous fashion. Relative to the notion that knowledge concerning practice and policy can be built through the agreement of a wider community by the application of traditions and standards, again we offer a critique suggesting that this idea rests on the ideal of a certain man, one who knows who he is and where he is headed, a Great Man (Yukl, 2002). Science in any form, and certainly research in education, is as much about uncertainty as it is about what works.

Efforts to embed SBR are not only limited to the development of programs and policy. NCLB legislation relies heavily on standardized testing to measure the competence of both K-12 students and those choosing to enter the teaching profession. As professors in the field of education, we do not argue that "loving children" provides a sufficient foundation for one to become a teacher, and that clearly, content knowledge and skill are important for prospective teachers. We do, however, argue that standardized tests alone cannot measure all that is necessary for quality teaching. Our argument is similar when we consider the notion of standardized measures of K-12 student learning.

Cheng (1999) argues that one mechanism through which hegemonic masculinity operates today is "the technical/professional form" (p. 3) that often results in domination. This form relies on the use of technical and professional skills in the new knowledge economy to "gain and maintain power over others" (Cheng, 1999, p. 3). In addition to the reliance on SBR, school reform today depends heavily on the notion of technical competence. Schools that are identified as "low-performing" and who do not improve in two years must receive technical assistance from the school district and undergo a variety of improvements, which might include major restructuring. School districts that do not raise scores and meet standards must receive technical assistance from the state. This reliance on "experts" and technical assistance creates a situation where hegemonically masculine traits are valued and rewarded, and through which the federal government can dominate states, districts, schools, teachers, and students, who must comply or face get-tough sanctions.

CLOSING IN ON A CONCLUSION

Kimmel (1994) argues that everywhere we look we see "the institutional expression" of masculine power (p. 136), including in the current school reform legislation and the rhetoric surrounding it. Today, more than ever, there exists a reciprocal relationship between school reform and hegemonic masculinity, similar to the relationship that Higate and Hopton (2005) argue exists between militarism and masculinity. On the one hand, politicians and the media utilize ideologies of hegemonic masculinity that valorize the idea of strength and science to gain support for get-tough school reform policies that measure students, teachers, and schools against each other. On the other hand, school reform today feeds into ideologies of masculinity through reliance characteristics such as competition, aggression, and technical competence.

School reform in America today focuses on accountability and standardization, relying on slogans like "no excuses" or "all students can learn to the same high standards" to promote the image of a commitment to public schooling and education for all children. However, what these slogans and the ideologies behind them really do is establish unrealistic goals that rely on a hegemonic norm that is damaging to students, teachers, schools, and communities. The coercive nature of both current school reform agendas and hegemonic masculinity makes them difficult to resist. As Swain (2005) argues, hegemonic masculinity "prefers to work by implicit *consent*, for, after all, the easiest way to exercise power and to gain advantage over others is for the dominated to be unaware of, and therefore be complicit in, their subordination" (p. 220). Schools today are in much the same situation, often unaware of how NCLB and other school reform efforts work to maintain unequal social relationships. Messner (1997) argues that masculine privilege and hegemonic masculinity comes "with a price tag" and at a high cost, which can "be lethal for men" (p. 6). We argue that as long as school reform legislation and rhetoric rely on hegemonically masculine standards and characteristics, they too come at a high cost that will be lethal for many of America's schools and students.

REFERENCES

Bass, B. (1990). *Handbook of leadership.* New York: The Free Press.

Cheng, C. (1999). Marginalized masculinities and hegemonic masculinity: An introduction. *Journal of Men's Studies, 7,* 295–317.

Connell, R. W. (1987). *Gender and power: Society, the person and sexual politics.* Stanford, CA: Stanford University Press.

Connell, R. W. (1995). *Masculinities.* Berkeley: University of California Press.

Darling-Hammond, L., & Youngs, P. (2002). Defining "highly qualified teachers": What does "scientifically based research" tell us? *Educational Researcher, 31,* 13–25.

Eisenhart, M., & Towne, L. (2003). Contestation and change in national policy on "scientifically based" education research. *Educational Researcher, 30,* (9) 13–25.

Erickson, F., & Guiterrez, K. (2002). Culture, rigor and science in education research. *Educational Researcher, 31,* 21–24.

Feuer, M., Towne, L., & Shavelson, R. (2002). Scientific culture and educational research. *Educational Researcher, 31* (8), 4–14.

Firestone, W. A., & Bader, B. D. (1992). *Redesigning teaching: Professionalism or bureaucracy?* Albany: State University of New York Press.

Firestone, W. A., & Riehl C. (2004). *A new agenda for research in educational leadership.* New York: Teachers College Press.

Higate, P., & Hopton, J. (2005). War, militarism, and masculinities. In M. Kimmel, J. Hearn, & R. W. Connell (Eds.), *Handbook of studies on men and masculinities* (pp. 432–447). Thousand Oaks, CA: Sage.

Karp, S. (2001). Bush plan fails schools. Milwaukee, WI: Rethinking Schools. Retrieved December 5, 2005, from http://www.rethinkingschools.org/special _reports/bushplan/Bush153.shtml

Kimmel, M. S. (1994). Masculinities as homophobia: Fear, shame, and silence in the construction of gender identity. In H. Brod & M. Kaufman (Eds.), *Theorizing masculinities* (pp. 119–141). Newbury Park, CA: Sage.

Leithwood, K., & Louis, K. S. (1998). *Organizational learning in schools.* Lissie: Swets and Zeitlinger.

Leithwood, K., Louis, K., Anderson, S., & Wahlstrom, K. (2004). *How leadership influences student learning.* New York: Wallace Foundation. Retrieved December 4, 2005, from http://www.wallacefoundation.org/WF/KnowledgeCenter/ KnowledgeTopics/EducationLeadership/HowLeadershipInfluences StudentLearning.htm

Mayer, R.E. (2000). What is the place of science in educational research? *Educational Researcher, 29,* 38–39.

Mayer, R.E. (2001). Resisting the assault on science: The case for evidence-based reasoning in educational research. *Educational Researcher, 30,* 29–30.

Messner, M. (1997). *Politics of masculinities.* Thousand Oaks, CA: Sage.

Miner, B. (2001, February). Bush's plan is shallow and ignores critical details. In Rethinking Schools. Retrieved May 9, 2007 from http://www.rethinking-schools.org/special_reports/bushplan/bush.shtml.

Newmann, F. M., & Associates (1996). *Authentic achievement.* San Francisco: Jossey-Bass.

Peurach, D. J., & Rowan, B. (1999, April). Organizational perspectives on instructional improvement. Paper presented at the annual meeting of the American Educational Research Association, Montreal, Canada.

Popkewitz, T. S. (2000). Reform and the social administration of the child: Globalization of knowledge and power. In N. Burbulus and A. Torres, (Eds.). *Globalization and Education.* New York: Routledge.

Scribner, J. P., Cockrell, K. S., Cockrell, D. H., & Valentine, J. W. (1999). Creating professional communities in schools through organizational learning: An evaluation of a school improvement process. *Educational Administration Quarterly, 35,* 130–160.

Swain, J. (2005). Masculinities in education. In M. Kimmel, J. Hearn, & R. W. Connell (Eds.), *Handbook of studies on men and masculinities* (pp. 213–229), Thousand Oaks, CA: Sage.

U.S. Department of Education. (2003). *Identifying and implementing educational practices supported by rigorous evidence: A user friendly guide.* Retrieved May 9, 2007 from www.excelgov.org

Yukl, G. (2002). *Leadership in organizations* (5th ed.). New York: Prentice Hall.

Chapter 21

Militarization

Kenneth J. Saltman and David Gabbard
DePaul University and East Carolina University

The militarization of schools in the United States involves a number of phenomena: the expansion of JROTC programs, the growth of public schools opened as or made into military academies, the expansion of the Troops to Teachers program that installs military personnel in public schools as teachers, and, perhaps most importantly, the intensification of military recruitment in schools. No Child Left Behind has drastically facilitated military recruitment, while youth inside and outside of public schools are targeted with sophisticated advertising techniques from Madison Avenue and old-fashioned pavement pounding by recruiters. Such recruitment has been linked to public school funding.

As the National Education Association reports,

> Buried deep within NCLB (No Child Left Behind) is Section 9528, which puts a school district at risk of losing NCLB funding if it doesn't give military recruiters home contact information for secondary school students. But this provision also allows parents to tell the district not to give out that information. And it requires districts to notify parents of this opt-out provision. (Jehlen and Winans, 2005)

Schools in Duval County, FL, punished those students whose parents opted them out of the program by refusing to publish their photographs in the school yearbook. The schools also refused to publish the names of those "opted-out" kids in athletic programs; they even refused to list the names of qualifying opted-out kids names on the honor roll. The school's punitive treatment to resistance indicates that the militarization of schools mirrors the broader militarization of culture.

Mother Jones reports that the impetus for this provision in NCLB stemmed from complaints from the military that up to 15% of the nation's high schools are "problem schools" for recruiters. In 1999, the Pentagon says, recruiters were denied access to schools on 19,228 occasions. Representative David Vitter, a Republican from Louisiana who sponsored the new recruitment requirement, says such schools "demonstrated an anti-military attitude that I thought was offensive" (Goodman, 2002).

Intensifying recruiting efforts, however, represents only one dimension of a much larger pattern of militarization in America's schools, particularly those serving working-class, poor, and non-White students. Neoliberal policies have dramatically increased the population of disposable youth who are marginalized from the economy and the political system. Rising youth poverty and unemployment targets not only working-class and poor students, but predominantly African American and Latino students. The neoconservative solution to the problem has entailed using militarization as a strategy for molding youth suffering grinding levels of poverty into obedient citizens.

As Pauline Lipman (2003) reports, Chicago Public Schools (CPS) "has established two public military high schools and expanded military programs in middle schools and neighborhood high schools" (p. 93). CPS located these schools in predominantly African American neighborhoods.

> Teachers wear military uniforms, and are called Captain.... In addition to the CPS Uniform Discipline Code, parents and students must sign a contract agreeing to obey the military discipline code with its own set of punishments for infractions of school rules and failure to complete school work (e.g., students must do push-ups, run laps, scrub walls). (Lipman, 2003, p. 93)

To enforce market principles of individualism, Lipman adds, "the schools teach competitive individualism and unquestioning obedience to a hierarchy of command" (Lipman, 2003, p. 94).

At Senn High School on Chicago's North Side, the newly formed Rickover Naval Academy functions as a magnet school skimming high-scoring minority students from other public schools around the city. These students learn subjects through a military curriculum while enduring a highly routinized and authoritarian day thoroughly at odds with democratic values of critical inquiry that links knowledge to questions of authority. The military academy was forced into one of Chicago's most culturally and linguistically diverse high schools, Senn, despite widespread opposition by teachers, parents, students, and local organizations.

Even nonmilitary schools in poor and predominantly minority neighborhoods are experiencing what Enora Brown (2003) describes as a "proliferation of JROTC (Junior Reserve Officers' Training Corps) programs" (p. 134). Brown quotes retired Rear General Eugene J. Carroll, deputy director of the Center of Defense Information, as stating the obvious: "It is appalling that the Pentagon is selling a military training program as a remedy for intractable social and economic problems in inner cities" (p. 135). As Howard Winant argues, U.S. militarism exploits working-class youth of color while it is financed by the attack on social programs that would otherwise be helping these same youth.

> The new imperialism has made a definite turn toward militarism as an instrument of global policy. Yet who does the fighting, and who pays for the war effort? The U.S. armed forces are predominantly composed of working-class youth. They are far more racially diverse than the higher (or even intermediate) reaches of the nation's occupational structure. While the upper-income and wealth-holding strata are doing their best to avoid taxation, they are leaving the burdens of financing military spending to the same working- and lower-middle-class families whose kids do the fighting. Simultaneously the Bush regime is hollowing out the social programs from which working-class and racially defined minorities most benefit: education, healthcare, housing, transportation, and childcare, not to mention welfare. (Winant, 2005, p. 127)

Winant's insight not only points to the fact that global war is inextricably woven with domestic policy, but also illustrates how neoliberal policies, designed to gut the caregiving role of the state, promote the punitive and repressive roles of the state.

While the Pentagon may be selling it as a remedy, advocates of neoliberal economic policies understand that no remedy is in sight for these youth. Otherwise, why would the rapidly growing and increasingly profitable prison industry use third-grade reading scores to project the number of prison cells needed within the ensuing 20 years? (Cappella & Bard, 2004, p. 1; New America Foundation, 2005). For this reason, we view these efforts to militarize schools as part of a broader program of "character education," defined best by Marvin Berlowitz and Nathan Long's description of JROTC's claim to impart leadership skills. "Manuals dealing with leadership," they report, "emphasize 'following the orders of those above you'" as their central message (Berlowitz & Long, 2003, p. 169). As an aide to President Bush told *New York Times* reporter Ron Suskind, "We're an empire now" (2004). So when Bush (2001) said shortly after his inauguration, "If this were a dictatorship, it'd be a heck of a lot easier, just so long as I'm the dictator," he was not kidding.

The militarization of schools can only be understood in relation to the broader cultural pedagogy of militarism and expanding authoritarianism that extends beyond formal educational institutions. Following September 11, 2001, the United States responded to terrorist attacks with a military response by declaring open-ended war not on an enemy nation-state but on terror — an instrument of fighting. Within this designation the enemy was an interchangeable constellation of ideologically incompatible entities: Al Qaeda, Stalinist North Korea, Islamist Iran, secular Syria, and Iraq. The declaration of endless war was symptomatic of a neoliberal denial of ideology that views the role of the United States as global enforcer of neoliberal globalization, and typifies the neoliberal denial of ideology and politics. Within this denial of ideology and politics, moralistic language of evil comes to replace meaningful debate over competing values and visions for the future. The enemy in the War on Terror is any regime or perspective that does not cohere with the singular version of capitalist democracy as expressed by the National Security Strategy of the United States. The "election" of the Bush administration in 2000 put in place a group of martial-minded crusaders whose hegemonist vision differed in strategy from that of the multilateralist neoliberals they replaced. The neoconservative hegemonists primed by the Project for a New American Century viewed the unipolar position of the United States following the collapse of the Soviet Union as an opportunity to expand U.S. power through the use of military force. Plans to invade Iraq began the moment the Bush administration came into the White House. September 11 provided an opportunity for the administration to trumpet the call to war by deceptively conflating the terrorist attacks with the fabricated threat of Iraq — a nation economically and militarily crippled by 12 years of sanctions and bombings since the end of the Gulf War. Some scholars have responded to these events by describing how the events consitute an overt grab for resources by an administration with deep ties to the oil industry. Others have emphasized the extent to which the crisis of neoblieral governance by the late 1990s left the U.S. hegemony with a weakened economic power and military power as its strong suite.

It is not only foreign policy that has been militarized. Mainstream publications such as the *New York Times* describe the Bush presidency as "imperial." Domestic policy has been transformed by dramatic expansion of the executive branch that has sought to undermine the constitution on the grounds of national security and the suspension of civil liberties and constitutional protections, including habeus corpus, protection from search and seizure, and privacy through such laws as the USA Patriot Act, made permanent in 2006. The executive branch has defied the Geneva convention and the constitution by inventing the prisoner-of-war designation "enemy combatant," holding suspects incommunicato and without leveling charges. The executive has secretly spied on the American people and lied about it, using the military apparatus to do so.

The militarization of civil society includes the militarization of culture as Jerry Harris describes:

Military culture has deep roots and influence. This covers everything from Civil War reenactments, movies, television, music, video games, comics, national mythology, toys, symbols, and dress. Much of this influence is indirect, simply affirming that evil exists in the world and that violence offers the best and quickest solution for security and safety. Other objects such as G.I. Joe action figures have specific and direct influence. Some of these cultural icons are used to quickly respond to political events. For example, Marvel's comic book her Captain America dresses in red, white, and blue and shortly after 9/11 was fighting terrorists lead by "Al-Tariq." Such mass popular culture helps maintain militarism as an embedded identity in U.S. society and can transform into widespread political support for aggressive policies during periods of crisis. (Harris, 2005, p. 150)

Militarism is clearly hostile to the development of a critical democratic public empowered to deliberate collectively over the future of culture, economics, and politics. The authoritarian aspects of current school reform, such as scripted lessons, standardized curriculum, high-stakes testing, and the myriad privatization initiatives that undermine public schooling, should be viewed as part of the broader crisis of democracy of which militarization is a central aspect. The struggle against militarization of society involves the struggle for public schools as places where democratic dispositions and social relations can be fostered.

REFERENCES

Berlowitz, M., & Long, N. (2003). The proliferation of JRTOC: Educational reform or militarization? In K. J. Saltman & D. A. Gabbard (Eds.), *Education as enforcement: The militarization and corporatization of schools.* New York: Routledge.

Brown, E. (2003). Freedom for some, discipline for others: The structure of inequity in education. In K. J. Saltman & D. A. Gabbard (Eds.), *Education as enforcement: The militarization and corporatization of schools.* New York: Routledge.

Bush, G. (2001). *Address to a joint session of Congress and the American People.* Retrieved January 17, 2006, from http://www.whitehouse.gov/news/releases/2001/09/20010920-8.html

Cappella, B. J., & Bard, G. E. (2004). *Project Flight Impact Statement.* Retrieved January 17, 2006, from http://www.nyking.org/Literacy/ProjectFlight_Impact_Abstract.pdf

Goodman, D. (2002, November/December). No child unrecruited. *Mother Jones.* Retrieved January 17, 2006, from http://www.motherjones.com/news/outfront/2002/11/ma_153_01.html

Harris, J. (2005). The military industrial complex in transnational class theory. In R. P. Appelbaum & W. I. Robinson (Eds.), *Critical globalization studies.* New York: Routledge.

Jehlen, A., & Winans, D. (2005). *No child left behind: Myth or truth?* National Education Association. Retrieved January 17, 2006, from http://www.nea.org/neatoday/0505/nclb.html

Lipman, P. (2003). Cracking down: Chicago school policy and the regulation of black and Latino youth. In K. J. Saltman & D. A. Gabbard (Eds.), *Education as enforcement: The militarization and corporatization of schools*. New York: Routledge.

New America Foundation. (2005). *Building a 21st century economy: The case for investing in early education reform*. Retrieved January 17, 2006, from http://www.newamerica.net/index.cfm?pg=event&EveID=527

Parsons, G. E. (2005). *How the Yellow ribbon became a national folk symbol*. The American Folklife Center. Retrieved January 17, 2006, from http://www.loc.gov/folklife/ribbons/ribbons.html

Suskind, R. (2004, October 17). Faith, certainty and the presidency of George W. Bush. *New York Times*. Retrieved May 9, 2007 from http://www.nytimes.com/2004/10/17/magazine/17BUSH.html?ex=1178856000&en=8006ed2 11522b41c&ei=5070

Winant, H. (2005). Globalization and racism: At home and abroad. In R. P. Appelbaum & W. I. Robinson (Eds.), *Critical globalization studies*. New York: Routledge.

ANTIEDUCATIONAL FOUNDATIONS: THE TRAP

Part III opens with the groundbreaking work of Philip Kovacs that reveals the too often hidden world of neoliberal think tanks, foundations, and institutes, that deploy neoconservative/Straussian techniques and a vast treasury of corporate funding in support of a national antischool movement that will ultimately, if the neoliberal/neoconservative agenda proves successful, effect transferring the management of schools from the public to private corporations. As Joel Spring explains, the agents of neoliberal conquest frequently "sell" this agenda to the public by using arguments stemming from the work of Milton Friedman, an intellectual icon within the circles of free-market fundamentalists. According to Friedman's argument, which he first articulated in the 1950s, improving the quality of education demands increasing competition among those institutions responsible for delivering it. This provides the ultimate rationale for privatizing schools, though George Schmidt and Ken Saltman provide ample evidence that neoliberalism's drive to transfer the management of schools from public hands to corporate hands is not guided by any altruistic concern for ensuring quality educational experiences for all American citizens. Schmidt's chapter on charter schools sheds an amazing light on how Bill Gates and other powerful players in Chicago's charter school movement have sold a false bill of goods to the public by offering up former private schools, now "charterized," serving affluent populations in affluent communities as the model of urban school reform. Meanwhile, carefully hidden from public view, charter schools in low-income and minority neighborhoods take on all the characteristics of authoritarian boot camps — hardly an approach amenable to celebratory ceremonies and public relations/propaganda campaigns. Schmidt's hard-hitting reporting from the front line in the struggle over public schools in Chicago confirms Saltman's contention that

> privatization is one of the most powerful tools of accumulation by dispossession, transforming publicly owned and controlled goods and services into private and restricted ones — the continuation of "enclosing the commons" begun in Tudor England. If neoliberalism came into crisis due to the excesses of capitalism (deregulation and liberalization yielding capital flight, de-industrialization, etc.), then the neoconservative response emphasizing control and order and reinvigorated overt state power makes a lot of sense not only for using state power to pillage productive forces for continued economic growth, but also to control populations through repression as inequalities of wealth and income are radically exacerbated, resulting in the expansion of a dual society of mobile professionals and everyone else.

As Marc Bousquet reports on how neoliberal principals have impacted life within our nation's colleges and universities, not even the hallowed halls of academia are immune from the spread of free-market fundamentalism. Bousquet's analysis gives us reason to wonder how long it will be before high-stakes testing, accountability, and other neoliberal/neoconservative measures of authoritarian control are imposed on college professors to stamp out their "liberal" bias that marks higher education as one of the last and strongest bastions of the threat of democracy. As Robert Bahruth helps us realize, we cannot separate the neoliberal/neoconservative assault on schools from the broader assault these convergence ideologies are registering on public life more generally. The assault on education represents one front in a larger war being waged against democracy and the Enlightenment principles and ideals upon which it rests. Privatizing schools will afford the plutocracy with a major victory in this struggle. Corporations already own and control the media. Controlling schools will allow them to control that much more of society's total information system, and that much more of the public mind.

Chapter 22

Think Tanks, Foundations, and Institutes

Philip Kovacs
University of Alabama–Huntsville

> The historical task and political purpose of neoconservatism would seem to be this: to convert the Republican party, and American conservatism in general, against their respective wills, into a new kind of conservative politics suitable to governing a modern democracy.
>
> **—Irving Kristol (2003)**

> ... the vast right-wing conspiracy has grown even more vast than liberals could imagine.
>
> **—Charles Krauthammer (2005)**

The neoconservative/neoliberal revolution is the evolving product of over 30 years worth of well-planned, well-funded, concentrated action. In terms of shaping policy and the world, both neoliberals and neoconservatives rely on think tanks, institutes, and foundations to make their ideological visions political reality, for these organizations provide funding, experts, research, connections, activists, advertisements, platforms, and staging grounds for the realization of their agendas. Central to both neoconservative and neoliberal agendas are U.S. public schools, which these ideologues see as sites for the creation of an efficient, malleable, hyperpatriotic workforce, capable of outpacing foreign competition for jobs in the postindustrial economy, but not critical enough to question power dynamics in either the United States or the world writ large.[1] It is in schools where these seemingly contradictory ideologies overlap, as neoliberalism, which requires constant surveillance and evidence of hard work and enterprise, "is ideally suited to the task of providing a mechanism for the neo-conservative attempts to specify what knowledge, values, and behaviors should be standardized and officially defined as 'legitimate'" (Apple, 2001, p. 416).[2]

FOUNDING FATHERS

The neoliberal/neoconservative think tanks, foundations, and institutes discussed in this chapter are best understood as advocacy organizations working together to reshape political landscapes to suit their ideological needs (see Rich, 2004).[3] Left-leaning think tanks, institutes, and foundations exist, but the far right has outspent them 3 to 1, using their money, connections, and influence more effectively (see Stefancic & Delgado, 1996, p. 142). "With resources that pale in comparison to centrist and liberal foundations, conservative funders have supported public policies that impact the entire nation" (Krehely, House, & Kernan, 2004, p. 4). While these conservative funders have given generously to shaping policy in numerous areas, the re-creation of America's educational landscape, from kindergarten through college, has been a goal of these organizations since their inception (Krehely, House, & Kernan, 2004, p. 9). Today, education receives a significant portion of their attention, with institutes like the Heritage Foundation, the American Enterprise Institute, and the Manhattan Institute spending millions annually to reshape America's schools (see Kovacs & Boyles, 2005).

In the decade following the defeat of Barry Goldwater, members of the far right reacted to what they perceived to be a growing threat, coordinated by a liberal intelligentsia, to the American way of life. Two individuals in particular, future Supreme Court Justice Lewis Powell and former Treasury Secretary William Simon, galvanized corporate leaders, wealthy philanthropists, and disaffected politicians, leading to the creation of what is today a well-oiled, well-funded network of organizations involved in all levels of policy creation and implementation. As part of a larger antischool movement (discussed Chapter 23), these organizations provide funding for research, the research itself, talking points, court briefs, and capital for selling "choice" to the American public.

Powell, concerned about college campuses, the media, academic journals, and the arts and sciences, circulated a memo detailing strategies for dealing with university-based "communists" and "new leftists," whom he believed to be destroying America (Johnson & Salle, 2004, p. 19). His suggestions for eliminating the growing threat included placing conservative scholars within universities, evaluating textbooks to make sure America was portrayed positively, using the media to advance conservative ideology, publishing in both popular and scholarly journals, and becoming active in courts at all levels of government (Krehely et al., 2004, p. 9). Following Powell's lead, William Simon, director of the ultraconservative John M. Olin Foundation, sought out business leaders and philanthropists to support and finance a "counterintelligentsia" that would stop the activities of "leftist" universities, which he considered to be dens of socialism and threats to the free market (see Spring, 2001, pp. 37–38). "The alliance between theorists and men of action in the capitalist world is long overdue," wrote Simon, who believed that there was "nothing more crucial" than funding intellectuals and writers fighting for capitalism (Simon, quoted in Spring, 2006, p. 209).

A core group of ultraconservative funders answered their calls, and today a handful of conservative foundations direct money to over 500 organizations nationwide (Johnson & Salle, 2004, p. 20). Between the years of 1999 and 2001 alone, conservative donors gave conservative think tanks, institutes, and foundations over $26 million targeted specifically toward shaping educational policy in the United States (Krehely et al., 2004, p. 22).[4]

CHANGING HEARTS AND MINDS

A significant portion of foundation money goes to the creation and dissemination of research supporting far-right ideology, and conservative funders give generously to think tanks, advocacy groups, and universities (both public and private) for their work. The Richard and Helen DeVos Foundation funds a number of academic organizations and universities, including the Intercollegiate Studies Institute, the Leadership Institute, and Calvin College; the DeVos Foundation also helped fund a new College of Education at Lee University (Krehely et al., 2004, p. 60, all of Appendix D). The Bradley Foundation funds conservative programs that include a Bradley Graduate and Post Graduate Fellowship Program as well as grants to the University of Chicago, Harvard, Marquette, and the University of Rochester. Additionally, Bradley funds the Collegiate Network, created to allow conservative ideologues to publish outside of the university presses, without university funding (Krehely et al., 2004, pp. 64–65). The Koch foundation (the same family that founded the Cato Institute) gave George Mason University over $23 million between 1985 and 2002 (Krehely et al., 2004, p. 65).

The John M. Olin Foundation alone has been responsible for millions of dollars worth of grants to a variety of universities and think tanks. The foundation gave four grants to Chubb and Moe (funneled through the Wisconsin Policy Institute and the Brookings Institution) for their work *Politics, Markets, and Schools,* a book claiming school privatization would better serve America (see Smith, Fey, Heinecke, Miller-Kahn, & Noble, 2003, p. 200). Additionally, the foundation gave Harvard's Paul E. Peterson

$850,000; Diane Ravitch received 17 grants totaling $2,100,650 (funneled through Columbia and New York Universities); and Chester Finn, while working at Vanderbilt University, the Hudson Institute, George Washington University, and the Manhattan Institute, received 10 grants totaling $961,000 (Smith et al., 2003).

Chester Finn, now head of the Thomas B. Fordham Foundation, a neoconservative, single-issue think tank currently operating a group of charter schools in Dayton, OH, deserves some extra attention (see Educational Excellence, 2004). The takeover of public schools by a private foundation is nothing short of a coup for the neoconservative/neoliberal movement as Finn achieves several shared goals at once. Democratically elected school boards, which Finn refers to as "worse than dinosaurs," are circumvented, and control of finances and hiring now lies with Fordham appointees (see Gehring, 2003). Given the right's constant refrain that teacher colleges and teachers are primarily responsible for the failure of U.S. schools, the ability to hire whomever they wish, credentialed or not, is another clear victory (see Moe, 2003; Hess, 2003). Finn's associates also control the schools' curricula, which, given Finn's defense of No Child Left Behind, can ignore issues of democracy and community in favor of creating hyperproductive knowledge workers (see Kovacs & Boyles, 2005). One may safely assume that Fordham reports such as *Terrorists, Despots, and Democracy: What Our Children Need to Know* also influence Dayton's children. This report, in addition to espousing a one-dimensional, narrow perspective of teaching American history, includes essays written by conservative scholars and politicians, including professor E. D. Hirsch and former Secretary of Education Lamar Alexander. The latter advocates forcing children to take oaths of allegiance, where they "agree to bear arms on behalf of the United States when required by the law" (Alexander, 2003).

Fordham's "in-house" scholarship indicates a major problem with most think-tank-sponsored research: The findings, bought and paid for, merely reveal what the contractors already know to be true. In a study of charter schools, for example, Fordham researcher Terry Ryan (2004) found that Dayton students attending charter schools outperformed students in district schools, performing "at a higher level in 2004 on every subject tested by state proficiency tests in grades 4 and 6." The nonpartisan National Assessment of Educational Progress (NAEP), in a nonpartisan national study, found no difference in scores, except for in mathematics, where charter schools performed at a lower level (see NAEP, 2004). Ryan's findings make perfect sense, given Fordham's heavy investment in Dayton's charter schools (see Kovacs & Boyles, 2005). No matter how objective, rational, or scientific think-tank-sponsored research appears to be, the research, bought and paid for by political ideologues, undermines any possibility of objective or scientifically based scholarship. Further reducing the credibility of foundation-purchased research is the suppression of research that does not suit their needs (see Wilmer & Vredenburg, 2003).[5]

Foundation-sponsored research is analogous to having a lawyer on retention. You know the lawyer is on your side; she has a number of "facts" and a large research staff to back her up, and she knows what information to leave out of her case, which is prepared before the opposition even knows what is going on. Most importantly, you know you can trust her because you pay her. Prepurchased research, questionable or misrepresented findings, and suppressed dissent help conservative scholars make a case for educational reform efforts ranging from replacing teachers and administrators with automatons to eliminating public education all together.

GETTING THE MESSAGE OUT

Neoconservative/neoliberal think tanks, foundations, and institutes have created a political infrastructure and network that allows for rapid dissemination of their research and ideology, giving these organizations the ability to influence policy at local, state, and national levels. While Chester Finn used his foundation to help him gain control of schools in Dayton, OH, parents in Boulder, CO, called on state and national support to help them pass pro-school choice initiatives in their community (Smith et al., 2003, pp. 86–93). When they knew they did not have enough votes to win, they switched their efforts to creating charter schools, and "advocates showered legislators with papers and briefs put out by various foundations and think tanks. They pushed newspapers to promote the values of choice [and] they sponsored a Charter School conference designed to win over enough legislators to pass the bill" (Smith et al., 2003, p. 96). When the state of Georgia decided to rewrite its history standards, the board of education hired Diane Ravitch as a consultant (see Manzo, 2004). The Walton Family Foundation, funded by the fortunes of Wal-Mart, generously supports a broad variety of initiatives at local levels, funding organizations in communities across the country. In 2003 the Florida School Choice Fund received $1,383,585, Floridians for School Choice received $337,750, the Knowledge is Power Program (KIPP) received over $300,000, and charter schools across America received well over $4.4 million.[6]

Think tanks are even more active, and arguably more influential, at the federal level, providing scholars for testimony before the House, Senate, and Supreme Court. Newt Gingrich, for example, represented the American Enterprise Institute, testifying before the Senate that failing to increase math and science scores was a national security threat second only to the detonation of an atomic bomb (see Gingrich, 2002). Krista Kafer of the Heritage Foundation spoke before the House Budget Committee Democratic Caucus, using think-tank-sponsored research to support her claim that an increase in funding will not help U.S. education (see Kafer, 2003). John Boehner (R-OH), chairman of the House Committee on Education and the

Workforce, used a Manhattan Institute "working paper" to attack "left-wing" criticism of No Child Left Behind (see Committee on Education and the Workforce, 2004). The author of that study, J. P. Greene, was cited four times in the Supreme Court's *Zelman v. Simmons-Harris* school voucher decision, which declared vouchers used at Catholic schools to be constitutional.

In addition to being well connected to political players, think tanks, foundations, and institutes are aggressive marketers, making sure their work finds its way into the mainstream media as well as a number of magazines and journals. "I make no bones about marketing," declared William Baroody of the American Enterprise Institute, "we pay as much attention to the dissemination of product as to the content" (cited by Spivak, 2005). The result of the right's focused attention is a "message amplification infrastructure [that] has a broad reach, repeating coordinated strategic messages through multiple communication channels" (see Johnson & Salle, 2004, p. 29). These channels include "conservative talk radio, Fox News, Internet sites like the Drudge Report, op-ed pieces in newspapers across the country, prefab letters-to-the-editor, books, pundits and columnists, talking points distributed to politicians and public speakers, advertisements, and newspapers such as *The Washington Times* and *The Wall Street Journal*" (Johnson & Salle, 2004, p. 39). Conservative-run magazines such as *Commentary*, *The Weekly Standard*, *City Journal*, and *Insight* provide further avenues for publication (see Alterman, 2005). Thanks in part to this vast infrastructure, the Manhattan Institute's J. P. Greene claims to have been cited on television, radio, or in print over 500 times in one year alone (see Cavanagh, 2004). That figure should not be too surprising, as think tank scholars are fond of (1) citing each other's work repeatedly in order to give their research the perception of credibility and (2) publishing the exact same article, word for word, in numerous venues at once (see Kovacs & Boyles, 2005; Johnson & Salle, 2004, p. 27).

The results of this well-financed media flooding are initially two-fold. First and foremost, the repetition of themes such as "the schools are failing" results in Americans buying into the argument regardless of whether it is valid. Story after story in newspapers and editorial after editorial on Fox News are bound to rub off on people, even if they live in neighborhoods with exceptional schools (see Kohn, 2004; Herman & Chomsky, 2002). The second result is that academics invested in using schools as sites for the creation and maintenance of a more democratic social order are kept on the defensive, having to respond to the charges of the right rather than explore new possibilities for U.S. schools. Constantly playing defense to the activities of the right allows neoconservative/neoliberal ideologues to frame educational debate, inhibiting discussion of more democratic educational discourse. "The very categories themselves — markets, choice, national curricula, national testing, standards — bring the debate onto the terrain established by neo-liberals and neo-conservatives. The analysis of 'what is' has led to a neglect off 'what might be'" (Apple, 2004, p. 40).

WHAT IS AND WHAT MIGHT BE

"Undoubtedly, conservative values, goals, ideas and ideals have become the norm in United States politics. It would be difficult to argue that the political right is not winning in this country, as it dominates at all levels and branches of government" (Krehely et al., 2004, p. 3). Neoconservative/neoliberal think tanks, foundations, and institutes have been instrumental in creating the "what is" in public education today. Recall Powell and Simon's goals for altering America's political landscape: (1) place conservative scholars in universities; (2) set up a counterintelligentsia to challenge leftist universities; (3) monitor textbooks to make certain America is portrayed in the best light; (4) use the media to frame and forward debate; (5) publish in scholarly and mainstream journals; and (6) become active in courts at all levels of government.

Each of these goals continues to be met, and in the field of educational policy, neoliberals and neoconservatives dominate agenda setting. Millions of dollars from conservative foundations go directly (and indirectly) to conservative scholars in both public and private institutions, effectively buying legitimacy for conservative causes. These researchers generate study after study to be used by activists and politicians at local, state, and federal levels. Thanks to the work of foundation-sponsored scholars like Diane Ravitch, E. D. Hirsch, William Bennett, Chester Finn, and the late Alan Bloom, as well as institutes and organizations scattered across America, U.S. textbooks have not only been monitored for pro-American bias, but they have been manufactured to engender certain ideological beliefs about America's past, present, and future.[7] The right effectively uses the mainstream media, as well as private and scholarly journals, to forward their neoliberal and neoconservative agendas. And if readers are to believe scholars like Joel Spring and Jonathan Kozol, the courts have been effectively used to undue 50 years' worth of desegregation efforts (see Spring, 2006, Chap. 3; Kozol, 2005).

Neoconservatives and neoliberals have manufactured the "what is" in educational policy today, a myopic focus on raising ideologically based standards with no mention of the development of a critical and engaged citizenry. Undoing their doings, the envisioning and realization of "what might be" will require efforts from the left similar to those of this power bloc. Making scholarship more accessible to the public, through publishing in more mainstream presses, visiting local PTAs, speaking with the media and political representatives, and directly challenging the right's propaganda campaign must occur immediately, in order to (1) counter the misinformation forwarded by neoconservative and neoliberal ideologues and (2) take the offense in terms of framing U.S. educational debate. While these are small, initial steps, they are essential for creating coalitions for challenging the think-tank-sponsored, neoliberal/neoconservative assault on U.S. public education in particular and on global democracy in general.

NOTES

1. For thorough treatments of the history and activities of these organizations, see Krehely, House, and Kernan (2004), Johnson and Salle (2004), Abelson (2002), and Rich (2004).
2. A full examination of the ways neoconservatives and neoliberals work together to form what Apple calls power blocks lies beyond the scope of this chapter. For more, see Apple (2004), Hursh (2001), and Giroux (2005).
3. These terms can generally be used interchangeably, as some foundations act as think tanks, and technically, both foundations and think tanks are institutions.
4. Krehely et al. (2004). The authors of the report estimate the figure to be much higher. My own search on Media Transparency's engine resulted in 3,135 grants under the term *education* for fiscal year 2003. The total sum of grants with the term *education* was $321,668,432. See www.mediatransparency. com. Given the amount of outside influence in U.S. schools, some question whether the term *public* should even be used (see Boyles, forthcoming).
5. They contend that the Fordham Foundation dismissed their research because it did not support the foundation's claim that charter schools outperformed other public schools.
6. These figures were obtained from Media Transparency's search engine. Retrieved September 9, 2005, from www.mediatransparency.com
7. Diane Ravitch recently received $10,000 (from the Hoover Institution) for her efforts in policing America's textbooks (see Hoover Institution, 2005).

REFERENCES

Abelson, D. E. (2002). *Do think tanks matter?* Montreal: McGill-Queen's University Press.

Alexander, L. (2003). Seven questions about September 11. In J. Agresto et al. (Eds.), *Terrorists, despots, and democracy: What our children need to know* (p. 44). Retrieved September 17, 2005, from http://www.edexcellence.net/foundation/publication/publication.cfm?id=316

Alterman, E. (2005). Neoconning the media: A very short history of neoconservatism. Retrieved September 17, 2005, from http://www.mediatransparency.org/story.php?storyID=2

Apple, M. W. (2001). Comparing neoliberal projects and inequality in education. *Comparative Education, 37,* 4.

Apple, M. W. (2004). Creating difference: Neo-liberalism, neo-conservatism and the politics of educational reform. *Educational Policy, 18,* 1.

Boyles, D. (2007). Already privatized: "Public" schools, privatization, and the public/private distinction. In S. Tozer & B. Guillegos (Eds.), *Handbook for the social foundations of education.*

Cavanagh, S. (2004, October 13). Greene machine. *Education Week.* Retrieved December 15, 2004, from www.edweek.org/ew/articles/2004/10/13/07jaygreene.h24.html

Committee on Education and the Workforce. (2004). New report debunks NEA-MoveOn.org excuses for poor school performance; Proves high standards are key to closing achievement gaps in education. Retrieved November 9, 2004, from http://edworkforce.house.gov/press/press108/second/09sept/nclb090904.htm

Educational Excellence. (2004). Thomas B. Fordham Foundation to sponsor charter schools in Dayton. Retrieved December 13, 2004, from www.edexcellence.net/foundation/about/press _release.cfm?id=11

Gehring, J. (2003, October 29). Essential or obsolete? Panel debates value, role of school boards. *Education Week.* Retrieved December 13, 2004, from www.edweek.org/ew/articles/2003/10/29/09board note.h23.html

Gingrich, N. (2002). We must expand our investment in science. Testimony before the Senate Committee on Commerce, Science, and Transportation. Retrieved November 9, 2004, from www.aei.org/include/news_ print.asp?newsID=15562

Giroux, H. A. (2005, Winter). The terror of neoliberalism: Rethinking the significance of cultural politics. *College Literature, 32,* 1.

Herman, E. S., & Chomsky, N. (2002). *Manufacturing consent.* New York: Pantheon Books.

Hess, F. M. (2003). Refining or retreating? High-stakes accountability in the states. In P. E. Peterson & M. R. West (Eds.), *No Child Left Behind? The politics and practice of school accountability.* Washington, DC: Brookings.

Hoover Institution. (2005). The Language Police by Diane Ravitch wins Hoover Institution's 2004 Uncommon Book Award. Retrieved September 17, 2005, from www.hoover.stanford.edu/pubaffairs/releases/2005/09ravitch.htm

Hursh, D. (2001). Neoliberalism and the control of teachers, students, and learning: The rise of standards, standardization, and accountability. Retrieved August 23, 2005, from www.eserver.org/clogic/4-1/hursh.html

Johnson, D. C., & Salle, L. M. (2004). Responding to the attack on public education and teacher unions. Menlo Park, CA: Commonweal Institute. Retrieved September 17, 2005, from www.commonwealinstitute.org

Kafer, K. (2003). The promise of No Child Left Behind. Testimony before the House Budget Committee Democratic Caucus, Senate Democratic Policy Committee. Retrieved November 9, 2004, from www.heritage.org/Research/Education/tst071703.cfm

Kohn, A. (2004). Test today, privatize tomorrow. *Education Digest, 70,* 20.

Kovacs, P., & Boyles, D. (2005). Think tanks, institutes, and foundations: Neoconservative influence on public schools. *Public Resistance, 1,* 1. Retrieved August 25, 2005, from www.publicresistance.org

Kozol, J. (2005). *The shame of the nation: The restoration of apartheid schooling in America.* New York: Crown.

Krauthammer, C. (2005). The neoconservative convergence. *Commentary, 120,* 1. Retrieved September 17, 2005, from www.frontpagemag.com/Articles/ReadArticle.asp?ID=18654

Krehely, J., House, M., & Kernan, E. (2004). Axis of ideology: Conservative foundations and public policy. National Committee for Responsive Philanthropy. Retrieved September 17, 2005, from www.ncrp.org

Kristol, I. (2003). The neoconservative persuasion. *The Weekly Standard, 8*, No. 47. Retrieved September 17, 2005, from www.weeklystandard.com/Content/ Public/Articles/000/000/003/000tzmlw.asp

Manzo, K. K. (2004, February 18). Ga. history plan stirs civil war fuss. *Education Week.* Retrieved September 17, 2005, from http://www.edweek.org/ ew/articles/2004/02/18/23civil.h23.html?querystring=ga%20history%20 plan%20stirs%20civil%20war%20fuss

Moe, T. M. (2003). Politics, control, and the future of school accountability. In P. E. Peterson & M. R. West (Eds.), *No Child Left Behind? The politics and practice of school accountability.* Washington, DC: Brookings.

National Assessment of Educational Progress. (2004). America's charter schools: Results from the NAEP 2003 pilot study. Retrieved January 9, 2005, from http://nces.ed.gov/nationsreportcard/pdf/studies/2005456.pdf

Rich, A. (2004). *Think tanks, public policy, and the politics of expertise.* Cambridge: Cambridge University Press.

Ryan, T. (2004). How are Dayton's charter schools doing? Retrieved January 9, 2005, from www.edexcellence.net/institute/publication/publication.cfm?id=334

Smith, M. L., Fey, P., Heinecke, W., Miller-Kahn, L., & Noble, A. (2003). *Political spectacle and the fate of American schools.* New York: Routledge/Falmer.

Spivak, L. (2005). The conservative marketing machine. Alternet. Retrieved January 15, 2005, from www.alternet.org/mediaculture/20946/

Spring, J. (2001). *Political agendas for education: From the Christian coalition to the religious right* (2nd ed.). Mahwah, NJ: Lawrence Erlbaum.

Spring, J. (2006). *American education* (12th ed.). New York: McGraw-Hill.

Stefancic, J. & Delgado, R. (1996). No mercy: *How conservative think tanks and foundations changed America's social agenda.* Philadelphia: Temple University Press.

Wilmer, J., & Vredenburg, D. (2003, October 29–November 2). When ideology sabotages the truth. Paper presented at American Educational Studies Association, Mexico City, Mexico.

Chapter 23

The Anti-School Movement

Philip Kovacs
University of Alabama–Huntsville

The Anti-School Movement (ASM) needs to be understood as a movement to control what and how American students learn. A broad coalition of individuals, alliances, corporations, foundations, and religious groups working alone and collectively to privatize public education, the ASM uses financial, social, and political capital to shape America's educational landscape according to its often overlapping needs. Since the needs of these ideologues are determined and met before a student even enters a classroom, the ASM can also be understood as an antivoice movement.

In public schools, and in the private, charter, and for-profit schools replacing them, standards shape students in particular ways regardless of who that student is or who that student might wish to become. Students, teachers, and, by default, communities have dwindling opportunities for engaging with subjects and pursuits that humanize, as revealed by decreased time allowed for music, art, play, exploration of self and other, innovation, creativity, reflection, debate, and the selection of goals, issues, and possibilities. If democracy requires collective participation in the institutions that shape our lives, then the ASM, and the privatization schemes that fall under its mantra of "choice," must also be understood as an antidemocracy movement, as the privatization of public education eliminates the possibility for citizens and communities to influence school goals. While parents can choose, their choice will ultimately be limited to schools sanctioned by corporate, and oftentimes fundamentalist, America.

The ASM contains elements of both neoliberal and neoconservative ideologies. Neoliberals seek to create educational systems suited to increasing economic productivity. Measuring productivity requires controlled conditions and repeated assessments, which exist today in the form of schools operating under multiple testing regimes. Neoliberals use these tests to claim schools are failing in a variety of ways. School failure, according to long-standing neoliberal logic, will result in America's loss of dominance in the global marketplace, a refrain kept alive since the early 1980s when the Reagan administration used *A Nation at Risk* to scare Americans into educational reform (see Gabbard, 2003 and 2004). The real irony behind the claim today is the World Economic Forum's research, which ranked America number one in global competitiveness for 2004 (see Bracey, 2005).

Neoliberals believe that embracing free-market reforms will save America's schools. Embarking on multiple media and political campaigns to color all schools failures (facilitated by a federal program that recently branded one of three American schools as failing [see Neill, Guisbond, & Schaeffer, 2004]), neoliberal educational "reformers" argue that parental choice will result in the best schools succeeding. Parents, informed through objective test scores, can select which schools they wish to support, thus determining which schools survive in the market. In order to create conditions suitable to an educational market, neoliberal educational reformers have funded various antischool initiatives such as vouchers, charters, and for-profit schools. Despite their rhetoric about the "free" market, neoliberals need a strong state to create and regulate markets. Neoliberal reformers have been successful at using the state to meet their demands, working with local, state, and federal judicial and legislative bodies to force privatization on citizens who are, by most accounts, happy with their schools (see Phi Delta Kappa/Gallup Poll, 2005). Once the market replaces the public, according to neoliberal reformers, the best schools, those with the highest test scores, will force the worst schools to shut down, and every American child will get a high-quality education, allowing America to retain its status as a global economic superpower.

Neoconservatives, like neoliberals, seek to use public schools to keep America leader of the free world. But while neoliberals focus on the economic function of schools, neoconservatives focus on moral and social issues. Neoconservatives believe America has lost its moral compass and that focusing on a common culture and hard work will return American society to the happy days before the culture wars, a time when, apparently, there were no problems with schools because everyone was working hard and attending church. Ignoring issues like class size, crumbling buildings, health care, funding, and a growing poverty rate, neoconservatives believe the problems with schools are the students, teachers, and administrators. Using terms like *mean accountability* and *coercive reform*, neoconservative educational reformers seek to replace teachers and administrators with individuals willing to indoctrinate students into particular ways of knowing (see Hess, 2003).

While neoconservatives favor increased federal involvement in local schools, seeking to regulate behavior and ways of knowing, they also favor privatization initiatives. Neoliberals seek the creation of an education market; neoconservative religious organizations seek money for their denominations. Neoconservatives heavily fund the voucher movement, as private religious schools stand to benefit most from the initiative (see People for the American Way, 2003). In Cleveland, for example, 97% of students using vouchers attend a church-affiliated school; 67% of Cleveland voucher money goes to Catholic schools specifically (Bracey, 2004, p. xi).

Evidence of both ideologies undergirds the No Child Left Behind Act (NCLB), which represents efforts by neoconservatives and neoliberals to reform and ultimately privatize public education. The legislation (1) regulates knowledge and meaning according to market and ideological demands, (2) provides participants for a competitive educational market by forcing failing schools to become charters or for-profits, and (3) directs public money to private corporations, organizations, and alliances in order to further undermine public education. Recall that both neoconservatives and neoliberals require a strong, regulatory state; neoconservatives need the state to reinforce norms of belief and ethics, and neoliberals need the state to regulate markets and mold the workforce according to market demands. NCLB, with its focus on standards, accountability, choice, and competition, serves both ends. As NCLB silences individual need and voice, turning public schools over to private alliances (either in curricular control or via outright privatization), the act must be understood as antischool, antivoice, and antidemocracy.

WHO IS THE ASM?

Members of the ASM include any organization, alliance, or individual working to undermine public education through choice initiatives. Foundations that provide millions of dollars annually to support privatization schemes, such as the Lynde and Harry Bradley Foundation, the Broad Foundation, the Adoph Coors Foundation, the Scaife Family Foundation, the John M. Olin Foundation, and the Walton Family Foundation, are part of the ASM (see Krehely, House, & Keran, 2004; Johnson & Salle, 2004). Think tanks, which produce and peddle policy, are part of the ASM. These include, but are not limited to, the Heritage Foundation, the Evergreen Freedom Foundation, the American Enterprise Institute, the Manhattan Institute, the Hoover Foundation, the Hudson Institute, the Thomas B. Fordham Institute, and the Heartland Institute. Various corporate alliances, such as Achieve and the Business Roundtable, which bring legislators and business leaders together to bash public schools, are part of the ASM (see Kovacs, 2005). The American Legislative Exchange Council, which delivers prefabricated privatization bills to legislators across the country, is part of the ASM. The Black Alliance for Educational Options, funded by the same neoconservatives who paid for *The Bell Curve*, is part of the ASM (see Black Commentator, 2002a). Reporters who produce work under the guise of objective journalism while at the same time parroting neoconservative scholars are part of the ASM (see Williams, 2005). Radio personalities who continuously attack public schools are part of the ASM. The Edison School Project and its attempt to make a profit from schools nationwide is part of the ASM. NCLB and its reliance on the market represents efforts by members of the ASM to open the door for private companies to run failing schools. Therefore, the federal government, under the current administration, is part of the ASM.

BRADLEY: ONE OF MANY

Essentially, members of the ASM use money, connections, and power to undermine confidence in public schools, ultimately seeking to end public education altogether. The ASM undermines public confidence through repeated attacks on schools, teachers, administrators, unions, and colleges of education; through the generation, transmission, and amplification of ideologically biased research; and with the use of propaganda, occasionally paid for by the public. The Lynde and Harry Bradley Foundation is one organization that makes all of these activities possible, giving large sums of money to alliances and individuals working to privatize schools. With total assets for 2004 topping $706,000,000, the Bradley Foundation can ensure its ideology thrives throughout the country (see Bradley Foundation, 2004). In 2004 alone, the Bradley Foundation spent nearly $7 million building intellectual infrastructure, money spent "to strengthen institutions and individuals which contribute to the nurturing of those ideas that form the cornerstone of our intellectual, cultural, and economic way of life" (Bradley Foundation, 2004, p. 25). The cornerstone is free-market capitalism, something public schools, according to neoliberals and neoconservatives, threaten.

Taking a closer look at how and where the Bradley Foundation operates proves instructive for understanding the network of organizations, individuals, and alliances constituting the ASM. One place to start is Marquette University's Institute for the Transformation of Learning (ITL). Since 1996 Bradley grants to ITL have topped $2 million, including $250,000 in 2004 alone.[1] Founded by Howard Fuller, a former superintendent of Milwaukee Public Schools, the ITL acts as a charter school incubator, providing research and developmental support for individuals and organizations seeking to start their own charter schools. ITL's research is indicative of most research conducted by members of the ASM, as it draws conclusions that, magically, support privatization initiatives. Relying heavily on the work of think-tank-housed researchers like the Manhattan Institute's

J. P. Greene, Gerard Robinson concludes ITL's "Survey of School Choice Research" with the assertion that school choice "improves academic performance, increases parent satisfaction and involvement, and appear[s] to have a positive impact on student achievement in public schools" (Robinson, 2005). There are, obviously, a number of researchers who argue otherwise (see Bracey, 2004).

Members of the ASM take biased research and use a well-funded message amplification system to broadcast their "science-based" research all over the country, framing the debate over school reform in ways favorable to privatization (see Haas, 2004). The Bradley Foundation helps keep the message amplification system fully operational, giving generously to various organizations in support of its media campaigns. One such organization is the Encounter for Culture and Education, "a tax-exempt, non-profit corporation dedicated to strengthening the marketplace of ideas and engaging in educational activities to help preserve democratic culture," which helps "preserve democratic culture" by publishing works such as J. Martin Rochester's *Class Warfare: Besieged Schools, Bewildered Parents, Betrayed Kids and the Attack on Excellence*, Myron Lieberman's *The Teacher Unions: How They Sabotage Educational Reform and Why*, Sandra Stotsky's *Losing Our Language: How Multiculturalism Undermines Our Children's Ability to Read, Write and Reason*, and Sol Stern's *Breaking Free: Public School Lessons and the Imperative of School Choice.*[2]

The neoconservative Heartland Institute, publisher of *School Reform News*, also benefits from Bradley grants, which allow the organization to disseminate pro-school choice propaganda all over the nation. Joseph L. Bast, president of Heartland, recently edited *Public Schools, Public Menace: How Public Schools Lie to Parents and Betray Our Children*, a polemic that misrepresents the past and present in its attempt to scare parents into taking their children out of public schools. Chapters include section headings like "Sexual Corruption of Children in Public Schools," "Turning Children Into Spies Against Their Parents," "Anti-Judeo-Christian Values," and "Pagan Religions in the Public Schools" (Turtel, 2005). The book, according to radio personality Dr. Laura Schlessinger, "is a must-read for every parent." She explains: "It is sad but true that the public school system in America threatens the values of families and the welfare of students. It is for that reason that Dr. James Dobson [of the ultraconservative Focus on the Family] and I urge parents to take their children out of public school...." (Turtel, 2005).

A more nonsecular attack on schools comes from individuals like Frederick M. Hess of the American Enterprise Institute and Terry M. Moe of the Hoover Institute; both institutes receive Bradley funding (see Moe, 2003; Hess, 2005). Hess and Moe believe schools fail because of the teachers and administrators within them (see Moe, 2003). According to Moe, schools suffer from a problem of "adverse selection." "They have not only attracted certain types of people to work for the school system," argues Moe, "but have actually attracted the *wrong* types and repelled the right types" (Moe, 2003, p. 84). Hess defines the *right* type of teachers; they are the ones willing to "teach the content and skills mandated by the state [or the private company running the school], regardless of their personal preferences" (Hess, 2003, p. 84). Since colleges of education produce the wrong type of teacher, members of the ASM seek to circumvent the institution, allowing anyone to teach in charter, for-profit, or private schools. Former Secretary of Education Rod "the NEA is a terrorist organization" Paige, another recipient of Bradley support, celebrated NCLB because the legislation "gives the green light to states that want to lower barriers to the teaching profession" (Finn, 2003). Here Paige is not only antischool, but also antilearning, as numerous researchers have argued for the importance of teacher colleges in helping to produce individuals capable of not only increasing achievement, but also building a more participatory democracy (see Darling-Hammond, 2002).[3]

Political connections are essential for the ASM, and the Bradley Foundation has done its part to influence policy makers nationwide. The American Legislative Exchange Council (ALEC), for example, received nearly a quarter of a million dollars from Bradley in the late 1980s and early 1990s.[4] Today, ALEC actively campaigns for privatization, offering publications and prefabricated bills in order to "help lawmakers fashion highly effective, constitutionally sound school choice legislation in their state" (Enlow & Ladner, 2005). In September 2005, ALEC hosted a two-day conference for legislators from 24 states. The press release is worth quoting at length:

> The legislators joined policy advisors and school choice experts for a full day of seminars on current school choice programs, litigation strategies, research conclusions, and successful policy development. The goal was to identify the facts and myths surrounding school choice issues and to provide lawmakers with the information and tools needed to successfully advance education options across the nation. (Drummer, 2005)

Present at the conference to discuss the "facts and myths" was the leader of the Alliance for School Choice, an organization that considers itself to be "the nation's vanguard organization for promoting, implementing and enhancing K-12 educational choice."[5] In January 2005, the alliance helped ALEC send model choice legislation to over 3,000 legislators across the country.[6]

In addition to supporting colleges, institutes, scholars, journals, privatizers, and politicians, the Bradley Foundation has given generously (over $2 million since 2000) to the Black Alliance for Educational Options (BAEO), an organization created to sell school choice initiatives to the African American community (see Black Commentator, 2002b). The chair of the organization, Howard Fuller, is also the head of the Institute for the

Transformation of Learning, which reveals a great deal about the incestuousness of the ASM. Individuals like Fuller might sit on six or seven different councils all funded by similar organizations with identical ideologies and missions, making the Anti-School Movement's "experts" look more impressive than they actually are. Fuller, married to the CCO of Edison Schools, also sits on the board of directors of Advocates for School Choice, the sister organization of the Alliance for School Choice. As Tom Siebold argues, the cloning of think tanks and organizations, the use of university space and prestige, and the subsequent manufacturing of experts helps buy credibility for the ASM, in this particular case making Fuller's BAEO look like more than it actually is, a neoconservative/neoliberal attempt to mislead black voters (see Siebold, 2005).

The BAEO has also received tax dollars; in 2002 the Department of Education gave the organization $600,000. Then Undersecretary of Education Gene Hickok (formerly a Bradley fellow at the Heritage Foundation) explained the purpose of the grant: "We want to change the conversation about parental choice by *positively influencing individuals who are resisting* parental choice options and get them to reconsider their outlook" (see Black Commentator, 2002a). This "full scale media campaign," according to the Department of Education's press release, "will use direct mail, television, radio, newspapers, the Internet and door-to-door visits" (see U.S. Department of Education, 2002). Essentially, tax dollars were spent on a media campaign for privatizing schools. Hickok, it should be noted, has also been accused of "positively influencing individuals" by withholding reports, commissioned by his own office, that are critical of charter schools. The *New York Times* had to use the Freedom of Information Act to gain access to one such report (Bracey, 2005).

In addition to funding the BAEO, the Bush administration attempted to positively influence individuals through the use of paid journalists, as was the case with black commentator Armstrong Williams. Williams, one of the founding directors for BAEO, received $240,000 to support NCLB, legislation that relies on choice for school improvement (Toppo, 2005). William's payment was part of a $1.3 million contract given to Ketchum Public Relations, and Ketchum's payment was part of a much larger campaign to sell NCLB to various American publics. According to the Office of the Inspector General, "media relations firms, advocacy groups, and other private companies received nearly $5 million in grants to help galvanize public support for [NCLB] without disclosing that they received taxpayer funds to do so" (see Murray, 2005). The ASM cannot survive without changing the hearts and minds of Americans across the country. When private foundations, alliances, and organizations are not enough to positively influence Americans, the ASM can use your tax dollars.

ANTISCHOOL, ANTIVOICE, ANTIDEMOCRACY

Perhaps the best way to understand the dangers of the ASM is to imagine an educational landscape dominated by private, charter, religious, and for-profit schools. What would choice offer Americans? Under corporate governance, under private control, parents will lose their increasingly shrinking ability to participate in the conversations that shape school goals. Teachers, in an educational landscape dominated by private interests, will lose the protection of the Constitution, as evidenced by teachers losing their jobs when their personal beliefs conflict with school operators' (see Rothschild, 2005; Associated Press, 2005). Students, in addition to losing highly qualified teachers, will lose innovation, diversity, and nuance as classrooms become increasingly scripted. Diane Ravitch (of the Brookings Institution, the Hoover Institution, and the Thomas B. Fordham Institute) believes "Americans must recognize that we need national standards, national tests and a national curriculum" (Ravitch, 2005). The for-profit Edison schools have already embraced the idea, seeking to have classroom lessons scripted to the point where every Edison student in the nation learns the same thing at the same time (see Saltman, 2005). As teachers nationwide regulate themselves according to corporate or national curricula, "teachable moments" will become a thing of the past, given that students and teachers will not have time to stop and reflect on their unique lives.

Benjamin Barber (2004) argues that public education "is the means by which a public is forged. It is how individuals are transformed into responsible participants in the communities of the classroom, the neighborhood, the town, the nation and (in schools that recognize the new interdependence of our times) the world to which they belong." Schools can be such spaces if, and only if, parents participate democratically in the agenda setting of those schools. Allowing corporate leaders, fundamentalists, and profiteers to control schools, and therefore the very mechanism that should be forging critical and engaged publics, is not only dangerous to students, but is dangerous to democracy. When corporate leaders shape public institutions according to their needs, countries move away from democracy and toward corporatism, a relative of, and arguably a precursor to, fascism. One obvious way of preventing such a move is to make public schools places where individuals can come together to determine, debate, and question what democracy, and fascism, mean. The conversation, long overdue, seems less likely to be had under increased corporate governance of America's public schools.

NOTES

1. For total giving to ITL, see www.mediatransparency.org. For fiscal year 2004, see the Bradley Foundation, "2004 Annual Report," p. 31.

2. To read excerpts of these works, visit http://www.encounterbooks.com/ main_web/catalog/education_family.html. Last accessed 11/18/05.
3. For evidence of coordination between Paige and Bradley see "U.S. Education Secretary to Mark 50th Anniversary of Brown Decision with Kennedy School Address." The press release is available online at http://www.ksg.harvard.edu/press/press%20releases/2004/paige_forum_042204.htm. See also http://www.aei.org/events/eventID.709,filter.all/event_detail.asp. Paige has also published work on AEI's Web site; see, for example, http://www.aei.org/ publications/pubID.19737,filter.all/pub_detail.asp.
4. See http://www.mediatransparency.org/recipientgrants.php?recipientID=585. Last accessed November 9, 2005.
5. Quote taken from the Alliance's home page. Available online at http://www. allianceforschoolchoice.org/about.aspx. Last accessed November 9, 2005.
6. Press release available online from http://www.allianceforschoolchoice.org/ public_policy.aspx. Accessed November 9, 2005.

REFERENCES

Associated Press. (2005). Christian school expels girl for having gay parents. ABCnews.com. Retrieved November 15, 2005, from http://abcnews.go.com/ US/wireStory?id=1151655

Barber, B. (2004). Taking the public out of education. *The School Administrator.* Retrieved November 18, 2005, from http://www.aasa.org/publications/ saarticledetail.cfm?ItemNumber=1375&snItemNumber=950&tnItemNumber=951.

Black Commentator. (2002a, July 11). Voucher tricksters: The hard right enters through the schoolhouse door. *The Black Commentator, 7.* Retrieved November 10, 2005, from http://www.blackcommentator.com/7_voucher_tricksters.html

Black Commentator. (2002b, November 14). Bush funds black voucher front group: Your tax dollars pay for propaganda blitz. *The Black Commentator, 16.* Retrieved November 18, 2005, from http://www.blackcommentator.com/16_thw.html

Bracey, G. W. (2004). *Setting the record straight: Responses to misconceptions about public education in the U.S.* Portsmouth, NH: Heinemann.

Bracey, G. W. (2005). The 15th Bracey report on the condition of public education. *Phi Delta Kappan, 87,* 2. Retrieved November 10, 2005, from www.proquest.com

Bradley Foundation. (2004). *2004 Annual Report.* Retrieved November 10, 2005, from http://www.bradleyfdn.org/publications.html

Darling-Hammond, L. (2002). Research and rhetoric on teacher certification: A response to "teacher certification reconsidered." *Educational Policy Analysis Archives, 10,* 36. Retrieved July 29, 2005, from http://epaa.asu.edu/epaa/ v10n36.html

Drummer, L. (2005). School choice academy spurs legislative interest. *School Reform News.* Retrieved November 9, 2005, from http://www.heartland.org/ Article.cfm?artId=17939

Enlow, R. C., & Ladner, M. (2005). *School choice: A reform that works.* Retrieved November 9, 2005, from www.alec.org/meSWFiles/pdf/0424.pdf

Finn, C. (2003). What's a "qualified" teacher and how can we get more of them? Retrieved August 20, 2005, from http://www.edexcellence.net/institute/gadfly/issue.cfm?id=110#1383

Gabbard, D. (2003). A Nation at Risk reloaded: Part I. *Journal for Critical Educational Policy Studies.* Retrieved November 10, 2005, from http://www.jceps.com/index.php?pageID=article &articleID=15

Gabbard, D. (2004). A Nation at Risk reloaded: Part II. *Journal for Critical Educational Policy Studies.* Retrieved November 10, 2005, from http://www.jceps.com/index.php?pageID=article&articleID=19

Haas, E. (2004). The news media and the Heritage Foundation: Promoting education advocacy at the expense of authority. *Journal for Critical Education Policy Studies, 2,* 2. Retrieved November 10, 2005, from www.jceps.com

Hess, F. M. (2003). Refining or retreating? High-stakes accountability in the states. In P. E. Peterson & M. R. West (Eds.), *No Child Left Behind? The politics and practice of school accountability.* Washington, DC: Brookings.

Hess, F. M. (2005). The case for being mean. Retrieved November 10, 2005, from http://www.aei.org/publications/pubID.19614/pub_detail.asp

Johnson, D. C., & Salle, L. M. (2004). Responding to the attack on public education and teacher unions. Menlo Park, CA: Commonweal Institute. Retrieved September 17, 2005, from www.commonwealinstitute.org

Kovacs, P. (2005). Bill Gates and the corporatization of U.S. schools. *Common Dreams.* Retrieved November 10, 2005, from http://www.commondreams.org/views05/0406-31.htm

Krehely, J., House, M., & Kernan, E. (2004). *Axis of ideology: Conservative foundations and public policy.* National Committee for Responsive Philanthropy. Retrieved September 17, 2005, from www.ncrp.org

Moe, T. M. (2003). Politics, control, and the future of school accountability. In P. E. Peterson & M. R. West (Eds.), *No Child Left Behind? The politics and practice of school accountability.* Washington, DC: Brookings.

Murray, C. (2005). Critics blast ED's "propaganda" probe. *eSchoolNews.* Retrieved November 9, 2005, from www.eschoonews.com/news/pfshowStory.cfm?ArticleID=5874

Neill, M., Guisbond, L., & Schaeffer, B. (2004). Failing our children: How "No Child Left Behind" undermines quality and equity in education. Cambridge, MA: Fair Test. Retrieved November 10, 2005, from http://www.fairtest.org/Failing_Our_Children_Report.html

People for the American Way. (2003). *The voucher veneer: The deeper agenda to privatize public education.* Retrieved November 18, 2005, from http://www.pfaw.org/pfaw/general/default.aspx?oid=11371

Phi Delta Kappa/Gallup Poll. (2005). The 37th annual Phi Delta Kappa/Gallup Poll of the public's attitudes toward the public schools. *Phi Delta Kappan, 87,* 1. Retrieved November 10, 2005, from www.proquest.com

Ravitch, D. (2005, November 7). Every state left behind. *New York Times,* Section A.

Robinson, G. (2005). Survey of school choice research. Retrieved November 10, 2005, from http://www.itlmuonline.com/content.asp?cat=2&id=60

Rothschild, M. (2005). Catholic high school teacher forced out over flag. *The Progressive.* Retrieved October 24, 2005, from www.commondreams.org/views05/1018-29.htm

Saltman, K. J. (2005). *The edison schools: Corporate schooling and the assault on public education.* New York: Routledge.

Siebold, T. (2005). A brief framework for understanding the anti-public school movement. Retrieved November 10, 2005, from http://susanohanian.org/show_
  commentary.php?id=294
Toppo, G. (2005, January 7). White House paid commentator to promote law.
  USA Today. Retrieved January 24, 2005, from www.usatoday.com/news/
  washington/2005-01-06-williams-whitehouse_x.htm
Turtel, J. (2005). *Public schools, public menace: How public schools lie to parents and
  betray our children*. New York: Liberty Books.
U.S. Department of Education. (2002). Education Department, BAEO form part-
  nership to reach parents about landmark No Child Left Behind Act. Retrieved
  November 10, 2005, from http://www.ed.gov/news/pressreleases/2002/10/
  10152002a.html
Williams, J. (2005). *Cheating our kids: How politics and greed ruin education*. New York:
  Palgrave Macmillan.

Chapter 24

Choice

Joel Spring
Queens College and Graduate Center at City University of New York

The word *choice* in education conjures up visions of democracy and free-dom-loving parents happily selecting from many educational alternatives. How was this vision distorted into an antidemocratic plan to allow parents to choose among schools teaching the same centrally determined curriculum? How did choice plans calling for less bureaucratic control result in greater bureaucratic control of the ideologies taught in public schools?

To answer these questions, I begin with a discussion of Austrian economics and the reaction of Protestant fundamentalists to the secularization of public schools. In the 1970s, Austrian economists supported the demands of the Protestant fundamentalists for the right of parents to choose between public and private schools. Christian fundamentalist organizations — the Moral Majority in the 1980s and the Christian Coalition in the 1990s — exerted political pressure on the Republican Party to support choice in education. From the 1970s to the 1990s, conservative think tanks and foundations popularized Austrian economics, which in turn influenced the Republican Party, the movement to reinvent government and the schools, and President Bill Clinton's New Democratic doctrines. In addition, the sharp reaction of the teachers' unions influenced choice plans in the Democratic Party.

Austrian economics is the best place to begin understanding the changing meaning of choice in education. Although originating in the 19th century, Austrian economics gained its foothold in the United States at the University of Chicago in the 1950s. During that period, noted Austrian economist Friedrich Von Hayek created what was later called the Chicago School of Economics (Boettke, n.d.; Hayek, 1994; Rothbard, 1970).

Choice is a key concept in Austrian economics. Austrian economists argue that all centrally planned economies are doomed to failure because of the difficulty in determining the price of goods. Price represents the value of a product to a society. Creating prices requires balancing demand with manufacturing and the availability of resources. How can a centrally planned economy, for instance, determine the price of televisions without a knowledge of public demand? The answer for Austrian economists is that in a centrally planned economy the bureaucrats fix prices in their own self-interest rather than in the interest of the public.

The solution, according to Austrian economists, is to have price determined by the workings of a free market. The assumption is that the "invisible hand of the marketplace" will establish prices and the production of goods that are more in line with the public interests as opposed to the interests of bureaucrats.

Austrian economists apply the same reasoning to ideas. A free market for ideas will allow the invisible hand of the marketplace to select ideas that are most compatible with the public interest. In a government-dominated society, bureaucrats select the ideas placed in textbooks and disseminated through public schools. The ideas selected by bureaucrats, according to Austrian economists, are those to promote the self-interest of bureaucrats. For instance, bureaucrats might want to ensure their jobs by distributing ideas through public schools that support the continuing existence of a welfare state.

Therefore, Austrian economists see the major problem with education as the existence of a public school monopoly controlled in the self-interest of educational bureaucrats. In this context, education choice means breaking up the public school monopoly, limiting the power of educational bureaucrats, and turning education over to the workings of the free market. It also means freedom of competition between ideologies in education.

In the 1960s, an influential member of the Chicago School, Milton Friedman, made the first proposal for a voucher system that would give parents a choice between public school districts. Friedman (1994) argues that school vouchers would allow children from some low-income families attending poor-quality city school systems to attend better schools in affluent suburbs. For Friedman, choice was a means of correcting the inequalities caused by the existence of rich and poor school districts. Based on similar arguments, Milwaukee and Cleveland in the 1990s initiated voucher plans to provide children from the low-income families the choice of attending private schools. In these voucher programs, the purpose of choice was to allow low-income families to have the same choice of private schooling as high-income families (p. 89).

Christian fundamentalists and conservatives rejected the emphasis of Austrian economists on the freedom to choose between competing ideologies. In the 1970s, Austrian economists and their political counterparts,

Libertarians, rushed to support Christian fundamentalists, who demanded having the choice at public expense to send their children to private, Christian academics. For both Austrian economists and Libertarians, the Christian revolt against public schools provided a chance to create competition between ideologies.

Christian fundamentalists welcomed the support but rejected the concept of ideological competition among schools. From their standpoint, public schools traditionally taught Protestant values. With continuing secularization, they argued, schools were now teaching the religion of secular humanism. Consequently, from their perspective, choice between public and private schools would allow parents to choose traditional schools based on Protestant values. Because they believe that Christianity is the only true religion, Christian fundamentalists are not interested in a public choice plan that allows choice at the public expense of Muslim or Afrocentric schools. Christian fundamentalists narrowed the meaning of choice in education from a free marketplace of ideas to the choice of a Christian alternative (see Buchanan, 1990; Delfatorre, 1992; Reed, 1996).

The meaning of choice was further narrowed by conservative foundations and think tanks, such as Hudson Institute, the Heritage Foundation, the Olin Foundation, and the American Enterprise Institute, and their scholars, Diane Ravitch, Chester Finn, Denis Doyle, and William Bennett (see People for the American Way, n.d.; Ricci, 1993; Simon, 1978; Smith, 1991). Traditionally, conservatives support government efforts to regulate social behavior through laws, police, and the schools. Conservatives support a strong role for government in regulating education. For instance, in the 1950s, President Dwight Eisenhower, a Republican and self-proclaimed progressive conservative, championed the National Defense Education Act, which greatly expanded the federal role in education (see Lind, 1996).

Therefore, it is not surprising that in the 1980s and 1990s, conservatives used Austrian economics to justify competition between schools while calling on the federal government to exert greater control over the curriculum of the nation's schools. The think-tank conservatives — Ravitch, Finn, Doyle, and Bennett — played active roles in the administrations of Republican conservatives Reagan and Bush in the 1980s and 1990s. The result was a combination of proposals for national standards and tests and plans for allowing parental choice between public and private schools (Finn & Ravitch, n.d.; Gerstner, Semerad, Doyle, & Johnston, 1994; Lawton, 1996).

The call for national academic standards eventually became part of President Bush's *America 2000* (1991). A major objective of *America 2000*, slightly revised and renamed before passing into legislation by President Bill Clinton in April 1994, was cooperation between state and federal governments in creating national academic standards and tests. In essence, these national standards, which were to be measured by national tests, would determine the content and curriculum in public schools. The resulting debate over history standards highlighted the issue of ideological control. What vision of American history should be represented in the history standards? Should the history curriculum emphasize Anglo-American traditions or a multicultural society? National standards would ensure the teaching of a common ideology (see Cody, Woodward, & Elliot, 1993; Cornbleth & Waugh, 1995; Diegmueller, 1995, 1996; Gluck, 1994; "Plan to Teach," 1994; Schlesinger, 1991).

What does choice mean if all schools conform to the same national standards? What happened to the original Austrian economics idea that choice included a competition of ideologies in a free marketplace? Conservatives answered these questions by turning the idea of choice into a management technique. In this context, choice became a method for imparting national standards to students. The invisible hand of the marketplace, conservatives hoped, would produce new forms of school organization and methods of instruction to more efficiently achieve national standards (see Cooper, 1991; Gerstner et al., 1994; Yang, 1991).

Of course, this conservative definition of choice denied the Christian fundamentalists' desire for parents to have the ideological choice of sending their children to Christian schools. Consequently, the influence of the Christian Coalition on the writing of the 1992 National Republican Platform forced Republican candidate Bush to withdraw support for national standards and simply advocate creating a plan to give parents a choice between public and private schools. In fact, the 1992 National Republican Platform not only abandoned support of national standards, but also called for the demise of the Department of Education (Niebuhr, 1996).

In contrast to the Republicans, the New Democrats under the leadership of Bill Clinton were strongly influenced by the arguments of David Osborne and Ted Gaebler (1993) in *Reinventing Government: How the Entrepreneurial Spirit Is Transforming the Public Sector.* New Democrats argue that competition between government agencies results in more efficiency in the provision of services to the public. This means that competition between public schools would supposedly result in cheaper and better instruction of students. In addition, the teachers' unions, who exercise major power within the Democratic Party, oppose choice plans that include private schools. Therefore, the New Democrats advocated plans that would allow parents to make choices between public schools, as opposed to choices among public and private schools. Similar to conservatives, the New Democrats advocated the establishment of national academic standards. Consequently, the New Democrats also reduced the idea of choice to a management tool to promote efficiency in achieving national standards (see Clinton, 1996; Clinton & Gore, 1992; Hale, n.d.; Riley, 1996; Smith, 1995; Weisberg, 1996).

In summary, major political groups have given the following meanings to choice in education:

- Choice to allow parental selection of private Christian school
- Choice between public and private schools to achieve more efficient attainment of national standards
- Choice to promote competition among government agencies, such as choice among public schools to promote efficient attainment of national standards
- Choice for low-income families in urban areas to attend private schools

None of these various political uses in education promote ideological freedom in public schools. The original Austrian economics idea of providing public choice of ideologies to be taught in school has disappeared from the debate. Conservatives and New Democrats have changed the meaning of choice into something antidemocratic. By reducing choice to a management tool for promoting efficiency in achieving national standards, conservatives and New Democrats have rejected the notion of freedom of ideas in public schools. How can there be meaningful democratic politics if everyone is taught the same ideology? In fact, if schooling influences future choices, then schooling with national standards could result in everyone's making the same political choices. In other words, conservative and New Democratic definitions of choice in education provide a new means of ideological control over the population.

Ironically, choice in education might mean the end of democratic choice of ideas. There is no meaningful freedom of thought if everyone thinks the same things. If choice combined with national standards results in uniformity of thinking in public schools, then democracy is dead. Interestingly, the Christian Coalition would like to impose its own brand of uniformity on the schools. Therefore, the Christian Coalition, conservatives, and the New Democrats have made choice an antidemocratic movement in education.

REFERENCES

America 2000: An education strategy. (1991). Washington, DC: U.S. Government Printing Office.

Boettke, P. (n.d.). *Friedrich A. Hayeck (1899–1992).* Department of Economics, New York University. Retrieved May 1, 2007 from www.econ.nyu.edu/user/boettke/hayek.htm

Buchanan, P. J. (1990). *Right from the beginning.* Washington, DC: Regenry Gateway.

Clinton, W. J., & Gore, A. (1992). *Putting people first: How can we change America.* New York: Times Books.

Clinton, W. J. (1996). *Between hope and history: Meeting America's challenges for the 21st century.* New York: Times Books.

Cody, C. B., Woodward, A., & Elliot, D. L. (1993). Race, ideology, and the battle over the curriculum. In C. Marshall (Ed.), *The new politics of race and gender.* Washington, DC: Falmer Press.

Cooper, K. J. (1991, April 19). *National standards at core of proposal: Model schools envisioned.* Compuserve Executive News Service, *Washington Post.*

Cornbleth, C., & Waugh, D. (1995). *The great speckled bird: Multicultural politics and education policy making.* Mahwah, NJ: Lawrence Erlbaum Associates.

Delfatorre, J. (1992). *What Johnny shouldn't read: Textbook censorship in America.* New Haven, CT: Yale University Press.

Diegmueller, K. (1995, October 18). Revise history standards, two panels advise. *Education Week,* p. 11.

Diegmueller, K. (1996, April 10). History center shares new set of standards. *Education Week.*

Finn, C., Jr., & Ravitch, D. (n.d.). *Educational reform 1995–1996: Introduction.* Retrieved May 1, 2007 from www.edexcellence.net

Friedman, M. (1994). *Capitalism and freedom.* Chicago: University of Chicago Press.

Gerstner, L., Jr., Semerad, R.D., Doyle, D.P., & Johnston, W. (1994). *Reinventing education: Entrepreneurship in America's public schools.* New York: Dutton.

Gluck, C. (1994, October 26). Let the debate continue. *New York Times,* p. 23.

Hale, J. (n.d.). *The making of the new democrats.* Democratic Leadership Council home page. Retrieved May 1, 2007 from www.dlcppi.com

Hayek, F. (1994). *The road to serfdom.* Chicago: University of Chicago Press.

Lawton, M. (1996, April 3). Summit accord calls for focus on standards. *Education Week,* pp. 1, 14–15.

Lind, M. (1996). *Up from conservatism: Why the right is wrong for America.* New York: The Free Press.

Niebuhr, G. (1996, September 16). Dole gets Christian Coalition's trust and prodding. *New York Times,* p. B8.

Osborne, G., & Gaebler, T. (1993). *Reinventing government: How the entrepreneurial spirit is transforming the public sector.* New York: Penguin.

People for the American Way. (n.d.). *Buying a movement: New report analyzes right-wing foundations.* Retrieved May 9, 2007 from http://www.pfaw.org/pfaw/general/default.aspx?oid=2052

Plan to teach U.S. history is said to slight white males (1994, October 26). *New York Times,* p. B12.

Reed, R. (1996). *Active faith: How Christians are changing the soul of American politics.* New York: The Free Press.

Ricci, D. M. (1993). *The transformation of American politics: The new Washington and the rise of think tanks.* New Haven, CT: Yale University Press.

Riley, R. (1996, February 28). *State of American education address.* Washington, DC: Office of the Secretary of Education.

Rothbard, M. N. (1970). *Man, economy, and state: A treatise of economic principles.* Los Angeles: Nash.

Schlesinger, A. M., Jr. (1991). *The disuniting of America.* Knoxville, TN: Whittle Direct Books.

Simon, W. (1978). *A time for truth.* New York: Readers Digest Press.

Smith, J. A. (1991). *The idea brokers: Think tanks and the rise of the new policy elite.* New York: The Free Press.

Smith, M. S. (1995). Education reform in America's public schools: The Clinton agenda. In D. Ravtich (Ed.), *Debating the future of American education: Do we need national standards and assessments?* Washington DC: Brookings Institute.

Weisberg, J. (1996). *In defense of government: The fall and rise of public trust.* New York: Scribner.

Yang, J. E. (1991, April 19). Bush unveils education plan: States, communities would play major role in proposed innovations. Compuserve Executive News Service, *Washington Post.*

Chapter 25

Charter Schools

George N. Schmidt
Editor, Substance

Can anyone with a critical eye imagine calling a community "inner city" in the United States where a family could not buy a home for less than $400,000? This is a community where a modest — say, two-bedroom — apartment rents for more than $1,000 a month, and a three-bedroom rental can cost as much as $2,400 a month. Can anyone imagine calling an urban community where there were almost no black people in a city that was half-black — and where most of the black children lived in Third World conditions of poverty — part of the inner city?

Yet the Chicago Board of Education has been doing just that — in a report to the nation on how to fix urban schools — since February 2005.

Sauganash is a very safe neighborhood in a town where huge stretches — square miles in some cases — are controlled by some of the nation's largest and best-organized drug gangs. Sauganash (and its adjoining neighborhood, Edgebrook) is an area where some of the city's wealthiest families — including former U.S. Secretary of Commerce William Daley (brother of Chicago's mayor; by early 2005, president of the phone company SBC) — live (or lived). In Sauganash, people are able to send their children to a private public school if they do not want to send those children to enormously expensive private schools or to relatively expensive parochial schools. And those children are able to play on the streets and in local parks without being in danger of the gunfire that punctuates play in other places in Chicago.

In Chicago in 2005 and 2006, the wealthiest man on earth — along with one of the most powerful Democratic Party politicians in the country and backed by the resources of some of the nation's largest news organizations — continued creating a virtual reality to frame public debate about public schools. By claiming that the Sauganash community was part of Chicago's inner city, a virtual reality about school reform was created as readily as *Grand Theft Auto* offers virtual driving. Bill Gates's goal was to speed up the privatization of public schools, mostly through charter schools and "small schools." This is heralded in expensive propaganda campaigns. By 2005, the work was shared by Chicago's mayor and the city's corporate CEOs. The majority of the city's residents fiercely opposed this privatization plan once they knew what the whole thing was about. Hence, the creation of the virtual reality to frame public debate: While privatization was victimizing the poorest children across Chicago's ghettos and barrios, the middle class was being assured that what was happening was a really good thing.

Within that virtual reality, a school in this privileged community of Sauganash, its students, and its community are called inner city. Then they are morphed with the help of as many of the billionaire's dollars as necessary into a model for solving the problems of urban public schools — other inner-city schools — across the United States. That is being done today mostly through eliminating traditional public schools and then through charterization, what many Chicagoans call "small school-ization" and the kind, risk-free "entrepreneurship" that characterized the privatization grabs that followed the end of Russian and Eastern European communism.

Much of this propaganda supporting all this is done with the help of hired PhDs from the largest education think tanks and most prestigious universities in the United States (in the case being discussed in this essay, WestEd). Most people trying simply to improve the public schools for their own children do not even realize how reality is being manipulated around them until it is too late.

The public debate over charter schools in Chicago (and by implication, in urban school districts across the United States, since Chicago has been on the cutting edge of corporate school reform for more than a decade) is scripted by media events as completely as the town hall meetings of George W. Bush were scripted during the 2004 election campaign. So far, however, media manipulations in favor of the privatization and charterization of public schools have met with much less media scrutiny than George W. Bush's attacks on the historical integrity of the "town hall meeting" or his later attacks on the promises of social security or the attacks by his corporate allies on, say, the pensions of their workers. While the manifestations may be different, however, the underlying realities are eerily similar.

Carefully framed to reflect only the privatization agenda, the debate about charter schools in Chicago takes place in carefully scripted events where informed and critical questions are ignored as completely as they were blocked out of the Bush campaign meetings. Part of the creation of this virtual reality is happening in Chicago today thanks to tens of millions of dollars from the Bill and Melinda Gates Foundation. (In six years, Gates poured more than $45 million into school reform in Chicago, and not one dollar of it went to improve a traditional public school.) Once the corporate scripts are compiled, they become "news." In Chicago, Gates is aided by a tightly controlled corporate media — dominated today by the Tribune Corporation, Hollinger International's *Chicago Sun-Times*, and Fox News. It is being imposed by a mayor who has what *Time* magazine in 2004 gushingly called "imperial" power over both the city and its public schools. The privatization campaign devotes millions of dollars a year to purchasing pseudo-scholarly research studies that are little more than propaganda for one side of a major policy debate, but which are reported as if they were as irrefutable as science. And this corporate agenda is supported not only by the city's traditional conservatives, but also by many self-described progressives who have been active in the neoliberal movement to privatize public schools through charterization, small schools, and other so-called reforms of the corporate era. To do these things, the proponents of reform have to ignore massive racial segregation. (In 2005, Chicago had 304 all-black public elementary and high schools; "all-black" in this case meant that 90% or more of the children in those schools were black. Another 70 schools were all-Latino by the same measure.) Those who promote corporate school reform also generally ignore the underfunding of traditional public schools in Illinois cities and the growing gap in pay and benefits between teachers (and other school employees) in Chicago and Chicago's wealthier suburbs. Instead of demanding smaller class sizes, they demand small schools and then repeat, as regularly as Bush administration spokesmen repeated the WMD talking points, a mantra about how schools will improve if only everyone believes "all children can learn." The reality has been that before the corporate attack on Chicago's public schools began in the mid-1990s, the majority of teachers and administrators in Chicago's schools were black. Translated, the rhetoric about the belief that all children can learn implies that the black teachers and principals they have been replacing did not believe the children in their schools could learn. But just as the reformers ignore massive segregation, so they ignore tens of thousands of black teachers, administrators, and other school workers who have been under attack.

One other thing is very important in this era of diversity politics. The majority of veteran teachers and administrators this movement displaces are black. They are being replaced by young (most often, white) educational classroom "entrepreneurs" who have been trained to talk the talk, but who have never had to walk the walk. They have as much understanding of inner-city educational praxis as their predecessors in corporate America did of real business during the days when a cool and visionary "business plan" became a substitute for the grittier reality of actually producing, marketing, and servicing a product or service in the real world. In fact, if America is looking for the successors of the glib, frenetic, arrogant dot.com hucksters who crashed the stock market bubble of 10 years ago

— amid a trillion dollars or more in fraud, incompetence, and loss to millions of average working people — it has to look no further than the outfits and individuals that are taking over corporate school reform in Chicago today. Just as the super-cool business plan of 1999 was a virtual reality that helped crash part of the economy, so today the charter school vision in Chicago is helping to crash public education. Veteran teachers are actually suspect, while the gushing literary effusions of novices are rewarded with million-dollar grants and multi-million-dollar contracts.

A MEDIA EVENT AT A CHICAGO CHARTER HIGH SCHOOL

At 10:00 on the cold morning of February 15, 2005, Chicago Public Schools' chief executive officer (CEO), Arne Duncan, spent more than an hour as the central spokesman for these virtual realities at a media event staged at a large, well-kept charter high school on Chicago's Far North Side.

The school, which still bore the sign "Good Counsel High School" over one of its entrances, is located at the corner of Peterson Avenue and Pulaski Road a mile south of Chicago's northwestern city limits. That school is at a location where Chicago meets its more affluent northern suburbs (including Lincolnwood, where single-family homes sell today for $1 million or more). For 75 years, Good Counsel had been a Catholic girls' school. By February 2005, it had not only become a public school in Chicago (or at least a school paid for with public education tax dollars), but it was about to become a model for urban school reform and inner-city education practice. Since February 2005, its supposed virtues have been spread nationwide through the Internet, in book form, and even with video and PowerPoint presentations.

For the 18 months prior to Arne Duncan's February 2005 visit, Good Counsel, under the short name Northtown Academy (the actual name — Chicago International Charter School–Northtown Campus — was required by the dodge used to evade a state law limiting the number of charter schools in Chicago), had been a public charter school. Most people in Chicago would have failed a test if asked what kind of school Good Counsel was in 2005. Most Chicagoans did not even know that Good Counsel had morphed into a "public" school by 2005, let alone that they had been paying for the last two years of what had amounted to a private school education for the girls who had attended the school in its parochial incarnation through 10th grade. As one commentator had long put it: "OIC — Only in Chicago."

After more than 75 years as a parochial school, Good Counsel quietly became a public school in September 2003. There had been no widely publicized public hearings, and the only recognition of the rather important change had been a bureaucratic proposal buried in the middle of dozens of others in the agenda for the Chicago Board of Education a few months earlier. But it had been known to generations on Chicago's North Side as Good Counsel High School, a Catholic girls' school. Under the terms of the conversion to a charter school, those students who were at Good Counsel remained there. Most of the staff also remained the same. The name changed, and over the next few years the school would have to add male students. The biggest change was that Chicago's taxpayers would now pay the budget, which had been covered by tuition.

Before and after its 2003 transformation into Chicago International Charter School–Northtown Campus, the school had been serving a clientele of Chicago's relatively privileged teenagers. Good Counsel girls were more middle class than very wealthy, but came from families that had the ability to pay tuition and a great deal more time and money than the average family whose children were attending Chicago's public schools. Most Good Counsel students had come from one of the six or seven wealthiest zip codes in Chicago. (Contrary to what many people believe about America's major cities, alongside some of the world's most vicious and heartbreaking child poverty on earth, cities like Chicago also have some of the world's most ostentatiously wealthy communities and vast stretches of middle-class homes and families.)

For the past 10 years, under the battle cry of "public housing reform," Chicago has been pushing poor people back from the shores of Lake Michigan, where property is most valuable. Other parts of the city had seen property appreciate as well. The homes north and west of Good Counsel do not compete with the $5 and $10 million luxury condominiums (or even a few brownstone mansions) overlooking Oak Street Beach on Chicago's "Gold Coast." It is possible to walk from Good Counsel past the local Starbucks to single-family homes — in Chicago — that cost more than $1 million, to conversions making already-luxurious Chicago homes into "McMansions," or to apartments that rent for more than many working families earn in a month. It is also possible from Good Counsel to walk, within 20 minutes, along safe Chicago streets north into a suburb where home prices begin at $1 million.

Prior to 2005, nobody in Chicago would have tried to claim that Good Counsel High School was comparable to the vast majority of the city's public high schools. Chicagoans simply do not talk about the Sauganash community on the Northwest Side in the same breath as Englewood, an all-black community on the city's South Side. Nobody in Chicago would have talked about the segregated all-black community about which Lorraine Hansberry wrote "A Raisin in the Sun" more than 50 years earlier and the wealthy white community 20 miles away as if they were the same, or even similar. And nobody would have thought to compare Englewood High School, 20 miles to the southeast of Good Counsel, with Good Counsel unless many qualifying realities were listed during the comparison. That all changed in February 2005, when Chicago's public school CEO

Arne Duncan and America's richest man Bill Gates did so on February 15, 2005. And they have continued to do so since using the enormous wealth of Gates to amplify the comparison.

On the morning of February 15, 2005, Arne Duncan was helping Bill Gates declare the North Side school a model for urban education reform while closing the South Side high school as a failure. More broadly, as many critics suggested at the time and which later proved true, Duncan and those who currently lead Chicago were in the process of turning a considerable number of Chicago schools — and tens of millions of dollars worth of public school buildings and operating budgets — over to private school operators, many of whom were Catholic school entrepreneurs.

The media event of February 15, 2005, might be called an extreme makeover. First, as CEO of CPS, Arne Duncan had transformed an exclusive Catholic school into an exclusive public school. On February 15, 2005, Gates and Duncan were about to transform Good Counsel into an inner-city school, which it was not and had never been. The times were like that. An era that could put Arne Duncan in charge of a public school system and turn George W. Bush into a war hero was capable of just about anything.

That transformation was for purposes of the media and the narrative about school reform and school choice they have been crafting. It was part of the virtualization of the debate over public education funded by Gates and others. Instead of confronting the huge injustices and inequities that created the vast stretches of poor children and families in the barrios and ghettos of Chicago, the "dominant narrative," as one scholar called it, was simply being changed. It was to become a narrative about how a supposedly successful educational model — one that relied on certain buzzwords and prejudices against public schools — could be transplanted from one part of town to another. One simply had to believe, ignoring obscene racial, economic, social, and religious differences at every step along the way. Just as a willful suspension of disbelief is necessary to the enjoyment of fiction, so a number of fiercely held beliefs — some would call them prejudices — had to be in place for the makeover and virtualization to work. Along the way, there would also be a lot of exhortations to belief and the repetition of well-worn cliches. Foremost among these was the mantra of the right and their progressive sidekicks: "All children can learn." Buried in the constant repetition of that phrase in propaganda, mission statements, and endless sound bites and talking points has been the implication that the teachers and principals — most of them black — in segregated all-black schools somehow had not thought of that. "If that's all it takes, anyone can do this job," more than one inner-city teacher had told me bitterly. The bitterness has increased over the years, as these phrases of right-wing propaganda have become the underlying clichés of education reform, ultimately elevated to the level of a spiritual mantra, relentlessly bashing teachers and public schools.

Behind that mantra lay more deeply rooted beliefs that had been drummed into people's heads for a generation, from both the pundits of the right (like Fox News) and the sages of the left (like the school reform gurus who were promoting both charter and small schools). Private is always better than public. Privatization and profit are always superior to public and service. In general (especially in places like Chicago), parochial is always superior to public in the education of the children of the poor.

Despite the claims, Chicago's charters are generally performing worse than comparable public schools. In order to sustain the meager gains they can show, the charters are kicking out large numbers of students every year, sending them back to the public schools, which have to be held account-able for their failure. The data are now available in required reports by the State of Illinois in summary form, despite the fact that every charter school contacted by this reporter has failed or refused to answer those specific questions about who it kicks out and why.

The two new public parochial schools for Englewood were among 15 approved at the November 2005 meeting of the Chicago Board of Educa-tion. Another (the first "virtual" Chicago charter school) was added two months later, adding 16 charter schools to those approved for Chicago by January 2006, with more to come.

But as charter schools proliferate in Chicago almost as fast as charter school propaganda comes out of the Gates Foundation and outfits like WestEd, at least some of Chicago's charter school activities are coming under closer scrutiny.

By January 2006, Chicago supposedly had only 30 charter schools, but at the time it was possible to drive across the city and stop at more than 50 locations where charter schooling was taking place, paid for by Chicago taxpayers.

Here is how that works.

When the first Illinois charter school law was approved by the Illinois General Assembly, it provided that the entire state should have no more than 45 charter schools. Fifteen of those were to be in Chicago, 15 in the Chicago suburbs (defined as certain counties around Chicago), and 15 across the remainder of the state.

In 2003, that law was amended to allow for the creation of 30 charters for Chicago. But the law was vague enough so that Chicago Board of Education lawyers, working with charter school operators, were able to proliferate the number of charter school locations in Chicago by declaring that already existing charter schools could form satellite campuses across the city.

By January 2006, a Chicago charter school might actually be as many as a dozen separate schools at different locations with nothing in common by the legal quirk that allowed the campus policy.

The Chicago International Charter School is by far the largest of these expanding charters. By January 2006, Chicago International Charter School had 5,608 students. Had all of these been attending one facility,

Chicago International would have dwarfed the largest city public schools (Lane Technical High School, which generally had 4,500 students). Given the fact that the Gates Foundation and Arne Duncan's office were also insisting that schools should be small (no more than 400 or 500 students), this would have been doubly questionable. But Chicago International was allowed (with the assistance of several lawyers providing legal opinions) to have more than a half-dozen campuses, including Northtown Academy. Chicago International now boasts nine campuses across Chicago.

Chicago International is not the only charter school in Chicago to be cloning itself. By January 2006, the Chicago Board of Education had approved three campuses for the Aspira charter schools (run by a Puerto Rican community organization with close ties to Mayor Daley's political organization). The Noble Street Charter Schools (whose anniversary was attended by Mayor Daley and other celebrities) were allowed to add campuses. Noble Street is also receiving millions of dollars in Gates Foundation money.

Another charter operator expanding across the city at various campuses is American Quality Schools, Inc., which is run by former Illinois Schools Superintendent (and gubernatorial candidate) Michael Bakalis. According to the American Quality Schools Web site, the corporation now has six campuses in Chicago, the latest of which is the Austin High School Business and Entrepreneurship Academy, located at what used to be Austin High School. Interested parties can find a copy of the application to the new Austin High School at the American Quality Schools Web site.

Other charter schools that have proliferated by opening additional campuses include Perspectives charter school, which now tells potential applicants they can apply to its two campuses in Chicago.

The second largest of Chicago's charter schools (in terms of student enrollment) is called Youth Connection. For the 2005–2006 school year, it claimed 2,500 students, which would make it one of Chicago's 10 largest schools. But it is difficult to find Youth Connection in the real world because, as one observer joked, it is "everywhere and nowhere." Youth Connection is apparently a string of small alternative school programs spread out across the city, some in schools and some located in coffee houses and other smaller locations. By one count, Youth Connection has more than 20 campuses.

But by 2006, there were more than 50 locations — and possibly 100 — in Chicago where charter schooling was taking place. What was going on?

Again, Northtown Academy serves as an instructive example.

Officially, Northtown Academy, despite WestEd and Bill Gates, is not even a school; instead, it is one of seven branches — campuses — of a thing called the Chicago International Charter School. Chicago International had seven campuses at the time WestEd touted it in February 2005 and had added two more by February 2006.

The Chicago Board of Education, like the boards of Hollinger International, Enron, WorldCom, and dozens of others, had somehow missed the fine print. Like the special-purpose entities of Enron, the various campuses of Chicago's charter schools enable the mayor (the real CEO of Chicago's privatization and charterization movement) to expand charters beyond the cap.

Like the deregulation of energy that led to Enron's corruption (and to the Enron manipulation of energy prices against the State of California two years before Enron's collapse), the deregulation of public schools in Chicago is creating unique problems.

The campuses of Chicago International are as diverse as the Star Wars entities created out of Enron. Chicago International Charter School–Longwood Campus is run by Edison schools, but not as a for-profit. Northtown Academy will graduate its last all-girls' class from its Good Counsel roots in June 2006.

The Gates Foundation has already given $45 million to promote charter schools and small schools in Chicago. But the Chicago Board of Education claims that it does not even have the power to tell the public what qualifies a person to serve as a principal or administrators at a charter school in Chicago, despite the fact that tax dollars are paying for these people. Nor does the Chicago Board of Education screen charter school employees for their professional and other qualifications. Deregulation supposedly forbids this. And Chicago has denied my request for the names and salaries of everyone working at Chicago's charter schools, something that is considered public information in all other public schools.

Charter schools in Chicago have already been collapsing through incompetence and corruption almost as quickly as the Bush administration — after all of its celebrity CEO propaganda — is dwarfing even its most corrupt and incompetent predecessors.

The stories about the corruption resulting from the deregulation of Chicago's public schools will be the subject of public discussion for decades to come, but the victims of that incompetence and corruption are real children who live today and whose futures are destroyed when public corruption attacks them.

Chapter 26

Privatization

Kenneth J. Saltman
DePaul University

The privatization of education involves the transformation of public school-ing on the model of the market. This transformation can be understood through three interrelated registers: economic, cultural, and political. In the first section, I briefly map the terrain of public school privatization in the United States through these three registers.[1] In the second section, I discuss how educational privatization relates to the broader neoliberal and neoconservative ideologies, policies, and political projects. This sec-tion contends that these authoritarian ideologies, policies, and political projects, which are global in nature, threaten the development of forms of education conducive to the expansion of democratic social relations.

In terms of economics, public school privatization has included intro-ducing business and for-profit endeavors into a realm that has historically been publicly owned and controlled. Profit-motivated initiatives include the steady rise of school commercialism, such as sponsored educational materials, advertisements in textbooks, in-class television news programs that show mostly commercials, soft drink vending contracts, and other attempts to hold youth as a captive audience for advertisers.

The most direct privatization initiatives include companies running public schools for profit. This is sometimes referred to as performance contracting, and it involves companies contracting with schools or school districts. Major privatization initiatives include for-profit charter schools, market-based voucher schemes, and the rise of the educational manage-ment organization (EMO), such as Michael Milken's Knowledge Universe, which is now going out of business. In addition to the aforementioned, these conglomerate companies hold a number of for-profit educational enter-prises, including test publishing, textbook publishing, tutoring services, curriculum consultancies, educational software development, publication, and sales, toy making, and other companies.[2]

In the United States the Elementary and Secondary Act (ESEA) law (No Child Left Behind [NCLB]) has fostered privatization by investing billions of public dollars in the charter school movement, which is pushing privatization, with over three-quarters of new charter schools being for-profit. NCLB is also requiring high-stakes testing, accountability, and remediation measures that shift resources away from public school control and into control by test and textbook publishing corporations and remediation companies. For example, because the Edison Schools failed to profit financially as a publicly traded company, the company has shifted investment toward remediation work through spin-off companies Newton and Tungsten. Despite a number of failed experiments with performance contracting in the United States in the 1980s and 1990s, for-profit education companies and their advocates have continued to claim that they could operate public schools better and cheaper than the public sector. This claim appears counterintuitive: After all, how could an organization drain financial resources to profit investors and still maintain the same quality that the organization had with the resources that could be paying for more teachers, books, supplies, and upkeep? Evidence appears on the side of intuition. To date, the evidence shows that it is not possible to run schools for profit while adequately providing resources for public education. This has been equally true whether the profit model is vouchers, charters, or performance contracting. Nonetheless, the business-sector, right-wing think tanks in and outside of academia, and corporate media continue to call for market-based approaches to public schooling. This has as much to do with ideology as with financial interest. For example, the Walton Family Foundation (the largest family-owned business in the United States is Wal-Mart) is the largest spender lobbying for public school privatization schemes. Assuredly, this has less to do with plans of the company to open Wal-Schools or interest in the public schools developing highly educated and thoughtful Wal-Mart greeters capable of union organizing to break the antiunion commitments of the company than it does with the ideological beliefs of the Walton family that business works for them, so business should be the model for schooling.

Privatization advocates depend upon on a number of arguments for their economic claims: (1) the larger the company becomes, the more it can benefit from economies of scale to save costs through, for example, volume purchasing; (2) the private sector is inherently more efficient than the public sector because for-profit companies must compete with other companies; and (3) the private sector is more efficient because the public sector is burdened by regulations and constraints, such as teachers' unions and the protections that they afford teachers, that only get in the way of efficient delivery of educational services. Proponents often justify commercialism and other for-profit initiatives on the grounds that they provide much needed income for underfunded public schools. However, even the business press by 2002 recognized that education is not good business: Schools have too many variable costs for economies of scale to work; business would have to be spectacularly efficient to allow for quality and skimming of profits for executives, while Enron, Worldcom, Martha Stewart, and the Edison Schools show just how inefficient business can be. Far from regulations being a hindrance, they provide necessary protections against abuse of teachers' labor while providing financial transparency. As the largest ever experiment in privatization, the Edison Schools overworked teachers, misreported earnings, misreported test scores, counseled out low-scoring students, cheated on tests to show high performance to potential investors, and, as they approached bankruptcy time and again, revealed just how precarious and unaccountable the market imperatives can be when applied to education (see Saltman, 2005). Meanwhile the argument for opening the school gates to commercialism cannot be divorced from broader questions of why schools need to open those gates, including issues of school funding, the inequitable distribution of educational resources, and the extent to which such distributions are interwoven with the economic distributive impacts of other industries, such as real estate markets, and imbricated with other social relations of oppression, such as white supremacy.

School commercialism is the most publicized aspect of public school privatization. This owes largely to liberal assumptions that commercialism taints the otherwise neutral and objective space of the school with business ideologies. From the progressive and radical traditions, such liberal horror at, for example, ads for junkfood in textbooks is naïve because the school is already understood as a political site and stake in struggles for hegemony by different groups, including classes, races, and genders.[3] For example, in the reproduction theories of the 1970s, the school reproduces social relations of capitalism necessary for continued capitalist reproduction. Schools teach the knowledge and skills necessary for students to take their places as workers and managers in the economy. Skills and know-how are taught in ideological forms conducive to social relations conducive to the reproduction of relations of production. In the 1970s this was dubbed the hidden curriculum: Students learn to be docile workers from teachers who emulate the boss. Tests and grades prepare students for understanding compartmentalized, often meaningless, tasks and numerically quantifiable rewards that are extrinsic. Earning grades prepares kids to work for money. School bells segment time in ways conducive to shift work, while desks are arrayed with the teacher/boss at the big desk and the students/workers at the little desks. All of this suggests that the space of school is hardly free of capitalist ideology from the outset. As Henry Giroux has recently suggested,[4] the hidden curriculum is no longer hidden. As neoliberal ideology has resulted in the triumph of market fundamentalism in an overt fashion to all realms of social life, schooling has been remade on the model of the market.

In addition to the above, the cultural aspect of privatizing education involves transforming education on the model of business, describing education through the language of business, and emphasizing what has been termed the "ideology of corporate culture," which involves making meanings, values, and identifications compatible with a business vision for the future. The business model appears in schools in the push for standardization and routinization in the form of emphases on standardization of curriculum, standardized testing, methods-based instruction, teacher de-skilling, scripted lessons, and a number of approaches aiming for efficient delivery of instruction. The business model presumes that teaching, like factory production, can be ever speeded up and made more efficient through technical modifications to instruction and incentives for teachers and students, like cash bonuses. Holistic, critical, and socially oriented approaches to learning that understand pedagogical questions in relation to power are eschewed as privatization instrumentalizes knowledge, thereby disconnecting knowledge from the broader political, ethical, and cultural struggles informing interpretations and claims to truth while denying differential material power to make meanings. Concomitant with neoliberal ideology, business metaphors, logic, and language have come to dominate policy discourse. For example, advocates of privatizing public schools often claim that public schooling is a monopoly, that public schools have failed, that schools must compete to be more efficient, and that schools must be checked for accountability, while parents ought to be allowed a choice of schools from multiple educational providers, as if education were like any other consumable commodity. Shifting public school concerns onto market language frames out public concerns with equality, access, citizenship formation, democratic educational practices, and questions of whose knowledge and values constitute the curriculum. Privatization threatens to undermine the public mission and public dimensions of public schooling by redefining schooling in private ways. This has potentially dire implications for societies theoretically committed to public democratic ideals by undermining civic education and collective public action. Instead, the market model fosters hyperindividualism, consumerism, and a social Darwinist ethic, thereby expanding the worst dimensions of the market into the public space of school. Market language and justifications for schooling eradicate the political and ethical aspects of education. For example, within the view of privatization, students become principally consumers of education and clients of teachers, rather than democratic citizens in the making who will need the knowledge and intellectual tools for meaningful participatory governance. Teachers become deliverers of services rather than critical intellectuals. Knowledge becomes discrete units of product that can be cashed in for jobs rather than something in relation to broader social concerns and material and symbolic power struggles, the recognition of which would be necessary for the development of genuinely democratic forms of education.

PUBLIC SCHOOL PRIVATIZATION: FROM NEOLIBERALISM TO NEOCONSERVATISM AND BACK AGAIN

Contemporary initiatives to privatize public schools can only be understood in relation to the intersections of neoliberal and neoconservative ideology that presently dominate politics (see Apple, 2001). Neoliberalism, alternately described as neoclassical economics and market fundamentalism, is an assemblage of economic, political, and cultural policy doctrine. Neoliberalism, which originates with Frederic Von Hayek, Milton Friedman, and the "Chicago boys" at the University of Chicago in the 1950s, redefines individual and social ideals through market ideals. Within this view individual and social ideals can best be achieved through the unfettered market. In its ideal forms (as opposed to how it is practically implemented), neoliberalism calls for privatization of public goods and services, decreased regulation on trade, loosening of capital and labor controls by the state, and the allowance of foreign direct investment. Public control over public resources should be shifted out of the hands of the necessarily bureaucratic state and into the hands of the necessarily efficient private sector. The collapse of the Soviet Union and the end of the Cold War were seized upon by neoliberals to claim that there could be no alternative to global capitalism. Within the logic of capitalist triumphalism, the only course of action would be to enforce the dictates of the market and expand the market to previously inaccessible places. As David Harvey (2005) has recently written, the financial record of neoliberalism is not one of success, but rather of failure. However, as he argues, it has been extremely successful at redistributing economic wealth and political power upward. For this reason, Harvey calls for understanding neoliberalism as a long-standing project of class warfare waged by the rich on the rest. Not only have welfare state protections and government authority to protect the public interest been undermined by neoliberalism, but these policies have resulted in wide-scale disaster in a number of places, including Argentina, forcing governments to rethink neoliberalism as it has been pushed by the so-called Washington consensus. Originally viewed as an off-beat doctrine, neoliberalism was not taken seriously within policy and government circles until the late 1970s and early 1980s in Thatcher's United Kingdom and in Reagan's United States. Chile under Pinochet was a crucial testing ground for these ideals. The increasing acceptability of neoliberalism had to do with the steady lobbying for neoliberals by right-wing think tanks, but also the right conditions, including economic crises facing the Keynesian model and Fordism in the late 1970s. Neoliberalism has a distinct hostility to democracy. As Harvey writes,

Neoliberal theorists are, however, profoundly suspicious of democracy. Governance by majority rule is seen as a potential threat to individual rights and constitutional liberties. Democracy is viewed as a luxury, only possible under conditions of relative affluence coupled with a strong middle-class presence to guarantee political stability. Neoliberals therefore tend to favour governance by experts and elites. A strong preference exists for government by executive order and by judicial decision rather than democratic and parliamentary decision-making. Neoliberals prefer to insulate key institutions, such as the central bank, from democratic pressures. Given that neoliberal theory centres on the rule of law and a strict interpretation of constitutionality, it follows that conflict and opposition must be mediated through the courts. Solutions and remedies to any problems have to be sought by individuals through the legal system. (2005, pp. 66–67)

In education, neoliberalism has taken hold with tremendous force, remaking educational common sense and pushing forward the privatization and deregulation agendas. The steady rise of all of the reforms and the shift to business language and logic mentioned in the first section can be understood through the extent to which neoliberal ideals have succeeded in taking over educational debates. Neoliberalism appears in the now-commonsense framing of education through presumed ideals of upward individual economic mobility (the promise of cashing in knowledge for jobs) and the social ideals of global economic competition. The TINA (there is no alternative to the market) thesis that has come to dominate politics throughout much of the world has infected educational thought, as the only questions on reform agendas appear to be how to best enforce knowledge and curriculum conducive to national economic interest and the expansion of a corporately managed model of globalization as perceived from the perspective of business. What is dangerously framed out within this view is the role of democratic participation in societies ideally committed to democracy and the role of public schools in preparing public democratic citizens with the tools for meaningful and participatory self-governance. By reducing the politics of education to its economic roles, neoliberal educational reform has deeply authoritarian tendencies that are incompatible with democracy. Educational language has been overrun with neoliberal terms that undergird the framing of educational issues through the ideals of achievement, excellence, and performance-based assessment. These nebulous terms falsely presume agreement over what is meant by these goals. Neoliberals have sought to lay claim to the meaning of democracy as well. John Chubb and Terry Moe wrote in their 1991 book *Politics, Markets, and America's Schools* that the market better facilitates democracy than does political involvement of the public. For Chubb and Moe the bureaucratic strictures of the public sector disable democratic administration while the market facilitates it. As liberal scholar Jeffrey Henig pointed out in his book *Rethinking School Choice*, Chubb and Moe's conception of democracy understands democracy through administrative procedure rather than collective public enactment of shared political and ethical commitments and visions. The limitations of the neoliberal managerial way of comprehending democracy are also nicely captured by none other than the godfather of the neoconservative movement, Irving Kristol:

> What I would call the "managerial" conception of democracy is the predominant opinion among political scientists, sociologists, and economists, and has, through the untiring efforts of these scholars, become the conventional journalistic opinion as well. The root idea behind this managerial conception is that democracy is a "political system" (as they say) which can be adequately defined in terms of — can be fully reduced to — its mechanical arrangements. Democracy is then seen as a set of rules and procedures, and nothing but a set of rules and procedures.... The purpose of democracy cannot possibly be the endless functioning of its own political machinery. The purpose of any political regime is to achieve some version of the good life and the good society. (pp. 175–176)

This quote by Kristol provides not only an incisive comment on the limitations of the neoliberal view for public democracy, but also an important difference between the two dominant political positions of the day and the two political persuasions most influencing educational policy. While neoliberalism in theory views the market as the best expression of politics and morality, neoconservatism in theory posits the need for strong political and moral vision and commitments to further liberal democracy. In this sense, that is, the refusal to reduce politics and morality strictly to the dictates of the market, neoconservatism shares with progressivism, liberalism, and the left radical tradition's faith in public democratic governance. Neoconservatives, however, differ vastly by focusing heavily on the notion that for citizens to participate democratically with others, they must first be educated in virtues. Unlike the neoliberals who in theory want the state out of the way for the market to work its magic, the neoconservatives see the state as having a central role in limiting individual behavior. As Kristol (2004) bluntly writes extolling what he understands as the ancient Greek conception of democracy, "If you want self-government, you are only entitled to it if that 'self' is worthy of governing" (p. 176). Consequently, Kristol and other neoconservatives believe, for example, in state censorship to control the appetitive passions. While the neoliberals, in theory, aim to reduce state involvement in all aspects of social life except repressive ones (police, military), the neoconservative movement embraces a large role for the state in limiting individual privacy, in protecting individuals from corrupting influences, in legislating morality, and in promoting democracy through hawkish militarism. Neoconservatives believe that their interpretation of democracy and freedom is the only way and the right way (exemplified in the National Security Strategy of the United States, 2002), and that on principle it must be achieved through the monopoly on state power and violence. If neoliberalism is a kind of market fundamentalism, then neo-conservatism is also a kind of fundamentalism, though politically oriented around a Eurocentric, masculinist, heavily racially coded, and nostalgic conception of the public good.[5] Individuals have to be educated into virtue and protected from corrupting influences (Kristol seems particularly fearful in this essay of the dangers of masturbation). These virtues are not negotiable but are rather universal. Culture either nurtures or corrupts in the neoconservative view. It is at this point that the neoconservative take on the individual and society appears as glaringly different than that of the progressive tradition. In the progressive tradition, public deliberation on matters of public importance are struggled over by citizens and groups. Culture in the progressive tradition is to be interrogated rather than worshipped or feared. What is common throughout the progressive tradition is the idea that acts of interpretation become central to acts of political intervention and participation. That is, in the progressive tradition the meaning of democracy and the contents of democracy, as well as the contents of the culture, are subject to interpretive struggle. The progressive tradition understands democracy as dynamic rather than static, as shot through with multiple power struggles, and as a quest and process rather than an achieved state that must be fixed and held and protected from corruption. In the progressive educational tradition a democratic society requires citizens capable of not just functional literacy but also critical literacies. Neoconservative ideology is dangerous to public democracy as it demonstrates a deep distrust of public governance and public deliberation and demands upon citizens for their allegiance to unquestionable dogma framed through jingoistic nationalism as well as much of the economism of neoliberal ideology. This was illustrated clearly when, following September 11, 2001, George W. Bush extolled citizens that the most patriotic thing they could do is to return to the malls and go shopping rather than partipating in the political work of deliberating on response. This neoconservative distrust of the people is illustrated in the vast new secrecy of the federal government, the USA Patriot Act, the marginalization of the public and the press from the workings of government, the hostility of the Bush administration to political dissent, the undermining of multiple constitutional protections and rights, and the justification for these on the basis of security. Neoconservative ideology is also dangerous to public democracy in the ways that its authoritarian tendencies lend themselves to reconciling the economic crisis facing neoliberal governance.

David Harvey offers a compelling economic argument for the general shift to repression explaining the shift from neoliberalism to neoconservatism: that neoliberal policy was coming into dire crisis already in the late 1990s as deregulation of capital was resulting in a threat to the United States as it lost the manufacturing base and increasingly lost service-sector and financial industry to Asia. For Harvey, the new militarism in foreign policy is partly about a desperate attempt to seize control of the world's oil spigot, as lone superpower parity is threatened by the rise of a fast growing Asia and a unified Europe with a strong currency. Threats to the U.S. economy are posed by not only the potential loss of control over the fuel for the U.S. economy and military, but also the power conferred by the dollar remaining the world currency and the increasing indebtedness of the United States to China and Japan as they prop up the value of the dollar for the continued export of consumer goods. For Harvey, the structural problems behind global capitalism remain the Marxian crisis of overproduction driving down prices and wages while glutting the market and threatening profits and the financialization of the global economy. Capitalists and states representing capitalist interests respond to these crises through Harvey's version of what Marx called primitive accumulation, "accumulation by dispossession."

> Put in the language of contemporary postmodern political theory, we might say that capitalism necessarily and always creates its own "other." The idea that some sort of "outside" is necessary for the stabilization of capitalism therefore has relevance. But capitalism can either make use of some pre-existing outside (non-capitalist social formations or some sector within capitalism — such as education — that has not yet been proletarianized) or it can actively manufacture it … the "organic relation" between expanded reproduction on the one hand and the often violent processes of dispossession on the other have shaped the historical geography of capitalism. This helps us better understand what the capitalist form of imperialism is about. (Harvey, 2003, pp. 141–142)

As Harvey explains, privatization is one of the most powerful tools of accumulation by dispossession, transforming publicly owned and controlled goods and services into private and restricted ones — the continuation of "enclosing the commons" begun in Tudor England. If neoliberalism came into crisis due to the excesses of capitalism (deregulation and liberalization yielding capital flight, de-industrialization, etc.), then the neoconservative response emphasizing control and order and reinvigorated overt state power makes a lot of sense not only for using state power to pillage productive forces for continued economic growth, but also to control populations through repression as inequalities of wealth and income are radically exacerbated, resulting in the expansion of a dual society of mobile professionals and everyone else.[6]

There is a crucial tension presently between two fundamental functions of public education for the capitalist state. The first involves reproducing the conditions of production: teaching skills and know-how in ways that are ideologically compatible with the social relations of capital accumulation. Public education, whether in the United States or Iraq (where a neoconservative-justified invasion aimed for a neoliberal remaking of the state), remains an important and necessary tool for capital to make political and economic leaders or docile workers and marginalized citizens, or even participating in sorting and sifting out those to be excluded from economy and politics completely. The second function that appears to be relatively new and growing involves the capitalist possibilities of pillaging public education for profit, whether in the United States, Iraq, or elsewhere. Drawing on Harvey's explanation of accumulation by dispossession, we see that in the United States the numerous strategies for privatizing public education from voucher schemes, to for-profit charter schools, to forced for-profit remediation schemes, to dissolving public schools in poor communities and replacing them with a mix of private, charter, and experimental schools follows a pattern of destroying and commodifying schools where the students are redundant to reproduction processes while maintaining public investment in the schools that have the largest reproductive role of turning out managers and leaders. These strategies of capitalist accumulation, dispossession, and reproduction appear to be at odds, yet they feed each other in several ways: Exacerbating differentiation and hierarchization in an ideological apparatus such as education or media through privatization and decentralization weakens universal provision, weakens the public role of a service, puts in place reliance upon expensive equipment supplied from outside, and then justifies further privatization and decentralization to remedy the deepened differentiation and hierarchization that has been introduced or worsened through privatization and hierarchization. The obvious U.S. example is the failure of the state to properly fund public schools in poor communities and then privatizing those schools to be run by corporations (see Saltman, 2000). Rather than addressing the funding inequalities and the intertwined dynamics at work in making poor schools, the remedy is commodification. Such a "smash and grab" approach to ideological state apparatuses appears in Iraq as infrastructure is devastated through sanction and war and followed up with neoliberal privatization and decentralization (Klein, 2005, p. 10; see Chatterjee, 2004). Harvey's and Klein's respective concepts of accumulation by dispossession and disaster capitalism help explain the relationship between a number of seemingly disparate national and international phenomena: For example, the U.S. Department of Education is in the process through NCLB of having the majority of schools in the nation designated as failed, which will require them to restructure in ways conducive to privatization, including charter and experimental models that will undermine unions and local democratically elected school councils and boards; following Hurricane Katrina in 2005, Margaret Spellings, secretary of the U.S. Department of Education, seized the opportunity to implement the largest experiment in publicly funded private vouchers without public oversight; following the U.S. invasions of Afghanistan and Iraq, the U.S. Agency for

International Development (USAID) gave a no-bid multi-million-dollar contract to for-profit corporation Creative Associates International, Inc., to rebuild education. The model has followed the conservative emphasis on charter schools and privatization (see Saltman, in press).

In the spirit of distrust of the public, the neoconservative perspective on knowledge and curriculum presumes that the right knowledge is given to students and teachers from above by those who know. Hence, the slew of pompous and didactic books by the neoconservative culture warriors, such as E. D. Hirsch's *Dictionary of Cultural Literacy* and William Bennett's *Book of Virtues,* that claim to have purchase on what students ought to know and how students ought to be. The neoconservatives and neoliberals share similar curricular values though for different reasons. Phonics, standardization of curriculum, and heavy standardized testing appear alluring to neoliberals because numerically quantifiable measures are easier to use to demonstrate achievement in the acquisition of knowledge. Critical questions for democratic schooling of whose knowledge matters and why and how claims to pedagogical authority relate to broader structures of power, social relations, and modes of subjectivity are generally seen by neoliberals as getting in the way of efficiency. Neoliberalism has seen the return to draconian forms of schooling that undermine creativity, intellectual curiosity, and critical capacities, all in the name of efficiency. Such a deep distrust of students to construct knowledge extends to the deep distrust of teachers' intellectual capacities as canned curriculum and scripted lessons described as "teacher proof" continue to spread. The exception to this is the appropriation of progressive educational approaches in elite communities where preparation for management requires group learning, creative exercises.

The neoliberal emphasis on efficiency intersects conveniently with the neoconservative desire to return to the "classics," the embrace of a high-low culture distinction, and the emphasis on discipline and character building. Neoliberals all too readily accept what neoconservatives put forth as the "right knowledge" because they can measure it. Neoconservatives readily accept the entrepreneurial spirit of neoliberalism because they can prostheletize through standardization. This intersection appears clearly in William Bennett's company K12. Bennett, secretary of education under Ronald Reagan, sells online curriculum to charter schools and homeschooling families through the company. The content is conservative and the format participates in the privatization of public schooling through the undermining of universal education in the form of the charter movement. If the content appeals to neoconservatives, the technology, standardization, and easy measurability of the program appeal to neoliberals. (Bennett's chief of staff while secretary of education was William Kristol, one of the leading neoconservative strategists.) The recent discovery of Bennett's multi-million-dollar gambling addiction and his statements on his radio program that aborting more black babies would certainly lower the crime rate suggest more than the possibility that Bennett may be a dubious authority when it comes to making claims about developing virtue in youth. It points to the broader matter of how truth and virtue, individual and social goods need to be understood as collectively arrived at through democratic dialogue and debate rather than received from above by self-proclaimed experts like Bennett, Hirsch, Ravitch, and others. Public schools are unique in that they hold the public potential to foster such democratic dialogue and debate rather than being reception centers for the knowledge, values, and virtues handed down by self-proclaimed experts. Public school privatization in its neoliberal and neoconservative forms threatens the possibility for public schools to develop as places where knowledge, pedagogical authority, and experiences are taken up in relation to broader political, ethical, cultural, and material struggles informing competing claims to truth. Struggles against these ideologies and their concrete political manifestations must link matters of schooling to other domestic and foreign policies. It is incumbent upon progressive educators and cultural workers to imagine new forms of public educational projects and to organize to take back privatized educational resources for public control.[7]

NOTES

1. This first section draws heavily on my entry in a forthcoming encyclopedia article on the marketization of schooling in Hare and Portelli (2005).
2. For the clearest and most up to date coverage of the terrain and scope of public school privatization and commercialization, see Molnar (2005). Molnar's theoretical perspective draws on Deweyan pragmatism and the institutional analysis typified by Edward Herman and Noam Chomsky's media analysis that focuses on the active role of the public relations industry in manufacturing consent to business dominance. Joel Spring's important historically sweeping *Educating the Consumer-Citizen* likewise offers essential institutional analysis. Such historical institutional analyses are crucial yet incomplete in that they need to be coupled with a more comprehensive cultural theorization as well as broader situating within global economic structural dynamics. The Educational Policy Studies Laboratory at Arizona State University issues regularly updated reports on business involvement in schooling. For important recent scholarship on a range of issues involved in privatization, see, for example, Boyles (2004), Spring (2003), and Kohn and Shannon (2002). See also Saltman (2003).
3. State-run schools in capitalist nations being a site and stake of struggle for hegemony appears in the work of Antonio Gramsci and is developed from Gramsci by Louis Althusser in, for example, his "Ideology and Ideological State Apparatuses" essay in *Lenin and Philosophy* (Althusser, Jameson, & Brewster, 2001) and more explicitly with reference to Gramsci in *Machiavelli and Us* (Althusser, Matheron, & Elliot, 1997). The limitations of the reproduction theories have been taken up extensively and importantly, for example, with regard to the theoretical problems of Marxism, including the legacies of scientism, class

reductionism, economism, and so forth. See, for example, Aronowitz and Giroux (1989). Despite these limitations, Althusser's work appears important for theorizing the state at the present juncture.

4. See, for example, Giroux's important discussion of the politics of No Child Left Behind in *Abandoned Generation* (2003).

5. *The Neocon Reader* includes essays in the tradition of racist sociology with its "culture of pathology" thesis, in which white police officers ideally do foot patrols of nonwhite communities to keep the natives in line. It is remarkable how feebly concealed is the racism here and in other neoconservative writings on culture, such as that of the Thernstroms. Nostalgia for education prior to the civil rights movement appears in the writing of Diane Ravitch. William Bennett admitted his belief on his radio program in 2005 that aborting black babies would lower the crime rate, but that this should not be done because abortion is immoral. Racism should be understood as endemic to neoconservative ideology, as difference generally is viewed with hostility.

6. The surging culture of religious right-wing populism, irrational new age mysticism, and endless conspiracy theorizing appears to symptomatize a cultural climate in which neoliberal market fundamentalism has come into crisis as both economic doctrine and ideology. Within this climate private for-profit knowledge-making institutions, including schools and media, are institutionally incapable of providing a language and criticism that would enable rational interpretation necessary for political intervention. Irrationalism is the consequence. Not too distant history suggests that this can lead in systematically deadly directions.

7. To date there have been few mass walkouts to regain control of public schools. I am aware of some in Illinois that succeeded in forcing the state to change testing rules. However, it is conceivable to imagine wide-ranging and multistate student-led rebellions and walkouts to take public schools back from the high-stakes testing, scripted lessons, standardized curriculum, and money-skimming profiteers.

REFERENCES

Althusser, L., Jameson, F., & Brewster, B. (2001). *Lenin and philosophy and other essays*. New York: Monthly Review Press.

Althusser, L., Matheron, F., & Elliot, G. (1997). *Machiavelli and us*. New York: Verso.

Apple, M. (2001). *Educating the "Right" way: Markets, standards, and inequality*. New York: Routledge.

Aronowitz, S., & Giroux, H. (1989). *Education still under siege*. Westport: Bergin and Garvey.

Boyles, D. (2004). *Schools or markets? Commercialism, privatization and school-business partnerships*. Mahwah, NJ: Lawrence Erlbaum Associates.

Chatterjee, P. (2004). *Iraq, Inc.: A profitable occupation*. New York: Seven Stories Press.

Giroux, H. (2003). *Abandoned generation: Democracy beyond the culture of fear*. New York: Palgrave.

Hare, W., & Portelli, J. P. (2005). *Key questions for educators*. Halifax: Ed Phil Books.

Harvey, D. (2003). *The new imperialism*. New York: Oxford University Press.

Harvey, D. (2005). *A brief history of neoliberalism*. Oxford: Oxford University Press.

Henig, J. (1995) *Rethinking School Choice: Limits of the Market Metaphor.* Princeton, NJ: Princeton University Press.

Klein, N. (2005, May 2). The rise of disaster capitalism. *The Nation.* Retrieved May 1, 2007 from www.thenation.com/doc

Kohn, A., & Shannon, P. (2002). *Education, Inc.* Portsmouth, NH: Heinemann.

Kristol, I. (2004). Pornography, obscenity, and the case for censorship. In I. Seltzer (Ed.), *The neocon reader* (pp. 169–180). New York: Grove.

Molnar, A. (2005). *School commercialism.* New York: Routledge.

Saltman, K. J. (2000). *Collateral damage: Corporatizing public schools — A threat to democracy.* Lanham, MD: Rowman & Littlefield.

Saltman, K. J. (2003). Essay review of Education, Inc. *Teachers College Record.* Retrieved May 9, 2007 from http://www.tcrecord.org/Content.asp?ContentId=11128.

Saltman, K. J. (2005). *The Edison Schools: Corporate schooling and the assault on public education.* New York: Routledge.

Saltman, K. J. (In press). Corporate education and democracy promotion in Iraq. *Review of education/pedagogy/cultural.* Creative Associates International, Inc.

Spring, J. (2003). *Educating the consumer-citizen.* Mahwah, NJ: Lawrence Earlbaum and Associates.

Chapter 27

The Corporate University

Marc Bousquet
Santa Clara University

The crisis in higher education today is increasingly addressed by way of something called the corporate university. By this term most commentators mean something obscene and everywhere tangible that has radically altered the quality of life in higher education for most people in it. But like other forms of obscenity, it is proving rather hard to define.

The notion of a corporate university combines two major lines of thought about the contemporary crisis in higher education — commercialization and managerialism. The commercialization discourse addresses the myriad institutional relations between higher education and actual business enterprise — the question of "corporate power in the ivory tower" and "universities in the marketplace." It also includes a large sector of education activities conducted by commercial entities for employee development or as a service in exchange for a fee. Many of the individual issues here will affect different kinds of campuses in different ways: the enclosure of intellectual property, for-profit education, control of curriculum and research. Nonetheless, every campus is enmeshed in a web of commercial activities, from the most basic purchasing decision to the provision of myriad services.

The second usage, invoking managerialism rather than commercialization, also involves nearly every campus. As employed by the discourse of academic labor, the term *corporate university* names the sweeping transformation of higher education *as a workplace* for millions of people, especially the internal structural rearrangement of the workplace on resource-maximizing organizational principles, especially the casualization and de-skilling of the workforce, and the institution of Toyotist or total-quality principles of continuously stressing the system in order to realize continuously greater savings on labor costs. The usage implies the historical rise to all-but-unchallenged dominance of management over other higher education constituencies, especially students, faculty, and staff (Bousquet, 2005). It also refers to the metastatic spread of *corporate culture* in and through higher education.

In the broader sense, what we mean by a spreading corporate culture can include general forms of corporate ideology and practice, including the complex of values and behaviors associated with neoliberalism. But it also has the narrower meaning of specific management philosophies that seek to perpetuate themselves by way of transforming worker cultures. Replacing earlier models of educational administration (Taylorist, bureaucratic, and human resources), the organizational culture school of academic management has intentionally targeted faculty and student culture with the intention of substituting a different kind of culture altogether, a culture scaffolded by the language of accountability, high performance, and excellence. The widespread dissemination of their management-engineered faculty culture is sometimes diagnosed as "academic capitalism" or "managed professionalism." As a result, even not-for-profit schooling transpires in a corporate ethos, exponentially multiplying the role of the university in disseminating corporate culture in society.

FOR-PROFIT EDUCATION: TOWARD THE EMO

The first line of thought on the corporate university, focusing on the question of commercialization, includes the most historical understanding of the term. In the narrow sense, the term *corporate university* used to designate the in-house training and continuing education operation of a business venture, chiefly meant for employees of the firm. IBM runs one. So does Xerox and hundreds of other major corporations. That kind of corporate university is growing steadily, though the employer often turns to outsourcing the internal training and continuing education operation, finding the cheap labor marshaled by local community colleges and for-profit contractors a better deal.

Another kind of corporate university has long been on Wall Street's radar — the for-profit higher education ventures led by the Apollo Group (University of Phoenix), Laureate (Walden University), the Career Education Corporation, ITT Education Services, Corinthian Colleges, Education Management Corp., DeVry, Inc., and Strayer, among others. The most recent federal statistics show at least 700,000 degree-seeking students annually enrolled in for-profit institutions, double the total of six years before. Between 2001 and 2003, with enrollment in these schools jumping 30% to 60%, the average annual return on publicly traded education corporations ranged from 63% to 75% (Cho, 2006). Currently, for-profits, according to consultants Eduventures, Inc., enroll about 8% of the 20 million students enrolled in financial-aid-eligible institutions, though only 2.4% of those are enrolled in degree-granting institutions (Blumenstyk, 2005c). They collect about 5% of the $395 billion spent on higher education in the United States. They remain strongest in distance and nondegree education, in the tradition of correspondence schools such as Donald Trump's 10,000-student "Trump University" (Osterman, 2006). However, their current growth in degree-granting activities suggests that in less than a decade for-profits may enroll 10% of the degree-seeking student body, unless a rash of re-regulation and support for public community colleges transforms their operating climate (Blumenstyk, 2005a).

The profits of education corporations are enormous. Following the success of University of Phoenix founder John Sperling, who went from labor organizer (and American Federation of Teachers [AFT] chapter president) to billionaire riding the wave of educational privatization, over 500 new for-profit campuses have been launched in the past two decades, more than a third of them offering four-year degrees. Ana Marie Cox contends that these profits come from "cheating" the student, pointing out that traditional institutions operate at a loss, with the deficit covered by public subsidy and private endowment: "Public universities sell a $10,150 education for $1,230; private schools sell a $15,310 education for $6,640" (2003, pp. 25–26). If she is right that in the commercial education sector "students get much less than they pay for, and that's not even considering the quality of education," it is a con game with a notably racial character, enrolling 8% of all postsecondary students; for-profits enroll 16% of all black students and 14% of all Hispanic students ("A Coming of Age," 2000). Nearly all of the major players in the vending of higher education have been under growing scrutiny, with ITT, Corinthian, and Apollo all enduring substantial federal or state investigation, and Career Education is under simultaneous investigation by the Department of Justice and the SEC, together with a handful of lawsuits from investors and employees (Morgenson, 2005; Blumenstyk, 2004). At press time (March 2006), the New York State Board of Regents had just placed a moratorium on new programs by for-profit institutions, after "perceived abuses" at the institutions enrolling 60,000 students receiving more than $100 million in aid from the state (Lederman, 2006).

In this context, the old oft-maligned DeVry Institute of Technology looks like Princeton. In fact, under the headline "An Exception to the For-Profit Rule," the *Chronicle of Higher Education* drapes a positively nostalgic aura around DeVry's relatively higher standards and commitment to students (Blumenstyk, 2005b). In addition to quick-buck entrepreneurs like Donald Trump, the education industry also attracts felons like junk-bond king Michael Milken, who mounted what the *New York Times* called his "comeback" on an encompassing vision of commercialized public education, a "Knowledge Universe," hoping to vertically integrate education profits from preschool through adult continuing education (Saltman, 2003). After his election to the leadership of the Republican House Majority in 2006, Rep. John Boehner was discovered, while chair of the House Education and Workforce Committee, to have been leasing his Washington apartment from a lobbyist employed by a number of companies with "stakes in legislation Boehner has co-written" and that he had overseen while committee chair (Edsall, 2006).

Higher education corporations so far generally operate on the fee-for-service model, funding themselves by aggressive lobbying of politicians like Boehner for loosened regulations on accreditation and student loan financing (Burd, 2004). Despite the obvious success of that model, there may be yet more insidious ways of profit-seeking stalking the campus today. The for-profit sector in K-12 has a different business model entirely. Patterned after the privatization structure of U.S. health care, K-12 education corporations style themselves after education management organizations (EMOs) and seek contracts to manage the public schools in such a way as to yield a profit. The best known player in the growing sector of K-12 privatization is Edison Schools, infamous for its 2002 decision to sell off schoolbooks, computers, lab equipment, and musical instruments from the Philadelphia public schools it managed in an effort to raise cash days before school was about to open, leaving students with books 10 years out of date and no equipment for activities (Saunders, 2002). While Edison's stock dropped to as low as 14 cents a share in that year, it has rebounded nicely in the current climate, and now Edison "partners" with states, charter organizations, and school districts "in 25 states, the District of Columbia and the United Kingdom" to manage the education of 330,000 students ("Edison Schools Overview," 2006). Despite a substantial record of underperforming existing public schools, much less meeting their own inflated promises, EMOs continue to acquire business the Bush way — by asking Republican legislatures to give it to them. In March 2005, the Texas legislature passed House Bill 2, which would have turned over 400 public schools for private education management (Smith, 2005).

How long before Edison and its ilk offers to turn around an underperforming state university system? Is there any reason to imagine that the 25 states who have turned some of their fourth-graders over to EMOs will object to a similar restructuring of their community colleges? How long before their four-year institutions follow? Why not Stanford?

THE UNIVERSITY AS VENDING MACHINE

A less literal but equally descriptive meaning of the term *corporate university* indicates the vast web of relationships between nonprofit institutions and commercial enterprise. This line of inquiry includes stockholder and executive influence over university boards, endowments, and other decisions; corporate sponsorship of research, curriculum, and facilities, not to mention eager collaboration in the privatization of socially useful knowledge; the sale of sports programming, distance education, continuing education, and other services to nonstudents; the manufacture of memorabilia; and provision of food services, health care, financial services, housing, books, supplies, computers, software, and so forth.

A nonprofit institution can still be a revenue-maximizing organization, and the overwhelming force of law and policy over the past 25 or 30 years has been to require institutions to maximize revenue from other-than-public sources.

In pursuit of maximum revenue and "optimum resource allocation," campus administrations have made some pretty unsavory deals with corporations and are functionally corporate actors themselves. Particularly egregious are the notorious deals made with sweatshop producers of apparel and shoes and the outsourcing of campus dining and custodial services to the likes of Sodexho Marriott, predatory employers that specialize in breaking unions and reducing hundreds of campus workers to benefitless positions below a living wage. The literature in this vein is voluminous, but hardly keeps pace with reality. As Lawrence Soley scathingly observed in 1995, "The story about universities in the 1980s and 1990s is that they will turn a trick for anybody with money to invest." The curriculum itself is for sale. Elite schools are more, not less, likely to be for sale, sometimes vending whole departments to corporate investors. Soley recounts how, in exchange for a $25 million basic research grant, UC Berkeley's Department of Plant and Microbial Biology gave first rights to Novartis to license much of the department's work (essentially whatever it found profitable), including work that was directly funded by the federal government. Novartis demanded, and received, multiple seats on the department's research advisory panel and the right to delay publication of the faculty's research for as long as four months. Additional instances include the funding of a journalism class in "reporting military affairs" at Boston University by a munitions manufacturer, pro-business economics classes designed for Gannon University and Springfield College by Hammermill paper, the agreement by Harvard to teach Islamic law in the wake of a $5 million gift from the Saudi government, and Newt Gingrich's PAC-funded course at Kennesaw State, a venture into the classroom for which the House Ethics Committee fined him $300,000 for "using tax-exempt contributions for political purposes" (Soley, 1995, 2000, pp. 29–30).

For Soley as well as more business-friendly observers of commercialization, such as the widely read and generally favorably received Derek Bok (2004) and David Kirp (2004), the locus classicus of the commercialization or commoditization discourse is the Bayh-Dole Act of 1980. This law gave universities and individual researchers property rights in their research, including the privilege of assigning those rights to others in exchange for money. This is an ironic locus classicus, however, because — as Jennifer Washburn and others observe — most universities actually lose money on technology-transfer efforts (2005a) (just as Murray Sperber's 2000 research on the marketing of college sports programming in *Beer and Circus* conclusively demonstrates that big-time college sports consistently lose money for the institutions, who then bury the expense of the sports program in questionable accounting).

Despite the fact that only a minority of schools net out a positive return on intellectual property deals, campus involvement in the privatization of socially useful knowledge is soaring. Before Bayh-Dole, universities produced about 250 patents annually. Today, the number is approximately 5,000 patents each year, in part because activist state legislatures require public research institutions to partner with private enterprise. But why? If higher education is not extracting net revenue from the process, what is going on here? As Soley, Washburn, and others make clear, just because higher education is not profiting from the enclosure of the intellectual commons does not mean nobody is. The industries that have most aggressively partnered with higher education have been handsomely rewarded. The major consequence of intellectual property deals for most campuses is ideological, creating an apparatus and a philosophy through which universities can be used "to further political or corporate objectives" (Soley, 2000, p. 30). Paramount among these objectives is the transfer of public resources into private hands. The pharmaceutical and biomedical industry has been particularly active in this regard, as Jennifer Washburn reports, with the result that U.S. medical schools have been "more infiltrated ... than any other sector of the university" (2005b). The consequences of enclosure for the public are enormous. As Washburn points out, researchers at the University of Utah, upon discovering a gene causing hereditary breast cancer, were prevented from sharing the knowledge with other researchers — first, by the university, which "raced to patent the gene," and second, from the genetics start-up, which bought monopoly rights to exploit the gene from the university (2005b). This despite that (1) the research was funded by nearly $5 million in taxpayer dollars; (2) if anything in the organic world deserves to be understood as collective human property, it is the human genome; and (3) the obvious, one might even say overriding, urgency of social application of this knowledge.

Higher education certainly plays a significant role in the transfer of public goods into private hands, but it is the role of Judas, who never actually enjoys his 30 pieces of silver. Rather than enriching the campus either intellectually or materially, as promised, the campus's forced partnership in the enclosure of the intellectual commons simply contributes to its own impoverishment. In seeking to understand the historical processes that brought us to this point, Jeff Williams (2006) names an earlier moment in

U.S. higher education "the welfare state university" so that he can grasp the present as its aftermath, a "post" welfare state university — the result of a planned and intentional assault on not just higher education, but all forms of social entitlement. This formulation grasps the contingency of the institutions of higher education, which, like the state itself, may have been turned for a time largely to advancing the social welfare but which for decades have been recaptured by private interest.

HOW THE UNIVERSITY WORKS

In Ana Cox's essay on for-profit education, she suggests that the for-profit institutions have a profound influence on the management of nonprofit higher education, that there is a "creeping for-profit ethos" spreading from the University of Phoenix "to the world." This is very commonsensical, but wrong in actuality. There are certainly some ways that the 4% market share of degree-seeking students enjoyed by the for-profits places pressure on certain segments of nonprofit education, especially community colleges. But it is hardly the case that the University of Phoenix is teaching nonprofit higher education how to deliver a vocationally oriented curriculum designed by secure administrators and implemented by a massively casualized instructional force. That practice was perfected by the nonprofits, long before the University of Phoenix sprang from the ashes of John Sperling's hopes to help realize faculty dignity by sitting on the national board of the AFT.

As I see it, for most of us working in higher education, when we speak of the corporate university, we are trying to articulate the ways the university actively participates in the global transformation of the work process. Instead of the high-wage, high-profit world of "knowledge work," most campus employees — including the vast majority of faculty — really work in the low-wage, low-profit sphere of the service economy. Seventy-five percent of university teachers are not eligible for tenure, and most of this untenurable majority work is for fast-food wages or less. Undergraduates are exploited, too. The business plans of global corporations such as UPS increasingly revolve around big-money relationships with campuses willing to provide them with thousands of cheap student workers. These corporations pay millions to build dormitories and subsidize fees, increasing their profits by using the undergraduate population as a low-cost, disposable workforce. More young people are working low-wage jobs for longer than ever before, and they spend more and more time in higher education (the average age of an undergraduate student is 26). For many, the extra years in school represent extra time spent as a temp worker on campus or for a nearby low-wage employer (Bousquet, 2002).

Fixing the problems of academic capitalism requires us to comprehensively address the ways U.S. higher education emulates and interlocks with the hyperexploitative employment patterns of global corporations. A core strategy of globalization is the quest for workforces that are low cost, but also underregulated (that is, not particularly well protected by employment law in the host country). The developed world has its own underregulated areas of the workforce — notably independent contractors and undocumented workers, as well as tens of millions who live by way of "off the books" economic activity. While some informal economic activity is traditionally illegal, such as prostitution, other informal activity, such as gypsy cab driving, unlicensed child care, and many forms of home work, would be legal if it transpired within regulatory boundaries. Other informal employment is better understood as semiformal, as in the regulatory transformation and institutionalization reflected in the way "illegal aliens" have morphed into "undocumented workers," with a new degree of radically limited, often contradictory participation in the regulatory "real."

Informality or semiformality designates profound differences in the political, material, and social entitlements of work. In an unprecedentedly stratified formal economy, which we might view in a series of tiers like a wedding cake, the global semiformal workforce is the base upon which all further stratifications rest.

Because of the traditional informality of campus employment, notably but not exclusively including the informality of the student-teacher learning relationship and the faculty-administration governing relationship, the work of both students and faculty is often similarly un-, under-, or semiregulated. For instance, university administrations have spent tens of millions defending the position that graduate employees are students and not workers. To university management, the informal designation "student" has tremendous implications for control of the workplace and the cost of doing business. Of particular importance, in many circumstances, persons formally recognized by law and policy as workers have the right to organize and bargain the terms of their work collectively; students generally do not.

At nearly all levels of the curriculum from high school to postdoctoral study, "student work" names a zone that falls outside of traditional worker rights and benefits. In most circumstances, students, like other members of the informal economy, can be put to work without health insurance, injury compensation, and unemployment protection; they can be asked to work odd hours without overtime and compelled to donate labor time under the guise of service or learning. In many cases, they will take out loans in order to subsidize scanty wages. Undergraduate employees are often particularly vulnerable and under pressure to stay on at jobs that are unhealthy, demeaning, or unpleasant. This pressure can be amplified when the employer is the university itself, or one of the university's corporate partners.

Graduate education, and its relationship to all forms of faculty work, including research, administration, and service, but especially teaching, is an area spectacularly devoid of regulation and oversight. Lacking any meaningful intervention by professional associations, accreditation bodies, or faculty unions, and only the occasional foray by state legislatures, campuses have since 1970 substituted student teachers and term workers, most of them also students or persons without the terminal degree but recently enrolled as students, for traditional faculty.

The semiformality of graduate employee labor radically affects the shrinking core of the formal professoriate: Assistant and associate professors teach more, serve more, and publish more in return for lower compensation than any previous generation of faculty. The fields where graduate employees and term workers are most widely employed are generally fields where faculty compensation is lowest. And there are widespread new informalities even within the sphere of formal professorial employment. In fields with the most casual workers, the stepped-up research and publication pressure is increasingly an informal demand: To remain formally employed, most administrations require the tenure eligible to do research, often quite expensive research, but without providing funds for the purpose, so that many faculty bear the entire cost of their research agendas out of their paycheck.

What can we do about this? Unionization makes a difference. As a result of the leadership provided by the self-organization of schoolteachers and other public employees, the majority of tenure-stream faculty at public institutions are unionized. Regrettably, it has been a flawed unionization that has been complicit in the perma-temping of everyone else. Private school faculty face Yeshiva; graduate employees at private schools face Brown. There is growth in organizing among the contingent faculty, who face smaller legal barriers but larger cultural obstacles. Twenty percent of graduate employees are unionized, a rate much higher than the typical U.S. worker.

So we also need regulation. We need to start imagining the overall arc of a career in higher education from a policy point of view.

Why not look at higher education faculty work the way we look at other occupations clearly recognized as in the public service, such as policing and firefighting, diplomacy, forestry, and the administration of health, welfare, and social security? In all of these and most other forms of public service, tenure is granted after a short period of probation, typically a year, rarely more than five. One has defined apprenticeship, usually a few months, generally at a pay rate within 90% of compensation awarded in the first year of formal employment, and one has defined periods of service, typically 20 or 25 years, with defined benefits for continuing in the public service a few years longer. Typically one is employed in a climate of affirmative action, with a greater degree of diversity than achieved in most academic disciplines. Higher education's requirement to donate one's labor for as long as a decade as a precondition of being considered for formal employment provides a poor return on education investment for those most affected by inequalities of wealth and income.

PLANNING FOR 25 YEARS

It has taken 25 years, since Yeshiva and Bayh-Dole, and the whole raft of privatization, to get us into our current hole. It could take 25 years more to get out. But I would like us to try. I would like for the academic associations and major unions to get together to come up with a clearly articulated vision of nationwide standards for an academic career, on the civil service model, with basic standards for pay grades, workloads, grievance procedures, and the like. It is not that these standards could be centrally enforced, but that we would be active in forming those standards and move toward implementing them through the variety of agencies available to us: bargaining, legislation, accreditation, public relations, and so forth. Of course, you are free to object that there is far too much variety in campus circumstance or between disciplines, and a simply overpowering need for flexibility, and such, like administrative propaganda, but the fact is that the federal government service (GS) grades, which are remarkably simple, cover far more diversity of work actions and local circumstances, and they do it just fine. Ditto for military pay grades. Neither system is perfect for figuring out the fair relationship between two extra years of training and various performances by various assessment standards, and it is certainly the case that some weapons specialists in grade 4 step 2 really feel that transportation specialists in the same grade and step are overpaid and have too much time off. But on the whole, military personnel and civil servants are a lot more satisfied with the way their pay and benefits are regulated than the vast majority of hyperexploited academic personnel.

That is, of course, because they are regulated, and they are regulated in large part because these other public servants demanded regularity, participate in regulation processes, and oppose efforts at deregulation on an organized basis. The past three or four decades have seen the progressive deregulation and informalization of higher education work. So let us plan on the same scale, develop a series of five-year plans for re-regulation. In short, let us substitute the figure of planning for the figure of market.

By accepting planning, rather than market, as the key to all professional mythologies, we would be enacting the demand of the graduate employee and other informal academic workers. It has often been claimed that graduate employee organizing is a symptom of a trauma other than graduate employee work itself, the wound of shrinking tenurable opportunity. I think that claim is false, because graduate employees darn well need representation, but also because organizing is the shortest path to raising the price of graduate employee labor to the point that it is cheaper to hire assistant professors, even though it may take 25 years to get there. But I also think that graduate employee organizing is a demand for, and long step toward, rationalization of the profession: insisting that organization, responsibility, and negotiated standards replace the propaganda circulating under the sign of the "market."

Ultimately, for me it is not a question of the plan one has, but who one thinks ought to do the planning. And in my view, it is the graduate employees who ought to do the planning, the graduate employees and other informal workers. Seriously, if graduate employee and other contingent-worker organizing is a symptom of an underlying demand — give us the secure, dignified jobs we have earned as a rational return on our years of dedication to the common well-being — that seems like the best sort of demand to plan toward.

REFERENCES

A coming of age. (2000, January 24). *Community College Week.* Retrieved March 1, 2006, from http://www.ecs.org

Blumenstyk, G. (2004, May 14). For-profit colleges face new scrutiny. *Chronicle of Higher Education.* Retrieved March 1, 2006, from http://chronicle.com

Blumenstyk, G. (2005a, November 25). Higher education 2015: For-profit outlook. *Chronicle of Higher Education.* Retrieved March 1, 2006, from http://chronicle.com

Blumenstyk, G. (2005b, April 22). An exception to the for-profit rule. *Chronicle of Higher Education.* Retrieved March 1, 2006, from http://chronicle.com

Blumenstyk, G. (2005c, November 25). For-profit education: Online courses fuel growth. *Chronicle of Higher Education.* Retrieved March 1, 2006, from http://chronicle.com

Bok, D. (2004). *Universities in the marketplace: The commercialization of higher education.* Princeton: Princeton University Press.

Bousquet, M. (2002). The informal economy of the information university. *Workplace: A Journal for Academic Labor, 5,* 1. Retrieved March 1, 2006, from http://www.workplace-gsc.com

Bousquet, M. (2005). The faculty organize, but management enjoys solidarity. *Symploke, 13,* 1–25.

Burd, S. (2004, July 30). For-profit colleges spend big and win big on Capitol Hill. *Chronicle of Higher Education.* Retrieved March 1, 2006, from http://chronicle.com

Cho, H. (2006, Februrary 28). For-profit schools at "tipping point." *Baltimore Sun,* Business, p. 1D.

Cox, A. M. (2003). None of your business: The rise of the University of Phoenix — and why it will fail us all. In B. Johnson, P. Kavanagh, & K. Mattson (Eds.), *Steal this university: The rise of the corporate university and the academic labor movement.* New York: Routledge, pp. 15–32.

Edison Schools' overview. (2006). Retrieved March 1, 2006, from http://www.edisonschools.com

Edsall, T., & Weisman, J. (2006, February 23). Boehner rents apartment owned by lobbyist in D.C. *Washington Post*, p. A3.

Kirp, D. (2004). *Shakespeare, Einstein, and the bottom line: The marketing of higher education.* Cambridge: Harvard University Press.

Lederman, D. (2006, January 23). N.Y. reigns in for-profit colleges. *Inside Higher Education.* Retrieved March 1, 2006, from http://insidehighered.com

Morgenson, G. (2005, May 15). Some things you just can't teach. *New York Times,* Sunday Business, p. 1.

Osterman, R. (2006, January 28). Trump's pitch: I'll teach you to be rich. *Sacramento Bee,* Business, p. D1.

Saltman, K. (2004). Rehabilitation for Milken's junk habit. In M. Bousquet & K. Wills, *The politics of information: the electronic mediation of social change.* An e-book from Alt-X Press. Retrieved March 1, 2006, from http://www.altx.com/ebooks/download.cfminfopol.pdf

Saunders, D. (2002, October 30). For-profit U.S. schools sell off their textbooks. *Toronto Globe and Mail.* Retrieved March 1, 2006, from http://www.commondreams.org

Smith, A. (2005, March 18). Public ed bill escapes the house — barely: First battle in Lege's schools package is contentious, narrow, and roughly partisan. *Austin Chronicle.* Retrieved March 1, 2006, from http://www.austinchronicle.com

Soley, L. (1995). *Leasing the ivory tower: The corporate takeover of academia.* Boston: South End.

Soley, L. (2000). The tricks of academe. In G. White (Ed.), *Campus Inc.: Corporate power in the ivory tower* (pp. 29–35). Amherst, NY: Prometheus Books.

Sperber, M. (2000). *Beer and circus: How big-time college sports is crippling undergraduate education.* New York: Henry Holt.

Washburn, J. (2005a). University, Inc.: 10 things you should know about corporate corruption on campus. *Campus Progress.* Retrieved March 1, 2006, from http://www.campusprogress.org

Washburn, J. (2005b, February). Studied interest: How industry is undermining academia. *American Prospect.* Retrieved March 1, 2006, from http://www.prospect.org

Williams, J. (2006). The post-welfare state university. *American Literary History, 18,* 190–216.

Chapter 28

Schooling

Robert A. Bahruth
Boise State University

It is hard to fight an enemy who has outposts in your head.

—Sally Kempton

It is abundantly clear to critical scholars that the incremental assault upon education since the 1983 *Nation at Risk* report (U.S. Department of Education, National Commission on Excellence in Education, 1983) demonstrates how schools increasingly function to serve the needs of corporations over the needs of children and the need for a critically educated electorate necessary for a strong representational democracy (Bowles & Gintis, 1976; Freire, 1998; Aronowitz, 2000). This leads to the necessary distinction between schooling and education in order to deepen understandings of what can only be deliberate harm to society accomplished through schooling defined by a ruling elite set on preserving the interests of a greedy minority while thwarting the interests of everyday citizens.

The work of Ivan Illich (1971) and Paulo Freire (1970) forewarned scholars of the purposes and dangers of "banking education" in ways that illustrated how schooling sorts citizens into winners and losers and indoctrinates all of its inductees into a logic of consumerism and self-interest. Illich (1992) later introduced the idea of the extinction of *Homo sapien* and the advent of "*homo miserablis*" or, as he translated it, "needy man" (p. 91). Gatto (1993), Molnar (1996, 2005), and Giroux (2000) decry the increased commercialization of the schooling experience where students are prepared for and targeted by marketing. According to Gatto:

Mass dumbness is vital to modern society. The dumb person is wonderfully flexible clay for psychological shaping by market research, government policy makers, public-opinion leaders, and any other interest group. The more pre-thought thoughts a person has memorized, the easier it is to predict what choices he or she will make. (1993, p. 4)

As Betto (2004) demystifies neoliberalism historically, it becomes increasingly evident that capitalism relies upon production, consumption, and maximizing profit through the exploitation of labor. The ideal products of schooling, then, consist of conforming consumer-debtors who will, rather than resisting their own exploitation, enthusiastically participate in their own entrapment by digging themselves a hole of debt by buying into the consumer logic — often accomplished through daily blatant or subliminal bombardments of advertising that now even permeate schools. Betto points out that before the industrial revolution people made things when they needed them. Since industrialization it is now possible to produce greater quantities of products that are not really needed. This requires a system of marketing to create a false need, ergo the neoliberal invention of *homo miserablis*. Martínez (1999) points out that neoliberal policies also violate all economic barometers for healthy growth. Unemployment figures above 10%, he claims, would be scandalous to Adam Smith, David Ricardo, and even Keynes (p. 23). His figures demonstrate worldwide unemployment as high as 41%! All of this is done in the name of development in a system of neoliberal globalization.

Although schools hold the potential for becoming sites of resistance, would-be educators are mostly complicit with the neoliberal agenda. Gabbard (1993) points out how the work of Ivan Illich was marginalized and silenced in mainstream educational journals of his day. Elsewhere, Bahruth (2005a) introduced a barometer for understanding potential for meaningful reform:

A scale of embracing or rejecting of ideas by the status quo serves as an indication of the potential for change the ideas represent. When ideas are embraced, it is because they pose no threat for change. When ideas are ignored, rejected, demonized, or dismissed as unscientific according to definitions of science established by the status quo, it is often because these ideas represent potential for change. (p. 510)

Sadly enough, the rejection of progressive innovations often comes from within the educational community, where most of the occupants of academe are also products of schooling. Schmidt (2000) goes so far as to say the more education, the deeper the indoctrination into the logic of the status quo. Chomsky (1997) states that self-policing away from critical discourse should come as no surprise:

People within them [universities], who don't adjust to that structure, who don't accept it and internalize it (you can't really work with it unless you internalize it, and believe it); people who don't do that are likely to be weeded out along the way, starting from kindergarten, all the way up. There are all sorts of filtering devices to get rid of people who are a pain in the neck and think independently. Those of you who have been through college know that the education system is very highly geared to rewarding conformity and obedience; if you don't do that, you are a troublemaker. (p. 10)

Gabbard (1997) also writes of his attempts to teach critically on a Crow reservation in Montana and how he was actually reprimanded by his dean and department chair for his progressive attempts at providing a critical educational experience to the students there. He also bemoans the already damaging effects of schooling by the sixth grade: "The secular gospel of compulsory schooling had already penetrated the consciousness of the Crow children" (p. 31).

SCHOOLING FOR NEOCONSERVATIVISM

There have always been great teachers operating in the best interests of their students to provide a critical education to the next generation of citizenry. However, recent trends in the neoconservative, corporate government, brought forth through mandates such as No Child Left Behind (NCLB) under the pretense of higher standards, have made it increasingly difficult and have even driven many excellent teachers out of the profession. The pseudo-science (see Shapiro, 1998; Coles, 2000; Freire & Macedo, 2000; Kozol, 2005) of a self-declared scientifically based literacy, standards, and testing agenda has become the main mechanism of repression of those teachers who choose to teach critically, rather than to be reduced to technicism and oppressive schooling practices. Kohn (2002) demystified the neoconservative agenda put forth by the architects of No Child Left Behind and the total disregard for science that contests their purposes. He claims that we may be living through the "most undemocratic" period ever in the history of American education. Along these lines, Arendt observed how education is employed by fascist governments: "The aim of totalitarian education has never been to instill convictions but to destroy the capacity to form any" (1968, p. 168). The relative strength of a democracy might be measured by how comfortable its citizens have become with lies and injustices, and how uncomfortable they have become with the truth.

The clarion call of these authoritarians asserts that whole language has produced an entire generation of children who cannot read and write. The historical amnesia required to make such a statement is aided by the fact that too few educators actually practiced and understood whole language as a philosophy. In addition, whole language has never been the dominant paradigm in schooling in America; behaviorism has always ruled. How ironic that scientifically based research conveniently ignores this fact and makes no linkage to the lack of literacy and the paradigm that produced it. Rather, authoritarians are insisting upon a redoubling of our efforts to resurrect a dead paradigm, and to harm the children who suffer from the antipedagogical experiences it creates in a place called school, especially children who are targeted to have literacy withheld from them through fragmentation and banking of skills, accompanied by a big-brother testing movement that lacks any dimension of validity among scholarly psychometricians and linguametricians (Allington, 2002). What these tests measure is privilege and ruling-class knowledge (Fehr, 1993; Kozol, 2005; Schmidt, 2000).

The results of this NCLB mandate will be the same five years from now, with the same children left behind as always. Schoolers who comply with the oppressive demands to teach to the test, who perform their duties as well-behaved servants of the empire, will find themselves painted into a corner with a bucket in one hand and a brush in the other and the accountability train bearing down upon them. It is not likely the architects (Paige and Spellings) will be showing up to say, "My bad." They will not be around to save anyone from the train wreck they caused. Herein lies the real accountability problem. What will have been accomplished through all of this is a justification to privatize public education employing corporate logic to hire and fire a new corps of schoolers who are guaranteed to be obedient to the purposes of capital over the needs of learners. One could easily argue that colleges of education may also become downsized or extinct as well.

On a broader scale, White (2003) illustrates the postmodern dilemma:

> From Adorno's perspective, the meaning of the Information Economy is the final victory of the organization of "facts" over truth. The brutal consequence of this victory is suffering and death for certain "administered populations" and, at the best in the First World, a great diminishment of what it means to be human.... The "end of history" that conservatives have celebrated becomes the end of hope for justice and universal well-being. (p. 176)

EDUCATION: FORMULATING A RESPONSE

The call for the intellectualization of teacher preparation has been issued throughout the literature on critical pedagogy (see especially Freire, 1970; hooks, 1994; Dykstra, 1995). Despite the fact that many university professors — still far too few — have accepted the challenge to raise the intellectual ante, the dominant paradigm continues to anchor itself in technicism through emphasis on lesson plans, methodologies, curriculum (without curriculum inquiry), and standardization. All of this is carried out in the guise of objectivity, yet as Macedo (1998) succinctly points out:

> Although many educators, particularly those who blindly embrace a positivistic mode of inquiry, would outright deny the role of ideology in their work, nonetheless, they ideologically attempt to prevent the development of any counter discourse within their institution. (p. xii)

When Giroux (1988) called for the intellectualization of teacher preparation programs, he signaled an imperative shift needed in order to contest capitalist logic; a logic of greed and exploitation. More recently, McLaren and Farahmandpur (2005) call for a "contraband pedagogy" (p. 68) for the desperate times we face under the neoconservative, anti-intellectual assault on education.

To see the depth of the times ahead may require a marginal field of education, such as bilingual education, as a ravaged context for such an understanding. This is not always the case, as evidenced by the lack of critical discourse in the field of "special education" — practices that should be termed "special schooling" (Ware, 2000). The connections between special education and No Child Left Behind are frightening, as it seems this militaristic, skill-driven, behaviorist paradigm has been generalized to the entire population, especially the poor (Kozol, 2005). This is the pseudoscience that provides labels — the language of schooling (Bahruth, 2005b) — to blame children who refuse to comply with the oppressive practices of behaviorism, and works in collusion with pharmaceutical companies to drug many of them into submission (p. 55). It would not take much investigation to discover that substantial evidence has linked every school shooting to these pharmaceuticals, and yet little is made of this in the media or in the field of special education. Critically literate people would be able to see the hypocrisy of drug-free school zones while pharmaceutical companies push their wares inside.

How ironic that many of the innovations that depart from the behaviorist paradigm, which has so obviously failed and continues to harm children, were born out of the "broken classrooms" where children of poverty were not responding to schooling based upon skill, drill-and-kill banking. Capitalism drives a system that confines children to poverty and rewards publishing companies that impede implementation of progressive pedagogy and pseudo-scholars who accept the bribes to be well behaved and mediocre.

To be fair, academic preparation of teachers in English as a second language and bilingual education has emphasized a methods/models approach, as evidenced by those who have been celebrated in the field for their innovative methods. While these methods represent a shift in paradigms, they fall short of being pedagogical in the political sense. TPR,

Silent Way, the Natural Approach, and other language teaching methods emphasized proficiency without consciousness. I wrote elsewhere:

> Let us suppose that we have a mean, greedy, dishonest person and it is our job to teach him or her a second language. To help a student to become communicatively competent in a second language without addressing ontological issues (for example, honesty, integrity, the importance of respecting others and our environment, sharing, passion and compassion), then what we end up with is a mean, greedy, dishonest person who can speak two languages. And now that person is even more dangerous! (Bahruth, 2000, p. 4)

The same can be said for the whole language movement in the United States. Teachers became more efficient in teaching reading and writing, without exploring the politics of literacy, who it was meant for and to what degree, as well as who was never intended to become "literate" through schooling (Macedo, 1994). Elsewhere, the limits of schooling as a form of "literalcy" (Bahruth, 2005a, p. 509) for privileged students — many of who become the acritical guardians of the master discourse of the ruling elite — shows how no one is left unscathed.

In my own development as a bilingual educator, it was up to me to broaden and deepen the methods into pedagogy through scholarship and conscientization (Freire, 1970). This came about through the nagging feeling that something was missing. Chávez Chávez (1997) relates a similar personal pedagogical process in his eulogy to Paulo Freire. As I prepare bilingual educators in the academy, conscientization is central to my pedagogy as we discuss the politics of schooling and institutionalized classism, racism, and sexism that prohibits or deters teacher-scholars from using what they have learned to democratize their classrooms. My students are then often able to recognize antipedagogical spaces that domesticate, and they complain about patriarchal professors who condescend and silence.

My students also complain about mandated reading programs that are seldom selected by scholars, are produced by textbook writers — perhaps the poorest genre of writing on the planet, if it is a genre at all — and are rejected by most self-respecting, knowledgeable, and capable teachers. The only teacher on the Reading First panel of the NCLB debacle refused to sign the final report and withdrew herself from participation (Berlak, 2005, p. 267). Yet, self-proclaimed CEOs of school districts, borrowing terminology from big business, with no pedagogical authority, assert their power over well-prepared teachers by making such mandates, treating their teachers as objects who are never included in the decision-making process. These teachers will receive salary increases for their academic advancements, but are prohibited or deterred from using what they have learned by people who have long since stagnated in their academic development and resort to policy making through power rather than through knowledge.

Authoritarianism trumps authority, leaving teacher-scholars with few options: Either conform to district policy, engage in "creative maladjustment" (Kohl, 1994) while escaping detection, or seek employment in a district where teachers are respected.

Bowles and Gintis (1976) argue that a social democracy must evolve through change in the economic order surrounding schools and that schools alone are limited in their ability to create change. The ways in which compulsory schooling requires a system of bribes, threats, and oppression should indicate the fundamental flaws of the system, unless it is understood through the logic of capitalism. Bowles and Gintis deconstruct the racist and classist arguments offered to account for student failure and argue that the main cause of failure in schools has one source: capitalism. They assert that all attempts at school reform in the long history of American education have failed because of a failure to address the economic order of American society. McLaren (2000b) more recently asserts:

> We cannot — we must not — think that equality can occur in our schools or society in general without at once and the same time demanding and participating in political and economic revolution. No sphere of domination must remain unassailed by the project of liberation. (p. 212)

Schools are an important part of the equation for change since they are within the "sphere of domination." To insist upon the distinction between schooling and education might help to clarify ways in which teachers are mandated to work hegemonically and how they might begin to work from a counterhegemonic praxis. Can education be fostered in a place called school? Leistyna (2005) documents the struggles of a critical educator working intensely with teachers trying to create change in schools. His story reflects the frustrations and realities of many progressive attempts for change. A sustained and consistent educational experience is not probable in institutions that encourage and support antipedagogical practices without question. However, although many would-be educators comply with the rules and regulations, there will always be teachers who refuse to accept classist, racist, and sexist explanations for failure, and who will work to democratize and humanize their classrooms through acts of "creative maladjustment" (Kohl, 1994, p. 127). The bright pedagogical moments in any teacher's or student's experiences in schools may be enough to undo the internalized oppression achieved through schooling, or to at least expose schooling through juxtapositions with genuine educational experiences.

As for colleges of education, preparing teachers must include an objective to place them in a moral dilemma created through making the clear distinctions between schooling and education. Hope and purpose, theory and philosophy, and a commitment to issues of social justice all factor into the preparation of teachers who assert a counterhegemonic praxis in an antihumane system. Many are out there, doing so right now, and college professors committed to the lofty goals of education continue to work to ensure that more are on the way. Illich's (1970, p. 89) distinction between a sophist and a philosopher might be helpful in understanding humanist philosophy as the source of strength for those educators who, in Freire's words (1997), "dare teach." Scholarship serves as an expression of caring and a means of resistance. We should also renew a spirit of boycotting products and corporations since we vote each time we spend a dollar in a capitalist society.

McLaren (2000a, p. 83) illustrates lifelong praxis through the unflinching example Che left us with:

> When Che lay wounded and exhausted on the dirt floor of the schoolhouse at La Higuera, he asked his captors to let him speak to the schoolteacher, Julia Cortez. In the final hours of his life, Che debated pedagogy. Taibo reports the following conversation between Che and Julia Cortez:
> "Ah, you're a teacher. Did you know that the 'e' in 'se' has an accent in 'ya sé leer?'" he said, pointing to the chalkboard. "By the way, they don't have schools like this in Cuba. This would be like a prison for us. How can peasants' children study in a place like this? It's anti-pedagogical."
> "Ours is a poor country."
> "But the government officials and the generals drive Mercedes cars and have a host of other things.... Don't they? That's what we're fighting against." (Taibo, 1997, p. 560)

AFTERWORD

I first read Ivan Illich in the 1970s. His book *Deschooling Society* was already well on its way to becoming the classic that it is today. It has taken me years and numerous re-readings to fathom his arguments therein. I finally got to see and hear Illich at a conference on education and technology at Penn State University when he was nearing the end of his lifelong struggle for democratic education as a deinstitutionalized intellectual. He slowly climbed onto the stage, his long grey locks shining in the lights, and he opened his talk with a line that surprised, captured, and delighted everyone there. "The very act of inviting me to speak at a conference on education and technology ... [he paused] ... demonstrates a complete misunderstanding of my life's work!"

Later on at the conference I saw him walking up to people making a final emphatic point about his views on schooling. He pointed at them with a gentle smile and said:

"School you! And, school you too!"

Everyone got the point.

REFERENCES

Allington, R. (2002). *Big brother and the national reading curriculum: How ideology trumped evidence.* Portsmouth, NH: Heinemann.

Arendt, H. (1968). *Totalitarianism.* New York: Harcourt, Brace, Jovanovich.

Aronowitz, S. (2000). *The knowledge factory: Dismantling the corporate university and creating true higher learning.* Boston: Beacon Press.

Bahruth, R. (2000, November 15). Changes and challenges in teaching the word and the world for the benefit of all of humanity. Keynote/Proceedings: International Conference of English Teacher's Association, Taipei, Taiwan.

Bahruth, R. (2005a). Critical literacy versus reading programs: Schooling as a form of control. *International Journal of Learning.*

Bahruth, R. (2005b). *El Pentagonismo: Idioma del Neoliberalismo,* Año 5, Numero 14, Agusto 2005.

Berlak, H. (2005). From local control to government and corporate takeover of school curriculum: The No Child Left Behind Act and the Reading First Program. In H. S. Shapiro & D. E. Purpel (Eds.), *Critical issues in American education: Democracy and meaning in a globalizing world* (3rd ed.). Mahwah, NJ: Lawrence Erlbaum Associates, pp. 227–235.

Betto, F. (2004). *¿Qué es neoliberalismo?* Sao Paolo, Brasil: Betto.

Bowles, S., & Gintis, H. (1976). *Schooling in capitalist America: Educational reform and the contradictions of economic life.* New York: Basic Books.

Chávez Chávez, R. (1997). *Taboo.* New York: Peter Lang Publishers.

Chomsky, N. (1997). What makes the mainstream media mainstream? *Z Magazine.* Retrieved May 9, 2007 from http://www.zmag.org/chomsky/articles/z9710-mainstream-media.html.

Chomsky, N., & Macedo, D. (2000). *Chomsky on miseducation.* Boulder, CO: Rowman & Littlefield.

Coles, G. (2000). *Misreading reading: The bad science that hurts children.* Portsmouth, NH: Heinemann.

Dykstra, D. (1995). Toward a scholarship of teaching: Against the dichotomy between research and teaching. Unpublished manuscript.

Fehr, D. (1993). *Dogs playing cards: Powerbrokers of prejudice in education, art and culture.* New York: Peter Lang.

Freire, P. (1970). *Pedagogy of the oppressed.* New York: Continuum.

Freire, P. (1998). *Teachers as cultural workers: Letters to those who dare teach.* Boulder, CO: Westview.

Freire, P., & Macedo, D. (2000). Scientism as a form of racism. In S. Steiner, M. Krank, P. McLaren, & R. Bahruth (Eds.), *Freirean pedagogy, praxis, and possibilities: Projects for the new millennium.* New York: Falmer Press, pp. 33–40.

Gabbard, D. (1993). *Silencing Ivan Illich: A Foucauldian analysis of intellectual exclusion.* San Francisco: Austin & Winfield.

Gabbard, D. A. (1997, Fall). The prairie is wide: Conrack comes to "The Rez." *Cultural Circles,* Vol. 1.

Gatto, J. (1993). Confederacy of dunces. *Sun Magazine,* 4–12.

Giroux, H. (2000). *Stealing innocence: Corporate culture's war on children.* New York: Palgrave Macmillan.

hooks, b. (1994). *Teaching to transgress.* New York: Routledge.

Illich, I. (1971). *Deschooling society.* London: Calder & Boyers, Ltd.

Illich, I. (1992). Needs. In W. Sacks (Ed.), *The development dictionary*. London: Zed Books, Ltd.

Kempton, S. (n.d.). The quotations page. Retrieved May 1, 2007 from www.quotationspage.com

Kohl, H. (1994). *I won't learn from you: And other thoughts on creative maladjustment*. New York: The New Press.

Kohn, A. (2002). Keynote address. AACTE, New York.

Kozol, J. (2005). *The shame of the nation: The restoration of apartheid schooling in America*. New York: Crown.

Leistyna, P. (2005). Revolutionary possibilities: Multicultural professional development in public schools. In M. Pruyn & L. Huerta-Charles (Eds.), *Teaching Peter McLaren: Paths of dissent*. New York: Peter Lang pp. 63–89.

Macedo, D. (1994). *Literacies of power: What Americans are not allowed to know*. Boulder, CO: West View Press.

Macedo, D. (1998). Foreword. In P. Freire, *Pedagogy of freedom*. Boulder, CO: Rowman & Littlefield.

Martínez, O. (1999). Neoliberalismo en crisis. *La Habana*.

McLaren, P. (2000a). *Che Guevara, Paulo Freire, and the pedagogy of the revolution*. Boulder, CO: Rowman & Littlefield, pp. 345–353.

McLaren, P. (2000b). Critical pedagogy. In D. Gabbard (Ed.), *Knowledge and power in the global economy: Politics and the rhetoric of school reform*. Mahwah, NJ: Lawrence Erlbaum Associates.

McLaren, P., & Farahmandpur, R. (2005). *Teaching against global capitalism and the new imperialism*. Boulder, CO: Rowman & Littlefield.

Molnar, A. (1996). *Giving kids the business: The commercialization of America's schools*. Boulder, CO: Westview Press.

Molnar, A. (2005). Commercial culture and the assault on children's character. In H. S. Shapiro & D. E. Purpel (Eds.), *Critical issues in American education: Democracy and meaning in a globalizing world* (3rd ed.). Mahwah, NJ: Lawrence Erlbaum Associates, pp. 72–89.

Schmidt, J. (2000). *Disciplined minds: A critical look at salaried professionals and the soul-battering system that shapes their lives*. Boulder, CO: Rowman & Littlefield.

Shapiro, S. (1998). Public school reform. *TIKKUN, 13*, No. 1.

Taibo, P. (1997). *Guevara: Also known as Che* (M. M. Roberts, Trans.). New York: St. Martin's Press.

U.S. Department of Education, National Commission on Excellence in Education. (1983). A nation at risk. Retrieved May 1, 2007 from http://www.ed.gov/pubs/NatAtRisk/risk.html

Ware, L. (2000). Inclusion. In D. Gabbard (Ed.), *Knowledge and power in the global economy: Politics and the rhetoric of school reform*. Mahwah, NJ: Lawrence Erlbaum Associates, pp. 111–120.

White, C. (2003). *The middle mind: Why Americans don't think for themselves*. San Francisco: Harper Collins.

CLASSROOM CONSEQUENCES

Kathleen Kesson's essay on teaching opens our eyes to the impact that neo-liberal and neoconservative policies have registered on the lives of teachers. While myopic policy makers pressure schools and colleges of teacher education to produce more graduates to offset the growing teacher shortage, Kesson allows us to understand the futility of this supply-side approach to the problem. It is like pouring water into an open sink. Policy makers fail or refuse to admit to how high-stakes testing and accountability have made teaching increasingly less appealing to anyone who truly values education and learning. Terry Atkinson provides a teacher's-eye -view of the consequences of the National Reading Panel's imperviousness to research on reading in mandating a phonics-based approach to reading in all classrooms and all schools. As Colin Lankshear and Michele Knobel point out, neoliberals approach literacy solely as a technical skill, not part of a much larger holistic process of interaction between the word and the world. After addressing the glaring contradictions in our national reading policy, Atkinson understandably questions whether contradictions even matter. Pat Hinchey's chapter on language arts education confirms her conclusions.

Again, facts seldom interfere with policy — an obvious truism reinforced
by Karen Cadiero-Kaplan and Margarita Berta-Avila in their discussion
of policy makers' aversion to funding bilingual education. In spite of the
magnanimous declaration to leave no child behind, we can only read the
refusal to support bilingual education in our schools as part of No Child
Left Behind's strategy to set schools up for failure, clearing the way for
privatization after 2014. As further testimony to the contempt for democracy that drives the neoliberal/neoconservative push to eliminate public
interference in establishing the goals of education, Wayne Ross's chapter on
social studies education provides crucial insights into why elites have always
feared an educated public committed to basic Enlightenment principles,
such as the rational deliberation of issues. "Deliberation," Ross writes,

> — rather than coercion, appeals to emotion, or authority — offers a means
> for resolving differences of opinion and a foundation for pedagogy that is
> attuned to the knowledge, skills, and values that citizens need in a society
> pursuing a democratic ideal.... Within a democratic community, members
> can disagree as long as they are willing to engage in a discussion about their
> beliefs, as long as their beliefs are consistent with the best available evidence,
> and they are open-minded about their beliefs.

Not only do Ross's observations hold great explanatory power for Atkinson's and Hinchey's concerns over the manner in which national reading
policy was created, but they also support John Jota Leaños & Anthony J.
Villarreal's perspective that equates the underfunding and obliteration of
arts education with the more general assault on any source of dissident
opinion. In the political climate ushered in by neoliberalism and neoconservatism, where there is no alternative to the market, dissent becomes a
national security risk. As they report, even defacing a picture of George
Bush will get you a visit from the FBI, as happened in the case of one North
Carolina student. Ross's observations on the neoliberal/neoconservative
opposition to rational thought within the public sphere receive further
support from Tom Munk and Dewey Dykstra in their treatments of math
and science education. In the name of character education, as addressed by
Four Arrows, neoconservatives promote the idea that the public mind must
be harnessed to irrational beliefs, not the powers of rational discernment
and deliberation. Thuy DaoJensen's chapter on abstinence-only sex education makes this point beautifully. In spite of the research that demonstrates
its counterproductive consequences, neoconservatives still counsel neoliberals to back abstinence-only curriculum in order to appease what Carl
Rove so cynically refers to as "our base," meaning the same people whom
Michael Scanlon — a business partner of Rove's friend Jack Abramhoff
— referred to as "the Christian wackos" in discussing the right's approach
toward mobilizing its supporters.

Chapter 29

Teaching

Kathleen Kesson
Long Island University

Teachers and the profession of teaching, as well as university-based teacher education, are all under great stress in these opening years of the new millennium. The causes are multiple, and the ramifications of current policies on teaching and teacher education are far-reaching. Understanding the many dimensions of the crisis requires a broad understanding of the macropolitical, economic, and cultural forces at work as well as a deep understanding of the historical aims of education and the role of teachers in a free, democratic society. The crisis in the teaching profession is not unrelated to the larger sociopolitical forces captured by the terms *neoliberalism* and *neoconservatism*. The requisite brevity of this chapter precludes examining the interface of these multidisciplinary streams of knowledge in great depth, so I will necessarily present in rather broad brush strokes what I perceive as the most pernicious attacks on teaching by the combination of neoliberal and neoconservative policies and positions. And though these streams of thought are global in their reach, this chapter will be limited to the impact on U.S. teachers, teaching, and public education.

From where I sit, the confluence of these streams of neoliberalism and neoconservatism has brought us to a very dangerous point in our short history as a nation. As I write, we in the United States live under the reign of a group of neoconservatives who have managed to keep the country in a perpetual state of war for the past five years. Social spending, in the wake of an unprecedented national disaster (Hurricane Katrina) and an enormous budget crisis, is in danger of severe cutbacks. We face the distinct possibility of a radically conservative Supreme Court, which is likely to continue the rollback of years of progressive policy decisions in the areas of environmental protection, women's rights, affirmative action, and so forth.

The past four years have brought us the Patriot Act, which has had a chilling effect on domestic dissent (teachers may recall Rod Paige's memorable naming of the National Education Association (NEA) as a "terrorist organization" in February 2004). There is a growing gap at home and abroad between the "haves" and the "have-nots," which has destabilizing effects (note the recent unrest in France, for example). In the United States we have witnessed the seamless integration of fundamentalist Christianity with politics and education, exemplified by the recent wrangling in Kansas, which may result in a mandate to teach the religiously based theory of intelligent design alongside scientific theories of evolution. Our national economy is in the grip of transnational corporations, virtually all aspects of our lives have been commodified by the integration of most services into the market economy, and those with imperialist ambitions dictate our foreign policy. Despite some political unraveling in the current White House and dissent among the ruling classes, the conservative restoration (Apple, 1988) shows no real signs of letting up, and I believe it is not hyperbolic to say that our democracy (which is, remember, barely 200 years old) is in crisis (see Henderson & Kesson, 2004).

It is in the context of this crisis that education policy has been subject to the most intense and intrusive federal intervention in the history of U.S. education. The No Child Left Behind Act (NCLB), a 2001 rewriting of the Elementary and Secondary Education Act (ESEA), received bipartisan (neoliberal and neoconservative) support. Under the guise of increasing schools' accountability for narrowing the achievement gap between poor and minority students and their mostly white suburban counterparts, the bill has instituted a regime of imposed standards and high-stakes testing alongside harsh and punitive measures for schools that do not measure up. The extreme measures in NCLB are not unconnected to larger political and economic forces or to the crisis in our democracy. "The glue," says Lois Weiner, "that held together the bipartisan endorsement of NCLB is the shared ideological support for neoliberalism's program for the global capitalist economy, a global transformation in education's character and role" (2005, ¶ 13).

At the risk of oversimplifying the intent and outcomes of the extraordinarily massive and complex bill, I will just address a few key features that concern the future of teaching. First is the support for the privatization of educational services embedded in the bill. Hinchey and Cadiero-Kaplan state: "School choice — the rationale for vouchers and charter schools — is an integral part of NCLB legislation. Although much of the choice rhetoric purports to focus on public schools, in fact the choice movement does a great deal to promote private schooling" (2005, ¶ 5). The privatization of schools through expanded school choice policies portends a vastly disempowered profession, one with decreased wages, benefits, security, and academic freedom. Private schools need not pay union wages, nor do they need to provide the level of employee benefits that the public sector does. They need not hire certified teachers and are not required to have a tenure system. Teachers as a collective entity would no longer have a say over such essentials as class size or curriculum.

Aside from the specter of school choice, there are a number of factors that favor private capital in the bill: the vastly increased and costly use of standardized tests developed by private corporations, the provision of services by for-profit companies (such as test-prep organizations), and the reliance on scientifically based programs of study created by private corporations such as McGraw-Hill, especially in literacy and mathematics. Hinchey and Cadiero-Kaplan highlight the case of McGraw-Hill:

> This corporation is profiting handsomely from the standards movement in general and from NCLB in particular. As the nation's largest manufacturer of K-12 classroom publications, with a total sales figure in 1999 of four billion dollars (Business Wire, 2001), the company said in a 2001 statement that SRA/McGraw-Hill had a "stellar year" in 2000, with its phonics-based reading programs capturing 37 percent of the $100 million spent on textbooks in Texas — when George W. Bush was governor. (2005, ¶ 21)

It is tempting to think that turning over educational products and services to the market might generate a great diversity of ideas and practices. However, the consolidation of control over the curriculum that is emerging at the intersection of national learning standards and high-stakes tests does not point to such diversification. And it is only logical to assume that corporate control over curriculum, tests, and professional development will favor business-friendly interests and content rather than information and perspectives that represent the public interest. Teachers in a democracy need access to a wide range of materials, created by scholars, educators, and nonprofit groups rather than by a few corporations. Most important, they need to reclaim their historic role as curriculum makers, sensitive to the needs and interests of the children in their care.

Another related aspect of NCLB that should concern us is the discourse on teacher quality. Universities have traditionally been the sites of teacher preparation and professional development. Teacher education, as constituted historically, has included a number of academic strands. Of course, it is important that teachers be grounded in the various liberal arts disciplines that they will be teaching. In addition to this, they study the foundations of education, including the history of education, the philosophical foundations of education, and the sociological dimensions of education, including the effects of culture, poverty, race, class, gender, and so forth on teaching and learning. Teacher candidates also study child development, learning theory, and content-specific pedagogy (methods) in order to learn how best to tailor their instruction to the specific children they work with.

Increasingly, in the professional field, there is an emphasis for both pre-service and in-service teachers on learning to inquire into their practice through various forms of classroom-based research and reflection in order to strengthen their capacities to make informed judgments. In teacher education, there is ongoing debate about the relative importance of these various academic demands, and programs vary across the country. However, scholars and teacher educators are in general agreement about the necessity for a broad, liberal-arts-based preparation that fosters critical thinking, reflective practice, and a commitment to equity and democratic schooling.

In this privatized environment, competition for the task of teacher preparation by private corporations (and by school districts) is under way. Many of the "alternative certification" options promise accelerated programs at lower cost than the traditional university route. Most of these programs require prospective teachers to have an academic background in a content area, and then they provide hasty and limited preparation in general teaching methods. The result of most of these programs is a kind of "on-the-job training" that often leads to a high attrition rate when underprepared teachers come up against some of the challenging realities of public schools. The emphasis in NCLB on certification in the content area is a quality indicator that few would argue. Most accelerated programs, however, ignore or neglect crucial aspects of teacher education, especially the foundations of education. It is perhaps no accident that in most accelerated programs the foundational academic disciplines that help teachers understand their profession from critical, historical, cultural, and political perspectives are eliminated in favor of inadequate teaching methods courses. The federal government offers incentives, including monetary support, for alternative routes into teaching, such as the Troops to Teachers program. It is perhaps telling that Troops teachers "view most problems facing teachers as less serious than teachers in general — *especially in such areas as compliance with the No Child Left Behind requirements, testing requirements* [italics added], extra duties, dealing with bureaucracies and administrators, discipline and class size" (p. 12, Profile of Troops to Teachers, National Center for Education Information). Clearly, the military provides a better background for teaching in this new era than does the university. As a constellation of proposals all related to teacher quality in NCLB, the combination of alternative (to university-based teacher education) pathways into the profession, proposals for expanded teacher testing, the reform of the tenure system, and merit pay based on student performances on tests, when understood in tandem with the narrowing of the curriculum to a standardized, testable range of basic facts and skills, promises to foster conformity and submission in the profession and the consolidation of bureaucratic control over the labor of teaching.

Another aspect of teacher quality is the new focus on professional development as "product implementation" (Hinchey & Cadiero-Kaplan, 2005).

Again, rather than enroll in graduate programs or courses that might perhaps introduce teachers to advanced theory, critical thinking, and sophisticated methods of teacher inquiry and classroom-based research, they are often encouraged, or mandated, to be trained by an ever-proliferating cadre of consultants whose services are tied to the corporate curricula that many teachers are now expected to implement in their classrooms. The implications for teacher quality and teacher development in this policy environment are troubling. Hinchey and Cadiero-Kaplan (2005) summarize it succinctly and well:

> Learning is to be measured by standardized tests — based on curricular materials designed by the same companies who make the tests. Good teachers will be those who most faithfully implement curricular materials so that students are well trained to take the tests. The standardized curriculum and tests form the center of this new educational universe, and all classroom actors and activities must revolve around them. (Section 6, ¶ 6)

Elsewhere I have written about the effects on teachers' labor of the regime of curriculum standardization and high-stakes testing (Kesson, 2004a, 2004b). Under the standardized management paradigm, in which the curriculum is scripted and oriented toward the accumulation of a narrow band of test-taking skills and content, and for which student responses are preprogrammed, teachers are deskilled and lose any sense of autonomy, creativity, and passion. The curriculum becomes reified, students become objectified, and the act of teaching becomes routinized and bureaucratized. The reasons for teacher attrition are multiple, but it is worth noting that in one survey (Tye & O'Brien, 2002) "the top-ranked reason for quitting teaching among those who had already left the profession is 'accountability' and the increasing use of high stakes, standards-based testing with the associated 'drill and kill' curricula that often come with it" (Buckley, Schneider, & Shang, 2004). We are losing many of our most experienced, creative, and professional teachers.

Teachers and those who educate teachers need to engage in the analysis of the connections between current policies that impact teaching and the larger currents in our society (and the world). If we accept the veracity of my proposition that our democracy is in crisis, and if we take seriously the notion that there is a relationship between democracy and education, and that teachers in a free society hold a great deal of responsibility for fostering this relationship, then I think we must agree that teachers and teacher educators are faced with some crucial choices about the direction of our profession. Will we assert our commitments to the democratic way of life and make the study of the dimensions of this a central aspect of our professional development? Will we devote ourselves to sustained and rigorous inquiry, not just about best practices in education, but also about the dimensions of the crises in our society? Will we become oppositional, in the sense of speaking truth to power about policies and practices that harm children or exacerbate inequities? Will we become more critical and refuse the unquestioned acceptance of curricula designed by politically affiliated consultants and corporations whose bottom line is more important than the authentic learning of our students? Will we ally ourselves with grassroots movements that are struggling for economic, racial, political, and educational justice (Anyon, 2005)? Will we adopt a critical pedagogy that recognizes the fundamentally political nature of all education, that aims to make explicit the relations of power that govern people's lives, and which is aimed toward democratic social transformation? Or will we become bureaucratic functionaries who do not question the aims and purposes of those above us in the hierarchy, and for whom reflection means "finding the most effective and efficient means to achieve ends and to solve problems that have largely been defined for [us] by others" (Grant & Zeichner, 2001, p. 104)?

This last position was expressed by a student teacher in one of my classes recently, who upon reading the journal article from which the preceding quote was taken, responded:

> I'm not sure that it is necessary for a teacher to be reflective about their work. When a person is given a clear set of instructions all they need to do is follow them. In today's classroom teachers are being given scripts and detailed curriculum that gives them minute-by-minute details of how the school day should go. If a teacher feels that his or her job is to teach what he or she is told to teach, one would have to ask, what is there to reflect on? After all, the course work has been reflected upon by various specialists before it is shoved down the throats of students and educators. The passage mentions the possibility of teachers forgetting the purpose of what they are teaching. How is this possible? Isn't the purpose given to the teacher with the curriculum each year?

As a teacher educator, I found this student's response troubling for a number of reasons. The student clearly feels disempowered in terms of her ability to control her own labor process. She accepts a hierarchical structure that dictates that her role will be the implementation of other's ideas, thus exemplifying the dissociation of conception and execution characteristic of alienated labor (Kesson, 2004a, 2004b). She does not really question the imposition of a rigid, prefabricated curriculum that leaves no room for teacher decision making in response to student needs or interests. She seems to have no understanding of the role of academic freedom in our society. There is a sense of despair and surrender to the inevitability of these conditions. And there is also anger, in her characterization of the curriculum as being "shoved down the throats of students and educators." It pains me to think about the kind of educational experience children have in the care of angry and disempowered teachers. I must add here that I teach in an urban university and virtually all of my students teach in underserved, inner-city schools. This student was student teaching in such a school. I have no doubt that the sort of deskilling represented by her perception is significantly more entrenched in poor schools that serve minority children than it is in wealthy suburban districts. In this sense, we must confront the possibility that teachers in poor schools that serve predominantly minority children are subjected to more severe control and surveillance mechanisms than are teachers in more privileged schools. However, I also know that these tendencies are becoming more and more the norm everywhere, and we need to take seriously the attrition of qualified veteran and promising new teachers who simply will not submit to the deskilling of their profession.

I have alluded to two competing visions of the future of teaching in this chapter. On the one hand, if there is no change in the direction things are going, teaching will become a profession in which teachers serve the interests of bureaucratic control and corporate interests: Curriculum will be designed by entrepreneurs and corporate entities who have no connection to children or local communities, and there will be little room in the day for activities that are not directly aligned to regular and repeated standardized tests. There will be little content that fosters critical understanding of the world we are living in, for such content would not be in the interests of the corporate world that creates the curricula and the tests. Teachers' work will be largely functionary — they will have scripts to read from that determine what is to be done minute by minute in the classroom, and correct student responses will be indicated by the script. There will be little opportunity to explore issues or topics of interest to either teachers or their students. Teacher labor will be monitored by managers who enter the classroom whenever they please and keep checklists of the extent to which the teacher is conforming to the pacing calendar (a document that dictates such things as how many minutes one should spend on accountable talk) and other bureaucratic requirements, such as where to place the "word wall" and what color the "Do Now" should be written in (I wish I were being playful here, but this is the reality of the surveillance in inner-city schools). Pay increases will be assessed based on the test scores of their students. Professional development will consist of training supplied by the corporate designers of the mandated curriculum. And should privatization become a reality, teaching will probably support a standard of living equivalent to that of the average Wal-Mart worker. Such teachers will be easy to control, for there will be a large pool of people with sufficient education to be able to follow directions and read the script waiting for the jobs. After all, these people — just a generation or two from now — will themselves have been the beneficiaries of such a dull, regimented education and will have no other model in mind.

On the other hand, there is the vision of an empowered profession (Jim Henderson and I describe this as a mature profession" [Kesson & Henderson, 2004]). In a mature profession, teachers with a strong sense of the relationship between democracy and education would reclaim their historic control over the curriculum (in collaboration with children and communities). They would ensure that the many cultures and perspectives of their students are reflected in their curriculum. They would be at least as interested in the development of critical, compassionate, and creative thinking as they are in getting students to pass tests of basic knowledge and skills. They would understand the necessity for students in a democracy to not only possess knowledge, but also question the authority of the knowledge they are presented with. Empowered teachers would pursue their own intellectual passions and creative interests and would bring these into the classroom in a meaningful way, hoping to spark the fire of similar passions in their students. They would be grounded in a set of eclectic inquiry practices that support the construction of professional knowledge through careful attention to experience as well as to the ideas of others. These inquiries would be directed toward their teaching practices as well as to broader questions having to do with the ethics and requirements of democratic living. Professional development would build capacity for such inquiry. Such teachers would consider themselves transformative intellectuals and would be committed advocates and activists who resist policies and practices that harm children or exacerbate inequality. They would, as Jean Anyon (2005) suggests, ally themselves with grassroots activists and create a social movement that might at last bring about the promises of democratic education.

It is possible that the vision of an empowered professional community of teachers is as inconsistent with the current focus on test scores, standardized curricula, and bureaucratic forms of accountability as are alternative social/economic models that offer strong protection for labor rights, human rights, the environment, and living wages with neoliberalism and neoconservatism. If so, we need to take the words of Hinchey and Cadiero-Kaplan seriously when they assert that "both the future of public schools and the future of teaching itself are now at stake — and with them, nothing less than the future of a genuinely democratic American society" (2005, ¶ 2). Connecting the dots in this way, teachers might recall their activist history and become, once again, leaders in the struggle for economic and social justice. Jean Anyon (2005) ends her important new book, *Radical Possibilities*, with just such a call to action:

> If those of us who are angry about injustice can recapture this revolutionary spirit of democracy, and if we can act on it together, then we may be able to create a force powerful enough to produce economic justice and real, long-term school reform in America's cities. (p. 200)

I believe that this is a vision worth pursuing.

REFERENCES

Anyon, J. (2005). *Radical possibilities: Public policy, urban education, and a new social movement.* New York: Routledge.

Apple, M. W. (1988). Redefining equality: Authoritarian populism and the conservative restoration. *Teachers College Record, 90,* 167–184.

Buckley, J., Schneider, M., & Shang, Y. (2004). *The effects of school facility quality on teacher retention in urban school districts.* National Clearinghouse for Educational Facilities.

Grant, C. & Zeichner, K. (2001). On becoming a reflective teacher. In Strouse, J.H. (ed.). *Exploring socio-cultural themes in education. Readings in social foundations.* Ohio: Merrill

Henderson, J., & Kesson, K. (2004). *Curriculum wisdom: Educational decisions in democratic societies.* Upper Saddle River, NJ: Merrill Prentice-Hall.

Hinchey, P.H., & Cadiero-Kaplan, K. (2005, October). The future of teacher education and teaching: Another piece of the privatization puzzle. *Journal for Critical Education Policy Studies, 3.*

Kesson, K. (2004a, March/April). Inhuman powers and "terrible things": The theory and practice of alienated labor in urban schools. *Journal for Critical Education Policy Studies, 2.* Retrieved May 9, 2007 from http://www.jceps.com/index.php?pageID=article&articleID=22.

Kesson, K. (2004b). An inhuman power: Alienated labor in low-performing schools. In Kesson, K. R., & Ross, E. W. (Eds.), *Defending public schools: Teaching for a democratic society.* Westport, CT: Praeger.

Kesson, K. R., & Henderson, J. G. (2004). Cultivating democratic curriculum judgments: Toward a mature profession. In Kesson, K. R., & Ross, E. W. (Eds.), *Defending public schools: Teaching for a democratic society.* Westport, CT: Praeger.

Tye, B. B., & O'Brien, L. (2002). Why are experienced teachers leaving the profession? *Phi Delta Kappan, 84,* 24–32.

Weiner, L. (2005, Winter). Neoliberalism, teacher unionism, and the future of public education. *New Politics,* Vol. X, No. 2, Whole No. 38. Retrieved May 1, 2007 from http://www.wpunj.edu/~newpol/issue38/weiner38.htm

Chapter 30

Reading

Terry S. Atkinson
East Carolina University

As a university professor who spent the majority of her career teaching in elementary school classrooms, it seems only fitting that a piece about politics and reading should begin with focus on an actual teacher — one who deals daily with the issues and decisions made by politicians and policy makers who, most likely, have never darkened the doors of a school. This particular teacher, one of my own graduate students, spends her days teaching first-graders in a rural county setting.

She recently contacted me after attending a daylong phonics workshop facilitated by reading specialists from a highly prestigious independent school in one of our state's largest metropolitan areas. A trained Reading Recovery®[1] teacher with most of her graduate-level reading coursework behind her, she agreed to attend the professional development session at the request of her district, fully expecting that she might be more informed about the teaching of phonics than her instructors. After the day concluded and her worst expectation had become reality, she asked me how it was possible for such a school, serving some of the most affluent children in the state, to pepper their workshop sessions with the cavalier refrain "research says, research says, research says" without sharing a shred of specific supporting evidence. Moreover, according to the presenters, "research" proved that children would transform into proficient readers if they learned a litany of complicated phonics rules and used them to read texts with controlled vocabularies, often characterized by rousing sentences such as "Dan ran and can fan the man, Jan."

This teacher, widely read and with years of teaching experience supporting struggling readers, was keenly aware that presenting phonics as the Holy Grail of reading was not only mandated by current federal-level policy makers, but also a regurgitated instructional approach that knew its first heyday in the early 1970s. Amazed that practitioners, policy makers, and politicians could all be so misguided, she aligned her dismay with that of other literacy experts, such as Richard Allington (2002), who states:

> There are days when I could swear that some sort of amnesia is running rampant. How is it that so many folks cannot see that the new, new educational reform plans are but recycled bad ideas? Ideas we have tried before. Ideas that had their chance. Ideas that fell flat on their faces thirty years ago. (p. vi)

The curious connections linking politics, policy making, and the teaching of reading offer insight into the reading amnesia that Allington describes. Garnering the attention of numerous writers and literacy experts, especially within recent years, related news stories, articles, commentaries, and entire books echo the implicit questions posed by the teacher in the previous scenario: Why did this happen? How can this be?

SLEIGHT OF HAND

Answers to the current questions posed by this teacher cannot be illuminated without looking several decades into the past. As far back as the late 1950s, the Russian launch of Sputnik led to increased federal scrutiny of public education that has since morphed into current federal mandates demanding state accountability and high-stakes testing. However, this scrutinous lens of educational reform has less to do with better serving the interests of American school children than it does with benefiting various politically motivated groups wielding power and status. Prestigious special-interest groups have historically not only suppressed or ignored educational reform evidence perceived to be contrary to their goals, but often fabricated supporting information (Berliner & Biddle, 1995; Jaeger, 1992; Linn, 1993; McDonnell, 1994; Tanner, 1993; Bracey, 2005). Consequently, negative media coverage of public schools has and continues to occur routinely, offering Americans a steady diet of information that is often incomplete, biased, and inaccurate.

Certain political groups, past and present, surreptitiously rely on sleight of hand to promote their own agendas in the name of educational reform. In many cases, the public remains almost wholly unaware of the deft moves and outcomes of such groups; this is especially true when the perpetrator responsible for misinformation or suppression of truth is the U.S. federal government. Historically, one of the most striking instances of such deception originated in the 1980s as the Reagan administration sought to promote the privatization of American schools by substantiating the pervasive inferiority of public school achievement. *A Nation at Risk: The*

Imperative for Educational Reform (National Commission on Excellence in Education, 1983) laid the groundwork for assuring the media, public, and top-level policy makers that the only way to ensure the United States a stronghold as an international economic competitor was to hold lax state governments accountable for student achievement. Reagan's educational goals morphed into those of his successor, George H. W. Bush. Soon after Bush took office, his America 2000 plan was enacted, detailing demands for higher national standards and increased school accountability. In early 1990, Adm. James Watkins, then secretary of energy, led a federally initiated charge to officially document the dreadful "state of public education." Three years later, Sandia National Laboratories completed a comprehensive study entitled *Perspectives on Education in America* addressing an extensive array of educational issues intending to underscore "the most pressing issues in American education" (Carson, Huelskamp, & Woodall, 1993, p. 259). Unexpected conclusive findings substantiated the necessity for none of the reforms detailed in Bush's America 2000 plan; in fact, on nearly every measure examined, "steady or slightly improving trends" (Carson et al., 1993, p. 259) were noted. Immediate administrative reaction led to serious questioning of the study's credibility. While numerous technical reviews identified no substantive flaws in the Sandia Report, its publication was prohibited until late 1993, when the study finally appeared in an academic journal far from the general public's view. Publication of the Sandia Report garnered little attention and was virtually absent from media or government reports, leading to the reality that many present-day educators still remain unaware of its findings or existence (Tanner, 1993).

With such a striking historical precedent in place, sleight-of-hand tactics employed in the case of the Sandia Report blossomed into more strategic deception as the 1990s progressed, ensnaring an even wider range of educational reform supporters, with affiliation across political party lines. Misleading reports about National Assessment of Educational Progress (NAEP) reading scores flooded the media and easily convinced a gullible public that a rampant pandemic of reading failure threatened to undermine America's future as a global competitor (Allington, 2002; Bracey, 2001; Taylor, 1998). A cunning political campaign was already in motion, meant to create a groundswell of nationwide support for the direct-instruction phonics-based reading programs that had failed in decades past.

Since wide distribution of several federally funded publications (including *A Nation at Risk*) had failed to shift *full-throttle phonics instruction* into gear within U.S. public schools, a wide network of well-funded conservative foundations and institutes successfully moved a series of bills through state legislatures during the 1990s supporting an outcome that would eventually have huge payoffs for powerful publishing lobbies (Goodman, 1998; Taylor, 1998). By defining direct-instruction programs as the only instructional reading methods based on scientific research, the pro-phonics campaign (including the Heritage Foundation, the Eagle Forum, and others; Goodman, 1998; Taylor, 1998) undermined and discounted more holistic approaches to teaching reading. Indeed, in the late 1980s David Pearson (2004) suggested that the whole-language movement[2] might eventually be doomed, not by its lack of instructional effectiveness, but by running "afoul of the powerful publishing lobbies in the United States" (p. 216). Additionally, and of wide-reaching importance, the tactics of this political campaign to validate scientific research strategically discredited the work of the reading research community. This was due in large part to the shift of reading researchers within the 1980s and 1990s to focus on studies that were from a "more qualitative, more interpretive, and more critical tradition" (Pearson, 2004, p. 225). As the campaign ensured passage of the Reading Excellence Act (HR 2614) in late 1997, this "crowning jewel" (Goodman, 1998) accomplishment represented the ultimate sleight-of-hand maneuver. By defining scientifically based reading research (SBRR) as the only viable basis for teaching schoolchildren to read, this covert network had effectively disqualified most of the reading research experts from consideration as policy-making players at the national level. Those who knew the most about teaching children to read had been rendered powerless by a political machine that relied upon misrepresentation, covert tactics, and distorted information to promote their own interests.

With the advent of the Reading Excellence Act, legislation was now in place to forward the experimental reading research that had gained momentum and support since the mid-1980s not only from powerful foundations, but also from millions of federal tax dollars granted by the National Institute of Child Health and Human Development (NICHD). Indeed, in late 1997 when NICHD's chief, Reid Lyon, was featured as speaker at a luncheon sponsored by the Heritage Foundation, invitations to the event described him as "chief of child development and behavior at the National Institute of Child Health and Human Development. The NICHD has conducted $200 million of research over 30 years showing that phonics is the most effective way to teach children who do not learn to read at home" (Taylor, 1998, p. 290).

Across the past three decades, NICHD had built a powerful network of *reading elite* who adhered to the clinical research model commonly used in the fields of science and medicine and had built a library of their own studies fitting their criteria of SBRR. In exceptional sleight-of-hand maneuvers, the work of NICHD's own chief, Reid Lyon, was funded repeatedly and often featured as seminal. Research agendas of those names that recur in the annals of NICHD's SBRR archives align closely with direct-instruction phonics teaching: Reid Lyon, Barbara Foorman, Jack Fletcher, Daniel Francis, Louisa Moats, Doug Carnine, Robert Sweet, and a host of other researchers (Taylor, 1998) who had benefited from the influence of NICHD and other political agendas. With NICHD (and thus the federal government) in the position of defining credible research, the bias inherent in research associated with the agency is hugely problematic, especially since it served as foundational for political decisions of the 1990s. Findings from significant studies funded by NICHD (including the Houston reading studies) have been found to be selectively reported or summarized as inconclusive. Denny Taylor provides extensive details about NICHD's sleight-of-hand research phenomena in her book *Beginning to Read and the Spin Doctors of Science: The Political Campaign to Change America's Mind About How Children Learn to Read* (1998).

CURIOUS CONTRADICTIONS

The questions posed by the teacher at the beginning of this piece — "Why did this happen? How can this be?" — might well be followed by "When will this end?"

This question surfaces regularly in the minds of classroom teachers who reel from the impact of continued federal dictums. They realize that the Reading Excellence Act transformed into No Child Left Behind in 2002 and "established Reading First [see Hinchey's "Language Arts Education" within this edition for further details] as a new, high-quality evidence-based program for the students of America" (U.S. Department of Education, 2005). With the demoralizing prospect of delivering scripted reading programs such as Open Court, teachers face the reality that they may soon be mandated to implement what one teacher termed "the new three Rs: readin', ritin', and rote" (Rice, 2006). With the future of reading instruction barreling headlong down a course charted by NICHD and its political backers, one might wonder why a number of curious contradictions that confound this national reading agenda have not garnered more attention from politicians, policy makers, educators, and the public.

Contradiction 1: *With "unbiased scientific truth" (Garan, 2001, p. 506) at the heart of its mission, why did Congress and NICHD use a grossly flawed research report as a basis for impacting classroom reading instruction?*

Passage of the Reading Excellence Act in 1997 initiated the appointment of a national panel of reading experts to be chosen from various federal agencies, including National Institute for Literacy, the National Research Council of the National Academy of Sciences, and the National Institute of Child Health and Human Development. While recommendations were made by these agencies, ultimate control of this National Reading Panel's membership was left to NICHD's chief, Reid Lyon (Goodman, 1998). With panel members representing the fields of accounting, pediatric medicine, physics, psychology, social science, and special education, only 4 of the 14 members were well-known researchers among academics in the reading community. One of the two former reading teachers on the panel, Dr. Joanne Yatvin, later became a vocal critic of the panel's tactics, claiming their work was "unbalanced, and, to some extent irrelevant" (Yatvin, 2002, p. 125).

The main charge given to the National Reading Panel (NRP), to produce a report assessing "the status of research-based knowledge, including the effectiveness of various approaches to teaching children to read" (U.S. Department of Labor, Health and Human Services, and Education and Related Agencies, 1998, Section 86), resulted in the publication of *Teaching Children to Read* in 1999 (National Institutes of Health and National Institute of Child Health and Human Development, 1999). Detailed in Elaine Garan's article "Beyond the Smoke and Mirrors: A Critique of the National Reading Panel Report on Phonics" (2001), this meta-analysis included only 38 studies of low-achieving students, defining a narrow student sample that is not a subset of the larger student population and classroom environment to which the NRP generalized its findings. Furthermore, the studies included did not assess the same conceptual outcome — a critical factor of sound meta-analyses. Purported to be an unbiased meta-analysis that "clearly articulates the most comprehensive review of existing reading research to be undertaken in American education" (Garan, 2001, p. 501), the study is seriously flawed. Elaine Garan's analysis of the NPR report published in *Phi Delta Kappan* in 2001 has received little, if any, media coverage — not surprising considering the political clout of the National Reading Panel. The report continues to be cited across the United States (and particularly in the opening teacher scenario) as the research used as the cornerstone for recommending the teaching of direct-instruction phonics-based reading programs in all American public schools.

DO FURTHER CONTRADICTIONS EVEN MATTER?

When shocking contradictions belie the fact that a government agency endorsing scientific truth employs valid research methods themselves, one might wonder if exploring further curious contradictions even matters. Indeed, if far-reaching deception is at the core of promoting the pro-phonics agenda in American schools, does it really matter that the publishers who have earned millions of dollars as a result of these reading reform efforts are huge contributors to conservative political campaigns (Metcalf, 2002; Trelease, 2005)? Does it really matter that the current stipulations imposed on teachers requiring that they be highly qualified do not apply to the highest-ranking education official in the United States, Margaret Spellings? (With a background in political science, she served as Bush's chief domestic policy aide prior to her appointment as the secretary of education in January 2005 [Lisman, 2004; Robelen, 2005].) Does it really matter that the impact of high-stakes testing and accountability is transforming students into automatrons whose perception of learning is framed by filling in bubble sheets and test scores rather than the processes most critical for life in the 21st century — critical analysis and problem solving (Brady, 2005; Levine, 2005)? Do these contradictions matter or is this *phonics obsession* simply more smoke and mirrors, more sleight of hand?

If so, then why? There must be an explanation that connects all of the dots. Theories are many, but when government scientists concoct stories about dangerous epidemics, tempt "scientists with lucrative deals to produce 'scientific treatments' which they can sell at enormous profit" (Taylor, 1998, p. xvi), and employ politicians to rant and rave about the importance of the scientific truth, then we all should be worried that the stakes are so high that something has gone wrong in Oz. Those who are at work behind the curtain are seeking a huge payoff, which from my perspective seems most logically explained in the words of literacy sage Kenneth Goodman:

> A successful reading campaign could be a vehicle for developing a blueprint for a campaign to control education at all levels through national law, an objective heretofore seemingly impossible under the constitution. How well this goal has been accomplished is witnessed in the muted voices of the right, who in the past always demanded local control and vigorously opposed imposition of educational policy through federal law.
>
> Am I saying the campaign was not about reading? That's right. Yes, many players had agendas that were about reading, at least tangentially. But I believe that from the anti–public education view of those who planned and carried through the campaign, the more harm the law eventually does to teachers, teacher educators, public schools, and the kids in those schools, the better. That's the amoral perspective of political campaigns anyway. Winning is its own justification. Privatization of schools depends on convincing the public that public education is a failed experiment. (Goodman, 1998, Section 3)

So with every ending, it must relate to where it began. What does this mean for the teacher who earlier looked to me for answers to her questions? What does this mean for her colleagues, both within her school and across the United States? Are we doomed to face the end of public schooling? Denny Taylor (1998) thinks not, if and only if educators at all levels organize and become politically active, exposing the sleight-of-hand manipulation of the campaign to undermine the future of all American schoolchildren. "Don't be silent. Resist the spin. We have the power if we speak out" (Taylor, 1998, p. 328). Taylor joins the ranks of other literacy educators such as Ken and Yetta Goodman, Elaine Garan, Donald Graves, Reggie Routman, Stephen Krashen, Patrick Shannon, Gerald Coles, and Richard Allington, who join her in writing, speaking, campaigning, and taking their activism seriously. It is you who determines whether you join their fight — you who determines whether you sit back and wait in silence for the lights to go out in public schools across America.

NOTES

1. An instructional approach meant to further the reading development of struggling first-grade readers within one-to-one and small-group settings. Based on the work of New Zealand reading researcher Marie Clay (see Gaffney & Askew, 2004), teachers receive extensive training in reading development, reading diagnosis, and responsive pedagogy within a coaching/mentorship setting.
2. An approach to teaching reading based on psycholinguistic and sociolinguistic theory where phonics instruction is embedded within human interaction about meaningful children's literature. According to Pearson (2004) roots of the approach are in "Deweyian-inspired, child-centered pedagogy and the integrated curriculum movements popular in England, Australia, and New Zealand" (p. 217).

REFERENCES

Allington, R. L. (2002). *Big brother and the national reading curriculum: How ideology trumped evidence.* Portsmouth, NH: Heinemann.

Berliner, D. C., & Biddle B. J. (1995). *The manufactured crisis.* New York: Addison-Wesley.

Bracey, G. W. (2001). The condition of public education. *Phi Delta Kappan, 83,* 157–169.

Bracey, G. W. (2005). The 15th Bracey Report on the condition of public education. *Phi Delta Kappan, 87,* 138–153.

Brady, M. (2005, December 17). "Straight-cut ditch" schools widen gap in education. *Orlando Sentinel, A21.*

Carson, C. C., Huelskamp, R. M., & Woodall, T. D. (1993). Perspectives on education in America: An annotated briefing. *Journal of Educational Research, 86,* 259–310.

Gaffney, J. S., & Askew, B. (2004). *Marie M. Clay.* Retrieved February 18, 2006, from http://www.readingrecovery.org/sections/reading/marieclay.asp

Garan, E. (2001). Beyond the smoke and mirrors: A critique of the National Reading Panel Report on Phonics. *Phi Delta Kappan, 82,* 500–506.

Goodman, K. (1998). *Comments on the Reading Excellence Act (U.S.).* Retrieved February 17, 2006, from http://www.readingonline.org/past/past_index.asp?HREF=../critical/act.html

Jaeger, R. M. (1992). World class standards, choice, and privatization: Weak measurement serving prescriptive policy. *Phi Delta Kappan, 67,* 118–128.

Levine, M. (2005). *Ready or not, here life comes.* New York: Simon & Schuster.

Linn, R. L. (1993). Educational assessment: Expanded expectations and challenges. *Educational Evaluation and Policy Analysis, 15,* 1–16.

Lisman, M. (2004). Spellings emerges from shadows to cabinet post. Retrieved December 27, 2005, from http://gseacademic.harvard.edu/~theappian/articles/fall04/spellings1204.htm

McDonnell, L. M. (1994). Assessment policy as persuasion and regulation. *American Journal of Education, 102*, 394–420.

Metcalf, S. (2002). Reading between the lines. Retrieved December 27, 2005, from http://www.thenation.com/doc/20020128/metcalf

National Commission on Excellence in Education. (1983). *A nation at risk: The imperative for educational reform.* Washington, DC: U.S. Government Printing Office.

National Institutes of Health and National Institute of Child Health and Human Development (1999). Teaching children to read: An evidence-based assessment of the scientific research literature on reading and its implications for reading instruction. Retrieved February 19, 2006, from http://www.nichd.nih.gov/publications/nrp/smallbook.htm

Pearson, P.D. (2004, January & March). The reading wars. In *Educational Policy,* pp. 216–252. Retrieved May 9, 2007 from http://seedsofscience.org/PDFs/PearsonReadingWars.pdf.

Rice, C. (2006). The new three Rs: Readin', ritin', and rote. IOBA Standard. Retrieved February 19, 2006, from http://www.ioba.org/newsletter/V12/IOBANL-Readin-Ritin-Rote-8-03.php

Robelen, E. W. (2005, January 19). Spellings' resume brings new twist to secretary post. *Education Week.* Retrieved May 9, 2007 from www.edweek.org/ew/articles/ 2005/01/19/19spellings.h24.html.

Tanner, D. (1993). A nation truly at risk. *Phi Delta Kappan, 75,* 288–297.

Taylor, D. (1998). *Beginning to read and the spin doctors of science: The political campaign to change America's mind about how children learn to read.* Urbana, IL: National Council of Teachers of English.

Trelease, J. (2005). All in the family: The Bushes and the McGraws. Retrieved December 27, 2005, from http://www.trelease-on-reading.com/whatsnu_bush-mcgraw.html

U.S. Department of Education. (2005). Reading First purpose. Retrieved February 19, 2006, from http://www.ed.gov/programs/readingfirst/index.html

U.S. Department of Labor, Health and Human Services, and Education and Related Agencies. (1998). Congressional charge to the National Reading Panel. Retrieved February 19, 2006, from http://www.nationalreadingpanel.org/NRPAbout/officialcharge.htm

Yatvin, J. (2002). Babes in the Woods: The Wanderings of the National Reading Panel. *Phi Delta Kappan, 83*(5), 364–369. Retrieved May 9, 2007 from http://www.pdkintl.org/kappan/k0201yat.htm.

Chapter 31

Bilingual Education

Karen Cadiero-Kaplan and Margarita Berta-Avila
San Diego State University and Sacramento State University

Presently in the United States there are 4.4 million English language learners (ELLs) in public school, with California public schools home to more than 40% of these students and with close to 50% of this total being Spanish speakers (Rumberger & Gandara, 2004). Research indicates that it takes an individual up to seven years to fully develop a second language (Collier, 1987; Krashen, 1994). However, in many schools across the country students are required to speak only English, to leave their mother tongue at home. The result: marginalization and silencing of students whose language and cultures are seen as a threat to the status quo. "When the minority language is seen as a suspicious characteristic that must be eradicated" (Garcia, 1995, p. 156), then policies are created that claim "English for the Children" and "No Child Left Behind."

As teachers we can assert that the of marginalization of language minority students is due partly to a lack of understanding and knowledge on how language is tied to one's own identity and sense of self, which is primary to a student's self-esteem and motivation to learn. We know, for example, that language and literacy are more than parts of speech (e.g., nouns, verbs, adjectives) and sound systems (e.g., phonemes, morphemes). We recognize that language is inherently tied to one's culture and community (Cummins, 1989). We also know that at home many of the students in our American classrooms will speak with parents and grandparents in languages other than English, and sadly and slowly these children will lose this ability when they are told to speak only English and when parents are told not to confuse children by using their native language in the home. In our efforts to leave no child behind, children quickly learn that their voice and words count in school only in English and to speak or write in another language is not a gift or sign of added benefit, but a deficit. A deficit that can only be corrected if they reject their mother tongue in school and "speak only English" — ah yes, "English for the Children," won't that save them? While we recognize the importance that students learn English, and that English is the language students must acquire, both socially and academically to be successful in school and our society, we also recognize that our current mandates do more harm than good when a student's native language is not recognized as a valuable asset to English language and literacy development. The real issue we argue is not about what is the appropriate pedagogy to best support the development of English for English language learners (ELLs), but rather to ask, as Tollefson (2001) does,

> In what sense is it empirically accurate to claim that English in the United States is central to "equality" or to "opportunity" or to "national unity?" For which groups does the dominance of English provide the greatest opportunity? For which groups is English a barrier to education or employment? For whom does it offer "equality"? Which groups does English unify or exclude? (p. 17)

At the same time a "myth of meritocracy" (Nieto, 1999, p. 24) exists in the United States that places education as a key factor to an individual's success in this country. This myth has been consciously and purposefully engrained in marginalized communities, fostering the belief that all people, regardless of race, culture, class, gender, age, or sexual preference, have equal access to a quality education as long as one is willing to work for it (Darder, 2002; Nieto, 1999). If one does not obtain this quality education, it is not due to lack of access or resources, or mediocre schooling received, but is because he or she did not take full advantage of opportunities presented. However, when we analyze the historical and current trends of education in the United States, its aim is not educational or even systemic equity, but rather, as Apple (2001) states, "conservative modernization" (p. 5). Apple (2001) describes this "rightward turn" (p. 37) toward conservative modernization as finding its strength from a broad-base conservative alliance consisting of neoliberals, neoconservatives, authoritarian populists, upwardly mobile professionals, and managerial new middle class. The success of their alliance is due to the following:

> This new alliance has been so successful in part because it has been able to win the battle over commonsense. That is, it has creatively stitched together different social tendencies and commitments and has organized them under its own general leadership in issues dealing with social welfare, culture, economy, and education. (Apple, 2001, p. 37)

Although Apple discusses four elements that comprise this alliance, neoconservatives have played a major role in promoting policies in education that have resulted in such things as mandatory curriculum, high-stakes standardized testing, and "revivification of the 'Western tradition'" (p. 47). It is this revivification that has fueled, as Apple (2001) states, a fear of the "other" — the "other" consisting of marginalized communities subjected to societal and educational policies that will limit their access to equity but maintain the hegemonic bloc. It is in this dichotomy of access and power that we see direct attacks, particularly on bilingualism/biliteracy and bilingual education.

As critical educators we are committed to a pluralistic vision of schools and society that includes the language, culture, and communities of all students and makes quality education for academic achievement available to all equitably and equally. The goal of this chapter is to first define bilingual education in the context of a society that views English as the language of opportunity and the languages and cultures of immigrants in particular as a threat to our national identity. We will then examine how the neoconservative agenda functions to suppress children and youth who come to school speaking a language other than English, and conclude with our work at the institutional and state levels to counter the hegemony of English.

BILINGUAL EDUCATION AND ENGLISH ONLY: A BRIEF HISTORY

In order to understand the policy informing bilingual education presently, we must first consider the history of the past. According to Hakuta (1986), one of the most fascinating aspects of bilingualism in the United States is the extreme instability, for it is a transitional stage toward monolingualism in English. "Each new wave of immigrants has brought with it its own language and then witnessed the erosion of that language in the face of the implicitly acknowledged public language, English" (p. 166). Bilingual education policies tend to reflect the politics of the times.

The most contemporary support toward bilingual education occurred at the same time the civil rights movement was gaining momentum in the United States, with a focus on cultural pluralism and equal educational opportunity. At this time the learning of foreign languages was promoted in schools and our society, which led to a degree of tolerance for ethnic languages (Dicker, 2001). This tolerance and the advent of the civil rights movement allowed for the passage of the Bilingual Education Act. Title VII of the Elementary and Secondary Education Act of 1965 set the policy guidelines for local school districts in states concerning the education of language minority students (Crawford, 1999). Within two years of this legislation, "twenty-one states had bilingual education programs concerned with Spanish, French, and Portuguese languages" (Kanoon, 1978, p. 23).

One of the key court cases that assisted the implementation of bilingual education programs occurred in 1974, with *Lau v. Nichols*. This lawsuit was filed on behalf of Chinese students in San Francisco who were failing in school because they could not understand the language of instruction. This case was taken to the Supreme Court because the state ruled that there was no segregation or disparate treatment of these students. The ruling of the state of California was: "If the Chinese children had a language deficiency, that was unfortunate, but the district was not to blame" (Crawford, 1999, p. 44). However, Justice Douglas held that "there is no equality of treatment merely by providing students with the same facilities, textbooks, teachers, and curriculum; for students who do not understand English are effectively foreclosed from any meaningful education" (Crawford, 1999, p. 566). While "*Lau v. Nichols* did not require a particular instructional approach, it did establish the right of students to differential treatment based on their language minority status" (Wiese & Garcia, 1998, p. 3). This court case set the precedent for policy and practice of bilingual education for the 1970s and 1980s, but this progress was short-lived.

Though gains were made, the authentic, democratic ideologies and empowering teaching pedagogies that were the foundation of most quality bilingual programs were seen as too liberal. In addition, language and culture were seen as assets to learning, and immigrant communities were becoming empowered. The 1980s saw the birth of the official English movement led by conservative business and political groups. These groups spearheaded voter proposition initiatives aimed at stemming the tide of immigration from the Mexico border. Two legislative proposals passed in California not only impacted educational policy and programming, but have received nationwide attention and are the fuel for controversy. The first, Proposition 187, was designed to prevent undocumented immigrants from receiving public services, including public school education (Adams, 1995; Escobedo, 1999). The second and most recent was Proposition 227, titled "English for the Children," which called for the elimination of bilingual education and required all public school students identified as limited English proficiency (LEP) to be taught "overwhelmingly" in English (Escobedo, 1999; Kerper-Mora, 2000a).

The first of these two measures, Proposition 187, passed in 1994 with over 60% of voter support. Ultimately, implementation of the measure was stopped by legal challenges in both state and federal courts on the grounds of civil rights violations (Escobedo, 1999), but the proposition and its passage had lasting effects. Of significance is the fact that this measure had such strong public support, that is, denying immigrants rights to health care and education, and that it led and supported a "climate of reprisal and fear for Latino immigrant families and their children in our schools" (Escobedo, 1999 p. 14). Unfortunately, the voter proposition process has forced the election process across the country to become a space where "voters express their disaffection, their alienation, and their fears, rather than their hopes, visions, or aspirations" (Adams, 1995, p. 17). The fear at the time was the knowledge that beginning in the 1990s the population of California would

> shift from having a white majority population to a majority of people of color. The registered electorate (as opposed to the population as a whole) at this time was 76 percent white. Therefore, proposition 187 served as the perfect vehicle for the overwhelmingly white electorate to express its unease with the increasing racial and linguistic diversity of its state. (Adams, 1995, p. 17)

Only a few short years after Proposition 187 came Proposition 227, "English for the Children," led by the wealthy software engineer Ron Unz, who has no background in education or linguistics. Unz is a supporter of U.S. ENGLISH, which "believes that the passage of English as the official language will help to expand opportunities for immigrants to learn and speak English, the single greatest empowering tool that immigrants must have to succeed" (http://www.us-english.org/inc/). At the same time, national and state professional education organizations such as Teachers of English to Speakers of Other Languages and the National Association of Bilingual Education came out in adamant opposition to such statements. Proposition 227 passed with 61% voter approval. The goals of this proposition are to "teach English as rapidly as possible, by heavily exposing ELLs to English; to reduce drop out rates among immigrants; and, to reverse low literacy rates and promote economic and social advancement for language minority students" (Kerper-Mora, 2000a). This proposition did not deny bilingual education, but it did not make it readily accessible either. Proposition 227 states that "alternatives to this proscriptive program [structured English immersion] may be provided pursuant to the initiative's 'parental exception waiver' provisions. These waivers can only be provided with prior written consent and are only available subject to certain prescribed criteria" (Escobedo, 1999, p. 15). In response to this, schools and districts in California created parental waivers so that those schools that had bilingual programs could maintain them, and parents who elected to have their children in bilingual education could do so (Escobedo, 1999; Kerper-Mora, 2000b).

According to Kerper-Mora (2000b), the reasoning provided by proponents of Proposition 227 to discount bilingual education is expressed in the language of the law itself, citing that

> Bilingual education is the reason for low levels of English proficiency among immigrant students, especially Latinos who are the group served by the vast majority of the bilingual programs. Bilingual education slows down the English language acquisition process or prevents English language learners from becoming fully proficient in English. Therefore, bilingual education contributes to the high dropout rates among Latinos. Since bilingual education is the problem, getting rid of it is the solution. (Kerper-Mora, 2000b)

Since the passage of this proposition and other similar measures in other states, the majority of ELLs have been placed in programs identified as structured English immersion. These programs are subtractive in nature, where "the learning of a majority second language may undermine a person's minority first language and culture, thus creating a subtractive situation" (Baker, 1996, p. 66). However, such subtractive models are gaining strength within the policy arena as the number of English language learners in schools increase across the country. Additionally, other states, including Arizona and more recently Massachusetts (the site of the first public mandated bilingual programs in the United States), have adopted even more restrictive measures than Proposition 227. Within one year, virtually all bilingual education programs in Arizona and Massachusetts were being dismantled and replaced with a compensatory education model of structured English immersion.

INSTITUTIONALIZED RACISM AND HEGEMONY

As this brief history indicates, curriculum and programming for students who are nondominant English speakers have always had more to do with fear of the "other" than of truly educating those of a less elite status. In fact, as a society we believe that education in English is not only the most viable, but also pedagogically the most suitable, language in which to learn. While critical pedagogists have put forth credible debates concerning "cultural democracy, social justice, and alternative ways of viewing the world, the question of language is, at best, rarely raised, and at worst, relegated to the margins" (Macedo, Dendrinos, & Gounari, 2003, p. 24).

Macedo et al. (2003) believe that it is this conservative agenda toward bilingualism/bilingual education that has promoted "the hegemony of English" as a way to maintain position of power. Thus, education has become one entity, among many, used to enforce this hegemony of language through a particular instructional delivery system in which the ultimate goal is to, as Macedo et al. describe, "deny effective education to millions of immigrant children in their native language" (p. 9) — ultimately perpetuating "linguistic racism" (Macedo et al., 2003, p. 12) by imposing the idea that the learning of English, in and of itself, is education. This type of imposition is a form of neocolonialism that strips children of various ethnicities from their own identity, language, and culture (Macedo et al., 2003).

The current neoconservative agenda regarding bilingual education is an example of such a correlation. As Macedo et al. (2003) explain:

> The real meaning of a language has to be understood through the assumptions that govern it and the social, political, and ideological relations to

which it points. Generally speaking, the issue of effectiveness and validity often hides the true role of language in the maintenance of the values and interests of the dominant class. In other words, the issues of the effectiveness and validity of a subordinate language becomes [sic] a mask that obfuscates questions about the social, political, and ideological order within which the subordinate language exists. (p. 13)

The issue, or lets say controversy, has never truly been the effectiveness of bilingual education. That argument has been used as a mask to hide the fear and threat of the other felt by the hegemonic bloc. Bilingual education is viewed as a threat to that romanticized yesteryear that, let us not forget, excluded marginalized communities from equitable access.

What is evident now is that there exist two prevailing political views of bilingual education that have a direct impact on how students are taught and how bilingual teachers are prepared. Brisk (1998) defines bilingual education as either "compensatory education" or "quality education." For many bilingual advocates the goal is not for students to just learn English but become bilingual/biliterate through a rigorous academic program, thus emphasizing a quality education. A *quality education* policy focuses on a student's right to a good education with the goal being "to educate students to their highest potential," where English is only a part of the educational goal. In a quality model, "bilingual learners access knowledge not only through English but through their native languages" (Brisk, 1998, p. xix); there is a recognition and value for their cultural experiences and knowledge. As a result, the teachers best prepared to meet the needs of students under a quality model are bilingual and most often from the same cultural or language group as the students for whom they are being prepared to teach.

For neoconservatives, the notion of providing a quality education, let alone a "quality bilingual education program," is not the goal. A quality education model poses a threat at many levels, not only language, as previously mentioned. What is advocated, according to Brisk, is a *compensatory education* policy that focuses on the choice of language, where the policy makers determine which language of instruction will be utilized. Within this model the overriding goal of education is to "teach students English as quickly as possible." Since "English is viewed as the only means for acquisition of knowledge, students' fluency in English is the essential condition to receiving an education" (Brisk, 1998, p. xviii). The irony that exists in this latter quote is the connection between English and success, for it does not take into account the English-only-speaking students who are not succeeding in school. In particular, African American students have had English as their primary language and yet are still subjected to systemic inequities that eventually lead them to be "pushed out" of their education (Macedo et al., 2003).

So, if you want to really hurt me, talk badly about my language. Ethnic identity is twin skin to linguistic identity — I am my language. Until I can take
pride in my language, I cannot take pride in myself (Anzaldúa, 1987, p. 59).

The danger that lies with this compensatory view of bilingual education
programs is that they are seen as the vehicle to assimilate students. Even
in the context of bilingual education there has to be a word of caution,
because compensatory programs promote an agenda of losing one's language. Many who are advocates of bilingual education often fall into this
belief system that they need to save their students from being identified
as English language learners, therefore perpetuating the power status of
English and devaluing the fact that these students are bilingual (Macedo
et al., 2003). In the eyes of the neoconservative it is not beneficial that students maintain their mother tongue, because they realize that it is through
language that communities are able to maintain their identity, and as a
result, their story stays alive. Often this is a story that counters what the
hegemonic bloc wants to identify as truth. Through the loss of one's language, the memory of values and beliefs can then be replaced with English. Through this process those losing their language/memory take on
what the dominant culture defines as the acceptable language and belief
system for that particular community (Macedo et al., 2003; Narayan, 1997).
Appropriating the language and culture of bilingual students eventually
makes it difficult to question the monolingual white hegemonic system,
because their process of socialization has made them believe that the existing norms are part of them. According to Narayan (1997), this is seen as
a betrayal of a value and belief system that has really been infiltrated into
the community.

This allows for the perpetuation of what hooks (2003) identifies as
"white supremacy." She explains as follows:

> I state my preference for using the word white supremacy to describe the sys-
> tem of race-based biases we live within because this term, more than racism,
> is inclusive of everyone. It encompasses black people/people of color who
> have a racist mindset, even though they may organize their thinking and act
> differently from racist whites. (p. 28)

Students are caught in a state in which they participate in their own
internalized oppression while believing the goal is to replicate their white
counterparts. This belief of replication allows for "white supremacy" to
perpetuate the notion that people of color are subject to serving Whites.
As hooks (2003) explains, "Embedded in this notion of service is that no
matter what the status of the person of color, that position must be config-
ured for the greater good of whiteness" (p. 33).

"For the greater good of whiteness" benefits those who place themselves as the "cognitive elite" to promote a compensatory bilingual education in order to prepare semiliterate individuals (Lincoln, 1997; Macedo, 1994). In doing so, students are only able "to read the word but not the world" (Macedo, 1994, p. 21). So, where do we go from here?

THE STRUGGLE FOR EQUITY CONTINUES

Though No Child Left Behind professes a desire for all students to succeed academically, it downplays (1) the punitive ramifications of high-stakes tests, (2) the reduction in the number of minority teachers stemming from increased testing requirements for those attempting to enter the field, and (3) the already marginalized status of those communities most negatively affected. By producing a small cadre of "cognitive elite" (Carspecken, 1997), while consigning the majroty to "lower cognitive" status further justifying their pre-existing condition of marginalization, NCLB enhances the policy of race-based, social partitioning advocated by Richard Herrnstein and Charles Murray in The Bell Curve (1994). This notion comes from the work of Herrnstein and Murray, authors of *The Bell Curve*, who make the case that social partitioning is not only class based, but also related to cognition and intelligence. They argue that those individuals who intellectually are cognitively low in intelligence are incompetent as citizens (p. 112). As Carspecen (1997) extrapolates, they are the ones with the highest unemployment, highest crime rates, and the highest number of dropouts. These are individuals who do not possess the cultural capital of English and represent lower-class immigrant groups. Therefore, it is in the best interest of the neoconservatives, who we contend are part of the cognitive elite, to maintain purity of intellect, but more importantly, to maintain power and control over those with lower cognition and lower socioeconomic status. The move to maintain communities within the "lower cognitive" is most evident when addressing bilingual education.

As teacher educators in bilingual teacher preparation programs we see that our students encounter greater demands financially and academically than those in mainstream teacher preparation programs. Our future teachers enter our programs with the ability to communicate socially and academically in English and Spanish, and sometimes three or more languages. When they exit our programs they have the knowledge, skills, and abilities to teach children both language and academics in two languages. Further, these young professionals are best able to communicate with parents and community members who do not speak English. Once hired, they become the cultural brokers for their colleagues and peers who are limited by only speaking English. It would seem that such skills would be highly valued and desired by policy makers. However, present policy not only makes it more difficult for these young men and women to enter the field of bilingual education, but it sends the message oftentimes that their language and community are not valued based on the racist and white supremacist ideologies addressed in this chapter. Many of these individuals are first-generation college students, are Latino, and have a desire to return to their home communities to teach. It is no coincidence then that we see a standardization movement within teacher education through NCLB, which makes no statement or mention of the need for bilingual educators, but rather for teachers to be prepared to meet the needs of English language learners. It is such a political language that is of concern and for which we now must focus our movements for equal education.

Based on our own collaborations with each other and colleagues, it is imperative that educators from the K-12 classrooms to universities go beyond recognizing and naming the politics of injustice, fear, and racism and become active voices in professional organizations and groups that advocate for educational justice. In California we are members of statewide groups that advocate for educational equality, such as the California Association for Bilingual Education and the California Association for Teachers of English to Students of Other Languages. While these organizations focus on appropriate curriculum and pedagogy, they are also have lobbyists at the state level. In addition, we have worked most recently with Californians Together, a statewide coalition of parents, teachers, education advocates, and civil rights groups committed to securing equal access to quality education for all children. We believe we must start at the grassroots level to organize and educate not just our future teachers, but parents and community members to understand and respond to policies that marginalize and silence. Presently through our activism we have been able to inform policy on the current status of the bilingual credential; through our efforts over the past year we were able to push our Commission on Teacher Credentialing to recognize the need to reevaluate the policy and processes for teacher certification. Our efforts have resulted in public hearings throughout the state where teachers, administrators, and community members will be able to have a voice in the process. This is still a battle we are currently waging, as the politics are not supporting our work, but through the process we are educating many. Finally, we have had to take risks in our classrooms and communities to instigate critical dialogue around issues of race, class, gender, and language; these risks, however, are necessary in a time of war and terrorism, where our officials promote fear over hope. As Paulo Freire (1995) states

> One of the tasks of the progressive educator, through a serious, correct political analysis is to unveil opportunities for hope, no matter what the obstacles may be. After all, without hope there is little we can do. (p. 9)

From Freire's statement we draw our inspiration as we find the way to work and walk together in solidarity for equality and justice:

Caminante no hay camino, se hace el camino al andar.
   Traveler, there is no road. The road is made as one walks.

—Antonio Machado (1982)

REFERENCES

Adams, J. (1995). Proposition 187 lessons. *Z Magazine,* Vol. 8, pp. 16–18.

Anzaldúa, G. (1987). *Borderlands — La frontera: The new mestiza.* San Francisco: Spinsters/Aunt Lute Book Company.

Apple, M. W. (2001). *Educating the "right" way: Markets, standards, God, and inequality.* New York: RoutledgeFalmer.

Baker, C. (1996). *Foundations of biligual education and bilingualism.* 2nd ed. Clevedon, PA: Multilingual Matters.

Brisk, M. (1998). *Bilingual education: From compensatory to quality schooling.* Mahwah, NJ: Lawrence Erlbaum Associates.

Carspecken, P. (1997). The setup: Crocodile tears for the poor. In J. Kincheloe, S. Steinberg, & A. Gresoson (Eds.), *Measured lies: The bell curve examined* (pp. 110–125). New York: St. Martins Press.

Collier, V. (1987). Age and rate of acquisition of second language for academic purposes. *TESOL Quarterly, 21,* 617–641.

Crawford, J. (1999). *Bilingual education: History, politics, theory, and practice* (4th ed.). Los Angeles: Bilingual Educational Services.

Cummins, J. (1989). *Empowering minority students.* Sacramento: California Association for Bilingual Education.

Darder, A. (2002). *Reinventing Paulo Freire: A pedagogy of love.* Boulder, CO: Westview Press.

Dicker, S. J. (2001). Official English and bilingual education: The controversy over language pluralism in U.S. society. In J. K. Hall & W. G. Eggington (Eds.), *The sociopolitics of English language teaching* (pp. 45–66). Tonawanda, NY: Multilingual Matters.

Escobedo, D. (1999, Summer). Propositions 187 and 227: Latino immigrant rights to education. *Human Rights Magazine,* pp. 13–15.

Freire, P. (1995). *Pedagogy of hope: Reliving pedagogy of the oppressed.* New York: Continuum.

Garcia, E. (1995). Spanish language loss as a determinant of income among Latinos in the United States: Implications for language policy in schools. In J. Tollefson (Ed.), *Power and inequality in language education* (pp. 42–160). Cambridge, MA: Cambridge University Press.

Hakuta, K. (1986). *Mirror of language: The debate on bilingualism.* New York: Basic Books.

Herrnstein, R., & Murray, C. (1994). *The bell curve: Intelligence and class structure in America.* New York: Free Press.

hooks, b. (2003). *Teaching community: A pedagogy of hope.* New York: Routledge.

Kanoon, G. D. (1978). The four phases of bilingual education in the United States. *TESOL Newsletter, 12,* 1, 23–24.

Kerper-Mora, J. (2000a). Policy shifts in language minority education: A mismatch between politics and pedagogy. *Educational Forum, 64,* 204–214.

Kerper-Mora, J. (2000b). *Proposition 227's second anniversary: Triumph or travesty?* Retrieved May 1, 2007 from http://coe.sdsu.edu/people/jmora/Prop227/227YearTwo.htm

Krashen, S. D. (1994). Bilingual education and second language acquisition theory. In C. F. Leyba (Ed.), *Schooling and language minority students: A theoretical framework* (pp. 51–79). Los Angeles: Evaluation Dissemination and Assessment Center, California State University–Los Angeles.

Lincoln, Y. (1997). For whom the bell tolls: A cognitive or educated elite? In J. Kincheloe, S. Steinberg, & A. Gresoson (Eds.), *Measured lies: The bell curve examined* (pp. 126–135). New York: St. Martins Press.

Macedo, D. (1994). *Literacies of power: What Americans are not allowed to know.* San Francisco: Westview Press.

Macedo, D., Dendrinos, B., & Gounari, P. (2003). *The hegemony of English.* Boulder, CO: Paradigm Publishers.

Machado, A. (1982). Proverb "se hace camino al andar." In *Selected poems* (Alan S. Trueblood, Trans., p. 143). Cambridge, MA: Harvard University Press.

Narayan, U. (1997). *Dislocating cultures: Identities, traditions, and third-world feminism (thinking gender).* New York: Routledge.

Nieto, S. (1999). *The light in their eyes: Creating multicultural learning communities.* New York: Teachers College Press.

Rumberger, R. W., & Gandara, P. (2004). Seeking equity in the education of California's English learners. *Teachers College Record, 106,* 2032–2056.

Tollefson, J. W. (2001). Policy and ideology in the spread of English. In J. K. Hall & W. G. Eggington (Eds.), *The sociopolitics of English language teaching* (pp. 7–21). Tonawanda, NY: Multilingual Matters.

Wiese, A. M., & Garcia, E. (1998). The bilingual education act: Language minority students and equal educational opportunity. *Bilingual Research Journal, 22,* 1–16.

Chapter 32

Language Arts Education

Patricia H. Hinchey
Pennsylvania State University

Among the many areas of education specifically targeted by recent educational reforms, language arts instruction has been one of the most intensely affected, in part because reading was one of the first targets of mandated high-stakes testing. Even before No Child Left Behind legislation was implemented, however, the administration's interest in — and agenda for — reading instruction became clear in its Reading First initiative. That initiative, based on a purportedly objective 2000 report from the National Reading Panel, linked federal grants specifically to the implementation of "scientifically based" reading instruction. Generally, the initiative equates scientifically based instruction with phonics-based instruction. In promoting this definition and policy—and doing so in the face of objections from a constellation of educators and researchers — the Reading First initiative launched what has been an ongoing assault on literacy instruction. Curricular change in response to the legislation has savaged not only language arts classrooms and teachers, but students as well.

READING FIRST AND MANDATED MATERIALS

Numerous scholars have challenged the National Reading Panel report findings, and many critics further charge that, in any case, the findings are far narrower than the government often claims (see Coles, 2003). Moreover, the recommendations based on the report fly in the face of decades of contradictory, solid research that argues for differentiated and authentic instruction (see National Council of Teachers of English, n.d.). Turning a deaf ear to critics, the administration has funded Reading First at over $1 billion annually, awarded via a competitive grant process that itself has also come under heavy criticism. Despite extensive criticism, however, many districts have felt constrained to apply for Reading First grants because of severe financial constraints they already suffer, and in doing so they have promoted extensive, and ill-advised, curricular change.

To date, Reading First grants have been awarded only to schools whose applications indicate that they will use one of a select group of commercial reading programs, all phonics based. Not surprisingly, given the cronyism of the current administration, many "experts" involved with awarding Reading First monies are also authors of the preferred materials or have close ties to the Bush administration (see Bracey, 2005). This bias in awards has been so obvious that a competitor was successful in prompting the Education Department to open a preliminary investigation into possible conflict of interest and mismanagement of funds (see Toppo, 2005). Ongoing complaints about government promotion of certain products have not, however, stopped funds from being awarded to favored programs, including Open Court and Direct Instruction; each of these are McGraw-Hill products, a notable fact in light of decades of close personal ties between the Bush and McGraw families.

Generally, Open Court, Direct Instruction, and similar products are based on the claim that the most effective way to teach reading is through phonics, through instruction first in letters and sounds, and then in blending sounds into word. *Cat*, or *c-a-t*, becomes *Kuh-aa-tuh*, for example. Often in the programs, the "words" students are asked to decode are "nonsense" words; *c-a-t* might be followed by *m-a-t*, or by *g-a-t* or *l-a-t*. This common practice indicates how completely sound takes the precedence over meaning and illustrates how a phonics approach teaches children that reading involves making *sounds* based on text — rather than making *meaning* based on text. This privileging of sound over sense is antithetical not only to the widely accepted definition of reading as a meaning-making activity, but also to the strong human impulse to impose meaning on experience.

Not surprisingly, teachers report that when a phonics approach stressing sound asks children to "read" a group of letters that may or may not add up to a real word, the children often try to impose sense within the nonsensical pedagogy. For example, when a script forced one teacher to present children with the nonword *schoolbun* (a variation based on *schoolbus*), one child asked for a definition of the word and another promptly answered, "Like, when you're at school, if they have hot dogs for lunch, they give it to you on a schoolbun" (Meyer, 2003). We can only speculate how activities that make no sense — and are not supposed to make sense — affect children's enthusiasm for schoolwork. And we can only speculate how much confusion such activities generate about what is and is not a word. In other areas, however, the impact of a mandated phonics-based approach is starting to become more clear.

Researchers are beginning to document the results of preferred programs in comparison to the results of more holistic and authentic approaches. For example, one recent study carefully monitored outcomes for similar classes using different programs (Reading Mastery, Open Court, and Guided Reading). It found that children in phonics-based programs did not perform better than children in literature-based programs in phonics use (either in or out of context), accuracy, or comprehension. However, children who were instructed in phonics were more willing to accept meaningless text and so kept reading through their mistakes, and they were in the habit of thinking that questions have one correct answer. In contrast,

> Children in literature-based programs, through their transactions with texts and immersion in rich discussions, attempt at every level to make sense of texts. They use what they know about language and the world, and integrate multiple strategies to construct meaning as they read. They focus on graphophonic cues, but do not rely solely on them. Because they demonstrate processing of both surface and deep structures of language, they are able to grapple with text and word-level processing and comprehension. This will enable them to develop independence as developing readers. (Arya et al., 2005)

Such specific efforts to subject Reading First-sanctioned strategies to the tests of research are beginning to yield still more evidence of how ill-advised this government dictate for curricula and pedagogy is. Phonics-based programs simply do not produce superior readers, the entire rationale for their imposition. Yet even as the favored programs fail this essential test, children are being denied access to a range of instructional options that might best nurture their potential as readers. Moreover, the imposition of government-sanctioned programs is draining the lifeblood out of classrooms and the teachers and students who live in them.

IMPOVERISHED CLASSROOMS, ALIENATED TEACHERS

As noted above, commercial phonics programs bring a great deal of nonsense into classrooms. Adding insult to injury, however, they mandate not only content, but also instructional process. Scripted programs not only tell teachers what to do during a class, but actually what to say. Each bit of an instructional sequence is laid out for the teacher, in a "Do this, now say this, now do this" format. The amount of time for each activity is carefully calibrated. The net effect is that, with the high-stakes test looming and administrators checking to be sure everyone is literally following the script, teachers are turned into what one has described as a "page-turning monkey" (Gensburger, 2005). The impact on teachers has been devastating.

First, many are frustrated by being forced to use methods they can see are not effective for their students, so that their entire reason for being in a classroom — to teach children — is undermined. Second, they are forbidden to use any of their own expertise, a situation that stifles their creativity and denies them any sense of professionalism. Like their students, teachers are force-marched through programs designed by distant "experts" with no firsthand knowledge of the individual human beings in any specific classroom context. Such severe curricular and pedagogical constraints have devastated faculty morale and are exacerbating the existing problem of staffing every classroom with a dedicated and highly skilled teacher.

The impact is felt most by the poorest schools — those most in need of talented and caring professionals. While some schools are in a position to reject government funds, and with them their curricular impositions, the poorest schools are the ones most vulnerable to problems generated by the phonics-based approach. Desperate for funds as well as good test scores, they are forced both to opt into materials geared to tests and to pursue Reading First money to buy those materials. Good teachers for poor classrooms are already difficult to find, and those that have somehow managed to find their way into them are now being driven out of them by scripted programs. One third- and fourth-grade public school teacher describes what is rapidly becoming a common experience:

> This is my 6th year teaching and frankly, most likely my last. The creativity and joy of teaching have been replaced by a cut and dry standards-based only education which, with unqualified results, fueled by a paranoid need for pushing NCLB at the expense of all else, has left us all staring blankly for some basic common sense.
>
> Just this week I was told that all non-adoption/non-core reading books were to be removed from my classroom — perfectly sound readers for reading-starved children that were paid for by parents, PTA, school and teachers over the years. The dictate is that since they are not included in the adoption they have no place in the classroom. In its place are the few readers that accompany the adoption which hardly offer the full richness of reading diversity that was previously available to students. (Gensburger, 2005)

At the very moment that government rhetoric insists on a qualified teacher for every classroom, contradictory policies are driving out the most professional teachers we have.

The issue here overflows into teacher education classrooms, where teacher educators are aware that their students are unlikely to be able to use the best practices their programs have stressed in the past. Are teacher educators to continue to teach what they know to be best practice — ensuring that new teachers are both frustrated at their impotence and unfamiliar with scripted programs? Or do they accommodate the reality of current conditions by abandoning all talk of methods they know to be in the best interest of children and focusing on prepackaged, prescripted curricula that they loathe — but which their students will need to use? A Solomon is sorely wanted by many teacher educators.

CHILDREN DENIED CURIOSITY — AND CHILDHOOD

Children's horizons are being limited at least as much as their teachers', with no hope of escape. Unlike teachers, they cannot simply walk away from mandated schooling, and they must suffer through whatever is inflicted upon them. Nonsense in much of their schoolwork and the loss of classroom libraries and other engaging materials certainly make the classroom less interesting and engaging. Additionally, since annual high-stakes tests focus on reading and math, other disciplines receive less — and often no — attention, further limiting students' experience. The more time spent on reading and math, the less time available for social studies, science, art, music, or anything else children themselves find interesting. This scaling back of curricular content not only narrows children's intellectual experiences, but it also translates to less opportunity for each child to explore his or her intrinsic interests, and less opportunity to shine and develop critical self-confidence. And, on the flip side of the coin, there is less opportunity for play, which is also central to children's development needs. There is nothing — not drawing a family, racing at recess, exploring how other people live and think, satisfying curiosity about how things work, experiencing the joy of a song well sung, or the exhilaration of an improvised dance — nothing that cannot be sacrificed to the god of higher test scores. Why would any child want to go to school?

Even the youngest children are being corralled into this joyless, standardized world of nonsensical, rote instruction. In 2003, the Bush administration announced that it was planning to mandate standardized testing to all 4-year-olds in Head Start programs to determine reading readiness — in effect, to mandate preschool high-stakes testing (Offman, 2004/2005). Given that many teachers have reported elementary-age children vomiting in response to the current testing environment, we can only imagine how testing mania affects preschoolers forced to forgo building with blocks so that they can chant *B, buh-buh-buh, B* ad nauseum. Their play time, too, is sure to be reduced despite their very young age, because of constraints placed on the instructor, who must keep the children focused on good test results in order to stay employed.

Nor is the impact on children only affective: Current reforms also, ironically, minimize children's opportunities to master literacy. Decades of research on language development indicate that writing plays a large part in children's developing language skills, certainly including reading. For example, writing provides an authentic lesson in how writers as well as readers employ phonics for real tasks, and writing also improves reading skills by focusing attention on how texts are constructed (Coles, 2003, p.

130). Because reform efforts focus on reading to the near exclusion of writing, and because teachers' instruction focuses nearly exclusively on tested domains, writing is among the areas now receiving less attention in classrooms. As a result, children are denied a major avenue of literacy growth that has long been an accepted part of effective pedagogy.

OUTCOMES: PRIVATE PROFIT, POOR PEDAGOGY, AND DISAFFECTED TEACHERS AND CHILDREN

Generally, No Child Left Behind and Reading First have had an enormous, and enormously harmful, effect on literacy education, especially in early years. Reading First monies have flowed into the pockets of cronies whose scripted products have received the administration's approval. Desperate to raise test scores and avoid sanctions, underfunded schools have felt constrained to apply for grants and implement those products, which, in any event, are likely tied to the mandated state assessment, since many states use test products from the same suppliers. Unable even to use their own voices in the classroom, let alone their professional skill and judgment, skillful teachers have become frustrated by the nonsense they have been forced to impose on children they genuinely care about, and often sufficiently depressed to leave a profession they once loved.

Even as they suffer methods more likely to impede their literacy growth than enhance it, children, meanwhile, are no longer expected to play much, if at all. Should they have curiosity about why a fish died after it was given new water, they have to satisfy it outside the classroom, where science has become a luxury the school can no longer afford. Nor should they ask the why of anything in the classroom — certainly not why they need to demonstrate they can pronounce *schoolbun*, which is not a real word, despite their efforts to make it so. They are to accept endless, meaningless, and nonsensical drills, being told repeatedly that the fate of their school and their teachers depends upon their filling in the right circles on a one-time test. If the pressure makes them ill, well, then, nausea is not fatal, and it is a small price for children to pay to ensure that the current political agenda favoring privatization is enacted.

And no child — except perhaps one lucky enough to be in a private school, where none of this legislation applies or is embraced — will be left out of this tortuous routine that has come to be called literacy education.

REFERENCES

Arya, P., Martens, P., Wilson, G. P., Altwerger, B., Laster, B., & Lang, D. (2005). Reclaiming literacy instruction: Evidence in support of literature-based programs. *Language Arts, 83*, 1. Retrieved December 10, 2005, from ProQuest database.

Bracey, G. (2005). *No Child Left Behind: Where does the money go?* Tempe, AZ: Educational Policy Research Unit, Arizona State University. Retrieved December 12, 2005, from http://www.asu.edu/educ/epsl/EPRU/documents/EPSL-0506-114-EPRU.pdf

Coles, G. (2003). *Reading the naked truth: Literacy, legislation, and lies.* Portsmouth, NH: Heinemann.

Gensburger, A. (2005). *Leaving the teacher behind.* Retreived March 4, 2005, from http://nochildleft.com/2005/feb05departing.html

Meyer, R. (2003, Summer). Captives of the script: Killing us softly with phonics. *Rethinking Schools Online.* Retrieved December 12, 2005, from http://www.rethinkingschools.org/special_reports/bushplan/capt174.shtml

National Council of Teachers of English. (n.d.). *NCTE guideline: Elementary school practices.* Retrieved December 10, 2005, from http://www.ncte.org/about/over/positions/category/inst/107653.htm

National Reading Panel. (2000). *Report of the National Reading Panel: Teaching children to read.* Retrieved December 12, 2005, from http://www.nationalreadingpanel.org/Publications/summary.htm

Offman, S. (2004/2005, Winter). All work and no play. *Rethinking Schools Online.* Retrieved December 12, 2005, from http://www.rethinkingschools.org/archive/19_02/work192.shtml;geturl=d+highlightmatches+gotofirstmatch;terms=sharna+olfman;enc=sharna%20olfman;utf8=on;noparts#firstmatch

Toppo, G. (2005, October 9). Reading program raises questions for lawmakers. *USA Today.* Retrieved October 10, 2005, from http://www.usatoday.com/news/education/2005-10-09-reading-program_x.htm

Chapter 33

Literacy

Colin Lankshear and Michele Knobel
James Cook University and Montclair State University

From the early 1990s educational reform discourse generally, and national education policy specifically, has emphasized five broad constructions of literacy. These can be identified as lingering basics, new basics, elite literacies, digital literacy, and foreign language literacy. With the exception of foreign language literacy, there is an overarching emphasis on standard English as the literacy medium.

At elementary and secondary school levels, *lingering basics* entails mastery of generalizable techniques and concepts for encoding and decoding text, presumed to be essential building blocks for subsequent education: acquiring content knowledge and higher-order skills. At the adult level, it refers to functional competence with everyday texts enabling citizens to meet basic needs for managing print and electronic media to the extent necessary for being integrated into the economic and civic mainstream. This construction lingers from the early 20th century and has been powerfully reasserted as the cornerstone of school education by the 2001 No Child Left Behind Act and, particularly, by the Reading First funding initiative in the United States.

New basics enshrines realization of the extent to which social practices have changed with major economic, social, and institutional transitions since the 1960s from an agroindustrial economy to a postindustrial information services economy, Fordism to fast capitalism, personal face-to-face communities to impersonal metropolitan and "virtual" communities, a paternal (welfare) state to a more devolved state requiring greater self-sufficiency, almost ensured (male) employment to greater reliance on personal entrepreneurship, and so on. Such shifts are seen to demand on the part of individuals qualitatively more sophisticated (smart), logical, symbolic, and strategic capabilities than were needed in the past. Hence, "the percentage of all students who demonstrate ability to reason, solve problems, apply knowledge, and write and communicate effectively [must] increase substantially" (Goals 2000, Goal 3 B, p. ii).

Elite literacies refers to higher-order scientific, technological, and symbolic practices grounded in excellence in academic learning. Here *literacy* denotes advanced understandings of the logics and processes of inquiry within disciplinary fields, together with command of leading-edge work in those fields. The ideal is one of high-level critique, innovation, diversification, refinement, and so on, through application of theory and research. The focus is knowledge work (Alvesson, 2004), construed as value-adding work and the source of commercially valuable intellectual property (Liu, 2004), as the base for competitive economic advantage.

Digital literacy is generally defined in terms of abilities or competencies to locate, use, and evaluate information presented via computing and communications technologies, often with an emphasis on work-related applications. With increasing globalization of work, initiatives have emerged to provide standardized operationalizations of digital literacy and devise global standards for Internet and computer literacy, such as the European Computer Driving Licence and Centriport's Internet and Computing Core Certification (IC³) program. The latter is endorsed by the Global Digital Literacy Council as providing a worldwide industry standard that accurately validates computer comprehension and skills in the workplace. Many operationalizations of digital literacy involve little more than showing proficiency with such functional tasks as copying to a clipboard, locating a designated Web site, compiling and modifying tables, and composing and sending an e-mail message. More demanding standards may require elementary proficiency with spreadsheets, online searching, presentation software, and the like.

Foreign language literacy refers to proficiency with oral communication and printed and visual texts integral to dealings within the new economic and strategic global order, thereby serving "the Nation's needs in commerce, diplomacy, defense, and education" (National Commission on Excellence in Education [NCEE], 1983, p. 26). This calls, minimally, for communicative competence allowing functional cross-cultural access to a range of social practices and, optimally, for levels of fluency and cultural awareness sufficient for being persuasive, diplomatic, and strategically effective within sensitive high-risk and high-gain contexts.

CHARACTERISTICS OF NEOLIBERAL CONSTRUCTIONS OF LITERACY

The Functional Symmetry of Literacies with New Conditions and Types of Work

A broad functional symmetry exists between the five constructions of literacy sketched here and trends within the new work order. The polarization of work between providing symbolic analytic services at one extreme and engagement in routine production and in-person service work at the other has intensified since the 1980s (Gee, Hull, & Lankshear, 1996). At the same time, companies aim to infuse a sense of responsibility for their success throughout the entire organization, and to integrate as many workers as possible into problem solving and creative innovation in the interests of efficiency and quality.

Symbolic analytic work is seen as "substantial value adding work" and is well paid (Reich, 1992, p. 177). It provides knowledge services, delivering concepts, words, high-end data, programs, and diverse visual and nonvisual representations. This is the work of research scientists, software programmers, systems analysts, editors, management experts, art directors, economists, architects and engineers, film producers, games designers, and the like. It draws on elite literacies involving symbolic manipulation, high-level problem posing, development of abstract designs and strategic thinking, and the application and extension of theory.

By comparison, routine production and in-person service work are represented as low value adding and are relatively poorly paid. Beyond demands for basic numeracy, the ability to read, and some facility with electronic machines, much routine work mainly calls for reliability, loyalty, willingness to take direction, and, in the case of in-person service workers, "a pleasant manner." The gulf between this and symbolic analytic work reflects the difference between elite literacies and the lingering basics.

Between these poles, work is impacted by the changed rules of manufacturing and competition associated with technological developments and global sourcing of labor and expertise. Front-line workers must increasingly solve problems as they arise, operate self-directed work teams, understand and apply procedures and concepts of quality assurance and control, and assume responsibility for many tasks and initiatives previously performed by lower-level management (Drucker, 2001). Such work is agreed to require higher-level basics than previously, together with functional digital literacy proficiencies.

The Push to Technologize Literacy

The frequent references to digital literacy and use of new technologies as learning technologies reflect the increasing mediation of daily routines in work, civic, and domestic life by digital texts and electronic communications. Toch (1991) cited claims that "alarming numbers of young Americans are ill-equipped to work in, contribute to, profit from, and enjoy our increasingly technological society" (p. 16). The February 1996 Technology Literacy Challenge package voted U.S.$2 billion over five years to mobilize "the private sector, schools, teachers, parents, students, community groups, state and local governments, and the federal government" to meet the goal of making all U.S. children "technologically literate" by "the dawn of the 21st century" (Winters, 1996). The Forum on the Future of Technology in Education convened by the U.S. Department of Education's Office of Educational Technology (1999) identified five key priorities. These were that "all students and teachers will have universal access to effective information technology in their classrooms, schools, communities, and homes"; "all teachers will effectively use technology"; "all students will be technologically literate and responsible cybercitizens"; "research, development and evaluation will shape the next generation of technology applications for teaching and learning"; and "education will drive the E-learning economy" (U.S. Department of Education, 1999). Most recently, the 2004 National Education Technology Plan established seven action steps and recommendations. These include supporting e-learning and virtual schools, encouraging continuous broadband access, and moving toward digital content and integrated interoperable data systems for the education sector (U.S. Department of Education, 2004).

Ensuring economic competitiveness is central to the technologizing of literacy and instruction. "Over the next decade, the United States will face ever increasing competition in the global economy [and] to an overwhelming extent, this competition will involve the mastery and application of new technologies in virtually every field of human endeavor" (U.S. Department of Education, 2004, Executive Summary). In addition, however, new technologies directly and indirectly comprise key products of new capitalist economies for which worldwide markets need to be generated and sustained. Educational reform agendas serve crucially here as a means to creating and maintaining enlarged markets for the hardware, software, and burgeoning service products (from repair to Internet access provision and Web site design) of the information economy. Besides exhorting educators to integrate new technologies into curriculum and pedagogy, reform discourse advocates extensive use of new technologies within administrative tasks of restructured schools (Kearns & Doyle, 1991; U.S. Department of Education, 2004).

Standard English as the "Bottom Line"

Within educational reform discourse literacy presumes standard English as the linguistic medium, with the sole exception of "foreign language literacy" (Goals 2000 Act, 1994; Kearns & Doyle, 1991; NCEE, 1983; No Child Left Behind Act, 2001). At formal and official institutional levels of economic, civic, business, and commercial life, standard English dominates. Mastery of standard English is regarded by policy makers as necessary if individuals are to participate in, benefit from, and advance personally through these institutionalized spheres of social practice.

Moreover, standard English continues to prevail as the global lingua franca of the information age. For almost 20 years now the number of

Chinese citizens studying English has exceeded the number of U.S. citizens. In times when maintaining competitive edge requires fine-tuning human resources for value-adding service in a global information/knowledge economy, maximizing the standard English proficiencies of non-standard-English-speaking citizens is seen as an urgent economic instrumentality.

This emphasis has been powerfully reasserted in Titles I and III of the No Child Left Behind Act. Under these provisions, limited English proficiency (LEP) students are to be assessed annually in listening, speaking, reading, and writing, and a score is also to be provided for comprehension. Moreover, LEP students are to be included in all state assessment scores, which intensifies the pressure on states to ensure that LEP students meet grade-level standards in literacy.

Literacy as "Standardized and Commodified"

Neoliberal educational reform standardizes literacy proficiency against accountability criteria and benchmarks predicated on broad goals of economic competitiveness, cultural cohesion, and national allegiance. The No Child Left Behind Act requires all states to employ either "a uniform set of assessments statewide" (U.S. Department of Education, Office of English Language Acquisition, 2003) or a combination of state and local assessments that can technically demonstrate measurement comparability and equivalence. As Popkewitz (1991) notes, a key reason for the drive to standardization relates to labor demands beyond the school, where the need is to produce standardized outcomes of uniform quality within a context where international quality assurance standards have been defined and agreed upon (p. 46).

Despite increased emphasis within workplaces on teamwork and communities of practice, literacy is seen to consist in the measured capacities of individual learners. This literacy is compiled into personal portfolios and reports. At a time when individuals must increasingly be prepared to move around to find employment, the idea of having a portable certified literacy competence is deemed useful.

This is currently being extended to digital literacy through the activities of supranational bodies like the Global Digital Literacy Council. The council's primary objective is to "review and update the Digital Literacy Standards based on input from subject matter experts worldwide" (Global Digital Literacy Council, 2003). It hosts summits where international stakeholders "collaborate, shape and define an emerging, vendor-independent, global standard for Internet and computer literacy" (Global Digital Literacy Council, 2003). Its preferred standard, the IC[3] certification, is recognized internationally as a baseline certification for ICT careers. The IC[3] program counts toward credit at almost 2000 degree-conferring colleges, universities, and other education-related institutions affiliated with the American Council on Education within the United States alone.

At the same time, literacy has become profoundly commodified under the neoliberal reform agenda. Testing and instructional packages abound. The Reading First provision of the No Child Left Behind Act provides funding for initiatives and program adoptions that are scientifically research based and focus on systematic and explicit instruction in phonemic awareness, phonics, fluency, vocabulary, and text comprehension. Popular examples of such comprehensive reading programs include Harcourt's Trophies program, the Houghton Mifflin Reading Program, and Open Court Reading by SRA/McGraw-Hill. More generally, literacy packages cover literacy assessment, evaluation and validation, remediation, instructional texts and other support resources, teacher professional development and in-servicing, adult and workplace literacy provision, requirements for translating curriculum frameworks and syllabus guidelines into classroom programs, and so on.

"Incorporated" Critique

To some extent neoliberal educational reform discourse endorses critical forms of literate practice. These, however, are typically couched in terms of a critical thinking component of effective literacy or as forms of problem solving mediated by texts. In such cases it is important to recognize the nature and limits of the critical literacies proposed. They are typically practices that involve subjecting means to critique while taking ends as given. The more closely literacy engages with the world beyond school, the more functional and instrumental critique becomes, with emphasis on finding new and better ways of meeting organizational or institutional targets (of productivity, quality, innovation, improvement), but where the targets themselves are beyond question. The mere fact that standards are specified so tightly within the current reform agenda, and that states are held accountable for ensuring their pursuit, carries an implication that the ends driving these standards are beyond critique.

LITERACY FROM A DIFFERENT POINT OF VIEW

One way of looking at the several constructions of literacy integral to neoliberal educational reform discourse is to say that they are all dedicated to recruiting different people from different walks of life to some role or other, and to some location or other, within a particular overarching conception of life as a worker-citizen. In the final analysis, each construction of literacy is bound to values, criteria, and procedures concerned with efficiency, measurable quality, competitive advantage, instrumental rationality, productivity, technological competence, and the like. This is antithetical to an educational philosophy that believes literacy should be integral to understanding how we are constituted through the discourses to which we are recruited; that if we are to live the lives we would "most choose to live," we need to develop points of view from which to understand and be capable of critiquing the discourses we belong to; and that it is the right of every person to be exposed to literacies that enable the development of such points of view.

Delgado-Gaitan (1990) provides a very useful way of looking at what is involved here through her discussion of literacy in relation to empowerment. She identifies and critiques a concept of empowerment that consists in "showing people how to work within a system from the perspective of [those] in power" (p. 2). This is how practically every discourse and literacy works, if we think of literacies as ways of reading and writing that are appropriate to wider social practices in which they are embedded. For example, the literacy involved in writing a doctoral thesis is very different from the literacy involved in corresponding with one's parents or siblings. Part of what is involved in getting someone through a doctorate is to empower them to read and write in the kinds of ways that meet the standards for conferring the degree. But these are standards that have been mastered and are upheld by people who are powerful within the worlds of their respective academic disciplines. If one wants to redefine the discipline to some extent, one will encounter the oppositional power of those who rule through it. This is the power that countless "newbies" have experienced when they first entered new cultures of computing, when they made an error of etiquette on a discussion list or received a mocking comment on their Web log for contributing to the "cheese sandwich effect" (Knobel & Lankshear, 2004, p. 1290). In other words, they read or wrote inappropriately according to the discourse police of the social practice in question. In reading and writing inappropriately, they failed to make the kind of move that would indicate they had been successfully recruited to that social practice or, at least, that they were on the way to being successfully recruited.

It is interesting to interrogate literacy from the standpoint of the idea of no child being left behind. Left behind *what*? Left behind in relation to *whom* and with respect to what *criteria*? Left behind in relation to what *goals and purposes*? *Whose* goals and purposes? When literacy education empowers children not to get left behind, what are these children being recruited to in various ways, and to varying degrees, and at varying levels of reward? What is their literacy education making them insiders to? And in doing so, what outsider positions are they being denied, from which they would envisage other ways of being, other goals and purposes? What kinds and qualities of literacy are pushed off the radar by the educational reform discourse that dominates school conceptions and practices of literacy? And if these other literacy practices are ruled out of reformed school learning programs and pedagogies, where can we look for them and how might we access them, apprentice ourselves to them, and employ them as standpoints from which to "critique other literacies [such as the very literacies to which neoliberal educational reform recruits us] and the ways they constitute us as persons and situate us in society" (Gee, 1996, p. 144)?

For insiders to understand the literacies shaped by neoliberal reform discourse for what they are, and to consciously embrace alternatives, involves using some other literacy as "a meta-language or a meta-Discourse (a set of meta-words, meta-values, meta-beliefs)" for understanding and evaluating them and what they recruit us to and make us into (Gee, 1996, p. 144). This other literacy provides a critical perspective outside the literacies of educational reform discourse. Such a perspective requires meta-knowledge as well as experience of this alternative literacy and its associated discursive values, beliefs, and ways of doing and being. From this standpoint one can build meta-knowledge of the literacy or literacies one is already "in," understand them for what they are, and choose whether and how to "move on."

The so-called new literacies of the Internet (Lankshear & Knobel, 2003) constitute a potentially powerful challenge to educational reform constructions of literacy, and we should (regretfully) continue to expect education policy makers and administrators to continue trying to circumscribe as closely as possible young people's online lives inside and outside of school. This is because in addition to providing opportunities to encounter diverse sets of values, opinions, activities, purposes, and affiliations (Gee, 2004), many online literacies also provide opportunities to obtain meta-level understandings of their associated communities and practices. A person who makes an inappropriate move in a game, a chat space, a discussion list, or an online trading transaction may well be "punished" or ostracized for the transgression. But they are equally very likely to get some coaching as to what went wrong and why it was wrong (e.g., newbies in online multiplayer games soon learn that begging for money or points, rather than earning them legitimately, is socially unacceptable within that space). From a more positive angle, newcomers are often met with very generous support when they join online communities. Fanfiction and gaming communities, for example, are renowned for sharing expertise, explaining procedures and conventions, giving feedback on moves and responses in relation to purposes, and so on. Events like the annual Bloggie Awards help to make explicit the criteria used by those who take it upon themselves to define and police what counts as successful and unsuccessful blogging performance. Discussion forums associated with online auction services provide advice on how to conduct oneself as a trustworthy and well-reputed buyer or seller online.

In such ways, recruits to online literacies are often in a position to grasp relationships between particular constructions of reading and writing (keying, imaging, file sharing, sampling, commenting, describing, etc.) and sets of values, commitments, purposes, forms of affiliation, ways of being, identities, types and qualities of relationships, and so on, that are organically associated with them (e.g., being technically proficient at playing a game is not sufficient to make one a well-respected gamer). In addition, recruits to these new literacies are also often overtly called to critique — to engage in critical evaluation — such as when invited to provide feedback on game design or challenged to create a better cheat or hack for an online game, or to provide or respond to feedback within a fanfiction community. These are the nuts and bolts of meta-level awareness of the relationship between a literacy and the larger discourse in which it is embedded: This kind of reading and writing goes with these kinds of people and processes, and this kind of quality of experience with these sorts of values and commitments. To the extent that participants in online affinity groups (Gee, 2004) can bring such thoughts and understandings to conscious recognition — and there is nothing especially profound about any of this; a lot of "metas" come "free" with online involvements — they can generate a perspective from which to understand and evaluate other literacies they engage in, and what these literacies commit them to and make them into. From the standpoint of this perspective they can make judgments and decisions: "I am at home with this; I am happy to be like this; I will stay here at least for now," or conversely, "I am not at home with this, etc." In addition, of course, they can evaluate this literacy itself — have a perspective on it, as well as draw on it to achieve a perspective on other literacies.

A literacy that opens itself up to critique as well as affording a perspective for critiquing other literacies might be said to empower us in a much deeper way than do literacies that enable us to perform effectively within discourses into which we have been incorporated. We might also say of such literacies that they are the fruits of an *education* and that they are in turn *educative*: They enable us to go on, to become more or, as Dewey (1944) would have had it, to grow.

Contrary to literacy ideals enshrined in educational reform discourse, educative or empowering literacy presupposes commitment to keeping options and critique open as a necessary condition for the free and democratic pursuit of the good life in any substantial sense of this ideal.

REFERENCES

Alvesson, M. (2004). *Knowledge work and knowledge intensive firms.* New York: Oxford University Press.

Delgado-Gaitan, C. (1990). *Literacy for empowerment.* London: Falmer Press.

Dewey, J. (1944). *Democracy and education: An introduction to the philosophy of education.* New York: Free Press.

Drucker, P. (2001). *Management challenges for the 21st century.* New York: HarperCollins.

Gee, J. P. (1996). *Social linguistics and literacies: Ideology in discourses* (2nd ed.). London: Taylor & Francis.

Gee, J. P. (2004). *Situated language and learning: A critique of traditional schooling.* London: Routledge.

Gee, J. P., Hull, G., & Lankshear, C. (1996). *The new work order: Behind the language of the new capitalism.* Boulder, CO: Allen & Unwin and Westview Press.

Global Digital Literacy Council. (2003). *Council objectives.* Retrieved December 10, 2005, from http://www.gdlcouncil.org/

Goals 2000: Educate America Act. (1994). Washington, DC: U.S. Government Printing Office.

Kearns, D., & Doyle, D. (1991). *Winning the brain race: A bold plan to make our schools competitive.* San Francisco: ICS Press.

Knobel, M., & Lankshear, C. (2004). Form and effect in weblogging. *International Journal of Learning, 11* pp. 2825–2830.

Lankshear, C., & Knobel, M. (2003). *New literacies: Changing knowledge and classroom learning.* Buckingham: Open University Press.

Liu, A. (2004). *The laws of cool: Knowledge work and the culture of information.* Chicago: University of Chicago Press.

National Commission on Excellence in Education (NCEE). (1983). *A nation at risk: The imperative for educational reform.* Washington, DC: U.S. Department of Education.

Popkewitz, T. (1991). *A political sociology of educational reform: Power/knowledge in teaching, teacher education, and research.* New York: Teachers College Press.

Reich, R. (1992). *The work of nations.* New York: Vintage Books.

Toch, T. (1991). *In the name of excellence.* New York: Oxford University Press.

U.S. Department of Education, Office of Educational Technology. (1999). *Report on the Forum on Technology in Education: Envisioning the future.* Washington, DC. Retrieved December 4, 2005, from http://www.air.org/forum/default.htm

U.S. Department of Education, Office of Educational Technology. (2004). *Toward a new golden age in American education: How the Internet, the law, and today's students are revolutionizing expectations.* Washington, DC. Retrieved December 4, 2005, from http://www.ed.gov/print/about/offices/list/os/technology/plan/2004/plan.html

U.S. Department of Education, Office of English Language Acquisition. (2003). *Final non-regulatory guidance on the Title III State Formula Grant Program: Standards, assessment and accountability* (Draft). Washington, DC. Retrieved December 4, 2005, from http://www.ed.gov/print/about/offices/list/oela/funding.html

Winters, K. (1996). *America's technology literacy challenge.* Washington, DC: U.S. Department of Education.

Chapter 34

Arts Education

John Jota Leaños and Anthony J. Villarreal
Arizona State University and University of California–Santa Cruz

The phrase "art censorship" might bring to mind parental advisory labels on gangsta rap albums, the decency clause covering National Education Association (NEA) funding put into place after the Robert Mapplethorpe controversy, or obscenity laws designed to protect us from pornography. However, the censorship of art is intimately linked to the censorship of political dissent. In order to begin a discussion of a theory and practice in arts education within a neoliberal context, we would like to invoke the present antidemocratic wave of state surveillance and censorship of people and ideas critical of U.S. government business policies; this repression functions to maintain not only a passive and reactionary public, but also limits of possibility of critical arts pedagogy.

As artists, educators, and cultural workers, we have used critical arts pedagogy and "social art practices" as discursive strategies to engage in the cultural and symbolic arenas of power in order to induce transformative shifts in understanding and knowledge. On the fringes and in the margins, social art practitioners working in the tradition of Paulo Freire, Augusto Boal, Martha Rosler, and Suzanne Lacy, among others, depart from the idea that not only is art beneficial to the cognitive and psychopersonal development of students, but also art practice serves fundamental social and democratic functions.

To engage in art practice and pedagogy in the midst of the current neoliberal hegemony, we must consider what institutional and pedagogical practices are considered valuable and desired and which are deemed irrelevant or unacceptable within the dominant discursive paradigms. From this understanding, we can begin to clearly challenge and dismantle the weighty ideological and social conditioning that normalizes unequal power

relations under what one might call the Judeo-Christian White Supremacist Heteronormative Capitalist Patriarchal Military Industrial Entertainment Prison University Complex.[1]

The silencing of dissent in the United States during times of war has an
unfortunately long history. From the Sedition Act of 1798, Lincoln's sus-
pending of habeas corpus, the internment of the Japanese during WWII,
McCarthyism of the Cold War, and the active political harassment of the
late 1960s' CointelPro operations, to today's War on Terror, "extraordinary rendition," and the renewel of the Patriot Act, the U.S. government
has with relative ease foregone democratic process in order to shield the
multitudes from unpopular views, "security threats," and ideas that prob-
lematize the terms of U.S. hegemony. Ideological censorship and surveillance have become an everyday practice in the United States, manifest not
only in the heart of corporate media, but also in the lives of average citizens, in the workplace, our neighborhoods, and, increasingly, our schools.
Take the example of the Currituck County, NC, student who was visited at
school by the FBI after workers at the local Wal-Mart reported his home-
work assignment, a photograph of President Bush with a thumbtack stuck
in his forehead.[2] In another instance, the FBI questioned and confiscated
the work of a student at Prosser High School, Prosser, Washington, because
of the art's antiwar message.[3] On still another occasion, the FBI investi-
gated a student at Calvine High School in Sacramento for writing the initials *PLO* in his notebook (2005).[4] These authoritarian reactions, coupled
with the surveillance, harassment, and indictments of politically engaged
professors and educators,[5] have become all too common in the midst of
the so-called infinite War on Terrorism. Discourse that challenges national
interests is considered blasphemous during times of war.

Hand in hand with the rise of the neoliberal surveillance state, the shift
toward privatization of public education since the 1980s[6] has established a
technocratic model that overvalues those skills that serve the needs of capital. At the university level, business, science, and technology are promoted
as prime economic generators for cities and institutions, supported by their
corporate-military partners, while the arts and humanities are generally
marginalized, underfunded, and expected to compete financially with the
for-profit sciences. It comes as no surprise, then, that President Bush's 2006
Federal Budget has completely eliminated funding for the Department of
Education's arts programming. Critical pedagogy in general, and critical
arts education in particular, have all but disappeared from school curriculums across the United States. At the same time, those art programs that
funnel students directly into the capitalist industries of advertising, television, and commercial film are thriving, conveniently silencing and filtering out counterhegemonic art practices.

For several decades, higher education has been organizing itself around
corporate, capitalist models wherein students are considered customers,

enrollment is compared to stock and investment, and academic departments are divisions or subsidiaries.[7] Policy makers across the United States preach a sermon based on the hegemony of math and science in the K-12 curriculum, reinforcing this ideology and sustaining the infrastructure of a militaristic, technological empire, but also slighting all other academic subjects, which are cast as too soft, too esoteric for the hard realities of global competition. As a result, very little funding and infrastructure are provided for the creative arts, such as painting, sculpture, ceramics, music, and dance, not to mention the new art forms, like digital media and performance. A potent recipe of conservative ideological surveillance and wartime national security, mixed with the marketization of the public sector, baked in a glaze of technological mythology, gives rise to an imperial substructure, serving up a main course that is toxic to the advancement of arts education. In the fog of authoritarianism, critical art pedagogy loses it footing.

I

However, the ascendancy of corporate influence over the arts, and by extension arts education, should not be seen as an unchallenged hegemony; culture, ideology, and power are never stable, but always "emergent," in a state of negotiation and flux (Williams, 1977; Hall, 1996). In order to better account for the ways in which arts production and consumption in the United States have been both sustained and contested at the level of human agency, a lens of "co-production" (Reardon, 2004) allows us to consider the simultaneous, mutually constitutive nature of the cultural, ideological, and material realms. Avoiding "vulgar" Marxist notions of ideology altogether, the "language [of co-production] allows one to step back from uncritical pronouncements about knowledge or assertions about power in order to ask a prior set of questions about how each is implicated in the formation of the other" (Reardon, 2004, p. 8).

In the United States, the cultural pecking order was first established in the early 20th century, through the creation of dominant economic and institutional structures of arts production and consumption that were born out of a European colonial legacy. Paul Dimaggio (1982/1991) writes:

> In almost every literate society, dominant status groups or classes eventually have developed their own styles of art and the institutional means of supporting them. It was predictable that this would happen in the United States, despite the absence of a hereditary aristocracy. (p. 381)

Going on to describe the creation of prestigious museums of fine art and symphonies, the "institutional means" of supporting elite influence of cultural production in the United States, Dimaggio (1982/1991) stresses that such organizations "created a base through which the ideal of high culture could be given institutional flesh" (p. 393). That is to say, the establishment of high culture as the norm reference for all cultural practices is an ideological process. Following Gramsci's (1973) conception of power, the maintenance of any historical hegemony requires both *coercion* and *consent.* In the case of arts education, consent is partly manufactured in the institutionalization of the high/low binary. As Dimaggio (1982/1991) describes:

> The alliance between class and culture that emerged was defined by, and thus inseparable from, its organizational mediation. As a consequence, the classification "high culture/popular culture" is comprehensible only in its dual sense as characterizing both a ritual classification and the organizational systems that give that classification meaning. (p. 394)

In sum, the full range of art activity occurs within a "cultural arbitrary" (Bourdieu & Passeron, 1977) that establishes elite aesthetics as the norm, a norm further enacted and enforced by the everyday practices of arts education that privileges beauty, form, and genius. As this high art aesthetic is central to the cultural arbitrary of traditional arts education in the United States, artistic contributions that fall outside of the narrow parameters of these norms, such as critical and politically engaged art practices, have been marginalized historically and are practically absent from official school curriculum. This ideologically formed arts education prevents social art practices from becoming valued as a vital form of democratic engagement.

II

Under the market logic of late capitalism, democratic engagement has been replaced by the concept of the *sovereign consumer,*[8] in which political citizenship is measured in terms of one's buying power. Key historical meta-narratives of the United States — democracy, liberty, justice, and equality — are repackaged in the form of limitless consumer choice. The consolidation of corporate media, greatly facilitated by the Federal Communications Act of 1996, has concentrated commercial control of the symbolic arena. These culture industries produce media representations of racial or gender equality, such as Asian newscasters, black sports stars, or Latina pop divas, that serve as "evidence" that equal opportunity and diversity exist, in stark contrast to a real world that remains profoundly stratified. Similarly, the commodity fetishism of consumer product choice hides the ongoing indentured servitude of third-world labor and the "Wal-Martization" of work in the United States.

While marginalized cultural forms, such as jazz, have only rarely been legitimized and made palatable to elite tastes, corporate media production of popular culture articulates a semblance of multiculturalism. Because independent cultural expression and the production of art always contain the potential for radical, progressive critique, a chance to express counterhegemonic discourse, or an anticapitalist logic — in short, a vision of alternatives — great resources are invested in the co-optation of certain popular forms of music, dance, and visual art. Not only does this amount to a kind of *pan y circo*,[9] in which popular media entertainment smoothes social antagonisms in an unequal society, but it also means that high culture can safely operate beyond the frame of the multitudes.[10]

This interplay between high art and media representations, and the separation between high art and the popular are central to the reproduction of the conditions necessary for capitalist arts education; media must constantly co-opt independent cultures, and high art must constantly renegotiate its place at the top. However, as in capitalism itself, there are inherent contradictions apparent in the maintenance of high art institutions. In order to legitimate the status of elites in the United States, through the superiority of their art, it is still necessary for them to share it. The contradiction resides in the difficulty elites face in attempting to socialize the multitudes through "institutions from which [the multitudes] are effectively barred" (Dimaggio, 1982/1991, p. 393). And so it is that independent, alternative, and indigenous art practices — the graffiti artists, custom bicycle and car builders, skateboarders, breakdancers, hip-hop DJs, rappers, street stencil guerrillas, zines, and everything in between — all the while must be assimilated, strategically ignored, or heavily policed and negatively sanctioned in order to maintain the terms of the hegemony. Because these regimes of status and taste in U.S. art practices are co-produced with economic, political, and cultural systems of stratification, these material arrangements and attendant discursive formations mediate how we experience race, class, gender, sexuality, and citizenship in the "imagined nation" (Anderson, 1991).

What, then, would a critical arts pedagogy look like? If media-generated hyperreality[11] is now the de facto cultural heritage of most Americans, in many ways transcending historical notions of race, ethnic, and nation-based identities, what would constitute a critical arts pedagogy? What would a radical, democratic arts education look like and what challenges would it confront? Along with the systematic legitimization of specific art forms comes the aggressive censorship and policing of counterhegemonic discourse through the arts. As long as art does not do anything besides act pretty or pretend it is deep, then its practice is allowed and even celebrated. However, when art practice begins to challenge historical narratives of oppression, question privilege and inequality, or disrupt fixed discourse of the hegemony, it is then that art practice begins to pose a threat within educational institutions, inevitably leading to meetings, classroom investigations, press conferences, death threats, or disciplinary action. In the next section, we present a case study of social art practice by co-author John Jota Leaños, which challenged the current militaristic hegemony of the imagined U.S. nation.

III

In the fall of 2004, Leaños taught a course entitled "Contemporary Chicana/o Art" at Arizona State University. The objective of the course was to engage students in the history of Chicana/o social art intervention in public spaces, from the mural movement and political postering to street theater and performance, while offering students a chance to engage in art intervention and media tactics. With wars raging in Iraq and Afghanistan, and an embattled presidential election coming to a head, Leaños and his students mounted an art campaign to be launched before the final presidential debate hosted at Arizona State University. With the international media's eyes focused on the upcoming debate, the students, most of them Chicana/os, reasoned that their ideas and perspectives were being ignored or misrepresented in the corporate media. The class decided, then, to become its own media by deploying traditional Chicana/o aesthetics of public postering combined with new media tactics of e-mail floods and press releases. Working with subject matter of the war in Iraq, the students created a range of artworks from condemnation of the "illegal" invasion of Iraq to calls for more debate on torture. Leaños created his own poster, a Días de los Muertos memorial to Arizona State University graduate, ex-Arizona Cardinal football player, and fallen U.S. Ranger Patrick Tillman.

Pat Tillman was a professional football player who gave up an NFL contract worth millions of dollars to enlist in the U.S. Rangers and fight the war on terror. In April 2004, Tillman was killed in Afghanistan. According to a military press release, Tillman died while fighting Taliban resistance. Tillman was immediately canonized as a great American war hero and deemed imperial martyr by the government-military-media complex. This was at a time when media discourse about the war dead was, for the most part, conspicuously absent. A few months later, a quiet Pentagon report released news stating that Tillman was "probably killed by 'friendly fire.'" The Pentagon, it turns out, lied about Tillman's death.[12]

By questioning the appropriation and canonization of Tillman's image by the government and the media (Tillman, the man, it turns out, was against the war in Iraq and an avid reader of Noam Chomsky[13]), Leaños committed a discursive intervention, challenging the framing of U.S. national identity based on war, hypermasculinity, and self-righteousness.

Such a critique was not tolerated and the backlash was immediate. Posters were torn down within hours of their hanging, and the Tillman poster was delivered to local and national television stations and to the president of the Arizona Board of Regents. It was evident that Chicana/o perspectives on the war in Iraq were not invited in the Arizona public sphere. The barrage of reactionary responses that ensued included thousands of hate e-mails, promises of violence, death threats, and investigations into Leaños's classroom activities. Ironically, the same digital culture that had made such art possible also facilitated the ideological surveillance that swarmed around what was seen as a blasphemous speech against an imagined American war hero.

The entire scenario became an arts teaching moment about free speech, militarism, and national identity, not only for Leaños's class and the university, but also for a country straddling the line between authoritarianism and democracy. Even though the immediate responses to the artwork were reactionary and mob-like, reflexive dialogue did develop in classrooms, on Internet blogs, and in the media.

IV

What is to be done? Unfortunately, for those of us concerned with creating a more egalitarian world, in arts education and beyond, we have no 12-step program for guaranteed progressive results from a critical arts pedagogy. Because any and all politics are "without guarantees" (Hall, 1996), the best we can hope for is increased debate, and the possibility of alternatives, put into play by counterhegemonic discourse, of which art can be a principal orator. Our critical educational pedagogy grows from the Ejército Zapatista de Liberación Nacional (EZLN) concept of an anti-(neoliberal) globalization movement based on "One No and Many Yes's," and we will offer some strategies for arts education in a time of infinite war.

First, we think artists need to take Indy Media's mantra to heart: "Don't hate the media, become the media."[14] Progressive, critical arts education must use the media's own strategies to disrupt media hegemony. This means making full use of digital technologies for counterhegemonic purposes. To some extent, this means culture jamming, but it also means understanding the limits of fighting representations with representations. While art is generally seen as symbolic, critical arts education must go beyond simply "ad busting" and address the structural inequalities of the material world.

We have also been unwilling to perform a "god-trick," as if this essay comes from nowhere,[15] so, we have inserted ourselves into this text, situating our knowledge in a particular sociohistorical context of global empire. Similarly, social art practices must be global-local, thinking globally, but acting locally, as it were, in order to make globalization's processes visible at the street level; no longer can we allow debate to treat neoliberal, modernist development schemes as something that only happens in Southeast Asian export processing zones or *maquiladoras* on the U.S.-Mexican border. Art's greatest potential to foster change is at the level of the microsocial, through tactical interruptions of *biopower*,[16] revealing the ways that we are complicit in the normalizing operations of power, opening up space for new forms of knowledge production, and spreading decolonial discourse. All of these tactics will depend on the local conditions of a given arts education program; however, as we have highlighted in this essay, the hegemony of high arts and media consolidation is a major obstacle blocking the creation of a truly democratic public sphere. It is toward these two areas that our efforts should work; we must muster the courage to speak truth to power in spite of the reactionary historical context in which we practice.

NOTES

1. This term attempts to embody the interconnected co-production of material and ideological structures, and owes much to bell hooks and Los Cybrids: La Raza Techno-Crítica.
2. See Rothschild, M. *Wal-Mart turns in student's anti-Bush photo, Secret Service investigates him.* Retrieved from http://progressive.org/mag_mc100405
3. See Parvaz, D., & George, K. *Secret Service confiscates anti-Bush drawings by 15-year-old at Prosser High.* Retrieved from http://seattlepi.nwsource.com/local/170992_prosser28.html
4. See Rothschild, M. *FBI talks to Muslim high school student about "PLO" initials on his notebook.* Retrieved December 23, 2005, from http://www.progressive.org/mag_mc122305
5. Right-wing zealot David Horowitz has circulated a list of the "100 Most Dangerous Professors in the U.S.," demonizing any and all academics who dare to question U.S. hegemony. See Stephen Kurtz and Critical Art Ensemble, Ward Churchill, John Leaños, and so forth, for the experiences of recent victims of this latest installment of the culture wars.
6. Michael W. Apple and Geoff Whitty have written extensively on privatization/marketization of public education. See, for example, Apple, M. W. (2001). Comparing neo-liberal projects and inequality in education. *Comparative Education, 37,* 409–423; Whitty, G., & Power, S. (2000). Marketization and privatization in mass education systems. *International Journal of Educational Development, 20,* 93–107.
7. See Slaughter, S., & Leslie, L. L. (1997). *Academic capitalism: Politics, policies, and the entrepreneurial university.* Baltimore: Johns Hopkins University Press. The so-called New American University of Arizona State is a prime example of a public institution taking on an explicit corporate structure.

The objectives of this and many institutions alike are to infinitely expand investments, capital, holdings, and customers. See http://www.asu.edu/president/newamericanuniversity/

8. Consumer sovereignty is a term used in economics to refer to the (disputed) notion of the rule or sovereignty of purchasers over producers in markets. See http://en.wikipedia.org/wiki/Consumer_sovereignty

9. *Pan y circo* (bread and circus) is a concept that expresses how Roman elites maintained order by offering the circus as entertainment and diversion to the masses of indentured servants, who subsisted mainly on bread.

10. Following Hardt and Negri (2001), we have chosen to use the term *multidudes* to invoke the great diversity of identities and social locations that have, in the past, been subsumed under modernist terminology, such as *public, the masses,* or *the people.*

11. Baudrillard, J. (1994). *Simulacra and simulation* (S. Faria Glaser, Trans.). Ann Arbor: University of Michigan.

12. To view the artwork and for a full account of this controversy, see http://leanos.net/Tillmantext.htm

13. See Zirin, D. (2005, October 24). Pat Tillman, our hero. *The Nation.* Retrieved May 1, 2007 from http://thenation.confdoc/20051024/zirin

14. See www.indymedia.org

15. Haraway, D. (1996). Situated knowledges: The science question in feminism and the privilege of partial perspective. In E. Fox Keller & E. E. Longino (Eds.), *Feminism and science* pp. 249–263, New York: Oxford University Press.

16. Here we are drawing on Foucault's conception of biopower; his two-part conception includes scientific *disciplinary knowledges* that categorize individuals, and *normalization* or the internalized surveillance through which each person disciplines himself or herself. Through discourses and practices, individuals are often unwittingly complicit. Rather than only concerning ourselves with power *over* us, as in domination, our tactics must reveal the ways that power runs *through* the body politic.

REFERENCES

Anderson, B. (1991). *Imagined communities: Reflections on the origin and spread of nationalism* (rev. ed.). London: Verso.

Bourdieu, P., & Passeron, J. C. (1977). *Reproduction in Education, Society, and Culture.* London: Sage Publications.

Dimaggio, P. (1991). Cultural entrepreneurship in nineteenth-century Boston: The creation of an organizational base for high culture in America. In C. Mukerji & M. Schudson (Eds.), *Rethinking popular culture: Contemporary perspectives in cultural studies.* Berkeley: University of California Press. (Original work published 1982.)

Gramsci, A. (1973). *Letters from prison* (selected, translated, and introduced by Lynne Lawner). New York: Harper and Row.

Hall, S. (1996). The problem of ideology: Marxism without guarantees. In D. Morley & K.-H. Chen (Eds.), *Stuart Hall: Critical dialogues in cultural studies.* London: Routledge. (Original work published 1986.)

Hardt, M., & Negri, A. (1991). *Empire.* Cambridge: Harvard University Press.

Reardon, J. (2004). *Race to the finish: Identity and governance in the age of genomics.* Princeton, NJ: Princeton University Press.

Williams, R. (1977). *Marxism and literature.* Oxford: Oxford University Press.

Chapter 35

Social Studies Education

E. Wayne Ross
University of British Columbia

Social studies education has had a relatively brief and contentious history as a school subject. The fundamental content of the social studies curriculum — the study of human enterprise across time and space — has always been at the core of education; however, there continues to be a lack of an agreed-upon definition of social studies.

One of the earliest uses of the term *social studies* to refer to school subjects is attributed to Thomas Jesse Jones in an article that appeared in the *Southern Workman* in 1905 in which he expressed his concern that young African Americans and Native Americans "would never be able to become integral members of the broader society unless they learned to understand that society, the social forces that operated within it, and ways to recognize and respond to social power" (Tabachnick, 1991, p. 725).

The roots of the contemporary social studies curriculum are found in the 1916 report of the Committee on Social Studies of the National Education Association's Commission on the Reorganization of Secondary Schools, which Jones chaired. The final report of the committee, *The Social Studies in Secondary Education*, illustrates the influence of previous National Education Association (NEA) (1916) and American Historical Association (1899) committees regarding history in schools, but it also emphasized the development of citizenship values in students and established the pattern of course offerings in social studies that has been consistent for most of the 20th century.[1]

Various reviews of the social studies curriculum have concluded that the apparent consensus that citizenship education is the primary purpose of social studies is "almost meaningless." Few social studies educators disagree that the purpose of social studies is "to prepare youth so that they possess the knowledge, values, and skills needed for active participation in society" (Marker & Mehlinger, 1992, p. 832). Arguments have been made that students can develop "good citizenship" through the study of history (Whelan, 2001), through the examination of contemporary social problems (Evans & Saxe, 1996) or public policy (Oliver & Shaver, 1966) or social roles (Superka & Hawke, 1982) or social taboos (Hunt & Metcalf, 1955) or by becoming astute critics of society (Engle & Ochoa, 1988).

Vinson and Ross (2001) argue the paradox of social studies education is that it is marked by both the *appearance of diversity* (e.g., the various traditions or categories proposed for social studies curriculum and instruction) and the *appearance of uniformity* (e.g., stable curricular scope and sequence and entrenched patterns of instruction).

The question, of course, is whether social studies should promote a brand of citizenship that is adaptive to the status quo and interests of the socially powerful or whether it should promote citizenship aimed at transforming and reconstructing society — a question that has fueled debates since Jones first employed the term *social studies* (see Hursh & Ross, 2000; Ross, 2006; Ross & Marker, 2005a).

SOCIAL STUDIES, CULTURAL TRANSMISSION, AND SPECTATOR DEMOCRACY

The tensions between an emphasis on transmission of the cultural heritage of the dominant society and the development of critical thought have produced a mixed history for social studies education — predominantly conservative in its purposes, but also at times incorporating progressive and even radical purposes (Stanley & Nelson, 1994). Various schemes have been used by researchers to make sense of the wide-ranging and conflicting purposes offered for social studies. Researchers essentially agree that social studies is used for three primary purposes: (1) socialization into society's norms; (2) transmission of facts, concepts, and generalizations from the academic disciplines; and (3) the promotion of critical or reflective thinking (see Vinson, 1998). These researchers also agree that citizenship transmission or conservative cultural continuity is the dominant approach practiced in schools.

The dominant pattern of social studies instruction is characterized as text-oriented, whole-group, teacher-centered approaches aimed toward the transmission of factual information. While many social studies educators have long advocated instructional approaches that include active learning and higher-order thinking within a curriculum that emphasizes gender equity, multiculturalism, environmentalism, and so forth, the dominant pattern has persisted. Social studies education is characterized, at least in part, by a pedagogy that produces students who are either unable or afraid to think critically (see Giroux, 1978; Ross & Marker 2005b). This pedagogy is the result of socioeconomic realities, beyond the direct control of teachers, that produce conditions such as classes with large numbers of students, a lack of planning time for teachers, the culture of teacher isolation, and a strong emphasis on standardized test scores as the only legitimate measure of educational achievement. The traditional pattern of social studies instruction is, however, also sustained by the fact that it is easier for teachers to plan and teach in accordance with a direct-instruction approach that focuses on information transmission and coverage of content and that encourages teachers' low expectations of students.

Reinforcing these tendencies is the conservative restoration of the past two decades, which have produced the educational excellence and standards movements, which have placed an emphasis on high-stakes testing and student recall and identification of social studies facts, persons, and events, diverting attention away from the ways in which the conditions of teaching and learning might be transformed to encourage critical, active, and democratic citizenship (Vinson & Ross, 2003).

HAS SOCIAL STUDIES GONE WRONG?

The Thomas B. Fordham Foundation, whose publications include *Where Did the Social Studies Go Wrong?* (hereafter *WDSSGW*; Leming, Ellington, & Porter, 2003) and *Terrorists, Despots, and Democracy: What Our Children Need to Know,* has sponsored one of the most visible recent efforts at social studies reform. These publications have sparked an aggressive and vigorous debate regarding the nature of social studies education. The authors of *WDSSGW* believe, among other things, that the current social studies curriculum "eschews substantive content and subordinates a focus on effective practice to educational and political correctness" (Leming & Ellington, 2003, p. ii).

In his foreword to *WDSSGW*, Chester E. Finn, Jr., president of the Fordham Foundation and former assistant secretary of education in the Reagan administration, states that an essential tenet of any decent social studies curriculum for young Americans is that "democracy's survival depends upon *transmitting* to each new generation the political vision of liberty and equality before the law that unites us as Americans" (p. vi, italics added). It is on this crucial point of *transmission*, and its primary role in education for democracy, that our differences with *WDSSGW* begin.

Even before the concept of social studies was invented, schools in America had been indoctrinating its youth; no other single factor has so characterized textbooks, curriculum materials, or classroom instruction. Teaching as "transmission of content" is alive and well in the contemporary social studies classrooms. However, indoctrination and transmission that result in an emphasis on artificial separate subjects, rote memorization of facts, and uncritical transmission of cultural values should not be an essential tenet of teaching for democracy. Rather, we should be focused on preparing informed, critically thoughtful citizens who are intent on improving our great experiment of democracy.

The current debate about social studies reform, and its incumbent tensions, indicates the need for social studies educators to begin a serious conversation that can help the field chart a deliberative, divergent, and flexible course for its curriculum. If the social studies is to continue to evolve, it must involve those interested in social studies in communicating areas of agreement as well as articulating philosophical differences.

The position of the self-described social studies "contrarians," as presented in *WDSSGW*, rejects the pluralism of the field of social studies and deliberation as the means to democracy. An examination of the table of contents of *WDSSGW* is illustrative of the desire of its authors to close off and limit the discussion: Chapters with titles such as "The Training of Idiots," "Garbage In, Garbage Out," and "Ignorant Activists" reflect a perspective that implies an inherent correctness and allows little room for scholarly discussion or reasoned disagreement (Ross & Marker, 2005a).

As we debate the reform of social studies, we should not move rashly to adopt a singular curricular perspective that is driven by ideology and special interests. Rather, we need to take the time to consider conscientiously a pluralism of viewpoints on social studies reform that could help to reinvent the social studies curriculum and make it relevant and flexible to meet the unknown demands of the future. A way to ensure that a pluralism of views on the nature and purposes of social studies education remains beneficial, and not factionalizing or destructive, is to embrace deliberation as the core idea of creating, maintaining, and teaching for democracy.

The Deweyan sense of democracy seems most useful here, that is, democracy as a "mode of associated living, or conjoint communicated experience" (Dewey, 1966, p. 87). As such, the social studies can avoid being understood in the either/or, dualistic terms of choosing education for social reproduction or social reconstruction. Rather, the pursuit of democracy (the purposes of citizenship education) becomes the process of creating communities with shared interests. What characterizes citizenship in this sense of democracy is not merely exercising the right to vote, but rather an obligation to engage in careful consideration and discussion of alternatives for the purpose of creating a better life.

Democracy so conceived presupposes what philosopher Brian Fay (1987) calls an "activist conception of human beings" — that is, human beings are (at least potentially) "broadly intelligent, curious, reflective and willful beings" (p. 64). Fay argues that these natural tendencies are made known in noncoercive contexts and result from rational deliberation and persuasion. It is through deliberation that we decide how to be and what to do.

Deliberation — rather than coercion, appeals to emotion, or authority — offers a means for resolving differences of opinion and a foundation for pedagogy that is attuned to the knowledge, skills, and values that citizens need in a society pursuing a democratic ideal. Fay points out that assuming rational deliberation is the basis for democratic communities does not presume that all members of a community agree on all things when the day is done. "To be rational is to have good reasons for one's beliefs, together with an openness to reconsider alternatives and a willingness to revise one's beliefs if evidence is adduced which fits better with an alternative system of beliefs" (1987, p. 179). Within a democratic community, members can disagree as long as they are willing to engage in a discussion about their beliefs, as long as their beliefs are consistent with the best available evidence, and they are open-minded about their beliefs. As Sandra Mathison (2000) notes, deliberation and democracy as described by Dewey and Fay,

> [are] concerned with a right action in particular contexts for particular people, given a specific set of details. The role of deliberation is not to settle a matter, to make a decision, or to take action that is definitive and immutable. It is a continuous process of assessing the particulars in order to move toward betterment with the implicit expectation that an ideal state does not exist and cannot be attained. (p. 237)

Deliberation then becomes the heart not only of education for democratic citizenship, but also of democracy itself.

IDEOLOGY OF NEUTRALITY AND SPECTATOR DEMOCRACY

The linkages among political agendas, classroom pedagogy, and research on teaching have been blurred and an "ideology of neutrality" has been internalized in the consciousness of both social studies researchers and teacher educators as well as classroom teachers (Marker, 2000). Many educational research studies accept the objectives pedagogical program and are organized to explain how the objectives were reached. For example, research on "effective teaching" extols the values of direct instruction over teaching that promotes student-to-student interaction, democratic pedagogy, and a learning milieu, which values caring and individual students' self-esteem. The results of such research do not question the assumed conception of student achievement — efficient mastery of content as represented by test scores. Left unquestioned are such issues as the criteria of content selection, the resultant mystification and fragmentation of course content, linkages between improved test scores and national economic prosperity, and the ways in which the social conditions of schooling might unequally distribute knowledge. And, as another example, critical thinking in social studies most often focuses on procedural problem solving (e.g., distinguishing facts from opinions) rather than problem posing. As a result, critical thinking stops short of equipping students to question, challenge, or transform society and serves to socialize students into accepting and reproducing the status quo (Marker, 2000; Whitson & Stanley, 1994).

Throughout the 20th century progressive intellectuals and media figures (e.g., Walter Lippmann, George Kennan, Reinhold Niebuhr, and many Deweyites) have promulgated spectator democracy — in which a specialized class of experts identify what our common interests are and then think and plan accordingly (Chomsky, 1997). The function of those outside the specialized class is to be spectators rather than participants in action. This theory of democracy asserts that common interests elude the general public and can only be understood and managed by an elite group. According to Lippmann, a properly running democracy is one in which the large majority of the population (whom Lippmann labeled "the bewildered herd") is protected from itself by the specialized class's management of the political, economic, and ideological systems, and in particular by the manufacturing of consent, for example, bringing about agreement on the part of the public for things that they do not want.

Spectator democracy is promoted in social studies classes through the traditional instructional patterns described above (which situate students outside the knowledge construction process as passive recipients of prepackaged information) as well as in the conceptions of democracy that dominate much of the content of social studies courses. For example, democracy is often equated with elections and voting. The procedure of allowing individuals to express a choice on a proposal, resolution, bill, or candidate is perhaps the most widely taught precept in the social studies curriculum. In this conception of citizenship, individual agency is construed primarily as one's vote, and voting procedures override all else with regard to what counts as democracy. Democracy, in this case, is not defined by outcomes but by application of procedures.

In social studies classes, exercising your right to vote is taught to be the primary manifestation of good citizenship; this, along with understanding the procedural aspects of government (e.g., how a bill becomes a law, the branches of government, separation of powers, etc.), becomes the primary focus of citizenship education. Democracy based on proceduralism leaves little room for individuals or groups to exercise direct political action; this is a function left to a specialized class of people such as elected representatives and experts who advise them. Yes, citizens can vote, lobby, and exercise free speech and assembly rights, but as far as governing is concerned, they are primarily spectators.

Perhaps the apparent consensus on the purpose of social studies as citizenship education is not, as has been suggested, meaningless.

Traditional liberal-democratic thinking, and the spectator democracy it engenders, has dominated the practice of both social studies teachers and teacher educators. Instead of a democratic society as one in which "the public has the means to participate in some meaningful way in the management of their own affairs and the means of information are open and free" (Chomsky, 1997, p. 5), we should have (and sustain through much of what occurs under the auspices of social studies education) a spectator democracy, in which the public is barred from managing their own affairs and the means of information is kept narrowly and rigidly controlled.

TRANSFORMING SOCIAL STUDIES EDUCATION

Achieving a democratic society in which members of the public are meaningful participants in the management of their own affairs requires moving beyond a brand of citizenship that is adaptive to the status quo and interests of the socially powerful. Social studies education for citizenship aimed at transforming and reconstructing society requires both socialization and countersocialization (Engle & Ochoa, 1988). Accomplishing this vision within the context of hierarchical, bureaucratic institutions like U.S. public schools, which reward passivity on the part of students and teachers, is no small challenge.

It should be no surprise that teachers are the key to transforming the aims and practices of social studies education. Students will never become meaningful participants (not mere spectators) in society unless they learn to understand society, the social forces that operate within it, and ways to recognize and *respond to social power in ways that are reconstructive of the old order, which privileges the rich and socially powerful*. Social studies education that is transformative and reconstructive can only be created by teachers that are practicing active, critical citizenship in their personal and professional lives.

The dialectical relationships among teachers' beliefs and actions and the contexts in which they work harbor a powerful, yet untapped, rejoinder to the top-down, centralized initiatives currently dominating school reform efforts. One reason for this is that teachers (and teacher educators) have traditionally understood their power to affect change as stopping at the classroom door and not extending into school-wide change or community-wide or national educational politics. True educational reform, however, involves engaging policy debates and other struggles beyond the classroom. As teacher Stan Karp (1994) argues,

> If we recognize that effective education requires students to bring their real lives into the classrooms, and to take what they learn back to their homes and

neighborhoods in the form of new understandings and new behavior, how can we not do the same? Critical teaching should not be merely an abstraction or academic formula for classroom "experimentation." It should be a strategy for educational organizing that changes lives, including our own. (p. 24)

There are many key educational issues that are determined in the larger context of community, state, and national politics (e.g., curriculum standards, voucher plans, privatization schemes). Teachers' efforts in the classroom are tied to broader endeavors to transform our society. If social educators (and others) truly want to transform schools, we must recognize and act on connections between classrooms and society. If we can find ways to link work for democratic reforms in both schools and society, both will be strengthened.

NOTES

1. The dominant pattern of social studies course offerings and topics in the United States has remained largely unchanged since 1916: K — self, school, community, home; Grade 1 — families; Grade 2 — neighborhoods; Grade 3 — communities; Grade 4 — state history and geographic regions; Grade 5 — U.S. history; Grade 6 — world cultures, Western hemisphere; Grade 7 — world geography or history; Grade 8 — U.S. history; Grade 9 — civics or world cultures; Grade 10 — world history; Grade 11 — U.S. history; and Grade 12 — government.

REFERENCES

Chomsky, N. (1997, October). What makes the mainstream media mainstream? *Z Magazine*. Retrieved May 9, 2007 from www.zmag.org/chomsky/articles/z9710-mainstream-media.html.

Committee of Seven, American Historical Association. (1899). *The study of history in schools*. New York: Macmillan.

Committee on Social Studies, National Education Association. (1916). *The social studies in secondary education* (Bulletin 28). Washington, DC: Government Printing Office.

Dewey, J. (1966). *Democracy and education*. New York: Free Press. (Original work published 1916.)

Engle, S., & Ochoa, A. (1988). *Education for democratic citizenship: Decision making in the social studies*. New York: Teachers College Press.

Evans, R. W., & Saxe, D. W. (Eds.). (1996). *Handbook on teaching social issues*. Washington, DC: National Council for the Social Studies.

Fay, B. (1987). *Critical social science*. Ithaca, NY: Cornell University Press.

Giroux, H. A. (1978). Writing and critical thinking in the social studies. *Theory and Research in Social Education, 6*, 34–95.

Hunt, M. P., & Metcalf, L. E. (1955). *Teaching high school social studies: Problems in reflective teaching and social understanding*. New York: Harper.

Hursh, D. W., & Ross, E. W. (Eds.). (2000). *Democratic social education: Social studies for social change.* New York: Falmer.

Karp, S. (1994). Beyond the classroom. *Rethinking Schools, 8,* 24.

Leming, J. S., & Ellington, L. (2003). Introduction: Passion without progress. In J. S. Leming, L. Ellington, & K. Porter (Eds.), *Where did the social studies go wrong?* Washington, DC: Thomas B. Fordham Foundation.

Leming, J. S., Ellington, L., & Porter, K. (2003). *Where did the social studies go wrong?* Washington, DC: Thomas B. Fordham Foundation. Retrieved May 1, 2007 from http://www.edexcellence.net/foundation/publication/publication. cfm?id=317#881

Marker, G., & Mehlinger, H. (1992). Social studies. In P. W. Jackson (Ed.), *Handbook of research on curriculum* (pp. 830–851). New York: Macmillan.

Marker, P. M. (2000). Not only by our words: Connecting the pedagogy of Paulo Freire with the social studies classroom. In D. W. Hursh & E. W. Ross (Eds.), *Democratic social education: Social studies for social change* (pp. 135–148). New York: Falmer.

Mathison, S. (2000). Promoting democracy through evaluation. In D. W. Hursh & E. W. Ross (Eds.), *Democratic social education: Social studies for social change* (pp. 229–241). New York: Falmer.

Oliver, D. W., & Shaver, J. P. (1966). *Teaching public issues in the high school.* Boston: Houghton Mifflin.

Ross, E. W. (Ed.). (2006). *The social studies curriculum: Purposes, problems, and possibilities* (3rd ed.). Albany: State University of New York Press.

Ross, E. W., & Marker, P. M. (2005a). (If social studies is wrong) I don't want to be right. *Theory and Research in Education, 33,* 142–151.

Ross, E. W., & Marker, P. M. (Eds.). (2005b, July/August, September/October). Social studies: Wrong, right, or left? *The Social Studies,* pp. 96–97.

Stanley, W. B., & Nelson, J. (1994). The foundations of social education in historical context. In R. Martusewicz & W. Reynolds (Eds.), *Inside/out: Contemporary critical perspectives in education* (pp. 266–284). New York: St. Martin's.

Superka, D. P., & Hawke, S. (1982). *Social roles: A focus for social studies in the 1980s.* Boulder, CO: Social Science Education Consortium.

Tabachnick, B. R. (1991). Social studies: Elementary school programs. In A. Lewy (Ed.), *International encyclopedia of curriculum* (pp. 725–731). Oxford: Pergamon.

Vinson, K. D. (1998). The "traditions" revisited: Instructional approach and high school social studies teachers. *Theory and Research in Social Education, 23,* 50–82.

Vinson, K. D., & Ross, E. W. (2001). In search of the social studies curriculum: Standardization, diversity, and a conflict of appearances. In W. B. Stanley (Ed.), *Critical issues for social studies research in the 21st century: Research, problems, and prospects* (pp. 39–71). Greenwich, CT: Information Age Publishers.

Vinson, K. D., & Ross, E. W. (2003). *Image and education: Teaching in the face of the new disciplinarity.* New York: Peter Lang.

Whelan, M. (2001). History as the core of social studies curriculum. In E. W. Ross (Ed.), *The social studies curriculum: Purposes, problems, and possibilities* (rev. ed., pp. 43–56). Albany: State University of New York Press.

Whitson, J. A., & Stanley, W. B. (1994). The future of critical thinking in the social studies. In M. R. Nelson (Ed.), *The future of the social studies* (pp. 25–33). Boulder, CO: Social Science Education Consortium.

Chapter 36

Math Education

Tom Munk
University of North Carolina–Chapel Hill

This chapter will be an attempt to investigate the possible equity consequences of the problem-solving-centered mathematics education reform movement led by the National Council of Teachers of Mathematics (NCTM), sometimes known as reform mathematics, sometimes as the standards movement because of the central role of a series of NCTM standards documents (National Council of Teachers of Mathematics, 1989, 1991, 1995, 2000). I will investigate first two definitions of equity: a limited definition implied by the No Child Left Behind Act and a more expansive one presented by Rochelle Gutiérrez. After a look at some hopeful progressive assessments of the equity potential for the math reform movement, I will look at the political roots of the reform, which seem more oriented to corporate profitability than to any kind of deeply egalitarian vision. If the supporters of reform — global capitalists and progressive activists — are strange bedfellows, then so are its opponents — mathematicians (at least initially) and cultural conservatives. Both groups have been disturbed by the advance of ambiguity into the realm of presumed objective truth, but this advance is central to the reform agenda. All students, not just white, middle-class males, must be allowed to solve true problems their way, not just replicate teachers' solutions as exercises. As the new field of ethnomathematics tackles these issues, critical pedagogies add a distinctly political dimension, suggesting that full cultural relevance is not achievable until the political realities that oppressed children understand through their life experiences are added to the problem sets with which they struggle. This is where the global capitalists part company with truly progressive reformers. They are looking for diverse workers good at solving problems, but they fully intend to maintain a monopoly on the problems posed. I will conclude with a look at some of the practitioners of an expansively equitable reform mathematics. To summarize, mathematics reform is worth the struggle, but to aim the reform in the direction of an expansive equity will require a struggle within a struggle.

LIMITED AND EXPANSIVE VISIONS OF EQUITY

The No Child Left Behind Act (NCLB) requires states, districts, and schools to bring all students, in all major subgroups, to the level of proficiency or above in mathematics by the year 2014 (Gingerich, 2003). While it can be argued that many of the authors of this act intend it as more of a battering ram against public education than as support for a diverse student population (see, for example, Emery & Ohanian, 2004), it represents a crystal-clear definition of equity. I will call it *limited equity*, as distinct from an *expansive equity* as defined by Rochelle Gutiérrez (2002).

Her definition comes in three parts. The first is "erasure of the ability to predict students' mathematics achievement and participation solely on characteristics such as race, class, ethnicity, sex, beliefs and creeds, and proficiency in the dominant language" (p. 154). This definition is very close to the limited equity of the NCLB legislation, differing only in that it requires equity throughout the achievement hierarchy, not just at the proficiency level. Larger differences appear with Parts 2 and 3 of her definition. Part 2 speaks to the nature of problems tackled by students: "erasure of the ability to predict among students the practice of mathematics to analyze, reason about, and especially critique knowledge and events in the world based solely on characteristics such as race, class, ethnicity, sex, beliefs and creeds, and proficiency in the dominant language" (p. 158). Gutiérrez is moving us from a vision of students technically prepared to solve problems posed for them by teachers or employers to one of students prepared to solve *and pose* problems of interest to themselves and their communities. She then takes us yet one step further: "erasure of inequities between people, mathematics, and the planet" (p. 165). In her vision, mathematics is no longer seen as a neutral tool, but as necessarily combined with an ethics of equality, humanity, and ecology. Like Gutiérrez, I will not be satisfied with a mathematics reform that serves only to provide more skilled problem solvers to meet the needs of global capital, even if this group of technical workers is more diverse than ever before. I want to work for an expansive equity that creates a diverse pool of numerate citizens, prepared to act ethically in support of equality, humanity, and the planet.

THE EQUITABLE POTENTIAL OF MATHEMATICS REFORM

Equity is one of the central principles of the standards movement. Most concretely, the movement proposes a single, high-level core curriculum for all students (National Council of Teachers of Mathematics, 2000). Mark Ellis and Robert Berry describe the reform as an

> on-going paradigm shift [that] holds the potential to change the look and outlook of successful learners of mathematics from what have historically been relatively small numbers of disproportionately "white" and middle class students, whose learning was focused on solving routinized problems by mastering procedural manipulations, to what should be large crowds reflective of the diversity found within the nation's public schools who learn to flexibly apply mathematical thinking to investigations of meaningful queries. (2005, p. 14)

A growing body of research demonstrates the possibility of such excellent and equitable results in a context of high-quality professional development, curriculum and testing alignment, and reform mathematics curricula (Schoenfeld, 2002). Malloy & Malloy (1998) and Stiff (1990) suggest that certain reform practices can be particularly helpful for African American students, but none of these references go far beyond the limited equity measured by test scores to speak to Gutiérrez's expansive definition of equity. Part of the reason may be the context from which the standards movement arose.

THE PROPONENTS OF MATHEMATICS
REFORM: STRANGE BEDFELLOWS

The first sentence on page 1 of the original standards document, *Curriculum and Evaluation Standards for School Mathematics* (National Council of Teachers of Mathematics, 1989), reads: "These standards are one facet of the mathematics education community's response to the call for reform in the teaching and learning of mathematics." The footnote reference is to *A Nation at Risk* (National Commission on Excellence in Education, 1983), an extremely influential Reagan-era document that powerfully focused the nation's attention on educational standards with incendiary phrases like: "If an unfriendly foreign power had attempted to impose on America the mediocre educational programs that exist today, we might well have viewed it as an act of aggression."

The argument shared by *A Nation at Risk* and the *Curriculum and Evaluation Standards* came from the point of view of global capital. It was that the United States is losing its competitive advantage in the global marketplace because its students (soon to be workers) are ill-prepared for the fierce competition of the coming information age. Results from international comparisons such as the Third International Mathematics and Science Study (TIMMS) were used to fuel the fear of falling behind (Schmidt et al., 1999). While there is no doubt that increasing the numbers of technically skilled students will increase the profits of global business, it is far from clear that much of that profit will trickle down to U.S. workers. Critics like Emery and Ohanian (2004) argue: "The truth that the corporate fat cats refuse to speak is that there are more highly skilled workers than there are jobs — and that's the way they like it. When you have lots of people competing for few jobs, workers are scared and compliant" (p. 20). They continue: "The crime is not that there isn't a workforce able and willing to do the jobs that need to be done; the crime is that so many of these jobs we need to make our country work don't come with a living wage" (p. 27).

The 1989 standards, however, appeared to buy the economic line completely. Three of the four "new social goals for education" (National Council of Teachers of Mathematics, 1989, p. 3) were framed in apocalyptic economic terms. "Mathematically literate workers" were needed for the new "information society" (p. 3); "lifelong learning" (p. 4) was required for workers who will be frequently changing jobs; equity was an "economic necessity" (p. 4). Even the single democratically oriented objective asked not for informed participants in a range of democratic processes, but just for an "informed electorate" (p. 4). With an argument that spoke to the equity concerns of progressives and to the training needs of global capital, who was left to object?

THE ENEMIES OF A PARADIGM SHIFT

In fact, there was no substantial objection to the notion of higher standards for all, but there was much objection to the nature of those standards. Global capital and mathematics educators agreed that with the advent of cheap computing power such as computers and calculators, student proficiency with paper-and-pencil computations was no longer the be-all and end-all of mathematics education. The goal was instead to inculcate "mathematical power, ... an individual's abilities to explore, conjecture, and reason effectively to solve nonroutine problems" (p. 5). Increasing emphasis on goals such as "learning to value mathematics," "becoming confident in one's own ability," and "learning to communicate mathematically" (pp. 5–6) led to a concern by some mathematicians and cultural conservatives that "basic skills" and "rigor" were being overlooked by "progressivist" education and replaced with "fuzzy math" (Wu, 1997; Allen, 1995; Mathematically Correct, 1996; Klein, 2003).

The concerns of the mathematicians were largely addressed in the 2000 standards document (Ross, 2000) and the growing research base suggesting that properly implemented reform increases conceptual understanding and problem-solving ability without sacrificing so-called basic skills (Putnam, 2003), but the "math wars" continue in skirmishes across the country (Becker, 2003; Choppin, 2005; Zimmerman, 2003). As Ellis and Berry (2005) note, conflict is to be expected when an epistemological paradigm shift of this magnitude is under way.

> If mathematics is a disembodied set of facts, skills, and procedures, it makes little sense to ask students to work collaboratively to construct understanding. Where would this knowledge come from? If mathematics is objective, it makes no sense to be concerned with learners' cultures and lived experiences. If mathematical achievement can be accurately and fairly measured with standardized tests of routinized items, it makes no sense to develop more "subjective" assessments of mathematical understanding. And if mathematics is inherently too difficult for many to master, it makes no sense to try to teach all students rigorous aspects of the discipline. (Ellis and Berry, 2005, p. 13)

In other words, the resistance to the reform is primarily the natural resistance to a challenge to the commonsense notions we were raised on.

THE EQUITY CONSEQUENCES OF WHAT WE THINK WE KNOW ABOUT MATHEMATICS

> If God speaks to man, he undoubtedly uses the language of mathematics.
>
> —Henri Poincare

It is common knowledge that the creation of mathematics is the defining realm of the super-intelligent, that these geniuses are rarely female or people of color, that the mathematics they create and use is an objective, culturally and politically neutral part of the nature of the world, and that the rest of us are best served by memorizing and copying the methods of these masters. Unfortunately, this "knowledge" is both false and deeply damaging to today's learners of mathematics. For at least two decades, the mathematics education research community has been painstakingly documenting the ways that each one of us must construct our own understanding of mathematics (Vadeboncoeur, 1997; Noddings, 1990; Glasersfeld, 1987, 1991; Piaget, 1970, 1964; Woods & Murphy, 2002; Ernest, 1991). More recently, the social and cultural nature of these constructions has been emphasized (Cobb & Yackel, 1995; Vygotsky, 1978; Zevenbergen, 2000; Gorgorio, Planas, & Vilella, 2000; Walkerdine, 1988). These changing ideas of the nature of mathematics and mathematics learning are centrally important to the ways that mathematics reform can increase both excellence and equity.

Part of the democratic potential of the NCTM reform comes from its reconstruction of the mathematics classroom. The teacher and textbook lose their roles as dispensers and judges of knowledge. In democratic fashion, the reform classroom becomes a mathematical community in which all participate in the creation and judgment of mathematical ideas (Malloy, 2002). As this happens, diverse students begin to see themselves as creators of mathematics and solvers of problems. Their mathematical potential is unleashed (Boaler, 2002, 2004; Malloy & Malloy, 1998; Stiff, 1990).

CULTURAL RELEVANCE IN MATHEMATICS EDUCATION

> A common misconception in the teaching of math has been, and still is, the belief that math can be taught effectively and meaningfully without relating it to culture or to the individual student. This, and not the difficulty of the subject, in my opinion, was, and still is, the main reason why math is considered meaningless, incomprehensible, and not a popular subject by the vast majority of students. (Fasheh, 1997, p. 281)

Before students can begin to believe in themselves individually as creators of mathematics, they must come to believe in the possibility that *people like them* can be a part of the world of mathematics. Ethnomathematics is a field of study designed to foster just that sense. Building on the notion that mathematics is a social construction, ethnomathematics argues that there is no unitary correct mathematics. An infinite number of mathematical systems are possible; school math and university math are but two of them (Gerdes, 1997a, b; D'Ambrosio, 1997a, b; Powell & Frankenstein, 1997a, b; Bazin & Tamez, 2002). Most of the mathematics done in the world has been devalued or destroyed in just the same manner that other parts of local cultures have been overwhelmed by colonial power (Powell & Frankenstein, 1997a, b; Harris, 1997; Gerdes a, b, 1997; Zaslavsky, 1997). One of the most powerful remaining myths of the colonial period is that mathematics is an exclusively European gift to the world. The true history includes Africa, Babylonia, India, and the Arab World, which preserved and expanded earlier mathematical contributions during Europe's Dark Ages (Joseph, 1997; Powell & Frankenstein, 1997a, b; Bernal, 1997; Lumpkin, 1997; Anderson, 1997). A diversification of the vision of who does and did mathematics is key to even a limited vision of equity.

PROBLEM SOLVING AND PROBLEM POSING: THE FORK IN THE ROAD

> Problem-solving must be the focus of school mathematics.

—National Council of Teachers of Mathematics (1989, p. 6)

The presence of the oppressed classes [is] a sine qua non for the real practice of democracy in a public, progressive school.

                                                    —Freire (1998b, p. 92)

In its most acceptable form, ethnomathematics provides a way to help students believe in themselves as problem solvers and creators of mathematics.
But true cultural relevance requires taking one more, crucially important
turn. This is the fork in the road that separates the interests of global capital from those of progressive educators. Both groups want a large, diverse
group of problem solvers, but capital wants to retain its monopoly on the
definition of the problems (Gabbard, 2000).

In her classic book *The Dreamkeepers* (1994), Gloria Ladson-Billings concludes that a culturally relevant school for African Americans must (1)
"provide educational self-determination," (2) "honor and respect the students' home culture," and (3) "help African American students understand
the world as it is and equip them to change it for the better." William Tate
(1995) echoes the third point with the statement that "African-American
students should be encouraged to use mathematics as an agent to change
their out-of-school realities" (p. 169), citing as an example the classroom of
Sandra Mason. While in a traditional classroom (and even in most reform
classrooms) the problems come from the textbook, in Mason's classroom
they are posed by the students, based on their real-life experiences and
situations. In one case, Mason's students used mathematically based lobbying to close some of the numerous liquor stores surrounding their school.

Examples of such expansive equity-based mathematics education are
increasing. Palestinian mathematics educator Munir Fasheh (1997) counts
as his best lessons those based on the lived experiences of his students, such
as comparisons of students' hand-drawn maps of their neighborhoods, yet
he is clear that there is always a political price to pay for deviation from the
rigid syllabus and absolute truth model. In their elementary mathematics
classrooms, Ball, Goffney, and Bass (2005) now see mathematics "as a critical lever for social and educational progress if taught in ways that make
use of its special resources" (p. 2). For Carol Malloy (2002), educator of
mathematics educators, "democratic education is a process where teachers and students work collaboratively to reconstruct curriculum to include
everyone" (p. 23). Eric Gutstein (1997) and his students added culturally
relevant material to a reform math curriculum with great success. Most
recently, Gutstein has teamed with Bob Peterson to collect a series of essays
and projects aimed at teachers called *Rethinking Mathematics: Teaching Social
Justice by the Numbers* (2005).

THE NCTM STANDARDS AS A TROJAN HORSE

> From the point of view of the dominant classes, ... it is fundamental to defend an educational practice that is neutral, that is content with pure teaching (if this actually exists), with the antiseptic transmission of subject matter content.
>
> **—Freire (1998b, p. 91)**

The standards movement in mathematics has been supported by a curious pair of partners — mathematics educators who are, for the most part, committed to the truly expansive vision of equity given by Rochelle Gutiérrez, and global capitalists who desire only the limited equity that increases their pool of technically trained workers. Global capital owes much to the National Council of Teachers of Mathematics for a problem-solving-based reform that "catalyzed a national standards movement" (Schoenfeld, 2002, p. 15). Yet there is subversive potential at the very core of the standards. Their student-centered nature is inconsistent with the neutral, antiseptic education preferred by the dominant classes. There is a chance that students empowered to create mathematics and solve interesting and relevant problems will also feel empowered to determine which problems are interesting to them. If students and their communities become the posers, as well as the solvers of problems, the problems may be more related to community needs than to the needs of employers or salespeople. Global capital is interested in creating workers and consumers, not democratic citizens, but diverse and empowered democratic citizens, capable of speaking back to the corporations in the powerful language of mathematics, may be the result of the reform that they helped birth. The realization of this possibility depends on the courage and clarity of teachers of mathematics and their students.

REFERENCES

Allen, F. (1995, March 25). A critical view of NCTM policies with special reference to the standards reports (open letter). Pomona, CA.

Anderson, S. E. (1997). Worldmath curriculum: Fighting Eurocentrism in mathematics. In A. B. Powell & M. Frankenstein (Eds.), *Ethnomathematics: Challenging Eurocentrism in mathematics education.* Albany, NY: SUNY, pp. 291–306.

Ball, D. L., Goffney, I. M., & Bass, H. (2005). The role of mathematics instruction in building a socailly just and diverse democracy. *The Mathematics Educator, 15,* 2–6.

Bazin, M., & Tamez, M. (2002). *Math and science across cultures: Activities and investigations from the Exploratorium.* San Francisco: Exploratorium.

Becker, J. (2003, March 2). New math programs are giving some parents anxiety. *Minneapolis Star Tribune.*

Bernal, M. (1997). Animadversions on the origins of Western science. In A. B. Powell & M. Frankenstein (Eds.), *Ethnomathematics: Challenging Eurocentrism in mathematics education*. Albany, NY: SUNY pp. 83–99.

Boaler, J. (2002). *Experiencing school mathematics: Revised and expanded edition*. Mahwah, NJ: Erlbaum.

Boaler, J. (2004). Promoting equity in mathematics classrooms: Important teaching practices and their impact on student learning. Paper read at ICME, Copenhagen.

Choppin, J. (2005, May 26). Teaching not only the how but the why of math is vital. *Rochester Democrat and Chronicle*.

Cobb, P., & Yackel, E. (1995). Constructivist, emergent, and sociocultural perspectives in the context of developmental research. Paper read at North American Chapter of the International Group for the Psychology of Mathematics Education, Columbus, OH.

D'Ambrosio, U. (1997). Ethnomathematics and its place in the history and pedagogy of mathematics. In A. B. Powell & M. Frankenstein (Eds.), *Ethnomathematics: Challenging Eurocentrism in mathematics education*. Albany, NY: SUNY pp. 13–24.

Ellis, M. W., & Berry III, R. Q. (2005). The paradigm shift in mathematics education: Explanations and implications of reforming conceptions of teaching and learning. *Mathematics Educator, 15*, 7–17.

Emery, K., & Ohanian, S. (2004). *Why is corporate America bashing our public schools?* Portsmouth, NH: Heinemann.

Ernest, P. (1991). *The philosophy of mathematics education*. Bristol, PA: Falmer.

Fasheh, M. (1997). Mathematics, culture, and authority. In A. B. Powell & M. Frankenstein (Eds.), *Ethnomathematics: Challenging Eurocentrism in mathematics education*. Albany, NY: SUNY pp. 273–289.

Freire, P. (1998a). The pedagogy of hope. In A. M. A. Freire & D. Maced (Eds.), *The Paulo Freire Reader*. New York: Continuum pp. 237–264.

Freire, P. (1998b). Public schools and popular education. In *Politics and education*. Los Angeles: UCLA Latin American Center Publications pp. 87–96.

Gabbard, D. A. (2000). Accountability. In D. A. Gabbard (Ed.), *Knowledge and power in the global economy: Politics and the rhetoric of school reform*. Mahwah, NJ: Lawrence Erlbaum Associates pp. 53–62.

Gerdes, P. (1997a). On culture, geometrical thinking and mathematics education. In A. B. Powell & M. Frankenstein (Eds.), *Ethnomathematics: Challenging Eurocentrism in mathematics education*. Albany, NY: SUNY pp. 223–247.

Gerdes, P. (1997b). Survey of current work on ethnomathematics. In A. B. Powell & M. Frankenstein (Eds.), *Ethnomathematics: Challenging Eurocentrism in mathematics education*. Albany, NY: SUNY pp. 331–371.

Gingerich, D. (2003). No Child Left Behind. *Currents, 6*, 1, 12–14.

Glasersfeld, E. von (1987). Learning as a constructive activity. In C. Janvier (Ed.), *Problems of representation in the teaching and learning of mathematics*. Hillsdale, NJ: Erlbaum pp. 3–17.

Glasersfeld, E. von (Ed.). (1991). *Radical constructivism in mathematics education*. Boston: Kluwer Academic Publishers.

Gorgorio, N., Planas, N., & Vilella, X. (2000). The cultural conflict in the mathematics classroom: Overcoming its "invisibility." In A. Ahmed, H. Williams, & J. M. Kraemer (Eds.), *Cultural diversity in mathematics (education): CIEAEM 51*. Chichester, England: Horwood pp. 179–185.

Gutiérrez, R. (2002). Enabling the practice of mathematics teachers in context: Toward a new equity research agenda. *Mathematical Thinking and Learning, 4,* 145–187.

Gutstein, E., Lipman, P., Hernandez, P., & de los Reyes, R. (1997). Culturally relevant mathematics teaching in a Mexican American context. *Journal for Research in Mathematics Education, 28,* 709–737.

Gutstein, E., & Peterson, B. (Eds.). (2005). *Rethinking mathematics: Teaching social justice by the numbers.* Milwaukee, WI: Rethinking Schools, Ltd.

Harris, M. (1997). An example of traditional women's work as a mathematics resource. In A. B. Powell & M. Frankenstein (Eds.), *Ethnomathematics: Challenging Eurocentrism in mathematics education.* Albany, NY: SUNY pp. 215–222.

Joseph, G. G. (1997). Foundations of Eurocentrism in mathematics. In A. B. Powell & M. Frankenstein (Eds.), *Ethnomathematics: Challenging Eurocentrism in mathematics education.* Albany, NY: SUNYpp. 61–81.

Klein, D. (2003). A brief history of American K-12 mathematics education. In J. Royer (Ed.), *Mathematical cognition.* Information Age Publishing. Retrieved May 1, 2007 from www.csun.edu/~vcmth00m/AHistory.html

Ladson-Billings, G. (1994). *The dreamkeepers: Successful teachers of African American children.* San Francisco: Jossey-Bass.

Lumpkin, B. (1997). Africa in the mainstream of mathematics history. In A. B. Powell & M. Frankenstein (Eds.), *Ethnomathematics: Challenging Eurocentrism in mathematics education.* Albany, NY: SUNY. (Original edition, I. Van Sertima [Ed.], *Blacks in science: Ancient and modern* [pp. 100–109]. New Brunswick, NJ: Transaction, 1983.)

Malloy, C. E. (2002). Democratic access to mathematics through democratic education. In L. English (Ed.), *The handbook for international research in mathematics education* Mahwah, NJ: Lawrence Ehrlbaum, pp. 17–26.

Malloy, C. E., & Malloy, W. M. (1998). Resiliency and algebra I: A promising non-traditional approach to teaching low-achieving students. *The Clearing House, 71,* 314–317.

Mathematically Correct. (2003). What is changing in math education? Retrieved May 1, 2007 from http://www.ed.gov/pubs/nata+risk/index.html.

National Commission on Excellence in Education. (1983). *A nation at risk.* Washington, DC: U.S. Department of Education.

National Council of Teachers of Mathematics. (1989). *Curriculum and evaluation standards for school mathematics.* Reston, VA: Author.

National Council of Teachers of Mathematics. (1991). *Professional standards for teaching school mathematics.* Reston, VA: Author.

National Council of Teachers of Mathematics. (1995). *Assessment standards for school mathematics.* Reston, VA: Author.

National Council of Teachers of Mathematics. (2000). *Principles and standards for school mathematics.* Reston, VA: Author.

Noddings, N. (1990). Constructivism in mathematics education. In R. B. Davis, C. A. Maher, & N. Noddings (Eds.), *Constructivist views on the teaching and learning of mathematics: Journal for research in mathematics education monograph #4.* Reston, VA: National Council of Teachers of Mathematics pp. 7–18.

Piaget, J. (1964). Development and learning. In R. E. Ripple & V. N. Rockcastle (Eds.), *Piaget rediscovered: A report of the conference on cognitive studies and curriculum development.* Ithaca, NY: Cornell University Press pp. 7–20.

Piaget, J. (1970). *Adaptation and intelligence: Organic selection and phenocopy.* Chicago: University of Chicago Press.

Powell, A. B., & Frankenstein, M. (1997a). Uncovering the distorted and hidden history of mathematical knowledge. In A. B. Powell & M. Frankenstein (Eds.), *Ethnomathematics: Challenging Eurocentrism in mathematics education.* Albany, NY: SUNY pp. 51–59.

Powell, A. B., & Frankenstein, M. (1997b). Reconsidering what counts as mathematical knowledge. In A. B. Powell & M. Frankenstein (Eds.), *Ethnomathematics: Challenging Eurocentrism in mathematics education.* Albany, NY: SUNY pp. 193–199.

Putnam, R. T. (2003). Commentary on four elementary mathematics curricula. In S. L. Senk & D. R. Thompson (Eds.), *Standards-based school mathematics curricula: What are they? What do students learn?* Mahwah, NJ: Lawrence Erlbaum Associates, pp. 161–178.

Ross, K. A. (2000). *The MAA and the new NCTM standards.* Retrieved May 1, 2007 from http://www.maa.org/features/ppsm.html.

Schmidt, W. H., McKnight, C. C., Cogan, L. S., Jakwerth, P. M., & Houang, R. T. (1999). *Facing the consequences: Using TIMSS for a closer look at U.S. mathematics and science education.* Dordrecht, The Netherlands: Kluwer Academic Publishers.

Schoenfeld, A. H. (2002). Making mathematics work for all children: Issues of standards, testing, and equity. *Educational Researcher, 31,* 13–25.

Stiff, L. V. (1990). African-American students and the promise of the *Curriculum and Evaluation Standards.* In T. J. Cooney & C. R. Hirsch (Eds.), *Teaching and learning mathematics in the 1990s: 1990 Yearbook.* Reston, VA: National Council of Teachers of Mathematics pp. 152–158.

Tate, W. F. (1995). Returning to the root: A culturally relevant approach to mathematics pedagogy. *Theory Into Practice, 34.*

Vadeboncoeur, J. (1997). Child development and the purpose of education: A historical context of constructivism in teacher education. In V. Richardson (Ed.), *Constructivist teacher education: Building a world of new understandings.* London: Falmer Press pp. 15–37.

Vygotsky, L. S. (1978). *Mind in society: The development of higher psychological processes.* Cambridge, MA: Harvard University Press.

Walkerdine, V. (1988). *The mastery of reason.* New York: Routledge.

Woods, B. S., & Murphy, P. K. (2002). Thickening the discussion: Inspecting constructivist theories of knowledge through a Jamesian lens. *Educational Theory, 52,* 43–59.

Wu, H. (1997). The mathematics education reform: Why you should be concerned and what you can do. *American Mathematical Monthly, 104,* 946–954.

Zaslavsky, C. (1997). World cultures in the mathematics class. In A. B. Powell & M. Frankenstein (Eds.), *Ethnomathematics: Challenging Eurocentrism in mathematics education.* Albany, NY: SUNY pp. 307–320.

Zevenbergen, R. (2000). Cracking the code of mathematics classrooms: School success as a function of linguistic, social, and cultural background. In J. Boaler (Ed.), *Multiple perspectives on mathematics teaching and learning.* Westport, CT: Ablex pp. 201–223.

Zimmerman, J. (2003, February 10). One way to end the math and reading wars. *Christian Science Monitor* (2003) 9.

Chapter 37

Science Education

Dewey I. Dykstra, Jr.
Boise State University

> There is no neutral pedagogical practice. Every single one is based on a given conception of the learning process and of the object of such a process. Most probably, those practices much more than the methods themselves are exerting the greatest lasting effects in the domain of literacy, as in any field of knowledge.
>
> **—Emilia Ferreiro (1991, p. 46)**

In this strange world we find those called neoconservatives working in concert with others called neoliberals to promote globalization of particular values, supremacy in the form of government, economic control, and ideology under the guise of promoting freedom; it appears the underlying lynchpin is reified in the notion of commodification. Levidow (2000) describes the central features of neoliberalism as "efficiency as progress," "commodification," and "globalization." But, when we look at these three central features applied to education, the efficiency is efficiency of transmission of a commodified knowledge. Globalization, as it applies to education, involves privatization so that free-market pressures can finance the transmission of this commodified knowledge. The commodified knowledge claimed to be objective turns out to merely support a neoliberal worldview, nothing else. Uncommodified, how could knowledge be transmitted and tested efficiently? How could capitalist free-market pressures apply to institutions that do not deal in a commodity?

The only commodified knowledge worth selling is fixed, objective, universal truth. This is what knowledge is in a realist's world. Even before there was the label, neoliberalism, knowledge in science instruction was presented as truth, or at least as close as we have come to truth so far. This way of describing the content in science instruction is so natural and uncontroversial, because it is one of the few lessons actually learned by all in typical science instruction. As a society we have bought this notion of the nature of knowledge in science. Having bought this lesson, it is hard to argue with this neoliberal agenda in science education, which was stated early in the famous report *A Nation at Risk: The Imperative for Educational Reform* (National Commission for Excellence in Education [NCEE], 1983). The recommendations involved hiring more science and mathematics teachers and paying them more. This brought many in science education on board at a time when all federal funds for science education were being eliminated.

The report weaves a message of the importance of intellectual capital and concern over decline in industrial productivity. The recommendations also called for the establishment of standards and strict enforcement. Nowhere in the report is what students actually understand as a result of the science instruction they experience examined. Nothing is stated about what they could possibly understand as a result of science instruction. At best, the findings address time on task in terms of numbers of courses taken. Some reference is made to comparative results of international tests in science and mathematics. Much of the findings used to justify the recommendations were from testimonial opinion and ideological stances apparently of the commissioners as authors of the report. Twenty years later the report has eerily foreshadowed major elements of the No Child Left Behind (NCLB) Act.

Meanwhile, a few students are experiencing truly revolutionary changes in understanding about the phenomena they study. That these changes in understanding are profound is not accidental. They are a routine student experience in a pedagogy that stands outside the bounds of realism, the box in which the neoliberals and neoconservatives remain confined, unaware, or aggressively rejecting that any other way of knowing the world might exist. The truly dangerous aspect of the neoliberal agenda is the forced institutionalization of the schools into an elitist-realist box via, among other mechanisms, utterly meaningless, factoid-driven high-stakes testing.

Since science knowledge in school has been a commodity transmitted to students for many decades, what is the result of schooling in science?

THE SPECTACULAR FAILURE OF SCHOOLING IN SCIENCE

Do Students Understand the Phenomena Studied?

Even though nearly all citizens of first-world countries have experienced schooling[1] in science, as have substantial additional numbers of other citizens of the world, they and their teachers have no idea what is possible as a result of this alternative pedagogy. In no small measure, any understanding of what is possible is lacking because neither the students nor their teachers nor the "trainers" of the teachers have themselves experienced

such changes in understanding of the phenomena studied. This is the outcome of standard science schooling: *no change in understanding of the phenomena studied for all students.* This is apparently the case indefinitely back
into the past.

> As we look for improved effectiveness in college science teaching and for the
> sources of our failures, experience makes it increasingly clear that purely
> verbal presentations — lecturing at large groups of students who passively
> expect to absorb ideas that actually demand intense deductive and inductive
> mental activity coupled with personal observation and experience — leaves
> [*sic*] virtually nothing permanent or significant in the student mind. (Arons,
> 1973, p. 771)

Taking cues from the experimental methods of the Swiss genetic episte-
mologist Jean Piaget and his co-workers (Inhelder & Piaget, 1958), since the
1970s science educators have been examining student conceptions of the
phenomena studied in science. In the 1980s bibliographies of publications
of these studies were developed. The bibliographic efforts were coalesced
into a single bibliography kept by Reinders Duit and his colleagues at the
Institute for Science Education at the University of Kiel in Germany (Duit,
2004). This bibliography, *Students' and Teachers' Conceptions in Science*, presently contains 6,413 entries. About a quarter of these studies document
evidence of change in students' conceptions as a result of science instruction. Uniformly, they indicate no change in conceptions of the phenomena
studied, in any science, for any age student, in any part of the world, in any
decade in the last century. Sadly, the neoliberals claim to be data driven,
but somehow this overwhelming body of findings is rejected as not proper
data. It seems the neoliberals have the right to "cherry-pick" through the
data to select only that which supports their view. Apparently if one has a
conclusion that is the truth, one is empowered to reject any data that does
not support the view, but still claim to be data driven.

In one example of this work, carried out by Dykstra (2005), a widely used,
carefully developed diagnostic of student conceptions of the nature of force
and its relationship to motion was employed in a pre- and postinstruction
strategy at the university level. The courses were in standard lecture-lab
format taught by regular physics faculty members with the aid of teaching
assistants who were graduate students in physics. The students were from
a number of large state institutions across the country over a period of
about 10 years. Nearly 600 students in introductory physics courses for science and engineering majors showed a shift from pre- to postscore on the
diagnostic of 0.56 standard deviation (effect size or Cohen's d) and a normalized gain of 15%. All of these students had studied force and motion at
least once before entering college, yet their prescores were in the range of
1 to 3 of 15. Their postscores at the university changed by only 15% of the

maximum possible gain from their prescores. In other words, their conceptions about force and its relationship to motion were essentially the same, at the end of this second or third round of instruction on motion and force by PhD physicists, as they were at the beginning.

Some students may be able to repeat the words transmitted and the algorithms drilled, but the meanings of these things cannot be what is intended, because the students have not changed their understanding of the phenomena. When exams go no deeper than the transmitted words and the algorithms drilled, the exams give no indication of the superficial façade or veneer. High-stakes exams written by the same people who write such exams only detect the mindless veneer, never deeper.

Those working in the schooling systems and the infrastructures of such systems (administrative agencies and teacher preparation institutions) are not in a position to understand the power, depth, and profundity of learning possible by all students in science instruction. They have never experienced such learning themselves. Lacking this understanding, all they can do is reproduce the same failure to construct new understanding of the phenomena studied.

> If colleges and universities do not try to solve the problem by assuming responsibility for the intellectual development of their students, but continue to look at their primary purpose as the transmission of information about several disciplines, the elementary and secondary schools will continue to fail in their mission of truly educating students. (McKinnon & Renner, 1971, p. 1052)

What Do Students Learn about Themselves?

It is not as though this schooling in science has no effect. There is one pervasive lesson of such science schooling: an elitist-realist view that rationalizes the spectacular failure of such standard science schooling. While studiously avoiding any sort of assessment that would indicate the presence of any understanding or lack thereof, the professionals explain the still dismal performance of students on mindless examinations of "transmitted fact" by the claim that "science is hard," as if only certain people are capable of science. The practitioners of this science schooling are so spectacularly successful at teaching this lesson that it is impossible not to find clear evidence of it in any setting populated by those citizens of the world who have experienced science instruction in school.

This elitist explanation at the same time lets both students and teachers off the hook. Girded by the elitist-realist view, teachers are exonerated of the fact that students do not really develop any new understanding of the phenomena studied. Only those few deserving students, capable of understanding science, have any obligation to work hard enough to get what is taught. Who can and who cannot get science is largely out of the teachers' hands. A little effort motivating the few deserving students is the only thing a teacher can do other than presenting the established canon to be learned in science. As for the rest of the students, too bad, but we cannot all be scientists. At the same time, students are exonerated for their dismal performance for the same reasons. No one need worry or question the status quo. Everyone accepts it. The resulting caste system need not be maintained by force or by law because no one challenges the elitist-realist view behind the explanation for the failure. The priesthood continues unchallenged.

PERPETUATING THE STATUS QUO

> It is the basic premise of the vast majority of introductory physics courses taught at the present time (be they general education courses for nonmajors or calculus-physics courses for majors and engineers) that, if one takes a huge breadth of subject matter and passes it before the student at sufficiently high velocity, the Lorentz contraction will shorten it to the point at which it drops into the hole which is the student mind.

> —Arons (1979, p. 650)

Preparing New Technicians Instead of Teachers

Of course the spectacular failure is preserved and propagated in how science teachers are prepared. The notion of developing deep understanding of the phenomena to be taught is completely missing from the preparation of science teachers. The ability to carefully explain problem solutions in terms of such deep understanding with attention to completeness is clearly out of the question. Teachers are prepared to do hardly more than repeat what they have heard or read in texts, often with little deeper understanding than their students. All this is justified with the notion that science is hard and not everybody can understand it.

We see in this description that, regardless of what the practitioners say,

> science teaching is the presentation of an established canon by approved methods for the benefit of the deserving. (Dykstra, 2005, p. 54)

We prepare teachers to do exactly this. The standard degree program to prepare teachers at the secondary level in science consists of three main components. First, the majority of the program consists of having the canon of the science to be taught transmitted to the teacher candidates. Typically this collection of courses on the canon is, as nearly as possible, the same as the courses taken by students being trained to be scientists. Next, in a single course, usually called a methods course, the approved methods are transmitted to the teacher candidates. Apparently, this is possible in a single course, because *in the end all the methods discussed are variations on the same thing, transmitting the canon.* Finally, some time is spent practicing the transmission methods under supervision. When a teacher candidate has demonstrated the ability to repeat back the canon in acceptable form and has demonstrated some facility with the approved methods of transmitting the canon, the candidate is certified or endorsed a bona fide teacher of science, ready and equipped to reproduce more of the same.

Even though many credit hours are spent in such a degree program transmitting the canon to teacher candidates, we know that in general their understanding of the phenomena advances very little (Duit, 2004). At least one program, which recognizes the importance of teacher candidates understanding the core phenomena to be taught in physics, has acknowledged this state of affairs and devised courses to develop the necessary deep understandings (University of Washington, 2006). A series of three 5-credit (quarter system) courses titled "PHYS 407–409: Physics by Inquiry II" are required for endorsement to teach physics from the University of Washington. These courses were devised by the Physics Education Group in the Physics Department of the University of Washington. The group is led by Lillian McDermott, who collaborated in writing the following:

> We know that, at the precollege level, there is much bad science teaching from abominable texts written by scientifically incompetent authors. The bad teaching, however, is being done by teachers whom we have educated in our colleges and universities in science courses that are, at that level, just as deficient pedagogically as the school books are deficient in correctness of subject matter.... Only a small minority of college science programs for future teachers give them the kind of exposure that develops the competence the majority intrinsically possess. The fault, Dear Brutus, is not in our stars. (Arons & McDermott, 1992, p. 103)

Since the deserving will get the transmission, if they have worked hard enough, and those not deserving will never really get what is transmitted, apparently looking closely to discover evidence of new understanding in the students is not necessary. As such, student understanding is not an issue in preparing science teachers. The elitist-realist view both explains and suppresses critical examination of the failure of the system. Because, for realists, this is the truth, then it is something to be accepted.

THE ELITIST-REALIST VIEW: IS IT THE OBJECTIVE TRUTH?

If the elitist-realist paradigm is the closest we know of to objective truth or is indeed the objective truth, then no other explanation for the nature of human knowing fits experience as well as it does. This being the case, then we apparently have in science education the best we can get at present. The question then comes down to: Is the elitist-realist paradigm the best explanation for the nature of human knowing in science education?

In the elitist-realist view described here it should not be possible for students who are not among the deserving to finish an instructional experience with an understanding of the phenomena closer to the canon than that of the more deserving students when the instruction is not even an attempt to transmit the canon. After all, even if they were among the deserving, how could they know, if they were not told?

In the study by Dykstra (2005) reported above, other groups of students, all nonscience, nonengineering majors, participated in a course that engages the students in making their own explanation of the phenomena, motion and force, subject to the criteria of fit to the phenomena. These students are generally considered as having a greater percentage who are not among the deserving. The course did not involve these students in formal mathematics at any time. The course is based in a different paradigm of the nature of human knowing. In this paradigm, understanding or meaning in explanatory knowledge is not transmittable by any means. *Instead, it can only be constructed by the knower.* This view, which grew out of the theoretical perspective of Jean Piaget (1980), is now referred to as radical constructivism (Glasersfeld, 1991).

The students in this different course took the same diagnostic on motion and force taken by the science and engineering students, pre- and postinstruction. There were 365 students distributed over five semesters. The average normalized gain for these students on the diagnostic was 63%, and the average shift for them was 2.5 standard deviations, pre to post.

There is clearly a major difference here from the results with standard instruction. We must question the notion that standard instruction is based on an explanation that is objective truth. How could those not among the deserving outstrip the deserving at developing their own knowledge equivalent to the canon? How could they do this without having the canon transmitted to them? How could there be learning results better than in courses based on the elitist-realist paradigm that claims to be the closest approach we have to objective truth?

When instruction rooted in this notion of commodified knowledge routinely results in essentially no change in understanding of the commodified knowledge, how can continuing the standard forms of teaching be justified? Do we not have an ethical obligation to the students and society to respond to the challenge posed by these results? If it is not necessary to transmit commodified knowledge, the canon, then what sense do standards for instruction and teacher preparation based on this notion make? When it can be demonstrated that ending a course with a genuine deeper understanding of the phenomena studied is not dependent on being among the deserving, how can the elitist features of the standard view be supported?

The elitist-realist view, on which the neoliberal agenda is based, does not have the status of objective truth, or even that of being the closest we have come to objective truth. Standard science instruction based on this elitist-realist view does not lead to learning anything about the phenomena, but *instead it results in learning about the ideology of elitist-realism,* as the opening quotation by Ferreiro suggests. The neoliberal agenda serves only to justify itself and the caste system it is based upon. It is not about education. Instead, it is about indoctrination and vocational selection and training. As such, it does not serve to promote the well-being of society, but to *preserve the illness of society.*

DRIVING THE NEOLIBERAL AGENDA
WITH HIGH-STAKES TESTING

Until recently the NCLB mandates did not require testing in science. Starting in 2007, to meet the NCLB Act requirements, states must test for achievement in science annually (Title 1 Directors, 2003; U.S. Department of Education, 2004). Until recently, only tests in reading and mathematics were mandated, and as a result, there were elementary schools that taught no science. Now that the mandate for tests in science is approaching, there is a head-on confrontation between the National Research Council (NRC), in collaboration with professional societies concerned with science education, and the designers of tests (Tomsho, 2006). The NRC, responsible for the development of the National Science Education Standards in conjunction with the professional societies, and the professional societies are unanimous in supporting inquiry-based instruction in science as superior to what is often called direct instruction. Direct instruction is the presentation of the established canon by approved methods for the benefit of the deserving. The exams developed treat knowledge in science as a commodity. Instead of testing for understanding, the exams test for student ability to give back chunks of the canon or repeat specified canonical performances of skills. Educators are now wondering how to teach.

Of course, the term *educator* must have a very narrow meaning here. Since they have not been trained in the scholarly aspects of teaching and they have no realization of the nature of understanding and how it might be developed in students, they are victims of their narrow preparation limited to the canon as a commodity and methods to transmit it. They are not the professional intellectuals they need to be, but deskilled technicians dependent on external motivation and external direction. As a result, they have little with which to analyze claims made about any aspect of teaching and its effect on student understanding. When conflicting messages are received, educators are left wondering how to respond, instead of being able to decide for themselves in a principled way, based on relevant data.

CLIMBING OUR WAY OUT OF THE HOLE

Having abandoned the moral high ground in favor of "our way is the right way" as dictated by neoconservative policy, we are working on *abdicating the intellectual high ground*. The groundwork for the loss of the intellectual high ground is accomplished via the hegemony of the elitist-realist paradigm in education, as can be seen particularly in science education. The loss is accelerated by explicitly applying the neoliberal agenda to schools in the form of the No Child Left Behind Act. When this process is complete, the only high grounds we will occupy are military and economic. We are already challenged in the case of the economic high ground. History suggests that the last remaining high ground is never held long.

Can we climb out of this hole? It may not be possible, given how long we have allowed the deck to stack. If it is possible, it will come in part because each of us acts with moral and intellectual integrity. The necessary changes in society are nothing short of fundamental and profound — a daunting task. Society has changed in the past. It will change in the future. Each of us must exert our own influence through our own dialectic with our students, our colleagues, and our society.

In science education it is known how to teach such that most students leave the experience having developed a new, deeper understanding of the phenomena. In the process these students advance in their abilities to critically analyze their world to develop an ever-deepening understanding of their experiences.

> A physics major has to be trained to use today's physics whereas a physics teacher has to be trained to see a development of physical theories in his students' minds. (Niedderer, 1992, p. 151)

We need to prepare teachers to assist students at this process in science, instead of the vocational selection, training, and indoctrination program that presently calls itself science education. We need to prepare teachers who themselves have developed a deep understanding of the phenomena that will be the subjects of their teaching. These teachers need to be able to discern the nature of their students' understandings and to allow this to drive the instructional process as suggested by Niedderer. It is known how to prepare such teachers, too. It requires that the teachers not be trained to present the established canon by approved methods for the benefit of the deserving, but instead to focus on the development of ever-deepening understanding — the intellectual development of the students.

We need to take action to produce such teachers who can become change agents in society by being public intellectuals who will enable our society to move back to the moral and intellectual high ground. To do this, we must become change agents ourselves, rejecting the elitist-realist paradigm in our work and our lives, and publicly reminding those around us of moral and intellectual high ground in our professional actions.

WHY KEEP TRYING?

Clearly, if the motivation is financial reward, education is not a sensible choice. If being acknowledged with awards for teaching were the motivation, examining the typical results of standard teaching closely and critically analyzing teaching are not wise moves. If one wishes to publish easily and frequently, then writing manuscripts that challenge the conventional notions of teaching and learning will result in disappointment. Why would one consider these unwise things important to do? Why continue to work for something that requires a fundamental change in society to be successful?

In my own case, it has always been about understanding the things around me and what I am doing. When I decided that science was about understanding the world, I was hooked on science. Through school, I thought that my teachers were attempting to get us to leave classes having developed new understanding. Eventually, I realized that this is how I wanted to contribute to society, to teach physics in such a way that my students left with a new understanding of the phenomena we studied. I discovered that such an enterprise could be pursued from a theory base with which to understand what was going on. I could not only engage the students in developing new understanding, but, while doing so, also develop a new understanding of the phenomena we were studying, a new understanding of the students' understandings of the phenomena, and a new understanding of understanding itself.

When I finally was able to free up my teaching in order to practice it under this program of developing new understanding, the die was cast and the mold thrown away. The rewards began to come in bundles and frequently. Routinely, I get to construct new understandings as I teach and reflect on my teaching. Routinely, I see students doing the same thing, and for me, the rewards are even richer.

Taking the responsibility of being a teacher who wishes students to leave the experience having constructed a new understanding is a substantial act. One is attempting to function in such a way that students leave changed — not just changed, but changed in a way they cannot understand before they change and changed in a way that they can never go back. One cannot get prior informed consent from the students. To give that consent the students would have to understand something they do not yet understand. Their parents usually do not yet understand it either. Once they have made the change, neither they, their parents, nor you can restore them to their original state. As this sort of teacher, if successful, one has induced an indelible change in the students.

Generally this change is not merely a change in understanding of the phenomena studied, but a change in the students' understandings of themselves and each other. What better contribution to society can one make than being responsible for students who have developed a deep understanding of their world, who have the skills and dispositions to continue developing a deep understanding of their world, who know how to work with others to develop these new understandings and are genuinely interested in understanding the ideas of others?

As this sort of teacher at the university, one can not only have this kind of effect on students, but also have the opportunity to develop new knowledge in the field, share it with others, and prepare teachers who can go out and induce their students to construct a new understanding. One truly is in a position to make valuable contributions to society. It is these joys and fulfillments that enable one to challenge the hegemony's incessant pressures to return to the mediocre and to the elitist-realist paradigm. Once one has experienced this "mountaintop," one's praxis cannot return to elitist-realism. One can see a better world and have the privilege of working toward making our world become that better world. Join us in this effort. You will be glad you did. Got change for a paradigm?

> I can't respect the teacher who doesn't dream of a certain kind of society that he would like to live in, and would like the new generation to live in; a dream of a society less ugly than those we have today; a society that is more open and less marred by prejudice. (Freire, 1996)

ACKNOWLEDGMENTS

Without students willing to allow me to understand their conceptions of the world, it would not have been possible to write this piece. My mentors over the years, Clayton Zeidler, Robert Little, Robert Fuller, Lee Rutledge, James Minstrell, and Ernst von Glasersfeld, have challenged me — and some continue to challenge me — to question my understandings, thereby deepening them. Valuable insights were gained while working in projects funded by the National Science Foundation. I also thank David Gabbard and Robert Bahruth for their valuable advice on this chapter. Anything of value in this piece is due in part to these influences. Ideas expressed are not necessarily those of any of these people or organizations.

NOTES

1. The term *schooling* is used here to distinguish students' experiences in school from education in the same sense that this distinction is made in Chapter 28, by Robert Bahruth.

REFERENCES

Arons, A. (1973). Toward a wider public understanding of science. *American Journal of Physics, 41*, 769–782.

Arons, A. (1979). Cognitive level of college physics students. *American Journal of Physics, 47*, 650–653.

Arons, A., & McDermott, L. (1992). Teachers of physics in our schools. *American Journal of Physics, 60*, 103.

Duit, R. (2004). Students' and teachers' conceptions in science. Kiel, Germany: IPN. Retrieved January 30, 2006, from http://www.ipn.uni-kiel.de/aktuell/stcse/stcse.html

Dykstra, D. I. (2005). Against realist instruction: Superficial success masking catastrophic failure and an alternative. *Constructivist Foundations, 1*, 49–60.

Ferreiro, E. (1991). Literacy acquisition and the representation of language. In *Early literacy: A constructivist foundation for whole language.* Washington, DC: NEA Professional Library pp. 31–56.

Freire, P. (1996). Keynote address. 51st Annual Conference of the Association for Supervision and Curriculum Development, New Orleans.

Glasersfeld, E. V. (1991). Knowing without metaphysics: Aspects of the radical constructivist position. In F. Steier (Ed.), *Research and reflexivity* (pp. 12–29). Newbury Park, CA: Sage. Retrieved January 30, 2006, http://www.kjf.ca/17-TAGLA.htm

Inhelder, B., & Piaget, J. (1958). *The growth of logical thinking from childhood to adolescence: An essay on the construction of formal operational structures.* Basic Books: New York.

Levidow, L. (2000). Marketizing higher education: Neoliberal strategies and counter-strategies. *Cultural Logic, 4.* Retrieved January 29, 2006, from http://eserver.org/clogic/4-1/levidow.html

McKinnon, J., & Renner, J. (1971). Are colleges concerned with intellectual development? *American Journal of Physics, 39*, 1047–1052.

NCEE. (1983). A nation at risk: The imperative of educational reform. Retrieved January 20, 2006, from http://www.ed.gov/pubs/NatAtRisk/index.html

Niedderer, H. (1992). What research can contribute to the improvement of classroom teaching. In International Conference on Physics Teachers' Education Proceedings (pp. 120–155), University of Dortmund, Dortmund, Germany.

Piaget, J. (1980). *The equilibration of cognitive structures: The central problem of intellectual development.* Chicago: University of Chicago Press.

Title 1 Directors. (2003). Assessment timeline: Phase three. Retrieved January 30, 2006, from http://www.ed.gov/admins/lead/account/standassess03/edlite-slide14.html

Tomsho, R. (2006, January 19). What's the right formula? Pressure from new tests leads educators to debate how best to teach science. *Wall Street Journal*, p. A9. Retrieved January 19, 2006, from http://online.wsj.com/article/SB113763977423350560.html

U.S. Department of Education. (2004). Stronger accountability: Facts about ... science achievement. Retrieved January 30, 2006, from http://www.ed.gov/nclb/methods/science/science.html

University of Washington. (2006). On-line course descriptions. Retrieved January 30, 2006, from http://www.washington.edu/students/crscat/phys.html

Chapter 38

Educational Technology

Patricia H. Hinchey
Pennsylvania State University

As widely noted, No Child Left Behind (NCLB) has gifted private enterprise with extensive new market opportunities and significant new profits (Bracey, 2005). Schools have been forced to divert huge portions of their often meager resources to meet legislative requirements, with for-profit vendors routinely providing not only tests, but also textbooks and consumables geared to the tests they produce, supplemental materials supporting test preparation, mandated tutoring, and professional development services for training teachers to use test-oriented materials. While much corporate income has come from paper products and in-person services, government policy has also created a significant and profitable role in reform for educational technology products and services, which build on earlier impositions.

In this role, educational technology will promote private schooling and increase its profitability while concurrently helping to undermine — and ultimately eliminate — public education. Advances in the use of educational technology to "deliver instruction" will not come alone. They will be accompanied by a new breed of thoroughly indoctrinated school personnel and by fully standardized curricula, eliminating any faint threat public schools may still pose to the continued production of a labor force — both within and outside of education — that accepts business interests as congruent with its own.

The ubiquitous imposition and acceptance of educational technology is a critical element of the agendas Hill (2003) has termed the "business agenda IN schools" — to produce ever more profit — and the "business agenda FOR schools" — to produce a compliant, ideologically indoctrinated workforce. A blueprint already laid out for enacting these agendas is evident in the 2005 National Education Technology Policy (NETP), which covers all necessary bases.

MANAGERS, NOT EDUCATORS; SOFTWARE, NOT TEACHERS; COMPUTERS, NOT CLASSROOMS

In January 2005, the Bush administration released its iteration of the National Education Technology Plan with great fanfare, boasting about its design having been informed by advice from some 200,000 school students, whom then-Secretary of Education Rod Paige characterized not only as having grown up with the World Wide Web at their fingertips, but also as representative of all school students (U.S. Department of Education, 2005). That only students with ready access to the Internet in schools offered this advice, and that children as young as 5 were invited to offer opinions on such topics as budget priorities, did not deter the administration from considering this student input reliable. Nor did the fact that the number of students having Internet access had been wildly inflated in government reports, so that these child "experts" were anything but representative (Hinchey & Clark, 2005). Moreover, insistent as it has been on school policy based on science, the plan offers no scientific evidence that increased use of technology enhances student learning. Instead, it uncritically accepts and promotes an unsubstantiated mantra of "more is better" for educational technology.

With no credible justification, the plan offers several confident recommendations to expand technology in schools, detailed in a set of seven action steps. Each step makes clear the intended expansion of market opportunity and ideology.

Step 1, strengthen leadership, calls for a new generation of tech-savvy administrators, to be trained in new ways so that they can specialize in "technology decision making" and "organizational change." To create this new breed of administrator, business, higher education, and schools are encouraged to form partnership projects. Since organizational change — most specifically from public to private and from in-person to online — is precisely what the entire reform agenda is pursuing, training a new generation of bottom-line school administrators in the mold of other for-profit managers is clearly in order. That higher education is to be a partner in producing administrators oriented to business — rather than to children — is neither a surprise nor an impediment, since in the interest of grant money, many institutions of higher education already routinely promote industry and government agendas, even as they equally routinely underfund colleges of education generally and teacher education programs specifically.

Even more important than a new type of administrator, however, is a new kind of teacher — one not only inclined to accept an enhanced role for technology, but also with fewer and fewer skills, more and more easily replaced. Experience with for-profit schools to date has been somewhat disappointing and frustrating for investors, who have not seen impressive returns. The largest impediment has been labor costs, which generally comprise 80% of a school's budget (Levin, 2001). Cutting labor costs is an imperative for private enterprise, and technology offers distinct advantages here.

Not surprisingly, then, Step 3 is a call to "improve teacher training" — with specific improvements helping to reshape teachers into a mold and mind-set more in accord with a for-profit model. This step insists that teachers themselves be guaranteed an opportunity to take online courses (already widely available from for-profit concerns as well as universities), helping to "normalize" electronic instruction in their own minds. As is well known, teachers often resist methodology unfamiliar to them while they replicate what they have experienced personally — even when such methods have not been particularly pleasant or effective. In this way, progress can be made toward promoting teachers' acceptance of computers as reasonable "delivery systems" for the educational process.

Even more importantly, however, NETP suggests that teachers must learn to "use data to personalize instruction" — a requirement also promoted in other moves to reform teacher education. This last may puzzle some teachers and teacher educators who believe that teachers already "use data to personalize instruction" when, based on student performance on classroom tasks, they assign some students more practice with subtraction, others more practice identifying verbs. However, an NETP-linked graphic titled "Online Testing" clarifies this confusion by showing that in the future, data will come exclusively from computers. In the graphic, a teacher is in charge of a classroom where each child is seated at a computer; apparently, the teacher's real task is to monitor interaction between student and software. Thus, the teacher must be sufficiently familiar with the standardized electronic curricula delivered via computer to understand what the computerized data say is the next appropriate electronic "lesson" for the child. Teachers for tomorrow's electronically improved schools, then, must above all be familiar not with children or content, but with software. For this reason, Step 3 also urges that new teachers specifically receive improved preparation in the use of technology.

This vision of classrooms as clusters of computers/teaching machines is a logical extension of current efforts to deskill teachers, which are evident in the scripted materials imposed upon teachers since the advent of high-stakes testing — and are evident even in the language of "teacher training" rather than "teacher education." While scripted materials now literally put words in teachers' mouths, in the electronic future teachers will lose even a preprogrammed voice in the classroom; scripted lessons will be delivered not by humans, but by machines.

When teachers are thus finally fully marginalized and silenced — that is, when media-giant publishers are fully in control of curricula, and when computers are the delivery mechanisms of choice and the only schoolroom agents posing questions to students — then business will no longer need to monitor schools to guard against "unpatriotic" materials. Thus, they will be spared the trouble of watching for and destroying seditious materials as, for example, William Randolph Hearst was forced to do decades ago when some textbooks by Harold Rugg suggested that consumers should think critically about claims made by advertisements.

When curricula are finally and totally in the hands of corporate publishers (who have already made lucrative product placement deals that feature candy in new math textbooks), there will be no need to fear unpatriotic teachers who actively (rather than rhetorically) support the Constitution and who might ask students to ponder such rogue and unhelpful questions such as why they probably do not know about — and do not care about — rBGH, or CIA complicity in drug smuggling and sales, or the purging of voter rolls in Florida in 2000. With the audience of children more captive than ever, advertising, market research, and indoctrination will proceed unfettered, with no impediments to the colonization of generations of American consumers and workers.

Despite NCLB's rhetorical insistence on the need for quality teachers, this vision for education, which simply and logically extends the advance wave of "teacher proof" materials that entered the classroom with standards and high-stakes testing, requires a teacher who actually needs less education than ever before. And if the planned robotic role drives talented and creative professionals from classrooms, as scripted materials are already doing, so much the better. An exacerbated teacher shortage would surely create a crisis that business will be ready to fill with candidates who have alternative types of certification, also promoted by NCLB.

During such a crisis, for example, a pool of paraeducators, or paraprofessionals, might provide replacements for teachers (if deemed necessary). Such a pool exists, and its members have extensive practice with the kinds of scripted materials that have begun spreading through all classrooms. Not coincidentally, perhaps, this pool — which stood at 450,000 in 1996 — is composed primarily of women and people of color who are paid a fraction of a teacher's salary and are currently working primarily in bilingual and special education in some of the nation's poorest schools. Twenty percent of them already function daily without a teacher's supervision (Haselkorn, 1996, p. 76).

Of course, a gradual elimination of in-person professional educators is not what the policy rhetoric suggests; in contrast, policy statements overtly emphasize "highly qualified" teachers and increased requirements for teacher certification and for paraeducators as well. Politically, the road to teacher deprofessionalization and marginalization — especially considering the strength of existing unions — must be gradual and must appear to be pursuing better education, not better profitability. Rhetoric notwithstanding, however, the destination of current reforms is the technological takeover of instruction. Other steps not only advance this goal, but offer additional evidence that the eventual disappearance of the professional educator is intended.

Steps 4 to 6 all advance the agenda of replacing teacher instruction with technological instruction. Together, they call for support for e-learning and virtual schools (Step 4), encouraging broadband access (Step 5), and moving toward digital content (Step 6).

NETP promotes the use of e-learning and virtual schools, alternatives to traditional brick-and-mortar schools, as one way to solve an existing dilemma — created by NCLB. That legislation includes provisions for children in "failing" schools to be allowed to transfer to another school. Just as critics warned, in many districts, transfer is not a feasible option because of capacity issues. Having created the problem by legislating an impossibility, government now suggests that districts can solve the problem by allowing students to attend "virtual schools." A supporting document linked to the recommendation explains that in e-learning, and so in virtual schools:

> Instruction can be provided by a subject matter expert, or a teacher guide, through collaborative exploration or largely through self-directed study. Instruction can also be facilitated by a "learning coach," often the role played by lab attendants in virtual high school classes and parents in K-8 settings, who provides the face-to-face counterpart for a virtual teacher. (Hassel & Godard Terrell, 2004, p. 2)

Despite the hype about highly qualified teachers, other segments of the plan already suggest that with the advent of e-learning, traditional teachers can be replaced by any number of others — including lab attendants and parents themselves. Additionally, e-learning and virtual schools have the cost advantage of not requiring a physical campus, reducing costly overhead for physical plants.

Step 5's promotion of a move to broadband access is offered with no justification except to support online learning — with content obviously being provided from remote sources, or such access would not be necessary. Broadband, however, is in fact the necessary infrastructure for Step 6, a move to digital content, justified by the claim:

> A move away from reliance on textbooks to the use of multimedia or online information (digital content) offers many advantages, including cost savings, increased efficiency, improved accessibility, and enhancing learning opportunities in a format that engages today's web-savvy students. (U.S. Department of Education, 2005)

Digital content goes hand-in-hand with e-learning and virtual schools, of course, and can help pave the way for the day when all learning is done via distance. The emphasis on the voices of students in the plan is explained a bit here as well, with the implication that no one can expect web-savvy students to engage in a format with a live — and therefore unengaging — teacher. Of course, corporations are already ahead of the curve in developing such content, which constitutes an enormous market for new products. Despite the claim of "increased efficiency," there is no explanation of how the move to online content — a move that requires both broadband access and technical support — will result in cost savings for schools.

Indeed, the only suggestion related to the need for schools to fund the proposed "ubiquitous access and connectivity for each student" is the recommendation for "innovating budgeting" proposed by Step 2, which calls primarily for reallocation of existing funds. Links from this step to supporting documents lead to a list of "facts" about federal spending for education that together stress how generous the federal government already is. Rather than any substantive suggestions about funding the extraordinary technological changes called for, supporting documents send the clear signal that schools should not look to the federal government for help. Innovation is the magic potion to remedy any shortfalls. That is, schools can certainly find ways to fund all this if they just try hard enough (just as teachers and students who try hard enough can certainly arrange for satisfactory test scores). And why is it again that all of this technology is worth the investment? Oh yes, because this administration, which reveres science-based policy, says so.

The final step, Step 7, promotes the need to "integrate data systems." An integrated system is computerized from start to finish, and it cuts across schools and districts and states and any other geographic boundary. Touted as a way for administrators to track progress in their own schools, interoperability more importantly provides a way to keep records on students who are widely dispersed in space and who are not asked to come together physically; it also facilitates the delivery of products to a wide variety of clients. Like broadband access, an integrated data system is necessary infrastructure for virtual schools, potentially perhaps the most profitable private option of all.

THE FUTURE IS NOW

A world without local schools, even in a time of mega-districts and their often warehouse-sized buildings, is likely unimaginable to anyone who has not carefully tracked discussions, proposals, and policies in education. The future described above, however, is well on its way to realization — much farther than is generally recognized outside the relatively small group of radical researchers and writers who have been working to sound alarms.

First, the elimination of teachers is an idea that appeared openly in a business publication as early as 1999. Discussing the appeal of a $600 billion educational "market" ("more than the Department of Defense"), one business writer noted the advantages of the move to technology "products" sure to saturate the field:

> Almost all of the new educational products and services now being marketed bear the stamp of technology. Such technology replaces teachers altogether or reduces their number, thus solving several critical weaknesses in traditional education. For instance, replacing teachers reduces the high cost of an excessively labor-intensive instructional process while still serving the same number of students. Then, too, it eliminates tenure, which unfortunately locks in instructors who do not have the training or knowledge to keep up with changing fields and new approaches. (Buchen, 1999)

Of course, tenure also protects the free speech of professional educators, a much greater problem for business than instructors who do not keep up with their fields. With the passage of NCLB, new technology products and services marginalizing teachers have been unfolding just as predicted, with wave after wave of new profit coming from products that take more and more of the instructional process out of teachers' hands. Within two years of NCLB's signing, the *Wall Street Journal* was already taking stock of its boon to business, in which technology featured prominently. In an article tellingly titled "Education Companies See Dollars in Bush School-Boost Law," the paper reported:

> No Child Left Behind also has created demand among schools for tools to help them track student progress and interpret the new data the law requires them to generate. Princeton Review is selling a Web-based product called Homeroom that lets teachers give frequent minitests to see whether their students are on track to pass the state exam. Test results come back immediately, identifying which youngsters are weak in, say, measurement or fractions, and providing exercises to help them improve their skills. The product costs $3,500 a school per year and is already in 3,000 schools, Princeton Review says.
>
> Similarly, Kaplan offers the Kaplan Achievement Planner that, for about $20 a student per year, analyzes each student, then gives teachers different lesson plans for their fast, slow and average learners. It also supplies instantly scored minitests that look and read like the state exam. Kaplan says revenue for its elementary and secondary-school division has doubled since No Child Left Behind passed.
>
> The law's emphasis on reading scores is also fueling new products to help youngsters, including struggling teenagers, learn to read. Scholastic Inc.'s Read 180 product uses videos to give youngsters background on the story they're about to read, then individually helps them through each chapter using computer software, and provides reading exercises to build their speed

and fluency. Scholastic's Read 180 was developed with National Institutes of Health funding, costs $30,000 for 60 students, and can be used over multiple years. Scholastic says Read 180 generated $40 million in sales last year, making it the company's fastest-growing education product. (Kronholz, 2003, p. B1)

Such products — funded with additional support from government — are already marginalizing teachers, providing them not only with the data NCLB and NETP stress, but also with prepackaged pretests and lessons tied to tests. Verbs once associated with teachers, like "gives youngsters background," "individually helps them," and "provides reading exercises," are now paired with software programs instead.

Left unchecked, these reform efforts will continue in breadth and depth until they eliminate the public school as a concept as well as neighborhood reality; they will replace professional educators with a staff of business managers and technology assistants, often housed in corporate offices at a distance from the children they purport to serve; and they will deliver all of America's young to private enterprise for whatever kind of job preparation — and worldview — the ownership class determines desirable for its own hegemony.

REFERENCES

Bracey, G. (2005). *No Child Left Behind: Where does the money go?* Tempe, AZ: Educational Policy Research Unit, Arizona State University. Retrieved November 12, 2005, from http://www.asu.edu/educ/epsl/EPRU/documents/EPSL-0506-114-EPRU.pdf

Buchen, I. (1999). Business sees profits in education: Challenging public schools. *The Futurist, 33,* 38–44. Retrieved November 12, 2005, from http://www.allbusiness.com/periodicals/article/258216-1.html

Haselkorn, D. (1996, August 7). Breaking the class ceiling. *Education Week.*

Hassel, B., & Godard Terrell, M. (2004). *How can virtual schools be a vibrant part of meeting the choice provisions of the No Child Left Behind Act?* Orlando, FL: U.S. Department of Education Secretary's No Child Left Behind Leadership Summit. Retrieved November 12, 2005, from http://www.nationaledtechplan.org/documents/Hassel-Terrell-VirtualSchools.pdf

Hill, D. (2003). Global neo-liberalism, the deformation of education and resistance. *Journal for Critical Education Policy Studies.* Retrieved November 12, 2005, from http://www.jceps.com/index.php?pageID=article&articleID=7

Hinchey, P., & Clark, S. (2005). The National Technology Plan: Bush contradicts himself again (and again). *Public Resistance.* Retrieved November 12, 2005, from http://www.publicresistance.org/journals/1.2-2NatlTechPlan2.htm

Kronholz, J. (2003, December 24). Education companies see dollars in Bush school-boost law. *Wall Street Journal,* p. B1.

Levin, H. (2001). Bear market. *Education Next.* Retrieved November 12, 2005, from http://www.educationnext.org/2001sp/6levin.html

U.S. Department of Education. (2005). *National educational technology plan.* Retrieved
    November 14, 2005, from http://www.nationaledtechplan.org

Chapter 39

Abstinence-Only Sex Education

Thuy DaoJensen
Arizona State University

> To educate, you have to be looking toward the future and believe in a better world. Better worlds, however, aren't profitable in the short term.
>
> **—Adrianna Puiggros (1996)**

Under the economic theory of neoliberalism, market profits are privileged over human beings. Beginning in the 1980s Reagan era, neoliberal economic policies have attacked public programs established by the federal government to provide for the poor and disenfranchised. Strengthened by a neoconservative political backlash, many of these social and welfare programs that provided relief for poor families were being dismantled. The rhetoric of neoliberalism is not limited to the idea of free markets for increased profits and privatization of social services; it also derides government as inefficient, too big, or out of control while simultaneously advocating for more personal responsibility. This symbiotic relationship does not encourage people to look to government for assistance, but demonstrates that government is part of the problem.

While the term *neoliberalism* is rarely named or discussed in mainstream American culture, the enactment of neoliberal economic policies has instilled a powerful ideology that undermines the idea that government has a responsibility for creating opportunities that enable and advance the collective good. Neoliberalism does not reside exclusively within a particular political party in American politics, and as I will later point out in this chapter, both Republican and Democratic presidents have instituted neoliberal policies that elevate and sustain the operation of corporatized markets and profits, leaving behind fragmented social programs for poor families and budget cuts to public schooling.

413

In this chapter, I will explore how the neoliberal logic of market competition converges with the politically neoconservative agenda of Christian right organizations by examining the hegemonic notions of personal responsibility in the public school curriculum. I will focus primarily on the implications for public schooling as federally funded abstinence-only sex education gained widespread appeal after it was included as a provision in welfare reform legislation, the Personal Responsibility and Work Opportunity Reconciliation Act of 1996 (PRWORA).

ABSTINENCE-ONLY SEX EDUCATION COMES OF AGE

Federal government funding for abstinence-only sex education programs has existed now for 25 years. Beginning in 1981, the Adolescent Family Life Act (AFLA), also commonly referred to as the "chastity law," created teen pregnancy prevention programs that instructed young women about sexual abstinence while simultaneously promoting adoption (instead of abortion) for teen mothers who were already pregnant.

Within two years, lawsuits charged that religious content in abstinence-only programs breached the establishment clause of the Constitution, which stipulates a separation of church and state. By 1993, the lawsuit was settled out of court with the agreement that AFLA-funded programs would not contain religious references (such as bringing Jesus Christ to chaperone while dating) and be medically accurate. Unfortunately, Christian-centered abstinence-only programs such as Sex Respect and Teen-Aid had been proliferating for several years by then, creating their own for-profit abstinence-only curricula.

The following year, Rep. John Doolittle (R-CA) tried unsuccessfully to introduce an amendment designed to limit the content of sexuality and HIV education. Part of the Christian right's agenda, it was an attempt to restrict gay and lesbian youth services. Since federal laws prohibit the federal government from mandating content of local community education programs, conservative Christian right lobbyists developed a strategy where they could influence program content through health policy and funding.

By 1996, during the period that welfare reform legislation was undergoing revisions, a mandated provision for abstinence-only sex education for $50 million annually for fiscal years 1998 to 2002 was hastily written into the law. The funds would be drawn from the Maternal and Child Health (MCH) Block Grant, which provides prenatal and neonatal services to low-income women. Funding for abstinence-only sex education in welfare reform legislation was granted entitlement status, which compelled Congress to fund it without requiring any debate.

Signed by President Clinton, PRWORA was lauded by the Democratic president, who proclaimed to "end welfare as we know it." Welfare reform law shifted Aid to Families with Dependent Children (AFDC) to Temporary Assistance for Needy Families (TANF). The name change was not merely superficial, it positioned single-family households (who are mostly headed by poor white women and women of color) as too dependent on government and, therefore, undeserving of public aid. Describing the intersections of neoconservative politics and neoliberal economics, Lisa Duggan (2003) writes:

> These legislative features emerged from decades of efforts to erode New Deal welfare state programs, especially AFDC, through the deployment of images of sexually promiscuous, lazy welfare queens breeding for the profit of an ever-enlarging welfare check. The specific neoliberal spin on this cultural project was the removal of explicitly racist, misogynist language and images, and the substitution of the language and values of privatization and personal responsibility. (Duggan, 2003, p. 16)

As part of PRWORA, single women raising families with welfare assistance were told to take "personal responsibility" for their poverty by returning to the workforce as low-wage workers. As a result of PRWORA, federal funding for abstinence-only sex education programs once intended to promote marriage to young unwed mothers and discourage sexual activity outside the confines of marriage was no longer limited to young, single mothers. The market competition for abstinence-only curricula was now open to all public school students.

FEDERAL GOVERNMENT'S DEFINITION OF ABSTINENCE-ONLY

Broadly viewed as a neoconservative attack on comprehensive sexuality education that encompasses contraception knowledge, abstinence-only sex education became an economic boon for Christian organizations as they competed to become federal grant recipients. The abstinence-only provision in PRWORA requires that for every $3 that states spend on abstinence-only sex education, federal funds will match it with $4. Under the guidelines, comprehensive sex education programs that mention the benefits of contraceptive usage toward preventing pregnancy, AIDS, and other sexually transmitted diseases do not qualify to receive federal funding.

The federal government defines abstinence-only sex education as meeting the following requirements:

- Has as its exclusive purpose teaching the social, physiological, and health gains to be realized by abstaining from sexual activity
- Teaches abstinence from sexual activity outside marriage as the expected standard for all school-age children
- Teaches that abstinence from sexual activity is the only certain way to avoid out-of-wedlock pregnancy, sexually transmitted diseases, and other associated health problems

- Teaches that a mutually faithful monogamous relationship within the context of marriage is the expected standard of human sexual activity
- Teaches that sexual activity outside of the context of marriage is likely to have harmful psychological and physical effects
- Teaches that bearing children out of wedlock is likely to have harmful consequences for the child, the child's parents, and society
- Teaches young people how to reject sexual advances and how alcohol and drug use increases vulnerability to sexual advances
- Teaches the importance of attaining self-sufficiency before engaging in sexual activity

As evident in the highly restrictive federal guidelines, states that prefer to allow a more comprehensive sex education program that includes prophylaxis would be excluded from receiving federal funds. The teaching of a mutually faithful monogamous relationship within the context of marriage and that sexual activity outside of the context of marriage is likely to have harmful psychological and physical effects eschews recognition of gay and lesbian sexuality and creates a hostile climate in which sex educators are silenced. Since gay and lesbian people are not allowed to legally marry in the United States, the avoidance of discussing gay and lesbian sexuality in a positive manner is an attempt to marginalize and render them invisible.

TAXPAYER DOLLARS FUNDING RELIGION

Despite the dubious effectiveness of abstinence-only programs to delay the onset of sexual activity or to lower pregnancy and STD rates, these programs have continued to enjoy increased matched state and federal funding. Funding for abstinence-only programs reached a record $500 million in the first five years, from 1998 to 2002. More recently, President Bush has requested a budget proposal for fiscal year 2006 to increase funding for abstinence-only sex programs to a record $206 million (Planned Parenthood, 2005).

In May 2005, the American Civil Liberties Union (ACLU) filed a lawsuit against the Department of Health and Human Services (DHHS), claiming that the abstinence-only program Silver Ring Thing (SRT) was "permeated with religion" and used "taxpayer dollars to promote religious content, instruction, and indoctrination." The Silver Ring Thing was awarded more than $1 million since 2003 for its three-hour abstinence-only programs, which include skits, flashing lights, video presentations, and a rally in which organizers quote Bible passages while students pledge to remain virgins. By August 2005, DHHS took action by withholding the remaining $75,000 in federal funds from SRT, claiming that the abstinence-only sex education curriculum, as implemented by SRT, contained religious activities that disqualified it from receiving federal tax dollars.

Similar to many abstinence-only programs, part of the SRT curricula involved organizing students to participate in a ritual of "virginity pledges." The virginity pledge, the brainchild social movement of the Southern Baptist Church since 1993, encourages adolescents to pledge to God that they will not engage in sexual intercourse before marriage (Gish, 2000; Neill, 2000; Todd, 1999). Abstinence-only programs have organized virginity pledges that range from a public document signing to participating in a mass ritual verbal pledge. It is an idea that appeals to adults because it encourages adolescents and teenagers to take personal responsibility by embracing the message of "just say no" to sexual intercourse. Many of the abstinence-only programs, most of which are overtly Christian and some that have secular language, include virginity pledges as part of the curricula:

> **Believing that true love waits, I make a commitment to God, myself, my family, my friends, my future mate, and my future children to a lifetime of purity including sexual abstinence from this day until the day I enter a biblical marriage relationship.** (True Love Waits, virginity pledge on a commitment card, sponsored by Lifeway Christian Resources)
>
> I, _____, am a (virgin, secondary virgin). I have made a choice to remain abstinent until _____. I will be accountable to _____ for this decision. (Teen-Aid, virginity pledge on personal commitment card)
>
> I, _____, promise to abstain from sex until my wedding night. I want to reserve my sexual powers to give life and love for my future spouse and marriage. I will respect my gift of sexuality by keeping my mind and thoughts pure as I prepare for my true love. I commit to grow in character to learn to live love and freedom. (Sex Respect, parent guide)

By 2000, over two-and-a-half-million adolescents had taken some form of the virginity pledge (Bearman & Brückner, 2000). In an updated study of adolescents who participated in virginity pledges, Brückner and Bearman (2005) used data from the National Longitudinal Study of Adolescent Health. Their findings point out that the difference between adolescents who made virginity pledges and those that did not was not statistically significant. In fact, the STD infection rates do not differ between pledgers and nonpledgers. The researchers have offered a possible explanation that "pledgers are less likely than others to use condoms at sexual debut and to be tested and diagnosed with STDs" (p. 271).

In the case of SRT, young adults are expected to wear a silver ring as a symbol of their virginity pledge, a ring that is inscribed with "God wants you to be holy, so you should keep clear of all sexual sin." Ironically, SRT denies any proselytizing aspects of its abstinence-only curriculum, yet for several weeks before and after DHHS announced it would cease to grant funds for SRT programs, an online ad for Silver Ring Thing programs on DVD advertised a forthcoming, not yet finished secular version of its current abstinence-only program. The Silver Ring Thing is an abstinence-only program run by John Guest Evangelistic Team, a Christian missionary organization.

A RELIGIOUS FAITH IN THE MARKET

Robert W. McChesney (1999 p. 8) writes that neoliberalism demands "a religious faith in the infallibility of the unregulated market." Based on the 19th-century concept of laissez faire, when businesses wanted minimal government interference, early conceptions of economic liberalism became a staple of American thinking by the early 20th century.

Although the ideas of economic liberalism fell out of favor after the stock market crash of 1929 and the ensuing Great Depression, they resurfaced again as neoliberalism by the end of the 20th century, with the mounting neoconservative backlash against many of the government-sponsored social programs. While one would expect the marketplace metaphor to describe an imaginary space in which competing ideas are discussed and contested, the conditions under neoliberalism are not hospitable to anything that challenges corporate profits. Within the unregulated marketplace metaphor, truth or claims to own the truth become just another commodity to be purchased and consumed.

In the unregulated marketplace of abstinence-only programs, Christian-based and neoconservative organizations have been given unprecedented access to millions of taxpayer dollars to set up medically inaccurate information on a federal government Web site while religious proselytizers have infiltrated American public schools in the guise of promoting morality and character building as they highlight the benefits of abstaining from premarital sexual activity. Since federal funds for abstinence-only programs have reached over $100 million annually, the competition for federal grants to implement an abstinence-only program has led some organizations to seek out fee-based consultative services in writing grants and proposals from more established abstinence-only organizations, such as Teen-Aid.

In their discussion of neoliberalism and the social changes that result, Fischman, Ball, and Gvirtz (2003) assert:

> The market, competitiveness, and choice involve not simply a new and more efficient mechanism for the delivery of public sector services, but also the basis for a new moral economy. It brings with it a new set of values and a new ethical framework within which relationships and practices in public sector organizations are reworked.

In the case of organizations that promote and design abstinence-only programs, the designation of nonprofit status serves to obscure the enormous profits generated as well as the benefactors who seek to establish a strategic agenda of less government regulation of business and more privatization of government (public) services. The "new moral economy" urges people to exert self-control over themselves and to not rely on government services. The Best Friends Foundation is an example of the ways in which neoconservatives and neoliberals have co-opted the nonprofit organization status to advance their own vision of the role (or lack of) of government.

Elayne Bennett is president and founder of Best Friends Foundation, a character-building program whose purpose is to "promote self-respect through the practice of self-control and provides participants the skills, guidance, and support to choose abstinence from sex until marriage and reject illegal drug and alcohol abuse." Best Friends Foundation creates abstinence-only programs that emphasize virtue and personal responsibility for students in elementary through secondary schools.

As the wife of William Bennett, former secretary of education during the Reagan administration and author of the popular and highly profitable *Book of Virtues: A Treasury of Great Moral Stories* (1993), Elayne has been able to profit from her husband's prominent business and political connections. Her Best Friends Foundation has 501(c)(3) status, a designation commonly given to nonprofit organizations.

During the years 1994 to 2003, Best Friends Foundation received $1,174,696 in charitable contributions. Public school districts that choose to implement the Best Friends abstinence-only and character-building curriculum must make a commitment to purchase the entire curriculum series from sixth grade to the high school level. Best Friends Foundation does not supply the abstinence-only curriculum for free. Instead, school districts are expected to secure funding or apply for federal abstinence funds. As a nonprofit organization, it is highly questionable why school districts would need to secure the majority of funding if Best Friends Foundation is highly successful in attracting Washington, D.C.'s elite and wealthy benefactors at its private fund-raising galas.

Upon closer examination of the Best Friends Foundation, one can see that its charitable organization status allows it to receive the majority of its funding from the Lynde and Harry Bradley Foundation, the country's largest and most influential right-wing organization. According to the Media Transparency Web site, the Bradley Foundation "supports the organizations and individuals that promote the deregulation of business, the rollback of virtually all social welfare programs, and the privatization of government services."

The Bradley Foundation's resolute commitment to financing organizations that privatize government services is incontrovertible. Its "philanthropic" financing of the Best Friends Foundation's character-building and abstinence-only sex education programs has targeted low-income public schools with a majority student population of African Americans.

Returning to Lisa Duggan's assertion that neoliberal economic policies mask racist and classist ideologies, the Best Friends Foundation serves as a private contractor to public schools, promoting a curriculum taught during school hours that emphasizes moral virtue and personal responsibility to young African Americans.

A tacit understanding of character-building and abstinence-only programs within this new moral economy (Fischman et al., 2003) is that the poor and working class need only look within themselves for economic stability, instead of analyzing the structures and systematic barriers of institutionalized racism and classism that have led to the continued defunding of public schools and other social support programs. The intersections of economic neoliberalism and social neoconservativism have overshadowed the danger to an engaged citizenry as private corporate interests, with some disguised as nonprofit organizations, dominate and compete for financial gain. It assumes that the market is the solution, that the market alone can solve, fix, or alleviate social inequalities that have been systematically formed for over three centuries.

Religious faith in rampant capitalism parallels religious faith in Christianity to provide solutions and salvation to young adults who have been shortchanged by decreased funding and budget cuts to their public education. The government funding and endorsement of abstinence-only programs should be looked at critically, especially because it privileges a particular religious morality over educating young adults with scientific knowledge about their sexual health. Abstinence-only sex educators, espousing covert Christian values of celibacy and self-control over the materiality of the physical world, have secularized their discourse on sexuality with key words such as "character building" and "personal responsibility" to emphasize that complex socioeconomic problems reside inherently within the individual. In other words, the "religious faith in the unregulated market" conceals the widening gap between rich and poor by offering virtue and personal responsibility as small consolation.

REFERENCES

Ball, S., Fischman, G., & Gvirtz, S. (Eds.) (2003). *Crisis and hope: The educational hopscotch of Latin America*. Routledge: New York.

Bearman, P., & Brückner, H. (2000). Promising the future: Virginity pledges as they affect transition to first intercourse. *American Journal of Sociology, 106*, 859–912.

Best Friends Foundation. Retrieved on September 10, 2005 from Best Friends Foundation website: www.bestfriendsfoundation.org/.

Brückner, H., & Bearman, P. (2005). After the promise: The STD consequences of adolescent virginity pledges. *Journal of Adolescent Health, 36*, 271–278.

Connolly, C. (2005, August 23). Federal funds for abstinence groups witheld. *Washington Post*. Retrieved November 30, 2005, from http://www.washingtonpost.com/wp-dyn/content/article/2005/08/22/AR2005082201230_pf.html

Duggan, L. (2003). *The twilight of equality? Neoliberalism, cultural politics, and the attack on democracy*. Boston: Beacon Press.

Fischman, G., Ball, S., & Gvirtz, S. (2003). Towards a neo-liberal education? Tension and change in Latin America. In S. Ball, G. Fischman, & S. Gvirtz (Eds.), *Education, crisis, and hope: Tension and change in Latin America*. New York: Routledge-Falmer.

Gish, J. (2000, February 7). "No sex, please, we're teens." *Evening Sun* (Hanover, PA).

Kaiser Family Foundation. (2000). *Sex education in America: A view from inside the nation's classrooms*. Menlo Park, CA: Henry J. Kaiser Family Foundation.

McChesney, R. (1999). Introduction to Noam Chomsky's *Profits over People*. New York: Seven Stories Press.

Media Transparency. Web site on Best Friends Foundation. Retrieved October 10, 2005, from http://www.mediatransparency.org/recipientgrants.php?recipientID=34

Neill, M. (2000, February 18). 544 high school students make promise of abstinence. The Times (Cullman, AL).

Planned Parenthood. (2005a). Abstinence-only "sex" education. Retrieved October 10, 2005, from http://www.plannedparenthood.org/pp2/portal/medicalinfo/teensexualhealth/fact-abstinence-education.xml

Planned Parenthood. (2005b). AIDS across America. Retrieved November 30, 2005, from http://www.plannedparenthood.org/pp2/portal/files/portal/webzine/eyeonextremism/eoe-041130-aids-america.xml

Puiggros, A. (1996, May/June). World Bank education policy: Market liberalism meets ideological conservatism (NACLA Report on the Americas). Retrieved October 21, 2005, from http://www.hartford-hwp.com/archives/40/031.html

SIECUS. (2004). A portrait of sexuality education and abstinence-only-until-marriage programs in the states (SIECUS State Profiles). Retrieved October 21, 2005, from http://www.siecus.org/policy/states/index.html

Todd, H. (1999, August 8). Abstinence workshop insertion criticized. *Herald Zeitung* (New Braunfels, TX).

Chapter 40

Character Education

Four Arrows
Fielding Graduate University

A neo-conservative/neo-liberal agenda for character education in schooling is an historical continuation of American cultural and educational hegemony, supported by the power of Christian orthodoxy when infused into governmental policies. As such, formal character education programs are generally rooted in anthropocentric and authoritarian ideologies that tend to oppose perennial wisdom and utilize cultures of fear.

—Martin Eigenberger (1998)

On April 11, 2005, I was surprised to find a book in my mailbox entitled *The Discourse of Character Education: Culture Wars in the Classroom.* In referring to my own character education text, *Teaching Virtues: Building Character Across the Curriculum,* the Smagorinsky and Taxel (2005) state:

Such facets of character as feeling humility, being at peace, being spiritual, seeing generosity as the highest expression of courage, and feeling connected with all life forms are absent from Western conceptions of character. As we will review in subsequent chapters, they are not surprisingly absent from proposals funded by OERI (Office for Educational Research and Improvement, p. 58) for character curricula.

The centerpiece of the authors' discourse is an analysis of proposals funded by the OERI in the latter half of the 1990s. They conclude that the dominant perspective on character education is based on "an authoritarian view in which young people are indoctrinated into the value systems of presumably virtuous adults through didactic instruction." Considering that between 1996 and 2000 the U.S. Department of Education awarded more than $25 million in character education renewable grant funds to 36 states and the District of Columbia, and that Bush requested $25 million more in 2004, this "authoritarian view" represents a considerable influence in American schools.

This current emphasis on character education may have been born when, in 1996, Texas Commissioner of Education Mike Moses sent out copies of "Building Good Citizens for Texas — Resource Guide" to all of the schools in the state, "highly encouraging" all teachers to use it in the classroom. Created by the Institute on American Values, the cover letter for the booklet was written by then-governor George W. Bush.

In "A Critique of Character Counts! As a Curriculum Model for Explicit Moral Instruction in Public Schools," Peggy Ruth Green (2001) describes the program as little more than an effort to ensure that children do not think critically and reflectively. "Character Counts!" is a product of the Josephson Institute of Ethics. A key tenant of this organization, which claims to be nonpartisan, is that negative social influences are usually overcome by the exercise of free will and, of course, good character. Perhaps an example of this relates to Bill Nielsen, a member of the Board of Governors. He is also vice president of Johnson & Johnson, a company currently in litigation for allegedly cheating the Indian government of millions in taxes (Indo-Asian News Service, 2003).

It is also interesting to note the identity of the financial sponsors, besides the U.S. government. For example, the Jacqueline Hume Foundation donated $130,000 to the Josephson Institute (Media Transparency, n.d.a). The Hume Foundation celebrates the free market. It is the founder of Citizens for America, a right-wing lobbying group aimed at bringing the message of the free market throughout the world. It is also the sponsor of the Foundation for Teaching Economics, an effort to teach the basic concepts of market economics in public schools. Of course, the Hume Foundation is also a large donator to the Republican Party and in 1998 made two $100,000 contributions to California for Paycheck Protection, an antiunion ballot initiative. They have also supported school voucher initiatives and antibilingual education (Bacon & Berkowitz, 1999).

The Character Education Partnership also plays a large role in promoting character education, formed during a conference of the Aspen Institute and organized as a coalition of character education organizations and Character Counts! International. The Aspen Institute is a global forum whose Board of Trustees includes Henry Kissinger and a number of other prominent global free marketers.

CHARACTER EDUCATION AND THE RELIGIOUS RIGHT

It would be difficult to separate the corporate and authoritarian goals for character education from the goals of the religious right in America. Numerous books have been written that reveal the powerful influence on education and society, such as *Onward Christian Soldiers: The Religious Right in American Politics* by Clyde Wicox; *The Christian Right in American Politics: Marching to the Millennium* by John Green; *Religion and Politics in the United States* by Kenneth D. Wald; and *Close Encounters With the Religious Right: Journeys Into the Twilight Zone of Religion and Politics* by Rob Boston. As a result of this use of God as ultimate authority and all the rewards and punishments that go along with Christian Fundamentalism's claims, a heavy dose of extrinsic motivation informs character education programs across the country. Alfie Kohn (1997), who has claimed that modern character education is little more than a pulpit for Christian religion and conservative ideology, also authored a book that exposes the educational problems relating to an overuse of rewards and punishments. In *Punished by Rewards* (1999), he refers to numerous research studies that show that extrinsic motivation encourages temporary obedience but ultimately leads to outcomes that contradict the original goals. For example, children who are rewarded or punished for being generous when young turn out to be less generous as adults.

There are a number of assumptions held by the religious right that support a kind of character education that in turn would move young people toward embracing the assumptions of neoliberalism. For the remainder of this chapter, I will address these assumptions as a way to look deeply into the issue before us. Until we understand the power of domination in terms of the religious fundamentalist mind-set that supports it, it may be difficult to effectively challenge the neoliberal and neoconservative agenda.

It Is Important To Believe Some Are Favored Over Others By God.

The Nicomachean Ethics (350 B.C.E./1998) is arguably the first character education text, one that precedes even the Bible. In it, Aristotle refers often to Olympic athletes as the model for good character. The Olympics were competitive games. Aristotle's influence on Christianity and on the idea of ethics was significant (Microsoft Encarta, 2005). For example, both conservative and democratic presidents refer to the goal of school in terms of becoming more competitive in the global marketplace.

> The Conservative Model of character education wants children to be socialized to conform to status quo authority and to employment market needs. The Liberal model focuses on questions of power in reaction to the injustices that result from the dog-eat-dog ethic of capitalism but still tends to view the world as competitive in nature.... In the Indigenous view, relationships are neither intolerant of nor competitive with others. Rather, aboriginal people experience themselves as part of others and see in nature, even in the fiercest struggles, examples of symbiosis, not survival of the fittest per se. (Four Arrows, 2004, p. 88)

What kind of character traits would be prominent in our citizenship? What success has the neoconservative ideology shown in terms of America's character? I will finish with this particular assumption by offering Currie's (1985) partial answer to this last question:

> Contemporary conservatives like those before them who have successfully posed as the guardians of domestic tranquility for decades typically promote social and economic policies that are in large part responsible for the level of crime and violence we suffer today. (p. 571)

Humans Are Weak And Ignorant And They Are Suspicious Of Their Own Nature And Require Such Authoritarian Mandates For Security Because They Do Not Trust In Their Potential For Virtuous Behavior Otherwise.

Neoliberalism rationalizes its globalization by subscribing to Aristotle's blank-slate philosophy or the assumptions that the masses must be controlled for their own good. Indigenous history proves the falsity of this (see Four Arrows, 2006).

The Ten Commandments legislation follows the logic of this assumption. In trying to legislate ways to improve the moral character of American youth, the federal government in 1999 gave states the right to choose if they want to mandate posting the Ten Commandments in public schools. In 2005, only Indiana, Kentucky, and South Dakota have passed such bills, but many states are waiting for the Supreme Court to weigh in on this sometime in 2005 for the first time since 1980, when it determined that the Ten Commandments could not be displayed in public schools because the children might read them and think that the government was encouraging children to follow them. Such mandates offer no room for critical thinking.

Aristotle even admits that rational thinking is a prerequisite for character building. Einstein believed that the intuitive mind is a sacred gift, but that the rational mind is a faithful servant and, unfortunately, that we have created a society that honors the servant and has forgotten the gift. Smagorinsky and Taxel (2005) found some rhetoric regarding the importance of critical thinking in the proposals funded by the government but say that the discourse was silent on the threat to authoritarian societies that may find it disrespectful or otherwise deficient in character to use critical thinking to challenge authoritarianism (p. 115).

The character education discourse may indeed be "silent" on this concern regarding critical thinking, but it is far from disregarded. The neoconservative promoters of character education are all too aware of this issue. Their morality is not a matter of right versus wrong, but of right versus left. William Bennett, author of the famous *Book of Virtues*, a book of stories emphasizing the "pick yourself up by your bootstraps" philosophy in various stories, is but one example. Former U.S. secretary of education under Reagan, he is considered one of the prime movers of the conservative movement (Media Transparency, n.d.). Bennett is a member of the conservative think tank, the Heritage Foundation. He has been a cabinet official in several Republican administrations. He is a senior fellow of the Freedom Works, a foundation dedicated to school vouchers (especially for religious schools). He helped form the Americans for Victory Over Terrorism, dedicated to keeping left-wing educators from misleading students about the nature of the war on terrorism. He is also a founder of Empower America, along with a former member of Reverend Moon's Unification Church, an organization that has paid huge sums of money to hire Bennett as a speaker. He was chairman of Hudson's Modern Red Schoolhouse Design Team for the New American Schools Development Corporation, a private, tax-exempt organization established by the National Business Roundtable and the National Association of Business. A major promoter of character education, Bennett's *Book of Virtues* has been compared to Chairman Mao's *Little Red Book* (Simonton, n.d.). Character education was at the heart of Chairman Mao's cultural revolution in Red China.

Bennett's goal entails the complete indoctrination of children into the values of the corporate-run global state (Simonton, n.d.). His, like many involved in the character education movement, continue to promote the free-market philosophy of "pick yourself up by the bootstraps" instead of the more liberal concept embraced by the phrase "there but for the grace of God go I."

Such character education programs that emerge from this controlling idea allow for the free market, but not for caring relationships between people. Referring again to *The Discourse of Character Education*:

> The emphasis on relationships runs counter to the discourse of the authoritarian society, which places students in subservient positions relative to adults. A relational approach to character education instead relies on mutual understanding and personal mentorship so that students are apprenticed into a caring community's value on joint activity and mutual assistance. (Smagorinsky & Taxel, 2005, p. 287)

Anyone Who Stands Against Anthropocentric Religiosity And For A Wisdom That Emerges From Nature Is Committing Political Suicide Or Worse.

Neoliberals and neoconservatives have taken anthropocentrism to the extreme in relation to our environment. Chet Bowers (1993), in *Education, Cultural Myths and the Ecological Crisis*, describes the problem in education:

Typically, textbooks represent natural resources — that interesting meta-phor that encodes so many cultural assumptions — as the "property" of a political unit. But since people make up the political unity, human needs remain the determining factor in what aspects of the environment are con-sidered a "natural resource." (p. 131)

Bowers (1993) also criticizes liberals, including critical thinkers who fight for social justice only in terms of human interests and the authority of rationality, as also contributing to a socialization process that prevents stu-dents from "understanding the limitations and consequences of embrac-ing certain values" (p. 144). The values he refers to relate to materialism and consumerism that leaves students with the message "you can have it all." Bowers (1993) again:

> The energy put into the politics of self-interest, as well as the older variety of interest group politics, becomes important as it erodes the sense of member-ship in a larger community. When the metaphor of community is extended to include the interdependence of species and other natural systems that constitute the bioregion, we can see the danger posed by increasing our reli-ance on the use of the political process. (p. 196)

Much of the Western, antinature worldview comes from Plato. Plato, Aristotle's teacher and the student of the father of Western philosophy, Socrates, quotes Socrates as saying, "I'm a lover of learning, and trees and open country won't teach me anything, whereas men in town do" (Plato, 360 B.C.E./1972). Until we realize that landscape is sacred, "embodying a divinity that it shares with everything from trees and rocks to birds and animals" (Four Arrows, 2004, p. 90), we will, especially under the leadership of neoconservative and neoliberal ideology and Eurocentric assumptions, reproduce the cultural orientation that threatens the sustainability of our planet.

You Are With Us Or You Are Against Us.

Jesus is reported to have said in Matthew 12:30, "He that is not with me is against me." Bush's use of this phrase in his speech on terrorism is not coincidental (see Thakur, 2002). This polarizing, absolutist statement is typically made by dictators in totalitarian regimes and shows neoliberal-ism's true colors. Furthermore, it is also a common strategy to weave such polarization into the fabric of a religious perspective, the very thing that Paine feared the most for America. Bush's born-again positioning and his "God is on our side" slogans are, or should be, a great warning. He told for-mer Palestinian Foreign Minister Nabil Shaath and former Prime Minister Mahmoud Abbas, now the Palestinian president, that "I'm driven with a mission from God. God would tell me, 'George, go and end the tyranny in Iraq' and I did" (Cornwell, 2005). Although his White House spokesman says he did not say it, it is likely that he did considering that Bob Woodward quotes him in his book *Plan of Attack* as telling him, when discussing Iraq War motives, "I pray that I will be as good a messenger of His will as possible" (Cornwell, 2005).

It should be obvious to the reader that Christian Fundamentalism and neoliberal, free-market ideology are using character education to ensure that Paine's message and his desire for a separation of church and state are at last buried forever. What is at stake is the complete loss of the commons. The goal is for everything, from drinking water and national forests to public gathering places and public education, to be privately owned. Bill Willers (2005), in his article "Breaking the Bank: The Right-Wing Road to America's Privatized Future," describes the strategies that have been in place since Reagan. Charter schools, vouchers, and character education are part of this strategy, as is the "private" use of Christian orthodoxy for political and financial gain.

In her book *The Fundamentals of Extremism: The Christian Right in America*, Kimberly Blaker (2003) opens her introductory chapter with a quote from James Dobson, former professor of pediatrics, founder of Focus on the Family, and host of a radio program that broadcasts on more than 2,000 stations. The quote is from Dobson's book *Children at Risk* (1990), which has a forward written by William Bennett.

> Those who control what young people are taught, and what they experience — what they see, hear, think and believe — will determine the future course for the nation. (Blaker, 2003, p. 27)

Blaker goes on to say that Dobson is

> known for his strong web of ties to the Christian right. In fact, his ability to wield power over the Republican Party suggests he is the Christian right. Dobson, an evangelical, a patriarch, an advocate of corporal punishment, is an opponent of reproductive choice, homosexual rights, free speech, liberal sex education, and the right to die with dignity. Yet, he has a remarkable ability to manipulate unsuspecting Americans who otherwise might not agree with his views. His sly maneuvering through the political arena unseen and unheard — except by those whose chains he pulls — has been a key to his power and success. (Blaker, 2003, p. 7)

Blaker's words rang true with the news of Karl Rove's secret conversations with Dobson about Harriet Meier's qualifications to be a nomination for the Supreme Court two days prior to Bush's announcement. Later Dobson confessed that the information was simply a confirmation of her very conservative religious views, which of course are a positive for the Bush administration (Family.org, 2005).

Even if news such as this eventually leads to indictments against the top members of the Bush administration, including Bush himself, the neoconservative/neoliberal agenda is too deep and too dependent upon the religious right to not remain a serious influence on the character education movement. Consider, for example, that the House of Representatives will soon debate legislation reauthorizing the historic antipoverty Head Start preschool education program. At that time, an amendment is likely to be offered that, for the first time, would permit Head Start programs run by religious organizations to engage in religious discrimination in hiring and firing of teachers and staff (Anti-Defamation League, 2005). Similarly, the neoconservative movement is pushing "intelligent design" into school curriculum. It continues to ensure that abstinence-only sex education dominates in spite of research that reveals its harm. Increasing use of vouchers for private religious schools, increased corporate encroachment into classrooms, and use of No Child Left Behind for military recruitment are but a few of the examples that parallel the untoward use of character education for purposes of the agenda.

One great irony in all of this is that honesty and integrity are universally touted as primary objectives of character education. That America continues to disregard the evidence surrounding the aforementioned concerns is in itself a sign of self-deception. The neoconservative, religious-right hypocrisy can only continue when we allow authoritarianism to overshadow our search for the truth and when our religious orthodoxy gives us false security that allows us to be led by authoritarian mandates "on high."

Daniel Goleman addresses how easily humans subscribe to self-deception in his book *Vital Lies, Simple Truths: The Psychology of Self-Deception* (1996):

> We live at a particularly perilous moment, one in which self-deception is a subject of increasing urgency. The planet itself faces a threat unknown in other times: its utter destruction. We live our lives oblivious to the consequences for the planet, for our own descendants, of just how we live. We do not know the connections between the decisions we make daily — for instance to buy this item rather than that — and the toll those decisions have on the planet. And for most of us, being oblivious to that relationship allows us to slip into the grand self-deception that the small and large decisions in our material lives are of no great consequence. Self-deception operates both at the level of the individual mind, and in the collective awareness of the group. To belong to a group of any sort, the tacit price of membership is to agree not to notice one's feeling of uneasiness and misgivings, and certainly not to question anything that challenges the group's way of doing things. The price for the group in this arrangement is that dissent, even healthy dissent, is stifled. (p. iii)

Before educators get too involved in implementing the federally granted character education programs, perhaps it is time for the educators themselves to become people of character and speak truth to the powers that are doing violence to both children and our world at large.

REFERENCES

Anti-Defamation League. (2005). The Ten Commandments controversy: A First Amendment perspective. Retrieved October 22, 2005, from http://www.adl. org/10comm/Prohibitions.asp

Aristotle. (1998). *The Nicomachean ethics.* New York: Oxford University Press. (Original work published 350 B.C.E.)

Bacon, D., & Berkowitz, D. (1999). San Francisco's Hume family: Building a right-wing empire on dried garlic and a busted union. Retrieved December 21, 2005, from http://dbacon.igc.org/Strikes/12Hume.htm#top

Blaker, K. (2003). The perils of fundamentalism and the imperilment of democracy. In Blaker, K. (Ed.) *The fundamentals of extremism: The Christian right in America* (p. 7). Plymouth, Michigan: New Boston Books.

Bowers, C. A. (1993). *Education, cultural myths and the ecological crisis.* Albany, NY: SUNY Press.

Cornwell, R. (2005, October 8). Bush: God told me to invade Iraq. *New Zealand Herald.* Retrieved December 21, 2005, from http://www.nzherald.co.nz/section/print.cfm?c_id=2&objectid=10349260

Currie, E. (1985). Fighting crime (Working Paper 9). In D. Stanley Eitzen & Doug A. Timmer (Eds.), *Criminology: Crime and criminal justice* (p. 571). New York: MacMillan.

Dobson, J. (1990). *Children at risk.* Nashville, TN: W. Publishing Group.

Eigenberger, M. E. (1998). Fear as a correlate of authoritariansim. *Psychological Reports, 83,* 1395–1409.

Family.org. (2005). Transcript of Dobson comments on Miers/Rove. Retrieved October 22, 2005, from http://www.family.org/welcome/press/a0038214. cfm

Four Arrows (Don Trent Jacobs). (2004). Character education: Coming full circle. In Kevin D. Vinson & E. Wayne Ross (Eds.), *Defending public schools* (p. 90). Westport, CT: Praeger Perspectives.

Four Arrows. (2006). Unlearning the language of conquest: Scholars expose anti-Indianism in America. Austin: University of Texas Press.

Goleman, D. (1996). Vital lies, simple truths: The psychology of self-deception. New York: Simon & Schuster.

Green, P. R. (2001). A critique of character counts! As a curriculum model for explicit moral instruction in public schools. Retrieved December 21, 2005, from http://www2.gsu.edu/~wwwsfd/2001/Geren.PDF

Indo-Asian News Service. (2003). Cheating charges against Johnson and Johnson executives. Retrieved December 21, 2005, from http://puggy.symonds.net/pipermail/corruption-issues/2003-June/000345.html

Kohn, A. (1997, February). How not to teach values: A critical look at character education. *Phi Delta Kappan.* Retrieved December 21, 2005, from http://www.alfiekohn.org/teaching/hnttv.htm

Kohn, A. (1999). *Punished by rewards: The trouble with gold stars, incentive plans, A's, praise, and other bribes.* Boston: Mariner Books.

Media Transparency. (n.d. a). Recipients by amount granted from Jaquelin Hume Foundation. Retrieved December 21, 2005, from http://www.mediatransparency.org/recipientsoffunderprint.php?funderID=16

Media Transparency. (n.d. b). William Bennett. Retrieved December 21, 2005, from http://www.mediatransparency.org/personprofile.php?personID=1

Microsoft® Encarta® Online Encyclopedia. (2005). Ethics. Retrieved December 14, 2005, from http://encarta.msn.com/encyclopedia_761555614_3/Ethics.html#p24

Plato. (1972). *Phaedrus* (R. Hackforth, Trans.). Cambridge: Cambridge University Press. (Original work published 360 B.C.E.)

Simonton, C. (n.d.). The Rockefeller-Heritage connection. Retrieved December 21, 2005, from http://watch.pair.com/rockefeller.html#rockefeller

Smagorinsky, P., & Taxel, J. (2005). *The discourse of character education: Culture wars in the classroom.* Mahwah, NJ: Lawrence Erlbaum.

Thakur, R. (2002, November-December). The peril of pre-emptive thinking (newsletter of the United Nations University 21). Retrieved December 21, 2005, from http://update.unu.edu/archive/issue21_1.htm

Willers, B. (2005, October 11). Breaking the bank: The right-wing road to America's privatized future. Retrieved October 13, 2005, from http://www.commondreams.org/views05/1011-22.htm

DEMOCRACY'S PATH

On one hand, an honest assessment of the public's chances to derail the neoliberal/neoconservative agenda in education leaves small room for optimism. Like the "coppertops" portrayed in *The Matrix* films, the public has yet to awake from its slumber. Even some of our colleagues in teacher education remain committed to helping schools try to win "the numbers game" of high-stakes testing. They fail to recognize that the deck has been squarely stacked against them. The policy aims to ensure failure as a pretext for justifying an otherwise hostile corporate takeover of public schools. Rejecting the neoliberal claim that "there is no alternative," the chapters in this final section offer an alternative vision. Takis Fotopoulos offers inclusive democracy as a more than viable alternative to the exclusive democracy currently operated of, by, and for the governing plutocracy of our market-dominated society. Sheila Landers Macrine's chapter on inclusive schooling supports Fotopoulos's notions of political democracy and social democracy by reminding us of our egalitarian commitments to equity as well as equality under the law. Curry Malott and Marc Pruyn's chapter on critical pedagogy, Juha Suoranta and Peter McLaren's chapter on socialist pedagogy, and Jeanne Brady's chapter on critical feminist pedagogy all help us reimagine education's potential as a source of political liberation and social transformation to help us shape and sustain a more vital democracy grounded in values other than domination and personal enrichment. Four Arrows, and Dana Stuchul and Madhu Suri Prakash, in their chapters on indigenous pedagogy and ecological literacy, respectively, remind us that we must turn our imaginations to nonmodern and non-Western cultural traditions for guidance in living our way to a world beyond the market if we are to avert the total collapse of our social and ecological systems. This does not require a rejection of "everything Western" as some fear-mongering neoconservatives would have the public believe. Mark Beatham and Marilyn Frankenstein would have us regard understanding the life-giving potential of our technologies and knowledge as just as important as understanding their life-denying and death-dealing potential. What will determine our future will be the principles and values that guide us in developing and implementing those technologies and knowledge. Will we pursue the market's path of individualism and heteronomy? Or will we pursue democracy's path of autonomy and community? In his chapter on deschooling, Matt Hern joins us in hoping that we will choose the latter. He would only have us stop and consider whether compulsory schooling is part of the solution or part of the problem.

Chapter 41

Inclusive Democracy

Takis Fotopoulos
International Journal of Inclusive Democracy

The starting point for the inclusive democracy project is that contemporary society, which presently takes the form of a market/growth economy and representative democracy everywhere, is undergoing a profound and widespread crisis. It is precisely the universal character of this crisis that constitutes the determining factor and differentiates it from other crises in the past while simultaneously calling into question practically every structure and value that supports contemporary heteronomous societies in East and West, North and South. Thus, the present crisis calls into question not just the political, economic, social, and ecological structures that came into being with the rise of the system of the market economy about two centuries ago, but also the actual values that have sustained these structures and particularly the post-Enlightenment meaning of progress and its partial identification with growth. This multidimensional crisis can be attributed to the very institutions of modernity, which today have been universalized. It is argued that the dynamics of the market economy and representative democracy have led to the present concentration of power at all levels, which in turn is the ultimate cause of every dimension of the present crisis.

THE MULTIDIMENSIONAL CRISIS

The Economic Dimension

The concentration of economic power, as a result of commodity relations and the grow-or-die dynamic of the market economy, has led to a chronic economic crisis that today is expressed mainly by a huge concentration of economic power. This is shown by the enormous income/wealth gap that separates not only the North from the South, but also the economic elites and the privileged social groups from the rest of society all over the world. Thus, the North has yet to recover from the crisis that surfaced in the mid-1970s as a result of the fundamental contradiction that was created, as I attempted to show elsewhere (see Fotopoulos, 1997, Chap. 1), by the internationalization of the market economy and the parallel expansion of statism, in the sense of active state control aiming at determining the level of economic activity. The transnational elite, which began flourishing in the context of the internationalization of the market economy process, embarked on an effort to shrink the state's economic role and to free and deregulate markets, which has already had devastating consequences for the majority of the population. This drastic reduction in statism turned the clock back to the period before the mixed economy and Keynesian policies were used to create a "capitalism with a human face." The result was an initial huge upsurge of open unemployment followed by today's period of massive low-paid and low-quality employment. This experience has been reproduced all over the North, particularly after the collapse of the alternative Rhineland model of "social market" capitalism in Germany and the replacement of Scandinavian social democracy by a kind of "social liberalism" (see Fotopoulos, 2005b).

The fierce competition among the countries in the triad (Free Trade Area of the Americas [FTAA], European Union [EU], and Far East) can safely be predicted to create conditions not so much of massive open unemployment, but of poor-quality employment everywhere. However, to my mind, the crisis of the market/growth economy in the North does not constitute the decisive element in the economic crisis. As long as the "two-thirds society" is somehow reproduced, the system may be stabilized when it moves to a new equilibrium resting on the exploitation of the technological advantages of the North and the low production cost of the new South, particularly China and India (see Fotopoulos, 2005a). We could therefore assume that the decisive element in the economic crisis consists of the fact that the system of the market economy is inherently incapable of transforming the market economy of the South into a self-sustaining growth economy, similar to the one already established in the North. This inherent incapability is the direct result of the fact that the concentration of economic power and the parallel growing inequality all over the world are not just consequences of, but also preconditions for the reproduction of the market/growth economy. This is because there is an absolute natural barrier that makes the universalization of the North's capitalist type of growth economy impossible. Assuming, for instance, that the world's population will be over 7 billion by 2015 (Human Development Report, 2005), for the inhabitants of our planet to reach the per capita energy use rates that those living in the rich countries now enjoy, world energy production would have to quadruple (or increase six times over for everybody to enjoy U.S. consumption standards).[1] No wonder the present Chinese growth "miracle" is accompanied by a huge rise in economic inequality that could somehow sustain the present growth rates (creating an environmental disaster in the process), but only at the expense of a growing social instability.

The Political Dimension

Concentration of political power has been the functional complement of the concentration of economic power. If the grow-or-die dynamics of the market economy have led to the present concentration of economic power, it is the dynamics of representative democracy that have led to a corresponding concentration of political power. Thus, the concentration of political power in the hands of parliamentarians in liberal modernity has led to an even higher degree of concentration in the hands of governments and the leadership of mass parties in statist modernity, at the expense of parliaments. In neoliberal modernity, the combined effect of the dynamics of the market economy and representative democracy has led to the conversion of politics into statecraft (see Bookchin, 1995; Castoriadis, 1991), with think tanks designing policies and their implementation. Thus, a small clique around the prime minister (or the president) concentrates all effective political power in its hands, particularly in advanced market economies that constitute major parts of the transnational elite. Furthermore, the continuous decline of the state's economic sovereignty is accompanied by the parallel transformation of the public realm into pure administration.

A crisis of politics has developed in the present neoliberal modernity that undermines the foundations of representative democracy and is expressed by several symptoms that frequently take the form of an implicit or explicit questioning of fundamental political institutions (parties, electoral contests, etc.). Such symptoms are the significant and usually rising abstention rates in electoral contests, particularly in the United States and United Kingdom, the explosion of discontent in the form of frequently violent riots, the diminishing numbers of party members, and the fact that respect for professional politicians has never been at such a low level, with the frequent financial scandals simply reaffirming the belief that politics, for the vast majority of politicians — liberals and social democrats alike — is just a profession, that is, a way to make money and enhance social status. Although the historical cause of the present mass apathy can be traced back to what Castoriadis (1997) called "the radical inadequacy, to say the least, of the programs in which [the project of autonomy] had been embodied — be it the liberal republic or Marxist-Leninist 'socialism'" (pp. 32–44), the crisis has become particularly acute in the last decade or so.

To my mind, the answer has to be found in the cumulative effect of the changes in the objective and subjective conditions that have marked the emergence of the internationalized market economy since the mid-1970s, namely, the growing internationalization of the market economy, which has effectively undermined the state's power to control economic events; the acute intensification of the struggle for competitiveness among the countries in the triad (European Commission [EC], United States, and Japan), which in turn has resulted in the collapse of social democracy and the establishment of the "neoliberal consensus"; and, last but not least, the collapse of "actually existing socialism," which has led to the myth of the "end of ideologies" and further enhanced the spreading of the culture of individualism promoted by neoliberalism.

The Social Dimension

The growth economy has already created a growth society, the main characteristics of which are consumerism, privacy, alienation, and the subsequent disintegration of social ties. The growth society, in turn, inexorably leads toward a nonsociety, that is, the substitution of atomized families and individuals in place of society, a crucial step toward the completion of barbarism. The social crisis has been aggravated by the expansion of the market economy into all sectors of social life, in the context of its present internationalized form. It is, of course, well known that the market is the greatest enemy of traditional values. It is not, therefore, surprising that the social crisis is more pronounced in precisely those countries where marketization has advanced the most. This becomes evident by the fact that neither campaigns of the "back to basics" type (Britain), nor the growth of religious, mystic, and other similar irrational tendencies (United States) has had any restraining effect on the most obvious symptoms of the social crisis: the explosion of crime and drug abuse that has already led many states effectively to abandon their "war against drugs" (see Fotopoulos, 1999).

The Cultural and Ideological Dimensions

The establishment of the market economy implied sweeping aside traditional cultures and values. This process was accelerated in the 20th century with the spreading all over the world of the market economy and its offspring, the growth economy. As a result, today there is an intensive process of cultural homogenization at work, which not only rules out any directionality toward more complexity, but also in effect is making culture simpler, with cities becoming more and more alike, people all over the world listening to the same music, watching the same soap operas on TV, buying the same brands of consumer goods, and so forth. The rise of neoliberal globalization in the last quarter of a century or so has further enhanced this process of cultural homogenization. This is the inevitable outcome of the liberalization and deregulation of markets and the consequent intensification of the commercialization of culture.

Furthermore, the changes in the structural parameters marking the transition to neoliberal modernity were accompanied by a parallel serious ideological crisis that put into question not just the political ideologies (what postmodernists pejoratively call emancipatory metanarratives), or even "objective" reason (see Kuhn, 1970; Lakatos, 1970; Feyerabend, 1975), but reason itself, as shown by the present flourishing of irrationalism in all its forms: from the revival of old religions like Christianity and Islam to the expansion of various irrational trends, such as mysticism, spiritualism, astrology, esoterism, neopaganism, and New Age.

The Ecological Dimension

The ecological crisis, as manifested by the rapid deterioration in the quality of life, is the direct result of the continuing degradation of the environment, which the market economy and the consequent growth economy promote. It is no accident that the destruction of the environment during the lifetime of the growth economy, in both its capitalist and state socialist versions, bears no comparison to the cumulative damage that previous societies have inflicted on the environment. The fact that the main form of power within the framework of the growth economy is economic, and that the concentration of economic power involves the ruling elites in a constant struggle to dominate people and the natural world, could go a long way toward explaining the present ecological crisis. In other words, to understand the ecological crisis, we should refer not simply to the prevailing system of values and the resulting technologies (as the environmentalists and the deep ecologists suggest), nor exclusively to capitalist production relations (as eco-Marxists propose), but to the relations of domination that characterize a hierarchical society based on the system of market economy and the implied idea of dominating the natural world.

In this context, humanity is faced today with a crucial choice between two radically different proposed solutions: sustainable development and what we may call the eco-democratic solution. The former seeks the causes of the ecological crisis in the dominant system of values and the technologies used and naively presumes that a massive change in them is possible, if only we could persuade people about the need for such a change. This solution is supported not just by the mainstream green movement, but also by the progressive parts of the transnational elite, as it takes for granted today's institutional framework of the market economy and representative democracy. Alternatively, the eco-democratic solution seeks the causes of the ecological crisis in the social system itself, which is based on institutionalized domination (not only economic exploitation) of human by human and nature by society. It is obvious that this solution requires forms of social organization that are based on the equal distribution of political and economic power. And this brings us to the relevance of the democratic project today.

INCLUSIVE DEMOCRACY AS THE WAY OUT OF THE CRISIS

If we accept the premise of the first section, that we face a multidimensional crisis, which is caused by the concentration of power in the hands of various elites, the clear implication is that the way out of it can only be found through a process of creating a form of comprehensive or inclusive democracy. Such a democracy should be based on a form of social organization that reintegrates society with economy, polity, and nature within an institutional framework that secures the necessary conditions for the equal distribution of all forms of power, that is, political democracy, economic democracy, democracy in the social realm, and ecological democracy. In this sense, an inclusive democracy is seen not as a utopia (in the negative sense of the word), but as perhaps the only way out of the present crisis.

Inclusive democracy is therefore a new conception of democracy that, using as its starting point the classical definition of it, expresses democracy in terms of direct political democracy, economic democracy (beyond the confines of the market economy and state planning), as well as democracy in the social realm and ecological democracy. The concept of inclusive democracy is not simply a theoretical construct but is derived from a synthesis of two major historical traditions, the classical democratic and the socialist, although it also encompasses radical green, feminist, and liberation movements in the South. It therefore expresses trends that have manifested themselves throughout history as expressions of the broader autonomy tradition, which has always been in implicit or explicit conflict with the alternative — and historically dominant — heteronomy tradition (see Fotopoulos, 1997, chap. 8; Castoriadis, 1995; Bookchin, 1991, chaps. 5 & 7).

Political or Direct Democracy

In the political realm there can only be one form of democracy: what we may call political or direct democracy, in which political power is shared equally among all citizens. Political democracy is therefore founded on the equal distribution of political power among all citizens, the self-instituting of society. This means that the following conditions have to be satisfied for a society to be characterized as a political democracy:

- Democracy is grounded on the conscious choice of its citizens for individual and social autonomy and not on any divine or mystical dogmas and preconceptions, or any closed theoretical systems involving natural or economic laws, or tendencies determining social change.
- No institutionalized political processes of an oligarchic nature. This implies that all political decisions (including those relating to the formation and execution of laws) are taken by the citizen body collectively and without representation.
- No institutionalized political structures embodying unequal power relations. This means, for instance, that where authority is delegated to segments of the citizen body for the purpose of carrying out specific duties (e.g., serving in popular courts or regional and confederal councils, etc.), the delegation is assigned, on principle, by lot and on a rotational basis, and it is always recallable by the citizen body. Furthermore, as regards delegates to regional and confederal bodies, the mandates should be specific.
- All residents of a particular geographical area (which today can only take the form of a geographical community), beyond a certain age of maturity (to be defined by the citizen body itself) and irrespective of gender, race, ethnic, or cultural identity, are members of the citizen body and are directly involved in the decision-making process.

The above conditions are obviously not met by parliamentary democracy (as it functions in the West), soviet democracy (as it functioned in the East), and the various fundamentalist or semi-military regimes in the South. All these regimes are therefore forms of political oligarchy, in which political power is concentrated in the hands of various elites (professional politicians, party bureaucrats, priests, the military, and so on). Similarly, in the past, various forms of oligarchies dominated the political domain, when emperors, kings, and their courts, with or without the cooperation of knights, priests, and others, concentrated political power in their hands.

However, several attempts have been made in history to institutionalize various forms of direct democracy, especially during revolutionary periods (for example, the Parisian sections of the early 1790s, the Spanish collectives in the civil war, etc.). Most of these attempts were short-lived and usually did not involve the institutionalization of democracy as a new form of political regime that replaces, and not just complements, the state. In other cases, democratic arrangements were introduced as a set of procedures for local decision making. The only historical example of an institutionalized direct democracy — apart from that of some Swiss cantons that were governed by assemblies of the people (*Landsgemeinden*) (see Hansen, 1991)

— in which, for almost two centuries (508/7 to 322/1 B.C.), the state was subsumed into the democratic form of social organization is the Athenian democracy. Of course, Athenian democracy was only a political democracy and, in fact, a *partial* one. However, what characterized it as partial was not the political institutions themselves but the very narrow definition of full citizenship adopted by the Athenians — a definition that excluded large sections of the population (women, slaves, immigrants) who, in fact, constituted the vast majority of the people living in Athens.

Economic Democracy

If we define political democracy as the authority of the people (*demos*) in the political sphere, implying the existence of political equality in the sense of equal distribution of political power, then economic democracy could be correspondingly defined as the authority of demos in the economic sphere, implying the existence of economic equality in the sense of equal distribution of economic power. And, of course, we are talking about the demos and not the state, because the existence of a state means the separation of the citizen body from the political and economic process. Economic democracy therefore relates to every social system that institutionalizes the integration of society and the economy. This means that, ultimately, the demos controls the economic process, within an institutional framework of demotic ownership of the means of production.

In a more narrow sense, economic democracy also relates to every social system that institutionalizes the minimization of socioeconomic differences, particularly those arising out of the unequal distribution of private property and the consequent unequal distribution of income and wealth. Historically, it is in this narrow sense that attempts were made by socialists to introduce economic democracy. Therefore, in contrast to the institutionalization of political democracy, there has never been a corresponding example of an institutionalized economic democracy in the broad sense defined above. In other words, even when socialist attempts to reduce the degree of inequality in the distribution of income and wealth were successful, they were never associated with meaningful attempts to establish a system of equal distribution of economic power. This has been the case, despite the fact that in the type of society that has emerged since the rise of the market economy, there has been a definite shift of the economy from the private realm into what Hannah Arendt called the "social realm," to which the nation-state also belongs. But, it is this shift that makes any talk of democracy that does not also refer to the question of economic power ring hollow, as it is clearly meaningless to talk today about the equal sharing of political power without conditioning it on the equal sharing of economic power.

On the basis of this definition of economic democracy, the following conditions have to be satisfied for a society to be characterized as an economic democracy:

- No institutionalized economic processes of an oligarchic nature. This means that all macroeconomic decisions, namely, decisions concerning the running of the economy as a whole (overall level of production, consumption and investment, amounts of work and leisure implied, technologies to be used, etc.) are taken by the citizen body collectively and without representation, although microeconomic decisions at the workplace or the household levels are taken by the individual producer and consumer, respectively.
- No institutionalized economic structures embodying unequal economic power relations. This implies that the means of production and distribution are collectively owned and controlled by the demos, the citizen body directly. Any inequality of income is therefore the result of additional voluntary work at the individual level. Such additional work, beyond that required by any capable member of society for the satisfaction of basic needs, allows only for additional consumption, as no individual accumulation of capital is possible, and any wealth accumulated as a result of additional work is not inherited. Thus, demotic ownership of the economy provides the economic structure for democratic ownership, while direct citizen participation in economic decisions provides the framework for a comprehensively democratic control process of the economy. The demos, therefore, becomes the authentic unit of economic life, since economic democracy is not feasible today unless both the ownership and control of productive resources are organized at the community level. So, unlike the other definitions of economic democracy, the definition given here involves the explicit negation of economic power and implies the authority of the people in the economic sphere. In this sense, economic democracy is the counterpart, as well as the foundation, of direct democracy and of an inclusive democracy in general.

Based on these general principles, we may draw an outline of a model of economic democracy, as an integral part of an inclusive democracy.[2] The dominant characteristic of this model, which differentiates it from similar models of centralized or decentralized planning, is that, although it does not depend on the prior abolition of scarcity, it does secure the satisfaction of the basic needs of all citizens, without sacrificing freedom of choice, in a stateless, moneyless, and marketless economy. The preconditions of economic democracy are defined in terms of *demotic* self-reliance, *demotic* ownership of productive resources, and confederal allocation of resources. The third condition in particular implies that the decision mechanism for the allocation of scarce resources in an inclusive democracy should be based at the confederal rather than the community level (i.e., at the level of the confederation of *demoi*), so that problems arising at the intercommunity level (energy, environment, transportation, communication, technology transfer, etc.) could be tackled effectively.

The mechanism proposed to allocate scarce resources aims to replace both the market mechanism and the central planning mechanism, both of which have failed historically. The former because it can be shown that the system of the market economy has led, in the 200 years since its establishment, to a continuous concentration of income and wealth at the hands of a small percentage of the world population and, consequently, to a distorted allocation of world resources. This is because in a market economy the crucial allocation decisions (*what* to produce, *how*, and *for whom* to produce it) are conditioned by the purchasing power of those income groups that can back their demands with money. The latter because it can be shown that centralized planning, although better than the market system in securing employment and meeting the basic needs of citizens (albeit at an elementary level), not only leads to economic irrationalities (which eventually precipitated its actual collapse) and ineffectiveness in covering nonbasic needs, but is also highly undemocratic.

The system of allocation proposed by the inclusive democracy project aims to satisfy the two-fold aim of:

- Meeting the basic needs of all citizens — which requires that basic macroeconomic decisions are made democratically
- Securing freedom of choice — which requires the individual to make important decisions affecting his or her own life (what work to do, what to consume, etc.)

Both the macroeconomic decisions and the individual citizen's decisions are envisaged as implemented through a combination of democratic planning, which involves the creation of a feedback process among workplace assemblies, demotic assemblies, and the confederal assembly — and an artificial market that secures genuine freedom of choice, without incurring the adverse effects associated with real markets. In a nutshell, the allocation of economic resources is made first on the basis of the citizens' collective decisions, as expressed through the community and confederal plans, and second on the basis of the citizens' individual choices, as expressed through a voucher system. The general criterion for the allocation of resources is not efficiency, as it is currently defined in narrow techno-economic terms. Efficiency should be redefined to mean effectiveness in satisfying human needs and not just money-backed wants. As far as the meaning of needs is concerned, a distinction is drawn between basic and nonbasic needs, and a similar one between needs and "satisfiers" (the form or the means by which these needs are satisfied). What constitutes a need — basic or otherwise — is determined by the citizens themselves democratically. Then, the level of need satisfaction is determined collectively and implemented through a democratic planning mechanism, while the satisfiers for both basic and nonbasic needs are determined through the revealed preferences of consumers, as expressed by the use of vouchers allocated to them in exchange for their basic and nonbasic work.

It is therefore clear that the project for an inclusive democracy refers to a kind of political economy that transcends both the political economy of state socialism, as realized in the ex-socialist countries of Eastern Europe, and the political economy of the market economy, either in its mixed economy form of social democratic consensus or in its present neoliberal form.

Democracy in the Social Realm

The satisfaction of the above conditions for political and economic democracy would represent the reconquering of the political and economic realms by the public realm — that is, the reconquering of a true social individuality, the creation of the conditions of freedom and self-determination, at both the political and economic levels. However, political and economic power are not the only forms of power, and therefore, political and economic democracy do not, by themselves, secure an inclusive democracy. In other words, an inclusive democracy is inconceivable unless it extends to the broader social realm to embrace the workplace, the household, the educational institution, and indeed any economic or cultural institution that constitutes an element of this realm.

Historically, various forms of democracy in the social realm have been introduced, particularly during the last century, usually in periods of revolutionary activity. However, these forms of democracy were not only short-lived, but seldom extended beyond the workplace (e.g., Hungarian workers' councils in 1956) and the educational institution (e.g., Paris student assemblies in 1968). The issue today is how to extend democracy to other forms of social organization, like the household, without dissolving the private/public realm divide. In other words, how, while maintaining and enhancing the autonomy of the two realms, such institutional arrangements are adopted that introduce democracy to the household and the social realm in general and, at the same time, enhance the institutional arrangements of political and economic democracy. In fact, an effective democracy is inconceivable unless free time is equally distributed among all citizens, and this condition can never be satisfied as long as the present hierarchical conditions in the household, the workplace, and elsewhere continue. Furthermore, democracy in the social realm, particularly in the household, is impossible, unless such institutional arrangements are introduced that recognize the character of the household as a needs satisfier and integrate the care and services provided within its framework into the general scheme of needs satisfaction.

Ecological Democracy

If we see democracy as a process of social self-institution in which there is no divinely or objectively defined code of human conduct, then there are no guarantees that an inclusive democracy would secure an ecological democracy in the sense defined above. Therefore, the replacement of the market economy by a new institutional framework of inclusive democracy constitutes only the necessary condition for a harmonious relation between the natural and social worlds. The sufficient condition refers to the citizens' level of ecological consciousness. Still, the radical change in the dominant social paradigm that will follow the institution of an inclusive democracy, combined with the decisive role that *paedeia* will play in an environmentally friendly institutional framework, could reasonably be expected to lead to a radical change in the human attitude toward nature. In other words, there are strong grounds for believing that the relationship between an inclusive democracy and nature would be much more harmonious than could ever be achieved in a market economy, or one based on state socialism.

Thus, at the political level, there are grounds for believing that the creation of a public space will in itself have a very significant effect on reducing the appeal of materialism. This is because the public space will provide a new meaning of life to fill the existential void that the present consumer society creates. The realization of what it means to be human could reasonably be expected to throw us back toward nature.

Also, at the economic level, it is not accidental that, historically, the process of destroying the environment en masse has coincided with the process of marketization of the economy. In other words, the emergence of the market economy and of the consequent growth economy had crucial repercussions on the society-nature relationship and led to the rise of the ideology of growth as the dominant social paradigm. An instrumentalist view of nature became dominant, in which nature was seen as an instrument for economic growth, within a process of endless concentration of power. If we assume that only a confederal society could secure an inclusive democracy today, it would be reasonable to assume further that once the market economy is replaced by a democratically run confederal economy, the grow-or-die dynamics of the former will be replaced by the new social dynamic of the latter: a dynamic aiming at the satisfaction of the community needs and not at growth per se. Furthermore, if the satisfaction of community needs does not depend, as at present, on the continuous expansion of production to cover the needs the market creates, and if the link between economy and society is restored, then there is no reason why the present instrumentalist view of nature should continue to condition human behavior.

Finally, democracy in the broader social realm could also be reasonably expected to be environmentally friendly. The phasing out of patriarchal relations in the household and hierarchical relations in general should create a new ethos of nondomination that would embrace both nature and society. In other words, the creation of democratic conditions in the social realm should be a decisive step in the creation of the sufficient condition for a harmonious nature-society relationship.

CONCLUSION

The institutionalization of inclusive democracy in terms of the above conditions is only the necessary condition for the establishment of democracy. The sufficient condition refers to the citizens' level of democratic consciousness, in which a crucial role is played by *paedeia* (see Fotopoulos, 2003) — involving not simply education, but character development and a well-rounded education in knowledge and skills, that is, the education of the individual as citizen, which alone can give substantive content to the public space.

NOTES

1. Calculations in the *World Development Report 2000/2001*, World Bank, Tables 1 and 10.
2. For a detailed description, see Fotopoulos (1997, chap. 6).

REFERENCES

Bookchin, M. (1995a). *From urbanisation to cities.* London: Cassell.

Bookchin, M. (1991). *The ecology of freedom.* Montreal: Black Rose Press.

Castoriadis, C. (1991). *Philosophy, politics, autonomy.* London: Oxford University Press.

Castoriadis, C. (1997). The retreat from autonomy. In D. A. Curtis (Ed.), *World in fragments* (pp. 32–43). Stanford, CA: Stanford University Press.

Feyerabend, P. (1975). *Against method.* London: Verso.

Fotopoulos, T. (1997). *Towards an inclusive democracy.* London/New York: Cassell/Continuum.

Fotopoulos, T. (1999). *Drugs: Beyond penalisation and liberalisation* (in Greek). Athens: Eleftheros Typos.

Fotopoulos, T. (2003, March). From (mis)education to *Paideia. Democracy and Nature, 9*. Retrieved May 1, 2007 from http://www.democracynature.org/dn/ vol9/takis_paideia.htm; also in D. A. Gabbard & W. Ross (Eds.), *Defending public schools* (Vol. I, Chap. 2). Westport, CT: Praeger.

Fotopoulos, T. (2005a, March 21). The neoliberal myths about globalisation. *The Inclusive Democracy Journal's Newsletter 11*. Retrieved September 14, 2005, from http:// www.inclusivedemocracy.org/journal/newsletter/neoliberal_myths.htm

Fotopoulos, T. (2005b, November 14). The European left and the myth of the European social model. *The Inclusive Democracy Journal's Newsletter 23*. Retrieved September 14, 2005, from http://www.inclusivedemocracy.org/journal/newsletter/ European_Left.htm

Hansen, M. H. (1991). *The Athenian democracy in the age of Demosthenes*. Oxford: Blackwell.

Human Development Report. (2005). Table 5.

Kuhn, T. S. (1970). *The structure of scientific revolutions*. Chicago: University of Chicago Press.

Lakatos, I. (1970). *Criticism and the growth of knowledge*. Cambridge: Cambridge University Press.

Chapter 42

Inclusive Schooling

Sheila Landers Macrine
St. Joseph's University

> The plight of persons with disabilities ... is a barometer for the "progress" or lack of it in our over-capitalized civilization. Disability and disability policy — past, present and future — is a tool for all to rate our present social order.
>
> **—Marta Russell**[1]

The concepts of equity, social justice, and democracy have become major concerns in education, acquiring a new intensity and urgency, particularly for students with learning disabilities in inclusive classrooms (Furman & Shields, 2003). This urgency is driven by increasing pluralism of Western industrialized societies and diversity in school populations (Goldring & Greenfield, 2002); the inadequate preparation of teachers to meet their needs (Carroll, 2003); and the achievement and economic gaps between mainstream and minoritized children, including the disabled (Coleman, 1990; Bowles & Gintis, 1976; Valenzuela, 1999). Additional factors include overrepresentation of students of color in special education, the racialized notions of ability (Ferri & Connor, 2005), and the growing injustices in schools, that is, national policies of accountability, standardized testing, and No Child Left Behind (Macrine, 2004); and neoliberal policies of downsizing and retrenchment (Pothier & Devlin, 2006; Furman & Shields, 2003; Larson & Ovando, 2001; Macedo, 1994). To address these concerns, models of educating disabled students must challenge inclusion and its inherent race, class, and gender exclusionary practices (Ferri & Connor, 2005). Only then can we aim to educate all children for participation in democracy (Giroux & Schmidt, 2004; Furman & Shields, 2003).

In this chapter, I argue that while inclusion purports to promote equity and social justice, it continues to segregate and marginalize students with learning disabilities along race, class, and gender lines. Interrupting these practices requires changes in how difference is perceived. By examining the tensions, I reveal that inclusion must advance via critical pluralism toward a social justice model of equity and access.

DISCOURSE ON DISABILITY

Some social theorists have argued that disability is constructed in relation to particular social and cultural practices independent of the loss of cognitive or physical function (Barton, 1996; Bérubé, 1996; Bogdan & Knoll, 1995; Fulcher, 1989, 1996; Goode, 1992; McDermott & Varenne, 1995). While in some cultures the meaning of disability is established by legal or professional institutions, in others these meanings emerge more from folk beliefs (Groce & Zola, 1993) and community understandings of people's roles (Edwards, 1997; Helander, 1995). In turn, societal values influence both models and meanings (Kalyanpu & Harry, 1999).

An analysis of education and inclusive practices also indicates differing interpretations of disability (Barton, 1996; Fulcher, 1989; Skrtic, 1995b). For instance, in many capitalist economies, nonproductive people — that is, those who do not contribute to the growth of the economy — are perceived as dependent or disabled (Hahn, 1986; Margonis, 2004). As Fulcher (1989, p. 24) pointed out, disability is contentious. Look at welfare state and education practices: Is this, or isn't it, a case of disability? And if so, how much, how disabled? Is this person feigning incapacity? Is this doctor working to lower the company's liability? Or is the doctor making an unbiased judgment? How should social institutions respond (segregate or integrate)? And how (with what resources)?

Disability discourses are broad ranging, with definitions underpinning fundamentals such as normalcy, health, bodily integrity, individuality, citizenship, and morality. Disabilities have been traditionally treated as medical or pathological conditions requiring intervention and correction. Naicker (1999) suggests that responses to inclusion are constructed by the various discourses on disability. Accordingly, Naicker (1999) cites four discourses of Fulcher's (1989): medical, lay, charity, and rights. Slee (1997) recognizes Fulcher's five discourses but suggested that five other theoretical perspectives — essentialist, social constructionist, materialist, postmodern, and disability — need to be added. For Skrtic (1995a) the framework of functionalist, interpretive, radical structuralist, and radical humanist is best to describe discourses around inclusion and disability. Finally, Dyson, Bailey, O'Brien, Rice, and Zigmond (1998) use three primary strands: critical, pragmatic, and rights (Van Rooyen, 2002).

Inclusion

While persons with learning disabilities are marginalized, the intent of reasonable accommodation is misunderstood, and the existence of the minority group — people with disabilities — in education is barely acknowledged (Rocco, 2002). Inclusion is supposed to provide equity and access for students with mental and physical disabilities, both academically and socially, in the general education classroom.

Historically, disabled students were segregated and mostly housed in institutions. A policy shift toward more options for inclusion for special needs students, who were denied access to the mainstream, came about through concerted efforts by parents, legislators (Miller, Strain, Boyd, Hunsicker, & Wu, 1992), and professional organizations (Division for Early Childhood, 1993). In 1975, Congress had determined that millions of disabled students were still not receiving an appropriate education, noting that more than half of the handicapped students did not receive the services that would enable them to have equal opportunity.[2] To fix this situation, Public Law (PL) 94-142 of 1975 was passed, providing all students with a Free and Appropriate Public Education (FAPE) and funding for disabled students in least restrictive environments (LREs) in special education programs.

Mainstreaming was adopted in an attempt to keep the LRE requirement in PL 94-142 and included disabled students participating in the nonacademic portions of the general education curriculum (Council for Exceptional Children [CEC], 2003). Students with special needs would receive their academic instruction in special classes and would spend lunch, art, recess, and so forth with their nondisabled peers. However, advocates for special education noted that mainstreaming provided far too little regular instruction, support, or accommodations for students with special needs (CEC, 2003).

In response, legislation called the Individuals with Disabilities Education Act Amendments of 1997 (IDEA 97; now PL 105-17) stated that students could not be excluded from the regular education classrooms because of their disabilities. The law requires that a continuum of services be made available for every student (CEC, 2003).

Out of this legislation, inclusion and collaboration evolved (CEC, 2003). Inclusion meant a commitment to every child, to the maximum extent, in the classroom he or she would regularly attend (Stainback & Stainback, 1990) — rather than pulling out the child for these services. So, inclusion was supposed to encompass all of the needs of every student with disabilities within the regular classroom (Hollaway, 1996). However, there have been a number of problems associated with special education diagnosis and placement in inclusive classrooms based on race, class, and gender.

Exclusion

The disproportion number of culturally and linguistically diverse students is among the most significant and intransigent problems of special education according to the National Research Council (NRC) (2002). Students of color (particularly male) and poor students are overidentified as having special needs, including learning disabled (LD), mildly or moderately mentally retarded (MMR), or emotionally disturbed (ED), and then easily deemed inappropriate for mainstreaming. Disabled students of color also experience inadequate special education services, low-quality curriculum and instruction, and unnecessary isolation from their nondisabled peers (Johnson, 2004). Moreover, inappropriate practices in both general and special education classrooms have resulted in overrepresentation, misclassification, and hardship for minority students, particularly black children (NRC, 2002). The continued significance of race as a predictor of special education disability identification, regardless of controls for a variety of other variables, leads to the contention that the process of special education referral and identification remains discriminatory (Ladner & Hammons, 2001; Losen & Orfield, 2002).

Social class or economic status also plays a significant role in overrepresentation of poor students in special education. It follows that minority children are disproportionately poor, and poverty is associated with higher rates of exposure to harmful toxins, including lead, alcohol, and tobacco, in early stages of development. Poor children are also more likely to be born with low birth weight and have poorer nutrition and environments less supportive of early cognitive and emotional development than their majority counterparts. The 18th Annual Report on Special Education to Congress suggested that poverty, and not ethnicity, is the most important factor influencing disproportion. Oakes and her colleagues explored how assumptions about race and class pervade school-based notions of ability as she quotes one teacher, "We all know that [tracking] has been a masquerade ... for institutional racism" (Oakes, Wells, Jones, & Datnow, 1997, p. 482).

Since the NCR report, much has changed in both general and special education. The proportion of minority students in special education has risen dramatically — to 35% in 2000 and an associated increase in the number of children served under IDEA. Many more of these students are receiving special education and related services in general education classrooms. Therefore, race, class, and gender play an important role in the construction of learning disabilities.

Segregation

To examine inclusion and segregation, we need to review the unfulfilled promises of two milestone pieces of legislation. Within the last two years, we have marked the 50th anniversary of *Brown v. Board of Education* (1954) and the 30th anniversary of IDEA (1975). The Supreme Court's *Brown v. Board of Education* decision concluded that in the field of public education the doctrine of "separate but equal" has no place and that separate educational facilities are inherently unequal. However, the Supreme Court left two glaring holes: It did not abolish segregation in other public areas (i.e., restaurants and restrooms), and it did not require the desegregation of public schools by any specific time. It did declare as unconstitutional the mandatory segregation that existed at that time in 21 states.

IDEA (1975), taking its cue from *Brown v. Board of Education*, was enacted to eliminate the public school segregation of children with developmental disabilities. Before Congress passed IDEA, nearly half of the nation's approximately 4 million disabled children were not receiving a public education (Losen & Orfield, 2002). The most recent reauthorization of IDEA in 2004 highlights the complex and contentious issues of overidentification and the disproportionate number of minority students in special education.

While the illegal practice of racial segregation in schools was challenged, dividing students according to ability has become a normalized category of marginalization for students of color (Ferri & Connor, 2005; Kauffman & Hallahan, 1995). Furthermore, students of color are overrepresented in 9 of the 13 disability categories and are more likely than white students to be placed in highly restrictive (exclusionary) educational settings (Losen & Orfield, 2002).

While race and disability histories overlap, they are distinct and support inclusion without connecting it to racial integration (Ferri & Connor, 2005). For example, white privilege and racialized concepts of ability have masked racial segregation. Today, students of color still face increased segregation, with most attending substandard schools in economically disadvantaged areas (Macrine, 2004; Orfield, Eaton, & Harvard Project on School Desegregation, 1996). *Brown v. Board of Education* highlighted the fact that segregation was harmful and unequal. Unfortunately, recent statistics are not encouraging and suggest that many gains in desegregation have been lost (Ferri & Connor, 2005). Despite the United States becoming more diverse in the 1990s, its schools also became more racially segregated (Frankenberg, Lee, & Orfield, 2003). The desegregation of black students, which increased continuously from the 1950s to the late 1980s, has now receded to levels not seen in three decades (Orfield, 2001). School desegregation and special education policies have both been criticized for contributing to two largely separate and unequal school systems (Linton, 1998; Lipsky and Gartner, 1996).

Nearly 30 years after the Education of All Handicapped Children Act (PL 94-142), many disabled students, especially a disproportionate number of students of color, remain separated from their peers because of culturally biased intelligence testing and unfair standardized achievement tests.

According to Ferri and Connor (2005), overt racially segregating school practices have led to covert forms, including some special education practices, for example, of overidentification of students of color as disabled. Furthermore, racism and ability discourses have converged, permitting racial segregation under the guise of "disability." Ferri and Connor (2005) locate the overrepresentation of students of color in segregated special education classrooms to the connected discourses of segregation and exclusion. Recent efforts to increase inclusion of disabled students in regular classrooms have resulted in similar resistance to school desegregation shortly after *Brown*.

Disability triggers racially disparate outcomes (Ferri & Connor, 2005). For white students, special education eligibility is more likely to guarantee access to extra support services, maintenance in general education classrooms, and accommodation for high-status examinations (Parrish, 2002). For students of color, however, the opposite can be the case (Oswald, Coutinho, & Best, 2002; Parrish, 2002; Fierros & Conroy, 2002; Osher, Woodruff, & Sims, 2002; Artiles, Rueda, Salazar, & Higareda 2002). These different outcomes are particularly problematic given the disproportionate number of black and Latino students identified as disabled and placed in highly segregated settings (Losen & Orfield, 2002). The intertwined histories of school desegregation and special education argue that race and disability should be understood as interactive social constructs and not distinct biological markers (Ferri & Connor, 2005).

Gender

Gender has been treated as either a nonissue or an organizational pathology in much of the disability literature (see Blackmore & Kenway, 1995, p. 237). Black males are more than twice as likely as Whites to be labeled mentally retarded (MR) in 38 states, emotionally disturbed (ED) in 29 states, and learning disabled in 8 states (Parrish, 2002). These labels continue to be overly ascribed to students of color, particularly black and Latino males (Osher et al., 2002). As a result, they are more likely to be removed from regular classrooms (Fierros & Conroy, 2002). In analyzing nationwide data collected by the Office of Civil Rights, Parrish (2002) concludes that white students are generally "only placed in more restrictive self-contained classes when they need intensive services. Students of color, however, may be more likely to be placed in the restrictive settings whether they require intensive services or not" (p. 26).

Cultural Politics

The sociopolitical context of education, particularly in light of the recent neoconservative tide, assumes that schools should produce human capital while legitimizing dominant definitions of knowledge and competence (Apple, 1996). Neoconservative reformers reason that, in an era of global competition and unprecedented economic growth, schools must produce a skilled and competitive labor force. Implied in this premise is that schools will have winners and losers (Apple, 1996; Varenne & McDermott, 1999). These policies have had dreadful consequences as they have become embodied in what some call "backlash pedagogies," with little awareness of human capacities and possibilities (Gutiérrez, Asato, Santos, & Gotanda, 2002).

As a result, schools and teachers have negative assumptions about students with disabilities. Disability is seen as a medical condition that prevents students from achieving high academic standards. Viewing disability as a medical condition existing within the individual leads to a pathological approach to assessment, diagnosis, prognosis, and intervention as necessary to identify and manage the disability (Burden, 1996; Archer & Green, 1996). The defective individual is subjected to diagnostic classification, regulation, and treatment (Slee, 1997). Adding to this notion of the defective individual, Naicker (1999, p. 13) states that the medical model constructs disability as an objective attribute, not a social construct, and as a natural and irremediable characteristic of the person. Van Rooyen (2002) continues that this construction — of people with impairments as disabled or unable and, because of this, disability as an objective characteristic of the person — leads to exclusion because they are seen as inadequate human beings who are unfit to be included in mainstream economic and social life. The medical discourse model links impairment with disability (Naicker, 1999).

In contrast, according to Van Rooyen (2002), organizations of disabled people clearly distinguish between *impairment,* as lacking part of a limb, organ, or mechanism of the body, and *disability,* as the disadvantage imposed by society's reactions (Sebba & Sachdev, 1997). Dyson & Forlin (1999) highlight the politicization of disability. They argue that historically, different cultures have constructed disability in different ways, but as modern states have used social policies to guide national responses to issues believed to be associated with disability (Van Rooyen, 2002).

The medical discourse is traditionally associated with institutionalization, differentiation, exclusion, regulation, dehumanization (Bèlanger, 2000), and special education practice (Kugelmass, 2001). Lloyd (2000) describes traditional medical models of disability as resulting in segregated educational provision based on treatment and remediation. However, within so-called inclusive education systems, the medical discourse is associated with exclusion within inclusion — the assessment of and provision for special needs.

Using this essentialistic medical model of disabilities fits with a functionalist perspective of modern social theorizing. Functionalism presupposes an objective, orderly, and rational social reality. Here, social problems or disabilities are storied as pathological or in need of fixing. Functionalist social scientists are rooted in positivistic methodologies to study disability (Skrtic, 1995), ascribing the individual as defective. This is critical in terms of instruction and how to meet the demands of the new standardization of curriculum. In this medical or defective model, the student with disabilities has little to offer society.

Critical Approach

In recent years, critical theorists have begun to examine the categorization of students, yet have omitted any mention of disability. Such omission gives credence to the continuation of two educational systems — one for disabled students and one for everyone else.

Critical pedagogy can address how relationships of inequality are (re)produced and transformed within educational institutions (Freire, 1972; McLaren, 1986, Weiler, 1991). The desire to challenge domination lies in the belief that education is where oppressive social relationships are played out in "the lived culture of individuals and groups" (Mohanty, 1994, p. 147). McLaren and Torres (1999) write that "critical pedagogy is about negotiating and transforming the relationship among classroom teaching, the production of knowledge, the institutional structures of the school, and the social and material relations of the wider community, society and nation-state" (p. 66).

Critical pedagogy challenges the inclusive classroom practices that oppress students, including how race, class, and gendered inequalities are (re)produced in schools (Althusser, 1971; Bowles & Gintis, 1976).

While some scholars address inclusion, their focus is on pluralism without examining the underlying power relations of how race and disability play out in schools. Some disability educators have addressed this (Johnson, 2004). Thousand et al. (1999) argue that Freirian perspectives can be used to promote inclusive education by eliciting voice from "students with special educational needs [who] often feel disempowered, disenfranchised, or silenced in school" (p. 324). Furthermore, Thousand et al. (1999), Erevelles (2000), and Gabel (2002) provide a starting point for exploring how inclusive practices can not only meet the immediate learning needs of students, but also lead to transformation and social justice. Erevelles (2000) contends that by addressing the insights of "materialist disability studies," the experience and understanding of all bodies/persons marked as "different" can be transformed. Furman and Shields (2003), when critiquing the role of schools in perpetuating inequality, argue that "injustice occurs when there is no space created into which students may bring their lived experiences, their whole selves inquisitive minds about the worlds and the words, when some voices are silenced and others privileged" (p. 17).

In a seminal book on the critical theory of disability Dianne Pothier and Richard Devlin (2006) argue that accommodating equality for the disabled is not a question of medicine/health, nor just an issue of sensitivity/compassion. Rather, it is a question of politics, of power and powerlessness, and that conventional notions of disability depend upon assumptions of misfortune and by implication privilege: "normal" over "abnormal." Thus, society is based on able-bodied and -minded norms and the best we can do is show sympathy/pity. This chapter supports a transformation of disability studies and urges a fresh understanding of participatory citizenship that includes the disabled, new policies to respond to their needs, and a new vision of their entitlements.

The interconnection of disability, race, class, gender, and sexuality is becoming more evident. Successful inclusion is based on the belief that, with commitment, all students can learn. Belief is not dictated by policy; it is based on experience, values, and a commitment to the success of all students (McGhie-Troff, 1999).

CONCLUSIONS

For full emancipation, disability culture, overall, must be relieved of the assumptions that marginalize it (Galvin, 2003). The paradox of disability culture may be stated as follows: How can we develop social justice models of equity and access regarding inclusive schooling for disabled students without falling into the same exclusionary practices that have served to create our divisive identifications in the first place? Conversely, how can we relinquish the practices (Galvin, 2003) of overidentification without losing the ability to claim identities? I argue, along with Galvin (2003), that by extricating disabilities and inclusive school practices from their origins in essentialist assumptions, disability culture and inclusive school practices can be reinvigorated and positively identified, ultimately creating educational experiences to educate all children to fully participate in democracy.

NOTES

1. Russell, M. (2005, April). Targeting disability. *Monthly Review, 56.*
2. Education for All Handicapped Children Act (EAHCA). (1998). Section 3(b)(3) as stated by the Council for Exceptional Children.

REFERENCES

Althusser, L. (1971). *Lenin and philosophy and other essays.* New York: Monthly Review Press.

Apple, M. W. (1996). *Cultural politics and education.* New York: Teachers College Press.

Archer, M., & Green, L. (1996). Classification of learning difficulties. In P. Engelbrecht, S. Kriegler, & M. Booysen (Eds.), *Perspectives on learning difficulties: International concerns and South African realities*. Pretoria: Van Schaik.

Artiles, A. J., Rueda, R., Salazar, I., & Higareda, J. (2002). *English learner representation in special education: Unpacking contextual influences in large urban school districts*. Cambridge, MA: Harvard Publishing Group.

Barton, L. (1996). *Disability and society: Emerging issues and insights*. Harlow, Essex: Addison Wesley Longman Ltd.

Bélanger, N. (2000). Inclusion of "pupils-who-need-extra-help": Social transactions in the accessibility of resource and mainstream classrooms. *International Journal of Inclusive Education 4*(3), 231–252.

Blackmore, J., & Kenway, J. (1995). Changing schools, teachers and curriculum: But what about the girls? In D. Corson (Ed.), *Discourse and power in educational organizations* (pp. 233–257). Toronto: OISE Press.

Bogdan, R. & Knoll, J. (1995). In E. L. Meyen & T. M. Skrtic (Eds.), *Special education and student disability: An Introduction. Traditional, emerging, and alternative perspectives* (4th ed., pp. 609–674). Denver, CO: Love Publishing.

Bogdan, R., & Knoll, J. (1995). The sociology of disability. In E. L. Meyen & T. M. Skrtic (Eds.), *Special education and student disability, an introduction: Traditional, emerging, and alternative perspectives* (4th ed., pp. 675–711). Denver, CO: Love Publishing.

Bowles, S., & Gintis, H. (1976). *Schooling in capitalist America: Educational reform and the contradictions of economic life*. New York: Basic Books.

Brown v. Board of Education. (1954). 347 U.S. 483.

Burden, R. (1996). Meaningful questions or meaningful answers: Worthwhile assessment in a changing world. In P. Engelbrecht, S. Kriegler, & M. Booysen (Eds.), *Perspectives on learning difficulties: International concerns and South African realities* (pp. 65–79). Pretoria: Van Schaik.

Carroll, A. (2003, Summer). The impact of teacher training in special education on the attitudes of Australian preservice general educators towards people with disabilities. *Teacher Education Quarterly*.

Coleman, J. S. (1990). *Equality and achievement in education*. San Francisco: Westview Press.

Division for Early Childhood (1993). DEC position statement on inclusion. *DEC Communicator, 19*(4), 4.

Dyson, A., Bailey, J., O'Brien, P., Rice, D., & Zigmond, N. (1998). *Inclusive education: A theoretical and comparative framework*. Newcastle-upon-Tyne: University of Newcastle-upon-Tyne.

Dyson, A., & Forlin, C. (1999). An international perspective on inclusion. In P. Engelbrecht, S. Kriegler, & M. Booysen (Eds.), *Perspectives on learning difficulties: International concerns and South African realities*. Pretoria: Van Schaik.

Education for All Handicapped Children Act (EAHCA). (1998). Section 3(b)(3) as stated by the Council for Exceptional Children.

Edwards, S. D. (1997). The moral status of intellectually disabled individuals. *Journal of Medical Philosophy, 22*, 129–142.

Erevelles, N. (2000). Educating unruly bodies: Critical pedagogy, disability studies and the politics of schooling. *Educational Theory, 50*, 25–48.

Ferri, B. A., & Connor, D. J. (2005) Tools of exclusion: Race, disability, and (re)segregated education. *Teachers College Record, 107*, 453–474. Retrieved February 11, 2006, from http://www.tcrecord.org

Fierros, E. G., & Conroy, J. W. (2002). Double jeopardy: An exploration of restrictiveness and race in special education. In D. J. Losen & G. Orfield (Eds.), *Racial inequity in special education* (pp. 39–70). Cambridge, MA: Harvard Education Press.

Frankenberg, E., Lee, C., & Orfield, G. (2003). *A multiracial society with segregated schools: Are we losing the dream?* (The Civil Rights Project). Cambridge, MA: Harvard University. Retrieved May 1, 2007 from http://www.civilrightsproject.harvard.edu

Freire, P. (1972). *Pedagogy of the oppressed.* New York: Penguin.

Gabel, S. (2002). *Breaking the silence: Disability studies in education.* New York: Peter Lang.

Galvin, R. (2003). The making of the disabled identity: A linguistic analysis of marginalisation. Disability Studies Quarterly, 23(2), 149–179. Retrieved May 1, 2007 from www.cds.hawaii.edu/DSQ/_articles_html.

Giroux, H., & Schmidt, M. (2004). Closing the achievement gap: A metaphor for children left behind. *Journal of Educational Change, 5,* 213–228.

Goldring, E., & Greenfield, W. (2002). Understanding the evolving concept of leadership in education: Roles, expectations and dilemmas. In J. Murphy (Ed.), *The educational leadership challenge: Redefining leadership in the 21st century* (NSSE Yearbook). Chicago: University of Chicago Press.

Goode, D. (1992). Who is Bobby? Ideology and method in the discovery of a Down syndrome person's competence. In P. M. Ferguson, D. L. Ferguson & S. J. Taylor (Eds.), *Interpreting disability: A qualitative reader* (pp. 197–212). New York: Teachers College Press.

Groce, N. E., & Zola, I. K. (1993). Multiculturalism, chronic illness, and disability. *Pediatrics, 91*(5), 1048–1055.

Gutiérrez, K., Asato, J., Santos, M., & Gotanda, N. (2002). Backlash pedagogy: Language and culture and the politics of reform. *The Review of Education, Pedagogy, and Cultural Studies, 24,* 335–351.

Hahn, H. (1986). Toward a politics of disability: definitions, disciplines and policies. *Disability, Handicap and Society, 1,* 121–138.

Helander, E. (1995). Sharing Opportunities: A Guide on Disabled People's Participation in Sustainable Human Development. Inter-Regional Programme for Disabled People. Geneva: United Nations Development Programme.

Holloway, F. (1996). Community psychiatric care: From libertarianism to coercion: Moral panic and mental health policy in Britain. Health *Care Analysis, 4,* 235–243.

Johnson, J. (2004). Universal instructional design and critical (communication) pedagogy: Strategies for voice, inclusion, and social justice/change. *Equity and Excellence in Education, 37,* 145–153.

Kalyanpu, M., & Harry, B. (1999). The legal and epistemological underpinnings of the construction of disability. In Kalyanpu, M. & Harry, B. (Eds.) (pp. 15–46), *Culture in Special Education.* Baltimore: Paul H. Brookes.

Kauffman, J. M., & Hallahan, D. P. (Eds.). (1995). *The illusion of full inclusion: A comprehensive critique of a current special education bandwagon.* Austin, TX: Pro-Ed.

Kugelmass, J. (2001). Collaboration and compromise in creating and sustaining an inclusive school. *International Journal of Inclusive Education, 5,* 47–65.

Ladner, M., & Hammons, C. (2001). Special but unequal: Race and special education. In C. E. Finn, A. J. Rotherham, & C. R. Hokanso (Eds.), *Rethinking special education for a new century* (pp. 85–110). Washington, DC: Thomas B. Fordham.

Larson, C., & Ovando, C. (2001). *Confronting biases: The color of bureaucracy.* Florence, KY: Taylor & Francis.

Linton, S. (1998). *Claiming disability.* New York: New York University Press.

Lipsky, D. K., & Gartner, A. (1996). Inclusive education and school restructuring. In W. Stainback & S. Stainback (Eds.), *Controversial issues confronting special education: Divergent perspectives* (pp. 3–15). Boston: Allyn & Bacon.

Lloyd, C. (2000). Excellence for all children — false promises! The failure of current policy for inclusive education and implications for schooling in the 21st century. *International Journal of Inclusive Education, 4*, 133–151.

Losen, D. J., & Orfield, G. (Eds.). (2002). *Racial inequality in special education.* Cambridge, MA: Harvard Education Press.

Macedo, D. (1994). *Literacies of power: What Americans are not allowed to know.* Boulder, CO: Westview Press.

Macrine, S. (2004). Cooking the books: Educational apartheid with No Child Left Behind. In D. Gabbard & E. W. Ross (Eds.), *Defending public schools* (pp. 141–156). Westport, CT: Praeger Press.

Margonis, F. (2004). From student resistance to educative engagement: A case study in building powerful student-teacher relationships. In C. Bingham & A. M. Sidorkin (Eds.), *No education without relation* (pp. 39–53). New York: Peter Lang.

McDermott, R. P., & Varenne, H. (1995). Culture, development, disability. In R. Jessor, A. Colby, & R. Shweder (Eds.), *Essays on ethnography and human development.* Chicago: University of Chicago Press.

McGhie-Troff, S. (1999). The "culture" of inclusion. Retrieved May 1, 2007 from http://www.ldonline.org/ld_indepth/legal_legislative/culture_of_inclusion.html

McLaren, P. (1986). Teacher education and the politics of engagement: The case for democratic schooling. *Harvard Educational Review, 56*, 213–238.

McLaren, P., & Torres, R. (1999). Racism and multicultural education: Rethinking "race" and "whiteness" in late capitalism. In S. May (Ed.), *Critical multiculturalism: Rethinking multtural and anti-racist education* (pp. 42–76). Philadelpha: Falmer Press.

Miller, G. (1997). *Becoming miracle workers: Language and meaning in brief therapy.* New York: Aldine de Gruyter.

Mohanty, C. (1994). On race and voice: Challenges for liberal education in the 1990's. In H. Giroux & P. McLaren (Eds.), *Between borders* (pp. 145–166). New York: Routledge.

Naicker, S. (1999). Inclusive education in South Africa. In P. Engelbrecht, S. Kriegler, & M. Booysen (Eds.), *Perspectives on learning difficulties: International concerns and South African realities.* Pretoria: Van Schaik.

National Research Council. (2002). National Council on Disability, back to school on civil rights: Advancing the federal commitment to leave no child behind. Author.

Oakes, J., Wells, A. S., Jones, M., & Datnow, A. (1997). Detracking: The social construction of ability, cultural politics, and resistance to reform. *Teachers College Record, 98*, 482–510.

Orfield, G. (2001). Schools more separate: Consequences of a decade of resegregation, Cambridge, MA, The Civil Rights Project, Harvard University.

Orfield, G., Eaton, S. E., & Harvard Project on School Desegregation. (1996). *Dismantling desegregation: The quiet reversal of Brown v. Board of Education.* New York: New Press.

Osher, D., Woodruff, D., & Sims, A. E. (2002). Schools make a difference: The overrepresentation of African American youth in special education and the juvenile justice system. In D. J. Losen & G. Orfield (Eds.), *Racial inequity in special education.* Cambridge, MA: Harvard Education Press.

Oswald, D. P., Coutinho, M. J., & Best, A. L. (2002). Community and school predictors of overrepresentation of minority children in special education. In D. Losen & G. Orfield (Eds.), *Racial inequity in special education* (pp. 194-206). Cambridge, MA: Harvard University Press.

Parrish, T. (2002). Racial disparities in the identification, funding, and provision of special education. In D. Losen & G. Orfield (Eds.), *Racial inequity in special education.* Cambridge, MA: Harvard University Press.

Pothier, D., & Devlin, R. (Eds.). (2006). *Critical disability theory: Essays in philosophy, politics, policy, and law.* Vancouver: University of British Columbia.

Riddell, S. (2005, August 1–4). *The classification of pupils at the educational margins: Shifting categories and frameworks.* Paper presented at Inclusive and Supportive Education Congress — International Special Education Conference Inclusion: Celebrating Diversity, Glasgow, Scotland.

Rocco, T. S. (2002, October 9–11). The invisible people: Disability, diversity, and issues of power in adult education. Paper presented at the Midwest Research-to-Practice Conference in Adult, Continuing, and Community Education, Northern Illinois University, DeKalb.

Sebba, J., & Sachdev, D. (1997). *What works in inclusive education, 2,* 29–43.

Skrtic, T. (1995a). *Disability and democracy: Reconstructing (special) education for postmodernity* (pp. 119–136). New York: Teachers College Press.

Skrtic, T. (1995b). The crisis in professional knowledge. In E. L. Meyen & T. M. Skrtic (Eds.), *Special education and student disability: An introduction.* Denver, CO: Love, p. 601.

Slee, R. (1997). Imported or important theory? *British Journal of Sociology of Education, 18,* 407–419.

Stainback, S., & Stainback, W. (1990). Inclusive schooling. In W. Stainback & S. Stainback (Eds.), *Support networks for inclusive schooling* (pp. 3–24). Baltimore: Paul H. Brookes.

Thousand, J., Diaz-Greenberg, R., Nevin, A., Cardelle-Elawar, M., Beckett, C., & Reese, R. (1999). Perspectives on a Freirean dialectic to promote inclusive education. *Remedial and Special Education, 20,* 323–327.

Valenzuela, A. (1999). *Subtractive schooling: U.S.-Mexican youth and the politics of caring.* Albany: SUNY Press.

Van Rooyen, B. (2002). In/exclusion and (dis)ability: (De)constructions of education white paper 6: Special needs education. Unpublished master's thesis, University of Stellenbosch, Stellenbosch.

Varenne, H. & McDermott, R. (1999). The Farrells and Kinneys at home: Literacies in action. In H. Varenne & R. McDermott (Eds.), *Successful failure: The school America builds* (pp. 45–62). Boulder, CO: Westview Press.

Weiler, K. (1991). Freire and a feminist pedagogy of difference. *Harvard Educational Review, 61,* 449–474.

Chapter 43

Critical Pedagogy

Curry Malott and Marc Pruyn
State University of New York–Buffalo and New Mexico State University

Marxists are not welcomed in academia. No big surprise there. But a new round of anti-Marxist "cleansing" has recently begun, and intensified, right along with the continued expansion of the neoliberal globalization project of Bush, Rumsfeld, Cheney, Blair, and capital in general. We need go no farther than looking at the case of one of the fellows cited above, Peter McLaren, and his recent chart-toping performance on UCLAProfs.com's list of the "Dirty Thirty" at UCLA (UCLAProfs.com, 2006a); the list generated by the neo-McCarthyite, and David Horowitz-inspired, "Students for Academic Freedom" (2006). UCLAProfs.com (2006a), also operating under the contested name of the "Bruin Alumni Association" (2006), even offered to pay students $100 to act as paid informants, going in to classes to take secret notes on left professors as part of their spying ring. While the offer of remuneration may no longer be on the table, the group continues to offer its sage advice to students on how to become model agents of capital (UCLAProfs.com, 2006b). And what is the crime? McLaren is accused not only of "poisoning" the minds of unsuspecting UCLA graduate students with his wacky ideas of social justice, civil rights, economic equity, and critique, but also of actually encouraging future teachers to propagate this lunacy in public schools. Imagine!

Here is the problem. Radicals and progressives of every stripe — Marxists (such as McLaren), anarchists (see the case of David Graber [Libcom.org, 2005]), feminists, antiracists (see the case of Ward Churchill [DemocracyNow.org, 2005]), antifascists (see the case of Colorado teacher Jay Bennish [ABC News, 2006]), and even evolutionists (Gibbons, 2006) — both within universities and in public schools, are under attack. They are undermining what Dave Hill (2003) has coined the "business plan *for* education."

Those of us in academia who do not have tenure, and especially those who contractually work semester by semester, are in particularly vulnerable positions and at the whims of increasingly business-dominated administrations (Zinn, 2005a). A result of this businessification, supra-regulation (No Child Left Behind [NCLB]), and intellectual "hit listing" is the not so subtle "push-back" (to borrow a term from Ronnie Reagan, back in the day) of academic freedom, freedom of speech, and unfettered intellectual exploration on college campuses and in the public schools. The critical/Marxist message to future teachers is "critique, analyze, and deconstruct," then "reconstruct, collectively and democratically, for social justice, equity, and community" (within schools, communities, and society). And to further silence this message is to support the current neoliberal trend of churning out unquestioning "good soldiers" for our global factories and armies of perpetual war.

In this chapter, we explore this most recent upturn in and intensification of "pogrom politics" against radicals in academia, and its implications for our collective pedagogical futures.

STAY IN SCHOOL

Glen Rikowski (2005) argues that rather than abandon schools, universities, and colleges because, with few exceptions, they serve as capital's training ground for their future labor force, Marxist educators in particular should work within them as agents of counterhegemony in an effort to transform their purpose against capital (refusing to serve as capital's hegemonists and propagandists), whether or not this risks our redundancy (i.e., "getting canned"). It has long been noted that Marxist and radical educators have been kept out of schools of education (and higher education generally) whenever possible, in an attempt to purposefully limit the range of possible discussion and debate on the efficacy of differing choices in terms of economic structures and political systems we might consider and advocate for among our students (Chomsky, 2000).

In a discussion on freedom within universities, and the lack thereof, Howard Zinn (2005a) argues that the "pluralism in thought that is required for truly free expression in higher education has never been realized. Its crucial elements — [such as] an ideologically diverse faculty ... have always been under attack from outside and from inside the colleges and universities" (p. 91).

In addition, we would add what Curry refers to as the "adjunctization" of the professoriate to Zinn's list of tactics used to keep counterhegemonic curricula and pedagogy out of higher education. In many colleges and universities throughout the United States, adjuncts currently teach as much as 80% of all undergraduate and graduate courses. Adjuncts are particularly vulnerable to punitive measures because they tend to work semester to semester, with no long-term contracts. Not only are adjuncts easy to dismiss, but they are also cost effective, earning far less than their tenured and tenure-track colleagues for comparable work.

Radical and revolutionary educators who make "class antagonisms" a focus of analysis in their teaching and scholarship, and who identify their politics with Marxism, are in constant danger of termination. But, more specifically, these scholars are also often viewed by both neoliberals and many on the non-Marxist educational left as being naïve, using outdated analyses. These critics often argue that class no longer exists and that Marxism is irrelevant (see McLaren & Farahmandpur, 2005). This, despite the fact that the wealthiest few in the world continue to amass ever-increasing concentrations of wealth via the thievery of the wage system; the reach of the capital's empire continues to extend almost without challenge; and we continue to be dragged into endless wars with endless "enemies" (McLaren & Farahmandpur, 2005). Given this, for many of us, Marxism and Marxist analyses are not only helpful, but necessary.

NCATE, THE BUSINESS PLAN FOR EDUCATION AND AN EXAMPLE OF REDUNDANCY

Once again, if we are "out" nontenured Marxists and stick to our principles, we are in constant danger of termination. This is the danger any revolutionary faces, a true soldier for the people, to paraphrase Huey P. Newton (1973/1995), co-founder and former defense minister of the revolutionary Black Panther Party, whose central focus was to "raise the consciousness of the masses through educational programs" (p. 16). That is, it is the responsibility of radical teachers to co-construct with the masses the tools for our collective liberation, critical thinking (way beyond Bloom), and class consciousness. As Marxists, these are the basic indispensable tools in the global struggle for emancipation from private property, the process of value production, and its divisive tendencies, such as white supremacy (Hill, 2003; Ignatiev, 1995; McLaren & Farahmandpur, 2005; Rikowski, 2005).

Otherwise, following state mandates, teachers serve the interests not of the many, but of the few, and are therefore at best naïve bystanders and at worst acting as enemies of the people, and thus not *educators* but *indoctrinators*. It is because true education is the freedom to question and to seek answers (Hill, 2003) that this is so. Without such opportunity for critical analysis, education becomes indoctrination and a hindrance to the liberation of people from the relationships that oppress them, namely, the labor-capital relationship.

Outlining capitalism's deleterious impact on education, focusing on how educations' *public* language, traditionally couched in hymns of duty and service, increasingly resembles the discourse of *private* capital, dominated by rantings on outcomes and performance (Hill, 2003). Even a superficial examination of the discourse of National Council for the Accreditation of Teacher Education (NCATE) quickly reveals the predominance of market rhetoric and the systems' business plan for teacher education. Such language and its manifestations in practice can now be observed invading schools of education like the smog of burning tires suffocating those who set them ablaze; like the oppressed Mexican worker, for example, suffering horrendous conditions engendered by the World Bank's "structural adjustment" policies and the North American Free Trade Agreement, in a desperate attempt to bear the bitter cold of a Mexican Borderlands winter under the flimsy shelter of cardboard and tin shacks (can you hum *"Casas de Cartón"*?). However, because the plight of relatively privileged radical professors pales in comparison to the conditions suffered by those toiling in Borderlands *maquiladora* factories, the responsibility for us to choose not to burn intellectual tires is great. In a classic essay on the responsibility of academics Chomsky (1966/1987) argues that

> intellectuals are in a position to expose the lies of governments, to analyze actions according to their causes and motives and often hidden intentions. In the Western world at least, they have the power that comes from political liberty, from access to information and freedom of expression. For a privileged minority, Western democracy provides the leisure, the facilities, and the training to seek the truth lying hidden behind the veil of distortion and misrepresentation, ideology, and class interest through which the events of current history are presented to us.... It is the responsibility of intellectuals to speak the truth and to expose lies. (p. 60)

While the freedom of academics that Chomsky highlights is currently under attack by right-wing corporate forces such as NCATE, it nevertheless remains true that professors within the United States, as well as other industrialized nations, remain in positions of privilege and therefore have a moral responsibility to use their power to academically rebel against the social form of value that has resulted in a material reality where "34.6 million Americans are living in poverty ... [and] 43.6 million Americans are lacking any access to health insurance" (McLaren & Farahmandpur, 2005, p. 8). While it is true that it is increasingly dangerous to be an untenured Marxist, even if we get "moved on" from time to time, we remain professors with PhDs and can usually always find part-time and even full-time teaching work that provides a standard of living well above the world's oppressed. As Antonia Darder and Gustavo Fischman noted at an American Educational Research Association (AERA) session a few years ago, "If you're a radical professor, and you haven't been fired a couple of times, you're not working hard enough!"

Let us now refocus on the accreditation association that is leaving a trail of burning tires wherever it goes. Again, the regulatory body driving teacher education programs to burn metaphorical tires, and away from its liberatory potential, we argue, is NCATE. In "Under Surveillance: NCATE and the Impoverishment of Education" (draft), Peter Taubman offers a rare and timely critique of the corporatizing impact of NCATE on teacher education programs. Summarizing the replacement of the language of education with the language of business Taubman argues that

> it is a system that translates students into "candidates," ways of evaluating and understanding students' and our own work into "targets" and "objectives," teaching into "delivery systems," intellectual engagement into "performances," understanding into "data aggregation" and "accountability," and schools of education and the colleges or universities in which they reside into "units." (p. 3)

In his analysis, Taubman takes special care to highlight NCATE's support for NCLB — a policy that has proven to serve the interests of the wealthy and the powerful, not the masses of people who comprise the working and middle classes. For example, Taubman cites Arthur E. Wise, who took control of NCATE in 1991, as arguing "accountability and high standards are empty promises without quality teaching.... NCATE welcomes President Bush's call that every child in America deserves a quality teacher" (p. 8). It has been well documented that the underlying motive behind NCLB is to hand public education over to private management companies for profit (see Coles, 2003; Karp, 2003; Miner, 2003). What such foci have ultimately meant for teacher education through NCATE is the dominance of the business plan for education.

Because education is arguably the primary method for creating indirect surplus value by creating workers willing to sell their labor power for a wage less than the value it produces, that is, as an ideological force of production, radicals tend not to be welcome candidates as future teachers. This is the driving force behind education policy for all levels, that is, the development of future workers willing to do whatever the job is required of them without talking back or asking the wrong questions. Highlighting this indoctrinating tendency of education Chomsky (2000) notes:

> Early on in your education you are socialized to understand the need to support the power structure, primarily corporations — the business class. The lesson you learn in the socialization through education is that if you don't support the interests of the people who have wealth and power, you don't survive very long. You are just weeded out of the system or marginalized. And schools succeed in the "indoctrination of the youth" — borrowing the Trilateral Commission's phrasing — by operating within a propaganda

framework that has the effect of distorting or suppressing unwanted ideas and information. (p. 17)

The idea Chomsky brings to the fore of being weeded out, if one does not take to capital's indoctrinating tendencies, is particularly relevant in the context of NCATE as Taubman stresses when he argues that "NCATE accreditation is all that stands between us and extinction" (p. 2). In other words, if schools of education do not comply with the terms NCATE has established and are not granted accreditation, then such teacher training programs could be weeded out, made redundant. The underlying message: Follow the party line or you will not be allowed to play the game. The hidden curriculum of NCATE, therefore, has a chilling effect and is engendering a culture of fear where professors tend to feel powerless at mounting an effective anti-NCATE resistance.

Given educators' relative economic privilege in capitalist societies such as the United States, it is not surprising that few, fearful of termination, choose the path of resistance. The power of the state therefore creates the conditions for self-censorship, which, in the long run, has the same toxic effect as burning tires. In this context, the question posed by Marxist educator, co-founder of the Rouge Forum, and former labor organizer Rich Gibson (2000), "How do I keep my ideals and still teach?" makes increasing sense. In other words, how do Marxist educators stay safe in increasingly impoverished business-dominated teacher education programs without burning tires, that is, without surrendering one's values and beliefs?

For many Marxist educators, such as Curry, the answer is that we move from job to job, surviving on public assistance and pieced-together part-time adjunct work, juggling various teaching loads across a wide range of urban universities and colleges. Resting just beneath the surface of the many short-term appointments littering our vitae are bruise patterns, the trace marks of the heavy hand of capital. Such description has been indicative of Curry's seven years of experience teaching at U.S. universities.

In the next section, we offer as a case study one of Curry's experiences (in the first person) in higher education of being moved on, in order to further analyze and explore the corporatization and NCATEization of education.

IN THE DEPARTMENT OF PEDAGOGY AND LEARNING AT SU

I held an instructor job teaching social studies methodology in the "Department of Pedagogy and Learning" (PL) at "Southwestern University" (SU). There I sharpened my skills at educating *against* oppression and *for* humanity, which, it turned out, required a lot of critical self-reflection (see Malott & Peña, 2004). One semester there came an ideologically disgruntled student, a student from the state's landed gentry. In the state where SU is located, such gentry — namely, large landholders, farmers, and ranchers — are most powerful. This gentry, as it so happens, also make up the majority of those who sit on SU's "Board of Governors," the ultimate governing body of the institution. So, this student wrote a letter — actually, later it came out that this student's mother had written the letter — to the president of SU and the chair of the Board of Governors, thus bypassing me (the instructor), the head of social studies education, the department, and the entire education college. In her letter, she complained that not only had I committed the cultural *couture* sin of wearing shorts to class, but also I had played a song in class that contained a naughty word: *fuck*.

I had played "Body Count" by rapper Ice-T. The song contained both the words *shit* and *fuck*, as well as sacrilegious language (*god damn*). What this European American female student actually took umbridge with, I believe, was the ideological discussion in our class of which this song was part. We had been discussing how, often, working-class people, and people of color in particular, perceive police as oppressive and their communities as prisons (not the road blocks, fences, and numbers of roofs). Since "Body Count" addresses some of these issues, I played it for the class, and we had a spirited and open discussion on the matter, a discussion where all points of view were presented and other examples from popular culture were referenced by the students. Ultimately, in my estimation, we had a rich, collectively constructed dialogue about working-class students and communities of color, and how issues of import to them might be made part of the official curriculum, problematized, and explored. But, of course, there was the issue of wearing shorts and the word *fuck*.

This woman's superficial and obfuscating complaints were enough to get me "reassigned" to a teacher/research assistant position, and effectively banned as an instructor from teacher education at SU. This reassigning occurred after I let all my supervisors and bosses know (the majority of who were and remain close allies) that I did not intend to water down my classes in any way. In other words, I let them know that under no circumstances would I burn tires. The official reason given to me for not being allowed to teach social studies methods courses was that I was not a certified public school teacher, which violated NCATE's law of who was allowed to teach classes required for certification, such as social studies methods.

Even though I had experience working with youth in public schools, I was deemed "unfit" because my work did not require that I become a certified public school teacher. However, such concerns were never an issue until I was put under scrutiny (as well as the fact that there were others at the institution working with future teachers without themselves having been certified teachers).

It was no secret that the complaining student never liked the focus of the course, which critiqued traditional social studies instruction and advocated for a critical multicultural social studies (CMSS), spending a considerable amount of time on what that CMSS might look like in practice (for more on CMSS, see the Borderlands Collective for Social Justice, 2006; Malott, 2005; Pruyn & Malott, 2001; Pruyn, Haworth, & Sánchez, 2004; Malott & Pruyn, 2006). It was also no secret that this student had no compunction with using naughty words herself. She was frequently overheard in the hallways outside of class using the word *fuck* in connection to a boyfriend who, it appeared, did not truly appreciate her. In the end, this case (one of several in my higher education teaching career) is an illuminating, and not uncommon, example of how NCATE is often used to exclude radical voices from our teacher preparation seminar rooms.

Contextualizing the SU Experience

While it remains true that more market friendly professors enjoy greater stability than their colleagues who teach and write against class, it is increasingly difficult, for even mainstream faculty, to toe the line, as NCATE influences teacher education programs to refocus attention from content and information to outcomes and so-called results. Before we get carried away with this technocratic analysis, let us not forget, of course, that content and pedagogy are not the only actors in this drama. Culture also plays a significant leading role in the dramatization of educational affairs. The culture of universities in general, and schools of education in particular, reflects a conservative, middle-class, "white" culture (McLaren, 1997) that tends not to take too kindly to infiltrators who do not value such homogenization or hegemonization, such as Curry, a Marxist punk rocker of European descent (Malott & Peña, 2004), or Marc, a tattooed European *estadounidense* activist and intellectual who draws on Marxism and anarchism.

NO CHILD LEFT BEHIND AND THE BUSINESS PLAN FOR PUBLIC EDUCATION

The connections between teacher education and public school policy in the United States are as clear as the connections between the process of value production and white supremacy. While capitalists rely on a divided, and thus weakened, working class unable to mount a unified resistance against their oppression, capitalist education is dependent on teacher education programs that will train teachers to support the capitalist imperative so they in turn teach their students to uncritically work within the system that exists. Leading the neoliberal charge to ensure public education serves the needs of capital through their business plan for education (Hill, 2003) is the Bush administration's No Child Left Behind Act of 2001 (McLaren & Farahmandpur, 2005).

It is argued by its creators and proponents that NCLB is a policy to increase the academic performance of underperforming schools, which disproportionately serve working-class students and students of color, through an increase in high-stakes standardized tests to ensure accountability. Not only do such tests have high stakes for students who face being held back if they do not pass, but the stakes are high for entire schools as they visage privatization if their student bodies do not pass such tests at high enough levels. Such has been the fate of many "failing" schools. The focus of NCLB testing is on math and reading, which has meant that if it is not on the test, it is not being taught. In many classrooms, the social studies — the content area that is the focus of our work in teacher education — as well as other important subjects have therefore been marginalized.

Uniquely, however, within the social studies there resides an overt potential for the co-creation of counterhegemonic knowledges and ways of viewing and action on the world. This is the case because social studies is the subject that directly concerns itself with citizenship formation. A critical multicultural social studies is envisioned as a potential way to counter the business plan for education, and other such ill-conceived antidemocratic shenanigans, through a Marxist and liberatory pedagogy where market forces are problematized as inherently undemocratic, challenging students to understand the role we play in our own oppression as workers, who produce, through our labor, that which oppresses us: capital. However, a focus on standardized testing limits teachers' ability to creatively employ their professionalism and potential counterhegemony, such as CMSS, as they are forced to "teach to the tests."

In addition to the testing craze, NCLB also endorses choice and vouchers, where students can opt out of attending failing schools and invest their state and federal education monies to privately run or charter schools, contributing to the privatization and commodification of public schools. School choice effectively transfers much needed funds away from already underfunded public schools that tend to serve working-class youngsters and students of color.

In New York City, for example, Mayor Michael Bloomberg's chancellor, Joel Klein, head of the city's Department of Education, in a 2004 address to the New York Charter School Association Conference, made it clear that "Charter Schools present a tremendous opportunity. I want them at the forefront of our reform effort here." The "tremendous opportunity" referred to by Klein becomes clear when one looks at his background. Klein, a transnational capitalist, was chief executive officer of Bertelsmann Inc., one of the world's largest media companies based in Germany, with annual revenue of $20 billion, employing over 76,000 people in 54 countries.

It is not surprising that Bloomberg — also a very wealthy capitalist — and Klein's ideas about education, among other things, represent the interests of their class, the ruling capitalist class. Likewise, it is similarly predictable that President George Bush's ideas about, and subsequent policies for, education serve the interests of his class, the ruling capitalist class, which is to maintain existing material relationships "expressed as an 'eternal law'" (Marx & Engels, 1996, p. 65).

RESISTANCE

Never has there been a more urgent time for teachers to refuse to burn tires and heed the challenge posed by capital's new imperialism, an imperialism that is threatening the democratic potential of a yet to be realized public education, uninfluenced by market forces and bourgeois politics.

A message needs to go out to radical/socialist/Marxist-friendly comrades able to give refuge to those professors and teachers unwilling to burn tires who have been pushed out of universities and public schools for what seem to be politically motivated reasons, as the system of education, under pressure from national accreditation associations such as NCATE and federal policies such as NCLB, restructures to fit the needs of global capital. Such trends have been observed by these two writers, from the NAFTA-ized Chihuahuan Borderlands of New Mexico (the *maquiladora/* sweatshop capital of the world) to Brooklyn, NY (indeed, the belly of the beast). It has been our intent that the teacher education classes that we teach consistently included uncompromising analyses of class, ethnicity, gender, sexuality, and their intersections. It has also been our intent to bring these stands and analyses to our scholarship (see Chávez Chávez, 2004; Malott, 2003; Malott & Carroll-Miranda, 2003; Malott & Peña, 2004; McLaren & McLaren, 2004; O'Donnell, Pruyn, & Chávez Chávez, 2004; Pruyn, 1999; Pruyn & Huerta-Charles, 2005). While continuing to support each other in whatever ways we can, we also need to continue to reiterate and expand on the reasons why it is important to be a radical teacher and uncompromisingly refuse to burn tires in this era of new imperialism (McLaren & Farahmandpur, 2005).

As a fundamental aspect of our professional and moral responsibility as academics and teachers, through our pedagogy and curricula both inside and outside of the classroom, we need to also support those people throughout the world who produce the cloths we dress ourselves with in the morning, who build the cars and trains we travel to work in, who grow the food that sustains our daily existence, who assemble the computers we write these very papers on — in short, those who directly produce all value. It is labor power that produces all value, the commodity that Rikowski (2005) argues is capital's weakest link, that is the substance of the social universe of capital. Because it resides in the hands of those relegated to the status of worker, it is capital's potential downfall. It is capital's business plan for education that requires future workers not to get the idea that they can unite with other oppressed people, take control of their labor power, and use it to create relationships and labor not based on creating value, but based instead on fulfilling human need in our own vision, to create nonalienated labor. Such materialization requires a humanizing education that will not materialize as long as tenured and nontenured radical educators alike, concerned with their own self-interests, willingly burn tires and pollute the educational environment, allowing their labor power to be contaminated with commodification and therefore alienation. We advocate Marxism against burning tires in this call to action.

REFERENCES

ABC News. (2006). Colorado teacher on leave for Bush comment: Students protest. Retrieved May 1, 2007 from http://abcnews.go.com/US/wireStory?id=1682341

Borderlands Collective for Social Justice. (2006). Critical multicultural social studies in the Borderlands. In V. Ooka Pang & E. W. Ross (Eds.), *Race, ethnicity and education: Principles of multicultural education.* New York: Greenwood.

Bruin Alumni Association. (2006). Retrieved May 1, 2007 from http://www.bruinalumni.com/

Chávez Chávez, R. (2004). Foreword. In Malott, C., & Peña, M. (Authors), *Punk rockers' revolution: A pedagogy of race, class and gender.* New York: Peter Lang.

Chomsky, N. (2000). *Chomsky on miseducation.* New York: Roman & Littlefield.

Chomsky, N. (1987). The responsibility of intellectuals. In James Peck (Ed.), *The Chomsky Reader* (pp. 59–155). New York: Pantheon. (Original work published 1966.)

Coles, G. (2003). Learning to read "scientifically." In L. Christensen & S. Karp (Eds.), *Rethinking school reform: Views from the classroom* (pp. 184–190). Milwaukee, WI: Rethinking Schools.

DemocracyNow.org. (2005). *The justice of roosting chickens: Ward Churchill speaks.* Retrieved May 1, 2007 from http://www.democracynow.org/article. pl?sid=05/02/18/157211

Gibbons, J. (2006, March 13). Evolution becomes hot topic at school board luncheon. *Missourian.* Retrieved May 1, 2007 from http://columbiamissourian. com/news/story.php?ID=18840

Gibson, R. (2000). Methods for social studies: How do I keep my ideals and still teach? *Renaissance Community Press.* Retrieved May 1, 2007 from http://www.pipeline. com/~rgibson

Hill, D. (2003). Global neo-liberalism, the deformation of education and resistance. *Journal for Critical Education Policy Studies, 1.* Retrieved May 1, 2007 from http://www.jceps.com/?pageID=article& articleID=7

Ignatiev, J. (1995). *How the Irish became white.* New York: Routledge.

Karp, S. (2003). Let them eat tests: NCLB and federal education policy. In L. Christensen & S. Karp (Eds.), *Rethinking school reform: Views from the classroom.* Milwaukee, WI: Rethinking Schools.

Libcom.org. (2005). Yale anarchist professor booted. Retrieved May 1, 2007 from http://libcom.org/forums/viewtopic.php?p=97376

Malott, C. (2003). The revolutionary potential of Sk8punk counter-cultural formations in an era of global capitalist exploitation and cooptation: A call to action. *Taboo: The Journal of Culture and Education, 7*, 95–102.

Malott, C. (2005). Karl Marx, radical education and Peter McLaren: Implications for the social studies. In M. Pruyn & L. Huerta-Charles (Eds.), *Teaching Peter McLaren: Paths of dissent.* New York: Peter Lang.

Malott, C., & Carroll-Miranda, J. (2003). PunKore scenes as revolutionary street pedagogy. *Journal for Critical Education Policy Studies, 1.* Retrieved May 1, 2007 from http://www.jceps.com/?pageID=article&articleID=7

Malott, C., & Peña, M. (2004). *Punk rockers' revolution: A pedagogy of race, class and gender.* New York: Peter Lang.

Malott, C., & Pruyn, M. (2006). Critical multicultural social studies: Marx and critical pedagogy. In E. W. Ross (Ed.), *The social studies curriculum: Purposes, problems and possibilities.* New York: SUNY.

Marx, K., & Engels, F. (1996). *The German ideology.* New York: International Publishers.

McLaren, P. (1997). *Revolutionary multiculturalism: Pedagogies of dissent for the new millennium.* Boulder, CO: Westview Press.

McLaren, P., & Farahmandpur, R. (2005). *Teaching against global capitalism and the new imperialism: A critical pedagogy.* New York: Roman & Littlefield.

McLaren, P., & McLaren, J. (2004). Afterword: Remaking the revolution. In Malott, C., & Peña, M. (Authors), *Punk rockers' revolution: A pedagogy of race, class and gender.* New York: Peter Lang.

Miner, B. (2003). For profits target education. In L. Christensen & S. Karp (Eds.), *Rethinking school reform: Views from the classroom* (pp. 176–182). Milwaukee, WI: Rethinking Schools.

Newton, H. (1995). *To die for the people: The writings of Huey P. Newton.* New York: Writers and Readers Publishing Group. (Original work published 1973.)

O'Donnell, J., Pruyn, M., & Chávez Chávez, R. (2004). *Social justice in these times.* New York: Information Age.

Pruyn, M. (1999). *Discourse wars in Gotham-west: A Latino immigrant urban tale of resistance and agency.* Boulder: Westview.

Pruyn, M., Haworth, R., & Sánchez, R. (2004). Critical multicultural social studies in the Borderlands: Resistance, contraband pedagogy and la lucha for social justice. In E. W. Ross & K. Vinson, *Defending public schools.* New York: Praeger.

Pruyn, M., & Huerta-Charles, L. (2005). *Teaching Peter McLaren: Paths of dissent.* New York: Peter Lang.

Pruyn, M., & Malott, C. (2001). Critical multicultural social studies: A teacher education case study. Paper presented at AERA, Seattle.

Rikowski, G. (2005). *The importance of being a radical educator. Students for academic freedom.* (2006). Retrieved May 1, 2007 from http://www.studentsforacademicfreedom. org/

Taubman, P. (Draft). *Under surveillance: NCATE and the impoverishment of education.*

Tucker, R. (1969). *The Marxian revolutionary idea: Essays on Marxist thought and its impact on radical movements.* New York: Norton.

UCLAProfs.com. (2006a). *The dirty thirty: Ranking the worst of the worst.* Retrieved May 1, 2007 from http://www.uclaprofs.com/articles/dirtythirty.html

UCLAProfs.com. (2006b). *UCLA students: Help UCLAProfs.* Retrieved May 1, 2007 from http://www.uclaprofs.com/studentshelp.html

Zinn, H. (2005a). *Howard Zinn on democratic education.* London: Paradigm Publishers.
Zinn, H. (2005b). *A people's history of the United States: 1492–present.* New York: Perennial.

Chapter 44

Socialist Pedagogy

Juha Suoranta and Peter McLaren
University of Tampere (Finland) and University of California–Los Angeles

Throughout history there have been numerous forms and practices of socialism and socialist pedagogies, often tightly confused with each other in the public debate. As much as we look forward to the day that capitalism will be described as part of the prehistory of socialist society, we readily acknowledge that the progenitors of socialism made their longest and most striking strides across the stage of world history during the Enlightenment (see Wilson, 2003).[1] Most modern forms of socialism consist of comprehensive, yet secular and often conflicting visions and worldviews with distinct views of society, human beings, education, and other earthly matters. But if there was one common idea in the vast array of different formulations of socialism, and their corresponding pedagogies, it had to do with the emphasis on the social and collective as well as the collaborative and equal character of societies and human beings.

Socialism throughout the 20th century has been largely seen as a casualty of Cold War politics. Western democracies and their vaunted political histories have often ignored or denigrated socialism as a desirable or even distinctive ideology, praxis, and philosophy. Particularly in North America, socialism and its pedagogical principles have often been viewed as ultimate threats to capitalist democracies, if not frequently demonized as a half-living, half-dead monstrosity still stalking humankind and the new world order. Part of this has to do with the failure of the political left in the United States, where establishment propaganda and political untruths have tended to become "part of the left's own intellectual apparatus" (Herman, 1997). But it is also because socialism has often been conflated with despotic regimes and totalitarian police states — Stalin's Soviet Union,

Mao's China, Pol Pot's Cambodia, and the current regime of North Korea being frequently cited examples.

Socialism and socialist pedagogy (as well as Marxism) have had several conceptual and historical uses both in social theory and in various political practices (see Burawoy & Wright, 2000). Sometimes — as in the above-mentioned cases — it has been propagated as a comprehensive worldview, often in the rigid forms of dogmatic enunciations. Other times socialism and socialist pedagogy have been dismissed as senseless and antiquated utopianism, with little relevance to social theory or praxis. Besides these uses, socialism has been treated as a worthy political philosophy containing ideas, insights, and arguments for social scientific analysis as well as for developing diverse social practices. In these contexts socialism has been defined not as a doctrine, body of ready-made truths, or ideology, but as an unfinished endeavor, an open "what if" category in need of reconstruction. In this sense the aim for truly critical social and educational theorists has always been to build arguments for socialist theory and pedagogy by seeing their promises, but also by understanding their limitations. Our own attempts to develop a radical humanistic socialism take the position that socialism and pedagogical socialist principles are not dead letters, but open pages in the book of social and economic justice yet to be written and rewritten by people struggling to build a truly egalitarian social order outside of capitalism's law of value.

AIMS OF SOCIALIST EDUCATION

While there is much talk about labor today and the decline of the labor movement, what is important for educators to keep in mind is *the social form that labor takes*. In capitalist societies, that social form is human capital (Rikowski, 2005). Schools are charged with educating a certain form of human capital, with socially producing labor power, and in doing so enhancing specific attributes of labor power that serve the interests of capital. In other words, schools educate the labor power needs of capital — for capital in general, for the national capital, for fractions of capital (manufacturing, finance, services, etc.), for sectors of capital (particular industries, etc.), or for individual capital (specific companies and enterprises, etc.) — and they also educate for functions of capital that cut across these categories of capitals (Rikowski, 2005).

It is important to note that Rikowski describes capital not only as the subsumption of concrete, living labor by abstract alienated labor, but also as a mode of being, as a unified social force that flows through our subjectivities, our bodies, our meaning-making capacities. Schools educate labor power by serving as a medium for its constitution or its social production in the service of capital. But schools are more than this, they do more than nourish labor power because all of capitalist society accomplishes that; in addition to producing capital in general, schools additionally *condition* labor power in the varying interests of the marketplace. But because labor power is a living commodity, and a highly contradictory one at that, it can be re-educated and shaped in the interests of building socialism, that is, in creating opportunities for the self-emancipation of the working class.

Labor power, as the capacity or potential to labor, does not have to serve its current master — capital. It serves the master only when it engages in *the act of laboring for a wage.* Because individuals can refuse to labor in the interests of capital accumulation, labor power can serve another cause — the cause of socialism. Socialist pedagogy can be used as a means of finding ways of transcending the contradictory aspects of labor power creation and creating different spaces where a de-reification, de-commodification, and decolonization of subjectivity can occur. Socialist pedagogy is an agonistic arena where the development of a discerning political subjectivity can be fashioned (recognizing that there will always be socially and self-imposed constraints).

From the angle of revolutionary critical pedagogy (a term coined by Paula Allman), socialist pedagogy is multifaceted in that it brings a Marxist humanist and socialist perspective to a wide range of policy and curriculum issues. The list of topics includes the globalization of capitalism, the marketization of education, neoliberalism and school reform, imperialism and capitalist schooling, and so on.

Revolutionary classrooms are prefigurative of socialism in the sense that they are connected to just social relations in the outside world. Classrooms based on socialist principles try to mirror in organization what students and teachers would collectively like to see in the world outside of schools — respect for everyone's ideas, tolerance of differences, a commitment to creativity and social and educational justice, the importance of working collectively, a willingness and desire to work hard for the betterment of humanity, and a commitment to antiracist, antisexist, and antihomophobic practices.

The core principles for a socialist pedagogy were set out by Karl Marx and Friedrich Engels in their *Communist Manifesto* in 1848: "Free education for all children in public schools. Abolition of children's factory labor in its present form. Combination of education with industrial production, etc." Marx did not write much about education as such, but since his time numerous authors in curriculum and policy making have appropriated from Marxist theory in advancing a critical pedagogy and socialist praxis.

The core idea of socialist pedagogy is its emphasis on the unity of human beings, and we are referring here to unity in the positive sense of "unity in diversity" as solidarity between people, or as a common good, and the equality of human beings irrespective of their class, race, gender, sexual orientation, or disabilities. An incipient socialist pedagogy can be seen in the following learning tasks of critical theory (Brookfield, 2005).

The first task, that of challenging ideology, is to set people free from the servitude of repressive ideas. But ideologies are hard to catch since they are tightly "embedded in language, social habits, and cultural forms that combine to shape the way we think about the world. Ideologies appear as common sense, as givens, rather than as beliefs that are deliberately skewed to support the interests of a powerful minority" (Brookfield, 2005, p. 41). A socialist pedagogy helps students to contest aspects of hegemony that affirm political control in the hands of the rich and powerful. Here Brookfield is using hegemony in the sense of "the way people learnt to accept as natural and in their own best interest an unjust social order" (Brookfield, 2005, p. 43). As he aptly points out, "the dark irony, the cruelty of hegemony, is that adults take pride in learning and acting on the beliefs and assumptions that work to enslave them. In learning diligently to live by these assumptions, people become their own jailers" (Brookfield, 2005, p. 44).

A socialist pedagogy is directed at unmasking power. This is accomplished by facilitating people to read the word and the world analytically and critically, and encouraging them to acknowledge and act on the power that they already possess (Brookfield, 2005, p. 48). A socialist pedagogy helps students overcome alienation and creates the context for the struggle for human freedom, which can only exist in a nonalienated world. As Brookfield (2005) notes, "alienation is antithetical to freedom, and the abolition of the former is essential to the realization of the latter" (p. 50). Alienation does not describe only capitalist conditions, but all the other forms of social life reducing human beings to commodities in the economics or infrastructure of capitalist society. A socialist pedagogy is also about learning about liberation. Although it emphasizes collective action, a place for reflective distancing is reserved in its pedagogical agenda. It thus sees momentarily reflective privacy not as retreat from collective solidarity, but a true revolutionary act, a deepening step into the real world (Brookfield, 2005, p. 51).

Yet another task for socialist pedagogy has to do with reclaiming reason (Brookfield, 2005, p. 56). An important element of reasoning is to direct it toward a good cause, to criticize inhuman circumstances, and to construct a better world. Reasoning concerns all spheres of life and can take various forms. In socialist pedagogy it can refer to basic literacy (reading, writing, math) and to economic, health, and media literacy. And finally, one of the central tasks of a social pedagogy is practicing democracy as part of the overall process of furthering political and economic transformation. Whatever the final purpose, socialist pedagogy is always political in a strict and concrete sense of the term: "It is intended to help people learn how to replace the exchange economy of capitalism with truly democratic socialism" (Brookfield, 2005, p. 351).

Socialist pedagogy aims at educating human beings as capable of thinking collectively, co-operatively, and in solidarity with their fellow human beings and often adopts an eco-socialist perspective with respect to the biosphere or nature. Socialist education fosters critical and analytical skills to comprehend the world, to read the world, and to act within and upon the world in ways that build the conditions necessary for a socialist society. In the context of socialist pedagogy, critical thinking does not refer to isolated cognitive faculties or new business liturgies found in management textbooks, but to social reality, in that its focus is on "common interests, rejecting the privatized, competitive ethic of capitalism, and preventing the emergence of inherited privilege" (Brookfield, 2005, p. 351). Critical thinking can thus lead to radical statements like the following by John Briggs (2005), a retired steel worker and WWII veteran: "Us capitalists, the wealthiest in the world, are at the same time the most savage, brutal, callous bastards since the Nazi regime, actual inheritors of their ideology and racism. Only a conscious working class can end the rationale that greed is good, that war is necessary evil.... There is no solution without a revolution by the workers of the world."

A more elaborated evaluation on working class's possibilities to change the world is given by Yates (2004), who states that organized labor needs to meet more consciously its racist bias, conservative, even antileft past (at least in the United States), and global challenges. The working class needs to educate itself, by creating more opportunities not only for labor education, but also for diverse literacy in economy, media, environment, health, culture, and aesthetics. This will eventually further to a working class and human way of looking at the world and ability to right measures to various sociopolitical matters. Furthermore, workers' self-education raises class consciousness and overall interest in being-in-the-world, a sense of a leftist and just culture.[2]

Furthermore, the working class needs to cooperate in building "more labor-intensive, smaller-scale, more localized, and energy-conserving production" (Yates, 2004). Other essential tasks for the workers of the world consist of "universal health insurance, meaningful job training, generous leave programs, universal education, and reduced working hours" (Yates, 2004). In addition, international solidarity and cooperation are high on the list of urgent tasks as well as environmental issues, for socialist pedagogy aims at balance among human beings and between human beings and nature.

What is needed more than ever today are pedagogies that connect the language of students', factory workers', cleaners', social workers', and so forth, everyday experiences to the larger struggle for autonomy and social justice.[3] And it is imperative that such pedagogies, as they are put into the service of building socialist communities of the future, do so in the spirit of pursuing genuine democracy and freedom outside of capital's law of value.

Many of today's socialist educators pursue locally rooted, self-reliant economies, designed to protect society from the corporate globalists. They work to decolonize cultural and political spaces and places of livelihood, to fight for antitrust legislation for the media, to replace indirect social labor (labor mediated by capital) with direct social labor, to live in balance with nature, and to replace the dominant culture of materialism with values integrated into a life economy.

Socialist educators develop a vision of the future that transcends the present but is still rooted in it, one that exists in the plane of immanence, and not in some sphere of mystical transcendence. It attempts to "speak the unspeakable" while remaining organically connected to the familiar and the mundane. Socialist educators acknowledge the presence of the possible in the contradictions that human beings live out daily in the messy realm of capital. They seek a concrete utopia where the subjunctive world of the "ought to be" can be wrought within the imperfect, partial, defective, and finite world of the "what is" by the dialectical act of absolute negation.

Socialist educators work toward a transformation of the social through a form of concrete as opposed to metaphysical transcendence, through entering into the subjunctive mode of what could be. Because they refuse to venture beyond the given, their quest for the transformation of the present into a new social order is not utopian but concrete utopian.

Not only must socialist educators understand the needs and capacities of human beings — with the goal of satisfying the former and fully developing the latter — but they need to express them in ways that will encourage new cultural formations, institutional structures, and social relations of production that can best help meet those needs and nurture those capacities to the fullest through democratic participation. Equally important is realizing through their self-activity and subjective self-awareness and formation that socialism is a collective enterprise that recognizes humankind's global interdependence, that respects diversity while at the same time building unity and solidarity. Socialist educators strive to bring about changes in the economic, social, and cultural order not by emptying out subjectivity, but by making possible the full development of human capacities for the benefit of all (Gulli, 2005).

Revolutionary critical pedagogy is a socialist pedagogy, but one that does not seek a predetermined form or blueprint of socialist society. Neither does it endorse the idea of the spontaneous self-organization of the multitude. Socialist educators seek to move beyond the struggle for a redistribution of value because such a position ignores the social form of value and assumes a priori the vampire-like inevitability of the market. Value needs to be transcended, not redistributed, since a socialist society cannot be built upon the principle of selling one's labor for a wage. Nor will it suffice to substitute collective capital for private capital. As Hudis (2004) argues, we are in a struggle to negate the value form of mediation, not produce it in different degrees, scales, or registers.

CONCLUSION

Socialist pedagogy defined as revolutionary critical pedagogy works within a socialist imaginary; that is, it operates from an understanding that the basis of education is political and that spaces need to be created where students can imagine a different world outside of capitalism's law of value (i.e., social form of labor), where alternatives to capitalism and capitalist institutions can be discussed and debated, and where dialogue can occur about why so many revolutions in past history turned into regimes of terror. It looks to create a world where social labor is no longer an indirect part of the total social labor but a direct part of it (Hudis, 2005a, 2005b); where a new mode of distribution can prevail not based on socially necessary labor time but on actual labor time; where alienated human relations are subsumed by authentically transparent ones; where freely associated individuals can successfully work toward a permanent revolution; where the division between mental and manual labor can be abolished; where patriarchal relations and other privileging hierarchies of oppression and exploitation can be ended; where we can truly exercise the principle "from each according to his or her ability and to each according to his or her need"; where we can traverse the terrain of universal rights unburdened by necessity, moving sensuously and fluidly within that ontological space where subjectivity is exercised as a form of capacity building and creative self-activity within and as a part of the social totality — a space where labor is no longer exploited and becomes a striving that will benefit all human beings, where labor refuses to be instrumentalized and commodified and ceases to be a compulsory activity; and where the full development of human capacity is encouraged.

NOTES

1. Some of these modern forms of socialism include but are not limited to African socialism, Christian socialism, communism, democratic socialism, guild socialism, humanist socialism, Islamic socialism, libertarian socialism, social democracy, syndicalism, utopian socialism, and their diverse variations in such orientations as Angka, Castroism, Juche, Leninism, Maoism, Situationism, Stalinism, and Trotskyism.
2. Working-class education has regained interest in both "new working-class studies" and radical adult education (Russo & Linkon, 2005; Nesbit, 2005). A multidisciplinary field of new working-class studies finds its foundations and inspiration from the early 20th-century worker education, Myles Horton's

and Don West's popular education and their fight for economic-social justice in the Highlander School, and Paulo Freire's (2005) pedagogy of the
oppressed. In radical adult education the very same approaches and figures
have long been part of the field's theory and practice, but often in rather
domesticated forms. The prolonged aversion of social class has nowadays
diminished in adult education discourse, and the concept of class has gained
new momentum.
  3. An expanded version of some of the ideas presented from here on can be
     found in Peter McLaren, "Fire and Dust," *International Journal of Progressive
     Education*, 1, 2005, retrieved from http://inased.org/mclaren.htm

REFERENCES

Briggs, J. (2005). Say you want a revolution. *The Progressive Populist, 12*, 4. Retrieved
    January 6, 2006, from www.populist.com/06.1.letters.html
Brookfield, S. (2005). *The power of critical theory.* San Francisco: Jossey-Bass.
Burawoy, M., & Wright, E. (2000). Sociological Marxism. Retrieved January 5,
    2006, from sociology.berkeley.edu/faculty/BURAWOY/burawoy_pdf/socio-
    logical.pdf
Freire, P. (2005). *Pedagogy of the oppressed* (30th anniv. ed.). New York: Continuum.
Gulli, B. (2005). The folly of utopia. *Situations, 1*, 161–191.
Herman, E. S. (1997). Pol Pot and Kissinger. On war criminality and impunity. Retrieved
    January 4, 2006, from www.zmag.org/zmag/articles/hermansept97.htm
Hudis, P. (2004). The death of the death of the subject. *Historical Materialism, 12*,
    147–168.
Hudis, P. (2005a, September 3). Organizational responsibility for developing a
    philosophically grounded alternative to capitalism. Report to National Ple-
    num of News and Letters Committees.
Hudis, P. (2005b, March 20). Directly and indirectly social labor: What kind of
    human relations can transcend capitalism? Presentation at Beyond Capital-
    ism series, Chicago.
Marx, K., & Engels, F. (1848). *Manifesto of the Communist Party.* Retrieved January 5, 2006,
    from www.marxists.org/archive/marx/works/1848/communist-manifesto/
Nesbit, T. (2005). *Class concerns: Adult education and social class (New Directions for
    Adult and Continuing Education 106).* San Francisco: Jossey-Bass.
Rikowski, G. (2005, February 14). Distillation: Education in Karl Marx's social uni-
    verse. Lunchtime Seminar, School of Education, University of East London,
    Barking Campus.
Russo, J., & Linkon, S. (2005). *New working-class studies.* Ithaca, NY: Cornell Uni-
    versity Press.
Wilson, E. (2003). *To the Finland station.* New York: Review Books. Retrieved May 1,
    2007 from en.wikipedia.org/wiki/To_the_Finland_Station
Yates, M. (2004). Can the working class change the world? *Monthly Review.* Retrieved
    May 1, 2007, January 6, 2006, from www.monthlyreview.org/0304yates.htm

Chapter 45

Critical Feminist Pedagogy

Jeanne F. Brady
St. Joseph's University

Immense social, economic, and cultural changes have occurred in our society in the last decade. Current events that have taken place globally have afforded those in power the opportunity to craft a political agenda that advances the neoliberal movement and revitalizes a neoconservative discourse nationally. In effect, the United States has, once again, re-emerged as an authoritarian, conservative society (Denzin & Lincoln, 2003; Duggan, 2003; Giroux, 2004). Neoliberalism, the dominant political economic ideology, which embraces free-market and corporate values over civic discourse and responsibility, is a broad-based cultural and political movement that poses a threat to democracy for many in our society. As Lisa Duggan (2003) suggests, "Neoliberalism cannot be abstracted from race and gender relations, or other cultural aspects of the body politic. Its legitimating discourse, social relations, and ideology are saturated with race, with gender, with sex, with religion, with ethnicity, and nationality" (p. 34). The corporate cultural values and discourses of neoliberalism have seeped into the educational context, with such practices as privatization, deregulation, and commercialization, in an effort to circumvent and ultimately supersede civic discourse and engagement. Sloan (2004) further reinforces this point when he states,

> Pushed aside by these corporate values and languages are discourses of social responsibility and public service. While cultivating profit-potential capabilities in schools may indeed increase stucritical, democratic education and civic responsibility. (p. 229)

In effect, this ideology has prompted a silent war against children in our schools, and in particular poor children and children of color.

Educators have important roles to play, and we must critically comprehend and actively challenge neoliberalism embedded within the educational context and reclaim schools as democratic public places for children and adults alike. Chandra Talpade Mohanty (2003) captures the expansive difficulties we face when she observes that "the political shifts to the right, accompanied by global capitalist hegemony, privatization, and increased religious, ethnic, and racial hatreds, pose very concrete challenges for feminists" (p. 34), in particular feminist pedagogues. While actively challenging neoliberalism, feminist theory and pedagogy may hold important lessons and promises for fostering democratic education and civic engagement in schools. To explore how pedagogy may contribute to the struggle against the neoliberal and conservative agendas, I will first present a brief overview of feminist theory and then address how a critical feminist pedagogy, linking feminist scholarship and political activism, can contribute to a more inclusive and democratic imperative in American education and school reform.

CONTEMPORARY FEMINIST THEORY

Feminist theory has evolved significantly over the past three decades and has formed a theoretically complex feminist practice. Feminism today, in its political, practical, and theoretical realms, represents various interpretations, signified by multiple theoretical perspectives, pedagogical approaches, and culturally diverse international movements (Braithwaite, 2002, pp. 335–344; Narayan, 1997; Nicholson, 1990; St. Pierre & Wanda Pillow, 2000). Transnational in nature, contemporary feminism affords spaces to embrace multiple positions so as not to define feminism as one conception or to create binarisms by placing one position in opposition to another. In practice, the commonalities of transnational feminism operate on a number of levels:

> At the level of daily life through the everyday acts that constitute our identities and relational communities; at the level of collective action in groups, networks, and movements constituted around feminist visions of social transformation; and at the level of theory, pedagogy, and textual creativity in the scholarly and writing practices of feminists engaged in the production of knowledge. (Mohanty, 2003, p. 5)

Transnational feminism allows for multiple positions of difference and diversity while at the same time supporting an overarching feminist philosophy that challenges us to think and act in particular ways. More specifically, it links the cultural politics of difference and identity with the social politics of justice and equality (Fraser, 1997; Fraser et al., 1998). In this sense, transnational feminism represents a politics in which people actively participate in the shaping of theories and practices of liberation by acknowledging both diversity and unity and at the same time focusing on the lives of the people who work and live in a multiracial and multicultural society.

Historically, the U.S. feminist debate was formulated in an attempt to identify and describe women's oppression, theorize its foundations and effects, and conceive ways to generate strategies for women's liberation (Hemmings, 2005; Brady, Dentith, & Hammett, forthcoming). It is no less important today that we acknowledge and challenge the specific gendered realities of oppression and exploitation. Yet, it is worth noting that focusing on shared forms of oppression is neither unproblematic nor the only basis on which feminists can develop a politics of solidarity. Rather, it is more important to emphasize that women should question their shared victimhood as the essential location of injustice since this reflects male supremacist thinking that to be female is to be victim. Instead, women should organize around their shared commonalities and their ability for self-determination and communal agency. Extending this point, it is important to emphasize that a politics of solidarity that allows for multiple positions of difference and diversity should also include men who are in opposition to logocentric and hierarchical values within the hegemonic patriarchal system. This is not to suggest that women should not represent themselves as much as it is to maintain that feminist politics is not limited to a specific gender.

One does not need to look too deeply to realize that the neoliberal agenda, embedded within present educational reform movements, does not address diversity and difference, but rather allows discrepancies based on gender as well as race identity, class location, ethnicity, and other forms of difference to continue. Contemporary educational reform, spurred by NCLB, even defined in terms of a gender-equitable one, does not promote the multiple spaces for all children to learn. Rather than point to the larger social structures that explain gender, race, and class inequities in schooling, such as accountability, high-stakes testing, gendered and ethnic division of labor, and the economy, NCLB adopts a premise that educational problems reside within the institution of schooling itself — believing that education can be the "great equalizer" capable of reforming society. This approach adheres to a dominant conception of schooling that supports a white, middle-class definition of knowledge. Children need to assimilate to be successful in this game by denying their own cultural identity, particularly poor children and children of color. In this sense, schooling for children in urban and rural communities is not connected to the larger multicultural society.

CRITICAL FEMINIST PEDAGOGY

As an educator I am interested in the relationship between transnational feminism and the politics of a critical pedagogy. A critical feminist pedagogy intersects a transnational feminism with critical praxis understood within the context of economic, political, and cultural constructs. Developing one's role as a critical feminist educator involves asking oneself questions about the nature of every theory and practice that determines the conditions of our environment. In this sense, theory as a form of both self- and cultural criticism is concerned with the issue of who speaks, for whom, under what conditions, and for what purpose. Theory in this case is not innocent. The bridging of these philosophies into a critical feminist pedagogy not only offers students and teachers the opportunity for raising questions about how the categories of race, class, and gender and other forms of oppression and privilege are shaped within the margins and centers of power, but also provides a new manner of reading history as a way of reclaiming power and identity. Moreover, a critical feminist pedagogy provides students and teachers with the opportunity to acknowledge the relevance and importance of different literacies, narratives, and experiences as part of a broader attempt to negotiate and transform the world in which they live. A critical feminist perspective, which incorporates multiple ways of knowing and understanding based on difference, can transform teaching and especially the interaction of knowledge, agency, and cultural identity that have been male biased and prescribed by white, middle-class, neoconservative values.

Guiding Principles of a Critical Feminist Pedagogy

To embrace the project of a critical feminist pedagogy, six guiding principles are addressed (Brady, 1995). First, a critical feminist pedagogy should engage in students' experience as central to teaching and learning. This means that educators need to accept that the learner is an active participant in the construction of knowledge in contrast to traditional educational experience, in which the learner is viewed as the receiver of knowledge. In this sense, a critical feminist pedagogy understands knowledge as something to be analyzed and understood by students and informed by their own experiences.

Second, students should be offered both the knowledge and skills that allow them to reclaim their voice and history so as to enable them to name new identities. By affirming students' experience and providing a safe space from which to speak of their own historical and cultural place, the opportunity can present itself for students to assume ownership and become active agents in their lives.

Third, students should be provided the opportunity to rewrite the relations between centers and margins as part of an effort to understand power and agency. Exploring the complexity of difference within power relations provides the opportunity to understand how these relations enable or silence different students who come out of diverse backgrounds.

Fourth, students should be given the opportunity to understand and reconstruct cultural differences, economic inequities, and social identities so as to produce knowledge and democratic practices. It is not enough to say that there will be unity with diversity, in which students will respect one another, but rather, a critical feminist pedagogy needs to allow for the creation of new forms of knowledge by breaking down old boundaries and permitting new connections that both legitimate and produce democratic social relations free of sexism, prejudice, and domination.

Fifth, students should be presented with a language of critique and possibility. In particular, a language needs to be developed that challenges sexist and racist assumptions and calls into question definitions of gender and other forms of domination. Furthermore, it should allow for the creation of imaginary possibilities to revise classroom praxis, enhance democratic education, and encourage civic engagement.

Finally, all of this must take place within the realm of teachers as engaged intellectuals that recognize the limits underlying their own views. To embrace the guiding principles of a critical feminist pedagogy in an attempt to include all children, educators need to acknowledge that their styles of teaching and interacting may need to change. This is not to say that educators are not well meaning or truly committed to high-quality education for all. But educators will need to shift paradigms from "banking education" that reduces learning to the dynamics of transmission and opposition, to the acknowledgment that there are multiple ways of knowing and create a space for constructive confrontation and critical interrogation. This challenges the assumption that knowledge flows in only one direction from teacher to student as though it were one-dimensional. Belief in this one-way flow of knowledge reflects the attitude that teachers cannot, or need not, learn from their students. When knowledge becomes more than information, that is, when it goes beyond the notion of banking education, it becomes connected to how one lives, behaves, and acts. Critical feminist pedagogy recognizes the power relationships that exist in the educational system, whether between student and teacher, teacher and principal, educational institutions and corporate values and imperatives, and so forth. This recognition allows authority to be unmasked and renegotiated, if need be, and within this the pedagogy becomes the means to empower the learner. It is within this realm that schools become a place to reinvent oneself and the world — from kindergarten through higher education. Schools and public spaces become sites of contention and conflict, and at times these ideas of (re)invention might run counter to the values and beliefs one learns from home. It also can place oneself at risk, challenging conformity and disrupting domination. In this sense, knowledge and practice become politicized.

Classrooms need to reflect a democratic setting, one that builds a community of difference that is safe — a zone of equality — which enhances intellectual rigor, promotes intellectual development, and encourages public service and civic engagement. Furthermore, knowledge needs to be rooted in respect for multiculturalism and difference. Knowledge and information must be made relevant so that they not only strengthen intellectual development, but also make a connection with the "every day," so as to expand our capacity to live more fully in the world.

CONCLUSION

Real-world thinking is a messy, multifaceted enterprise. A critical feminist pedagogy offers a different approach to educational theory and practice that calls for a revision of schooling so as to embrace a future that is more just, and to organize and act in a democratic way that embraces civic engagement in multiple sites. Included in these sites are multiple cultures represented by gender, race, ethnicity, sexual orientation, age, class, and a wide range of subcultures. A feminist critical pedagogy not only offers students and teachers the opportunity for raising questions about how these categories are shaped within the margins and centers of power, but also provides them with a new manner of reading and working as a way of reclaiming power and identity. Moreover, a critical feminist pedagogy provides students and teachers with the opportunity to acknowledge the relevance and importance of different experiences as part of a broader attempt to critically negotiate and transform the world in which they live.

Critical feminist pedagogy aims for education as the practice of freedom. It intends to rupture neoliberal/neoconservative discourses and present social and cultural practices. It is a philosophy of schooling directed at restructuring the relations of power in ways that enable all children to speak and act as subjects within democratic social relations. Its purpose is to end oppression while challenging the politics of domination. Difference and gender discourses not only provide new analyses for understanding how subject positions are constructed, but also reclaim the importance of linking the personal with the political.

REFERENCES

Brady, J. F. (1995). *Schooling young children: A feminist pedagogy for liberatory learning.* Albany: State University of New York Press.

Brady, J. F., Dentith, A., & Hammett, R. F. (Forthcoming). Feminisms and theories of leadership. In F. English (Ed.), *The Sage encyclopedia of educational leadership and administration.* Thousand Oaks, CA: Sage.

Braithwaite, A. (2002). The personal, the political, third-wave and postfeminisms. *Feminist Theory, 3*, 335–344.

Denzin, N., & Lincoln, Y. (Eds.). (2003). *9/11 in American culture.* Lanham, MD: Rowman & Littlefield.

Duggan, L. (2003). *The twilight of equality: Neoliberalism, cultural politics, and attack on democracy.* Boston: Beacon Press.

Fraser, N. (1997). *Justice interruptus: Critical reflections on the postsocialist condition.* New York: Routledge.

Fraser, N. & Honneth, A. (1998). *Redistribution of recognition? A political philosophical exchange.* London: Verso.

Giroux, H. A. (2004). *The terror of neoliberalism: Authoritarianism and the eclipse of democracy.* Boulder: Paradigm.

Hemmings, C. (2005). Telling feminist stories. *Feminist Theory, 6,* 2.

Mohanty, C. T. (2003). *Feminism without borders: Decolonizing theory, practicing solidarity.* Durham, NC: Duke University Press.

Narayan, U. (1997). *Dislocating cultures: Identities, traditions, and third-world feminism.* New York: Routledge.

Nicholson, L. (Ed.) (1990). *Feminism/postmodernism.* New York: Routledge.

Sloan, K. (2004). Curriculum and pedagogy and neoliberalism: Reclaiming public, democratic life in schools. *Journal of Curriculum and Pedagogy, 1,* 41.

St. Pierre, E., & Pillow, W. (Eds.) (2000). *Working the ruins: Feminist poststructural theory and methods in education.* New York: Routledge.

Chapter 46

Indigenous Pedagogy

Four Arrows
Fielding Graduate School

Most public K-16 education fosters the ideology behind neoliberalism. Tacit support for privatization and loss of the commons resonates throughout the educational system. The rule of the market, deregulation, and a quest for being more competitive in the global marketplace have become unchallenged assumptions that define the purpose of education in classrooms across the country. In concert with media propaganda and the religious right, our nation's education has managed to hypnotize people into believing there is no alternative to all of this. For example, in my own teacher education classes, the great majority of my soon-to-be teachers feel it would be "un-American" to have any kind of caps on CEO salaries that would allow for increased wages among lower-level workers. After a recent viewing of a documentary exposing the partisan deceit of Fox News, a number of people rationalized that network owner Rupert Murdock could have people say anything he wants on his programs because he owns it. As for knowledge regarding many of the most vital issues facing the world today, most are clueless and many could care less. They simply trust their national leaders.

The Association of American Colleges and Universities (AAC&U) recently called attention to this disinterest. In its announcement for a conference entitled "Liberal Education in an Era of Global Competition, Anti-Intellectualism, and Disinvestment," held in conjunction with the 62nd Annual Meeting of the American Conference of Academic Deans in January 2006, it states that "many students lack deep understanding of the world and of how global forces are shaping their futures — and AAC&U research suggests they actually lack interest in acquiring such understanding" (Association of American Colleges and Universities, 2006). Of course, neoliberals could easily use the AAC&U's announcement to support its own agenda. They would likely define this "lack of deep understanding" in terms of corporate profitability. However, in a statement defining what it means by a liberal education, the AAC&U does not define education in terms of global competition and profit, but rather sees a truly liberal education as one that

> prepares us to live responsible, productive, and creative lives in a dramatically changing world. It is an education that fosters a well grounded intellectual resilience, a disposition toward lifelong learning, and an acceptance of responsibility for the ethical consequences of our ideas and actions. Liberal education requires that we understand the foundations of knowledge and inquiry about nature, culture and society; that we master core skills of perception, analysis, and expression; that we cultivate a respect for truth. (University of Southern Maine, 2004)

The problem is that the Euro-centric model of education simply cannot achieve these holistic outcomes. Einstein said this often with such quips as "The only thing that interferes with my learning is my education." He recognized that education limits what American Indian educator Gregory Cajete (1994) calls "creative acts of perception." Einstein also believed that the highest purpose of education was to do service for the community. This emphasis is the hallmark of indigenous education. It is about thinking with the head and the heart. It is not less about money and more about spirit. It is about leaving a beautiful, healthful world to the seventh generation.

These are not romantic notions. In spite of rigorous efforts by a number of academics to discredit genuine accomplishments and potential contributions of indigenous worldviews and philosophy (Four Arrows, 2006), many others have endorsed the relevance and importance of them for a healthful future. A short list of these latter scholars would include, in addition to many indigenous researchers, such non-Indian notables as Patrick Slattery, Parker Palmer, Edward DeRoche, Noam Chomsky, Chet Bowers, Thom Hartmann, Ron Miller, Larry Bendtro, Lenneal Henderson, and David Gabbard.

What is it that these educators recognize as important and applicable for modern-day education, and how might indigenous pedagogy counter the harm done by the neoliberal paradigm? For starters, consider the generalized differences between typical Western values and typical indigenous ones and think about which ones are more likely to support the neoliberal agenda in terms of pedagogical applications. The following list is my own, with adaptations from the work of Robert Rhodes (1988) and others:

Western	Indigenous
Knowledge is always good	Mystery is often more appropriate
Competition reflects the natural order	Cooperation reflects the natural order
Possessions are important and good	People are important and good
Individual ownership is best	Group sharing is best
Frugality is valued	Generosity is valued
Technology rules	Relationships rule
Mastery over environment	Cooperation with environment
New ways always sought	Old ways may be more important
Emphasis on linear time	Emphasis on timelessness or circular time
Money is main goal	Helping is main goal
Standardization is best	Fitting the situation is best
Boss others	Let people decide for themselves
Leaders lead	Leaders advise
Women are minimized	Women are crucial
Mythology is not applicable to life	Mythology is applicable to life
Do something now	Wait until you understand before acting
Work and school are paramount	Family and relationships are paramount
Try if you are not sure	Be sure through observation and thinking
Books are a source of information	Memory is a source of information
Graduation is good	Learning is good
Learn theory, then apply	Learn in context
Ideas can be separated	It is all part of the whole
Control children	Allow children to learn for themselves
Teacher is authority	Teacher is facilitator
Discipline is external	Discipline is internal
Win-lose perspective	Win-win perspective
Pride is important	Humility is important
Rights emphasized	Responsibility emphasized
Art is entertainment	Art is a vehicle of connecting to the sacred[a]
One size fits all	Each person's way is honored
Authority is external	Authority is internal
External testing is important	Internal assessment is important

[a] More, A.J. (1987). Native Indian learning styles: A review for researchers and teachers. *Journal of American Indian Education*, 27, 17–29.

Being careful to note the problem of duality represented by this overly simplistic comparison and realizing that there are a number of cross-over relationships, it is still useful to use such a comparison to reflect on our current situation. With this in mind, which column most likely contains concepts that would support neoliberal objectives, and which would challenge them? Which would more likely lead to a happier, healthier world? Which best represents the ideals of democracy? Thomas Paine, Thomas Jefferson, and Benjaman Franklin answered this question long ago. For example, Paine (1797) said:

> Among the Indians there are not any of those spectacles of misery that poverty and want present to our eyes in the towns and streets of Europe.

Paine also learned from observing the First Nations that the European concept of land ownership was flawed. Paine admired the native way of equally distributing property. A major debate on this issue resulted in the word *happiness* being substituted for *property* in our Declaration of Independence.

Paine's study of the American Indian way of life helped him realize a number of ideas that today stand in the way or are destroyed by neoliberalism. For example, he learned that caring for the elderly should be a responsibility of the society. From observing Indian treatment of the elderly, he proposed a retirement pension for Americans who reached the age of 50. Paine opposed slavery and was one of the few founding fathers who refused to own slaves. He was against capital punishment and a champion of public education and a guaranteed minimum wage. He advocated for many other radical ideas that stem from a citizenry characterized by what are generally the stated goals of character education — generosity, caring, honesty, humility, courage, and respect — traits he saw the native people practicing without the need of legal repercussions for acting otherwise.

Paine's belief that First Nations offered the social capital for creating a new American society was shared by other founding fathers. Thomas Jefferson (1784/1955), referring directly to the concept of morality, wrote that Native Americans had never

> submitted themselves to any laws, any coercive power and shadow of government. Their only controls are their manners, and the moral sense of right and wrong.

Writing to Edward Carrington, Jefferson (1787) again connected character to social organization, citing American Indians as exemplary:

> The basis of our government being the opinion of the people, our very first object should be to keep that right; ... I am convinced that those societies [as the Indians] which live without government enjoy in their general mass an infinitely greater degree of happiness than those who live under European governments.

Jefferson knew the American Indians were not just running free and "wild in the woods,"[1] but were highly organized in societies guided by guidelines that rested upon the good character of the people. Unfortunately, unlike Paine, who neither owned slaves nor used his power for financial gain, Jefferson's actions as a slave owner did not match the character of his language.

Benjaman Franklin also had spent many hours with the First Nations people. He truly believed that happiness was more likely to come from the kind of societies he witnessed in First Nations than those he witnessed in Europe. He said, "No European who has tasted savage life can afterwards bear to live in our societies" (1770, p. 381).[2]

What Paine, Jefferson, and Franklin understood then, and Chomsky, Bowers, and Slattery understand now, about the American Indian or indigenous aboriginal worldview is what may be responsible for the policies of U.S. education that have continually tried to annihilate Indian thinking, from boarding school days to No Child Left Behind legislation. Most people now know about how boarding schools did this, but few consider how NCLB ignores the more healthful assumptions that would deter neoliberal policies. Taking just a few of the ideas from the indigenous side of the above table, I attempt to briefly identify how NCLB does this dirty work:

- *Cooperation is emphasized over competition.* NCLB emphasizes competition among students and between teachers, administrators, and schools. Worse, such competition ensures that there will be losers. Standardized tests ensure that half the children will always be "below average." Recent laws in Denver and elsewhere now tie test scores to teachers' salaries.
- *The arts are important.* NCLB virtually ignores the visual arts, and standardized tests focus almost exclusively on logical expression. Art and music are integral to indigenous peoples' learning, yet the high-stakes focus on math and reading have all but eliminated these from the curriculum. One second-grade test asks students to choose which of three photos illustrated will best help a person remember a visit to a national park. One photo is of a big camera on a tripod. Another is a throw-away camera. The third is a pad with colored pencils. The "correct" answer is the throw-away camera.
- *People are more important than possessions.* NCLB presupposes that certain skills and knowledge may ensure a certain degree of material success for some, yet it ignores the traditional indigenous belief that each person become who he or she is in ways that have little to do with material gain. Further, the labeling of students and their schools as "low performing" violates the doctrine of respect held by most indigenous people.

- *Generosity and sharing are vital.* The more extrinsic are the rewards and punishments used to motivate learning, the less generous will be the learner. NCLB relies on the leverage of rewards and punishments at every turn, and thus violates one of the most important cultural rights of American Indians and Alaskan natives, the right to grow into a generous person. This is because research shows that the more extrinsic rewards and punishments that are used to encourage virtues like generosity, the less likely these virtues will become a part of the individual's priorities.

- *Mythology is as important as history.* NCLB calls for states to ultimately develop history standards, but whose history? The current level of educational hegemony is such that most college students still do not know the atrocities associated with the Christopher Columbus legacy. What oppressive histories will be required knowledge on NCLB tests developed by states? As for the important cultural mythologies that are revealed in storytelling and the arts, they are entirely ignored by NCLB standards.

- *Timelessness makes more sense than time.* NCLB has specific and urgent timelines for student learning, yet traditional indigenous cultures see the world more in terms of place than linear time. Time perspectives are more circular, and the very notion of learning according to a rigid time schedule is counterintuitive to Indian people. Such timelessness relates to a better understanding of life and death than that which emerges from an overemphasis on timeliness.

- *The group is a priority.* NCLB ultimately is another form of rugged individualism that ensures that the "haves" will keep having and the "have-nots" will keep falling behind. Further, schools that are successful outside the narrow definitions of NCLB are to be disbanded under the law, thus hurting the larger community but promoting privatization.

- *Information should be relevant.* Indigenous learning makes sense when it is relevant to present life. Standardized tests and the kind of learning that generally precedes them relate to the unique circumstances and important issues facing the test takers or their communities. Even issues with global relevance, like the Iraq War or global warming, are blatantly absent from state tests attempting to comply with NCLB.

- *Holistic perspectives come before related details.* Indian cultures tend to see the larger, interconnected world as the priority in learning, before related details are learned. NCLB generally deals with fragmented information and seldom connects it to the larger picture (Rhodes, 1988, pp. 27, 21–29).

- *Testing is a self-reflective process.* NCLB and high-pressure mandates teach children that testing is mainly an external process out of the hands of learners. This is just the opposite view of indigenous approaches to teaching and learning that lead to authentic mastery.

- *Authentic humility is valued.* The very idea of becoming better than another school or group of students counters the indigenous understanding that each person and group has significance, and trying to be better violates this understanding.
- *Discipline is internal.* The ultimate authority for indigenous people comes from intrapersonal reflection on one's personal experience. Although ostracizing is a common external discipline used in extreme cases, even this ultimately results in the violator's self-discipline and reflection. The hallmark of NTSB is its extrinsic, punitive mandates from "on high."

Once educators begin to understand the value of indigenous values and educational philosophies, perhaps more people will come to value indigenous cultures and people themselves. NTSB, like most educational policies and practices, tends to ignore the many contributions to America. For example, two-thirds of all the vegetables now consumed in the world were cultivated by American Indians prior to the arrival of Columbus (Jaimes, 1991, pp. 7, 34–44), but it is unlikely any test questions on state exams will ever reflect this. There are many other contributions that indigenous ways of thinking about teaching and learning can offer to counterbalance the out-of-control destruction perpetrated by the current neoliberal way of thinking. It is past time for rethinking the antagonistic dualisms that allow American hegemony to dominate current approaches to the world's many challenges. If this rethinking does not occur in education, there will be little hope for future generations to cope with the terrible legacy we have already guaranteed them. It is time for curriculum to follow Patrick Slattery's advice:

> Curriculum development in the postmodern era also includes attention to the wisdom embedded in Native American spirituality, for it is in the very sacred land of the native people that American education now finds its home. (Slattery, 1995, p. 79)

NOTES

1. As mentioned earlier, a number of books continue to be written that disparage First Nations that have obvious neoliberal agendas. Consider, for example, Whelan's *Wild in the Woods: The Myth of the Noble Eco-Savage*, sponsored by the Institute of Economic Affairs, a right-wing think tank.
2. For a thorough listing of quotes from the founding fathers that praise the worldview of the native indigenous people of their times, see Johansen, B. E., & Grinde, D. A. (1991). *Exemplar of liberty: Native America and the evolution of democracy.* Omaha: University of Nebraska.

REFERENCES

Association of American Colleges and Universities. (2006). Conference announce-
ment for January 25–28, 2006, entitled "Liberal Education in an Era of Global
Competition, Anti-Intellectualism, and Disinvestment." Retrieved November
12, 2005, from http://www.aacu-edu.org/meetings/annualmeeting/index.cfm
Cajete, G. (1994). *Look to the mountain: An ecology of indigenous education.* Durango,
CO: Kavaki Press.
Four Arrows. (2006). *Unlearning the language of conquest: Scholars expose anti-Indianism
in America.* Austin, TX: University of Texas Press.
Franklin, B. (1770). Marginalia. In Labaree L.W. (Ed.), *The Franklin Papers* (Vol.
17) New Haven, CT: Yale University Press.
Jaimes, M. A. (1991). The stone age revisited: An indigenous view of primitivism,
industrialization, and the labor process. *Wicazo Sa Review,* 33–34.
Jefferson, T. (1955). *Notes on the state of Virginia* (W. Peden, Ed.). Chapel Hill: Uni-
versity of North Carolina Press. (Original work published 1784.)
Jefferson, T., to Carrington. (1787, January 16). In Boyd (Ed.), *Jefferson Papers*
(Vol. 11).
Johansen, B. (1982). *Forgotten founders: Benjamin Franklin, the Iroquois, and the ratio-
nale for the American revolution.* Boston: Harvard Common/Gambit.
More, A. J. (1987). Native Indian learning styles: A review for researchers and
teachers. *Journal of American Indian Education, 27,* 1.
Paine, T. (1797). Agrarian justice. Retrieved November 12, 2005, from http://www.
ssa.gov/history/paine4.html
Rhodes, R. W. (1988). Holistic teaching/learning for Native American students.
Journal of American Indian Education, 27, 21–29.
Slattery, P. (1995). *Curriculum development in the postmodern era.* New York:
Garland.
University of Southern Maine. (2004). *A liberal education defined.* Retrieved November
12, 2005, from http://www.usm.maine.edu/davis-grant/liberallearning.pdf
Whelen, R. (1999). *Wild in the woods: The myth of the noble eco-savage.* London: The
Environment Unit, Institute of Economic Affairs.

Chapter 47

Ecological Literacy

Dana L. Stuchul and Madhu Suri Prakash
Pennsylvania State University

We are all connected. Such is the lesson taught by ecology. We drive a car. The waste products of internal combustion float into the atmosphere. In the atmosphere, these materials are changed chemically, falling back to the ground as acid rain, remaining and joining a layer of gases that act as a giant pane of glass, much like that which warms a greenhouse.

To make the car go, we need more and more gasoline. No matter whether the engine is "efficient" or "hybridized," it takes fuel. To secure this fuel, ever increasingly risky and oftentimes violent measures are needed. Off-shore drilling. On-shore drilling. Military persons for the protection of the point of extraction. Everything is connected. The factories to refine the fuel, the factories to manufacture and assemble the vehicle, the infrastructure of concrete, asphalt, and steel to justify its use.

By means of the car or the bus, we buy food at the nearby grocery store. Food that has toured one or several nations. Food that has been sprayed, injected, packaged. Most of this food, having undergone some mysterious transformation called processing, is likely to contain substances that over time, and when joined with the other substances that we will drink, breathe, or absorb, will harm us. More connections.

Looking a little further into this food that will find its way onto our table and into our bodies, we will soon find that to grow it, in some distant or not so distant place, farm workers are likely to be enslaved. Poisoned, or made sterile. To compete, some of these workers will grow for "market," their efforts stretched to grow for their own subsistence. Others will be compelled to join the "economy," where their products — a function of comparative advantage — are likely over time to yield increasingly smaller returns.

To "get ahead," some of these workers, perhaps even to qualify for work, will require schooling. There they will learn the language of commerce, their own language falling into marginal utility. Their own understanding of local soils, growing conditions, seed variety, and more will be, in a few generations, forgotten.

Our food connected to the loss of languages? Our driving connected to military expansion? The economy connected to altered landscapes, communities in decline, large-scale highways, and the superstores whose logic rests on fuel and vehicles? Connections everywhere.

Back in our own communities, cars, roads, and fuel will soon betray their relationship to prisons, landfills, and waste incineration. Pollution, cancers, depression, wars. We have learned well the core lesson provided by ecology: interconnection. Or have we?

Ecological and environmental science/studies, ecological literacy, environmental education, sustainability studies, education for the commons — these contemporary iterations of older efforts that include nature studies, outdoor education, and conservation education (Wenden, 2004, p. 11) — have revealed what had formerly been concealed: connections or relationships. Prior to the late 1940s, a predominantly mechanistic understanding of the world with a consequent identification, definition, and analysis of its parts presided. In the preceding six decades, our thoughts, our thinking, and our actions have been colonized by systems.

The epistemological shift — from knowing that focuses on the parts within the whole, on the phenomena in themselves — to how the presence or absence of each phenomenon alters or relates to other observed differences and to the whole is what we have named the systems shift. With this shift, relationships among parts that are themselves systems within larger systems are central. Dynamics, exchanges, regulation, emergence, and so forth are the new matter that matters. Arney (1991) writes,

> Systems thinking is offered as a corrective to the kind of vision that apprehends the complexity of a thing by seeing it, as Descartes taught the West to do, in terms of the simple parts that compose it and in terms of the simple relations that drive it. To see the world from a systems perspective, one must see connectedness instead of boundaries and irreducible organization instead of well-articulated, interacting parts. Systems thinking gathers everything together without discrimination or prejudice. (p. 48)

With the systems shift, a collection of concepts — feedback, control, information, complexity, self-organization, self-reproduction, autonomy, networks, connectionism, and adaptation (Heylighen & Joslyn, 2002) — are applicable to all relationships, as there is no reality or entity that cannot be understood as a system. Fields such as biology, psychology, cybernetics, management, and mathematics have provided particularly fruitful soils for growth of systems thinking catalyzed by the systems shift. Education endeavors to keep pace. Education partnered with ecology makes substantial use of the systems shift in its compulsion to explain and effect "purposiveness or goal-directed behavior, an essential characteristic of mind and life, in terms of control and information" (Heylighen & Joslyn, 2002, p. 3).

Our taken-for-granted, imperceptible means for apprehending the world now focus on the gooey in between, the interstitial zones, the traverses, crevices, gaps, and translations. In seeking to understand connections or relationships, relationships among relationships, the systems shift has abandoned the quest for complete control of anything. Given the inherent incomprehensibility and irreducible uncertainty of relationships, control is sacrificed to management. In monitoring parameters and information loops, the systems analyst makes adjustments, "tweaking" a system toward favorable ends. Neither conquerors nor controllers, as Meadows (2001) states, we "dance with systems."

To dance, systems thinkers dream up models, conjecture about inputs, perform analysis of feedback, manage information, and adjust parameters. Whether the system is a field, a city, a curriculum, a government, a neighborhood, a pond, or a body, management of information about the system in the direction of the system's stabilization is possible utilizing systems thinking. Yet, within all-encompassing systems, who is the dancer who dances?

Laszlo (1972), Meadows (2001), Bowers (2003), and Capra (1996, 2005) — among the more recognizable proponents of ecological consciousness, education for sustainability, ecological literacy, and so forth — promote what Arney (2000) names the eco-cratic discourse. In this discourse, the systems shift features prominently. Rather than the eco-cratic discourse and its heavy inflection of systems concepts and language, we propose a return to common sense. Consideration of language, thought, and re-embodiment is central to this return.

Our difficulties with the systems shift begin with its implied ethical orientation. Proponents claim that thought and action that elevate holism, interconnection, and complexity necessarily suggests social egalitarianism. Meadows (2001) writes,

> The real system is interconnected. No part of the human race is separate either from other human beings or from the global ecosystem. It will not be possible in this integrated world for your heart to succeed if your lungs fail, or for your company to succeed if your workers fail, or for the rich in Los Angeles to succeed if the poor in Los Angeles fail, or for Europe to succeed if Africa fails, or for the global economy to succeed if the global environment fails.... As with everything else about systems, most people already know the interconnections that make moral and practical rules turn out to be the same rules.

Consider, following Meadows's optimism about moral and practical rules, how the systems thinker might respond. Having recognized a connection between car driving and cultural annihilation within the underdeveloped world, the systems thinker might construct new ways of thinking about cars, communities, and cultures. Soon, the systems thinker *qua* car driver of the North — given new awareness of her connection to and inherent equality with the indigenous *campesino* of the South — no longer understands driving as morally neutral. In driving her car, the connection between her action and the cultural survival of the *campesino* becomes more clear. In time, to drive becomes untenable. The Northerner is now compelled to make practical her moral conviction against car driving.

In the less than optimistic counterposition, aware of the connections between driving and death (of cultures), this same systems thinker *qua* car driver recognizes that feedback within the system (earth) will soon yield adjustments that include a degree of "die-off." Lynn Margulis, an early promoter of the systems shift, further clarifies this morbid evolutionary direction.

> This has always been the way of the world. If stress is severe enough, only tolerant organisms survive. ... Darwinian natural selection is the ultimate ancient Gaian feedback system upon which all the newer technological and behavioral ones are based. ... If catastrophe strikes, as it regularly has in life's history, some options will no longer be viable. But their expiration, in the form of death or extinction, makes the biosphere as a whole stronger, more complex, and more resilient. (Excerpt in Sachs, 1993b, p. 191; L. Margulis & D. Sagan, M*icrocosmos: Four Billion Years of Evolution From Our Bacterial Ancestors* [New York: Summit Books, 1986], pp. 263–265.)

In the latter case, the moral dilemma made conscious via the systems shift finds its resolution in systems feedback, complexity, and resiliency. The car driver need not alter her practice given the ability of systems to adjust, regulate, and evolve. Solidarity between Northerner and Southerner notwithstanding, moral rules suggest only that relationships (e.g., the loss of cultures) will change over time. Systems thinking, rather than providing a moral imperative to change one's own practice, evokes a calm assuredness that the earth system in its totality will become stronger over time despite catastrophe. The moral dilemma is resolved.

Rather than promoting "moral rules," our contention is that the systems shift suggests moral ambiguity. Though recognizing connectedness, the actor soon recognizes that her embeddedness within a complex weave of systems yields little actual room to affect any of the systems. She exists apart of systems ad infinitum. Her immune system lies within a body system within an ecosystem within a geosystem within a planetary system.

Connections everywhere. And changes within a given subsystem necessarily affect every other system. Such is the nature of interconnection.

With authority given to the "abstractions of information exchange," this "'grand theory' or universal framework" fails, however, in its concern for individual humans. A version of "antihumanistic" sociology, systems thinking "denies the ability of individuals and institutions to guide social change consciously" (Strijbos & Mitcham, 2005, p. 1883). Complexity within systems and the tendency of systems toward autopoiesis (self-creation) can no longer accommodate "actors." Yet, unaware of this epistemological trap — a recognition of connectedness with a concomitant loss of an ability to act — systems thinkers expend unlimited energy on efforts to affect or manage the organizing tendency of a given system. This is the only action available. Management of one's immune system is inextricably linked to management of the globe and its systems.

In both scenarios, the Northerner, in acquiring a new awareness of her connectedness to the Southerner, evolves from human person into global citizen replete with new responsibilities. The new being, *homo systematicus*, must oversee global indices and monitoring mechanisms while discerning her actions in light of system parameters. She is ever-more connected to everything though at the same time unable to actually affect anything.

With the advent of global citizenship, responsibility to act paradoxically achieves a previously unknown imperative. If the earth system is threatened, no limit to interventions, mandates, policies, and bodies with global reach and oversight will be accepted. "Can one imagine a more powerful motive for forcing the world in line than that of saving the planet?" (Sachs, 1993a, p. 19) Resources, decisions, rights, and so forth — all relational — will of necessity for global survival provide impetus for worldwide surveillance and management. A dubious globalism settles in.

Further, the co-optation — given the worldwide dominance of economics — of natural systems into economic systems extends this globalism. The systems shift opens the path for the commodification of every systems part. Water, forest, atmosphere, knowledge, genes, and organs are all transformed equally into either resource or sink. All are available as forms of capital needing more sophisticated controls within systems management. Natural and social capital advocates (Hawken, Lovins, & Lovins, 1999) wittingly contribute to the expansion of markets in the advocacy of new measures of living standards, social equity, and communalism. In essence, these new measures — a function of the systems shift — are universalizable, suggestive of one best way to live, to suffer, and to die. Also, these suggest a new, more insidious path of progress.

In this emerging context, development has a completely renewed meaning. In the eyes of certain eco-technocrats, this process is not just yesterday's debate on liberal economic reductionism destroying the traditional cultures all over the globe, but in addition, it appears as the embryonic-like development of a planetary organism and even entity. A techno-natural "Global Golem" is being built up through the Northern activity — or, if we are pessimistic, a Leviathan or a Big Alien.

This process, according to the geocrats, must not be hindered or delayed because it is perceived as the sense of the earth, the fruit of the whole life evolution, and thus of the billions and billions of lives that have ever animated the biosphere. Hence, it is no longer the moment to criticize development but, through its last green and sustainable version, to fulfill its mission. "'Real Teihardianism' is on the move" (pp. 186–187).

Real Teihardianism — the evolutionary convergence of all minds into a singular and global consciousness — is technological and socioeconomic development taken to its fullest conclusion. The purpose of history is revealed in this convergence, also known as the omega point. In the relationship between human beings and the natural world, feedback enables progress toward coevolution. Troubling is the inclusion of all tools or technologies as natural. The runaway development of increasingly complex and autonomous technologies is cited as evidence of the positive feedback loop that is accelerating the inevitable march toward the omega point (Smart, 2003). In this future moment, the human will be utterly eclipsed by technology. The enfleshed human who is alive will be no more. "Functions [such] as human language, self-awareness, rational-emotive insight, ethics, and consciousness, complex and carefully-tuned processes that we consider the essence of higher humanity, are likely to become fully accessible to tomorrow's technologic systems" (Smart, 2003). The systems shift accelerates the advance of science and technology, specifically the acceleration of computational capacity that portends the eclipse of the human/mind by the incomprehensibly faster, self-correcting, and self-creating computational system. With this eclipse, the systems shift places the human dancer, who no longer leads, in the role of perennial follower. Postbiological human ascends the evolutionary ladder.

SUMMARY

The lesson learned from ecology — connections — we contend has been anything but well learned. The infusion of systems language and thinking into education and ecology, while optimistically said to clarify moral and practical rules given an awareness of innumerable ecological and social ills, is revealed as morally ambivalent. While systems thinkers promote an epistemological stance that purportedly offers guidelines for action, this stance may less optimistically suggest deference, indifference, and inaction in the face of these same ills. While promoting awareness, relationships, even self-limitation (a decidedly ethically derived orientation), the combination of eco-literacy with systems thinking contributes to the advance of an all-encompassing globalism, management, and diminution of human action. The eco-discourse creates a stage for human action that is simultaneously hubris ridden in its global and globalizing aspirations and dehumanizing as human beings lose the evolutionary race to their technologies.

In his short address "Computer Literacy and the Cybernetic Dream," Ivan Illich (1997) wrote about the correspondence between the "computer-boggled mind-state" and a new "disembodied mode of perception." Illich, citing Merleau-Ponty, wrote, "Cyberneticism has become an ideology. In this ideology human creations are derived from natural information processes, which in turn have been conceived on the model of man-as-a-computer" (p. 2). Illich continued, "In this mind-state, science dreams up and 'constructs man and history on the basis of a few abstract indices' and for those who engage in this dreaming 'man in reality becomes that *manipulandum* which he takes himself to be.'" As systems-beings, living becomes management of one's body systems' indices, which are a subset of innumerable other systems requiring further management vigilance.

In our plea for a return to common sense, we follow Illich in his renunciation of the total incorporation of our being, our bodies, our living, suffering, and dying into the global system. This incorporation — the body as system within the ecological system — generates normative categories, such as health, responsibility, and so forth, each requiring maintenance. Saying a firm no to health as his responsibility in light of the systems shift, Illich explained,

> In a world which worships an ontology of systems, ethical responsibility is reduced to a legitimizing formality. The poisoning of the world, to which I contribute with my flight from New York to Frankfurt, is not the result of an irresponsible decision, but rather of my presence in an unjustifiable web of interconnections. It would be politically naïve, after health and responsibility have been made technically impossible, to somehow resurrect them through inclusion into a personal project; some kind of resistance demanded.... The new health requires the smooth integration of my immune system into a socio-economic world system. Being asked to take responsibility is, when seen more clearly, a demand for the destruction of meaning and self. And this proposed self-assignment to a system that cannot be experienced stands in stark contrast to suicide. It demands self-extinction in a world hostile to death. (Tijmes, 2002, pp. 212–213)

To have learned a disembodied connection to atmosphere, soil, and the other who stands nearby via the systems shift promoted within ecological literacy is to have not learned any ecological lesson. "Plugged in," with neither an Archimedean point nor "the concepts that would allow us to relate virtue to common soil, something vastly different from managing behavior on a shared planet," we forfeit the "bonds" to soil, "the connections that limit action, making practical virtue possible as modernization insulated us from plain dirt, from toil, flesh, soil and grave" (Illich, Groeneveld, & Hoinacki, 1991). A return to common sense, to sensing that is felt, shared, suffered, and attentive not to the abstract individual whose systems parameters are managed, but to the person in whose face one comes to know and to be known, requires an epistemological *askesis* of systems concepts, language, and thinking. Ecological literacy or awareness, a knowledge and stewardship of *oikos* (Greek *eco-*, meaning "home"), suggests that those struggling against the neoliberal/neoconservative agendas abandon systems and return to their common sense.

REFERENCES

Arney, W. R. (1991). *Experts in the age of systems*. Albuquerque, NM: University of New Mexico Press.

Arney, W. R. (2000). Experts and critics and the "eco-cratic" discourse. In W. R. Arney (Ed.), *Thoughts out of school* (pp. 149–157). New York: Peter Lang.

Bowers, C. A. (2003). *Mindful conservatism: Rethinking the ideological and educational basis of an ecologically sustainable future*. Lanham, MD: Rowman & Littlefield.

Capra, F. (1996). *The web of life: A new scientific understanding of living systems*. New York: Anchor Books, 1996.

Capra, F. (2005). How nature sustains the web of life. (preface). In M. Stone & Z. Barlow, *Ecological literacy: Educating our children for a sustainable world* (pp. xiii–xvi). San Francisco: Sierra Club Books.

Hawken, P., Lovins, A., & Lovins, L. H. (1999). *Natural capitalism: Creating the next industrial revolution*. Boston: Little, Brown & Co.

Heylighen, F., & Joslyn, C. (2002). Cybernetics and second-order cybernetics. In R. A. Myers (Ed.), *Encyclopedia of physical science and technology* (3rd ed., pp. 2–24), St. Louis, MO: Academic Press.

Illich, I. (1997, February). Computer literacy and the cybernetic dream. Unpublished lecture, Second National Science, Technology, and Society Conference, Washington, DC.

Illich, I., Groeneveld, S., & Hoinacki, L. (1991, Summer). Declaration on soil. *Whole Earth Review*. Retrieved May 1, 2007 from www/wholeearthmag.com/ArticleBin/238.html

Laszlo, E. (1972). *The systems view of the world: The natural philosophy of the new developments in the sciences*. New York: G. Braziller.

Meadows, D. (2001). Dancing with systems. Retrieved February 12, 2006, from http://www.sustainabilityinstitute.org/pubs/Dancing.html

Sachs, W. (1993a, March/April). Global uniformity. *Resergence, 151*, 18–19.

Sachs, W. (1993b). "Gaia": The globalitarian temptation, interview with Guy Beney. In W. Sachs (Ed.), *Global ecology: A new arena of political conflict* (pp. 179–193). London: Zed Books.

Smart, J. (2003). Considering the singularity: The coming age of autonomous intelligence. Retrieved February 12, 2006, from http://omegapoint.org

Strijbos, S., & Mitcham, C. (2005). Systems and systems thinking. In C. Mitcham, (Ed.), *Encyclopedia of science, technology, and ethics* (Vol. 4, pp. 1880–1883). Detroit: Macmillan Reference.

Tijmes, P. (2002). Ivan Illich's break with the past. In L. Hoinacki & C. Mitcham (Eds.), *The challenges of Ivan Illich: A collective reflection* (pp. 205–217). Albany, NY: SUNY Press.

Wenden, A. L. (2004). Introduction. In A. Wenden (Ed.), *Educating for a culture of social and ecological peace*. Albany, NY: SUNY Press.

Chapter 48

Technological Literacy

Mark D. Beatham
State University of New York at Plattsburgh

Teaching technological literacy for over a decade has revealed discernible patterns of thought from students about technology. To a great degree, these naive assumptions mirror common misunderstandings about technology in the general public. These patterns could be generally described as the following:

1. That technology means "hi-tech," that is, anything with a circuit board and nothing less.
2. That one can easily be a technophile or a technophobe (and each consistently divides itself simply this way, with few in between), and that technophobes can "take it or leave it."
3. That technology is neutral. This takes two common forms:
   a. It is politically neutral.
   b. Technology is one-way: One can use it without being used by it.

These naive assumptions are dangerous because they perpetuate an ignorance that threatens to undermine productive cognitive and social processes. People living in a technological culture must understand how that culture is constituted by its technologies. More specifically, people must understand how culture itself is constituted by its technology. This chapter addresses these misunderstandings about technology, points to more productive definitions, and uses these definitions to suggest more profitable ways of understanding digital technologies for the present and future cultures. Technology, I argue, is a relationship, *a mediation, and it goes all the way down.* The more that one can recognize this "ethic," the

511

more one can productively reconsider appropriate technologies in terms of clearly defined personal and social criteria.

TECHNOLOGY, THE ATOMISTIC WORLD, AND THE FORCED COLLECTIVE

Toward the end of his life, Laurens Van der Post (1994), South African ecologist, adventurer, and writer, wrote what was as close to an autobiography as his conscience would allow. In *The Voice of the Thunder*, Van der Post tried to account for the loss of what he considered the ethically superior, mythically richer way of the Bushman of his youth at the hands of modern "civilizing" forces of the West. But instead of blaming the loss on simple cultural ignorance or on a failure to adapt to material, technological, or cultural change, Van der Post identified something deeper, more constitutional in each culture's ethos. Van der Post characterized the Westerner ethos in this way:

> It is shown so clearly in the language he uses today and in what he writes with such a marked and strained rational obsession with that which is external, visible and felt through the senses and at best weighed in instruments of his own design. His vocabulary is increasingly desiccated and deprived of colour; and something, for which one can only use the antique word "magic," that was invested in the living word when it first burst like a star in the night into the consciousness of the first man, has vanished from his thought. The magic of the living word, *which depends on its closeness to the image that gave it birth,* and the distance which the person who uses the word today has put between himself and that moment are there for all to see [italics added]. (pp. 51–52)

Van der Post (1994) contrasts the Westerner's ontological and linguistic habits with the Bushman's primitive way of being, which animated his language:

> The most ancient of stone-age societies to which we still had access in my youth *stayed integrated when it was rooted in its own myths, legends and stories, in contrast to the disintegration that has followed* almost everywhere in the great primitive societies of Africa when they lost their story, and junior lecturers from the proliferating universities in Europe took over from witchdoctors and seers and prophets, with their own rational and moth-eaten ideologies *that could not be honourably lived* [italics added]. (p. 55)

Van der Post's distinctions illustrate an essential relationship at the heart of the argument presented here. One of the primary ways that "primitives" and "moderns" are identified is through their respective type and use of technology. But as Van der Post implies above, each group's *ontology* is connected to its technology, in this case, its communication technologies. He contrasts two ways of perceiving and living in the world: the Bushman's oral tradition with its vital integration of "word and world" (to borrow Paulo Friere's dynamic phrase) and the "desiccated" written word of the modern First Worlder and her essentially pinched sensibilities. And these sensibilities, these two types of ethos, are inextricably integrated with the technologies. First, technology must be defined more precisely.

TECHNOLOGY DEFINED

The ecologist Jeremy Rifkin (1991) defines technology as "appendages of [human] physical and mental processes, providing ... greater power to affect, control, and overcome the limitations of time and space" (p. 27). Marshall McLuhan (1964) defines technology as "extensions" and says that "whether [they are] of skin, hand, or foot, [they] affect the whole psychic and social complex" (p. 4). These definitions encompass material implements as simple as knives and as abstract and complex as fire and computers. But these definitions also recognize technology in their non-material forms, as ideas, concepts, and methods. These extensions would thus include such nonmaterial yet prodigious elements as language (i.e., pictographs, phonemes, syntax, etc.), the alphabet, and algorithms. This amplifies the definition considerably and affords the opportunity to see *technology as a distinct mediation.*

From the beginning, human implement making has been more a symbolic than a literal enterprise, involving the representation of dreams, hopes, and ideals. Lewis Mumford (1972) spent much of his professional life exploring how human artifacts such as tools and buildings symbolize human beliefs and values about the world and their place in it. He claims that humans are "pre-eminently a mind-using, symbol-making, and self-mastering animal," and that the earliest human "technics," or extensions, were intended more "to bring order and meaning into every part of ... life" than to master the external environment (p. 81). These first extensions were mostly religious symbol making and life centered, not work, power, or production centered. The works of Mumford, McLuhan, and Rifkin help change the way that technology is viewed and evaluated: not in terms of isolated machines, or even in terms of all of the physical "extensions of humans" combined, but as integrated with and key facilitators of human symbolic ambitions. McLuhan (1964) shows how the feudal system was a social extension of the stirrup from the eighth century, and how the printed word burst the bonds of the monasteries and guilds, "creating extremist patterns of enterprise and monopoly" (p. 23). Mander (1991) helps to overturn the naive belief that technologies are stand-alone implements or solitary machines by pointing to modern examples of how modern technologies enable one another — indeed, they make sense of one another. For example, Mander shows how skyscrapers became possible with the invention of the telephone, and multinational corporations with the invention of the computer. Suburbs are inextricably linked to cars, roads, and supply stores, as well as Middle East politics and concepts of time and distance.[1] Mander talks about this modern technical integration and the paradox it has produced:

> While we walk on pavement, or drive on a freeway, or sit in a shopping mall, we are unaware that we are enveloped by a technological and commercial reality, or that we are moving at technological speed. We live our lives in reconstructed, human-created environments; we are inside manufactured goods. (p. 31)

There are significant consequences of this envelopment, this integration. And what Mander says of the more obviously human-created environments of manufactured goods applies to all human environments, even the most primitive. As extensions, technology becomes the environment, what Bateson (2002) defines as a component of mind.

It is simply nonsense to assume that technology stands alone and can be left alone. But let us continue where we have been heading: to the sense-making ethic that connects the technologies to human consciousness.

Technology in Technique

Much of the modern sensibility in materialism, atomism, and mechanism is frequently attributed to the hegemony of modern materialist science. Other sources are less well known. But as Jacques Ellul (1965) and Lewis Mumford (1972) have separately argued, civilizations began to steer toward atomistic and mechanical approaches very early in their inception, long before the rise of materialist science. Mumford argues that the Egyptians constructed the very first "machine" over 5000 years ago; it was a *social* mechanization, a "Mega-machine" comprised of *human parts*. It was the world's first significant, highly organized social stratification of human society for the purpose of controlling mass quantities of people and resources on a grand scale and to construct Egyptian material culture. The pattern has been used by nearly every civilization since the Egyptians to a greater or lesser extent. This technical arrangement of culture (what Ellul calls "technique" — the belief in the importance of social conditioning along technical lines) is a philosophy embraced as much by modern citizens and bureaucrats as by any ancient ruler.

One way of considering technique is to imagine two fundamentally different ways of organizing groups of living things, be they cells, plants, animals, or humans. The first way is to do it exogenously. This could be called a *forced collective*. It is based purely on pressure from outside, forcing the components inside into some type of order. This is essentially what the cultural theorist Riane Eisler means when she describes a "domination hierarchy" (1988). Those occupying the apex of the hierarchy enforce the hierarchy for their own benefit. There is some modest benefit to nearly all in the hierarchy, but clearly those who occupy the upper echelons reap the greatest reward. Technique is a domination hierarchy. Its main tools are abstraction, determinism, categorization, and bureaucratization in order to efficiently predict and control. Science is both a product and enforcer of technique, but so are bureaucracies of all sorts.

The other type of collective could be referred to as a *synergistic collective*, where the organization comes from the bottom up or the inside out. Integration is the operative principle. Here, the various components, many of them dissimilar, cooperate for the purposes of survival, in the initial stages, and for flourishing in the mature or emergent levels. Eisler's version of this is the "actualization hierarchy." An ecosystem, an ideal family or support group, and the planet are excellent actualization hierarchies, for they function to maximize the benefit to all, in relationship. The "parts" in an actualization hierarchy are not atomized. Rather, they are more like "nodes in the field," to borrow ecologist Neil Evernden's phrase (1985). They function in dynamic relation to one another, ultimately developing emergent properties that cannot easily be predicted from an abstract accounting of the properties of the parts. Synergistic collectives will be described more in the next section. Here a brief description will suffice in order to contribute to understanding technical or domination hierarchies by contrast.

The social effects of technical or domination hierarchies did not escape the poets, artists, and critics of the age, especially when the mechanical metaphors lined up so easily in the Industrial Age in the West. English poet and mystic William Blake referred to the industrial turbines as the culture's "wheels tyrannic." English poet Mary Shelley (1969) warned a blinkered culture about the dangers of scientific and technological hubris in her prescient classic *Frankenstein*. The 19th-century writer and social critic Henry David Thoreau (1994) quipped that we do not ride on the train, but rather the train rides on us, to highlight both the literal fact of dead immigrant laborers buried beneath the train tracks and his concern with the likely imminent social disintegration resulting from the culture's fevered embrace of this new technology. Twentieth-century American playwrights Elmer Rice (1923; *The Adding Machine*) and Arthur Miller (1999; *Death of a Salesman*) recognized the dulling effects of life as a "company man."

The Technology of Language

Science and technical domination hierarchies have long controlled the sensibilities of the civilized. But there are still other major cultural tones to identify. One resonates and organizes more deeply the civilized conscious-ness and its predilection for control. It has two aspects: to fix language's relationship to meaning and to fix language itself in the form of print. The first is best illustrated by a sharp philosophical division between two eminent Chinese philosophers 2,500 years ago and their distinct reactions to the instability of their times. Lao-Tzu and Confucius were both quite dis-turbed by the constant warring and corruption in the China of their day. They chose very different ways of addressing those problems, however. The story goes that Lao-Tzu became convinced that the corruption so prevalent in his time (the Warring Period in China) was the result of man's estrange-ment from nature. Therefore, he sought to return to human origins in nature and find there the organic and authentic premises for human thought and action.[2] He authored Taoism, the world's only major nature-based religion (philosophy, really). Lao-Tzu represents his understanding of this original sensibility in the following from the *Tao Te Ching*:

> When the great Tao was lost,
> there came (ideas of) humanity and justice.
> When knowledge and cleverness arrived,
> there came great deceptions.
> When familial relations went out of harmony,
> there came (ideas of) good parents and loyal children.
> When the nation fell into disorder and misrule,
> there came (ideas of) loyal ministers. (99c,
>   Quoted in Watts, 1977, p. 112)

The recovery of the original sensibility, the Tao (nature/spirit), would fund the social imagination, which would in turn animate proper language and action. Lao-Tzu sought to put the horse in front of the cart. In his eyes, Confucius wanted it the other way around.

It was Confucius's idea about humanity, justice, obedience, and loyalty that Lao-Tzu complains about. Ever the devout technician, Confucius decided that the way to bring order and obedience to a corrupt Chinese society was through what he called "the rectification of names." That is, Confucius sought to render permanent the signification of value in specific words and social roles, to determine meaning and implication in advance, and to establish an absolute and objective moral order.[3] This type of forced collective — order imposed from the outside by language — was to be ensured by the indoctrination of the young in unquestioned obedience to the imposed order, yet another type of forced collective. Confucius's tech-nical feat was to order by "calling things by their right names," in order to avoid all of the rattling social chaos of open debate.

The second aspect of this linguistic enforcement was through the invention of the written word. The quotation from Van der Post above implies what has been argued by many language and media scholars through the centuries (i.e.,

Plato (1937), Eric Havelock (1978), Marshall MacLuhan, Neil Postman (1986), and others). Taking speech, a live verbalization, and freezing it in abstract symbolic forms is more than a magician's trick. Taken seriously, it induces the literate consciousness to consider the world by way of descriptions, prescriptions, and proscriptions. It changes thought and action, indeed, entire societies. As Eric Havelock has argued, justice did not exist, for all intents and purposes, in the ancient Greece that Homer described in the *Iliad* and *The Odyssey*. It took Plato and the other literate Greeks of his day to forge it into an abstract, foundational concept, making it a central pillar in Greek and Western edification. The predominance of writing as a cultural resonation affects law making and court systems, constitutions and governments, sciences and institutions of knowledge, and storage and learning. It also changes the heavens, making God a God of the Word, a God of Law and Order, whose Way is known through print. As Ivan Illich said, even the illiterate of Medieval Europe believed that they lived in a scripted world. They believed that God, the Great Accountant, was recording all of their deeds in his Great Book, and that the tally would be read to them by Saint Peter upon their death.

A god of law makes no sense to oral peoples, whose relationship with the spirit world must be continuously replenished by invocations, propitiations, and correct action. The live "give and take" of conversation with the spirit world reflects the expected give and take of everyday conversation to maintain relationships in the material world. Keeping one's word in oral cultures is tantamount to maintaining these vital relationships in both worlds.[4] Literacy discourages that same type of immediacy, diffusing the sensibilities in abstractions about the world through frozen speech. Van der Post (1994) says,

> [Writing] exposed the word to a kind of betrayal in which the pen and the rationalism of the day gave an undue role to calculation, deliberation and all the many adjectives which contribute to an exercise of the rational hubris in the intellectually ambitious fashion of the day, and obeisance to the power as opposed to the feeling and immediacy of the word. (pp. 53–54)

As ecologist David Orr (1994) has argued of higher education, the secondhanded nature of the knowledge is the key to its mediocrity.

But as history has well established, forced collective, or technical, societies, constructed as they are on artificial and abstract concepts of order, soon become oppressive and overly encumbered by their endless and convoluted rules and policies. Alan Watts, the man who introduced much of the Oriental religious and philosophical traditions to the West, summarized the problem with Confucian-like/techno-rational control consciousness quite well. Watts (1977) said, "The conscious control of life seems to involve us in ever more bewildering webs of complexity so that, despite their initial successes, technics create more problems than they solve" (pp. 112–113).

DIGITAL TECHNOLOGY: REMIXING THE CULTURE

The major advances in civilization are processes that all but wreck the societies in which they occur.

—**Alfred North Whitehead**[5]

If the message of the printed word is frozen speech and sequential analysis, which in turn produces abstraction, rules, laws, science, and a law-making god, what kind of message is digital technology and what type of mediation might it produce? Digital technology is evident principally in computing technology, but its ubiquity increases daily as it rapidly supplants the concrete metaphors of print. Media ecologist Raymond Gozzi Jr. (1999) explains that "first, a particular medium's form is internalized as a metaphor, and encourages certain cognitive habits on the part of its users.[6] ... Second, a medium tends to favor certain types and patterns of symbolization, and exclude others" (p. 20). Perkinson (1995) said that new media recode the culture and allow it to be criticized. McLuhan was one of the first to recognize the metaphorical power of media to translate experience into new forms. McLuhan (1964) is in league with what Van der Post (1994) revealed about language as a technology:

> The spoken word was the first technology by which man was able to let go of his environment in order to grasp it in a new way. Words are a kind of information retrieval that can range over the total environment and experience at high speed. Words are complex systems of metaphors and symbols that translate experience into our uttered or outered senses. They are a technology of explicitness. (p. 57)

We are still quite familiar with the word-based technologies and the mechanized environment they fostered. Delbanco (1995) shows how easily someone like General U. S. Grant could become an archetypal hero in the age of the machine and a model of the "modern, dead-eyed, murdering twentieth century man" (p. 139). Grant, Delbanco says, "was a man ... [with] no ground for faith ... [who was] at home in the mechanized world, thinking about men as bodies capable of obedient motion." He "doesn't think ... [he just] surrenders his spirit, grateful to have a function ... an alienation in the midst of action" (pp. 139–140). Grant was a product of his media environment.

Cultures founded on the reductive, abstract, concretizing metaphors of frozen speech are bound for revolutions when digital metaphors supersede. Speaking of this changing metaphor in terms of the advent of electric circuitry back in the 1960s, McLuhan and Fiore (1967) argued,

> Electric circuitry profoundly involves men with one another. Information pours upon us, instantaneously and continuously. As soon as information is

acquired, it is very rapidly replaced by still newer information. Our electri-
cally-configured world has forced us to move from the habit of data classification to the mode of pattern recognition. We can no longer build serially,
block-by-block, step-by-step, because instant communication insures that all
factors of the environment and of experience coexist in a state of active
interplay. (p. 63)

Gozzi, McLuhan and Fiore, and Postman argue that digital technology
mediates *myth* and *metaphor* itself, not sequential analysis. McLuhan and
Fiore (1967) describe this tension between these two poles felt so keenly in
contemporary times:

> Myth is the mode of simultaneous awareness of a complex group of causes
> and effects. Electric circuitry confers a mythic dimension on our ordinary
> individual and group actions. Our technology forces us to live mythically,
> but we continue to think fragmentarily, and on single, separate planes. (p.
> 114)

Digital technology signals the breakdown of *form*, away from *product* and
toward *process*, and thus relationship. The Age of Information should not be
considered in its word-bound manner of specific, immutable, and objective
facts and solutions, but rather as McLuhan and Fiore (1967) have characterized it, as "all factors of the environment and of experience coexist[ing]
in a state of active interplay" (p. 63).

So, in spite of the organization required to deliver and maintain it,
digital technology constantly threatens to undermine institutions. Institutions — bureaucracies especially — are technical institutions designed to
reduce, slow, and standardize information. They are the de facto word pro-
cessors in a print-centered society, in the form of courts, schools, churches,
corporations, and various government bodies. One can do word processing on digital technology, but the technology apes the effort. It is not about
words; it is about processing. It is not about hardware; it is about software.
When digital technology keeps information "in a state of active interplay"
— when it is all about "remixing" (Gaiman et al. 2005), not standardizing
and controlling — then institutions are at sea. All of those "frozen speech"
institutions will be stressed to adapt to an increasingly hostile environment.
While it is doubtful that institutions will disappear completely — since they
do serve a human need for certainty — they are likely to appear less and
less relevant, more a burlesque.

Traditional political and social categories of conservative, liberal, and
radical, and all other political categories and agendas must change as well.
Conservatives see an opportunity in digital technology to expand control
and order, while liberals fret about the intrusion on individual privacy and
freedom. Then again, liberals promote the technology as a way to expand

freedom and opportunity, while conservatives worry about the breakdown of tradition and social order. Both are correct about the negative and positive possibilities, but they miss the point. Both see the technology in traditional terms and misunderstand how digitization undermines both projects and categories. In the initial stages, all of these groups act conservatively by trying to use the technology to advance their own agendas, considering it a mere tool. As McLuhan and Fiore (1967) say, "In the name of 'progress,' our official culture [strives] to force the new media to do the work of the old" (p. 81). These sections of official culture believe, with my naive students, that they can use the technology without being used by it, that they are truly separate from it. But since digital technology as a medium becomes the environment, as McLuhan says, all political, social, and economic contexts change.

Gozzi (1999), Mander (1991), and Rheingold (2002) correctly argue that digital technology can increase the weapons of surveillance and control (the Panopticon)[7] and that one must properly distinguish ordinate and subordinate functions. Mander makes this point ominously by indicating the link between computers and the possibility of worldwide holocaust:

> Every military in the world has attached itself to computers, and all military strategies are now computer based. The programs are written, the computers are ready to act. In the face of this reality, to speak of computers helping you edit your copy or run your little business seems a bit absurd. (p. 74)

But the essential message of digital technology also contradicts the type of order that they and others argue is inevitable. The new world order sponsored by digital technology is globalism, but a globalism based less on multinational capitalism than on ever-increasing patterns of information flows. As McLuhan and Fiore (1967) argue, "Electric circuitry is Orientalizing the West. The contained, the distinct, the separate — our Western legacy — are being replaced by the flowing, the unified, the fused" (p. 143).

Electric circuitry has overthrown the regime of "time" and "space" and pours upon us instantly and continuously the concerns of all other men. It has reconstituted dialogue on a global scale. Its message is Total Change, ending psychic, social, economic, and political parochialism. The old civic, state, and national groupings have become unworkable. Nothing can be further from the spirit of the new technology than "a place for everything and everything in its place." You can't *go* home again. (p. 16)

THE NEAR FUTURE OF DIGITAL TECHNOLOGY

Digital technology is currently experiencing a major revolution of its own. The movement from large, mainframe computers to personal computers has put the power of digital technology into the hands of millions more potential experimenters, which is radically altering how ordinary people live, work, and recreate. Now digital technology has gone mobile on a large scale. More and more common individuals are participating in what Howard Rheingold calls "the next social revolution" — *smart mob technology*. Smart mob technologies are essentially handheld, wireless computers — in the form of cell phones, PDAs, Pocket PCs, GPSs, and so forth, often integrated with one another — that are always on and connected to multiple networks. Rheingold sees in this technology an exponential leap (an *emergent property*) beyond personal computing,[8] which promises to take the technology and society to untold dimensions. Smart mob technologies create "virtual clouds of information" or "swarm intelligence" as "they enable people to act together in new ways and in situations where collective action was not possible before" (Rheingold, 2002, p. xviii). Rheingold cites examples of smart mob organization of protests against GATT talks in Seattle, of peaceful, revolutionary protests in Panama, and of terrorism all around the globe to point out the burgeoning social and political effects of smart mobs. The United States' War on Terrorism represents well the incongruity of these older and newer technologies. On one side there is a large centralized nation-state comprised of multiple, extensive, and poorly communicating bureaucratic armed services trying to pursue and capture the other side, which is not so much an enemy as a series of decentralized extremely mobile and adaptive clouds of information. Rheingold's ambivalence is evident throughout the book, on the one side highlighting the potential for significant cultural breakthroughs as a result of the free-flow potential of swarm intelligence, and on the other clearly acknowledging the potential for significant loss of personal privacy through participation in these multiple networks.

There are reasons to remain cheerful about the potential of digital technology in general and smart mob technology specifically, in spite of the dire warnings about big brother and the ubiquity of global technique. For all that digital technology threatens to direct, control, and manipulate data — indeed, to turn everything into data — its metaphor is *metamorphosis*, which implies a possible return in some remarkably familiar way to an ethos of process, relationship, and reciprocity, which Van der Post so keenly acknowledged and admired in oral peoples of his boyhood.[9]

Ultimately, human and planetary welfare is best served by recognizing that technology is so integral to human cognition and understanding that it is indispensable. Technology goes all the way down and mediates our experience and understanding of ourselves and the world around us. Far from neutral, it establishes an environment that favors particular ways of thinking and behaving and discourages or eliminates others. More attention to how technologies mediate — what they say and prefer — will go a long way toward affirming and promoting the technological relations that affirm and promote what is best in us.

NOTES

1. The assumption of technology use influences language at the conceptual level. When I tell my students that my home is 10 minutes away, they always assume that I mean by car. As will be discussed below, McLuhan would say that car technology has mediated American culture — that it has become the environment.
2. This resembles Van der Post's own spiritual recapitulation, investigating the Bushman following his trials in WWII.
3. One could argue that the "signification of value" is the daily business of a vigorous culture, and that rendering the signification permanent leads to cultural morbidity.
4. Remnants of this type of "honorable living" are evident still in literate cultures, although its ethical force is certainly weakening.
5. Quoted in McLuhan and Fiore (1967, pp. 6–7).
6. For example, St. Peter standing at the entrance to the pearly gates with a written record of each person's sins and virtues in a book makes sense in a literate culture, even among the illiterate.
7. Rheingold (2002) takes this concept from Foucault and defines it as applying mental, knowledge-based power through constant observation (p. 189), something for which digital technology is well suited.
8. Rheingold's example of the telephone as an exponential leap from telegraphy illustrates this point and indicates the expected difference between mere computing and mobile computing.
9. In fact, in addition to McLuhan (1964) and McLuhan and Fiore (1967), Ong (1982) argued a likely return to orality from the influence of computing technology.

REFERENCES

Bateson, G. (2002). *Mind and nature: A necessary unity.* New York: Hampton.

Delbanco, A. (1995). *The death of satan: How Americans have lost the sense of evil.* New York: Farrar, Strauss, & Giroux.

Eisler, R. (1988). *The chalice and the blade: Our history, our future.* New York: Harper Collins.

Ellul, J. (1965). *The technological society.* New York: Knopf.

Evernden, N. (1985). *The natural alien: Humankind and environment.* Toronto: University of Toronto.

Gaiman, N., Gibson, W., Lam, B., Pinkser, B., Arcuni, P., Boulware, J., Pollack, N., & Stauer, E. Remix Planet (2005). *Wired, 13.07,* 112–129.

Gozzi, R. (1999). *The power of metaphor in the age of electronic media.* Cresskill, NJ: Hampton.

Havelock, E. (1978). *The Greek concept of justice: From its shadow in Homer to its substance in Plato.* Cambridge, MA: Harvard University.

Mander, J. (1991). *In the absence of the sacred: The failure of technology and the survival of the Indian nations.* San Francisco: Sierra Books.

McLuhan, M. (1964). *Understanding media: The extensions of man.* New York: McGraw-Hill.

McLuhan, M., & Fiore, Q. (1967). *The medium is the massage: An inventory of effects.* New York: Bantam.

Miller, A. (1999). *Death of a salesman: 50th anniversary edition.* New York: Penguin.

Mumford, L. (1972). Technics and the nature of man. In C. Mitcham & R. MacKey (Eds.), *Philosophy and technology* (pp. 77–85). New York: Free Press.

Ong, W. (1982). *Orality and literacy.* London: Routledge.

Orr, D. (1994). *Earth in mind.* Washington, DC: Island Press.

Perkinson, H. (1995). *How things got better.* Westport, CT: Bergin & Garvey.

Plato. (1937). *The dialogues of Plato.* New York: Random House.

Postman, N. (1986). *Amusing ourselves to death: Public discourse in the age of show business.* New York: Viking.

Rheingold, H. (2002). *Smart mobs: The next social revolution.* New York: Basic.

Rice, E. (1923). *The adding machine: A play in seven scenes.* Garden City, NY: Doubleday, Page & Co.

Rifkin, J. (1991). *Biosphere politics.* San Francisco: Harper.

Shelley, M. (1969). *Frankenstein, or the modern Prometheus.* Oxford: Oxford University Press.

Thoreau, H. (1994). *Walking.* San Francisco: Harper San Francisco.

Van der Post, L. (1994). *The voice of the thunder.* New York: W. Morrow & Co.

Watts, A. (1977). *Tao: The watercourse way.* New York: Pantheon.

Chapter 49

Quantitative Form and Arguments

Marilyn Frankenstein
University of Massachusetts–Boston

Many people argue that too much data about the injustices in our world make us numb to the realities of those situations in people's lives. Wasserman's editorial cartoon about the Israeli occupation of Palestine makes this point:[1]

FIGURE 49.1   Courtesy of Tribune Media Services, Inc. Reprinted with permission.

However, I argue that we do need to know the meaning of the numbers describing our realities in order to deepen our understandings of our world. One of my proudest academic moments was when *The Nation* published an edited version of the following letter I wrote responding to an article by Howard Zinn in which he argues that the numerical descriptions of the deaths from the U.S. war on Afghanistan can obscure those horrors.

February 11, 2002

To the Editor:

Howard Zinn's article ("The Others," February 11) is a powerful reminder of the horrors that are perpetrated in the world on all the days in addition to 9/11. I, too, cried as I saw the portraits of the 9/11 victims. I, too, was crying not only for them, and not only for the victims of the wars the USA and other powers create, but also for the millions who die every year because of economic terrorism — from unsafe working conditions that kill "by accident," to unjust working conditions that result in death from preventable causes such as hunger.

Binu Mathew reports in Z Magazine (January 2002) that at this point in time the original death toll of 8,000, caused by the Bhopal gas leak at Union Carbide's factory, has increased to 20,000, growing every month by 10–15 people succumbing to exposure-related diseases. Union Carbide management delayed sounding the public siren for 15 hours, and continues to obstruct full revelations which would have helped decrease some of this horrific toll. I, too, wondered, if detailed, in-depth TV and newspaper portraits of these victims, and of, say, the 12 million children who die from hunger every year (Food First Backgrounder, "12 Myths About Hunger," Summer 1998), would wake up our collective consciousness.

Zinn makes another important point that I stress with my Quantitative Reasoning classes at the College of Public and Community Service (University of Massachusetts/Boston): statistical data can distance us from a deep empathy and understanding of the conditions of people's lives. Of course, the data are important because they reveal the institutional structure of those conditions. But, also, quantitatively confident and knowledgeable people can use those data to deepen their connections to humanity. Those 12 million children are dying faster than we can speak their names.

In essence, the quantitative point of my letter is about the form in which we put numerical information.[2] Changing the form can help us make sense of quantities whose significance we cannot grasp. Changing the form through basic calculations can allow us to feel the impact of those quantities through better understandings. Further, knowing the most effective form in which to present those quantities in arguing for creating a just world is an important skill to teach in a criticalmathematical[3] literacy curriculum. I would go so far as to argue that knowing the most meaningful quantitative form in which to express information is necessary in order to understand what is going on.

CHANGING THE FORM TO UNDERSTAND LARGE QUANTITIES

In the Globe magazine article "Playing With Billions" (Denison, 2002) the author did not use my favorite ways of making sense of the size of 1 billion.[4]

Try to guess, without calculating, the answers to the first two questions to get a sense of how little sense we have about the meaning of large numbers.

- About how long, at the nonstop rate of one number per second, would it take to count to 1 billion?[5]
- About how long, at the nonstop rate of $1,000 per hour, would it take to spend $1,000,000,000?[6]

And the *Globe Magazine* article certainly did not use a more political and real meaning of these numbers by asking us to think about such questions as the following: What human services programs could we fund from various items in the military budget of the United States? In 1997, was "a B-2 bomber[7] worth more than twice the $800 million currently being saved by cutting 150,000 disabled children with insufficiently severe disabilities? Is $248 billion for the military and $31 billion for education a proper balance in the use of federal funds?" (Herman, 1997, p. 43)

KEY DOMESTIC PROGRAMS VERSUS MAJOR MILITARY PROGRAMS[8]

Fiscal 1998 Budget

Domestic Program	Military Program
Home heating assistance for low-income families ($1 billion)	Cost of 1 Arleigh Burke destroyer ($1 billion)
Raise Pell grants to $3,000 ($1.7 billion)	Cost of 1 B-2 bomber ($2.1 billion)
Head Start for young children ($4.3 billion)	Cost for 1 Seawolf attack submarine ($4.3 billion)
Drug prevention programs ($2.2 billion)	Request for F-22 fighter program ($2.2 billion)

Source: Center for Defense Information, quoted in Herman (1997, p. 43).

Further, other seemingly large numbers are not so large when placed in context, in a different quantitative form. Dean Baker (2005) even argues that without proper context, people's lack of quantitative understanding results in their voting against their own interests. For example, in the mid-1990s a Kaiser poll found that 40 % of people ranked welfare for those with low incomes as one of the two largest items in the federal budget — the number, even according to the government statistics that mislead in a way that underestimates human services, was under 4%. Baker blames this on the way these numbers are reported — $16 billion sounds gigantic, but in context it is only 0.6% of total federal spending. He feels that when people have such an exaggerated view of current welfare spending, they are unlikely to support increases in programs for those with low incomes.

QUANTITATIVE FORM IN ARGUMENTS

One consideration in understanding, evaluating, and constructing arguments whose claims are supported by quantitative evidence is the form in which this evidence is presented. Is it clear, or is it misleading? Is it powerful, or is it likely to be ignored? In this section of the chapter, I am going to focus on examples in which the latter question is explored.[9] Below are a number of examples from my curriculum that illustrate various ways I ask students to reflect upon how the forms of quantitative data affect the meanings we take from information.

- We discuss the table below from *The Nation* (1991): Is the numerical form of this counter to the first Bush's claim about our former wars, in particular our war on Vietnam, powerful? What might be more powerful forms in which to express the numbers supporting this counterargument?

What Does He Mean?

"Our troops ... will not be asked to fight with one hand tied behind their back."

—President Bush, national address, January 16[, 1991]

Tons of bombs dropped on Vietnam by the U.S.: 4,600,000[a]
Tonnage dropped on Cambodia and Laos: 2,000,000[a]
Tonnage dropped by the Allies in World War II: 3,000,000[b]
Gallons of Agent Orange sprayed: 11,200,000[c]
Gallons of other herbicides: 8,000,000[c]
Tons of napalm dropped: 400,000[c]
Bomb craters: 25,000,000[d]
South Vietnamese hamlets destroyed by the war: 9,000
(out of 15,000)[e]
Acres of farmland destroyed: 25,000,000[e]
Acres of forest destroyed: 12,000,000[e]
Vietnamese killed: 1,921,000[f]
Cambodians killed (1969–1975): 200,000[f]
Laotians killed (1964–1973): 100,000[f]
Vietnamese, Cambodians & Laotians wounded: 3,200,000[f]
Total refugees by 1975: 14,305,000[f]
American troops who served in Vietnam: 2,150,000[g]
American troops killed: 57,900[h]

---

[a] Jim Harrison, "Air War in Vietnam," recent conference paper

[b] Howard Zinn, author, *A People's History of the United States*

[c] Jim Harrison, "Air War in Vietnam," recent conference paper

[d] Marilyn Young, *The Vietnam Wars*

[e] Noam Chomsky, *Manufacturing Consent*

[f] "Indochina Newsletter," Nov–Dec 1982

[g] Lawrence Baskir and William Strauss, *Chance and Circumstance*

[h] National Archives. Thanks for inspiration to "Harper's Index."

- As part of understanding Helen Keller's argument below, students are asked to discuss how she uses numbers to support her claim, to evaluate whether that support makes her claim convincing, and to reflect on the form of her data — why she sometimes uses fractions, other times uses whole numbers, and whether there are alternative ways of presenting her quantitative evidence that would strengthen her argument.[10]

  > In 1911, Helen Keller wrote to a suffragist in England: "You ask for votes for women. What good can votes do when ten-elevenths of the land of Great Britain belongs to 200,000 people and only one-eleventh of the land belongs to the other 40,000,000 people? Have your men with their millions of votes freed themselves from this injustice?" (Quoted in Zinn, 1995, p. 337)

- Another example of considerations about quantitative form comes from an argument we study about the globalization of workers in the garment trades. As part of that argument Gonzalez (1995, p. 148) compares the Leslie Fay Company's Honduran workers' earnings with the company's sales receipts. Specifically, he expresses the quantities as a "grand total of $300" that all assembly-line workers in Honduras cost Leslie Fay for one day (and he includes the information that this comes from 120 workers paid $2.50 per day), and $40,000 in retail sales that the company takes from the skirts those workers make in that one day. He does not say how many skirts they each make (another quantity that could reveal a different aspect of the exploitation)[11]. He does not calculate the workers' yearly pay and compare it to the yearly retail sales of those Leslie Fay skirts.

- One of the points brought out in our discussions is that if he had just focused on the average worker's daily pay and the average amount the company made from selling the skirts she made, he would have compared $2.50 to $333. We speculate that he felt, even though the numbers for 1 worker are in the same proportion as the numbers for 120 workers, the $333 figure would not appear as outrageous to the reader as the $40,000. Also, most readers can relate to $40,000 in terms of their yearly income — most would have a yearly income that is somewhere between half and double that figure. Since Leslie Fay is grossing that amount of money in one day, that adds to the outrageousness Gonzalez wants us to feel. If he had calculated the yearly sales — $14,600,000 — since most readers could not deeply grasp the meaning of such a giant number, its impact would have been less than when readers can think "Leslie Fay makes more in one day than I make in a year!" And even minimum-wage workers in the United States could think, "In one day, they are paying their workers less than I make in half an hour — could it cost that much less to live decently in Honduras?"

- The following is an argument supported by quantitative evidence, and four forms of similar quantitative information that could have been used to support the claim.[12] Students are asked to identify the claim, the reasoning, and the evidence Wuerker and Sklar are making in their editorial graph below. Then we compare the different forms of the quantitative evidence given in each of the related arguments. Students reflect on which quantitative form provides the most powerful support for the claim. What other kinds of numerical data would further strengthen the claim? What data or reasoning would a counterargument present?

  - The argument from Sklar (1999):

FIGURE 49.2   "CEO vs. Worker Pay" chart by Matt Weurker and Holly Sklar, 1999.
Reprinted with permission.

- Another presentation of similar quantitative evidence from Jackson (2001): If the minimum wage had risen at the same level pace as executive pay since 1990, it would be $25.50 an hour, not $5.15; if average pay for production workers had risen at the same level as CEO pay since 1990, the annual salary would be $120,491, not $24,668.

- Another presentation from United for a Fair Economy (Sklar, 1999, p. 63): "If the real 555-foot Washington Monument reflects average 1998 CEO pay, then a scaled-down replica representing average worker pay would be just 16 inches tall — 5 inches shorter than in 1997. Back in 1980, the Workers Monument was over 13 feet tall — reflecting a CEO-worker wage gap of 42 to 1."[13]
- Another presentation from Wasserman (1999):

FIGURE 49.3   Tribune Media Services, Inc. Reprinted with permission.

- Another presentation from Wasserman (1996):

FIGURE 49.4   Tribune Media Services, Inc. Reprinted with permission.

QUANTITATIVE FORM IN ARTISTS' ARGUMENTS

In addition to various written and graphical forms of quantitative information, the arts present different kinds of opportunities for people to understand and use quantities in arguments. As Toni Morrison states: "Data is
not wisdom, is not knowledge" (quoted in Caiani, 1996, p. 3.) Caiani goes
on to add:

> In contrast to stories told in a living language filled with images taken from
> the human world, facts, statistics, data and bits of information, valuable as
> they are, slide in and out of memory without fully engaging sustained, power-
> ful connections to the whole being. Data are important, are necessary, but not
> all by themselves, not alone. Analysis and facts are not able to give a face, eyes,
> a body to the suffering, joy, love, anguish of the people.... Art, I am convinced
> (as indeed have been many scientists like Pascal and Einstein), is at least as
> necessary as the sciences in grasping reality if we are ever to effect the change
> we seek in our long struggle to be human.... Our efforts to make a better
> world through a narrow, reductive, isolated, scientific method which relies on
> the accumulation of data and its business-like interpretation, will fail. (p. 3)

The following examples of art encode quantitative information in ways
that make us understand — What does this amount mean? The numbers
are the data of our world — our wars; the art allows us to understand the
quantities in ways we could not understand from the numbers alone.

1. "'The other Vietnam Memorial' (by artist Chris Burden, USA) refers
   to the famous memorial in Washington, D.C. by artist Maya Lin which
   lists the names of 57,939 Americans killed during the Vietnam War.
   In this work, Burden etched 3,000,000 names onto a monumental
   structure that resembles a Rolodex standing on its end. These names
   represent the approximate number of Vietnamese people killed
   during U.S. involvement in the Vietnam War, many of whom are
   unknown. Burden reconstructed a symbolic record of their deaths
   by generating variations of 4000 names taken from Vietnamese telephone books. By using the form of a common desktop object used to
   organize professional and social contacts, Burden makes a pointed
   statement about the unrecognized loss of Vietnamese lives" (notes
   from the Museum of Contemporary Art in Chicago).
2. Artist Alfredo Jaar (born in Chile, works in New York City) went to
   Rwanda in 1994 to try to understand and represent the slaughter of
   "possibly a million Tutsis and moderate Hutus" during three months of
   Prime Minister Jean Kambanda's term. "Even after 3000 [photographic]
   images, Jaar considered the tragedy to be unrepresentable. He found
   it necessary to speak with the people, recording their feelings, words

FIGURE 49.5   "The other Vietnam Memorial." Chris Burden, artist; James Isberner, photo. Courtesy of Museum of Contemporary Art, Chicago, Illinois. With permission.

and ideas.… In Jaar's Galerie Lelong installation, a table containing a million slides is the repetition of a single image, The Eyes of Gutete Emerita." The text about her reads: "Gutete Emerita, 30 years old, is standing in front of the church. Dressed in modest, worn clothing, her hair is hidden in a faded pink cotton kerchief. She was attending mass in the church when the massacre began. Killed with machetes in front of her eyes were her husband Tito Kahinamura (40), and her two sons Muhoza (10) and Matriigari (7). Somehow, she managed to escape with her daughter Marie-Louise Unumararunga (12), and hid in the swamp for 3 weeks, only coming out at night for food. When she speaks about her lost family, she gestures to corpses on the ground, rotting in the African sun." The art review ends with a comment about the numbers:

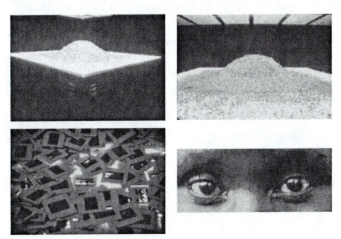

FIGURE 49.6   The Eyes of Gutete Emerita, 1996. Courtesy of Alfredo Jaar.
With permission.

"The statistical remoteness of the number 1,000,000 acquires an objective presence, and through the eyes of Gutete Emerita, we witness the deaths, one by one, as single personal occurrences" (Rockwell, 1998).

ADDITIONAL CONSIDERATIONS ABOUT QUANTITIES IN ARGUMENTS

In addition to quantitative form, there are other kinds of considerations about quantities that are important in understanding, evaluating, and making powerful arguments that challenge the global imperialism that has trickled down into every corner of our world. In addition to the more typical ways of classifying various misleading statistical accounts (like mistaking correlation for causation), I think two overarching questions are important to consider: What are the political, as opposed to scientific/mathematical, aspects involved in the data presented? Is the measure chosen the most accurate way of describing or analyzing the situation, or in other words, is the correct answer being given to the wrong question?

It is important to understand which aspect of quantitative evidence is mathematical fact and which is political, and therefore subject to debate. Much data are presented as if they were neutral descriptions of reality, masking the political choices that produced the data. For example, once the government determines which categories of workers count as part of the labor force and which categories of workers count as unemployed, rewriting that information in percent form is a mathematical algorithm for which there is only one answer and about which it does not make sense to argue. The politics about which we can (and I would argue should) argue come in decisions made by the government, such as to count part-time workers who want full-time work as fully employed, and to not count workers who have looked for over a year and not found a job as unemployed.[14]

It is also important to determine which quantitative measure gives the most accurate picture of a particular issue. For example, the ultraconservative Heritage Foundation argues that our progressive federal income tax is terribly unfair because of facts such as in 1997 the top 1% income group paid 33.6% of all federal income taxes, while the share of all taxes paid by the bottom 60% was only 5.5%. But, a left (and even a liberal) perspective would argue that is the wrong measure by which to judge tax equity. It makes much more sense to look at what happens to the share of total pretax and total after-tax income. That picture reveals only a small progressivity: a slight upward shift for the bottom four quintiles, and a slight downward shift for the top income quintile. Ellen Frank (2002) then argues:

> If one believes that Ken Lay deserved no less than the $100 million he collected from Enron last year, while the burger-flippers and office cleaners of America deserve no more than the $6.50 an hour they collect, then a progressive tax would seem immoral. But if one believes that incomes are deter-

mined by race, gender, connections, power, luck and (occasionally) fraud,
then redistribution through the tax system is a moral imperative. (p. 44)

Frank goes on to discuss the impact of other kinds of federal taxes, such as
social security taxes (which are capped at $90,000), excise taxes, and so on,
which are regressive, as well as state and local regressive levies like sales taxes.
She hypothesizes that adding all these taxes together would "almost certainly
find that the U.S. tax system, as a whole, is not progressive at all" (p. 44).[15,16]

CONCLUSION

In "Scenes from the Inferno," Alexander Cockburn (1989) wrote about some
of the realities behind the so-called worldwide triumph of capitalism. One
of his illustrations is particularly relevant to understanding how the wrong
quantitative measure has real consequences in people's lives. He relates how
in some neighborhoods of Santiago, Chile, "the diet of 77 to 80 percent of the
people does not have sufficient calories and proteins, by internationally established standards, to sustain life." Under Pinochet, the dictator of Chile during
that country's period of "triumphant capitalism," malnutrition was measured
in relation to a person's weight and height, in contrast to the usual comparison
of weight and age. "So a stunted child is not counted as malnourished, and
thus is not eligible for food supplements, because her weight falls within an
acceptable range for her height" (p. 510). I argue that the overarching goal
underlying a criticalmathematical literacy curriculum is to explore the connections between understanding the outrageousness of collecting such statistics and struggling to change the outrageousness of such conditions.

This chapter, however, focused on the importance of the form in which
the measures are actually expressed. I argue for the importance of criticalmathematical literacy curricula also consisting of reflections on questions such
as whether it is more powerful to state that "The wealthiest 1% of Americans
control about 38% of America's wealth" (Jackson, 1999) or that, in the United
States, "The richest 1% owns more than the poorest 92% combined" (Food First,
1998). Part of struggling to change our world in the direction of more justice is
knowing how to clearly and powerfully communicate the outrageousness.

NOTES

1. Of course, there is more here than just that interpretation. My colleague,
   Rutgers University Professor Arthur B. Powell, who provided many helpful
   suggestions about this manuscript, read the cartoon as saying that as time
   goes on, people tend to lose interest in protesting injustices, and as a consequence, perpetrators of injustices eventually can act with impunity.

2. Another publication of which I am very proud is an edited version of the following letter responding to an editorial in the *Boston Globe*. To my delight, they titled it "Secretary of Death" and included a drawing of Kissinger, which made the letter the central one on the editorial page. In this case, the focus is on how a particular quantitative form can be correct, but highly misleading.

November 30, 2002

Dear Editor:

I commend the *Globe* for writing an editorial questioning the appointment of Henry Kissinger to lead what is supposed to be an independent commission investigating intelligence failures in the September 11, 2001 attacks.

However, as a teacher of Quantitative Reasoning, I was dismayed to see your misleading presentation of numerical data. You mention Kissinger's responsibility for "thousands" of civilian deaths in Indochina, Bangladesh and East Timor. In facts, very clearly documented by Christopher Hitchens' review of USA government declassified documents detailing Kissinger's legal crimes (*The Trial of Henry Kissinger*, London and New York: Verso, 2001), Pentagon figures for deaths in Vietnam during the period under which Kissinger's deceits and policies prolonged that war are: 31,205 of our citizens, 86,101 South Vietnamese, and 475,609 Vietnamese "enemy." The US Senate Subcommittee on Refugees estimated that during that time more than 3 million civilians were killed, injured or made homeless (p. 41). In Bangladesh, "the eventual civilian death toll has never been placed at less than half a million and has been put as high as 3 million" (p. 46). In East Timor, 200,000 people, approximately one-third of the population, were slaughtered as a direct result of the "green light" then United States Secretary of State Kissinger gave to Indonesian dictator General Suharto (p. 93).

Although your statement that Kissinger's policies resulted in "thousands" of civilian deaths is technically accurate, clearly it presents a misleading picture. In a conservative tallying from just these three areas of the world, Kissinger is responsible for *more than one million* deaths, *hundreds of thousands* of them civilian deaths.

3. Broadly speaking, criticalmathematics [one word] defines a pedagogical perspective that connects education in mathematics with critical analyses of social, economic, cultural, and political issues and with movements for social change. Criticalmathematics educators teach for understanding rather than memorization, start with the mathematical knowledge of students, and engage students to reflect critically on both the substance and process of their learning. In agreement with ethnomathematics, this perspective counters Eurocentric historiography of mathematics and considers the interaction of culture and mathematical knowledge. Moreover, criticalmathematics

attends to the dynamics of power in society to understand the effects of racism, sexism, ageism, heterosexism, monopoly capitalism, imperialism, and other alienating, totalitarian institutional structures and attitudes. Finally, criticalmathematics educators attempt to develop commitment to build more just structures and attitudes and personal and collective empowerment needed to engage these tasks. For an elaboration on these ideas and the history of the Criticalmathematics Educators Group, see Frankenstein (1983, 1998) and Powell (1995).

4. There are also some really interesting ways of getting a sense of the size of finite numbers larger than one billion. For trillions, one of my favorites is:

> Our blood contains tiny red corpuscles, each like a circular disc somewhat flattened in the center and about 0.007 mm in diameter and 0.002 mm thick. In a drop of blood (1 cubic mm) there are about 5 million of these corpuscles. An average adult has about 3,500,000 cubic mm of blood. If all these corpuscles were strung out in a single chain, about how many times could this chain be wound around the earth's 25,000 mile equator? (Note: 1 mile = 5280 feet; 1000 mm = 1 meter; 1 meter is approximately 3 feet.) (Answer: about 3 times)

Also, a fascinating science fiction story whose theme is making sense of super-gigantic finite numbers is "The Universal Library" (Kurd Lasswitz, pp. 237–243 in Clifton Fadiman [Ed.], *Fantasia Mathematica* [New York: Simon & Schuster, 1958]), as well as "Postscript to 'The Universal Library'" (Willy Ley, pp. 244–247 in the same collection).

5. Answer: about 32 years — most people guess way too little or way too big.

6. Answer: over one century — 114 years rounded to the nearest year.

7. The General Accounting Office found that this bomber deteriorates in rain, heat, and humidity and "must be sheltered or exposed only to the most benign environments." These special shelters are not available at the very military bases at which the plane was proposed to be located. The plane also needs as much as 124 hours of maintenance time for each hour in the air. In 74% of the trial missions its radar "could not tell a rain cloud from a mountainside." Further, since the early 1980s its theoretical mission to evade Soviet radar to penetrate to targets in the former Soviet Union has ended with the end of the Cold War. Finally, the then-claim of Soviet military superiority used to justify requests for 21 of these bombers has been challenged (Herman, 1997).

8. Thad Williamson, in *Dollars and Sense* (July/August 2004, p. 12), provided a number of different ways of looking at what the money spent by the United States in the war on Iraq — $151 billion by the end of 2004 — could have been used for. Of interest to readers of this book on the effects of what some people call globalization, and others insist is a current euphemism for imperialism, is his calculations that in the developing world (which my colleague Munir Fasheh has pointed out that Gustavo Esteva and Madhu Prakesh call the "two-thirds world" in *Grassroots Post-Modernism: Remaking the Soil of Cultures*), for two years, this money could have provided:

• Food for half of the malnourished people in the world

- A comprehensive, global HIV/AIDS treatment/prevention program
- Clean water and sanitation to all who lack them
- Immunizations for all children

9. In a later section I will briefly discuss some considerations that address the question of misleading quantitative evidence. Some references to investigate this further are Frankenstein (1994) and Griffiths, Irvine, and Miles (1979).

10. When considering this example, I also include information about the politics of knowledge. When Helen Keller became an active socialist, the *Brooklyn Eagle*, a newspaper that had previously treated her as a hero, wrote "her mistakes spring out of the manifest limitations of her development." Howard Zinn relates that the *Eagle* did not print her reply in which she wrote that when she had met the editor of the *Eagle*, he had complimented her lavishly

> but now that I have come out for socialism he reminds me and the public that I am blind and deaf and especially liable to error.... Oh, ridiculous *Brooklyn Eagle*! What an ungallant bird it is! Socially blind and deaf, it defends an intolerable system a system that is the cause of much of the physical blindness and deafness which we are trying to prevent.
>
> ... The *Eagle* and I are at war. I hate the system which it represents.... When it fights back, let it fight fair.... It is not fair fighting or good argument to remind me and others that I cannot see or hear. I can read. I can read all the socialist books I have time for in English, German and French. If the editor of the Brooklyn *Eagle* should read some of them, he might be a wiser man, and make a better newspaper. If I ever contribute to the Socialist movement the book that I sometimes dream of, I know what I shall name it: Industrial Blindness and Social Deafness. (Zinn, 1995, pp. 337–338)

11. In Las Vegas, for example, in a unionized hotel laundry shop (with much better pay and other conditions than the nonunionized shops), workers count and bundle 1,800 washcloths an hour; other workers separate stained and ripped sheets from the total and feed the good sheets, "310 an hour, into a machine that irons and folds them. The pillowcase feeder has to complete 900 an hour; the napkin feeder, 1300" (Wypijewski, 2002). The workers in the "soil sort need to sort 700 to 1050 pounds of dirty linen an hour." For this they get paid $9.09 to $10.45 an hour plus benefits.

12. It is particularly challenging to analyze visual arguments, which is one reason I include them in my curriculum. The next section on artists' arguments carries this kind of critical visual thinking even further.

13. Recently, I came across a similar presentation in Johnston (2003), an important book revealing the details of how the U.S. current tax structures transfer money not only from the poor to the wealthy, but even from the upper middle classes to the top 0.1% wealthiest. To visualize what he calls the enormous chasm in incomes ("just 28,000 men, women and children had as much income in 2000 as the poorest 96 million Americans" [p. 41]), he suggests

we "imagine these two groups in geographic terms. The super rich would occupy just one-third of the seats at Yankee Stadium, while those at the bottom as the equivalent of every American who lives west of Iowa — plus everyone in Iowa" (p. 41).

14. And, of course, there is the Wal-Mart example, where many of their counted-as-employed-in-the-unemployment-statistics full-time workers earn so little that, even under the current stinginess of our government, they are eligible for various kinds of public assistance. The Democratic Staff of the House Committee on Education and the Workforce (2004) estimated that "one 200-person Wal-Mart store may result in a cost to federal taxpayers of $420,750 per year — about $2,103 per employee. Specifically, the low wages result in the following additional public costs being passed along to taxpayers:

- $36,000 a year for free and reduced lunches for just 50 qualifying Wal-Mart families.
- $42,000 a year for Section 8 housing assistance, assuming 3 percent of the store employees qualify for such assistance, at $6,700 per family.
- $125,000 a year for federal tax credits and deductions for low-income families, assuming 50 employees are heads of households with a child and 50 are married with two children.
- $100,000 a year for the additional Title 1 expenses, assuming 50 Wal-Mart families qualify with an average of two children.
- $108,000 a year for the additional federal health care costs of moving into state children's health insurance programs (S-CHIP), assuming 30 employees with an average of two children qualify.
- $9,750 a year for the additional costs for low income energy assistance." (p. 9)

Further kinds of costs that Wal-Mart extracts from taxpayers are detailed in Robert Greenwald's new documentary, *Wal-Mart: The High Cost of Low Price* (2005).

15. Another example that illustrates how to shift the argument by using more appropriate measures involves what Paul Krugman (2005) called the right-wing's "little black lies" about social security for African Americans. Of course, the whole premise of the argument that social security privatization would be fairer to Blacks since their life expectancy is shorter than Whites, so they collect fewer benefits, speaks volumes about racism in our society. Imagine stating this outrageous fact and then remaining silent about the obvious health care and other programs that would eliminate that fact. But, in addition to this moral consideration, as Spriggs (2004) argues, there are problems with using the life expectancy measure to calculate the benefits collected. One key concern he discusses is that since social security "also serves families of workers who become disabled or die, a correct measure would take into account all three risk factors — old age, disability, and death. Both survivor benefits and disability benefits, in fact, go disproportionately to African Americans" (p. 18).

16. Another example involves the actual creation of a measure to counter the argument that heavily populated countries with many poor people are ruining our environment. Holtzman (1999) relates that Mathis Wackernagel and William Rees, community planners at the University of British Columbia,

developed a measure of the impact of each country on the world's resources. "The ecological footprint measures the resources consumed by a community or a nation, whether they come from the community's backyard or from around the globe.... Wackernagel and Rees ask how many hectares ... are needed per person to support a nation's consumption of food, housing, transportation, consumer goods, and services. They calculate how much fossil energy use, land degradation, and garden, crop, pasture, and forest space it takes to produce all that consumers buy." Using this measure, each person in the United States consumes 5.1 hectares, while each person in India only consumes 0.4 hectares. So, even with a population four times that of the United States, India has only one-third the impact on our global environment that the United States does.

REFERENCES

Baker, D. (2005, May 9). Numbers before politics. *In These Times*, p. 33.

Caiani, J. (1996, July/August). Art, politics, and the imagination. *Resist*, Vol. 5, No. 6, pp. 1-3, 11.

Cockburn, A. (1989, April 17). Scenes from the inferno. *The Nation*, pp. 510–511.

The Democratic Staff of the House Committee on Education and the Workforce. (2004, February 16). Everyday low wages: The hidden price we all pay for Wal-Mart. U.S. House of Representatives, Rep. George Miller (D-CA), Senior Democrat. Retrieved May 1, 2007 from http://edworkforce.house.gov/democrats/WALMARTREPORT.pdf

Denison, D. C. (2002, December 29). Playing with billions. *Boston Globe*, pp. 20–23, 29–31.

Esteva, G. & Prakash, M.S. (1998). *Grassroots postmodernism: Remaking the soil of culture*. London: Zed Books.

Food First. (1998, December 21). Should America be measured by its 3.5 million millionaires ... or by its 30 million hungry? (advertisement). *The Nation*, pp. 20–21.

Frank, E. (2002, September/October). Ask Dr. dollar. *Dollars and Sense*, p. 44.

Frankenstein, M. (1983). Criticalmathematics education: An application of Paulo Freire's epistemology. *Journal of Education*, *165*, 315–340. Reprinted in Shor, I. (Ed.), *Freire for the classroom* (pp. 180–210). Porthsmouth, NH: Boynton/Cook.

Frankenstein, M. (1994). Understanding the politics of mathematical knowledge as an integral part of becoming critically numerate. *Radical Statistics*, *56*, 22–40.

Frankenstein, M. (1998). Reading the world with math: Goals for a criticalmathematical literacy curriculum. In E. Lee, D. Menkart, & M. Okazawa-Rey (Eds.), *Beyond heroes and holidays: A practical guide to K-12 anti-racist, multicultural education and staff development*. Washington, DC: Network of Educators on the Americas.

Gonzalez, J. (1995). *Roll down your window: Stories from a forgotten America*. London: Verso.

Greenwald, R. (2005). *Wal-Mart: The high cost of low price* (DVD). Retrieved May 1, 2007 from www.walmartmovie.com

Griffiths, D., Irvine, J., & Miles, I. (1979). Social statistics, towards a radical science. In J. Irvine, I. Miles, & J. Evans (Eds.), *Demystifying social statistics* (pp. 340–381). London: Pluto.

Herman, E. S. (1997, November). Privileged dependency and waste: The military budget and our weapons culture. *Z Magazine*, pp. 41–44.

Holtzman, D. (1999, July/August). Economy in numbers: Ecological footprints. *Dollars and Sense*, p. 42.

Jackson, D. (2001, August 31). Who's better off this Labor Day? Numbers tell. *Boston Globe*, p. A27.

Johnston, D. C. (2003). *Perfectly legal: The covert campaign to rig our Tax system to benefit the super rich — and cheat everybody else.* New York: Penguin.

Krugman, P. (2005, January 25). Race and social security: Little black lies. *New York Times*.

The Nation. (1991, February 18). What does he mean? (table).

Powell, A. B. (1995). Criticalmathematics: Observations on its origins and pedagogical purposes. In Y. M. Pothier (Ed.), *Proceedings of 1995 Annual Meeting of the Canadian Mathematics Education Study Group* (pp. 103–116). Halifax, Nova Scotia: Mount Saint Vincent University Press.

Rockwell, S. (1998, Fall). Alfredo Jaar at Galerie LeLong in New York. *Art International*, Vol. 1, No. 3, pp. 3, 12–13.

Sklar, H. (1999, July/August). For CEO's, a minimum wage in the millions: The wage gap between CEO's and workers is ten times wider than it was in 1980. *Z Magazine*, pp. 63–66.

Spriggs, W. E. (2004, November/December). African Americans and social security: Why the privatization advocates are wrong. *Dollars and Sense*, pp. 17–19, 32–33.

Wasserman, D. (1996). Op-ed cartoon. *Boston Globe*.

Wasserman, D. (1999, September 2). Op-ed cartoon. *Boston Globe*.

Wypijewski, J. (2002, February). Light and shadow in the city of lights. *The Progressive*, pp. 26–29.

Zinn, H. (1995, updated from 1980). *A People's History of the United States: 1492-Present.* New York: Harper-Collins.

Chapter 50

Deschooling

Matt Hern
Institute for Social Ecology and Crank *magazine*

> Two institutions at present control our children's lives: television and school-ing, in that order. Both of these reduce the real world of wisdom, fortitude, temperance and justice to a never-ending, non-stop abstraction.... Schools are intended to produce, through the application of formulas, formulaic human beings whose behaviour can be predicted and controlled.
>
> **—John Gatto (1992)**

After a little more than 150 years of compulsory schooling in North Amer-ica one thing has become manifestly clear: Schools do not need reform. They need a fundamental rethinking of their role, structure, assumptions, and mandates. They need to be radically reimagined.

There is a deep antagonism to mandatory schooling (what is more cli-ché than "kids hate school"), and yet our culture clings to a salvific notion of schools: that compulsory education is the solution to many of our most pressing social problems. It is common to ask whether schools are working,[1] but I believe it far more pressing to ask fundamental questions about the nature of schools and the experience of kids within them. The point is to look closely at the nature of our children's everyday lives and ask whether schools are helping our kids and our culture thrive.

Would anyone in their right mind argue that the best way for a child to grow up and flourish is to be institutionalized 6 hours a day, 5 days a week, 10 months a year, for 12 years of their youth? To spend the vast majority of their days confined to single rooms with 30 of their peers and one adult? To be force-fed material that neither they nor their teacher has had any significant role in choosing? To change activities at the sound of a bell? To swallow petty authority, testing, surveillance, and monitoring as a way of life? If not, then what are we doing?

Thinking about the future of education is a trap and a question worth rejecting. As soon as we begin to speak about what all kids need, or what education as a supposed universal good should look like, we engage in logic that is antagonistic to the reality of everyday life. What kids need to thrive is necessarily a local question: an ongoing collection of conversations that has to be held among neighbors, friends, and families, one that has to be about specific kids, the kids right in front of us, not the abstract children.

I want to argue that there is no such thing as necessary knowledge, nothing that we can insist all kids have to know to grow up right. What kids need is an intensely complex stew of circumstance, place, time, family, interest, competencies, and so much else. It is only individuals, families, and local communities that can make everyday, real decisions about how kids should be spending their days and what they should be learning.

> And they aint teachin us nothin related to
> Solvin our own problems, knowhatimsayin?
> Aint teachin us how to get crack out the ghetto
> They aint teachin us how to stop the police from murdering us
> And brutalizing us, they aint teachin
>   us how to get our rent paid
> Knowhatimsayin? They aint teachin our families how to interact
> Better with each other, knowhatimsayin? They just teachin us
> How to build they shit up, knowhatimsayin?
>   That's why my niggas
> Got a problem with this shit, that's why
>   niggas be droppin out ...
> Until we have some shit where we control
>   the fuckin school system ...
> And I love education, knowhatimsayin?
> But if education aint elevatin me, then
>   you knowhatimsayin it aint
> Takin me where I need to go on some
>   bullshit, then fuck education

(DEAD PREZ, 2000)

In some ways it is easy to make sense of the security apparatuses surrounding schools today: the cameras, security guards, compulsory attendance, ID tags, surveillance, threats, coercion. They are extensions of normative school logics that suggest the means are always subservient to the ends of curriculum delivery. It is exactly the same stance that makes possible standardized curriculums and their attendant mechanisms of grading and (inter)national standards.[2]

The compulsory school project is necessarily evolving toward a universalized curriculum that will embrace all children everywhere, a process that is clearly well under way. When local knowledge, local epistemologies, and local pedagogies are conflated and entirely displaced by nationalized (and rapidly globalized) curriculums, the possibilities for understanding what it will take for a child to flourish are catastrophically reduced. That is to say, when we expect that children learn the same things at the same rates and in the same sequences,[3] we reduce child rearing, an activity that lies at the heart of human existence, to an industrial activity governed by probability theory.

Children are not production units, and the factors necessary for a child to flourish are inherently enigmatic and dependent on such a wide range of factors that standardized testing bears no significant relationship to reality, nor does it indicate anything in particular about the child's needs or capacities. But to reverse the trend toward global compulsory schooling,[4] we have to root the logic out at its source.

The core discourses of schooling are all about the fundamentalist belief that professionalized institutions simply know what is best for people who they have assumed need to be under their care. They are what Ivan Illich has termed disabling professions, roles that actively remove power from individuals and toward professionalized service providers who are convinced that value and meaning are necessarily created only with their intervention.

Many students, especially those who are poor, intuitively know what the schools do for them. They school them to confuse process and substance. Once these become blurred, a new logic is assumed: The more treatment there is, the better are the results; or, escalation leads to success. The pupil is thereby "schooled" to confuse teaching with learning, grade advancement with education, a diploma with competence, and fluency with the ability to say something new. His imagination is schooled to accept service in the place of value (Illich, 1970, p. 1).

Much like the urge to control nature, schools necessarily seek to standardize the lives of children with a globalizing logic that reduces self and local self-reliance, a very poor sister to professional service. School people, by identifying a specific and comprehensible Western canon of knowledge and mandating it as necessary, are thereby encumbered with providing that knowledge by almost any means necessary. Schools are then perceived as essential, and child rearing is governed by a series of calculations, like manipulating a stock portfolio, making the least risky choices.

Much of contemporary schooling can be viewed as exercises in *governmentality*: a term and an idea with Foucauldian origins (see Burchell, Gordon, & Miller, 1991) that draws on the same historiography as Ian Hacking:

the management and regulation of populations based on statistical information gathering.

The systematic collection of data about people has affected not only the ways in which we conceive of a society, but how we describe our neighbor. It has profoundly transformed what we choose to do, who we try to be, what we think of ourselves (Hacking, 1990, pp. 2–3).

Contemporary schools take it upon themselves to collect massive amounts of data on their students[5] and to categorize, manage, and stream children overwhelmingly on the basis of statistical evidence. Schools both reflect and construct our culture and the reliance on expert-driven population management continues to fundamentally inform both.

> I kept making the same mistake, and it was a serious one: I kept wanting to teach. I wanted our school to be more relevant to the needs of the boys. And they, of course, kept throwing me off. What they needed, and obviously craved, was a dose of the big world. (George Dennison, 1969, p. 163)[6]

The basic aspects of everyday school life have emerged and continue to evolve not as a response to the needs of students, but as driven by institutional needs. Contemporary pedagogical thinking is almost entirely constrained by classroom requirements, and it is of little use for teachers to ask broad questions about their students' well-being. Students are required to fit into the apparatus of school days, times, schedules, agendas, curricula, and class order, and it is their flexibility and adaptivity that is assumed, not the institutions'. Why do we demand that children fit into schools and not the other way round?

Forcing children to adapt to a predescribed institutional model has given rise to a whole teaching industry of carrots and sticks, bribes, threats, rewards, surveillance, monitoring, drugging, therapy, counseling, and much more, desperately trying to ensure that all students can learn the same curriculum, in the same fashion, at the same rate. The reality is that all kids are uniquely enigmatic creatures with constantly changing learning patterns, needs, interests, passions, family circumstances, capacities, and quirks.

Pedagogically, this is exactly where schools run into trouble. Compulsory state schooling has posited itself as capable of being all things to all people — collapsing all children into consensual canonical agreement. Compulsory state schooling suggests that it can provide that which all students need to grow up right, and that the state, and only the state, is a reasonable arbiter of necessary knowledge. As society becomes ever more diverse and complex, that position becomes more and more difficult to maintain, as the canon comes under continual attack and the range of student needs, demands, and expectations becomes increasingly diverse.

The implied expectations of a school are brought into question and teachers/administrators become ever more leery of experimentation, innovation, and risk as they are compelled to teach more and more tightly to the curriculum and are constrained by national and international standards, testing, and grading. As the range of subjects becomes restricted, monitoring becomes increasingly globalized, and teachers are held accountable for student performance, the possibilities for anomalous experience shrink vastly.

Plainly put, kids should spend their days being challenged intellectually, socially, and physically, and that, as anyone who has spent any time in schools knows, is rarely the case. They challenge students' patience, their capacity to accept petty authority, their ability to negotiate bureaucracies, their ability to follow orders, but only the very best schools actively attempt to challenge their students' best capacities: It is simply too dangerous.

The curricular requirements schools are burdened with and their institutional size (even for very small schools) almost always mean that lasting personal relationships are at a premium. It is very difficult for staff to be able to develop and create the kinds of individualized and enigmatic circumstances that children need to be genuinely challenged. The pace, curriculum, subject matter, teaching style, time schedules, frequency of breaks, disciplinary measures, time outside, and everything else have to be standardized in schools or else their mandates become impossible.

Thus, schools retreat into the most basic and standardized kinds of pedagogies that allow for very little deviance, and the school experience retreats into the same haze of mall, television, video games, and movies that so much of childhood has been reduced to today.

Viewed broadly, the whole security apparatus surrounding schools[7] is the functional expression of the belief that educational bureaucracies are capable of defining what people need to know. Once schools start with that premise, and compulsory state schools necessarily do, then the enforcement is all self-justifying.

That is to say that schools start with the premise that they are the keepers of necessary knowledge; thus, education becomes a for-your-own-good process of instilling a very certain canonical knowledge as quickly and as efficiently as possible. It is what Paolo Freire called the banking method of education.

Education thus becomes an act of depositing, in which the students are depositories and the teacher is the depositor. Instead of communicating, the teacher issues communiqués and makes deposits, which the students patiently receive, memorize, and repeat. This is the banking method of education, in which the scope of action allowed to the students extends only so far as receiving, filing, and storing the deposits. They do, it is true, have the opportunity to become collectors or cataloguers of the things they store. But in the last analysis, it is the people themselves who are filed away through the lack of creativity, transformation, and knowledge in this (at best) misguided system. For apart from inquiry, apart from the praxis, individuals cannot be truly human. Knowledge emerges only through invention and reinvention, through the restless, impatient, continuing, hopeful inquiry human beings pursue in the world, with the world, and with each other.[8]

The everyday ubiquity and acceptance of what Freire describes came home to me some years ago when I was taking a train from Montreal to Prince Edward Island (PEI). I was sharing my compartment with four older ladies who were returning home after a weekend of gambling in Quebec. They were giddy and fun to be with. In time they found out I was heading to PEI to teach a course called "The Philosophy of Education." They were delighted: All were former teachers. As one of them said to gales of laughter, "I taught seventh grade for almost forty years, honey. And there's only one thing you need to know: Sometimes you can't pour a gallon into a cup."

If we accept the exigency of the canon and adopt the educative stance, then virtually anything can be justified. If we really believe that canonical inculcation is "for their own good," then logically we would be amiss if we were to leave any stone unturned in our efforts to ensure that all kids accept as many deposits as they can possibly hold. School people are able to convince themselves that the ends justify virtually any means.

> Trust is always the condition of experimentation, of taking chance. Trust must be created for things to change. (Isabelle Stengers, 2002)

I think school "choice" is treacherous ground. Reducing the raising of children to a series of options, as if families were stock portfolios to be artfully maneuvered into the most productive scenarios, is a grim way to walk through life. Considering how our kids can flourish has to be far more variegated and nuanced than simply picking between A, B, and C, as if child rearing were a risk management exercise.

What makes a good school? Refusing to answer the question, and instead building local places that look at the kids that are there and asking "What will it take for these kids to flourish?" The questions are complex and meandering and look much more like parenting questions. It is imperative for people who want to work with kids to turn their backs on the manipulative intents of education, wash themselves of the impulse to mold students in an idealized image, and begin to create community institutions that are flexible enough to evolve with the needs of participants.

And that is why it is impossible to describe what a good school might look like, as if it were a magic formula that could be applied and reapplied anywhere. It is the technocratic fantasy of imposing industrial production models everywhere. Kids need places to gather and places to meet interested and interesting adults who care about them and their lives. Beyond that, there is an endless array of possibilities, and how these places are constructed is a matter for local discourse and debate. Kids and families need to come together and create the kinds of institutions that best serve their children, their families, and their communities. The resources, the facilities, the people, the knowledge, and the skills are all in place. The only things missing are the political and cultural will to renounce compulsory state schooling, and the trust in local places and people.

So what could one say makes a good place for kids? How about using the same criteria that describe libraries, parks, pools, plazas, bike trails, community centers, and rinks, places that people all over the world use and love? These are public places in the real sense of the word, widely available, open for a variety of uses, free when possible, and not having a coercive agenda. These institutions are community resources and widely admired for their utility and broad value. I think libraries are a very good potential starting point for the transformation of schools.

Every community needs to engage in an ongoing conversation with local families and kids about what kinds of places are needed for people to thrive in. We have to talk about building institutions where all kids, especially those from the least privileged families, can begin to legitimately explore what it will take to flourish. The specifics are not important, but every community should have as wide a range of places as possible — schools, learning centers, homeschooling support, travel, work, internship, anything and everything — and all kids should have as many choices as possible in front of them.

The important thing is for every family, every kid, every neighborhood to start thinking about flourishing, and imagining and reimagining what institutions can be built to help that happen.

NOTES

1. Maybe they are, maybe not, depending on what you think the purpose of schools is. If you want to argue that schools make kids smarter and more competent, that is a tough one. Did you know, for example, that literacy levels in Massachusetts, where compulsory schooling first took root on this continent, were 95% in 1850, two years before sending kids to school was made law? It has never reached those levels since. Or that in the United States, a country that has so enthusiastically and bombastically swallowed the compulsory school pill, still only 32% of fourth graders can read at grade level? Einstein said that the definition of insanity is doing the same thing over and over again and expecting different results. It is a suggestion that leaps to mind often when I think about compulsory education.

2. There is a huge and growing interest in global standards, measuring school performance in various countries against one another. You probably see this most readily in your local paper when you read that Japanese students

are ahead of Canadian kids in math, who are behind Scandinavians in science, and so forth. UNESCO is perhaps the largest force in this project. See, for example, the UNESCO Institute for Statistics (UIS), Global Education Digest, retrieved from http://www.uis.unesco.org/ev.php?ID=5728_201&ID2=DO_TOPIC: "The UIS strives to help countries collect timely data of integrity which meet the dual requirements of relevance to national policies and compliance with international data standards. This will permit regional and global pictures to be drawn and cross-national comparisons to be made. Improving the quality of education statistics takes time since many of the statistics can only be collected as by-products of sound administrative systems which are often under-resourced. Nonetheless, we believe that this digest represents a significant improvement since last year in terms of coverage, timeliness, international comparability and validity."

3. Which is what the No Child Left Behind Act in the United States, and in Canada provincial examinations for all high school students specifically intend.

4. As The 1948 Universal Declaration of Human Rights, Article 26, states: "Elementary education shall be compulsory." UNESCO, writing in 1951, "the principle of universal compulsory education is no longer questioned." More recently, the April 2000 World Education Forum in Dakar, including 1,100 delegates from 164 countries, adopted the Dakar Framework for Action, calling for "free and compulsory education of good quality for all by 2015."

"The practice of compulsory schooling is animated and sustained by an almost universal prevailing public consensus that the practice is in the child's interest.... Indeed in so far as it confers a right to education as well as an obligation to make use of it, the law making education compulsory could be said to be one of the achievements of civilization.... After all disagreement is common about such issues as capital punishment, the right to carry firearms, divorce, abortion, etc., but not regarding compulsory education." (Williams, K., In Defence of Compulsory Education, *Journal of Philosophy of Education*, 24, 285–295, 1990)

5. Have you ever visited any of the U.S. Education Department's statistical storage sites? It is awesome and mind boggling. See the National Center for Education Statistics, for example, http://nces.ed.gov/

6. Dennison, G., *The Lives of Children: The Story of the First Street School* (New York: Vintage, 1969), p. 163.

7. By this I am referring to the whole constellation of tools, technologies, and techniques enforcing school attendance, legitimate behavior, and social relationships within, from truant officers to attendance sheets and so much else.

8. Friere, P., The "Banking" Concept of Education, in Friere, P., and Macedo, D. (Eds.), *The Paolo Friere Reader* (New York: Continuum, 1998), pp. 67–68.

REFERENCES

Burchell, G., Gordon, C., & Miller, P. (Eds.). (1991). *The Foucault effect: Studies in governmentality*. Hemel Hempstead, U.K.: Harvester Wheatsheaf.

Dead Prez. (2000). They schools. On *Lets Get Free* (compact disc). Jonesboro, AK: Relativity.

Dennison, G. (1969). *The lives of children: The story of the first street school.* New York: Vintage.

Gatto, J. (1992). *Dumbing us down.* Gabriola Island, British Columbia: New Society.

Hacking, I. (1990). *The taming of chance.* Cambridge: Cambridge University Press.

Illich, I. (1970). *Deschooling society.* New York: Harper & Row.

Stengers, I. (2002). *Hope: New philosophies for change.* New York: Routledge.

Index